Mary Berry's
COMPLETE COOKBOOK

Mary Berry's

COMPLETE COOKBOOK

Contents

Introduction

Mary Berry's Complete Cookbook has been the reliable, trusted companion of home cooks for many years. But much has changed since it was first published. We lead busier lives, fulfilling greater dreams. We entertain less formally than in the past, but so much more comfortably, often in the warmth of a cosy kitchen where guests can chat with the cook and enjoy the fun of preparing a meal together. Travel has broadened our horizons, and given us a taste for different foods.

Now, we know what it means to eat well in the modern sense, downplaying butter and sugar and rich sauces, preparing healthier meals using natural ingredients, and letting their flavour and freshness shine through. Fortunately, there's an abundance of good foods available – seasonal fruits and vegetables; fresh fish and lean meat; locally produced cheeses and interesting artisan breads not mass produced but lovingly formed by hand and baked in the traditional way. Supermarkets as well as small neighbourhood shops have responded to our more adventurous tastes – acquired during holidays to exotic destinations – and provide us with all manner of unusual ingredients, including the herbs, spices, and flavourings that enhance the appeal of simple ingredients.

This new edition of the book takes account of all these changes while retaining the features that made the original one so special. In preparing the book, I've been enormously helped by my assistant, Lucy Young, who helped to develop the new recipes and lent her youthful view to the enterprise. My grateful thanks.

Mary Berry

Buckinghamshire

Hot and chilled soups

In this chapter...

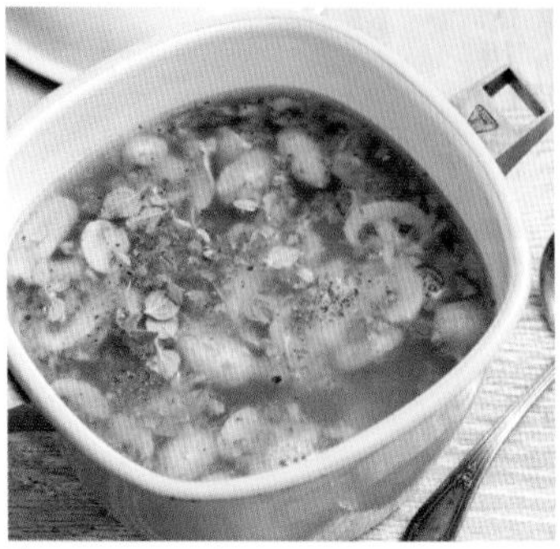
Somerset mushroom soup
page 14

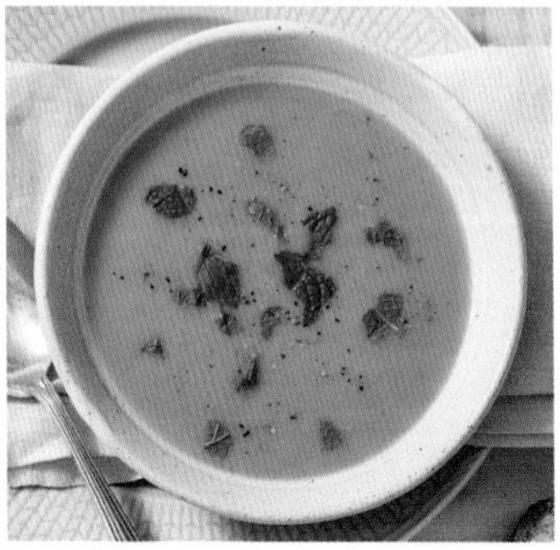
French pea soup
page 14

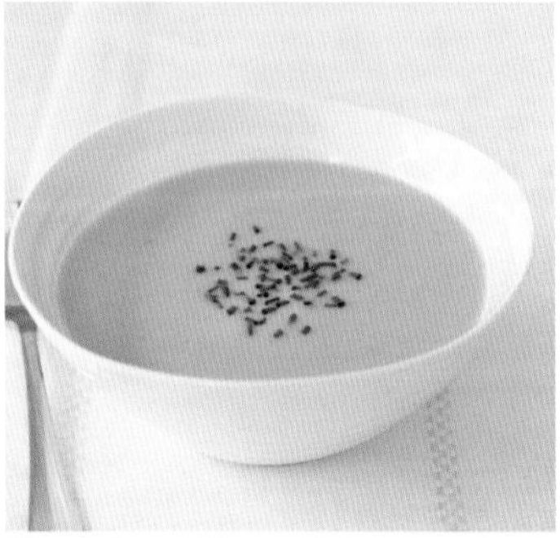
Curried parsnip soup
page 15

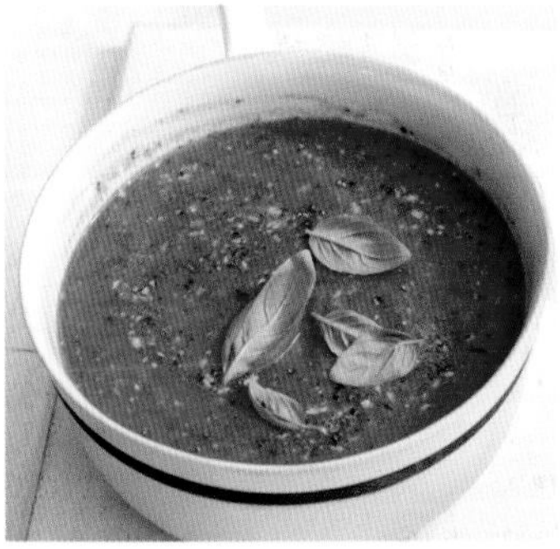
Tomato soup
page 15

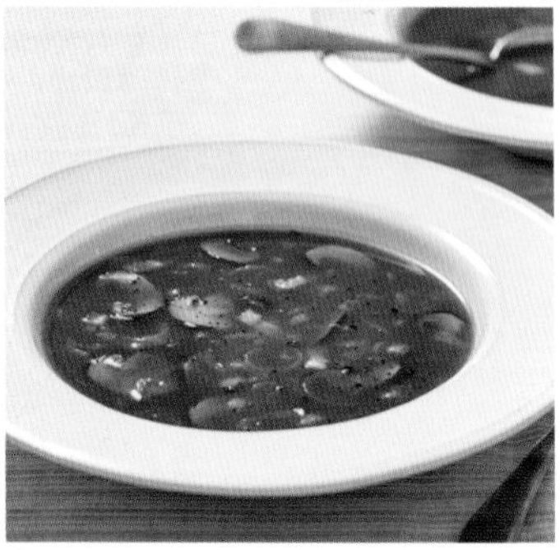
Game soup
page 16

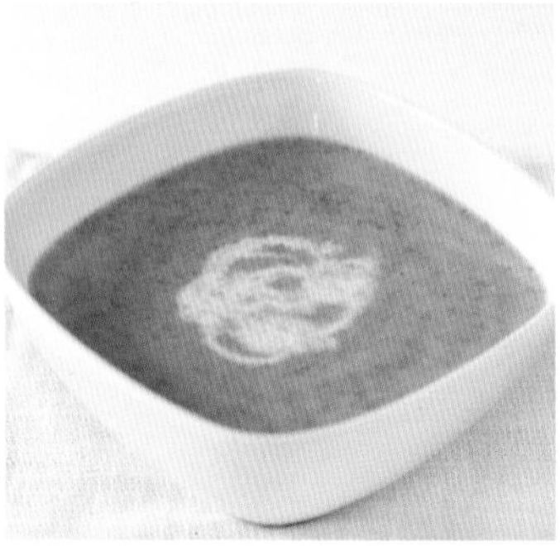
Watercress soup
page 16

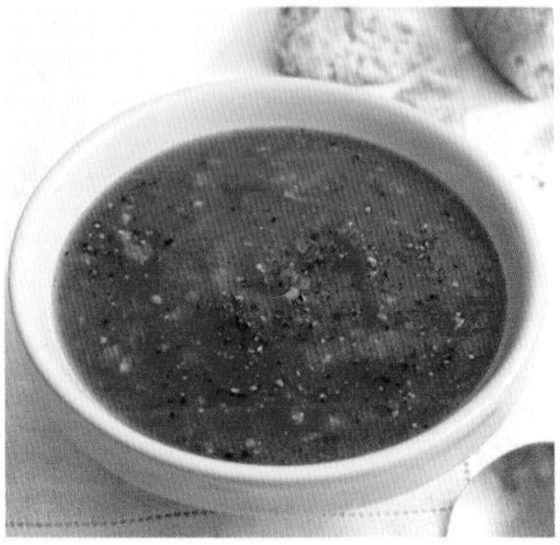
Roasted tomato and garlic soup
page 17

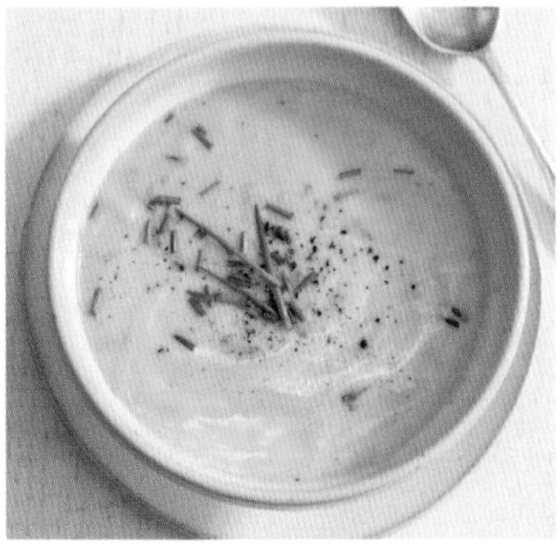
Creamy carrot and orange soup
page 17

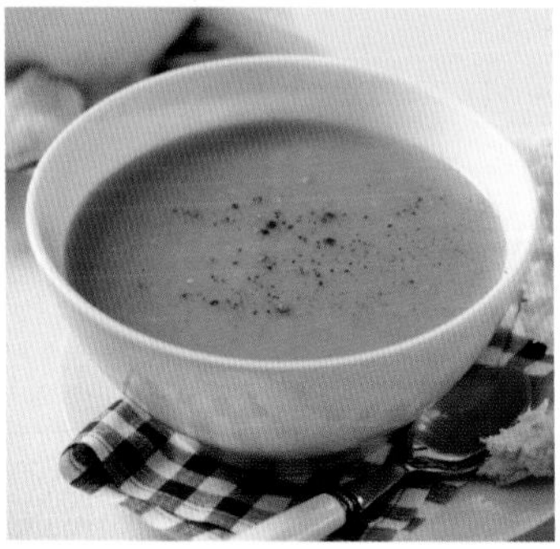
Butternut squash soup
page 18

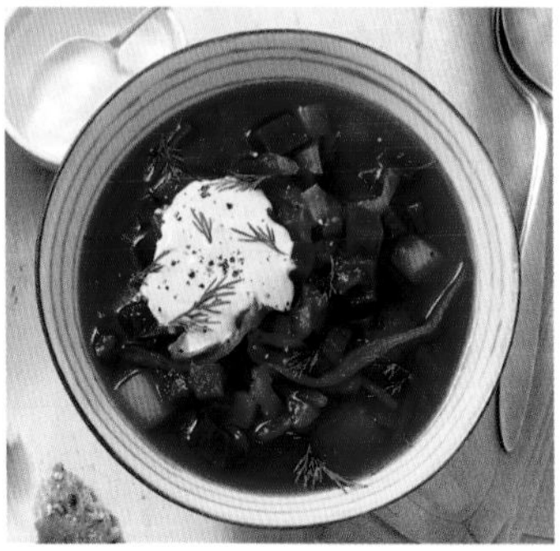
Borscht
page 18

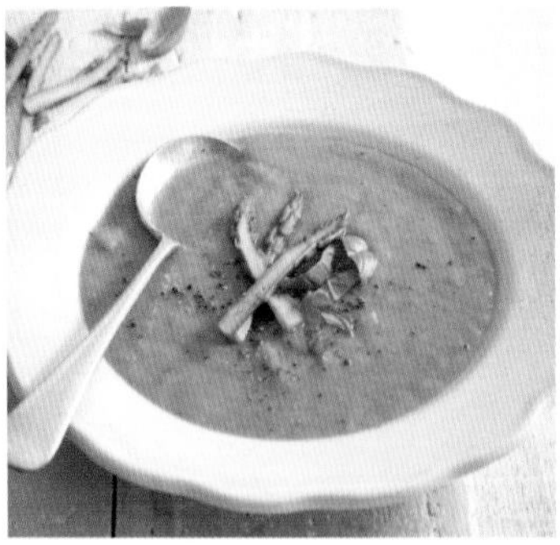
Asparagus soup
page 20

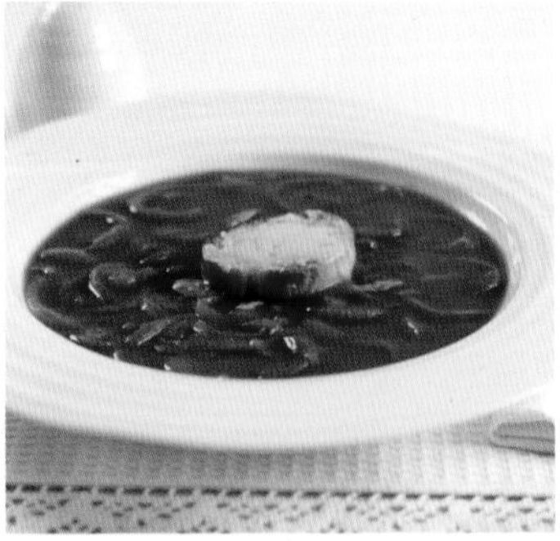
French onion soup
page 20

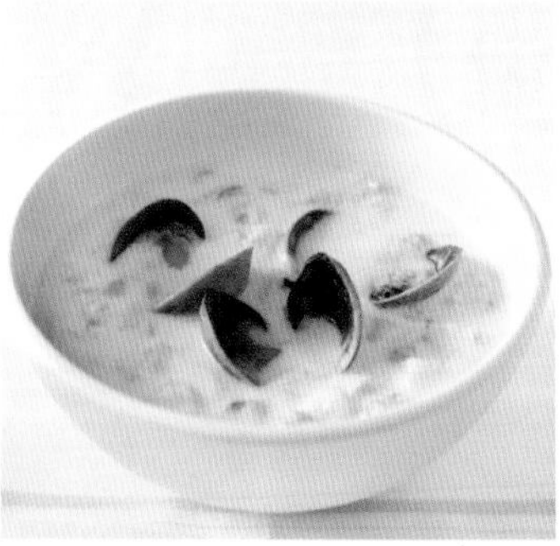
Clam chowder
page 21

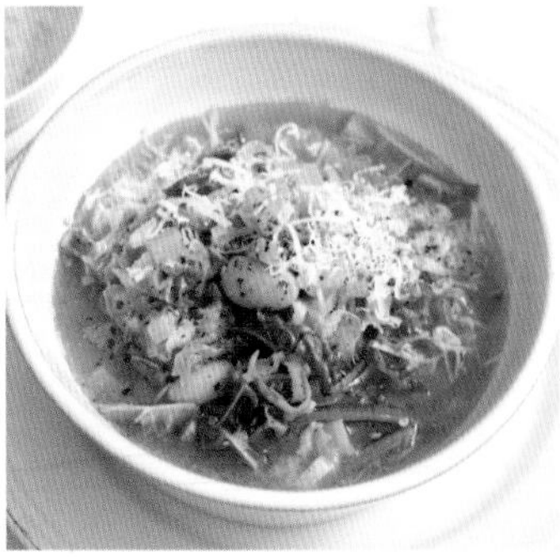
Vegetable minestrone
page 21

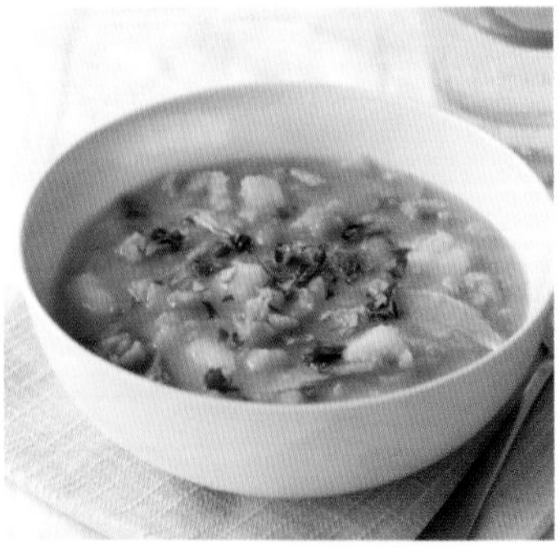
Split pea and gammon soup
page 22

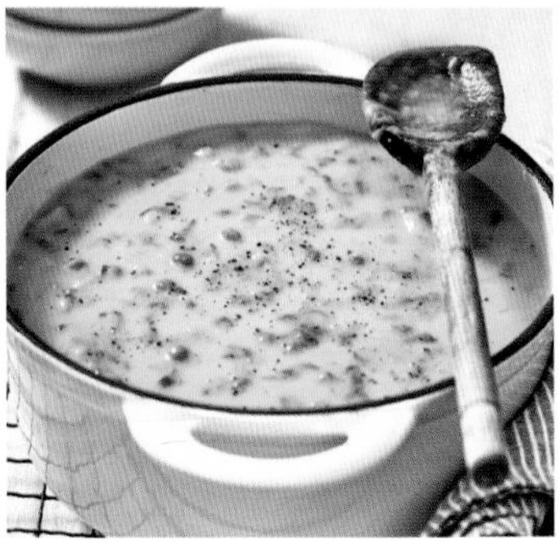
Pumpkin soup
page 22

Lentil and bacon soup
page 24

Goulash soup
page 24

Blue Stilton and onion soup
page 25

Winter vegetable soup
page 26

Spiced autumn soup
page 26

Lobster bisque
page 28

Bouillabaisse
page 29

Chinese crab and sweetcorn soup
page 30

Thai spiced soup
page 30

Chicken noodle soup
page 32

Gazpacho
page 32

Tzatziki soup
page 34

Vichyssoise
page 34

Chilled curried apple and mint soup
page 35

Soups know-how

A batch of soup in the fridge is one of the best convenience foods ever, highly nutritious and wonderfully versatile. On a cold day, a bowl of soup is warming and sustaining, and with a sandwich or just some bread it can make a well-balanced lunch or supper. Soup is great for entertaining too, the ideal prepare-ahead starter. And soup is comforting at bedtime or, indeed, at any time of day.

There are all kinds of soups: light and delicate or rich and hearty; simple and quick to prepare or cooked long and slow to extract maximum flavour from the ingredients; velvety smooth in texture or full of delicious pieces of meat, vegetables, pulses, or pasta. Soups may be served hot or chilled, in a mug, a bowl, or a soup plate, plain or attractively garnished. There are even sweet and fruity soups that can double up as desserts.

Stocks

A well-flavoured stock forms the base of many soups, and nothing tastes as good as home-made stock. Stock is economical to make because it is based on meat, poultry, or fish bones and trimmings, and vegetables. Although it usually takes time to make stock – several hours of gentle simmering for meat and poultry stocks – it is easy to prepare, and can be made well in advance and in large quantities. It can then be frozen until needed. Recipes for stocks can be found on pages 105, 154–55, 232, and 317. If you don't have any home-made stock, there are fresh stocks available in the chilled cabinets in supermarkets, or you can use stock made from bouillon powder or a cube. Remember, though, that stock cubes are often strong and salty, so go easy on the salt. Another quick alternative is to use canned consommé.

Clarifying stock

Skimming will make a stock quite clear (see below), but for crystal-clear results it needs to be clarified. When cold pour into a large pan. For each 600 ml (1 pint), add an egg white and crushed egg shell. Heat slowly, whisking. When frothy and starting to rise up, stop whisking and remove from the heat to subside. The crust that forms will act as a filter, collecting all the impurities. Repeat the rising up and subsiding two or three times, then simmer gently for 45 minutes. Strain through a muslin-lined sieve, holding back the crust.

Skimming soups

As a soup is brought to the boil, foam or scum may form on the surface. This is most likely with soups that contain meat or poultry, particularly on the bone, or root vegetables and pulses. This foam, which contains impurities, should be removed as it forms.

Use a large metal spoon or skimmer (slotted if there are herbs and whole spices in the soup) to skim off the foam.

If there is a lot of fat on the surface of a soup, skim it off with a large metal spoon, or blot it with paper towels, before serving.

Thickening soups

Many soups can be slightly thickened simply by being puréed to a smooth consistency. Puréed soups that contain starchy ingredients such as rice, pasta, and potatoes will be even thicker.

In some soup recipes, flour is used as a thickener. Normally it is added to the softened vegetables, to bind the fat and juices together. The mixture is then cooked to remove the raw flour taste before the stock is stirred in. Flour can also be added to puréed soups at the end of cooking if they are not thick enough: blend the flour with cold stock, whisk in and simmer until thickened.

Adding cream and yogurt

Double and whipping cream and full-fat crème fraîche can be added to a hot soup and heated further, with no danger of curdling.

Single cream, soured cream, and yogurt will curdle if overheated, so add them just before serving and warm through over a low heat. For chilled soups, add cream or yogurt once the soup has been chilled, before serving.

Garnishes

An attractive garnish can lift a soup, adding a contrast in colour, texture, and flavour. Here are some ideas.

- Fresh herbs, either chopped or as whole leaves – mint, chives, thyme, parsley, basil, tarragon, and coriander are all popular. Choose a herb that complements or mirrors any herbs in the soup, and add at the last minute so that it retains its freshness.
- Grated or crumbled cheese
- Chopped hard-boiled egg
- Fine shreds of citrus zest or whole berries
- Crisp pieces of bacon; diced meat or poultry
- Toasted nuts; sunflower seeds
- Croûtons
- Chopped, diced, sliced, or grated vegetables such as spring onions, cucumber, carrots, peppers, and fennel
- A spoonful of a sauce such as pesto
- A blob or decorative swirl of cream or yogurt (see box, below)

Garnishing with cream

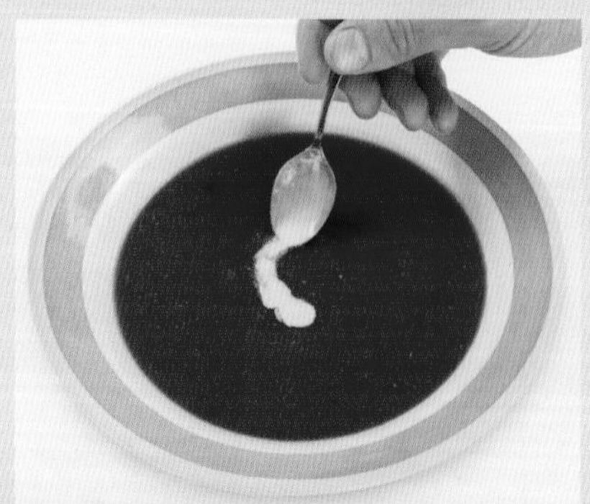

Use a teaspoon to quickly swirl single or whipping cream in a spiral on each serving.

Freezing

Soups taste best if freshly made, but most can be frozen without impairing flavour or texture. Avoid freezing soups containing ingredients such as pasta, potatoes, and rice as they become mushy. It is always best to underseason, as further seasoning can be added when reheating. Add any cream, eggs, and milk at the reheating stage, as freezing could cause separation or curdling.

To thaw a soup to be served hot, heat from frozen in a heavy saucepan over a low heat, stirring occasionally. If the soup appears to be separating, whisk briskly until smooth or work in a blender or food processor, or with a hand-held blender, for a few seconds. Thaw soup to be served cold in its freezer container, in the refrigerator.

Microwaving

For many soups, a microwave cannot give the same results as conventional long, slow cooking, but it can produce light vegetable soups in minutes. And it is useful for thawing frozen stocks and soups, and for reheating soups. The most efficient way of heating soup in the microwave is to transfer the soup to individual bowls or mugs, because soup in larger containers will take longer to heat up than it would in a pan on top of the stove. For cooking soup in the microwave, use a container that is large enough to allow the soup to rise up slightly. Stir once or twice during cooking or heating, and just before serving, as the soup at the edge will be hot and bubbling long before that in the centre. Add single cream, soured cream, or yogurt and any garnish just before serving.

Puréeing soups

Soups are often puréed to give them a velvety-smooth texture. This also gives them a thicker texture. Starchy vegetables and a little flour will help to thicken them even more.

Blender or food processor

Either of these can be used to process the cooked ingredients in batches. Scrape the sides of the container once or twice to ensure there are no solid pieces left unprocessed.

Hand-held blender

Use this to purée directly in the saucepan (which should be deep to prevent splashes). It's not useful for large quantities, but is ideal for blending in a final addition of cream or yogurt.

Sieve

To make a puréed soup ultra smooth, and remove any fibres, seeds, or skins, work it through a fine sieve with a wooden spoon. This is much easier to do if the soup is first puréed in a blender or food processor.

Somerset mushroom soup

SERVES 4–6 **CALS PER SERVING** 109–73

30 g (1 oz) butter
1 small onion, finely chopped
1 garlic clove, crushed
500 g (1 lb) mushrooms, sliced
1.25 litres (2 pints) vegetable or chicken stock
150 ml (¼ pint) dry white wine
2 tsp chopped fresh marjoram
1 tsp chopped fresh thyme
salt and black pepper

1 Melt the butter in a large saucepan, add the onion and garlic, and cook gently, stirring occasionally, for a few minutes until soft but not coloured. Add the mushrooms and cook, stirring from time to time, for 10 minutes.

2 Pour in the stock and wine, then add the marjoram and half of the thyme, and season with salt and pepper. Bring to a boil, cover, and simmer gently for 10 minutes or until the mushrooms are tender.

3 Taste for seasoning and serve hot, sprinkled with the remaining fresh thyme.

French pea soup

SERVES 4–6 **CALS PER SERVING** 179–119

30 g (1 oz) butter
1 large onion, coarsely chopped
1 tbsp plain flour
500 g (1 lb) frozen peas
1.25 litres (2 pints) vegetable or chicken stock
½ tsp caster sugar
2 large mint sprigs
salt and black pepper
shredded fresh mint, to garnish

1 Melt the butter in a large saucepan, add the chopped onion, and cook very gently, stirring occasionally, for about 10 minutes until soft but not coloured.

2 Sprinkle in the flour and stir for a further 1–2 minutes, then add the frozen peas, stock, caster sugar, and sprigs of mint.

3 Bring to a boil, cover, and simmer gently, stirring occasionally, for 5 minutes or until the peas are soft. Do not simmer any longer than this or the peas will lose their fresh green colour.

4 Remove the mint sprigs and discard. Purée the soup in a food processor or blender until smooth.

5 Return the soup to the rinsed-out pan, reheat, and add salt and pepper to taste. Serve hot, garnished with shredded fresh mint.

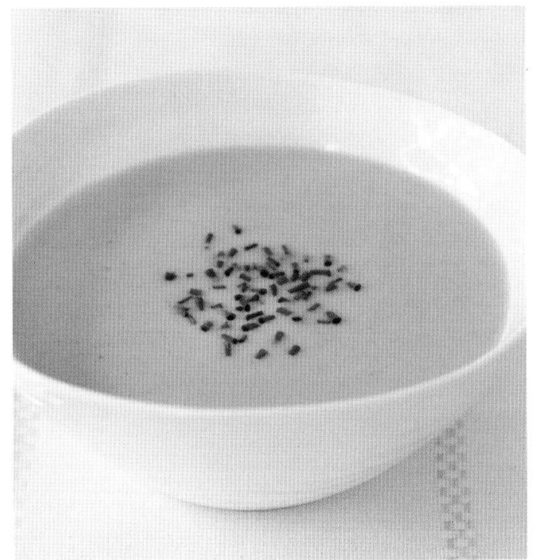

Curried parsnip soup

SERVES 6–8 **CALS PER SERVING** 197–147

30 g (1 oz) butter
750 g (1½ lb) parsnips, coarsely chopped
1 large onion, chopped
1 large garlic clove, crushed
2 tsp mild curry powder
1.8 litres (3 pints) vegetable or chicken stock
salt and black pepper
200 ml (7 fl oz) single cream
snipped fresh chives, to garnish

1 Melt the butter in a large saucepan, add the chopped parsnips, onion, and crushed garlic, and cook gently, stirring occasionally, for 5 minutes or until the onion is softened but not coloured.

2 Stir in the curry powder, and cook for 1 minute, then blend in the stock, and season with salt and pepper. Bring to a boil, stirring, then cover, and simmer gently for 20 minutes or until the parsnips are tender.

3 Purée the soup in a food processor or blender until smooth. Return the soup to the rinsed-out pan, heat gently to warm through, stirring constantly, then taste for seasoning.

4 Stir in the single cream and reheat gently. Serve at once, garnished with fresh chives.

Tomato soup

SERVES 6–8 **CALS PER SERVING** 134–101

30 g (1 oz) butter
2 onions, coarsely chopped
1 garlic clove, crushed
1 tbsp plain flour
1.25 litres (2 pints) vegetable or chicken stock
2 x 400 g cans tomatoes
1 bay leaf
salt and black pepper
4 tbsp ready-made pesto
single cream (optional) and fresh basil leaves, to garnish

1 Melt the butter in a large saucepan, add the onions and garlic, and cook gently, stirring from time to time, for a few minutes until soft but not coloured.

2 Add the flour to the pan and cook, stirring constantly, for 1 minute.

3 Pour in the stock, then add the tomatoes and their juice and the bay leaf. Season with salt and pepper. Bring to a boil, cover the pan, and simmer gently for 20 minutes.

4 Remove the bay leaf and discard. Purée the soup in a food processor or blender until smooth.

5 Return the soup to the rinsed-out pan, add the pesto, and heat through. Taste for seasoning.

6 Serve at once, garnished with cream (if you like) and fresh basil leaves.

QUICK TOMATO SOUP

Passata, Italian sieved tomatoes, makes a beautiful, deep red soup. Substitute 750 ml (1¼ pints) of bottled or canned passata for the canned tomatoes and then cook as directed.

Game soup

SERVES 4 **CALS PER SERVING** 223

30 g (1 oz) butter
125 g (4 oz) smoked streaky bacon rashers, rinds removed, diced
1 onion, sliced
125 g (4 oz) chestnut mushrooms, sliced
1 tbsp plain flour
1.25 litres (2 pints) game stock (page 154)
salt and black pepper
1 tbsp redcurrant jelly

Orange-herb bouquet

6 parsley stalks
pared zest of 1 orange
1 bay leaf
1 large thyme or marjoram sprig

1 Make the orange-herb bouquet (see box, right) and set aside.

2 Melt the butter in a large saucepan, add the bacon, and cook over a high heat, stirring occasionally, for 5–7 minutes until crisp.

3 Lower the heat, add the onion to the pan, and cook gently, stirring from time to time, for a few minutes until softened but not coloured.

4 Add the mushrooms to the pan, and cook for about 5 minutes, then add the flour and cook, stirring constantly, for 1 minute. Add the stock and the orange-herb bouquet, season with salt and pepper, and bring to a boil. Cover and simmer for 30 minutes.

5 Discard the bouquet, then stir in the redcurrant jelly. Taste for seasoning before serving.

Orange-herb bouquet

Tie the parsley, orange zest, bay leaf, and thyme or marjoram with a piece of white string. Leave a length of string to tie to the saucepan handle, so that the bouquet can be easily lifted from the pan at the end of cooking.

Watercress soup

SERVES 6 **CALS PER SERVING** 140

30 g (1 oz) butter
1 onion, finely chopped
2 potatoes, coarsely chopped
125 g (4 oz) watercress, tough stalks removed
900 ml (1½ pints) vegetable or chicken stock
300 ml (½ pint) milk
1 bay leaf
salt and black pepper
single cream, to garnish (optional)

1 Melt the butter in a large saucepan, add the onion, and cook gently, stirring from time to time, for a few minutes until soft but not coloured.

2 Add the potatoes and the watercress to the saucepan and cook for about 5 minutes until the watercress is wilted.

3 Pour in the chicken or vegetable stock and milk, add the bay leaf, and season with salt and pepper.

4 Bring the mixture to a boil, cover, and simmer very gently for 15 minutes or until the potatoes are tender.

5 Remove the bay leaf and discard. Purée the soup in a food processor or blender until smooth. Return the soup to the rinsed-out pan, reheat, then taste for seasoning.

6 Serve hot, garnishing each bowl with a little single cream if you like.

Roasted tomato and garlic soup

SERVES 4 **CALS PER SERVING** 127

1 kg (2 lb) ripe tomatoes
2 tbsp olive oil
1 onion, chopped
3 garlic cloves, coarsely chopped
1.5 litres (2½ pints) chicken or vegetable stock
salt and black pepper
pesto, to serve

1 Cut the tomatoes in half and arrange them, cut-side down, in a roasting tin. Roast in a preheated oven at 220°C (200°C fan, Gas 7) for 15 minutes or until the skins are charred.

2 Remove the tomatoes from the oven and leave until they are cool enough to handle, then peel off the skins and discard them. Chop the flesh coarsely, retaining the juice.

3 Heat the oil in a large saucepan, add the onion and garlic, and cook gently, stirring occasionally, for a few minutes until soft but not coloured.

4 Add the stock and the tomato flesh and juices, and bring to a boil. Lower the heat and simmer for 5 minutes, then add salt and pepper to taste.

5 Serve the soup hot, with a bowl of pesto so everyone can stir in a spoonful before they eat.

Creamy carrot and orange soup

SERVES 6–8 **CALS PER SERVING** 308–231

30 g (1 oz) butter
1 onion, coarsely chopped
1 kg (2 lb) carrots, thickly sliced
1.5 litres (2½ pints) vegetable stock
grated zest of ½ orange
300 ml (½ pint) orange juice (squeezed fresh or from a carton)
salt and black pepper
300 ml (½ pint) full-fat crème fraîche
3 tbsp snipped fresh chives

1 Melt the butter in a large saucepan, add the onion, and cook gently, stirring occasionally, for a few minutes until soft but not coloured. Add the carrots, cover, and cook gently, stirring from time to time, for 10 minutes.

2 Add the stock and bring to a boil. Cover and simmer, stirring from time to time, for 30–40 minutes until the carrots are soft.

3 Purée the soup in a food processor or blender until smooth. Return the soup to the rinsed-out pan, add the orange zest and juice, and salt and pepper to taste. Stir in the crème fraîche and then gently reheat the soup.

4 Stir in half of the snipped chives, and garnish individual servings with the remaining chives.

Butternut squash soup

SERVES 6 **CALS PER SERVING** 197

3 small butternut squash, about 1.7 kg (3½ lb) total weight
2 tbsp olive oil
grated nutmeg
salt and black pepper
30 g (1 oz) butter
1 large onion, roughly chopped
2 large carrots, roughly chopped
2 large celery stalks, roughly chopped
1.2–1.3 litres (2–2¼ pints) vegetable stock
crusty bread, to serve

1 Cut each squash lengthways in half, then scoop out and discard the seeds and stringy fibres. Arrange the squash halves cut-side up in a roasting tin just large enough to hold them in a single layer. Drizzle the olive oil over the flesh of the squash, and season with nutmeg, salt, and pepper. Pour 150 ml (¼ pint) cold water into the tin around the squash. Roast in a preheated oven at 200°C (180°C fan, Gas 6) for about 1 hour until tender. Remove from the oven, and set aside until cool enough to handle.

2 Meanwhile, melt the butter in a large saucepan, and add the chopped vegetables. Cook over a high heat for a few minutes until lightly coloured, stirring constantly. Pour in the stock, season with salt and pepper, and bring to a boil. Cover, and simmer gently for 20 minutes or until the vegetables are tender. Remove from the heat.

3 Scoop the flesh from the squash skins into the soup in the pan, then purée in a food processor or blender until smooth. (If using a food processor, purée the vegetables with a little of the liquid first, then add the remaining liquid and purée again.) Return the soup to the rinsed-out pan, reheat, and taste for seasoning. Serve hot, with crusty bread.

Borscht

SERVES 4 **CALS PER SERVING** 244

175 g (6 oz) white cabbage, coarsely shredded
200 g (7 oz) waxy potatoes, peeled and diced
1 x 225 g can chopped tomatoes
1 small carrot, chopped
1 small onion, chopped
1.5 litres (2½ pints) vegetable or chicken stock, more if needed
500 g (1 lb) cooked beetroot, peeled and diced
3–4 dill sprigs, chopped
30 g (1 oz) sugar
2 tbsp wine vinegar
salt and black pepper
crusty bread, to serve
soured cream and dill sprigs, to garnish

1 Put the cabbage, potatoes, tomatoes, carrot, and onion into a large pan with the stock.

2 Bring to a boil, then simmer for 30–40 minutes until the vegetables are very tender. Add extra stock if necessary.

3 Add the diced beetroot, dill, sugar, and vinegar, and simmer for 10 minutes to let the sweet–sour flavours develop. Add salt and pepper to taste, and more sugar and vinegar if necessary.

4 Serve at once with crusty bread, garnished with spoonfuls of soured cream and sprigs of dill.

Asparagus soup

SERVES 6 **CALS PER SERVING** 96

250 g (8 oz) potatoes, chopped
1.5 litres (2½ pints) vegetable or chicken stock
500 g (1 lb) asparagus
2 garlic cloves, crushed
2 tbsp chopped fresh basil (optional)
salt and black pepper
30 g (1 oz) butter (optional)

1 Put the potatoes into a large saucepan, add the stock, and bring to a boil. Cover and simmer for 15 minutes or until the potatoes are tender.

2 Meanwhile, cut any woody ends off the asparagus and discard. Cut off the tips and chop the stalks into chunks.

3 Add the asparagus and garlic to the pan, and cook for 5 minutes, stirring from time to time, until the asparagus is tender. Remove nine tips and reserve for the garnish.

4 Purée the soup in a food processor or blender until smooth.

5 Return the soup to the rinsed-out pan and reheat. Add the basil, if using, and salt and pepper to taste. Slice the reserved asparagus tips lengthways in half. Serve the soup hot, garnished with the asparagus tips, and small nuggets of butter, if wished.

ARTICHOKE SOUP

Use 1 x 400 g can artichoke hearts or bottoms, drained and diced, instead of the asparagus, and garnish with basil.

French onion soup

SERVES 8 **CALS PER SERVING** 353

45 g (1½ oz) butter
1 tbsp sunflower oil
1 kg (2 lb) large white onions, thinly sliced
2 tsp caster sugar
30 g (1 oz) plain flour
1.8 litres (3 pints) vegetable, chicken, or beef stock
salt and black pepper
8 Gruyère croûtes (page 28)

1 Melt the butter with the oil in a large saucepan, and caramelize the onions with the sugar (see box, right). Sprinkle the flour into the pan and cook, stirring constantly, for 1–2 minutes.

2 Gradually stir in the stock and bring to a boil. Season with salt and pepper, then cover and simmer, stirring from time to time, for 35 minutes.

3 Taste the soup for seasoning, then ladle into warmed bowls. Float a Gruyère croûte in each bowl and serve at once.

Caramelizing onions

Cook the onions in the butter and oil for a few minutes until soft. Add the sugar and continue cooking over a low heat, stirring occasionally, for 20 minutes or until the onions are golden brown.

Clam chowder

SERVES 4 **CALS PER SERVING** 497

500 g (1 lb) fresh clams in their shells, cleaned (page 105)
250 ml (8 fl oz) fish stock
45 g (1½ oz) butter
1 onion, chopped
3 unsmoked bacon rashers, rinds removed, diced
2 tbsp plain flour
2 potatoes, peeled and diced
750 ml (1¼ pints) milk
1 bay leaf
salt and black pepper

1 Put the clams into a large saucepan, add the fish stock, and bring to a boil. Lower the heat, cover, and cook over a medium heat for 5–8 minutes until the clam shells open.

2 Discard any clams that have not opened. Set aside 12 clams in their shells for garnish and keep warm. Remove the remaining clams from their shells. Discard the shells and strain the cooking juices.

3 Melt the butter in a large pan, add the onion, and cook gently for a few minutes until soft but not coloured. Add the bacon and the flour, and cook, stirring, for 1–2 minutes.

4 Add the potatoes, milk, strained clam juices, and bay leaf to the pan. Bring to a boil, then lower the heat and simmer for 15 minutes. Add the shelled clams, and heat gently for about 5 minutes. Remove the bay leaf and discard.

5 Add salt and pepper to taste. Serve hot, garnished with the reserved clams in their shells.

Vegetable minestrone

SERVES 4–6 **CALS PER SERVING** 250–167

2 tbsp olive oil
1 onion, chopped
2 celery stalks, chopped
2 carrots, finely diced
1 x 400 g can chopped Italian plum tomatoes
1 tbsp tomato purée
1 garlic clove, crushed
salt and black pepper
1.5 litres (2½ pints) chicken or vegetable stock
1 x 400 g can cannellini or red kidney beans, drained
250 g (8 oz) leeks, trimmed and finely sliced
125 g (4 oz) Savoy cabbage, finely shredded
2 tbsp arborio (risotto) rice
grated Parmesan cheese, to serve

1 Heat the oil in a large saucepan, add the onion, celery, and carrots, and cook gently, stirring, for 5 minutes.

2 Add the tomatoes, tomato purée, and garlic, and season with salt and pepper. Stir, then pour in the stock and bring to a boil over a high heat.

3 Cover the pan and lower the heat so the soup is gently simmering. Cook for 15 minutes, stirring occasionally.

4 Add the beans, leeks, cabbage, and rice, and simmer for a further 20 minutes. Taste for seasoning.

5 Serve hot, with a bowl of grated Parmesan cheese for everyone to help themselves.

Cook's know-how

If you haven't got arborio or any other type of risotto rice, use broken spaghetti instead. You will need 30 g (1 oz).

Split pea and gammon soup

SERVES 8 **CALS PER SERVING** 338

500 g (1 lb) green split peas
500 g (1 lb) gammon knuckle
2.5 litres (4 pints) water
1 large onion, finely chopped
4 celery stalks, finely chopped
3 potatoes, peeled and diced
3 leeks, trimmed and sliced
salt and black pepper
2 tbsp chopped parsley, to garnish

1 Put the green split peas and the gammon knuckle into separate large bowls and cover generously with cold water. Leave to soak overnight.

2 Drain the split peas and gammon knuckle, then put them both into a large saucepan with the measured water. Bring to a boil, then simmer, uncovered, for about 1 hour.

3 Add the onion, celery, potatoes, and leeks to the pan, cover, and simmer gently for 2½ hours until the gammon is tender and the peas are cooked. Add more water, if needed, during cooking.

4 Skim the surface if necessary. Remove the gammon knuckle from the saucepan and let it cool slightly. Pull the meat away from the knuckle bone, discarding any skin and fat.

5 Coarsely chop the meat and return it to the saucepan. Add salt and pepper to taste, then heat gently to warm the meat through. Serve hot, garnished with a sprinkling of fresh parsley.

Cook's know-how

Gammon knuckles are meaty yet inexpensive. Your butcher will have them, if you can't get one at the supermarket.

Pumpkin soup

SERVES 6 **CALS PER SERVING** 329

1.5 kg (3 lb) pumpkin
150 g (5 oz) butter
2 leeks, trimmed and sliced
1 litre (1¾ pints) chicken or vegetable stock
¼ tsp grated nutmeg
salt and black pepper
30 g (1 oz) fresh or frozen peas
250 g (8 oz) spinach leaves, finely chopped
300 ml (½ pint) single cream

1 Cut out the flesh from the pumpkin, discarding the seeds and fibres. Cut the flesh into 2 cm (¾ in) chunks.

2 Melt 100 g (3½ oz) of the butter in a large saucepan. Add the leeks, and cook very gently, covered, for 10 minutes or until soft.

3 Add the stock, pumpkin chunks, and nutmeg, and season with salt and pepper. Bring to a boil, cover, and simmer for 30 minutes or until the vegetables are very soft.

4 Meanwhile, cook the peas in boiling salted water for 5 minutes. Drain thoroughly.

5 Melt the remaining butter in a saucepan. Add the spinach, cover, and cook gently for 3 minutes until wilted.

6 Purée the soup in a food processor or blender until smooth, in batches if necessary. Return to the pan and stir in the cream. Stir the peas and spinach into the soup, heat through, and serve hot.

Cook's know-how

You could serve the soup in small hollowed-out pumpkins, scalloping the edges. Other possibilities include leaving the soup chunky rather than puréeing it, using double the amount of spinach and omitting the peas, and halving the butter and cream to reduce the fat content.

Lentil and bacon soup

SERVES 4–6 **CALS PER SERVING** 301–201

30 g (1 oz) butter
1 onion, chopped
1 carrot, diced
1 celery stalk, diced
3 garlic cloves, crushed
2–3 lean back bacon rashers, rinds removed, diced
175 g (6 oz) red lentils
about 125 g (4 oz) potatoes, swede or turnip, peeled and diced
2 bay leaves
2 litres (3½ pints) vegetable or chicken stock
salt and black pepper
chopped parsley, to garnish

1 Melt the butter in a large saucepan, add the onion, carrot, celery, and garlic, and cook, stirring, for 5–6 minutes until soft and lightly coloured.

2 Add the bacon, lentils, potato, swede or turnip and bay leaves. Cook for 15 minutes.

3 Pour in the stock and bring to a boil, then simmer gently, uncovered, for about 20 minutes or until the lentils and vegetables are tender. Add salt and pepper to taste.

4 Remove the bay leaves and discard. Serve hot, sprinkled with chopped parsley.

LENTIL AND FRANKFURTER SOUP

For a hearty main meal soup, add 250 g (8 oz) frankfurters. Chop them into 1 cm (½ in) pieces and add to the soup about 5 minutes before the end of the cooking time, so that they warm through but do not overcook. Smoked sausages can also be used.

Goulash soup

SERVES 6 **CALS PER SERVING** 363

2 red peppers or 4 pieces of roasted red pepper from a jar, drained
2 tbsp sunflower oil
500 g (1 lb) stewing beef, trimmed and cut into 3.5 cm (1½ in) pieces
2 large onions, thickly sliced
1 tbsp plain flour
2 tsp paprika
1.5 litres (2½ pints) beef stock
1 x 400 g can chopped tomatoes
2 tbsp tomato purée
1 tbsp red wine vinegar
1 garlic clove, crushed
1 bay leaf
salt and black pepper
750 g (1½ lb) potatoes, peeled and diced
dash of Tabasco sauce
soured cream and snipped fresh chives, to garnish (optional)

1 Roast and peel the fresh red peppers (page 426) if using. Cut the roasted pepper flesh into chunks.

2 Heat the oil in a large pan. Add the beef and brown all over. Add the onions, peppers, flour, and paprika, and stir over a high heat for 1–2 minutes.

3 Add the stock, tomatoes, tomato purée, vinegar, garlic, and bay leaf, and season with salt and pepper. Bring to a boil, cover tightly, and simmer for 1½ hours.

4 Add the potatoes and cook for 30 minutes or until the beef and potatoes are tender. Remove the bay leaf and discard.

5 Add a little Tabasco sauce and taste for seasoning. Serve hot, garnished with soured cream and snipped chives if you like.

Blue Stilton and onion soup

SERVES 8 **CALS PER SERVING** 255

600 ml (1 pint) milk
2 bay leaves
¼ tsp grated nutmeg
90 g (3 oz) butter
2 large onions, finely sliced
75 g (2½ oz) plain flour
1.5 litres (2½ pints) vegetable or chicken stock
salt and black pepper
150 g (5 oz) blue Stilton cheese, coarsely grated
single cream, to serve (optional)
crusty bread, to serve

1 Pour the milk into a saucepan, add the bay leaves and nutmeg, and bring almost to a boil. Remove from the heat, cover, and leave to infuse for 20 minutes.

2 Meanwhile, melt the butter in a large pan, add the onions, and cook very gently, stirring occasionally, for about 10 minutes or until they are soft but not coloured.

3 Add the flour, and cook, stirring, for 2 minutes. Strain the milk and gradually blend it into the onion and flour. Add the stock, and season with salt and pepper. Bring to a boil and simmer, half covered, for 10 minutes.

4 Add the cheese and stir over a very low heat until it melts (do not boil or the cheese will be stringy). Taste for seasoning, and stir in a little cream if you wish. Serve hot, with crusty bread.

Winter vegetable soup

SERVES 6 **CALS PER SERVING** 153

45 g (1½ oz) butter
1 leek, trimmed and diced
1 onion, chopped
1 celery stalk, diced
1 small potato, peeled and diced
1 turnip, diced
1 small carrot, diced
3 garlic cloves, crushed
1.5 litres (2½ pints) vegetable or chicken stock
250 g (8 oz) spinach, coarsely shredded (see box, right)
3 spring onions, thinly sliced
salt and black pepper

1 Melt the butter in a large saucepan, add the leek, and cook gently, stirring occasionally, for 5 minutes or until softened. Add the onion, celery, potato, turnip, carrot, and garlic, and cook for 8 minutes.

2 Pour in the stock, and bring to a boil. Cover and simmer, stirring occasionally, for 25 minutes or until the vegetables are tender.

3 Add the spinach and spring onions, and cook for just 3 minutes until the spinach is wilted but still bright green. Season well, and serve hot.

Shredding spinach

Remove the stalks and stack several spinach leaves. Roll up tightly, and cut crosswise into shreds.

Spiced autumn soup

SERVES 8 **CALS PER SERVING** 171

60 g (2 oz) butter
2 large onions, coarsely chopped
2 potatoes, coarsely chopped
2 carrots, coarsely chopped
3 garlic cloves, crushed
pared zest and juice of 1 orange
2 tsp mild curry powder
1.8 litres (3 pints) vegetable or chicken stock
2 x 400 g cans chopped tomatoes
2 eating apples, peeled and chopped
salt and black pepper
herb croûtes (page 28), to serve

1 Melt the butter in a large saucepan, add the onions, potatoes, carrots, garlic, and orange zest, and cook gently, stirring from time to time, for about 5 minutes.

2 Add the curry powder, and cook, stirring constantly, for 1–2 minutes.

3 Add the stock, orange juice, tomatoes, and apples, and season with salt and pepper. Bring to a boil, cover, and simmer gently for 30 minutes or until the vegetables are tender. Discard the orange zest.

4 Purée the soup in a food processor or blender until smooth. Return to the rinsed-out pan, reheat, and taste for seasoning. Serve hot, with herb croûtes.

Paring orange zest

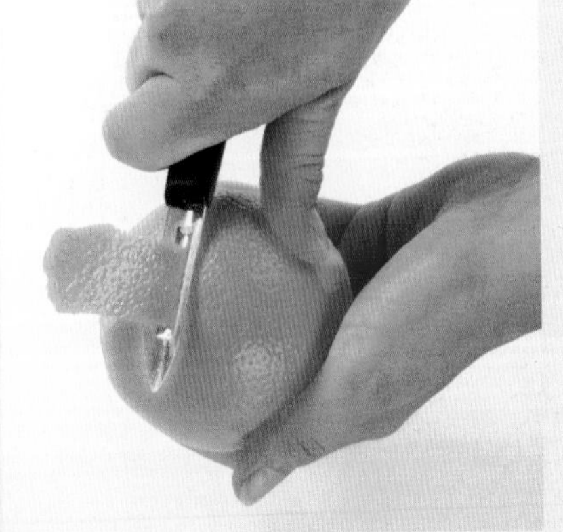

With a vegetable peeler, remove strips of zest, excluding the bitter white pith.

Croûtes and croûtons

These need not be reserved for special occasions. They can turn the most basic of everyday soups into a complete meal.

Herb croûtes
Trim the crusts from slices of bread. Cut each slice into a square or decorative shape. Heat a very thin film of oil in a non-stick frying pan, add the bread, and brown on both sides. Finely chop some parsley or separate into small sprigs. Drain the croûtes on paper towels. Roll the edges of the croûtes in the parsley or put a leaf on top of each one.

Garlic croutons
Trim the crusts from slices of bread and cut into 1 cm (½ in) cubes. Heat a very thin film of oil in a non-stick frying pan. Peel and crush 1 garlic clove and cook for 1 minute. Add the bread cubes and cook, stirring occasionally, until brown all over. Remove, and drain on paper towels.

Gruyère croûtes
Cut slices from a baguette and toast on one side under a hot grill. Remove from the heat and turn the slices over. Grate Gruyère cheese evenly over the untoasted sides of the bread slices. Return to the grill and cook until the cheese has melted and is gently bubbling.

Lobster bisque

A bisque is a purée flavoured with brandy, white wine, and cream, prepared by a complex process that brings out the maximum flavour. When made with lobster, it is perfect for a special occasion. This lighter and healthier version of the traditional recipe is just as delicious.

SERVES 6 **CALS PER SERVING** 192

30 g (1 oz) butter
6 shallots, coarsely chopped
½ carrot, finely chopped
1 cooked large lobster
pinch of cayenne pepper
½ tsp paprika
juice of 1 small lemon
4 tbsp brandy
300 ml (½ pint) dry white wine
1.5 litre (2½ pints) fish stock
60 g (2 oz) long-grain rice
about 3 tbsp single cream (optional)
snipped chives, to garnish

1 Melt the butter in a large saucepan, add the shallots and carrot, and cook gently for about 5 minutes until softened.

2 Using a mallet or wooden rolling pin, crack the lobster shells, remove the cooked meat (page 107), and set aside. Reserve a single large piece of the shell to add to the bisque, and discard the rest.

3 Slice the meat from the large claws and tail of the lobster, reserving a few pieces for garnish.

4 Add the cayenne, paprika, lemon juice, and brandy to the shallots and carrot in the pan, and reduce over a high heat to about 2 tablespoons.

5 Add the wine, fish stock, rice, and reserved lobster shell to the pan, and cook for about 15 minutes until the rice is tender. Remove the lobster shell, and discard.

6 Add the lobster meat (except the garnish) to the pan, and season lightly with salt and pepper. Cook the soup over a low heat just until the lobster is heated through, about 5 minutes.

7 Purée the soup in a food processor or blender until smooth. Pour the purée through a sieve to remove any tiny pieces of lobster shell.

8 Return the purée to the pan, and add the cream if using. Taste for seasoning, and adjust if necessary.

9 Serve the soup at once, garnished with the reserved lobster slices and a sprinkling of snipped chives.

Bouillabaisse

Bouillabaisse, the classic fish soup–stew with the authentic flavours of Provence, is one of the most satisfying and delectable dishes you can bring to your table. In France it is traditionally served with thick slices of toasted bread spread with rouille, a chilli-flavoured mayonnaise.

SERVES 8 **CALS PER SERVING** 337

- 2 tbsp olive oil
- 1 large onion, chopped
- 1 small fennel bulb, sliced
- 4 garlic cloves, crushed
- 1 tbsp chopped parsley
- 1 bay leaf
- 1 litre (1¾ pints) water
- 600 ml (1 pint) fish stock
- 500 g (1 lb) ripe tomatoes, finely chopped
- a strip of orange zest
- ¼ tsp fennel seeds (optional)
- 2–3 potatoes, cut into chunks
- 500 g (1 lb) assorted fish, cut into bite-sized pieces
- 500 g (1 lb) assorted shellfish, shelled
- pinch of saffron threads
- salt and black pepper
- 8 toasted baguette slices, to serve

Rouille

- 3 garlic cloves
- 125 ml (4 fl oz) mayonnaise
- 2 tsp paprika
- 1 tsp mild chilli powder
- 3 tbsp olive oil
- 1 small fresh red chilli, halved, deseeded, and finely chopped
- 1 tbsp lemon juice
- salt

1 Heat the olive oil in a large, heavy saucepan. Add the onion, fennel, garlic, parsley, and bay leaf, and cook, stirring occasionally, for 5 minutes.

2 Add the water, stock, tomatoes, orange zest, and fennel seeds (if using). Bring to a boil, cover, and simmer for 30 minutes.

3 Meanwhile, make the rouille (see box, right). Chill until needed.

4 Add the potatoes to the soup, cover, and simmer for 10 minutes. Do not stir or the potatoes will break up.

5 Add the fish, shellfish, and saffron, and season with salt and pepper. Cover and cook for a few minutes, just until the fish turns opaque.

6 Remove the bay leaf and orange zest, and discard. Serve the bouillabaisse with slices of toasted baguette spread with the rouille.

Making rouille

Use a knife blade to crush the garlic to a paste. Mix in a bowl with the mayonnaise, paprika, and chilli powder.

Pour in the olive oil, drop by drop, whisking constantly as the oil is absorbed into the spicy mayonnaise.

Add the red chilli and lemon juice to the sauce; add salt to taste, and stir well to combine.

Thai spiced soup

SERVES 4–5 **CALS PER SERVING** 238

90 g (3 oz) thin egg noodles
salt and black pepper
500 ml (16 fl oz) chicken stock
1 x 400 g can coconut milk
1 small carrot, coarsely chopped
30 g (1 oz) French beans, cut into 1 cm (½ in) pieces
3 spring onions, thinly sliced
250 g (8 oz) cooked lean boneless and skinless chicken, shredded
125 g (4 oz) mixed green leaves, such as spinach and pak choi, shredded
30 g (1 oz) bean sprouts
2 tbsp fish sauce
2 tsp Thai curry paste (green or red)
¼ cucumber, cut into matchstick-thin strips, and coriander sprigs, to garnish

1 Cook the noodles in boiling salted water for 2–3 minutes, or according to packet instructions, until just tender. Drain and rinse in cold water. Set aside while preparing the soup.

2 Put the stock, coconut milk, carrot, French beans, and spring onions into a large saucepan; bring to a boil.

3 Lower the heat, add the chicken, green leaves, bean sprouts, fish sauce, and spice paste, and cook for 2 minutes or until the green leaves are just wilted. Season to taste with salt and pepper.

4 To serve, divide the cooked noodles among warmed bowls. Ladle the hot soup over the noodles, and garnish with cucumber strips and coriander sprigs.

Chinese crab and sweetcorn soup

SERVES 4 **CALS PER SERVING** 216

375 g (12 oz) frozen sweetcorn kernels
1 litre (1¾ pints) hot chicken stock
3 spring onions, thinly sliced
1 cm (½ in) piece of fresh root ginger, peeled and grated
1 garlic clove, crushed
1 tbsp light soy sauce
250 g (8 oz) cooked crabmeat
1 tbsp cornflour mixed with 2 tbsp cold water
salt and black pepper
sesame oil and coriander sprigs, to serve

1 Purée the sweetcorn with one-quarter of the hot stock in a food processor or blender until smooth.

2 Pour the remaining stock into a pan, and add the spring onions, ginger, garlic, and soy sauce. Heat until bubbles form at the edge.

3 Add the crabmeat and the sweetcorn purée, and continue to heat until bubbles form again. Blend the cornflour mixture into the soup, and cook, stirring occasionally, for 10 minutes or until it thickens slightly. Season to taste with salt and pepper.

4 Pour the soup into bowls, drizzle a little sesame oil over each serving, and garnish with coriander. Serve hot.

Cook's know-how

For a vegetarian version, omit the cooked chicken and use a vegetable stock instead of the chicken stock. You can also vary the vegetables, but their cooking times may be different. Try shredded white cabbage instead of the green leaves and mangetout instead of French beans. Shredded Swiss chard would also be good in this soup, as would a small quantity of sweetcorn kernels or peas, and even a little diced aubergine.

Chicken noodle soup

SERVES 6 **CALS PER SERVING** 261

500 g (1 lb) chicken thighs
500 g (1 lb) carrots, sliced
½ head celery, chopped
1 small onion, peeled but left whole
2–3 garlic cloves, coarsely chopped
a few parsley sprigs
1.75 litres (3 pints) chicken stock
salt and black pepper
125 g (4 oz) thin noodles
chopped fresh dill, to garnish

1 Put the chicken thighs into a large saucepan with the carrots, celery, onion, garlic, and parsley. Pour in the stock and bring to a boil. Using a slotted spoon, skim off the foam that rises to the top of the pan.

2 Lower the heat and season with salt and pepper. Cover and simmer gently for 30 minutes.

3 Skim any fat from the surface of the soup. With a slotted spoon, lift out the parsley, onion, and chicken. Discard the parsley. Chop the onion, and shred the chicken meat, discarding the skin and bones. Set aside.

4 Break the noodles into 5 cm (2 in) pieces and drop them into the soup. Bring to a boil, cover, and simmer for about 10 minutes or until tender.

5 Return the onion and chicken to the soup, heat through, and taste for seasoning. Serve hot, garnished with dill.

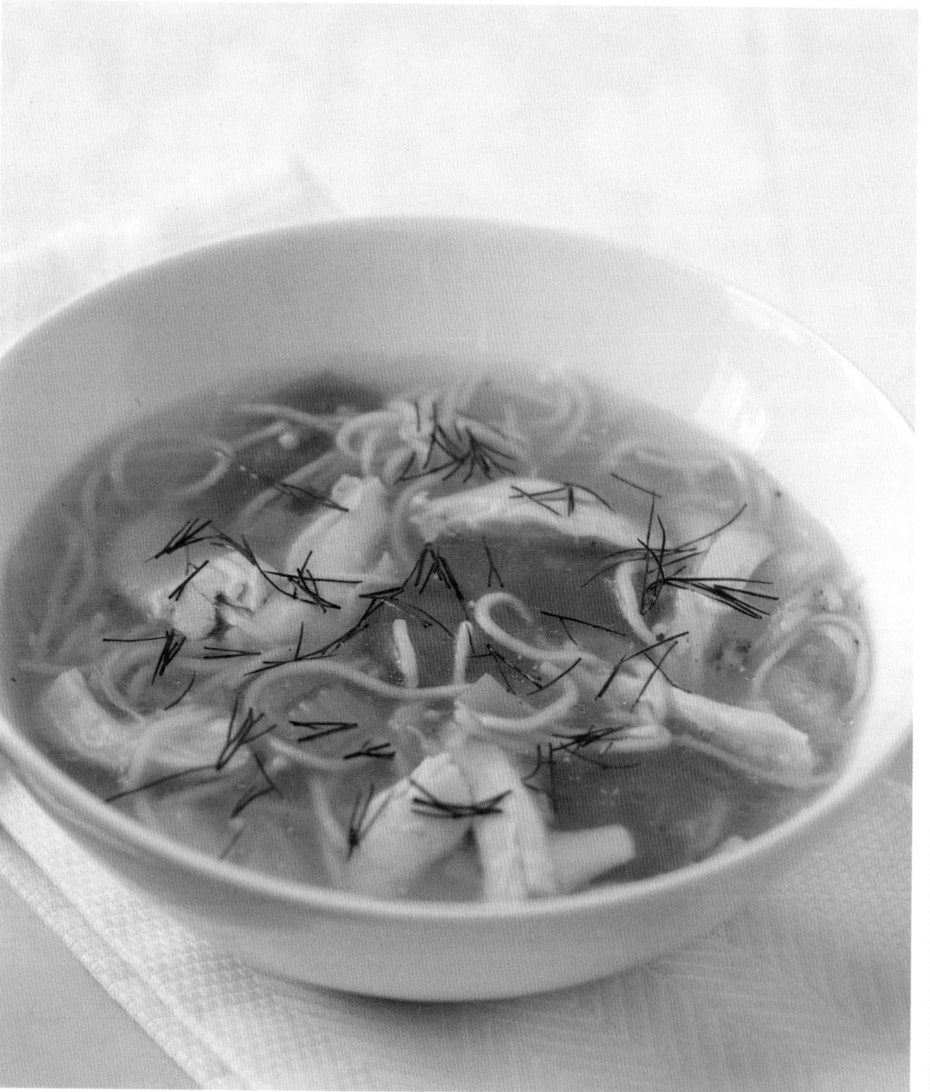

Gazpacho

SERVES 4–6 **CALS PER SERVING** 249–166

1 kg (2 lb) tomatoes, peeled (see box, below), quartered, and deseeded
1 large Spanish onion
1 x 200 g jar roasted peppers (in oil or brine), drained
2 large garlic cloves
600 ml (1 pint) cold vegetable or chicken stock
75 ml (2½ fl oz) olive oil
4 tbsp red wine vinegar
juice of ½ lemon
salt and black pepper

To serve

½ cucumber, diced
1 small green pepper, halved, deseeded, and diced
ice cubes
garlic croûtons (page 28)

1 Coarsely chop the tomatoes, onion, peppers, and garlic. Purée in a food processor or blender with the stock, oil, and vinegar until smooth.

2 Turn the mixture into a bowl and add the lemon juice, and salt and pepper to taste. Cover and chill for at least 1 hour.

3 Serve the soup well chilled in bowls, each one garnished with spoonfuls of diced cucumber, green pepper, garlic croûtons, and a few cubes of ice (if wished).

Peeling tomatoes

Cut the cores from the tomatoes and score an "x" on the base. Immerse the tomatoes in boiling water for 8–15 seconds until their skins start to split. Transfer at once to cold water. When the tomatoes are cool enough to handle, peel off the skin with a small knife.

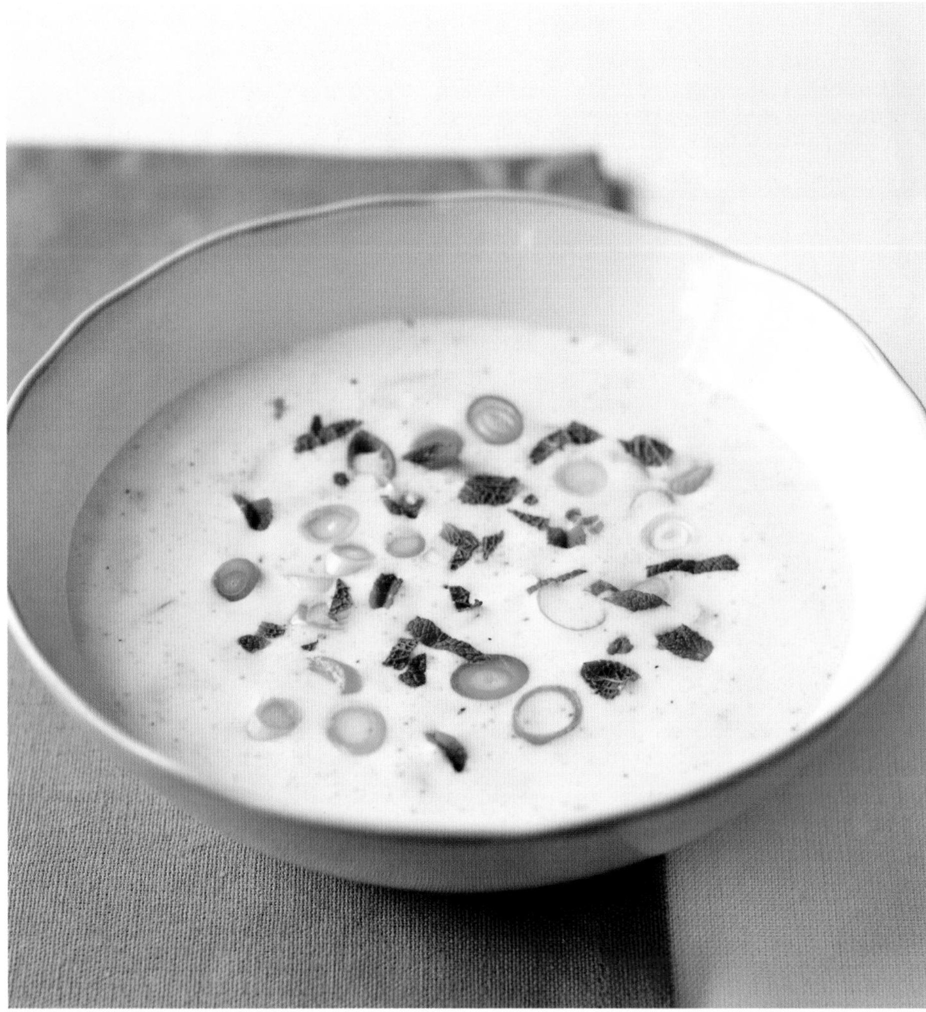

Tzatziki soup

SERVES 4–6 **CALS PER SERVING** 138–92

1 cucumber, deseeded (see box, right) and diced
4 garlic cloves, coarsely chopped
600 g (1 lb 3 oz) plain yogurt
250 ml (8 fl oz) water
1 tbsp olive oil
1 tsp white wine vinegar
1 tsp chopped fresh mint
salt and black pepper
2–3 tbsp chopped fresh mint and 3 spring onions, thinly sliced, to garnish

1 Put one-quarter of the diced cucumber in a food processor or blender. Add the garlic, yogurt, measured water, oil, vinegar, and mint, and purée until smooth. Season well with salt and add pepper to taste.

2 Transfer the soup to a large bowl and stir in the remaining cucumber. Cover and chill for at least 1 hour.

3 Taste for seasoning. Sprinkle the soup with chopped fresh mint and spring onions before serving.

Deseeding a cucumber

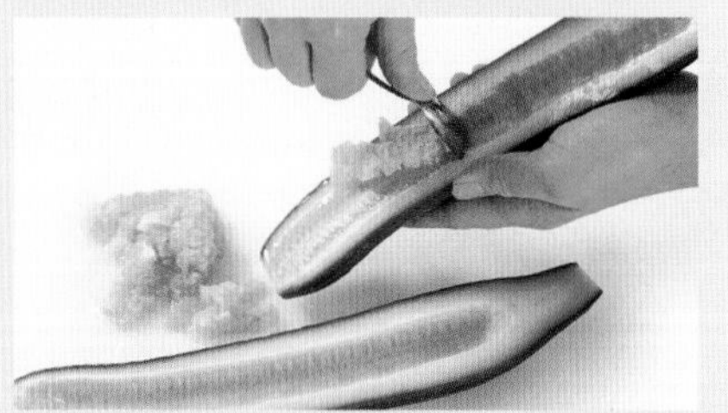

Trim the cucumber with a small knife, then cut it in half, lengthways. With a teaspoon, scoop out and discard the seeds from each cucumber half.

Vichyssoise

SERVES 4–6 **CALS PER SERVING** 251–167

60 g (2 oz) butter
3 large leeks, trimmed and sliced
1 small onion, chopped
2 potatoes, peeled and coarsely chopped
1.25 litres (2 pints) chicken stock
salt and black pepper

To serve

150 ml (¼ pint) single cream
milk (optional)
2 tbsp fresh snipped chives

1 Melt the butter in a large saucepan, add the leeks and onion, and cook very gently, stirring occasionally, for 10–15 minutes until soft but not coloured.

2 Add the potatoes, stock, and salt and pepper to taste, and bring to a boil. Cover and simmer gently for 15–20 minutes until the potatoes are tender.

3 Purée the soup in a food processor or blender until smooth. Pour into a large bowl or pass through a sieve for a smoother finish. Cover and chill for at least 3 hours.

4 To serve, stir in the cream. If the soup is too thick, add a little milk. Taste for seasoning. Garnish with snipped chives before serving.

Chilled curried apple and mint soup

SERVES 6 **CALS PER SERVING** 110

30 g (1 oz) butter
1 onion, coarsely chopped
1 tbsp mild curry powder
900 ml (1½ pints) vegetable stock
750 g (1½ lb) cooking apples, peeled, cored, and coarsely chopped
2 tbsp mango chutney
juice of ½ lemon
7–8 fresh mint sprigs
salt and black pepper
100 g (3½ oz) plain yogurt
a little milk, if needed

1 Melt the butter in a large saucepan, add the onion, and cook gently, stirring occasionally, for a few minutes until soft but not coloured. Add the curry powder and cook, stirring constantly, for 1–2 minutes.

2 Add the stock and chopped apples and bring to a boil, stirring. Cover and simmer for 15 minutes or until the apples are tender.

3 Purée the apple mixture, mango chutney, and lemon juice in a food processor or blender until very smooth.

4 Strip the mint leaves from the stalks, reserving six small sprigs for garnish. Finely chop the mint leaves.

5 Pour the soup into a large bowl, stir in the chopped mint, and add salt and pepper to taste. Cover and chill in the refrigerator for at least 3 hours.

6 Whisk in the yogurt, then taste for seasoning. If the soup is too thick, add a little milk. Garnish with the reserved mint before serving.

Cook's **know-how**

This soup is equally delicious served hot. After puréeing, return the soup to the rinsed-out pan and reheat it gently, stirring occasionally. Stir in the chopped mint, then remove from the heat and swirl in the yogurt. Serve at once.

First courses

In this chapter...

Sardine pâté
page 56

Smoked salmon roulade
page 57

Salmon quenelles
page 58

Smoked salmon terrine
page 59

Asparagus and quails' egg salad
page 60

Asparagus with quick hollandaise
page 60

Chick pea and red pepper salad
page 61

Mozzarella, tomato, and basil salad
page 61

Avocado with tomatoes and mint
page 62

Baked figs with Camembert
page 62

Summer melons
page 63

Prawn cocktail
page 64

Smoked chicken salad with walnuts
page 64

Warm salad with bacon and scallops
page 65

Scallops with cheese sauce
page 66

Moules marinière
page 66

Sardines with coriander
page 67

Jumbo prawns with aïoli
page 69

Seafood blini
page 69

Gravadlax
page 70

Ceviche with tomato and avocado salsa
page 70

Canapés

Home-made canapés are an excellent accompaniment for drinks, or they can be served as an appetizer before dinner. These use toasted bread as a base, but if you prefer, fry the bread in a mixture of oil and butter instead.

SERVES 4 **CALS PER SERVING** 251

4 slices of white bread, crusts removed

Cheese topping

30 g (1 oz) full-fat soft cheese
2 spring onion tops, very finely sliced
4 capers

Anchovy topping

1 tbsp mayonnaise
1 or 2 spring onion tops
8 anchovy fillets, drained
4 prawns, cooked and peeled

Salami topping

15 g (½ oz) butter
2 slices of salami
4 slices of gherkin

Asparagus topping

1 tbsp mayonnaise
6 asparagus tips, cooked and drained
2 slices of radish
a few parsley leaves, to garnish

1 Make the canapé bases: toast the white bread lightly on both sides. Leave to cool.

2 Make the cheese topping: spread one piece of toast with soft cheese and cut into four squares. Arrange the spring onion slices diagonally across the cream cheese. Place a caper on each square.

3 Make the anchovy topping: spread one piece of toast with mayonnaise and cut into four squares. Cut the spring onion tops into four pieces, then make vertical cuts to separate each piece into strands. Cut the anchovies in half and arrange in a lattice pattern on each square. Place a prawn on top, and garnish with the spring onions.

4 Make the salami topping: butter one piece of toast and cut into four rounds with a pastry cutter. Cut each slice of salami in half to make two half-moon-shaped pieces. Roll each piece to form a point at the straight end so that a cornet shape is made. Put one cornet and one piece of gherkin on each canapé.

5 Make the asparagus topping: spread one piece of toast with mayonnaise and cut into four squares. Halve the asparagus tips lengthways. Halve the radish slices and cut away the centres to form four crescents. Put two halved asparagus tips on each square, and arrange a radish slice on top.

Cook's know-how

Ring the changes with different types of salami. The Danish salami used here is mild in flavour, but you may prefer spicier Italian salami, such as *salame di Milano* or *salame di Napoli*.

Sun-dried tomato crostini

SERVES 8 **CALS PER SERVING** 165

1 baguette
2 garlic cloves, crushed
about 3 tbsp olive oil
4 sun-dried tomatoes in oil
30 g (1 oz) butter
salt and black pepper
12 pitted black olives, chopped
¼ tsp fresh rosemary, chopped

1 Cut the baguette into 24 thin slices and arrange them on two baking trays. Add the garlic to the olive oil, then brush about half of the mixture on to the slices of bread. Bake in a preheated oven at 180°C (160°C fan, Gas 4) for 10 minutes.

2 Remove the baking trays from the oven, turn the slices of bread over, brush with a little more garlic oil, and bake for a further 10 minutes or until crisp and golden. Leave to cool.

3 Dry the sun-dried tomatoes with a paper towel and cut them into pieces. Put the tomatoes and butter in the small bowl of a food processor and work until finely chopped (or pound them with a mortar and pestle). Season with salt and pepper to taste.

4 Spread the sun-dried tomato purée over the crostini, arrange the chopped olives on top, and sprinkle with rosemary.

Chèvre croûtes

SERVES 4 **CALS PER SERVING** 450

½ baguette
about 2 tbsp pesto
1 log-shaped goat's cheese
olive oil, for sprinkling
black pepper
radicchio and frisée leaves, to serve (optional)
chervil sprigs, to garnish

1 Cut the baguette into eight slices, 1 cm (½ in) thick, and toast under a hot grill on one side only. Lightly spread the untoasted sides of the baguette slices with the pesto.

2 Cut the goat's cheese into eight slices, 1 cm (½ in) thick, and arrange on top of the pesto. Toast the topped croûtes under the hot grill, 7 cm (3 in) from the heat, for 3 minutes or until the cheese just begins to soften. Remove the grill pan from the heat.

3 Lightly sprinkle a little olive oil and grind a little pepper over each cheese croûte. Return the croûtes to the hot grill, close to the heat, for 3 minutes or until the cheese begins to bubble and is just tinged golden brown.

4 Line a serving platter with radicchio and frisée leaves if you wish, arrange the croûtes on top, and garnish with chervil sprigs. Serve at once.

ITALIAN BRUSCHETTA WITH GOAT'S CHEESE
Substitute eight slices of Italian ciabatta for the baguette. After toasting the topped croûtes in step 3, sprinkle chopped pitted black olives over them and drizzle with extra virgin olive oil. Serve sprinkled with fresh basil leaves.

Brioches with wild mushrooms and watercress

SERVES 6 **CALS PER SERVING** 295

30 g (1 oz) butter
250 g (8 oz) wild mushrooms, trimmed and sliced
60 g (2 oz) watercress, finely chopped, plus extra to garnish
4 tbsp double cream
squeeze of lemon juice
salt and black pepper
6 brioches (page 459)

1 Melt the butter in a large frying pan, add the mushrooms, and cook over a high heat, stirring from time to time, for 3 minutes or until all the liquid has evaporated. Add the watercress, cream, lemon juice, and salt and pepper to taste, and cook until the watercress is just wilted.

2 Hollow out the brioches (see box, right). Spoon in some of the mixture.

3 To serve, transfer the brioches to warmed serving plates and replace the brioche tops. Spoon the remaining mushroom and watercress mixture on to the plates beside the brioches, and garnish with watercress sprigs.

Preparing brioches

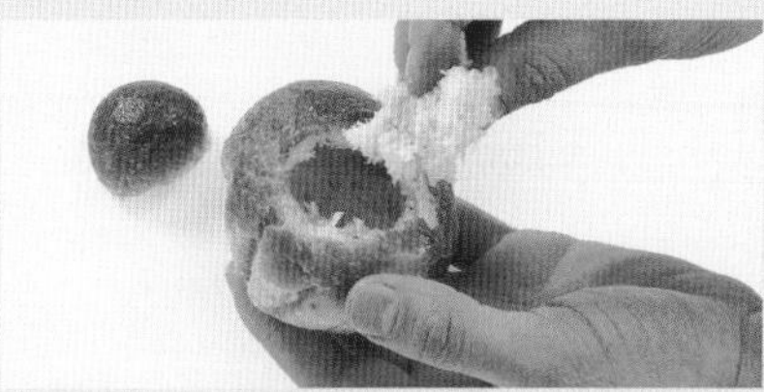

Remove the top of the brioche and set aside. Using your fingers, pull out the soft inside, leaving a 5 mm (¼ in) crust. Repeat with the remaining brioches.

Cheese and olive bites

SERVES 4 **CALS PER SERVING** 317

175 g (6 oz) mature Cheddar cheese, grated
90 g (3 oz) plain flour
15 g (½ oz) butter, plus extra for greasing
1 tsp paprika
½ tsp mustard powder
20 pimiento-stuffed green olives
cayenne pepper and parsley sprigs, to garnish

1 Work the cheese, flour, butter, paprika, and mustard powder in a food processor until the mixture resembles fine breadcrumbs.

2 Flatten the dough mixture, and wrap around the olives (see box, right).

3 Butter a baking tray. Add the wrapped olives and bake in a preheated oven at 200°C (180°C fan, Gas 6) for 15 minutes until the pastry is golden.

4 Remove the cheese and olive bites from the baking tray and leave to cool slightly.

5 Serve warm or cold, sprinkled with cayenne pepper and garnished with parsley sprigs.

Wrapping the olives in the dough

Take a thumb-sized piece of the dough mixture and flatten on a work surface. Place an olive in the middle of the dough. Wrap the dough around the olive, pressing to make it stick. If the pastry is too crumbly and will not stick, add a little water. Repeat with the remaining dough and olives.

Smoked chicken tart

SERVES 6 **CALS PER SERVING** 290

250 g (8 oz) ready-made shortcrust pastry
15 g (½ oz) butter
½ small onion, finely chopped
60 g (2 oz) mushrooms, thinly sliced
60 g (2 oz) baby spinach, washed
salt and black pepper
200 ml (7 fl oz) full-fat crème fraîche
2 large eggs
2 tbsp chopped parsley
90 g (3 oz) cooked smoked chicken, sliced into thin strips
30 g (1 oz) Cheddar cheese, grated

18 CM (7 IN) FLAN DISH OR TIN

1 Roll out the pastry, and use to line the flan dish or tin. Prick the bottom of the pastry with a fork. Line the pastry shell with foil or greaseproof paper, and fill with baking beans, rice, or pasta.

2 Place the dish or tin on a heated baking tray, and bake in a preheated oven at 220°C (200°C fan, Gas 7) for about 15 minutes, removing the foil and beans for the final 5 minutes. Remove from the oven and turn the temperature down to 180°C (160°C fan, Gas 4).

3 Melt the butter in a frying pan, add the onion, cover, and cook gently for 10–15 minutes until soft. Remove the lid, increase the heat, add the mushrooms, and cook for 1–2 minutes. Add the spinach and cook until just wilted, then season and leave to cool.

4 Mix the crème fraîche, eggs, and parsley in a bowl, and season with salt and pepper. Mix the chicken with the cold spinach, spread over the pastry base, and top with the grated cheese. Pour the egg mixture over the top and bake for 25–30 minutes until golden brown and set. Serve warm.

Salmon and prawn filo purses

These crisp, golden purses and their creamy sauce are ideal for a party as they can be prepared up to 24 hours ahead, kept covered with a damp tea towel in the refrigerator, and cooked at the last minute. For a really special occasion, use scallops instead of prawns.

MAKES 8 **CALS PER SERVING** 448

- 500 g (1 lb) tail end of salmon, boned, skinned, and cut into bite-sized pieces
- 250 g (8 oz) cooked peeled prawns
- lemon juice, for sprinkling
- salt and black pepper
- 1 x 250 g packet filo pastry
- 60 g (2 oz) butter, melted
- butter, for greasing
- lemon slices and dill sprigs, to garnish

White wine sauce

- 100 ml (3½ fl oz) dry white wine
- 300 ml (½ pint) double cream
- 1 tsp chopped fresh dill

1 Combine the salmon pieces and prawns. Sprinkle with lemon juice, and add salt and pepper to taste. Set aside.

2 Cut the filo into sixteen 18 cm (7 in) squares. Brush two squares with a little of the melted butter, covering the remaining squares with a damp tea towel. Make a filo purse (see box, right). Repeat to make eight purses.

3 Line a baking sheet with non-stick paper and brush with butter. Add the filo purses, lightly brush with the remaining melted butter, and bake in a preheated oven at 190°C (170°C fan, Gas 5) for 15–20 minutes, until crisp and golden.

4 Meanwhile, make the sauce: pour the wine into a saucepan, and boil rapidly until it has reduced to about 3 tbsp. Add the cream and simmer until it reaches a light coating consistency. Remove from the heat and add the dill, and salt and pepper to taste.

5 Pour the sauce into a bowl. Garnish the purses with the lemon slices and dill sprigs and serve with the warm sauce.

Making a filo purse

Place one-eighth of the salmon and prawn mixture in the middle of one buttered filo pastry square.

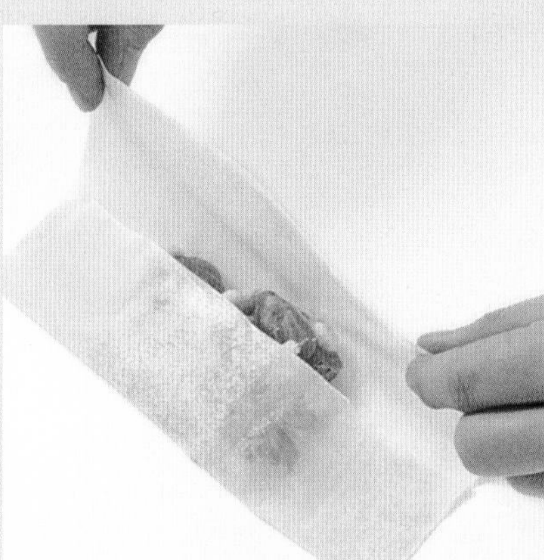

Fold two sides of filo pastry over the mixture to form a rectangle. Take the two open ends and fold one over the filling and the other underneath.

Place this parcel on the second buttered pastry square and draw up the edges. Squeeze and twist the pastry close to the filling.

Herbed mini sausage rolls

MAKES 36 **CALS EACH** 83

knob of butter
1 large onion, finely chopped
500 g (1 lb) pork sausagemeat
finely grated zest and juice of ½ lemon
2 tbsp chopped parsley
1 tsp chopped fresh thyme
salt and black pepper
375 g (12 oz) ready-made puff pastry
2 tsp sun-dried tomato paste
beaten egg, to seal and glaze

1 Melt the butter in a frying pan, and fry the onion gently for about 8 minutes until soft. Set aside to cool.

2 Put the sausagemeat, lemon zest and juice, and herbs into a bowl. Add the onion, season with salt and pepper, and mix with your hands until thoroughly combined.

3 Cut the pastry in half, and roll out each piece on a lightly floured surface to a 25 x 30 cm (10 x 12 in) rectangle. Cut each rectangle lengthways into three strips – so you have six long strips.

4 Spread a little tomato paste along the middle of each strip. Divide the sausagemeat mixture into sixths, then spread one-sixth over each line of tomato paste to cover it completely from one end to the other. Brush the pastry around the filling with beaten egg, fold over the pastry lengthways to enclose the filling, and seal the long edges by pressing with a fork. Lay the strips on two baking trays lined with baking parchment, and chill for 30 minutes.

5 Slice each strip crosswise into six pieces to make 36 sausage rolls, and separate the pieces a little. Brush with beaten egg, and make two small slashes in the top of each piece. Bake in a preheated oven at 200°C (180°C fan, Gas 6) for 25–30 minutes until golden. Serve warm.

Nachos grande

SERVES 6 **CALS PER SERVING** 396

2 tbsp sunflower oil
1 onion, finely chopped
½ green pepper, chopped
3 garlic cloves, crushed
1 x 225 g can chopped tomatoes
½ –1 fresh green chilli, halved, deseeded, and finely chopped
½ tsp chilli powder
½ tsp paprika
1 x 400 g can refried beans
75 ml (2½ fl oz) water
1 x 75 g packet tortilla chips
¼ tsp ground cumin
175 g (6 oz) Cheddar cheese, grated
extra paprika, to garnish

1 Heat the oil in a frying pan, add the onion, green pepper, and garlic, and cook gently, stirring occasionally, for 5 minutes or until softened.

2 Add the tomatoes and chilli, and cook over a medium heat for a further 5 minutes, or until most of the liquid has evaporated.

3 Stir in the chilli powder and paprika, and cook for 3 minutes, then add the refried beans, breaking them up with a fork. Add the measured water and cook, stirring from time to time, for 8–10 minutes, until the mixture thickens.

4 Spoon the beans into a baking dish, arrange the tortilla chips around the edge, and sprinkle with cumin. Sprinkle the cheese over the beans and tortilla chips.

5 Bake in a preheated oven at 200°C (180°C fan, Gas 6) for 15–20 minutes until the cheese has melted. Sprinkle paprika on top before serving.

Spicy meatballs

SERVES 8 **CALS PER SERVING** 481

1 kg (2 lb) lean minced beef
1 small onion, grated
2 garlic cloves, crushed
1 egg, beaten
90 g (3 oz) fresh breadcrumbs
2 tbsp tomato purée
2 tbsp paprika
2 tbsp chopped fresh coriander
salt and black pepper
3 tbsp olive oil, for frying
chopped parsley, to garnish
crudités, to serve

Sesame dip

2 tbsp soy sauce
2 tbsp sesame oil
1 tbsp rice wine or sherry
1 spring onion, thinly sliced
1 tbsp sesame seeds, toasted

1 Make the sesame dip: whisk all the ingredients together and set aside.

2 Combine the meatball ingredients in a bowl. Using your hands, roll the mixture into little balls.

3 Heat the oil in a frying pan, and cook the meatballs, in batches, over a medium heat for 5 minutes or until browned, firm, and cooked through. Garnish, and serve warm with the sesame dip and crudités.

Spicy chicken wings

SERVES 4–6 **CALS PER SERVING** 206–137

500 g (1 lb) chicken wings
2 tbsp sunflower oil
1 tsp lemon juice
1 tbsp paprika
1 tsp ground cumin
½ tsp marjoram
½ tsp mild chilli powder
black pepper
parsley sprigs and cress, to garnish

To serve

½ red pepper, cut into strips
½ celery head, cut into sticks, plus leaves
blue cheese dressing (page 397)

1 Cut the chicken wings in half and put the pieces in a shallow dish.

2 In a large bowl, combine the oil, lemon juice, paprika, cumin, oregano, chilli powder, and black pepper. Brush the mixture over the chicken, cover, and leave to marinate at room temperature for at least 1 hour.

3 Line a large baking tray with foil and place a rack on top. Lay the chicken wings in a single layer on the rack, and cook in a preheated oven at 200°C (180°C fan, Gas 6) for 40 minutes, or until browned, sizzling, and crispy.

4 Remove the chicken from the rack and drain on paper towels. Serve with red pepper strips, celery sticks, and blue cheese dressing, and garnish with parsley and cress.

Andalucian mushrooms

SERVES 4 **CALS PER SERVING** 92

250 g (8 oz) button mushrooms
2 tbsp olive oil
6 shallots, chopped
3 garlic cloves, crushed
30 g (1 oz) serrano ham, cut into strips
¼ tsp mild chilli powder
¼ tsp paprika (preferably sweet smoked)
1 tsp lemon juice
90 ml (3 fl oz) dry red wine
4 tbsp chopped flat-leaf parsley, to garnish

1 Pull the mushroom stems from the caps. Heat the olive oil in a frying pan until hot, add the shallots and half of the garlic, and cook, stirring, for about 5 minutes until soft but not coloured. Add the mushroom caps and stems, and cook, stirring, for 3 minutes until lightly browned.

2 Add the serrano ham, chilli powder, and paprika, and cook, stirring constantly, for 1 minute.

3 Add the lemon juice, and cook over a high heat for a few minutes until the liquid has almost evaporated and the mushrooms are just tender.

4 Add the red wine and continue to cook over a high heat until the liquid is reduced and flavourful. Stir in the remaining garlic, sprinkle with the chopped parsley, and serve at once.

Caponata

SERVES 4–6 **CALS PER SERVING** 297–198

about 4 tbsp olive oil
1 large aubergine, cut into 1 cm (½ in) chunks
½ head celery, diced
2 onions, thinly sliced
125 g (4 oz) tomato purée
60 g (2 oz) sugar
125–175 ml (4–6 fl oz) red wine vinegar
125 g (4 oz) pitted green olives
30 g (1 oz) capers (optional)
1–2 garlic cloves, crushed
30 g (1 oz) parsley, chopped
salt and black pepper

1 Heat 3 tbsp of the oil in a large saucepan, add the aubergine, and cook gently, stirring, for 8 minutes or until tender. Remove the aubergine from the pan with a slotted spoon.

2 Heat the remaining oil in the pan, add the celery, and cook gently, stirring occasionally, for 7 minutes or until browned.

3 Return the aubergine to the pan with the onions, tomato purée, sugar, and vinegar. Cook over a medium heat for 10 minutes to reduce the harshness of the vinegar. Add a little water if the mixture becomes too thick and starts sticking to the pan.

4 Remove from the heat, and add the green olives, capers, if using, garlic, and half of the parsley. Add salt and pepper to taste. Cover and leave to cool. Sprinkle with the remaining parsley, and serve.

Hummus

SERVES 6 **CALS PER SERVING** 150

2 x 400 g cans chick peas, drained
2–3 garlic cloves, coarsely chopped
1 tbsp tahini paste, or to taste
3 tbsp olive oil, or to taste
juice of 1 lemon, or to taste
salt and black pepper

1 Purée the chick peas, garlic, tahini paste, oil, and lemon juice in a food processor or blender until smooth.

2 Add salt and pepper to taste, and more oil, tahini, and lemon juice if you think it needs it, then purée again.

3 Spoon into dishes. If you like, garnish with rosemary, red pepper, and olives.

Aubergine dip

SERVES 4 **CALS PER SERVING** 179

750 g (1½ lb) aubergines
salt and black pepper
2 shallots, halved
1–2 garlic cloves
4 tbsp lemon juice
4 tbsp olive oil
4 tbsp chopped parsley
2 tbsp tahini paste
olive oil and chopped parsley, to garnish (optional)

1 Cut the aubergines in half lengthways. Score the flesh in a lattice pattern, sprinkle with salt, and leave to stand for 30 minutes.

2 Rinse the aubergine halves with cold water, and pat dry with paper towels. Place on a baking tray and bake in a preheated oven at 200°C (180°C fan, Gas 6) for 20 minutes.

3 Add the shallots and garlic to the baking tray, and bake for 15 minutes.

4 Purée the aubergines, shallots, and garlic with the lemon juice, oil, parsley, tahini paste, and salt and pepper to taste in a food processor until smooth.

5 Turn the dip into a bowl. Cover and chill for at least 1 hour before serving. If you wish, add a splash of olive oil and sprinkle with parsley just before serving.

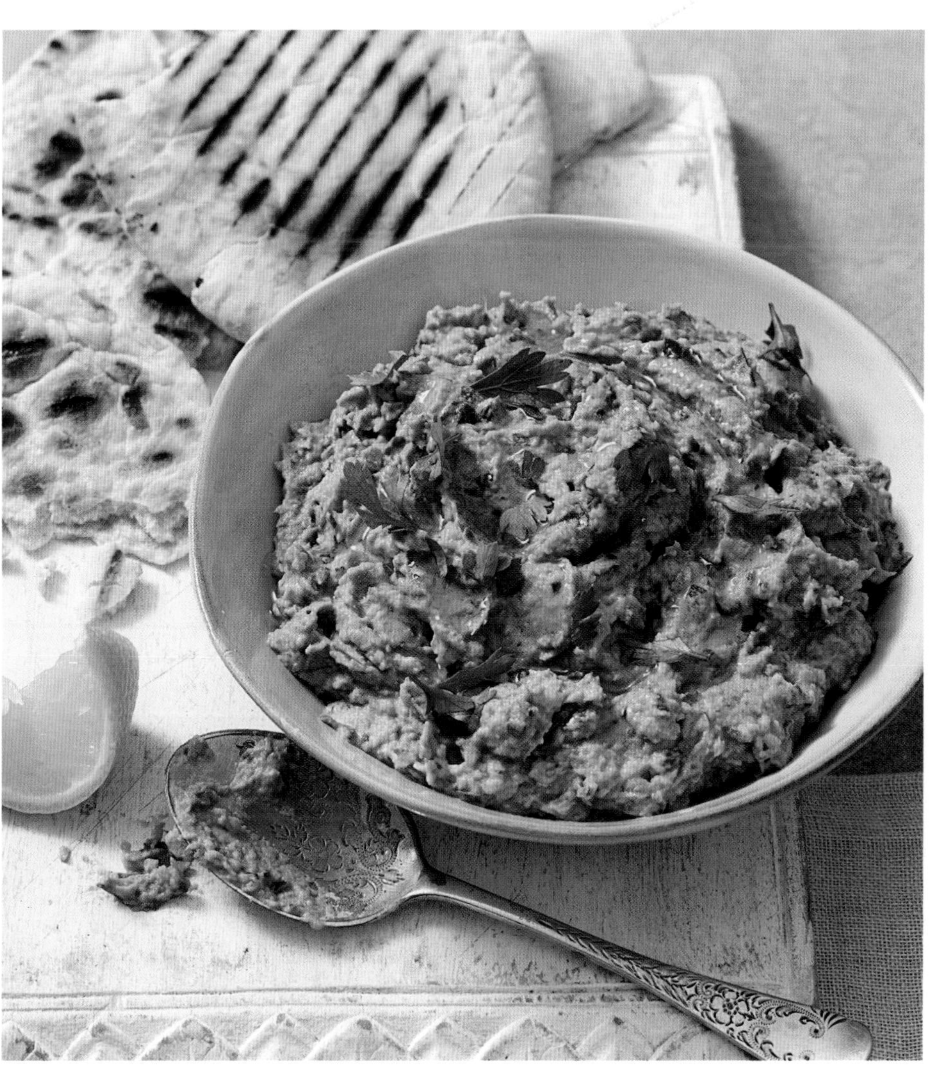

Taramasalata

SERVES 4 **CALS PER SERVING** 714

500 g (1 lb) smoked cod's roe, skinned and coarsely chopped
4 small slices of white bread, crusts removed
4 tbsp lemon juice
1 large garlic clove, coarsely chopped
250 ml (8 fl oz) olive oil
salt and black pepper

1 Purée the cod's roe in a food processor or blender until smooth. Break the bread into a bowl, add the lemon juice, and let the bread soak for 1 minute. Add to the cod's roe with the garlic, and purée until smooth.

2 Pour the oil into the mixture, a little at a time, and purée until all the oil has been absorbed. Add salt and pepper to taste. Turn the taramasalata into a bowl. Cover and chill for at least 1 hour before serving as a dip or pâté.

Classic olive tapenade

SERVES 4 **CALS PER SERVING** 188

1 garlic clove, roughly chopped
juice of 1 lemon
3 tbsp capers, drained and chopped
6 anchovy fillets in olive oil, drained and chopped
250 g (8 oz) black olives, pitted
20 g (¾ oz) fresh flat-leaf parsley, roughly chopped
about 3 tbsp olive oil
salt and black pepper

1 Put the garlic, lemon juice, capers, and anchovies into a food processor or blender, and purée for about 10 seconds until quite smooth.

2 Add the olives and parsley, and purée again. With the machine running, add enough olive oil to make a paste. Taste the tapenade, and season with salt and pepper if necessary.

3 Serve at once, or refrigerate in a covered container for up to 3 days and allow to come to room temperature before serving.

Brandied chicken liver pâté

SERVES 8 **CALS PER SERVING** 268

125 g (4 oz) bread, crusts removed
1 garlic clove, coarsely chopped
125 g (4 oz) streaky bacon rashers, rinds removed, coarsely chopped
2 tsp chopped fresh thyme
500 g (1 lb) chicken livers, trimmed
1 egg
4 tbsp brandy
½ tsp grated nutmeg
salt and black pepper
60 g (2 oz) butter, melted

1 KG (2 LB) LOAF TIN OR TERRINE

1 Line the loaf tin with foil, leaving 5 cm (2 in) foil overhanging on each side.

2 Cut the bread into thick chunks, and work them with the garlic in a food processor to form fine breadcrumbs. Add the bacon and thyme, and work until finely chopped.

3 Add the chicken livers, egg, brandy, and nutmeg, season with salt and pepper, and purée until smooth. Add the butter and purée again.

4 Put the pâté mixture into the prepared loaf tin, level the surface, and fold the foil over the top. Place in a roasting tin, pour in boiling water to come about halfway up the side of the loaf tin, and bake in a preheated oven at 160°C (140°C fan, Gas 3) for 1 hour.

5 Test the pâté for doneness (see box, below). Leave the pâté to cool completely, then cover, and leave to chill in the refrigerator overnight. To serve, cut the pâté into slices.

Is it cooked?

Insert a skewer into the middle of the pâté. If it comes out hot and clean, the pâté is cooked.

Pan-fried pâté

These little bacon-wrapped chicken liver and spinach pâtés are easy to make, and they are at their most delicious when served with a tangy salad of sliced tomatoes and chopped onions in a herb vinaigrette dressing.

SERVES 4 **CALS PER SERVING** 392

30 g (1 oz) butter
125 g (4 oz) chicken livers
5 shallots, coarsely chopped
125 g (4 oz) lean bacon rashers, rinds removed, coarsely chopped
60 g (2 oz) spinach leaves, shredded
2 tbsp chopped parsley
1 tsp chopped fresh thyme leaves
1 garlic clove, crushed
salt and black pepper
8 streaky bacon rashers, rinds removed
toasted bread and cornichons, to serve

1 Using a pair of kitchen scissors, trim the chicken livers, cutting away any membranes. Melt half of the butter in a frying pan, add the livers, and cook gently, stirring occasionally, for 3 minutes or until they are browned on the outside but still pink inside.

2 Purée the chicken livers in a food processor until smooth. Turn into a large bowl and set aside.

3 Melt the remaining butter in the frying pan, add the shallots, and cook gently, stirring occasionally, for a few minutes until soft but not coloured.

4 Add the shallots to the chicken livers with the chopped bacon, spinach, parsley, thyme, and garlic. Season with salt and pepper. Purée half of this mixture until smooth, then stir it into the remaining mixture in the bowl.

5 Shape and wrap the chicken liver pâtés (see box, opposite).

6 Heat a frying pan, add the pâtés, and cook them gently until browned all over. Lower the heat, cover, and cook over a very gentle heat for 35–40 minutes.

7 Serve the pan-fried pâtés either warm or at room temperature, accompanied by the toast and cornichons.

Shaping and wrapping the pâtés

Mould the pâté mixture into eight equal-sized oval shapes, using your hands.

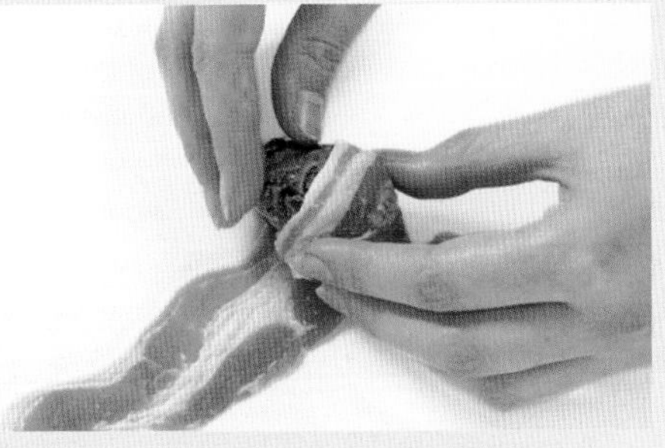

Lay a bacon rasher flat, put a pâté oval at one end and roll the bacon around it.

Twist the rasher around the ends to enclose the pâté, then tuck it in underneath to secure. Repeat with the remaining bacon rashers and pâté.

Three fish terrine

Three kinds of smoked fish – trout, salmon, and mackerel – are blended with soft cheese, arranged in layers, then wrapped in smoked salmon for a subtle variety of flavours. The finished terrine can be frozen for up to 1 month.

SERVES 10 **CALS PER SERVING** 424

sunflower oil, for greasing
175–250 g (6–8 oz) smoked salmon slices
salt and black pepper
watercress, to garnish

Trout pâté

175 g (6 oz) smoked trout
90 g (3 oz) butter
90 g (3 oz) full-fat soft cheese
1½ tbsp lemon juice

Salmon pâté

125 g (4 oz) smoked salmon pieces
60 g (2 oz) butter
60 g (2 oz) full-fat soft cheese
1½ tbsp lemon juice
1 tbsp tomato purée
1 tbsp chopped fresh dill

Mackerel pâté

175 g (6 oz) smoked mackerel
90 g (3 oz) butter
90 g (3 oz) full-fat soft cheese
1½ tbsp lemon juice

1.2 LITRE (2 PINT) LOAF TIN OR TERRINE

1 Make the trout pâté: remove the skin and bones from the trout and purée with the butter, cheese, lemon juice, and salt and pepper to taste in a food processor until smooth and well blended. Turn into a bowl, cover, and chill.

2 Make the salmon pâté: purée the smoked salmon pieces, butter, cheese, lemon juice, tomato purée, dill, and salt and pepper to taste in a food processor until smooth and well blended. Turn into a bowl, cover, and chill.

3 Make the mackerel pâté: remove the skin and bones from the mackerel and purée with the butter, cheese, lemon juice, and salt and pepper to taste in a food processor until smooth and well blended. Turn into a bowl, cover, and chill.

4 Assemble the terrine (see box, right). Cover and chill overnight.

5 To serve, carefully turn out the terrine, cut into thick slices, and arrange on individual serving plates with a watercress garnish.

Assembling the terrine

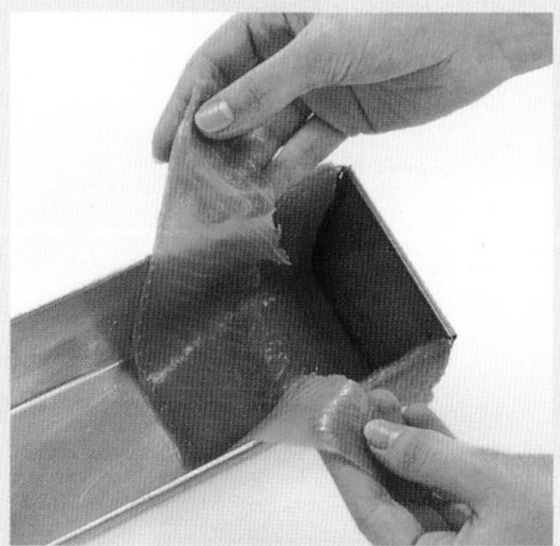

Oil the loaf tin and line with overlapping slices of smoked salmon. Arrange them crosswise and allow 3.5–5 cm (1½–2 in) to overhang the sides of the tin.

Turn the trout pâté into the loaf tin and spread it evenly with a palette knife, levelling the surface. If necessary, wet the knife to prevent sticking. Add the salmon pâté in the same way, and then top with the mackerel pâté.

Fold the smoked salmon over the mackerel pâté, tucking in the ends.

Double salmon tian

SERVES 6 **CALS PER SERVING** 232

650 g (1 lb 5 oz) fresh salmon fillet, skinned
200 g (7 oz) full-fat soft cheese
4 tbsp chopped fresh dill
salt and black pepper

To serve

6 small slices of smoked salmon, total weight about 200 g (7 oz)
50–60 g (1½–2 oz) fresh rocket or mizuna leaves
6 lemon wedges, to serve

6 X 7.5 CM (3 IN) METAL RINGS OR 150 ML (5 FL OZ) RAMEKINS

1 Wrap the fresh salmon tightly in foil, and bake in a preheated oven at 190°C (170°C fan, Gas 5) for 15–20 minutes or until just cooked. Leave to cool in the foil.

2 Mix the cheese and dill in a large bowl until smooth. Flake the cooled salmon into the bowl, including any fish juices and jelly, but discarding any bones. Season well with salt and pepper, and fold gently together.

3 Put the metal rings on a flat plate or baking tray (if using ramekins, line them with cling film). Divide the salmon and cheese mixture among them, smoothing the surface with the back of a metal spoon. Cover and refrigerate for at least 2 hours, overnight if possible.

4 Lift each ring filled with salmon using a fish slice. Place on a serving plate, then carefully ease off the ring. (If using ramekins, invert the salmon onto the plate and gently remove the cling film.) Top each tian with a loosely curled piece of smoked salmon. Divide the salad leaves among six plates and serve with lemon wedges for squeezing.

Smoked haddock mousse

SERVES 6 **CALS PER SERVING** 217

250 g (8 oz) smoked haddock, skinned
juice of ½ lemon
salt and black pepper
250 g (8 oz) full-fat soft cheese
2 tbsp reduced-calorie mayonnaise
1 tbsp turmeric

6 SMALL BOWLS

1 Line a baking sheet with a long, wide piece of foil, and place the haddock on it. Sprinkle the fish with the lemon juice, and season with pepper. Bring the long edges of the foil together, and fold to seal. Bring each of the short edges together, and fold to seal, forming a parcel.

2 Bake the fish in a preheated oven at 160°C (140°C fan, Gas 3) for 7–10 minutes, or until the fish is just cooked and flakes easily with a fork. Set aside in the foil parcel until cold.

3 Flake the fish, removing any bones. Place in a food processor or blender, adding any juices that are left on the foil. Add the cheese, mayonnaise, and turmeric. Season lightly with salt.

4 Process or blend the mixture until smooth, then check and adjust the seasoning if necessary.

5 Lightly oil the bowls and spoon in the fish mixture. Cover and chill for at least 3 hours, when the mixture will be set to a soft mousse.

6 Serve with a sprig of parsley and slices of plain wholemeal toast (the cheese adds richness so no butter is needed).

Sardine pâté

SERVES 8 **CALS PER SERVING** 197

2 x 125 g cans sardines in oil, drained, bones removed
125 g (4 oz) butter, softened
125 g (4 oz) low-fat soft cheese
3 tbsp lemon juice
black pepper
lemon twists and parsley sprigs, to garnish

1 Purée the sardines, butter, cheese, and lemon juice in a food processor until almost smooth. Add pepper and more lemon juice to taste.

2 Divide the sardine mixture among eight small ramekins (or put into one large bowl) and level the surface. Cover and chill in the refrigerator for at least 30 minutes.

3 Serve chilled, garnished with lemon twists and parsley sprigs.

PRAWN PÂTÉ

Substitute 250 g (8 oz) cooked peeled prawns for the sardines.

Smoked salmon roulade

The richness of the cheese and smoked-salmon layers is offset by a thin layer of tomatoes that provides a fresh and tangy contrast. Here the roulade is served in slices, but you could serve it whole, with just a few slices cut at one end.

SERVES 4–6 **CALS PER SERVING** 407–271

15 g (½ oz) butter
1 garlic clove, crushed
150 g (5 oz) spinach leaves, cooked, squeezed dry, and chopped
4 eggs, separated
1 tsp chopped fresh rosemary
pinch of grated nutmeg
salt and black pepper
salad leaves and lemon slices, to garnish

Filling

200 g (7 oz) full-fat soft cheese
3 tbsp Greek-style yogurt or 2 tbsp milk
4 spring onions, thinly sliced
125 g (4 oz) thinly sliced smoked salmon
2 ripe tomatoes, thinly sliced

23 X 33 CM (9 X 13 IN) SWISS ROLL TIN

1 Make the roulade: line the Swiss roll tin with a sheet of baking parchment, cutting the corners of the paper so that it fits snugly into the tin.

2 Put the butter into a saucepan, add the garlic, and cook gently until the butter melts. Remove from the heat. Stir in the spinach.

3 Add the egg yolks, rosemary, and nutmeg, season to taste, and beat into the spinach mixture.

4 In another bowl, whisk the egg whites until firm but not dry. Fold 2–3 spoonfuls into the spinach mixture, then fold in the remainder.

5 Spread the mixture in the Swiss roll tin, and bake in a preheated oven at 190°C (170°C fan, Gas 5) for 10–12 minutes until the mixture feels firm. Remove from the oven, cover with a damp tea towel, and leave to cool.

6 Meanwhile, make the filling: beat the cheese and yogurt or milk together until smooth, then stir in the onions.

7 Turn out the cooled roulade and peel off the paper. Fill and roll the roulade (see box, right).

8 Wrap the roulade in foil, then overwrap with a damp tea towel, and chill overnight.

9 To serve, trim off the hard edges of the roulade, cut into thick slices, and arrange on a serving platter. Garnish with salad leaves and lemon slices.

PARMA HAM ROULADE

Substitute 125 g (4 oz) thinly sliced Parma ham for the smoked salmon.

Filling and rolling the roulade

Arrange the slices of smoked salmon on top of the roulade, leaving a 2.5 cm (1 in) border on each side.

Spread the cheese filling over the salmon, using a palette knife. Arrange the tomato slices over half of the cheese filling, looking at it widthways.

Roll up the roulade, starting from the end where the tomato slices have been placed.

Cook's **know-how**

This roulade can be prepared up to the end of step 8 up to 2 days ahead, making it ideal for a dinner party or other special occasion.

Salmon quenelles

Quenelles are delicate little dumplings, traditionally oval but sometimes round, which can be made with fish, meat, or chicken. The name comes from Knödel, the German word for dumpling. They are simple to make, and yet they look elegant and impressive as if they require professional skills.

SERVES 6 **CALS PER SERVING** 511

500 g (1 lb) salmon fillet, skinned, boned, and cut into chunks
2 egg whites
salt and white pepper
150 ml (¼ pint) double cream
lemon slices and flat-leaf parsley sprigs, to garnish

Asparagus sauce

90 ml (3 fl oz) dry white wine
250 g (9 oz) young asparagus, trimmed, woody parts removed
300 ml (½ pint) double cream

1 Make the quenelles: purée the salmon, egg whites, and salt and pepper to taste in a food processor until completely smooth.

2 With the machine still running, pour in the cream in a steady stream until it is thoroughly blended. Turn the mixture into a large bowl, cover, and chill for about 2 hours.

3 Bring a saucepan of salted water to a simmer. Shape and cook the quenelles (see box, right). Keep the quenelles warm while you make the sauce.

4 Make the asparagus sauce: pour the wine into a saucepan and boil rapidly for about 2 minutes until it is reduced to a thin syrup.

5 Cook the asparagus in a pan of boiling salted water for 3–5 minutes until tender. Drain, then cut off the asparagus tips, and reserve them for garnish.

6 Purée the reduced wine and the asparagus stalks until very smooth.

7 Boil the cream in a saucepan for 4 minutes or until it is thick enough to coat the back of a metal spoon. Stir in the purée, and taste for seasoning.

8 Pour the sauce on to warmed plates, arrange the quenelles on top, and garnish with the reserved asparagus tips, and the lemon slices and parsley sprigs.

Cook's know-how

Take care not to overprocess the purée when blending the quenelle mixture. If you work it too hard, this could cause the cream to curdle.

Shaping and cooking the quenelles

Dip a dessertspoon into the simmering water, then take a spoonful of the chilled quenelle mixture. Using a second warm, wetted dessertspoon or your fingers, mould into an oval. Repeat with the remaining mixture.

Lower some quenelles into the simmering water and cook for 6–10 minutes until they are firm when pressed with a finger. Do not put too many into the pan at one time.

Remove the quenelles with a slotted spoon, drain well, and keep them warm while you cook the remainder.

Smoked salmon terrine

SERVES 8 **CALS PER SERVING** 186

275 g (9 oz) thinly sliced smoked salmon
black pepper
250 g (8 oz) low-fat soft cheese
125 g (4 oz) unsalted butter, softened
2 tbsp creamed horseradish
4 canned anchovy fillets (more if you wish)
1–2 tbsp chopped fresh parsley or dill, or a mixture of the two

To serve

salad leaves, tossed in your favourite dressing
lime or lemon wedges

500 G (1 LB) LOAF TIN

1 Dampen the loaf tin and line with cling film, letting it overhang the sides. Divide the smoked salmon into four equal piles. Cover the base of the tin with a quarter of the salmon and sprinkle with black pepper.

2 Put the soft cheese, butter, horseradish, anchovies, and parsley or dill into a blender or food processor, season with black pepper, and work to a very smooth paste. Do not add salt. (If you haven't got a blender or food processor, beat the mixture vigorously with a wooden spoon.)

3 Spread a third of the paste over the salmon in the tin and cover with a second layer of salmon. Continue alternating the layers, finishing with salmon. Tightly pull the cling film over the top and press down firmly. Refrigerate for at least 6 hours, preferably overnight.

4 To serve, put the terrine in the freezer for 30 minutes (this will make it easy to slice). Turn it out of its tin and discard the cling film, then cut into 16 thin slices. Serve 2 slices on each plate, on a bed of dressed salad leaves, with lime or lemon wedges for squeezing.

Asparagus and quails' egg salad

SERVES 6 **CALS PER SERVING** 222

12 quails' eggs
18 asparagus spears
1 x 340 g jar roasted artichoke hearts in oil

To serve
1 tbsp balsamic vinegar
salt and black pepper
about 30 g (1 oz) Parmesan shavings

1 Put the eggs in a pan of cold water, bring to a boil, and boil for 3 minutes (start timing as soon as the water comes to a boil). Drain and rinse under cold running water, then peel immediately. The shells come off very easily when the eggs are just cooked.

2 Peel the asparagus stems with a potato or vegetable peeler if they are woody, then cut the asparagus into 5 cm (2 in) lengths. Cook in boiling salted water for about 2 minutes until only just tender. Drain into a sieve and rinse thoroughly under cold running water, then pat dry with kitchen paper.

3 Drain the artichoke hearts, reserving the oil. Cut the artichokes and eggs lengthways in half. Divide the artichokes and asparagus among six plates, and top each serving with four egg halves.

4 Make a dressing by mixing 3 tbsp of the reserved oil from the artichoke jar with the balsamic vinegar, and season with salt and pepper.

5 To serve, drizzle the dressing over the salad, top with Parmesan shavings, and serve with crusty rolls.

Asparagus with quick hollandaise

SERVES 4 **CALS PER SERVING** 384

625 g (1¼ lb) asparagus
salt and black pepper
lemon twists, to garnish

Quick hollandaise
1 tbsp lemon juice
1 tbsp white wine vinegar
4 egg yolks, at room temperature
150 g (5 oz) unsalted butter, melted

1 Cut any woody ends off the asparagus and discard. Lay the spears flat in salted boiling water in a shallow pan (a sauté pan or frying pan is ideal), and simmer gently for 3–4 minutes until the asparagus is tender but still firm.

2 Meanwhile, make the quick hollandaise: three-quarters fill a food processor or blender with hot water from the kettle and pulse or process briefly, to warm the bowl. Pour the water away and dry the bowl.

3 Put the lemon juice and vinegar into the warm bowl of the food processor or blender, add the egg yolks, and pulse or process briefly.

4 With the machine running, gradually pour in the hot melted butter, and process until thick and creamy. Season to taste.

5 To serve, drain the asparagus. Ladle the hollandaise sauce on to warmed plates, arrange the asparagus on top, and garnish with lemon twists.

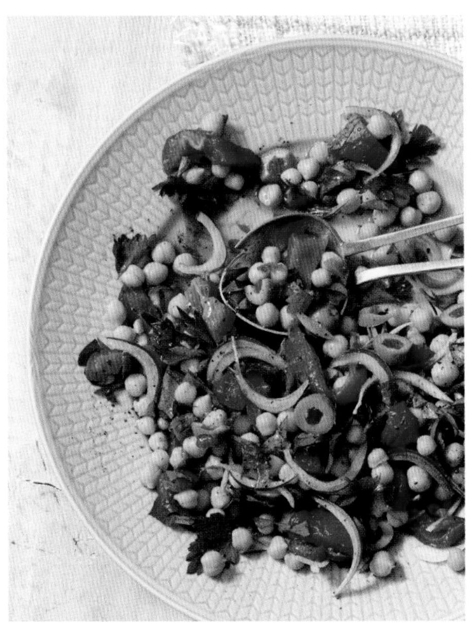

Chick pea and red pepper salad

SERVES 4 **CALS PER SERVING** 158

1 x 400 g can chick peas, drained
½ red onion or 3 spring onions, chopped
3 garlic cloves, crushed
3 tbsp olive oil
2 tbsp white wine vinegar
salt and black pepper
a bunch of flat-leaf parsley
1 red pepper, roasted and peeled (page 426)
about 12 pimiento-stuffed olives

1 Combine the chick peas with the onion, garlic, oil, vinegar, and salt and pepper to taste. Remove the parsley leaves from the stems, chop them roughly and stir in.

2 Cut the red pepper into small chunks and chop the olives if you like. Stir into the chick pea mixture until evenly mixed.

Mozzarella, tomato, and basil salad

SERVES 8 **CALS PER SERVING** 147

4 slicing or beefsteak tomatoes
250 g (8 oz) mozzarella cheese
4 tbsp shredded fresh basil
4 tbsp olive oil
1 tbsp balsamic vinegar
salt and black pepper
basil sprig, to garnish

1 Peel the tomatoes: cut out the cores and score an "x" on the base of each one, then immerse in boiling water until the skins start to split. Transfer at once to cold water; when cool, peel off the skin. Thinly slice the tomatoes.

2 Slice the mozzarella and arrange with the tomato slices alternately on a plate, overlapping one another.

3 Just before serving, sprinkle with the basil, olive oil, and vinegar, and salt and pepper to taste. Garnish with a basil sprig.

Avocado with tomatoes and mint

SERVES 4 **CALS PER SERVING** 232

4 small firm tomatoes
2 ripe avocados
1 tbsp chopped fresh mint
mint sprigs, to garnish

Dressing
2 tsp white wine vinegar
1 tsp Dijon mustard
2 tbsp olive oil
1 tsp caster sugar
salt and black pepper

1 Peel the tomatoes: cut out the cores and score an "x" on the base of each one, then immerse in a bowl of boiling water until the skins start to split. Transfer at once to a bowl of cold water. Peel, seed, and then coarsely chop the tomato flesh.

2 Make the dressing: in a small bowl, whisk together the vinegar and mustard. Gradually whisk in the oil, then add the caster sugar, and salt and pepper to taste.

3 Halve and stone the avocados. Brush the flesh with a little dressing to prevent discoloration.

4 Combine the tomatoes, chopped mint, and dressing. Pile the tomato mixture into the avocado halves, garnish with mint sprigs, and serve at once.

Baked figs with Camembert

SERVES 6 **CALS PER SERVING** 180

175 g (6 oz) Camembert cheese
6 just-ripe large figs
12 slices of Parma ham

To serve
6 tbsp olive oil
3 tbsp white wine vinegar
1 tsp Dijon mustard
2 tsp clear honey
salt and black pepper
125 g (4 oz) mixed green salad leaves

1 Put the Camembert into the freezer, and freeze for about 30 minutes until hard. This will make it easier to cut the cheese into neat slices.

2 Sit the figs on a board, remove their stalks, and cut a cross in the stalk end of each one to come about halfway down the fruit. Cut the cheese into six thin slices, and push one slice into each cross so that the cheese sits inside the fig.

3 Wrap each fig in two slices of ham and place them on a baking tray.

4 Bake in a preheated oven at 200°C (180°C fan, Gas 6) for 10–12 minutes or until the ham is crisp and the cheese just beginning to melt.

5 Meanwhile, whisk the olive oil and vinegar in a salad bowl with the mustard and honey, and season with salt and pepper. Add the salad leaves, and toss until they are coated in the dressing.

6 Divide the salad leaves among six plates, and sit a fig in the middle of each pile of leaves. Serve immediately.

Summer melons

SERVES 4 **CALS PER SERVING** 282

2 x 750 g (1½ lb) ripe melons with different coloured flesh (see Cook's know-how, right)
500 g (1 lb) tomatoes
1 tbsp chopped fresh mint
mint sprigs, to garnish

Dressing

90 ml (3 fl oz) sunflower oil
2 tbsp white wine vinegar
¼ tsp caster sugar
salt and black pepper

1 Cut the melons in half, and remove and discard the seeds. Using a melon baller or a knife, cut balls or neat cubes of flesh into a bowl.

2 Peel the tomatoes: cut out the cores and score an "x" on the base of each one, then immerse in a bowl of boiling water until the skins start to split. Transfer at once to a bowl of cold water. Peel and seed the tomatoes, then cut the flesh into long strips. Add the strips to the melon.

3 Make the dressing: in a small bowl, whisk together the sunflower oil and vinegar, then add the caster sugar, and salt and pepper to taste. Pour the dressing over the melon and tomato mixture. Cover and chill for at least 1 hour.

4 To serve, stir the chopped mint into the melon and tomato mixture, spoon the salad into chilled bowls, and garnish each serving with a mint sprig.

Cook's know-how

Choose two or three varieties of melon to make an attractive colour combination. Honeydew has pale greenish yellow flesh, cantaloupe has either pale green or orange flesh, Ogen and Galia have pale yellow or green flesh, while Charentais melons have deep orange flesh.

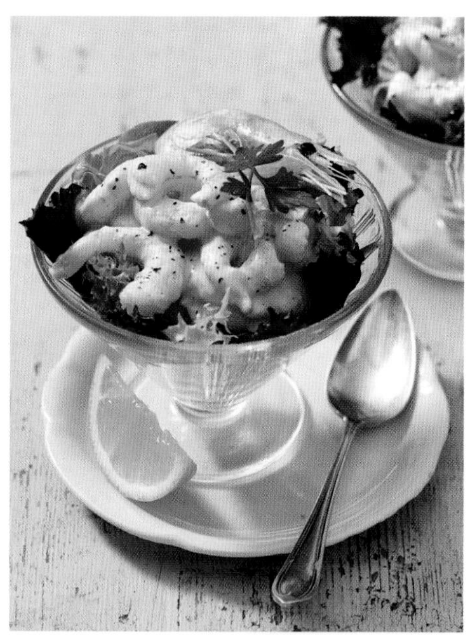

Prawn cocktail

SERVES 4 **CALS PER SERVING** 338

150 ml (1/4 pint) mayonnaise
2 tbsp creamed horseradish
1 tbsp lemon juice
1 tsp Worcestershire sauce
1 tsp tomato purée
1/4 tsp caster sugar
a few drops of Tabasco sauce
black pepper
250 g (8 oz) cooked peeled prawns
salad leaves, to serve
thin lemon wedges, parsley sprigs, and 4 large cooked prawns in their shells, to garnish

1 Make the dressing: in a medium bowl, combine the mayonnaise, creamed horseradish, lemon juice, Worcestershire sauce, tomato purée, caster sugar, and Tabasco sauce, and season well with a little black pepper.

2 Add the peeled cooked prawns and stir to coat with the dressing.

3 Line four individual glass serving bowls with the salad leaves and top with the prawn mixture. Garnish each serving with a thin lemon wedge, a parsley sprig, and a large prawn.

Smoked chicken salad with walnuts

SERVES 6 **CALS PER SERVING** 472

450 g (1 lb) cooked smoked chicken breasts
100 ml (3½ fl oz) sunflower oil
2 tbsp walnut oil
75 ml (2½ fl oz) orange juice
1/4 tsp ground coriander
1/4 tsp caster sugar
salt and black pepper
375 g (12 oz) mixed salad leaves
4 oranges, peeled and segmented
60 g (2 oz) walnut pieces

1 Cut the chicken breasts into thin, neat slices. Put the slices into a shallow non-metallic dish.

2 In a small bowl, combine the sunflower and walnut oils, orange juice, ground coriander, and sugar. Season with salt and pepper. Pour the mixture over the chicken slices and toss them gently until evenly coated.

3 Arrange the salad leaves, orange segments, and chicken slices on individual serving plates, scatter the walnut pieces over the top, and serve immediately.

WARM DUCK SALAD

Substitute 375 g (12 oz) smoked duck or turkey breast for the chicken. Gently heat the poultry slices in the dressing, and add warm garlic croûtons (page 28) to the salad.

Warm salad with bacon and scallops

SERVES 4 **CALS PER SERVING** 276

375 g (12 oz) mixed salad leaves, such as radicchio, lamb's lettuce, frisée, and rocket
8 shallots, finely chopped
1 tbsp sunflower oil
250 g (8 oz) lean unsmoked bacon rashers, rinds removed, diced
12 scallops, halved
3 tbsp white wine vinegar
2 tbsp walnut oil
salt and black pepper

1 Put the salad leaves into a large bowl and sprinkle with half of the shallots.

2 Heat the oil in a frying pan, add the bacon, and cook quickly, stirring occasionally, for 5 minutes or until crisp. Add the scallops and cook quickly for 1–2 minutes until just opaque. Remove from the pan and keep warm.

3 Add the remaining shallots and cook for 1 minute. Add the vinegar and boil rapidly, stirring to incorporate the pan juices.

4 Sprinkle the walnut oil over the salad leaves and toss together until the leaves are evenly coated and shiny. Add the bacon and scallops, hot vinegar and shallots, and season to taste.

Cook's know-how

Stirring vinegar into the frying pan loosens and dissolves the flavoursome juices on the bottom of the pan so they are not wasted. This is called deglazing.

Scallops with cheese sauce

SERVES 4 **CALS PER SERVING** 297

8 scallops, with 4 shells if possible
150 ml (¼ pint) water
4 tbsp medium dry white wine
1 bay leaf
salt and black pepper
lemon wedges and chopped coriander, to garnish

Mornay sauce

45 g (1½ oz) butter
3 tbsp plain flour
4 tbsp single cream
60 g (2 oz) Gruyère cheese, grated

1 Cut each scallop into 2–3 pieces. Put the measured water, wine, and bay leaf into a small pan, and season with salt and pepper. Bring to a boil, then lower the heat and add the scallops.

2 Poach for 1 minute or until the scallops are just tender when tested with the tip of a knife. Lift out the scallops with a slotted spoon, strain the cooking liquid, and reserve.

3 Make the Mornay sauce: melt the butter in a saucepan, add the flour, and cook, stirring, for 1 minute. Gradually stir in the reserved cooking liquid, and bring to a boil, stirring constantly, until the mixture thickens. Simmer gently for about 5 minutes. Lower the heat, and stir in the cream and half of the grated cheese. Taste for seasoning.

4 Stir the scallops into the sauce, divide among the shells, and sprinkle with the remaining cheese.

5 Place the filled shells under a hot grill, 7 cm (3 in) from the heat, for 5 minutes or until the cheese has melted and the sauce is golden and bubbling. Garnish with lemon wedges and chopped coriander.

Moules marinière

SERVES 6 **CALS PER SERVING** 302

90 g (3 oz) butter
1 small onion, finely chopped
1 garlic clove, crushed
3 kg (6 lb) mussels, cleaned (page 105)
450 ml (¾ pint) dry white wine
6 parsley sprigs
3 thyme sprigs
1 bay leaf
salt and black pepper
1 tbsp plain flour
3 tbsp chopped parsley, to garnish

1 Melt two-thirds of the butter in a large saucepan, add the onion and garlic, and cook gently, stirring occasionally, for a few minutes until soft but not coloured.

2 Add the mussels, wine, parsley, thyme, and bay leaf, and season with salt and pepper. Cover the saucepan tightly and bring to a boil.

3 Cook, shaking the saucepan frequently, for 5–6 minutes or until the mussels open.

4 Throw away any mussels that are not open. Transfer the open mussels to a warmed tureen or large serving bowl.

5 Strain the cooking juices into a small pan and boil until reduced by one-third.

6 Mix the remaining butter and the flour on a plate to make a paste (beurre manié).

7 Whisk the beurre manié into the cooking liquid, and bring to a boil, stirring constantly. Taste for seasoning, and pour over the mussels. Garnish with chopped parsley and serve at once.

Sardines with coriander

SERVES 4 **CALS PER SERVING** 511

12–16 large sardines
olive oil, for brushing
salt and black pepper
lime wedges and chopped flat-leaf parsley (optional), to garnish

Coriander lime butter

2 tbsp fresh coriander
60 g (2 oz) unsalted butter, at room temperature
1½ tsp lime juice
1 shallot, finely chopped
¼ tsp finely grated lime zest

1 Scale the sardines with the back of a kitchen knife. With a sharp knife, cut the stomachs open, and scrape out the contents, particularly any dark blood.

2 Rinse the sardines inside and out, and pat dry. Brush all over with oil, and sprinkle with salt and pepper.

3 Prepare the coriander lime butter: combine the coriander, butter, and lime juice and whisk until thick. Stir in the shallot and lime zest, and season with salt and pepper.

4 Place the sardines under a hot grill, 10 cm (4 in) from the heat, and grill for 1½–2 minutes on each side until they begin to feel firm.

5 Transfer the sardines to a serving plate and spread a little coriander lime butter on each one. Garnish with lime wedges and flat-leaf parsley sprigs (if you like), and serve at once.

Jumbo prawns with aïoli

SERVES 4 **CALS PER SERVING** 482

2 tbsp olive oil
12 uncooked jumbo prawns in their shells
chopped parsley and lemon wedges, to garnish

Aïoli

2 garlic cloves, coarsely chopped
salt and black pepper
1 egg yolk
1 tsp mustard powder
150 ml (¼ pint) olive oil
1 tbsp lemon juice

1 Make the aïoli: in a small bowl, crush the garlic with a pinch of salt until it forms a smooth paste. Add the egg yolk and mustard powder, and beat well. Beat in the oil, drop by drop, whisking constantly until the mixture is thick and smooth, and all the oil has been absorbed. Beat in the lemon juice, and add pepper to taste.

2 Heat the oil in a large frying pan, add the prawns, and toss over a high heat for 3–4 minutes, just until the shells turn bright pink. Remove the prawns from the frying pan and drain on paper towels.

3 To serve, arrange the prawns on warmed plates and garnish with chopped parsley and lemon wedges. Serve with individual bowls of aïoli.

Cook's know-how

Uncooked, or raw, prawns are usually grey in colour – it is only when they are cooked that they turn into the pink prawns we are more familiar with. The golden rule when cooking prawns is never to overcook them, so remove them from the heat as soon as they turn pink. Overcooked prawns are rubbery, chewy, and tasteless.

Seafood blini

Blini are small Russian pancakes made with yeast and buckwheat flour. Buckwheat flour is available at health food shops but if you cannot find any, use wholemeal flour instead. This mixture makes about 24 blini.

SERVES 6–8 **CALS PER SERVING** 369–227

Blini

125 g (4 oz) plain flour
125 g (4 oz) buckwheat flour
½ tsp salt
½ tsp fast-action dried yeast
450 ml (¾ pint) milk, warmed
1 egg, separated
sunflower oil, for frying

To serve

2 x 75 g jars lumpfish roe (1 red, 1 black)
125 g (4 oz) cooked peeled prawns
125 ml (4 fl oz) crème fraîche
lemon segments and fresh chives, to garnish

1 Put both types of flour into a large bowl. Add the salt and yeast, then stir together until evenly mixed.

2 Gradually beat in the warm milk to make a smooth batter. Cover the bowl and leave in a warm place for about 40 minutes until the mixture is frothy and has doubled in volume.

3 Beat the egg yolk into the flour and yeast mixture. Put the egg white into a clean bowl and whisk until stiff but not dry, then fold into the mixture.

4 Heat a large non-stick frying pan or griddle, brush with oil, and heat until the oil is hot. Spoon about 2 tbsp batter into the pan for each blini (you should be able to cook three or four at a time), cover, and cook over a moderate heat for 2–3 minutes, or until bubbles rise to the surface and burst.

5 Turn the blini over with a palette knife and cook for a further 2–3 minutes until golden on the other side. Wrap the cooked blini in a tea towel and keep them warm.

6 Cook the remaining batter in batches until all the batter is used up, lightly oiling the pan between each batch.

7 To serve, arrange the blini on warmed plates, with spoonfuls of red and black lumpfish roe, prawns, and crème fraîche. Garnish with lemon segments and snipped fresh chives.

Cook's know-how

If you buy ready-made blini, they will need to be gently warmed through before serving.

Gravadlax

You can buy this Scandinavian "pickled" salmon, but it is easy (and less expensive) to make it yourself – and your guests will be very impressed. Serve it with thin slices of sourdough rye bread (page 445). You will find the gravadlax easier to slice if it has been frozen for about 4 hours beforehand.

SERVES 16 **CALS PER SERVING** 395

2.25 kg (4½ lb) whole fresh salmon, boned, and cut lengthways in half into 2 fillets (ask your fishmonger)
dill sprigs and lemon segments, to garnish

Pickling mixture

75 g (2½ oz) granulated sugar
4 tbsp coarse sea salt
4 tbsp chopped fresh dill
salt and black pepper

Mustard dill sauce

3 tbsp Dijon mustard
2 tbsp caster sugar
1 tbsp white wine vinegar
1 egg yolk
150 ml (¼ pint) sunflower oil
2 tbsp chopped fresh dill

1 Make the pickling mixture: put the granulated sugar, sea salt, and chopped fresh dill into a small bowl, season generously with black pepper, and stir well to mix.

2 Sandwich the salmon fillets together (see box, right).

3 Wrap the fillets in a double thickness of foil and place in a large dish. Weigh down with kitchen weights or heavy cans, and keep in the refrigerator for 24 hours. Halfway through this time, turn the salmon over.

4 Make the mustard dill sauce: in a medium bowl, whisk together the mustard, sugar, vinegar, and egg yolk, then whisk in the oil a little at a time. The sauce should have the consistency of mayonnaise. Add salt and pepper to taste, and stir in the chopped dill.

5 Unwrap the gravadlax. A lot of sticky, salty liquid will drain from the fish when it has been pickled: this is quite normal. Remove the fish from the pickling liquid, and dry well. Separate the two salmon fillets.

6 To serve, slice each fillet on the slant, cutting the flesh away from the skin. The slices should be a little thicker than for smoked salmon and each one should have a fringe of dill. Garnish with dill sprigs and lemon segments, and serve with the mustard dill sauce.

Sandwiching the salmon fillets

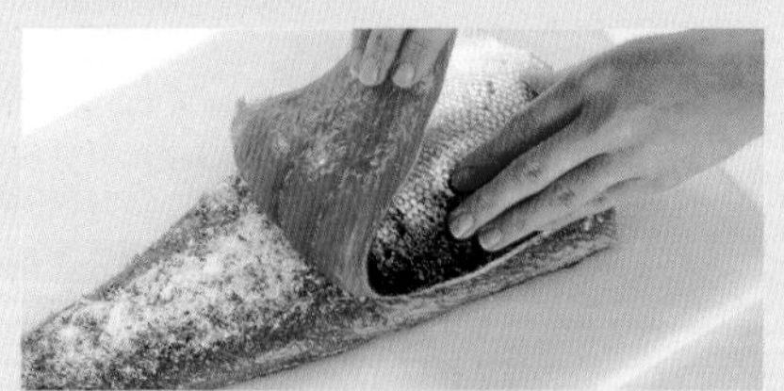

Put one salmon fillet skin-side down on a board, cover the surface with the pickling mixture, and place the second fillet on top, skin-side up.

Ceviche with tomato and avocado salsa

SERVES 6 **CALS PER SERVING** 328

3 large scallops (with or without corals according to taste), sliced horizontally in half
200 g (7 oz) cleaned squid, cut into thin strips
125 g (4 oz) skinless salmon fillet, cut across the grain into wafer-thin strips
juice of 2 limes

Salsa

3 tomatoes, peeled, deseeded, and cut into thin strips
3 spring onions, finely chopped (including a little of the green leaves)
1 fresh green chilli, halved, deseeded, and finely chopped
1 large avocado, halved, stoned, peeled, and finely chopped
salt and black pepper
125 ml (4 fl oz) olive oil
juice of 1 lime
2 tbsp chopped parsley

1 Put the scallops, squid, and salmon into a bowl. Add the lime juice, and stir gently until the fish is coated in juice. Cover, and chill for 4–5 hours until the fish is opaque.

2 Meanwhile, make the salsa: put the tomatoes, spring onions, chilli, and avocado into a bowl, and season with salt and pepper. Add the olive oil and lime juice, and stir gently to mix. Cover, and chill with the ceviche.

3 To serve, drain the juice from the fish, and mix the juice gently into the salsa with the chopped parsley. Arrange the fish on six plates, and spoon the salsa on top.

Cook's know-how

It is essential to use very fresh fish for ceviche, because the fish is marinated and served raw, not cooked. Really fresh raw scallops are translucent and creamy grey in colour, not as white as they appear when cooked. Do not leave the ceviche to marinate for any longer than the recipe states or it will begin to lose its texture and colour, and always serve chilled, straight from the refrigerator.

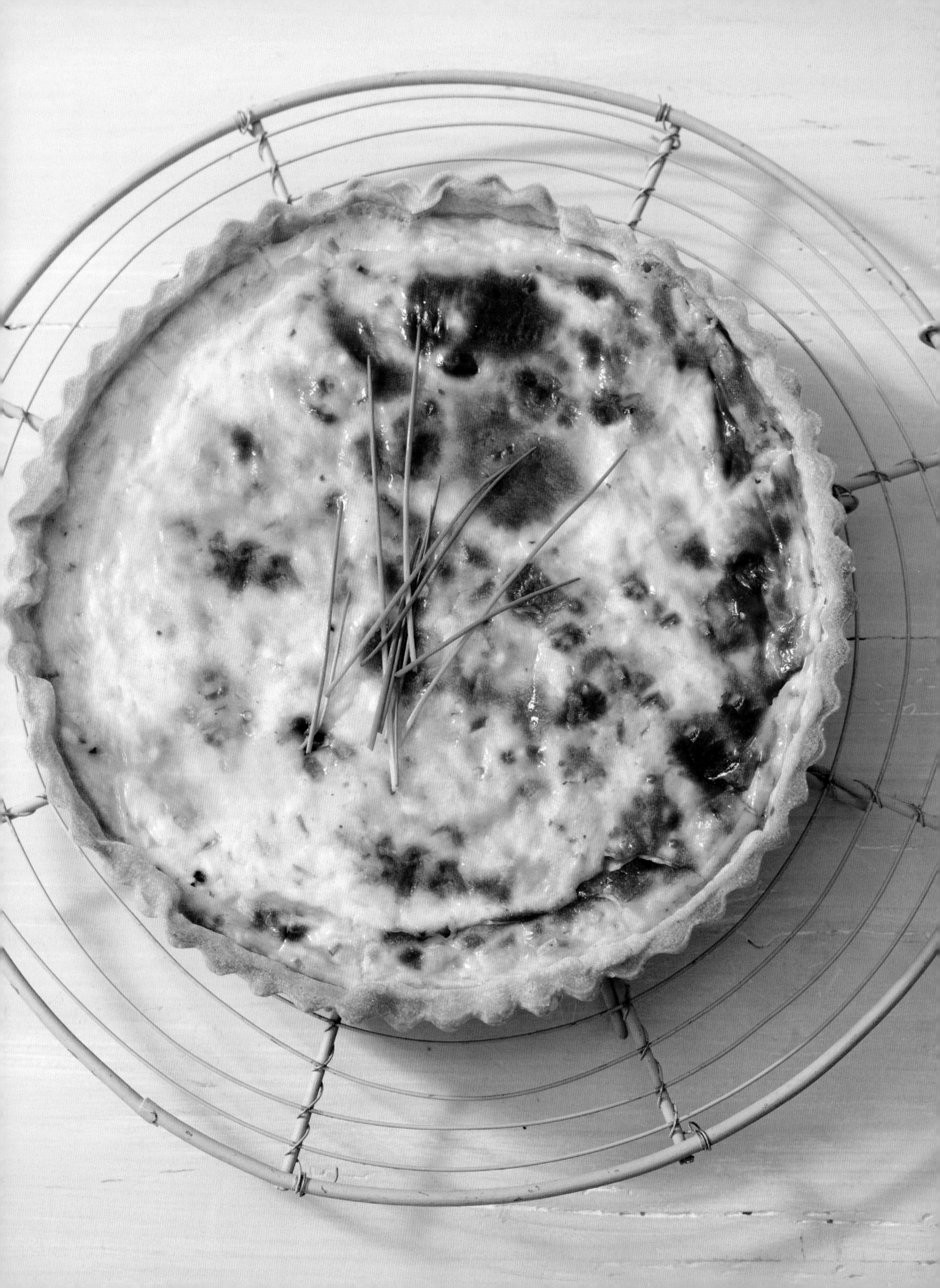

Eggs and cheese

In this chapter...

Mushroom omelette with ciabatta
page 79

Mexican omelette
page 79

Spanish omelette
page 80

Savoury soufflé omelette
page 80

Eggs Benedict
page 80

Eggs Florentine
page 82

Spinach and mushroom frittata
page 82

Oeufs en cocotte
page 83

Courgette and Parma ham frittata
page 83

Quiche Lorraine
page 84

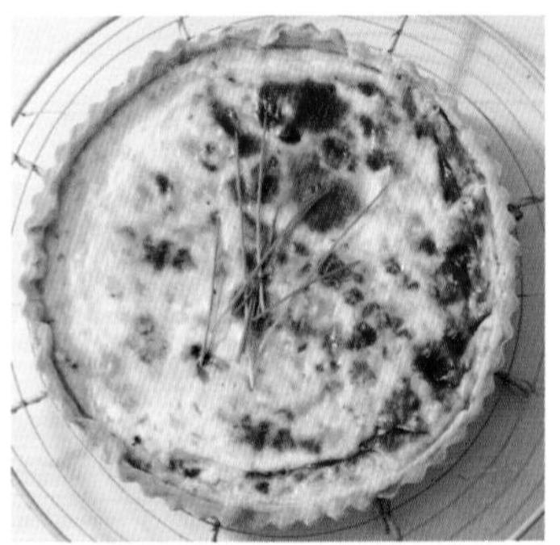
Roquefort quiche
page 85

Smoked salmon and asparagus quiche
page 86

Bacon and Gruyère galette
page 86

Pizza tartlets
page 88

Spinach, leek, and Gruyère tart
page 89

Classic cheese soufflé
page 90

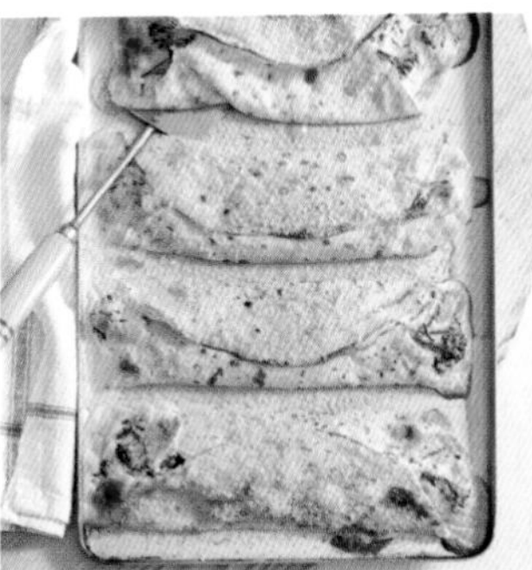
Soufflé pancakes with broccoli and cheese
page 90

Swiss double cheese soufflés
page 92

Stilton and broccoli soufflés
page 93

Garlic and goat's cheese soufflés
page 94

Creamy seafood crêpes
page 95

Chicken pancakes florentine
page 96

Croque señor
page 96

Cheese fondue
page 97

Raclette
page 97

Eggs and cheese know-how

Eggs are one of the most useful foods in a cook's repertoire. They can be cooked in many delicious ways, from simple boiling, poaching, and scrambling to omelettes and soufflés that require a little more skill. Eggs are also used to enrich pastries and doughs, give volume and moistness to cakes and many puddings, thicken sauces and custards, bind mixtures ranging from burgers to pâtés, and provide a coating for foods to be fried.

Cheese has countless culinary uses. Apart from its everyday use as a sandwich filling, it is found in sauces, fondues, and pizza toppings; it flavours savoury pastries, doughs, and quiche fillings; it is essential in many pasta dishes; and it is popular in puddings such as cheesecake and tiramisu.

Buying and storing

Most of the eggs we eat are hen's eggs, although there are also tiny quail's eggs, large duck eggs, and even larger goose eggs. Hen's eggs are usually described according to the farming method used – for example, "free-range", "barn", "from caged hens" (ie the battery system), and "organic" – and these descriptions guarantee that the eggs have been produced according to certain rules. Wherever possible, opt for organic or free-range eggs: not only is this the most ethical choice, but the higher welfare standards also produce tastier eggs. Whichever you buy, choose the ones with the longest "use-by" date, and check that none is damaged or cracked. Store eggs in their box in the refrigerator (away from strong foods so that they do not absorb flavours and odours through their shells). If you place them pointed end down, the yolk will remain centred in the white. Always use them by their use-by date.

Cheese deteriorates once cut, so do not buy it in a large piece unless you know it will be used up quickly. Keep all cheeses well wrapped in the refrigerator or in a cool larder (soft cheeses must be stored in the refrigerator and used within a few days).

All about eggs

Hen's eggs are graded by weight. Those weighing 73 g and over are classified as "very large"; eggs weighing 63–73 g are "large"; eggs weighing 53–63 g are "medium"; and eggs below 53 g are "small".

The shell – usually brown or white, but now also blue, green, pink, or speckled – is a result of the breed of hen.

The colour of the yolk depends on the hen's diet and added natural or artificial colourants.

Freezing

Shelled raw eggs freeze very successfully, and can be stored for up to 6 months. If whole, whisk gently to mix the yolk and white; add a little salt to whole eggs and egg yolks for use in savoury foods or sugar for use in sweet dishes (nothing needs to be added to whites). Thaw at room temperature. Egg-based dishes such as quiches, custards, and mousses can also be frozen.

Hard and firm cheeses freeze well, as do soft ripened cheeses such as Brie. Store them for up to 1 month. Thaw in the refrigerator before use. Note that the texture of hard cheeses may change after freezing, becoming more crumbly, making the cheeses suitable only for cooking. Soft fresh cheeses and soft blue-veined cheeses do not freeze well.

Microwaving

Never microwave an egg that is still in its shell as it will burst. Even out of its shell, a whole egg may burst, so always pierce the membrane on the yolk with a toothpick before cooking. The yolk cooks more quickly than the white, so standing time should be allowed to let the white continue cooking. Where yolks and whites are combined, as for scrambled eggs, the mixture will appear undercooked but will firm up during standing time.

Cheeses melt quickly in the microwave, so take care not to overcook or burn them. Hard or firm mature cheeses and processed cheeses are the best. Frozen soft ripened cheeses can be softened and brought to room temperature in the microwave before serving.

Cooking with cheese

Cheese needs to be cooked with care as heat can spoil its texture, making it rubbery or stringy. Hard and firm cheeses can withstand heat best, melting and blending smoothly. When adding cheese to a sauce, do this at the end of cooking and melt gently; do not boil. If grilling a cheese topping, cook as briefly as possible.

Separating eggs

For best results, take eggs straight from the fridge so they are well chilled.

1 Holding an egg over a bowl, break open the shell. Carefully transfer the yolk from one half shell to the other, letting the egg white run into the bowl. Repeat several times.

2 Put the yolk in another bowl. Remove any yolk from the white with the tip of a spoon (the white will not whisk if there is any trace of yolk).

Cooking eggs

Eggs are one of the cheapest sources of protein and could not be easier to cook. Once you have mastered the basic techniques you will be able to produce a wide range of nutritious meals in minutes.

Boiling

Use eggs at room temperature (the shells are less likely to crack). Put the eggs into a pan of simmering water. Bring back to a boil, then simmer gently. Cooking times are calculated from the time the water comes back to a boil, and can vary according to individual taste and on the size and freshness of the eggs. For soft-boiled eggs, simmer gently for 4–5 minutes; for hard-boiled eggs, allow 8–10 minutes. After cooking hard-boiled eggs, lift them out of the water and crack the shell to allow steam to escape, then plunge the eggs into iced water. Peel when cool enough to handle. (An unsightly black line may form round the yolk if you cook them too long, or keep them in the shell.) Use straight away or keep in a bowl of cold water in the refrigerator for up to 24 hours.

Soft-boiled eggs

Hard-boiled eggs

Frying

Fresh eggs are essential for successful frying because they keep their shape during cooking. Fry the eggs in your favourite oil, adding a knob of butter for extra flavour if you like.

1 Heat a thin layer of oil in a non-stick frying pan. When the oil is very hot and starting to sizzle, slip in an egg and cook over a medium heat.

2 Spoon the oil over once or twice to give a white top. Remove and serve, or turn over and cook for a few seconds, to set the yolk a little more.

Scrambling

Scrambled eggs can be served plain, or flavoured with herbs, cheese, ham, or smoked salmon. Allow 2 eggs per person.

1 Lightly beat the eggs with salt and pepper to taste and a little milk, if you like. Melt a knob of butter in a pan. Add the eggs.

2 Cook over a medium heat, stirring constantly with a wooden spatula or spoon, until almost set – they will continue to cook after they have been removed from the heat. Serve at once.

Poaching

The classic method for poaching eggs is in a pan of simmering water. Use the freshest eggs possible, as they will keep a neat shape.

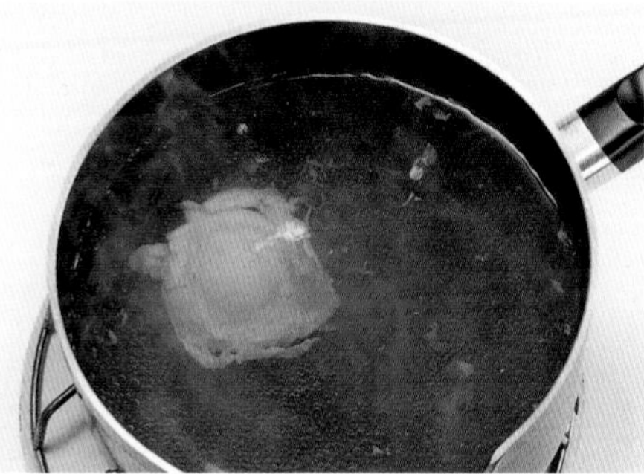

1 Bring a wide pan of water to the boil. Lower the heat so that the water is simmering, and slide in an egg. Swirl the water round the egg to give it a neat shape. Simmer for 3–4 minutes until the egg is cooked to your taste.

2 Lift out the egg with a slotted spoon and drain briefly on paper towels. To keep them warm, or to reheat them if they have been prepared ahead, immerse them in a bowl of hot water (they will take 1 minute to reheat).

Making pancakes

The quantities given here will make enough batter for about 12 thin pancakes (the kind that the French call crêpes), using an 18–20 cm (7–8 in) pan. Do not worry if the first pancake or two is a failure: it acts as a test for the consistency of the batter and the heat of the pan, and if you are new to pancake-making you may prefer to make them slightly thicker, to be on the safe side, in which case you may only make eight pancakes. Any uneaten pancakes will keep in a stack for 24 hours, or they can be frozen.

1 Sift 125 g (4 oz) plain flour into a bowl and make a well in the middle. Whisk together 1 egg, 1 egg yolk, and a little milk taken from 300 ml (½ pint), then pour into the well. Whisk with a little of the flour.

2 Gradually whisk in half of the remaining milk, drawing in the rest of the flour a little at a time, to make a smooth batter. Stir in the remaining milk. Cover and leave to stand for about 30 minutes.

3 Heat the frying pan and brush with a little oil. Ladle 2–3 tbsp batter into the pan and tilt the pan so that the batter spreads out evenly over the bottom.

4 Cook the pancake over a medium–high heat for 45–60 seconds until small holes appear on the surface, the underside is lightly browned, and the edge has started to curl. Loosen the pancake and turn it over by tossing or flipping it with a palette knife. Cook the other side for about 30 seconds until golden.

5 Slide the pancake out of the pan. Heat and lightly grease the pan again before making the next pancake. Serve the pancakes as they are made, or stack them on a plate and reheat before serving. (If the pancakes are hot when stacked they will not stick together; there is no need to interleave them with greaseproof paper.)

Making an omelette

Omelettes are best made in a special pan kept solely for the purpose, so that they are less likely to stick. If you do not have one, use a small frying pan, no more than 20 cm (8 in) in diameter.

1 Beat 2–3 eggs with salt and pepper, plus chopped fresh herbs if you like. Heat the pan, then add a knob of butter. When the butter is foaming, tilt the pan to coat the bottom. Pour in the eggs.

2 Cook over a medium heat. As the eggs begin to set, lift and pull back the edge of the omelette towards the middle, and tilt the pan so the liquid egg runs underneath.

3 Continue cooking until the omelette is just set and the underside is golden. Tilt the pan, loosen the edge of the omelette and flip over in half, to fold it. Slide on to a plate to serve.

Omelette know-how

Gently stir to combine the yolks with the whites: vigorous beating will make the omelette rubbery. Make sure the pan is hot and the butter foaming when you add the eggs. The omelette will continue to cook after you remove it from the heat, so the middle should still be a little moist.

Mushroom omelette with ciabatta

SERVES 2 **CALS PER SERVING** 673

4 eggs
salt and black pepper
30 g (1 oz) butter
60 g (2 oz) shiitake mushrooms, sliced
1 tbsp snipped fresh chives
1 loaf of ciabatta bread, warmed and split lengthways

1 Break the eggs into a small bowl, season with salt and black pepper, and beat with a fork.

2 Melt half of the butter in a small frying pan, add the mushrooms, and cook over a high heat for 3–5 minutes until all the liquid has evaporated. Remove from the heat, stir in the chives, season with salt and pepper, and keep hot.

3 Heat an omelette pan or a small frying pan until very hot. Add the remaining butter and swirl the pan to evenly coat the base and sides. When the butter is foaming, pour in the seasoned egg mixture.

4 Cook the omelette over a medium heat, pulling back the edge as the eggs set, and tilting the pan to allow the uncooked egg to run to the side of the pan. Continue until the omelette is lightly set and the underside is golden. Remove from the heat.

5 Scatter the mushrooms over half of the omelette, then flip the uncovered half over them. Fill the warmed split ciabatta with the omelette, cut the ciabatta in half crosswise, and serve at once.

Mexican omelette

An omelette is one of the most useful of all egg dishes, quick and easy to make, and nutritious either plain or with a filling. This recipe combines a classic French omelette with a piquant filling, but you can add whatever filling you like.

SERVES 2 **CALS PER SERVING** 547

6 eggs
30 g (1 oz) butter
chopped parsley, to garnish

Filling
2 tbsp olive oil
1 onion, finely chopped
1 garlic clove, crushed
1 green pepper, halved, deseeded, and finely chopped
2 ripe tomatoes, skinned, deseeded, and finely chopped
125 g (4 oz) button mushrooms, thinly sliced
¼ tsp Worcestershire sauce
a few drops of Tabasco sauce
salt and black pepper

1 Make the filling: heat the oil in a frying pan, add the onion and garlic, and cook for 5 minutes or until softened. Add the pepper, and cook, stirring, for 5 minutes.

2 Add the tomatoes and mushrooms, and cook, stirring, for 10 minutes. Add the Worcestershire and Tabasco sauces, season with salt and pepper, and simmer for about 5 minutes. Keep warm.

3 Beat 3 of the eggs in a bowl with salt and pepper. Heat an omelette pan or small frying pan and add half of the butter.

4 When the butter is foaming, add the eggs, and cook over a medium heat, pulling back the edge as the eggs set, and tilting the pan so the liquid egg runs underneath. Continue until lightly set and golden.

5 Spoon half of the filling on to the half of the omelette farthest from the pan handle. With a palette knife, lift the uncovered half of the omelette and flip it over the filling.

6 Slide the omelette on to a warmed plate, and garnish with chopped parsley. Make the second omelette in the same way, reheating the pan before adding the butter.

MUSHROOM OMELETTE
Substitute 175 g (6 oz) sliced button mushrooms for the filling. Cook in a little melted butter, and season with salt and pepper.

SMOKED CHICKEN OMELETTE
Substitute 125 g (4 oz) diced smoked chicken and 1 tbsp snipped fresh chives for the filling.

TOMATO OMELETTE
Substitute 5 finely chopped ripe tomatoes for the filling. Cook the tomatoes in a little butter for 2–3 minutes. Season well, and stir in a few snipped fresh chives.

Spanish omelette

SERVES 4 **CALS PER SERVING** 389

3 tbsp olive oil
2 large potatoes, diced
2 large onions, chopped
6 eggs
salt and black pepper
1 tbsp chopped parsley

1 Heat the oil in a frying pan, add the potatoes and onions, and stir until coated with the oil. Cook gently for about 10 minutes until golden brown. Pour the excess oil from the pan.

2 Break the eggs into a bowl, season with salt and pepper, and beat with a fork.

3 Pour the eggs into the pan, and mix with the vegetables. Cook for about 10 minutes until the eggs are almost set, then brown the top of the omelette under a hot grill for 1–2 minutes.

4 Slide the omelette on to a warmed plate, and cut into quarters. Sprinkle with chopped parsley and serve warm or cold.

MIXED BEAN OMELETTE
Lightly cook 60 g (2 oz) French beans and 125 g (4 oz) shelled broad beans. Add to the pan in step 3, when mixing the potatoes and onions with the eggs.

Savoury soufflé omelette

SERVES 2 **CALS PER SERVING** 479

4 eggs, separated
30 g (1 oz) butter

Filling
2 tbsp olive oil
½ onion, thinly sliced
1 garlic clove, crushed
1 courgette, sliced
1 red pepper, halved, deseeded, and sliced
1 x 200 g can chopped tomatoes, drained of juice
1 tbsp chopped fresh thyme leaves
salt and black pepper

1 Make the filling: heat the oil in a frying pan, add the onion and garlic, and cook gently for 5 minutes or until softened. Add the courgette and red pepper, and cook for about 2 minutes. Add the tomatoes and thyme, season with salt and pepper, and simmer for about 20 minutes.

2 Whisk together the egg yolks and season with salt and pepper. Whisk the egg whites until stiff, then fold into the yolks.

3 Melt half of the butter in an omelette pan. When it foams, add half of the egg mixture, and cook over a gentle heat for 3 minutes. Add half of the filling, fold the omelette in half, and serve. Repeat with the remaining eggs and filling.

Eggs Benedict

SERVES 4 **CALS PER SERVING** 602

8 lean back bacon rashers, rinds removed
2 muffins, halved
4 eggs
butter, for spreading
fresh flat-leaf parsley, to garnish

Hollandaise sauce
2 tsp lemon juice
2 tsp white wine vinegar
3 egg yolks, at room temperature
125 g (4 oz) unsalted butter, melted
salt and black pepper

1 Cook the bacon under a hot grill, 7 cm (3 in) from the heat, for 5–7 minutes until crisp. Keep the bacon warm.

2 Toast the cut sides of the muffin halves under the grill. Keep warm.

3 Make the hollandaise sauce: put the lemon juice and wine vinegar into a small bowl, add the egg yolks, and whisk with a balloon whisk until light and frothy.

4 Place the bowl over a pan of simmering water and whisk until the mixture thickens. Gradually add the melted butter, whisking constantly until thick. Season. Keep warm.

5 Poach the eggs: bring a large pan of water to the boil. Lower the heat so that the water is simmering, and slide in the eggs. Swirl the water round the eggs to make neat shapes. Simmer for about 4 minutes. Lift out with a slotted spoon.

6 Butter the muffin halves and put on to warmed plates. Put two bacon rashers and an egg on each one, and top with the sauce. Serve at once, garnished with parsley.

SPICY LIME HOLLANDAISE
Substitute 2 tsp lime juice for the lemon juice in the hollandaise sauce, and add ½ tsp each of paprika and mild chilli powder.

Eggs Florentine

SERVES 4 **CALS PER SERVING** 475

250 g (8 oz) spinach leaves
3 spring onions, thinly sliced
2 tbsp double cream
4 eggs
3 tbsp grated Parmesan cheese

Cheese sauce

30 g (1 oz) butter
30 g (1 oz) plain flour
250 ml (8 fl oz) milk
175 g (6 oz) mature Cheddar cheese, grated
pinch each of cayenne pepper and grated nutmeg
salt and black pepper

1 Rinse the spinach, and put into a medium saucepan with only the water that clings to the leaves. Cook for about 2 minutes until tender. Drain, and set aside.

2 Make the cheese sauce: melt the butter in a saucepan, add the flour, and cook, stirring, for 1 minute. Remove from the heat and gradually blend in the milk. Bring to a boil, stirring constantly until the mixture thickens. Simmer for 2–3 minutes.

3 Stir in the Cheddar cheese, add the cayenne pepper and nutmeg, and season with salt and pepper. Keep warm.

4 Combine the spinach in a bowl with the spring onions and cream, and season with salt and pepper. Set aside.

5 Poach the eggs: bring a large pan of water to a boil. Lower the heat so that the water is simmering, and slide in the eggs, one at a time. Swirl the water round the eggs to make neat shapes. Lift out with a slotted spoon.

6 Divide the spinach and spring onion mixture among four warmed flameproof dishes. Arrange the poached eggs on the spinach, and spoon the cheese sauce over the eggs.

7 Sprinkle the grated Parmesan cheese over the sauce, then place the dishes under a hot grill, 7 cm (3 in) from the heat, until the cheese has melted and is lightly browned, and the whole dish is heated through. Serve hot.

Spinach and mushroom frittata

SERVES 3 **CALS PER SERVING** 449

3 tbsp olive oil
60 g (2 oz) thick-cut smoked bacon rashers, rinds removed, diced
250 g (8 oz) chestnut mushrooms, quartered
125 g (4 oz) spinach leaves, coarsely chopped
6 eggs
salt and black pepper
2 tbsp grated Parmesan cheese

1 Heat the oil in a large frying pan. Add the bacon and mushrooms and cook over a high heat, stirring, for about 7 minutes or until the bacon is crisp. Add the spinach and turn it in the oil for 1–2 minutes. Do not allow the spinach to wilt. Lower the heat.

2 Break the eggs into a bowl, season with salt and pepper, and beat with a fork.

3 Pour the eggs over the mushrooms and spinach and cook over a medium heat for 10 minutes. As the eggs set, lift the frittata with a spatula and tilt the pan so the uncooked egg runs underneath.

4 When the eggs are set, sprinkle with grated Parmesan, and place the pan under a hot grill, 10 cm (4 in) from the heat, for 1–2 minutes or until the top is golden brown and firm when pressed. Serve at once.

Courgette and Parma ham frittata

SERVES 4 **CALS PER SERVING** 270

2 tbsp olive oil
625 g (1¼ lb) small courgettes, thinly sliced
6 eggs
salt and black pepper
60 g (2 oz) Parma ham, diced
shredded fresh basil or chopped flat-leaf parsley, to garnish

1 Heat the oil in a large frying pan. Add the courgettes and cook gently for 5 minutes or until just tender.

2 Break the eggs into a bowl, season with salt and pepper, and beat with a fork.

3 Add the ham to the courgettes in the frying pan, then pour in the eggs.

4 Cook over a medium heat for about 10 minutes. As the eggs set, lift the frittata with a spatula and tilt the pan to allow the uncooked egg to run underneath. Continue until almost set and the underside is golden brown.

5 Place the pan under a hot grill, 10 cm (4 in) from the heat, for 1–2 minutes or until the top is a light golden brown, the egg is cooked through, and the frittata is quite firm when pressed.

6 Cut the frittata into wedges, and lightly garnish with fresh basil or parsley. Serve hot or cold.

Cook's know-how

Courgettes have a mild flavour and soft texture that works well with salty Parma ham. Choose the smallest, youngest courgettes you can find.

Oeufs en cocotte

SERVES 4 **CALS PER SERVING** 176

15 g (½ oz) butter
4 eggs
salt and black pepper
4 tbsp double cream
1 tbsp chopped parsley

4 SMALL RAMEKINS

1 Melt the butter, and pour a little into each ramekin.

2 Break each egg into a saucer, then slide into a prepared ramekin. Sprinkle with salt and pepper, and top each egg with 1 tbsp cream.

3 Place the ramekins in a roasting tin and pour in boiling water to come halfway up the sides of the ramekins. Cover with foil.

4 Bake in a preheated oven at 200°C (180°C fan, Gas 6) for 10 minutes or until the whites are opaque and firm but the yolks still soft. Or, put the ramekins into a large frying pan, add boiling water to come halfway up the sides, cover, and cook over a medium heat for 10 minutes, letting the water boil and gently steam the eggs.

5 Sprinkle a little parsley over each baked egg 1–2 minutes before the end of cooking time.

FETA CHEESE COCOTTES

After pouring the butter into the ramekins, divide 125 g (4 oz) diced feta cheese, marinated in chopped fresh herbs and diced fresh red chilli, among the ramekins. Proceed as directed, substituting 2–3 thinly sliced spring onions for the parsley.

Quiche Lorraine

This most famous of all quiches is named after the area from which it comes – Alsace-Lorraine in north-eastern France – where it was traditionally served on May Day, following a dish of roast suckling pig.

SERVES 6 **CALS PER SERVING** 504

30 g (1 oz) butter
1 onion, chopped
175 g (6 oz) unsmoked streaky bacon rashers, rinds removed, diced
125 g (4 oz) Gruyère cheese, grated
250 ml (8 fl oz) single cream
2 eggs, beaten
salt and black pepper

Shortcrust pastry

175 g (6 oz) plain flour
90 g (3 oz) butter
1 large egg, lightly beaten

20 CM (8 IN) LOOSE-BOTTOMED FLUTED FLAN TIN
BAKING BEANS

1 Make the pastry with the flour, butter, and water (see box, right). Wrap in cling film and chill for 30 minutes.

2 Roll out the pastry on a lightly floured work surface, and use to line the flan tin. Prick the bottom of the pastry shell with a fork.

3 Line the pastry shell with a sheet of foil or greaseproof paper, and fill with baking beans (or rice or pasta if you have no beans). Place the flan tin on a heated baking tray and bake the shell in a preheated oven at 220°C (200°C fan, Gas 7) for 15–20 minutes, removing the foil and beans for the final 10 minutes.

4 Meanwhile, make the filling: melt the butter in a frying pan, add the onion and bacon, and cook gently, stirring occasionally, for 10 minutes or until the onion is golden brown and the bacon is crisp.

5 Spoon the onion and bacon into the pastry shell, and sprinkle the cheese on top. Mix the cream and eggs in a jug, season with salt and pepper, and pour into the pastry shell.

6 Reduce the oven temperature to 180°C (160°C fan, Gas 4), and bake the quiche for 25–30 minutes until the filling is golden and set. Serve warm or cold.

Making shortcrust pastry

Tip the flour into a bowl and rub in the butter lightly with your fingertips until the mixture looks like fine breadcrumbs.

Add the egg and mix with a round-bladed knife to form a soft but not sticky dough.

Roquefort quiche

SERVES 6 **CALS PER SERVING** 336

90 g (3 oz) Roquefort or other blue cheese, crumbled
175 g (6 oz) full-fat soft cheese
2 eggs, beaten
150 ml (¼ pint) full-fat crème fraîche
1 tbsp snipped fresh chives
salt and black pepper

Shortcrust pastry

175 g (6 oz) plain flour
90 g (3 oz) butter
1 large egg, lightly beaten

20 CM (8 IN) LOOSE-BOTTOMED FLUTED FLAN TIN

BAKING BEANS

1 Make the pastry: tip the flour into a bowl and rub in the butter with your fingertips. Add enough egg to bind to a soft dough. Wrap in cling film and chill for 30 minutes.

2 Roll out the shortcrust pastry, and use to line the flan tin. Prick the bottom of the pastry shell with a fork.

3 Line the pastry shell with foil or greaseproof paper, and fill with baking beans (or rice or pasta if you have no beans). Place the tin on a heated baking tray, and bake in a preheated oven at 220°C (200°C fan, Gas 7) for 15–20 minutes, removing the foil and beans for the final 10 minutes.

4 Meanwhile, make the filling: mix the Roquefort and full-fat cheese in a bowl, then beat in the eggs, crème fraîche, and chives, and season with salt and pepper. Take care not to add too much salt as blue cheese is quite salty.

5 Pour the mixture into the pastry shell, reduce the oven temperature to 180°C (160°C fan, Gas 4), and bake the quiche for about 30 minutes until golden and set. Serve warm or cold.

Smoked salmon and asparagus quiche

SERVES 6–8 **CALS PER SERVING** 321–241

- 125 g (4 oz) fine asparagus, cooked, drained, and cut into 3.5 cm ($1\frac{1}{2}$ in) lengths
- 100 g ($3\frac{1}{2}$ oz) smoked salmon, cut into strips
- 300 g (10 oz) Greek yogurt or full-fat crème fraîche
- 2 eggs
- 1 tbsp chopped fresh dill
- black pepper

Shortcrust pastry

- 175 g (6 oz) plain flour
- 90 g (3 oz) butter
- 1 large egg, beaten

23 CM (9 IN) LOOSE-BOTTOMED FLUTED FLAN TIN

BAKING BEANS

1 Make the pastry: tip the flour into a bowl, rub in the butter with your fingertips, then add enough egg to bind to a soft dough. Wrap in cling film and chill for 30 minutes.

2 Roll out the pastry, and use to line the tin. Prick the pastry with a fork. Line the pastry shell with foil or greaseproof paper, and fill with baking beans (or rice or pasta if you have no beans).

3 Place the tin on a heated baking tray and bake in a preheated oven at 220°C (200°C fan, Gas 7) for 15–20 minutes, removing the foil and beans for the final 10 minutes.

4 Arrange the asparagus and half of the salmon in the pastry shell. Mix the yogurt or crème fraîche, eggs, dill, and plenty of pepper, and pour into the shell. Arrange the remaining salmon on top.

5 Reduce the oven temperature to 180°C (160°C fan, Gas 4), and bake for 35 minutes or until golden and set. Serve warm or cold.

Bacon and Gruyère galette

SERVES 6 **CALS PER SERVING** 472

- 200 g (7 oz) smoked streaky bacon rashers, rinds removed, chopped
- 2 onions, roughly chopped
- 375 g (12 oz) ready-made puff pastry
- 1 x 290 g jar roasted peppers, drained and thinly sliced
- 2 tomatoes, thinly sliced
- salt and black pepper
- 150 g (5 oz) Gruyère cheese, grated

1 Fry the bacon in a frying pan over a high heat for a few minutes until the fat runs, then add the onions and fry for a further minute. Turn the heat down to low, cover, and cook for 15 minutes or until the onions are soft. Remove the lid, increase the heat to high, and fry for a few minutes to evaporate any liquid, stirring frequently. Set aside to cool.

2 Put a large baking tray in the oven, and preheat the oven to 220°C (200°C fan, Gas 7).

3 Roll out the pastry on a lightly floured surface until about 5 mm ($\frac{1}{4}$ in) thick. Cut out a 28 cm (11 in) round, using a dinner plate or frying pan as a guide. Place the pastry round on a sheet of baking parchment, and prick all over with a fork.

4 Spread the bacon and onions over the pastry, and top with the peppers and tomatoes. Season with salt and pepper, and sprinkle with the cheese.

5 Carefully lift the galette on the paper, and place it on the hot baking tray. Bake for 20–25 minutes until the cheese and pastry are golden brown. Slice into six wedges, and serve hot or warm.

Pizza tartlets

These tartlets, with their traditional pizza flavours, will serve four people as a light lunch or supper dish, accompanied by a crisp, green salad. They also make a tasty appetizer to serve with pre-dinner drinks. They taste just as good cold as warm, so they can be prepared well in advance.

MAKES 12 **CALS EACH** 198

- 90 g (3 oz) green pesto
- 250 g (8 oz) ripe tomatoes, finely chopped
- 2–3 garlic cloves, crushed
- 9 black olives, pitted and quartered
- 125 g (4 oz) Fontina or mozzarella cheese, grated
- 2–3 tbsp grated Parmesan cheese
- 2 tsp chopped fresh marjoram

Shortcrust pastry

- 175 g (6 oz) plain flour
- 90 g (3 oz) butter
- 1 large egg, beaten

1 Make the pastry: tip the flour into a bowl and rub in the butter with your fingertips. Add enough egg to bind to a soft dough. Wrap in cling film and chill for 30 minutes.

2 Make the tartlet shells (see box, right).

3 Spread the pesto in the tartlet shells, then fill the shells with the tomatoes, garlic, black olives, and Fontina cheese.

4 Sprinkle the grated Parmesan cheese over the tartlets, covering the pastry edges as well as the filling. Sprinkle the chopped marjoram on top.

5 Bake the tartlets in a preheated oven at 200°C (180°C fan, Gas 6) for 20–30 minutes until the edges are a golden brown colour and the cheese topping has melted and become crispy. Serve the tartlets warm or cold.

GOAT'S CHEESE TARTLETS

Cut a log of goat's cheese into 12 slices and use instead of the grated Fontina or mozzarella.

Making tartlet shells

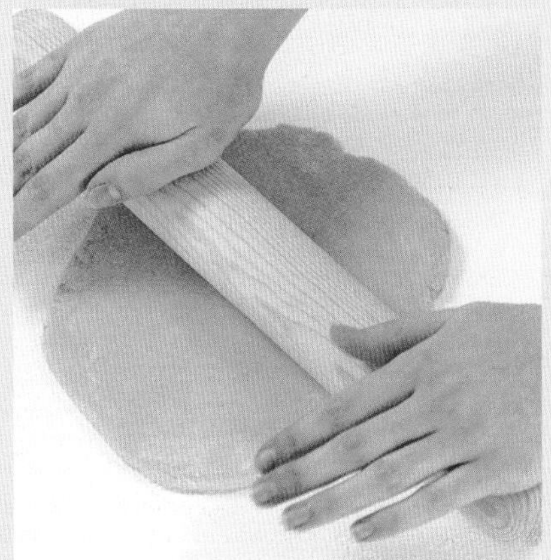

Sprinkle the work surface with flour, then roll out the shortcrust pastry until 3–5 mm (1/8–1/4 in) thick.

Cut out 12 rounds from the pastry, using a 10 cm (4 in) pastry cutter or the rim of a glass or saucer.

Fold up the edges of the rounds to form rims; put the rounds on a baking tray.

Spinach, leek, and Gruyère tart

SERVES 6 **CALS PER SERVING** 480

30 g (1 oz) butter
175 g (6 oz) leeks, trimmed and finely sliced
250 g (8 oz) young spinach leaves, coarsely chopped
2 eggs, beaten
150 ml (1/4 pint) each double cream and milk, or 300 ml (1/2 pint) milk
90 g (3 oz) Gruyère cheese, grated
salt and black pepper

Shortcrust pastry

175 g (6 oz) plain flour
90 g (3 oz) butter
1 large egg, lightly beaten

23 CM (9 IN) LOOSE-BOTTOMED FLUTED FLAN TIN
BAKING BEANS

1 Make the pastry: tip the flour into a bowl and rub in the butter with your fingertips. Add enough egg to bind to a soft dough. Wrap in cling film and chill for 30 minutes.

2 Roll out the pastry on a lightly floured work surface, and use to line the flan tin. Prick the bottom of the pastry shell with a fork.

3 Line the pastry shell with foil or greaseproof paper, and fill with baking beans (or rice or pasta if you have no beans). Put the tin on a heated baking tray, and bake in a preheated oven at 220°C (200°C fan, Gas 7) for 15–20 minutes, removing the foil and beans for the final 10 minutes.

4 Meanwhile, make the filling: melt the butter in a frying pan, add the leeks, and cook over a high heat for 5 minutes or until just beginning to turn golden brown. Add the spinach and cook for about 2 minutes until it just begins to wilt. Spoon the filling into the pastry shell.

5 Mix together the eggs, milk, cream, and Gruyère cheese in a jug, season with salt and pepper, and pour into the pastry shell.

6 Reduce the oven temperature to 180°C (160°C fan, Gas 4), and bake for 25 minutes or until the filling is golden and set. Serve warm or cold with crisp salad leaves and cherry tomatoes.

Classic cheese soufflé

SERVES 4 **CALS PER SERVING** 363

300 ml (½ pint) milk
1 bay leaf
a few parsley stalks
½ onion, peeled
pinch of cayenne pepper
salt and black pepper
45 g (1½ oz) butter, plus extra for greasing
45 g (1½ oz) plain flour
3 eggs, separated
1 tbsp Dijon mustard
125 g (4 oz) mature Cheddar cheese, grated

1.25 LITRE (2 PINT) SOUFFLÉ DISH

1 Bring the milk to a boil in a saucepan with the bay leaf, parsley stalks, and onion half. Remove from the heat, cover, and leave to infuse for about 20 minutes. Strain, then add the cayenne and season with salt and pepper.

2 Melt the butter in a large pan, add the flour, and cook, stirring, for 1 minute. Remove from the heat, slowly blend in the milk, then bring to a boil. Simmer for 2–3 minutes, stirring, until thickened, then remove from the heat. Leave to cool for about 10 minutes.

3 Beat the egg yolks in a bowl. Stir them into the cooled white sauce, then stir in the mustard and all but 15 g (½ oz) of the Cheddar cheese.

4 Whisk the egg whites until they form firm but not dry peaks. Fold 1–2 tbsp egg whites into the cheese mixture until evenly combined, then fold in the remaining egg whites.

5 Lightly butter the soufflé dish, pour in the soufflé mixture, and sprinkle with the remaining cheese

6 Bake on a preheated baking sheet in the top half of a preheated oven at 180°C (160°C fan, Gas 4) for about 25 minutes, or until just set in the middle. Serve at once.

Soufflé pancakes with broccoli and cheese

MAKES 8 **CALS EACH** 200

8 pancakes (page 78)
butter, for greasing
2 tbsp grated Parmesan cheese

Filling

125 g (4 oz) tiny broccoli florets
salt and black pepper
45 g (1½ oz) butter
45 g (1½ oz) plain flour
300 ml (½ pint) milk
½ tsp Dijon mustard
125 g (4 oz) mature Cheddar cheese, grated
4 eggs, separated

1 Make the filling: blanch the broccoli florets in boiling salted water for 1 minute. Drain, rinse under cold running water, and drain again.

2 Melt the butter in a small saucepan, add the flour, and cook, stirring occasionally, for about 1 minute.

3 Remove the pan from the heat, and gradually blend in the milk. Bring to a boil, stirring until thickened. Remove from the heat, add the mustard and cheese, and season with salt and pepper. Stir, then leave to cool slightly.

4 Beat the egg yolks into the sauce. In a large bowl, whisk the egg whites until soft peaks form, then fold into the cheese sauce with the broccoli.

5 Lay the pancakes on two lightly buttered baking trays. Divide the soufflé mixture among the pancakes, arranging it down the middle of each one. Fold the sides of each pancake loosely over the top of the filling, and sprinkle with grated Parmesan cheese.

6 Bake in a preheated oven at 200°C (180°C fan, Gas 6) for 15–20 minutes, until the soufflé mixture has risen and the pancakes are crisp.

Swiss double cheese soufflés

SERVES 6 **CALS PER SERVING** 465

- 45 g (1½ oz) butter, plus extra for greasing
- 45 g (1½ oz) plain flour
- 300 ml (½ pint) milk
- 60 g (2 oz) Gruyère cheese, grated
- 2 tbsp snipped fresh chives, plus extra to garnish
- salt and black pepper
- 3 eggs, separated
- 60 g (2 oz) Parmesan cheese, grated
- 300 ml (½ pint) double cream

6 X 150 ML RAMEKINS

LARGE SHALLOW GRATIN DISH

1 Melt the butter in a large saucepan, add the flour, and cook, stirring, for 1 minute. Remove from the heat and gradually blend in the milk. Return to the heat and bring to a boil, stirring until the mixture thickens.

2 Remove the pan from the heat and beat in the Gruyère cheese and chives. Season with salt and pepper, and stir in the egg yolks.

3 Whisk the egg whites until stiff but not dry. Stir 1 tbsp into the mixture, then fold in the rest.

4 Generously butter the ramekins, and divide the mixture equally among them. Place the ramekins in a small roasting tin, and pour boiling water into the tin to come halfway up the sides of the ramekins.

5 Bake the soufflés in a preheated oven at 220°C (200°C fan, Gas 7) for 15–20 minutes until golden and springy to the touch. Leave the soufflés to stand for 5–10 minutes; they will shrink by about one-third.

6 Butter the gratin dish. Sprinkle half of the Parmesan cheese over the bottom. Run a palette knife around the edge of each soufflé, unmould carefully, and arrange on top of the Parmesan in the gratin dish.

7 Season the cream with salt and pepper, then pour over the soufflés. Sprinkle the remaining Parmesan over the top, and return to the oven for 15–20 minutes until golden. Garnish with snipped chives.

Stilton and broccoli soufflés

SERVES 8 **CALS PER SERVING** 182

45 g (1½ oz) butter, plus extra for greasing
45 g (1½ oz) plain flour
250 ml (8 fl oz) hot milk
150 g (5½ oz) broccoli florets
salt and black pepper
1 tbsp olive oil
1 large banana shallot, finely chopped
1 tsp Dijon mustard
pinch of grated nutmeg
75 g (3 oz) blue Stilton cheese, grated
4 eggs, separated

8 SMALL RAMEKINS

1 Melt the butter in a saucepan. Add the flour and cook, stirring, for 30 seconds. Pour in the hot milk and whisk until thickened and boiling. Remove from the heat and leave to cool for 10 minutes.

2 Cook the broccoli in boiling salted water for 2–3 minutes until just tender. Drain and rinse under cold water. Drain well, then chop coarsely.

3 Heat 1 tbsp of oil in a saucepan. Add the shallot and cook gently until soft.

4 Add the mustard, nutmeg, Stilton cheese, seasoning, and egg yolks to the mixture. Stir until well mixed, then fold in the broccoli.

5 Whisk the egg whites until stiff but not dry. Fold in 2 tbsp of the egg whites into the cheese mixture, then gently fold in the remaining egg whites. Prepare the ramekins (see box, below), then carefully spoon in the mixture and run your finger around the edge.

6 Place on a baking sheet and bake in a preheated oven at 220°C (200°C fan, Gas 7) for 15 minutes, until the soufflés are well-risen and lightly golden brown, but still soft and moist in the middle.

Preparing the ramekins

Butter the bottoms and sides of the ramekins. Sprinkle with a thin layer of grated Parmesan cheese.

Garlic and goat's cheese soufflés

SERVES 6 **CALS PER SERVING** 267

1 head of garlic
250 ml (8 fl oz) milk
125 ml (4 fl oz) water
45 g (1½ oz) butter, plus extra for greasing
45 g (1½ oz) plain flour
150 g (5 oz) goat's cheese, diced
6 eggs, separated
salt and black pepper
fresh chives, to garnish

6 X 150 ML (¼ PINT) RAMEKINS

1 Separate and peel the garlic cloves. Put the milk, measured water, and all but one of the garlic cloves into a saucepan. Bring to a boil, then simmer for 15–20 minutes until the garlic is tender and the liquid has reduced to 250 ml (8 fl oz). Leave to cool. Lightly mash the garlic in the milk.

2 Melt the butter in a saucepan, add the flour, and cook, stirring, for 1 minute. Remove from the heat, and gradually blend in the garlic milk.

3 Return to the heat and bring to a boil, stirring constantly, until the mixture thickens. Simmer for 2–3 minutes. Transfer to a large bowl and leave to cool for about 10 minutes. Chop the remaining garlic clove.

4 Add the chopped garlic, diced goat's cheese, and egg yolks to the cooled sauce. Season with salt and pepper.

5 In a large bowl, whisk the egg whites until stiff but not dry. Stir 1 tbsp of the egg whites into the garlic and cheese mixture, then fold in the remaining egg whites.

6 Lightly butter the ramekins, pour in the soufflé mixture, and bake in a preheated oven at 180°C (160°C fan, Gas 4) for 15–20 minutes. Serve at once, garnished with chives.

Filling and folding the crêpes

Put a pancake on a serving plate. Put 2–3 spoonfuls of the seafood filling on to one half and spread it to within 5 mm (¼ in) of the edge.

Fold the unfilled half of the pancake over the seafood filling to enclose it.

Fold the pancake in half again, to form a triangle. Keep warm. Repeat with the remaining pancakes and filling.

Creamy seafood crêpes

The succulent filling of prawns and white fish in a herby cream sauce makes these crêpes really rich and special – ideal for a weekend lunch served with a crisp green salad. You could also serve them as a dinner party first course, allowing just one per person. The unfilled crêpes can be made in advance and stored in the freezer for up to 1 month.

SERVES 6 **CALS PER SERVING** 308

Filling

250 g (8 oz) cod fillet, skinned
375 g (12 oz) cooked prawns in their shells
2 tbsp olive oil
1 small onion, finely chopped
1 garlic clove, crushed
4 tomatoes, finely chopped
1 tbsp chopped fresh dill
salt and black pepper
3 tbsp single cream
2 tbsp chopped fresh basil
basil and lemon, to garnish

Pancakes

125 g (4 oz) plain flour
1 egg, plus 1 egg yolk
300 ml (½ pint) milk
sunflower oil, for frying

1 Make the pancake batter: sift the flour into a large bowl, and make a well in the middle. Add the egg, extra egg yolk, and a little of the milk.

2 Gradually blend in the flour, beating until smooth. Add the remaining milk to make a thin, creamy batter. Leave to stand while you make the filling.

3 Cut the cod fillet into 1 cm (½ in) pieces. Reserve 12 prawns for the garnish, and peel the remainder.

4 Heat the oil in a medium saucepan, add the onion and garlic, and cook very gently, stirring occasionally, for about 10 minutes until soft but not coloured.

5 Add the cod, tomatoes, and dill, and season with salt and pepper. Cook over a medium heat, stirring, for 10 minutes or until thick.

6 Stir in the cream and prawns and heat gently. Remove from the heat and stir in the basil. Keep warm.

7 Make the pancakes. Heat a small frying pan, and brush with a little oil. Stir the batter, ladle about 3 tbsp into the pan, and cook for 1 minute until the underside is golden. Turn and cook the second side, then slide out of the pan and keep hot. Repeat to make 12 pancakes.

8 Fill the pancakes with the seafood mixture, and fold (see box, opposite). Garnish with basil and lemon, and the reserved prawns.

Chicken pancakes florentine

SERVES 8 **CALS PER SERVING** 360

500 g (1 lb) spinach leaves, coarsely chopped
30 g (1 oz) butter
pinch of grated nutmeg
8 pancakes (page 78)
125 g (4 oz) Gruyère cheese, grated

Filling

60 g (2 oz) butter
375 g (12 oz) chestnut mushrooms, quartered
45 g (1½ oz) plain flour
300 ml (½ pint) chicken stock
375 g (12 oz) boneless and skinless cooked chicken, cut into bite-sized pieces
1 tbsp chopped fresh tarragon
salt and black pepper

1 Make the filling: melt the butter in a heavy pan, add the mushrooms, and cook, stirring often, for 2–3 minutes.

2 Add the flour, and cook, stirring, for 1 minute. Remove the pan from the heat, and gradually blend in the stock. Bring to a boil, stirring, and simmer for 2–3 minutes. Add the chicken and tarragon, and season with salt and pepper.

3 Rinse the spinach and put into a saucepan with only the water that clings to the leaves. Cook for 2 minutes or until tender. Drain well, squeezing to extract any excess water, then stir in the butter and nutmeg. Spoon into a shallow ovenproof dish.

4 Divide the chicken and mushroom mixture among the eight pancakes. Roll up the pancakes, and place them in a single layer on top of the spinach.

5 Sprinkle with the cheese, and bake in a preheated oven at 190°C (170°C fan, Gas 5) for about 25 minutes until golden. Serve hot.

Croque señor

SERVES 4 **CALS PER SERVING** 413

8 slices of white bread
4 slices of mature Cheddar cheese
4 slices of ham
30 g (1 oz) butter, softened
lemon wedges and coriander sprigs, to garnish

Spicy tomato salsa

3 ripe but firm tomatoes, finely chopped
1 red pepper, halved, deseeded, roasted, and peeled (page 426), finely chopped
1 garlic clove, crushed
2 spring onions, thinly sliced
1 fresh green chilli, halved, deseeded, and chopped
1 tbsp red wine vinegar
salt

1 Make the salsa: combine the tomatoes, red pepper, garlic, spring onions, chilli, and vinegar in a bowl. Season with salt and set aside.

2 Put 4 slices of bread on to a board, and arrange the cheese and ham slices on top. Spoon the salsa over the ham.

3 Lightly spread the butter over one side of the remaining slices of bread and put them, butter-side up, on top of the salsa.

4 Heat a heavy frying pan, and cook each sandwich, butter-side down, over a medium–high heat until the cheese begins to melt and the bread becomes golden. Lightly spread the second side of each sandwich with butter. Turn over and cook the other side until golden.

5 Garnish with lemon wedges, coriander sprigs, and any remaining spicy tomato salsa. Serve hot.

Cheese fondue

SERVES 6 **CALS PER SERVING** 813

1 large loaf of crusty bread, crusts left on, cut into 2.5 cm (1 in) triangles
250 g (8 oz) Gruyère cheese, coarsely grated
250 g (8 oz) Emmental cheese, coarsely grated
30 g (1 oz) cornflour
500 ml (16 fl oz) dry white wine
1 garlic clove, lightly crushed
2 tbsp kirsch
pinch of grated nutmeg
salt and black pepper

To serve (optional)

2 eating apples, quartered and sliced
60 g (2 oz) sesame seeds, toasted
30 g (1 oz) cumin seeds, toasted

1 FONDUE SET

1 Place the pieces of bread on a large baking tray and put into a preheated oven at 160°C (140°C fan, Gas 3) for 3–5 minutes until dried out slightly.

2 Put the Gruyère and Emmental cheeses into a medium bowl, and toss with the cornflour.

3 Put the wine and garlic into a fondue pot and boil for 2 minutes, then lower the heat so that the mixture is barely simmering. Add the cheese mixture, a spoonful at a time, stirring constantly with a fork and letting each spoonful melt before adding the next.

4 When the fondue is creamy and smooth, stir in the kirsch, nutmeg, and salt and pepper to taste.

5 Stand the fondue pot over the burner, with the heat low so the mixture barely simmers. Offer the baked bread round for dipping into the fondue, with apple slices, sesame seeds, and cumin seeds if you like.

Raclette

SERVES 4 **CALS PER SERVING** 446

1 kg (2 lb) new potatoes, halved
salt
250 g (8 oz) Swiss raclette cheese, cut into 16 thin slices
1 red onion, thinly sliced
12 cornichons or small gherkins
12 cocktail pickled onions

1 Cook the potatoes in boiling salted water for 12–15 minutes until just tender. Drain, and keep the potatoes warm.

2 Put four heavy, ovenproof serving plates into a preheated oven at 240°C (220°C fan, Gas 9) to warm for 3–5 minutes.

3 Divide the potatoes among the plates, and arrange 4 slices of raclette cheese on top of each serving. Return the plates to the oven for 1–2 minutes until the cheese is melted and sizzling.

4 Divide the red onion slices, gherkins, and pickled onions among the plates, and serve at once.

Fish and shellfish

In this chapter...

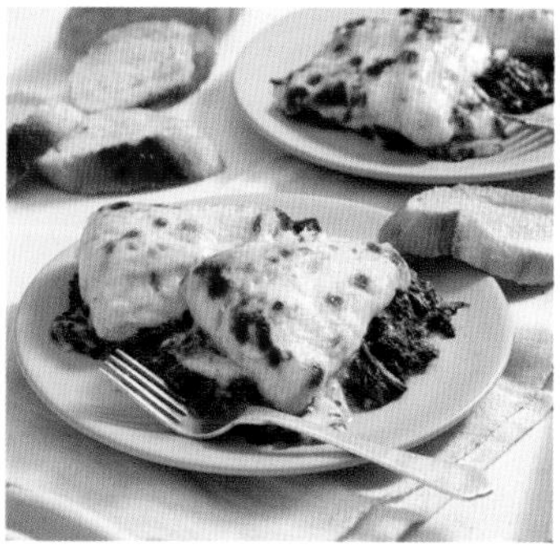
Lemon sole florentine
page 108

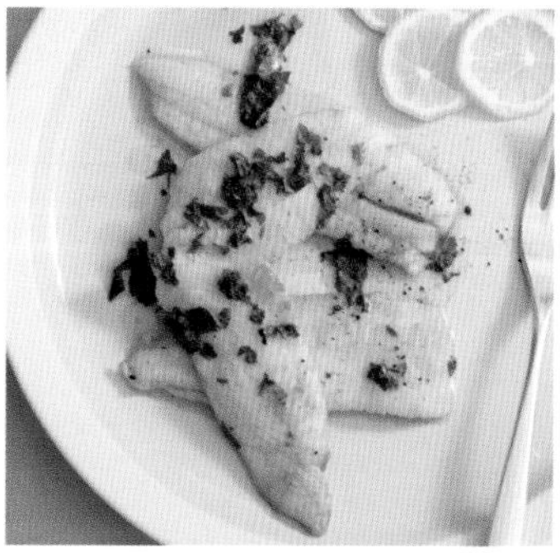
Fillets of sole meunière
page 109

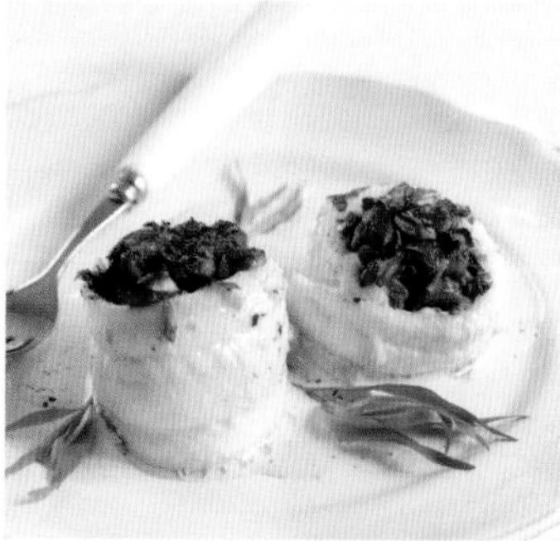
Mushroom-stuffed sole fillets
page 109

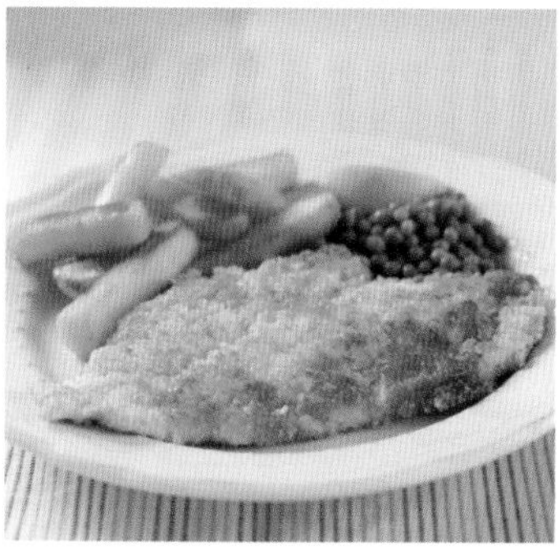
Best-ever fried fish
page 110

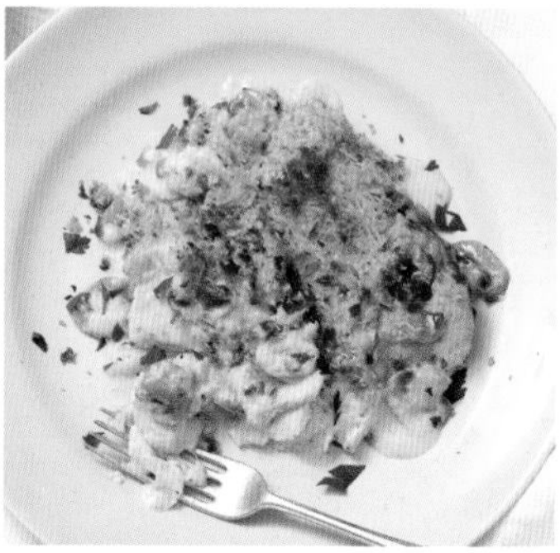
Haddock with mushrooms and cream
page 111

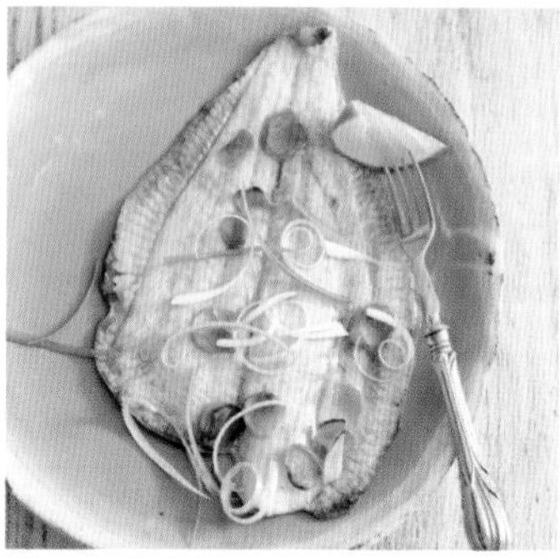
Gingered plaice
page 112

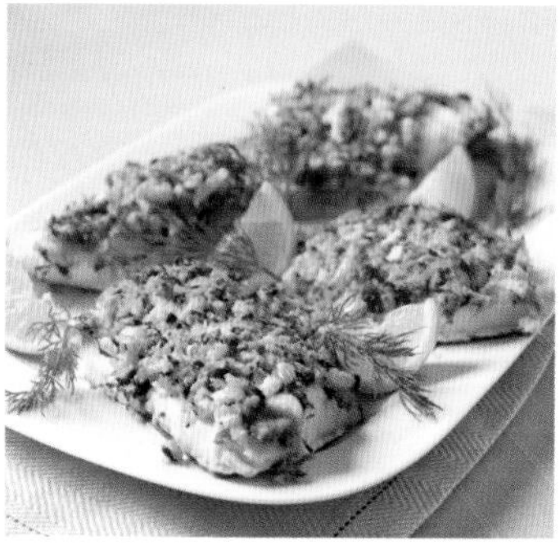
Cod steaks with anchovy and fennel
page 112

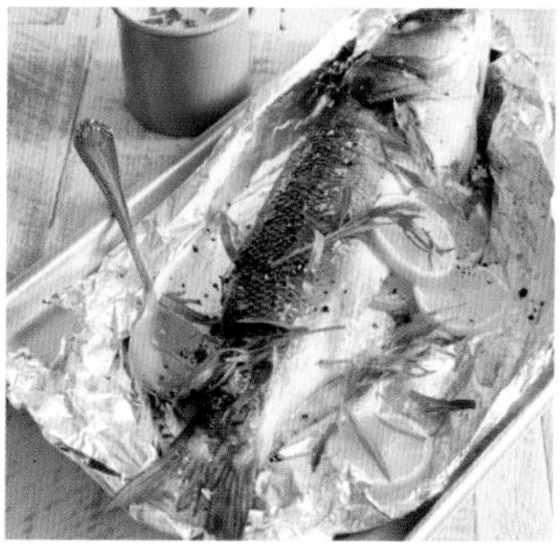
Sea bass with lemon butter sauce
page 113

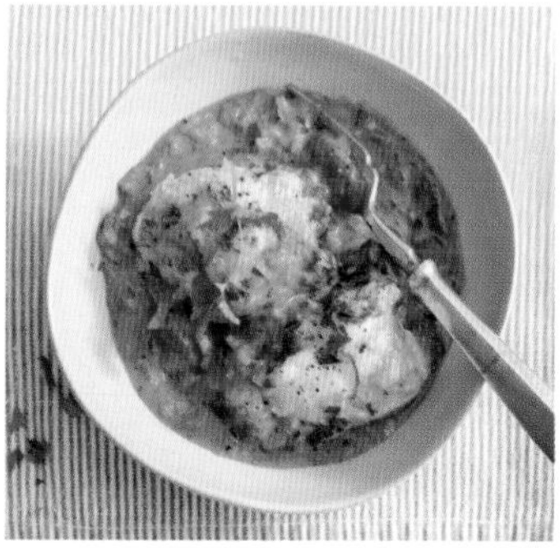
Spiced fish with coconut
page 113

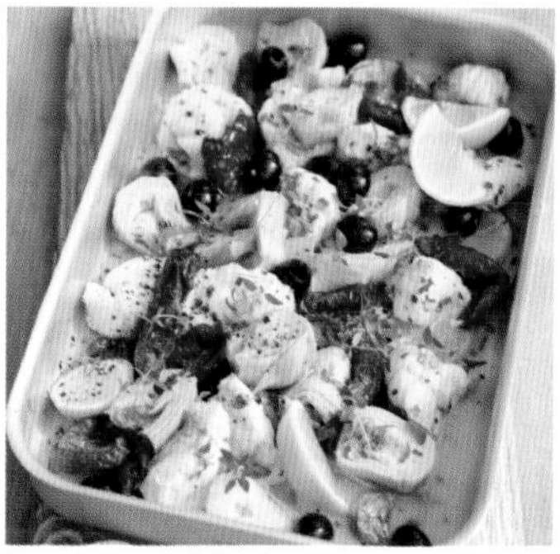
Roast monkfish niçoise
page 114

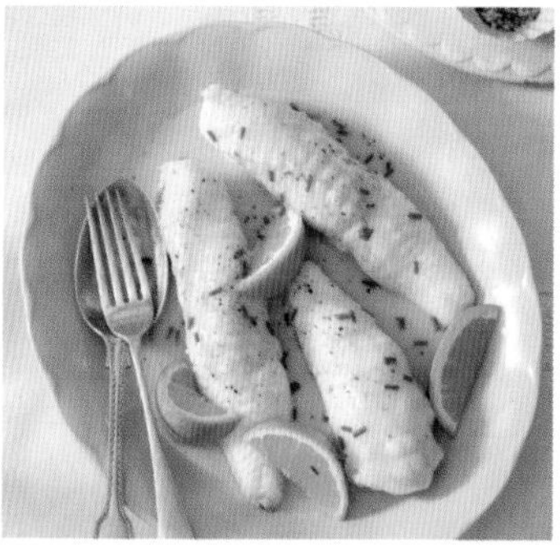
Monkfish with ginger-orange sauce
page 114

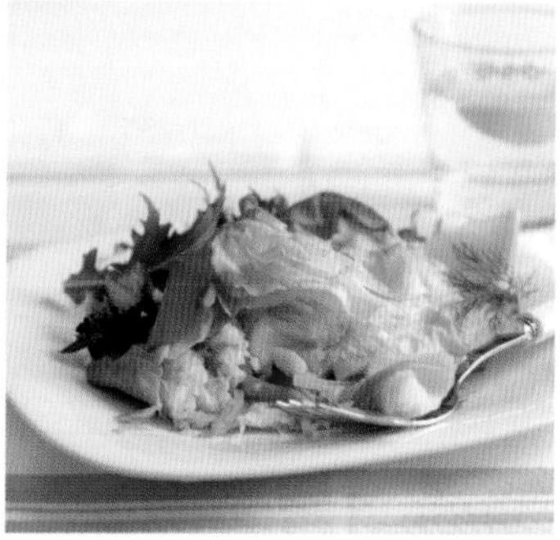
Halibut in filo parcels
page 116

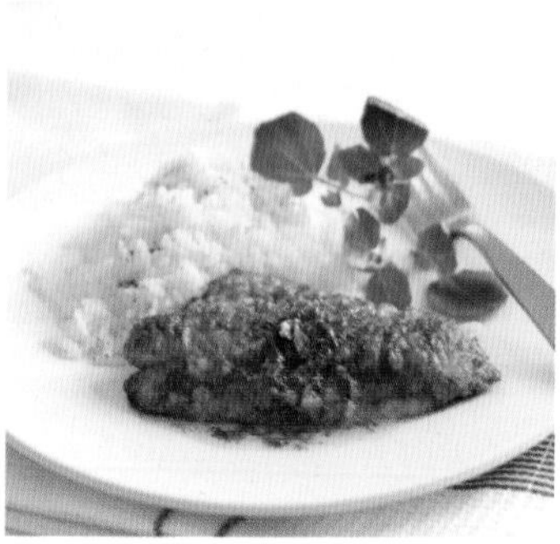
Cajun-spiced red snapper
page 117

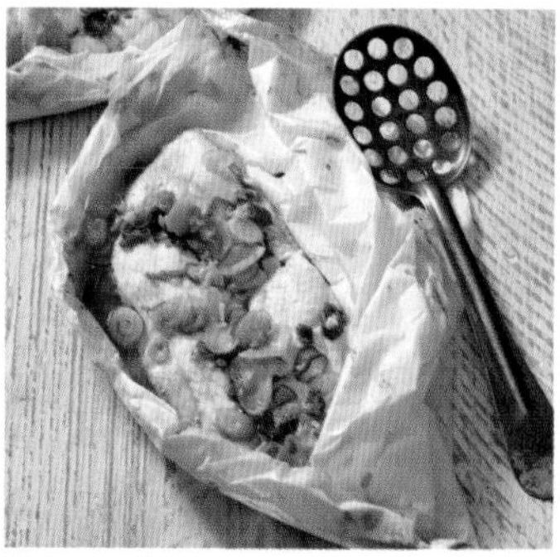
Oriental fish parcels
page 117

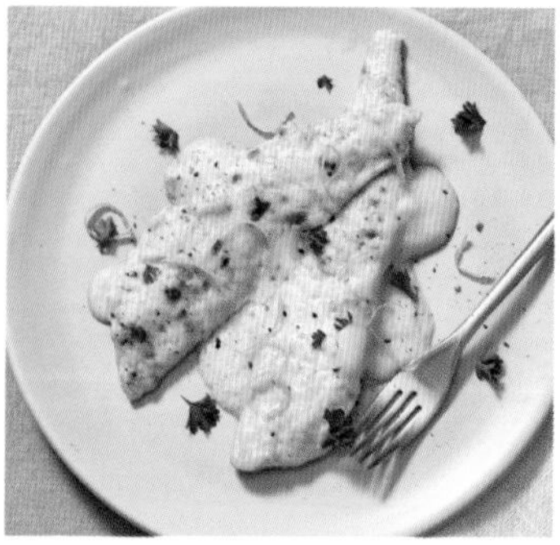
Cheese-topped baked bream
page 118

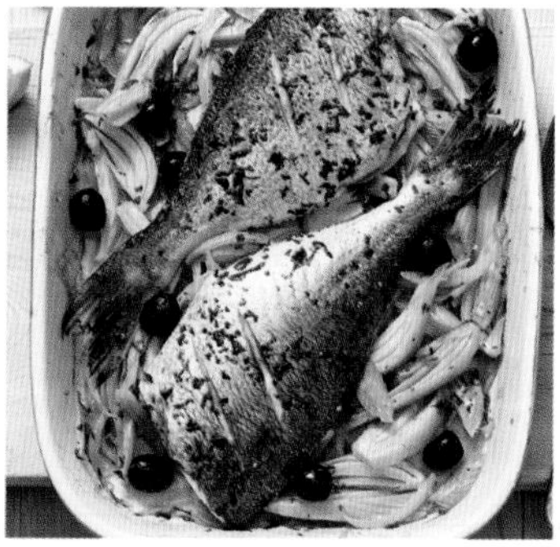
Sea bream niçoise
page 118

Koulibiac
page 120

Salmon with spinach salsa
page 121

Golden fish cakes
page 121

Salmon en croûte
page 122

Severn salmon
page 122

Warm honeyed salmon salad
page 122

Salmon with avocado
page 123

Classic buffet party salmon
page 124

Griddled salmon tranches
page 126

Herb-roasted salmon
page 126

Thai chilli salmon
page 128

Baked trout with orange
page 128

Smoked trout bake
page 129

In this chapter... *continued*

Tiger prawns with tarragon sauce
page 139

Thai prawn stir-fry
page 141

Devilled crab
page 141

Spicy clams with coriander dressing
page 142

Classic steamed clams with parsley
page 142

Lobster tails with black-eyed bean salsa
page 143

Chinese-style oysters
page 144

Lobster tails with mango and lime
page 143

Mediterranean stuffed squid
page 144

Mussel gratin
page 146

Scallops with asparagus and lemon
page 146

Fish and shellfish know-how

Seafood is delicious, versatile, and quick to cook. Compared with other protein foods it is excellent value for money as there is usually little wastage. In addition, it is very nutritious: all fish and shellfish are good sources of essential vitamins and minerals, but oily fish are particularly rich in vitamins A and D and also provide beneficial omega-3 fatty acids.

Seafood is divided into two broad categories: fish and shellfish. Fish may be white (its oil is found mainly in the liver) or oily (the oil is distributed in the flesh); white fish are further sub-divided according to body shape (round or flat). Of the shellfish, crustaceans (crab, prawns) have shells and legs; molluscs (mussels, scallops) just have shells. Squid is a mollusc with an internal "shell".

Cleaning and boning round fish

Round fish such as trout, mackerel, herring, and salmon are often cooked whole, and boning makes them easier to serve and eat. When boned they can also be stuffed. Fishmongers will prepare the fish for you, but if you want to do it yourself, here's how.

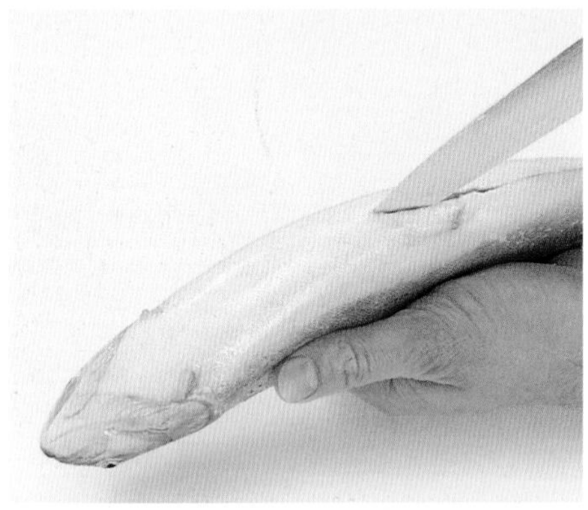

1 To clean the fish, first snip off the fins. Cut along the belly, from the vent end to just below the head. Remove the innards, scraping away any dark blood. Lift the gill covering and remove the concertina-shaped gills. Rinse well.

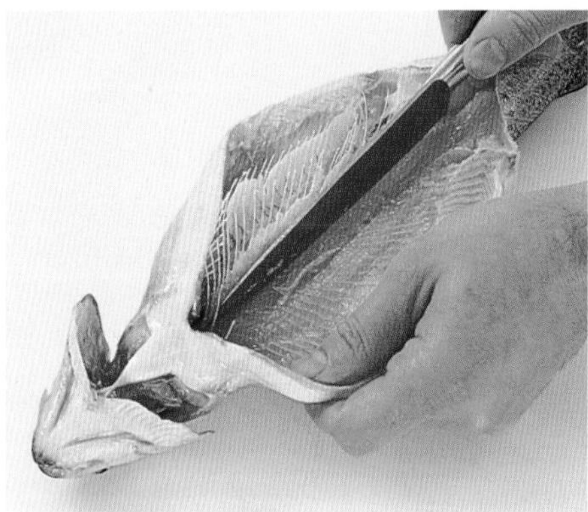

2 To bone, extend the belly opening so that it goes all the way to the tail. Hold the belly open and carefully run the knife between the flesh and the bones along one side, from tail to head, to cut the flesh from the ribcage.

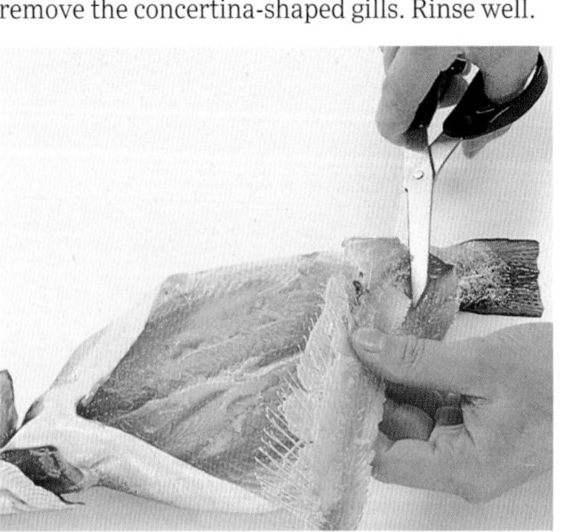

3 Turn the fish around and cut the flesh from the ribcage on the other side. Snip through the backbone at each end and gently pull it away from the flesh, removing it with the ribcage in one piece.

4 If the head and tail have been cut off, open out the fish and lay it skin-side up. Press along the backbone to loosen the bones. Turn over and lift or cut out the ribcage and backbone. The fish is now "butterflied".

Buying and storing

Always buy sustainable fish from a reliable source. Let aroma and appearance be your guides for freshness. Seafood should have the clean smell of the sea. If it has an unpleasantly "fishy" or ammonia-like odour, it is not fresh.

Whole fresh fish should have clean, red gills, the scales should be firmly attached, and it should be covered in a clear slime; the flesh should feel firm and springy. The flesh of fillets and steaks should be firm, moist, and lustrous. If at all possible ask for steaks to be cut while you wait. If buying pre-packaged fish, check the colour of any liquid that has accumulated in the pack: it should not be cloudy or off-white.

Shellfish is sold both in the shell and shelled, raw and cooked. The shells of crabs, lobsters, and prawns become pink or red when cooked. Live shellfish, such as mussels, clams, and oysters, should have tightly closed shells. If any shells are open they should close if lightly tapped; if they do not, the shellfish is dead and should be discarded. Shelled oysters, scallops, and clams should be plump; scallops should smell slightly sweet. Prawns should also smell faintly sweet, and feel firm.

Keep the fish or shellfish cool until you get home, then unwrap it, cover with a wet cloth or wet paper towels, and store in the coldest part of the refrigerator. Use oily fish and shellfish the same day; keep white fish no more than 24 hours.

Freezing

It's best to buy fish ready-frozen, as it will have been processed and frozen at very low temperatures immediately after being caught – while still at sea – to prevent there being any deterioration.

If you have fish to freeze yourself, clean it and wrap tightly. For the best flavour, store white fish for no longer than 3 months, oily fish and shellfish for 2 months. (When buying, be aware that some seafood sold as “fresh” may have been frozen and then thawed, so it should not be frozen again at home.)

Fish fillets and some shellfish can be cooked very successfully from frozen, but if you need to thaw seafood before cooking, do so slowly in the refrigerator or quickly in the microwave.

Microwaving

One of the best uses for a microwave is for cooking or thawing fish: they retain their texture and all of their flavourful juices. However, you should only cook fillets of fish. Whole fish have delicate areas, such as the tail and head, which can get overcooked in the microwave. For the same reason, do not cook or defrost shellfish in the microwave, as there is no way of protecting the delicate flesh.

Scaling

Unless skinning a fish before cooking, the scales should be removed. Dip your fingers in salt to ensure a firm grip and grasp the fish tail. Using the blunt side of a knife, with firm strokes scrape off the scales, from tail to head. Rinse well. Or ask your fishmonger to do this.

Fish stock

Ask your fishmonger for heads, bones, and trimmings from lean white fish (not oily fish, which make a bitter-tasting stock).

Rinse 750 g (1½ lb) bones and trimmings and put them into a large pan. Add 1 litre (1¾ pints) water and 250 ml (8 fl oz) dry white wine. Bring to a boil, skimming the surface.

Add 1 sliced onion, 1 sliced carrot, 1 chopped celery stalk, 1 bay leaf, a few parsley sprigs, and a few black peppercorns. Simmer for 20–25 minutes. Strain. Use immediately, or cool, cover, and refrigerate to use within 2 days. It can also be frozen for up to 3 months.

Filleting flat fish

Either two wide or four narrow fillets can be cut from a small flat fish. Larger flat fish will yield four good-sized fillets. Keep the bones for making stock.

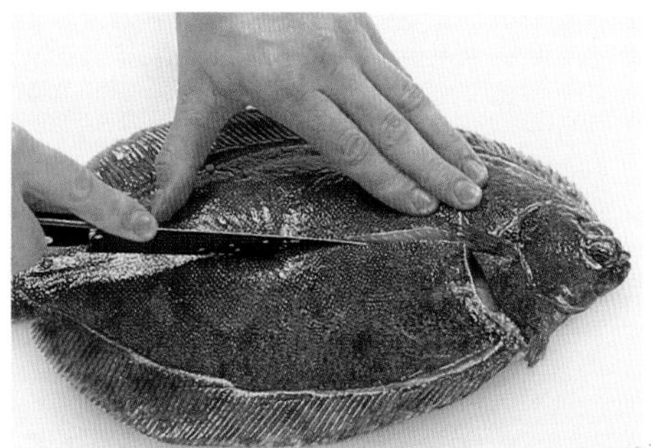

1 Make a shallow cut through the skin around the edge of the fish, where the fin bones meet the body. Cut across the tail and make a curved cut around the head. Then cut down the centre of the fish, cutting through the flesh to the bone.

2 Insert the knife between the flesh and the bones on one side at the head end. Keeping the knife almost parallel to the fish, cut close to the bones, loosening the flesh to detach the fillet in one piece.

3 Repeat to remove the second fillet on the same side. Then turn the fish over and remove both of the fillets from the other side. Check the fillets for any stray bones, pulling them out with tweezers.

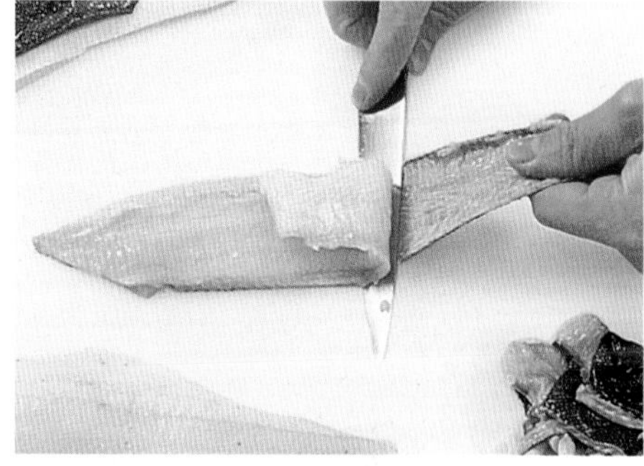

4 To skin, lay each fillet skin-side down and hold the tail with salted fingers to ensure a firm grip. Cut through the flesh at the tail end, then holding the knife at an angle and cut the flesh from the skin.

Preparing mussels and clams

Most mussels and clams are sold live and are cooked by steaming in their shells. They must be scrubbed before cooking. The anchoring threads found on mussels, known as beards, must also be removed.

1 To clean the shells of mussels and clams, hold under cold running water and scrub with a small stiff brush. Use a small knife to scrape off any barnacles.

2 To remove the beard from a mussel, hold the beard firmly between your thumb and the blade of a small knife and pull the beard away from the shell.

Preparing a cooked crab

The meat inside a crab is of two types – a soft, rich, brown meat and a flaky, sweet, white meat. When a crab is "dressed", the meat is removed from the shell, with the two types being kept separate, and then arranged back in the shell for serving.

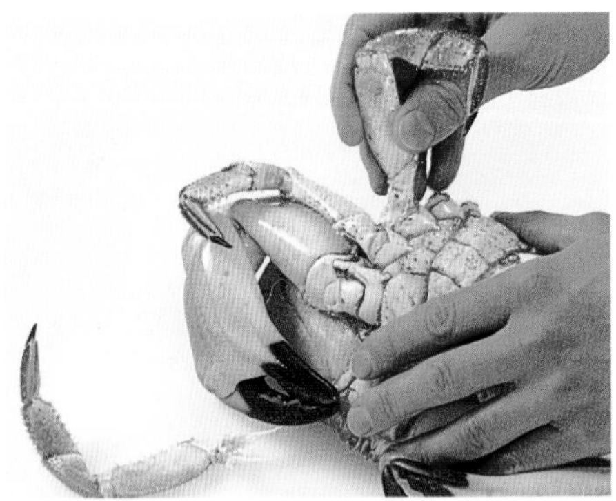

1 Put the crab on its back and twist off the legs and claws, close to the body.

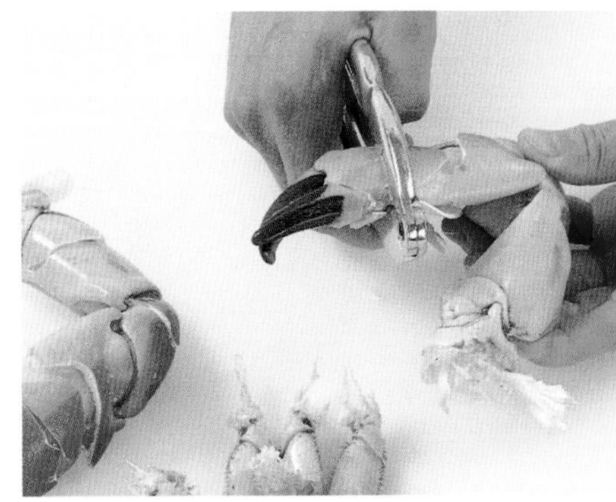

2 Using nutcrackers, a small hammer, or a rolling pin, crack the shells of the claws without crushing them. Break open the shells and carefully remove the meat, using a small fork or skewer.

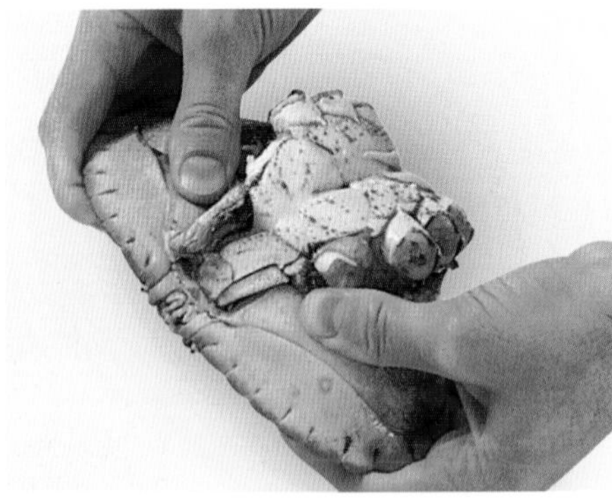

3 Press your thumbs along the "perforation" to crack the central section of the shell and prise it apart. Remove and discard the "apron" flap from the underside of the body.

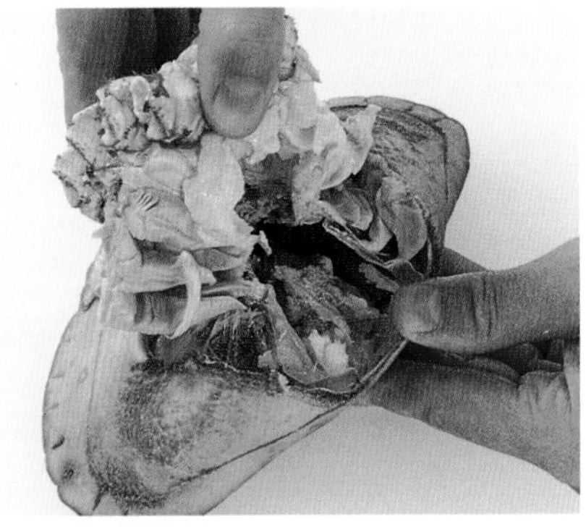

4 Pull the central body section up and away from the shell. Scoop the creamy-textured brown meat out of the shell and put it into a bowl (keeping it entirely separate from the white claw and leg meat). Scoop out any roe. Discard the stomach sac, which is located between the eyes.

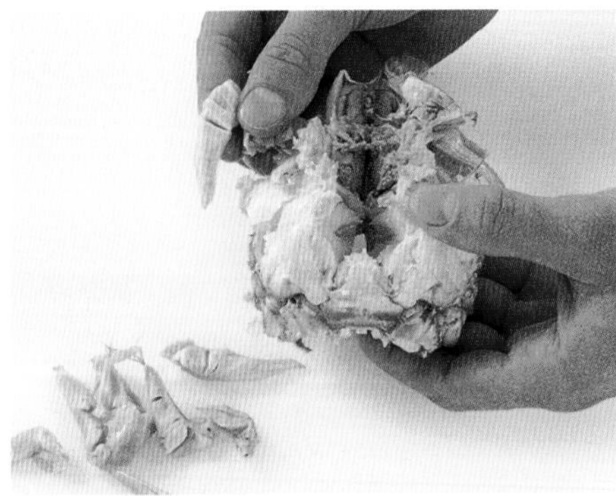

5 Pull the spongy gills (known as "dead man's fingers") from the body and discard them.

6 Cut the body in half with a large knife and pick out all the white meat from the crevices. Add to the white meat from the claws.

Preparing prawns

Both raw and cooked prawns can be used successfully in a variety of tasty dishes. When buying, take into account that prawns lose at least half of their weight when the heads and shells are removed.

1 Gently pull off the head and then the legs. Peel the shell from the body, leaving on the last tail section of shell if you like.

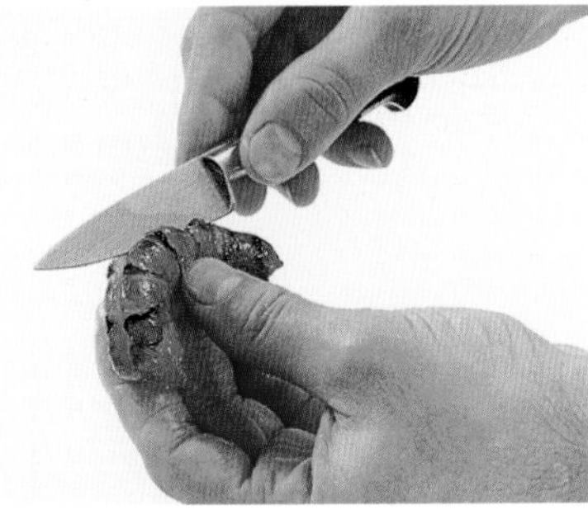

2 Make a shallow cut along the centre of the back of the prawn. Lift out the black intestinal vein and rinse the prawn under cold running water.

Preparing oysters

To shuck oysters, use an oyster knife or a small, sturdy knife.

Hold oyster round-side down, and insert the knife near the hinge. Lever the shells apart. Slide in the knife to sever the top muscle. Lift off the shell. Run the knife under the oyster to loosen it.

Preparing a cooked lobster

Ready-cooked lobster meat can be added to cooked dishes for a brief heating, or it can be served cold with mayonnaise (most attractively in the shell) or in a salad.

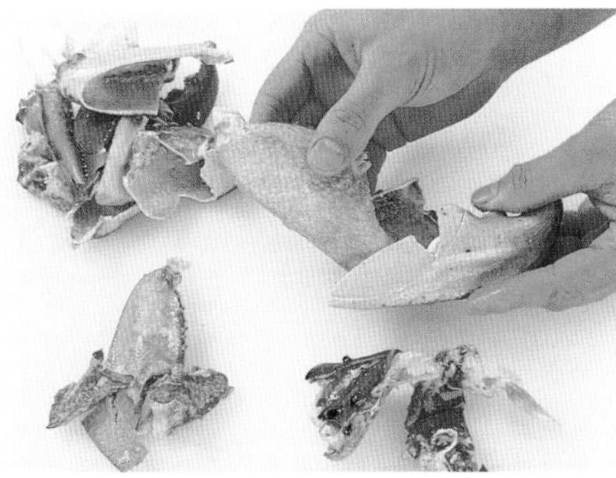

To remove the meat

1 Twist off the large claws. Using a sturdy nutcracker, a small hammer, or a rolling pin, crack the shells of the claws without crushing them. Pick out the meat in one or two large pieces. If the shell is not to be used for serving, pull apart the body and tail. Twist off the small legs, crack them, and remove the meat with a skewer or lobster pick.

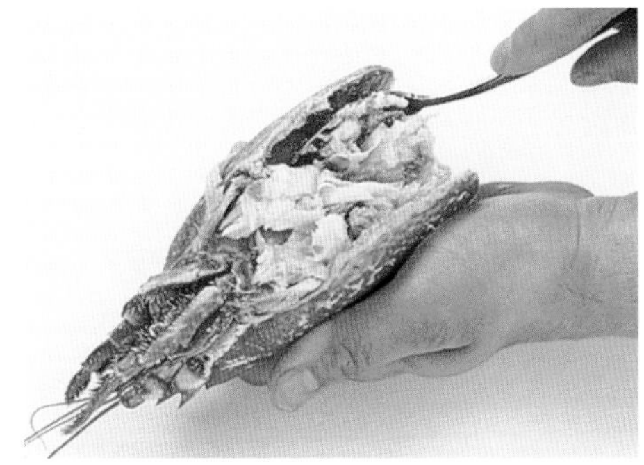

2 Lift off the top of the body shell. Scoop out the grey-green liver (tomalley) and any coral-coloured roe, both of which are edible, and reserve. Discard the stomach and spongy gills ("dead man's fingers").

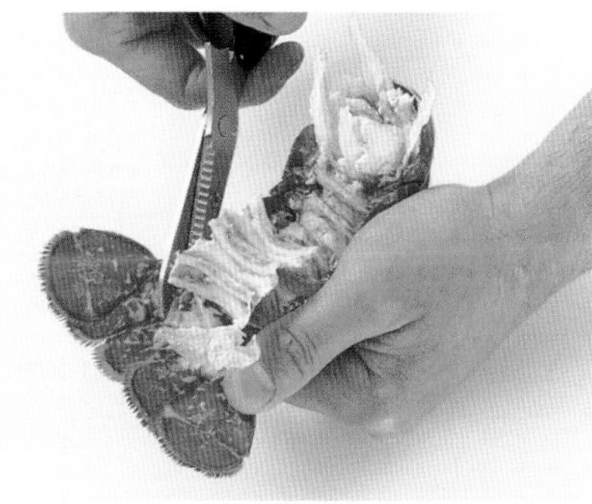

3 With scissors or a sharp knife, cut along the soft underside of the tail.

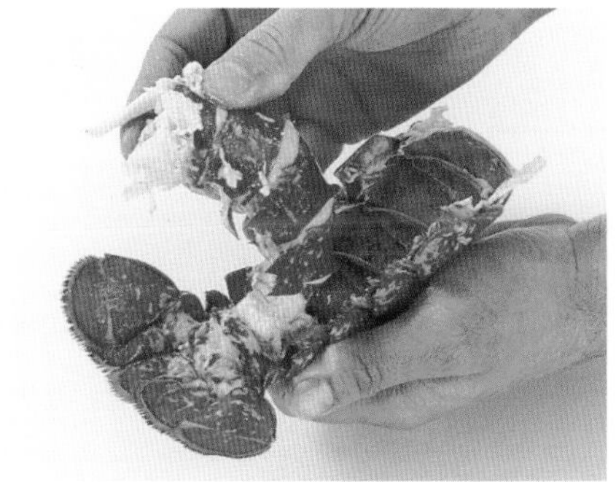

4 Bend back the flaps and carefully remove the tail meat, keeping it in one piece. Remove and discard the intestinal tract that runs through the centre of the tail meat. Slice the tail meat, or prepare as required, and serve with the claw and leg meat.

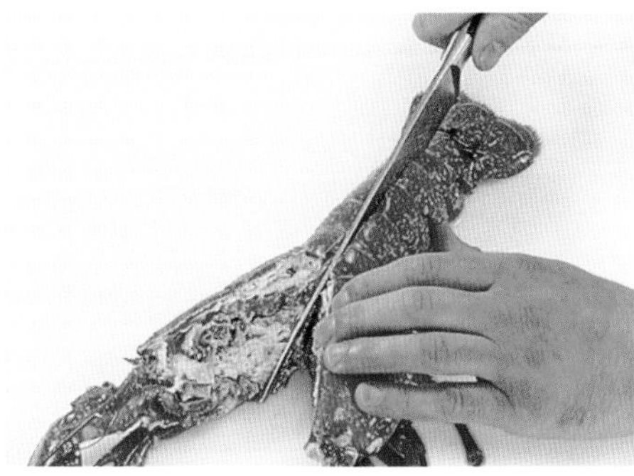

To serve in the shell

1 Use a sharp, heavy knife to split the lobster in half lengthways, cutting from the head to the tail. Pull the halves apart.

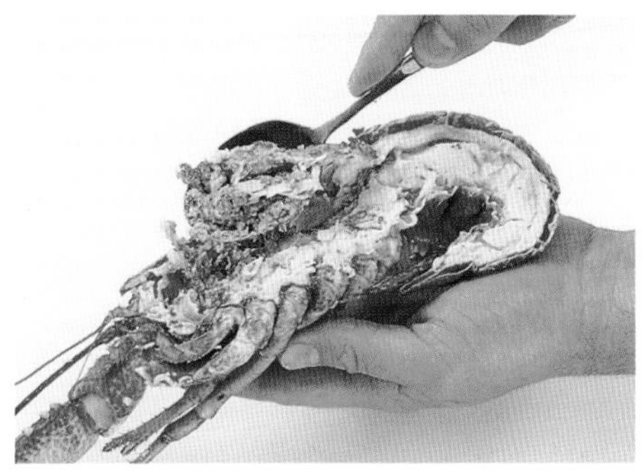

2 Scoop out the liver and roe, and discard the intestine. Twist off the legs and claws (remove the meat). Loosen the meat in the shell.

Preparing a squid

Once cleaned, fresh squid yields a tube-like body, which can be stuffed or sliced, and separate tentacles. You can buy it already cleaned or do this yourself as shown here.

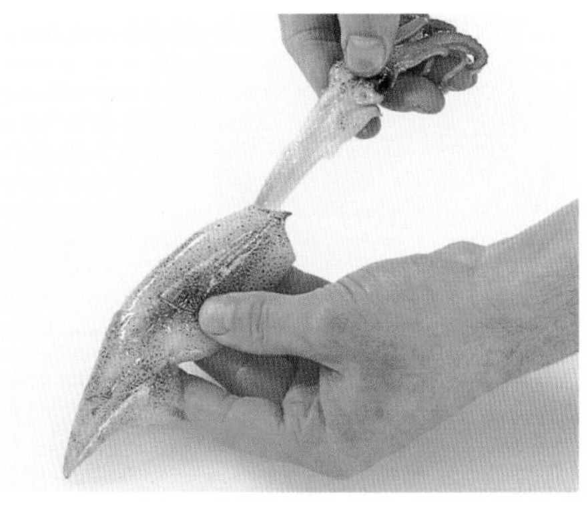

1 Pull the head and tentacles away from the body (the innards will come away with the head as will the long, narrow ink sac if it is present). Cut off the tentacles, just in front of the eyes.

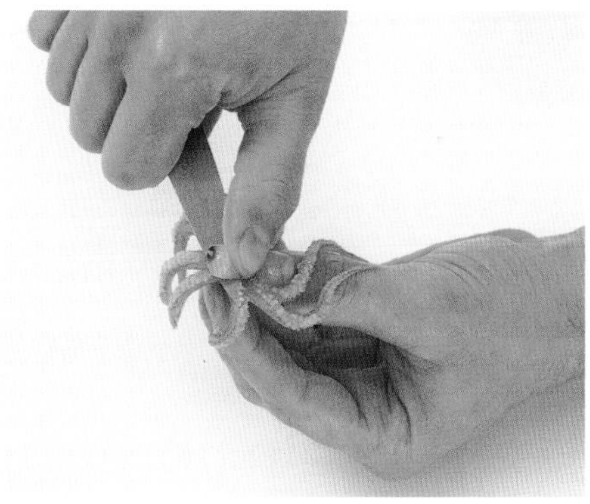

2 Squeeze the tentacles near the cut end so that the hard beak can be removed. Discard it. Rinse the tentacles well and set aside. Discard the head and innards (and the ink sac unless using it in a sauce).

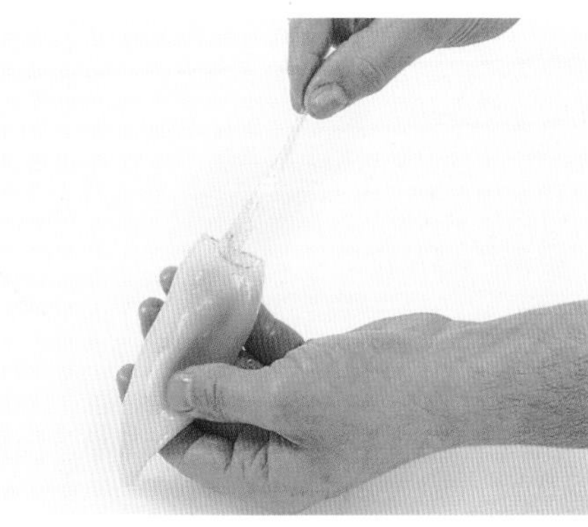

3 Peel the skin from the body. Pull the long piece of cartilage (quill) out of the body and discard. Rinse the body thoroughly, inside and out, and pull off the two flaps (slice these for cooking).

Lemon sole florentine

Fillets of lemon sole are topped with a cheese sauce and baked on a bed of spinach, so they stay moist while cooking. Slices of hot lemon bread – an interesting variation of garlic bread – make an unusual accompaniment.

SERVES 4 **CALS PER SERVING** 422

- 4 large lemon sole, each cut into 4 fillets and skinned (page 105)
- juice of ½ lemon
- salt and black pepper
- 45 g (1½ oz) butter
- 45 g (1½ oz) plain flour
- 450 ml (¾ pint) milk
- 750 g (1½ lb) spinach leaves
- 30 g (1 oz) Parmesan cheese, grated
- hot lemon bread, to serve (see box, right)

1 Sprinkle the lemon sole fillets with the lemon juice and salt and pepper. Fold the fillets in half widthways, and set aside.

2 Melt the butter in a saucepan, add the flour, and cook, stirring, for 1 minute. Remove from the heat and gradually blend in the milk. Bring to a boil, stirring constantly until the white sauce mixture thickens. Simmer for 2–3 minutes, then add salt and pepper to taste.

3 Wash the spinach and put into a pan with only the water remaining on the leaves. Cook for 2 minutes or until wilted. Drain well.

4 Stir half of the sauce into the cooked spinach and spoon into a shallow ovenproof dish. Arrange the sole on top. Pour the remaining sauce over the top and sprinkle with the cheese. Bake in a preheated oven at 200°C (180°C fan, Gas 6) for 30 minutes. Serve hot, with hot lemon bread.

Hot lemon bread

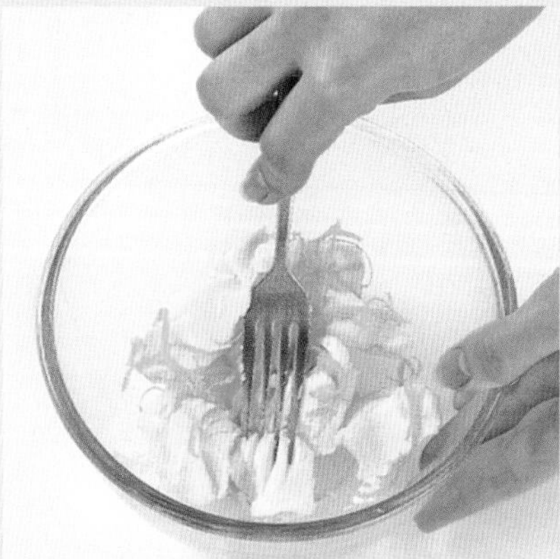

Beat the grated zest of ½ lemon into 125 g (4 oz) softened butter, using a fork. Work in the juice of ½ lemon, and salt and pepper to taste.

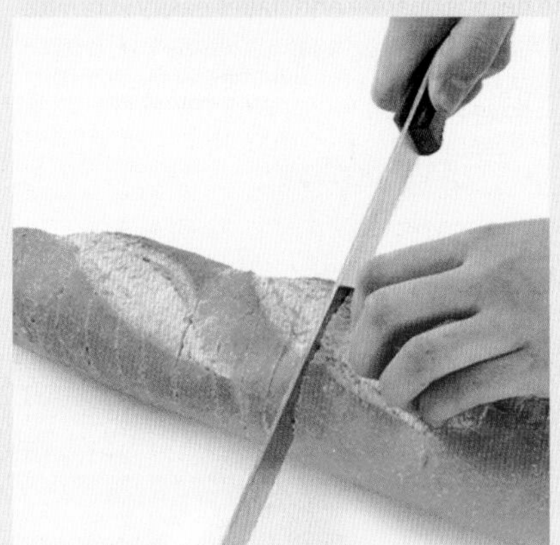

Cut 1 baguette into 1 cm (½ in) slices, leaving the slices attached underneath.

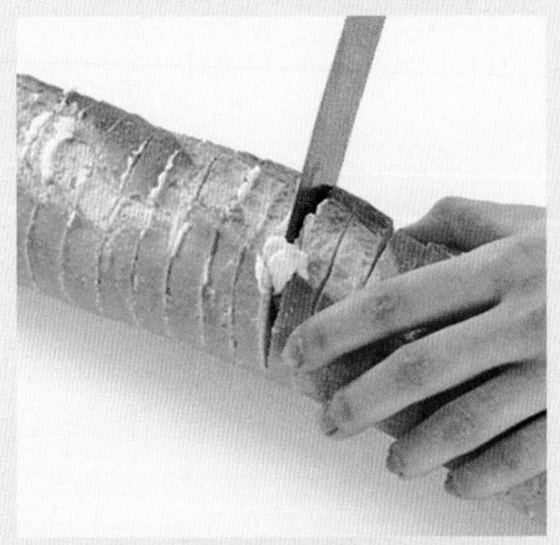

Spread the butter in between the slices, and a little on top. Wrap in foil and bake in a preheated oven at 200°C (180°C fan, Gas 6) for 20 minutes, opening the foil for the last 5 minutes to crisp the top.

Fillets of sole meunière

SERVES 4 **CALS PER SERVING** 274

60 g (2 oz) plain flour
salt and black pepper
4 small lemon sole, each cut into 4 fillets and skinned (page 105)
60 g (2 oz) butter
1 tbsp chopped parsley
juice of ½ lemon
lemon slices and parsley sprigs, to garnish

1 Sprinkle the flour on to a plate and season with salt and pepper. Dip the 16 fillets into the seasoned flour and shake off any excess.

2 Melt half of the butter in a large frying pan. When it is foaming, add the fillets, and cook for 2 minutes on each side or until the flesh is opaque and flakes easily. Transfer to warmed serving plates and keep warm.

3 Wipe the pan with paper towels. Melt the remaining butter and heat quickly until golden. Stir in the parsley and lemon juice, then pour over the fillets. Serve hot, garnished with lemon slices and parsley sprigs.

Mushroom-stuffed sole fillets

SERVES 4 **CALS PER SERVING** 568

60 g (2 oz) butter
1 onion, finely chopped
375 g (12 oz) mushrooms, finely chopped
2 large lemon sole, each cut into 4 fillets and skinned (page 105)
250 ml (8 fl oz) dry white wine
2 tsp chopped fresh tarragon
salt and black pepper
250 ml (8 fl oz) double cream
squeeze of lemon juice
fresh tarragon sprigs, to garnish

1 Melt half of the butter in a saucepan, add the onion and mushrooms, and cook gently for 5 minutes.

2 Roll the fillets (see box, right), with the skinned sides facing inwards. Stand them in a shallow baking dish, and fill with the mushrooms and onion.

3 Add the wine, tarragon, and salt and pepper to taste. Cover and bake in a preheated oven at 180°C (160°C fan, Gas 4) for 15 minutes or until the fish is opaque and flakes easily.

4 Remove the fish from the dish and keep warm. Pour the juices into a saucepan and boil for 3 minutes or until reduced by half. Stir in the cream and lemon juice, heat through gently, and taste for seasoning before serving, garnished with sprigs of fresh tarragon.

Rolling the fillets

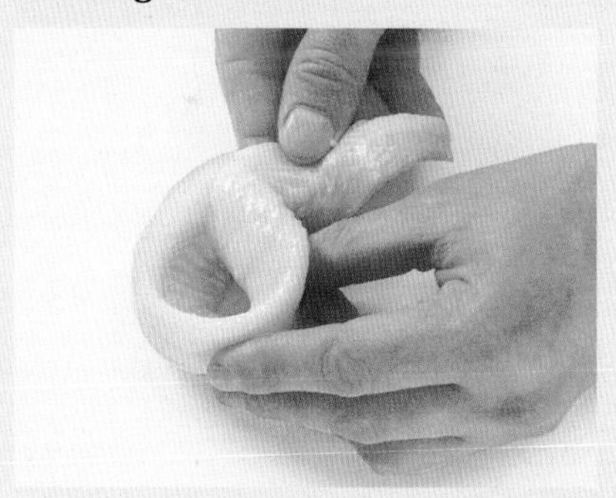

Bring round the two ends of each fillet to form a circle, with the smaller tail end on the outside.

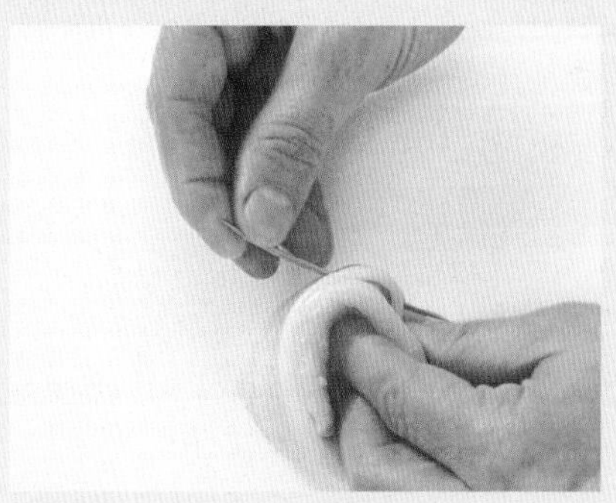

Thread a wooden cocktail stick through both ends of each fillet, to secure.

Best-ever fried fish

These plaice fillets are shallow-fried in a crisp coating of fresh breadcrumbs. This is far superior to a batter coating in both flavour and texture, and it protects the fish from the heat of the fat and keeps it moist, in the same way as batter.

SERVES 4 **CALS PER SERVING** 298

3 tbsp plain flour
salt and black pepper
1 large egg, beaten
30 g (1 oz) fresh white breadcrumbs
4 large plaice fillets, skinned
2 tbsp sunflower oil
lemon wedges, to garnish

1 Sprinkle the flour into a shallow dish and season with salt and pepper. Pour the beaten egg into another dish, and sprinkle the breadcrumbs into a third.

2 Lightly coat the fish fillets with breadcrumbs (see box, right).

3 Heat the oil in a large frying pan, add the coated fillets, in two batches if necessary, and fry over a high heat for 2–3 minutes on each side until they are crisp, golden, and juicy inside.

4 Lift the fillets out of the frying pan with a fish slice and then leave to drain briefly on paper towels. Serve the fish at once, garnished with the lemon wedges and accompanied by petits pois and chipped potatoes.

Coating a fish fillet

Dip the fillet into the seasoned flour, to coat. Shake off any excess.

Dip the floured fillet into the beaten egg, letting any excess drain off.

Dip the fillet into the breadcrumbs, making sure it is evenly coated.

Sauces for fish

Dill cream sauce Purée 300 ml (½ pint) single cream, 90 g (3 oz) butter, 1 egg yolk, the juice of 1 lemon, and 1 tsp plain flour in a food processor until smooth. Transfer the mixture to a small saucepan and heat very gently, stirring constantly, until the sauce has thickened and will coat the back of a spoon. Add salt and pepper to taste, then stir in 2 tbsp chopped fresh dill and 1 tbsp snipped fresh chives.

Tartare sauce Purée 1 egg, 1½ tsp sugar, ½ tsp mustard powder, and salt and pepper to taste in a food processor or blender until smooth. Add 300 ml (½ pint) sunflower oil, pouring in a steady stream, and purée until the mixture is very thick and all of the oil has been incorporated. Add the juice of 1 lemon, and purée. Transfer to a bowl, and stir in 1 tbsp each chopped gherkins, capers, and parsley, and 2 tbsp chopped fresh tarragon. Cover and leave to stand for at least 1 hour to allow the flavours to blend.

Haddock with mushrooms and cream

SERVES 4–6 **CALS PER SERVING** 429–286

300 ml (½ pint) milk
1 slice of onion
6 black peppercorns
1 bay leaf
60 g (2 oz) butter, plus extra for greasing
750 g (1½ lb) haddock fillet, skinned
salt and black pepper
squeeze of lemon juice
250 g (8 oz) button mushrooms, sliced
30 g (1 oz) plain flour
3 tbsp single cream (optional)
30 g (1 oz) fresh white breadcrumbs
30 g (1 oz) Parmesan cheese, grated
chopped parsley, to garnish

1 Put the milk into a small saucepan with the onion, peppercorns, and bay leaf, and bring just to a boil. Remove from the heat, cover, and leave to infuse for 10 minutes. Lightly butter a shallow ovenproof dish.

2 Cut the haddock into 7 cm (3 in) pieces, and place in a single layer in the dish. Sprinkle with salt and pepper.

3 Melt half of the butter in a saucepan, add the lemon juice and mushrooms, and season with salt and pepper. Cook gently, stirring occasionally, for 3 minutes or until just tender. Remove the mushrooms with a slotted spoon and put them on top of the fish.

4 Strain the infused milk and set aside. Melt the remaining butter in a saucepan, add the flour, and cook, stirring, for 1 minute. Remove from the heat and gradually blend in the infused milk. Bring to a boil, stirring until the mixture thickens. Simmer for 2–3 minutes. Stir in the cream, if using, and season with salt and pepper.

5 Pour the sauce over the fish and mushrooms, then sprinkle with the breadcrumbs and Parmesan. Bake in a preheated oven at 190°C (170°C fan, Gas 5) for 25–30 minutes until the fish is cooked and the top is golden and bubbling. Garnish with parsley, and serve at once.

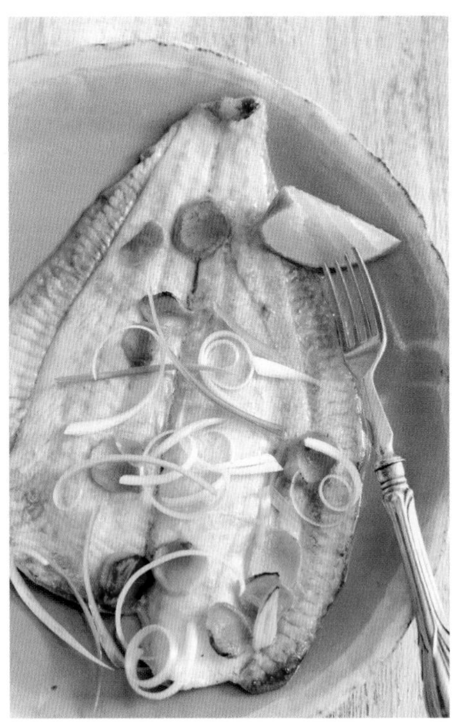

Gingered plaice

SERVES 4 **CALS PER SERVING** 247

4 large plaice fillets
spring onions, to garnish (optional)

Ginger marinade

2.5 cm (1 in) piece of fresh root ginger, peeled and finely sliced
1 large garlic clove, sliced
2 tbsp sunflower oil
1 tbsp sesame oil
1 tbsp dry sherry
1 tbsp balsamic vinegar
2 tsp light soy sauce

1 Put the plaice fillets into a shallow non-metallic dish.

2 Make the marinade: combine the ginger, garlic, sunflower and sesame oils, sherry, vinegar, and soy sauce, and pour over the fish.

3 Cover the fish and leave to marinate in the refrigerator, turning once, for 30 minutes.

4 Grill the fillets, skin-side down, under a hot grill, 7 cm (3 in) from the heat, for 4–5 minutes, until the fish is opaque and flakes easily. Serve hot, garnished with spring onions if you like.

Cod steaks with anchovy and fennel

SERVES 4 **CALS PER SERVING** 429

1 x 60 g can anchovy fillets
30 g (1 oz) butter, plus extra for greasing
1 small onion, finely chopped
1 small fennel bulb, finely chopped
30 g (1 oz) parsley, chopped
125 g (4 oz) fresh white breadcrumbs
salt and black pepper
4 x 250 g (8 oz) cod steaks
dill sprigs, lemon wedges, and watercress sprigs, to garnish

1 Drain the anchovy fillets, reserving the oil. Cut the anchovies into small pieces and set aside.

2 Melt the butter in a pan, add the onion and fennel, and cook over a medium heat, stirring, for 5 minutes or until soft but not browned. Remove from the heat, stir in the anchovies, parsley, and breadcrumbs. Season with salt and pepper.

3 Put the cod steaks into a buttered ovenproof dish and top each one with the anchovy and fennel mixture, pressing it down firmly with your hand.

4 Drizzle a little of the reserved anchovy oil over each steak. Bake the steaks in a preheated oven at 200°C (180°C fan, Gas 6) for 10–15 minutes until the cod is opaque and the flesh flakes easily from the bone.

5 Transfer to a warmed serving plate. Garnish the cod steaks with dill sprigs, lemon wedges, and watercress sprigs, and serve at once.

COD STEAKS WITH SUN-DRIED TOMATOES

Omit the anchovies, fennel, parsley, and breadcrumbs. Chop 4 ripe but firm tomatoes. Drain 30 g (1 oz) sun-dried tomatoes in oil, and snip them into small pieces. Add both types of tomato to the softened onion in step 2, with 12 pitted and chopped black olives. Season with salt and pepper. Drizzle the cod steaks with 1 tbsp olive oil, top with the tomato mixture, and bake as in step 4.

Sea bass with lemon butter sauce

SERVES 4 **CALS PER SERVING** 363

sunflower oil for greasing
1.1 kg (2¼ lb) sea bass, cleaned and butterflied (page 104)
4 tarragon sprigs
1 lemon, sliced
salt and black pepper
2 tbsp dry white wine

Lemon butter sauce

150 ml (¼ pint) single cream
juice of ½ lemon
45 g (1½ oz) butter, melted
1 egg yolk
1 tsp plain flour
white pepper
1 tsp chopped fresh tarragon

1 Put a large piece of foil on to a baking tray and brush lightly with oil. Put the sea bass on to the foil, tuck three of the tarragon sprigs and all but 1–2 of the lemon slices inside the cavity, and sprinkle with salt and black pepper.

2 Season the outside of the fish, and lift up the sides of the foil. Pour the wine over the fish, then seal the foil into a loose parcel. Bake in a preheated oven at 200°C (180°C fan, Gas 6) for 30 minutes or until the flesh is opaque and flakes easily.

3 Meanwhile, make the sauce: whisk the cream in a pan with the lemon juice, butter, egg yolk, and flour until mixed. Heat very gently, stirring constantly, until the mixture is thick enough to coat the back of a spoon. Season with salt and white pepper, and stir in the tarragon. Keep warm.

4 Remove the sea bass from the foil and arrange on a warmed serving dish. Pour over the cooking juices. Garnish with the remaining lemon slices and tarragon sprig, and serve at once. Serve the warm lemon butter sauce separately.

Spiced fish with coconut

SERVES 4 **CALS PER SERVING** 389

750 g (1½ lb) monkfish fillets, skinned
30 g (1 oz) plain flour
salt and black pepper
2 tbsp sunflower oil
1 onion, finely sliced
1 garlic clove, crushed
1 tsp ground coriander
1 tsp ground cumin
½ tsp turmeric
150 ml (¼ pint) canned coconut milk
1 x 400 g can chopped tomatoes
3 tbsp chopped fresh coriander
coriander sprigs, to garnish

1 Cut the monkfish into 5 cm (2 in) pieces. Season the flour with salt and pepper. Lightly coat the monkfish with the flour.

2 Heat the oil in a large frying pan, add the onion, garlic, coriander, cumin, and turmeric, and cook gently, stirring from time to time, for 3 minutes or until the onion begins to soften.

3 Pour in the coconut milk and tomatoes, stir well, and bring to a boil. Simmer for about 5 minutes.

4 Add the monkfish, cover, and cook gently, stirring occasionally, for 10 minutes or until the fish is opaque and the flesh flakes easily. Add the chopped coriander, and taste for seasoning. Serve hot, garnished with coriander sprigs.

Roast monkfish niçoise

SERVES 4 **CALS PER SERVING** 448

3 tbsp olive oil
1 head of garlic, separated
1 lemon, thickly sliced
500 g (1 lb) monkfish fillets, skinned and cut into chunky pieces
1 tbsp mixed chopped fresh thyme and parsley, and snipped chives
250 ml (8 fl oz) dry white wine
125 ml (4 fl oz) fish stock
1 x 400 g can artichoke hearts, drained and rinsed
15 pitted black olives
10 sun-dried tomatoes in oil, drained
squeeze of lemon juice
salt and black pepper
lemon wedges and thyme sprigs, to garnish

1 Put 1 tbsp of the oil into an ovenproof dish, add the garlic cloves, and roast in a preheated oven at 190°C (170°C fan, Gas 5) for about 10 minutes until softened.

2 Arrange the lemon slices in the dish, and put the garlic and monkfish on top.

3 Sprinkle with the remaining oil and the herbs, and pour in the wine and stock. Return to the oven for 10 minutes.

4 Add the artichoke hearts, olives, and sun-dried tomatoes, and cook for 5 minutes to heat through.

5 Transfer the fish and vegetables to a serving dish, discarding the lemon slices. Keep warm.

6 Pour the cooking juices into a small saucepan, and boil for about 8 minutes until reduced to about 125 ml (4 fl oz). Add the lemon juice, season with salt and pepper, and pour over the fish. Garnish with lemon and thyme, and serve at once.

ROAST MONKFISH BASQUAISE

Instead of the artichokes, use 2 peppers (1 red and 1 yellow), halved, deseeded, and cut into strips, and roast with the garlic cloves.

Monkfish with ginger-orange sauce

SERVES 4 **CALS PER SERVING** 221

1 orange, washed and thinly sliced
1 onion, chopped
1 cm (½ in) piece of fresh root ginger, peeled and grated
500 g (1 lb) monkfish fillets, skinned
4 spring onions, chopped
250 ml (8 fl oz) fish stock
grated zest of ½ lime
75 ml (2½ fl oz) lime juice
salt and cayenne pepper
60 g (2 oz) unsalted butter, chilled and cubed
sugar or honey, to taste (optional)
orange and snipped chives, to garnish

1 Put the orange slices, onion, and ginger into a pan. Add the monkfish, spring onions, and stock. Bring to a boil, and simmer, without stirring, for 10 minutes or until the fish is firm. With a slotted spoon, transfer the fish to a serving dish. Keep hot.

2 Put a sieve over a bowl, tip in the remaining contents of the pan and press hard with the back of a spoon to extract all the juices.

3 Pour the juices into a small saucepan and boil rapidly, uncovered, for about 12 minutes until the liquid has reduced to about 2 tbsp.

4 Add the lime zest and juice, season with salt and cayenne, and heat gently, stirring, until warm. Remove from the heat and finish the sauce (see box, below).

5 Pour the sauce over the fish, garnish, and serve at once.

Finishing the sauce

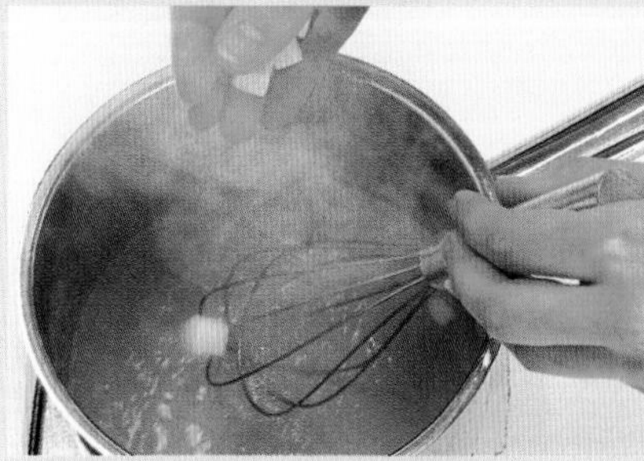

Add the cubes of butter one at a time, whisking between each addition until the butter melts. The sauce will become glossy at the end. Taste, and add a little sugar or honey if you like.

Halibut in filo parcels

Halibut is a very fine fish with a delicate flavour and firm texture. Enclosing the halibut steaks in filo parcels with matchstick-thin vegetables keeps the fish moist and seals in all the flavours, while the pastry trimmings on top provide an attractive, crunchy finish.

SERVES 4 **CALS PER SERVING** 564

2 x 375 g (12 oz) halibut steaks, skinned and boned
1 carrot
1 leek, trimmed
150 ml (1/4 pint) fish stock
2 tbsp dry white wine
2 tsp lemon juice
3 strands of saffron or 1/4 tsp turmeric
salt and black pepper
8 large sheets of filo pastry
60 g (2 oz) butter, melted
lemon slices and dill sprigs, to garnish

1 Cut the halibut steaks crossways so you have four equal-sized pieces. Cut the carrot and leek into matchstick-thin strips.

2 Put the vegetables into a pan with the stock, wine, lemon juice, and saffron.

3 Bring to a boil, and cook, uncovered, for 5 minutes or until the vegetables are just tender. Drain, and then season with salt and pepper.

4 Cut the filo pastry into eight 25 cm (10 in) squares, and reserve the trimmings. Brush one square with a little melted butter, put a second square on top, and brush with more melted butter. Make a filo parcel (see box, right). Repeat to make four filo parcels.

5 Place the filo parcels on a baking tray, and bake in a preheated oven at 200°C (180°C fan, Gas 6) for 20 minutes or until golden and crispy. Garnish with lemon slices and dill sprigs, and serve at once with a simple babyleaf salad.

SALMON IN FILO PARCELS

Substitute skinned salmon fillets for the halibut, and 1 courgette and 4 spring onions, both cut into matchstick-thin strips, for the carrot and leek.

Cook's know-how

Sheets of filo pastry are usually sold in a roll, fresh or frozen. The size of the sheets may vary with different brands, so don't worry if they are slightly smaller than 25 cm (10 in) wide – just be sure there is sufficient pastry to cover the filling.

Making a filo parcel

Spoon one-quarter of the vegetable mixture into the middle of the pastry square. Put one piece of halibut on top of the vegetable mixture.

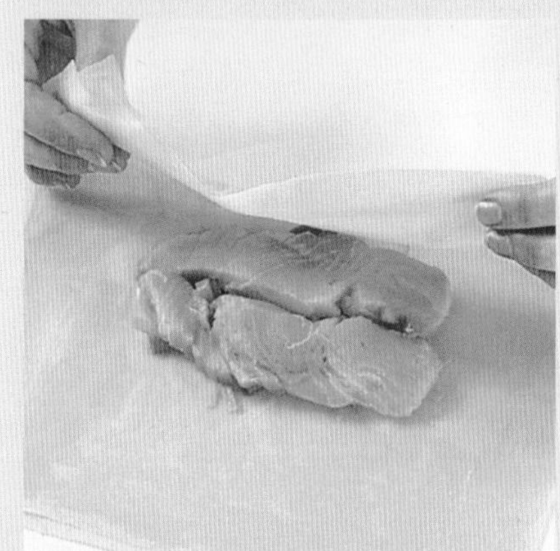

Fold two sides of the filo pastry over the halibut and vegetables, and tuck the remaining two ends underneath to form a neat parcel. Brush the top of the parcel with a little melted butter.

Crumple some of the reserved filo trimmings, and arrange them on top of the filo parcel. Brush with melted butter.

Cajun-spiced red snapper

SERVES 4 **CALS PER SERVING** 258

4 x 150–175 g (5–6 oz) red snapper fillets
30 g (1 oz) butter
coriander butter (page 246) and watercress sprigs, to serve

Cajun spice mixture
30 g (1 oz) plain flour
1 garlic clove, crushed
1 tbsp paprika
1 tsp ground cumin
1 tsp hot chilli powder

1 Make the Cajun spice mixture: combine the flour, garlic, paprika, cumin, and chilli powder.

2 Rub over the red snapper fillets, cover, and leave to marinate in the refrigerator for about 30 minutes.

3 Melt the butter in a large frying pan, add the fillets, and cook gently for 2–3 minutes on each side until the fish is opaque and the flesh flakes easily.

4 Top the fillets with pats of coriander butter, garnish with watercress, and serve hot with boiled rice (page 354).

Cook's **know-how**

You can buy ready mixed Cajun seasoning, but it tends to include dried garlic and onion salt, both of which overpower the spices in the mix. This simple version uses chilli powder, which is not just ground dried chillies as its name suggests, but a special fiery mixture of chilli with herbs and spices. Check the label before buying.

Oriental fish parcels

SERVES 4 **CALS PER SERVING** 312

45 g (1½ oz) butter
4 x 250 g (8 oz) white fish fillets, such as sole or plaice, skinned
2 cm (¾ in) piece of fresh root ginger, peeled and thinly sliced
3 spring onions, thinly sliced
2–3 garlic cloves, crushed
2 tbsp dark soy sauce
1 tbsp mirin (Chinese rice wine)
½ tsp sugar

NON-STICK BAKING PARCHMENT

1 Cut eight sheets of baking parchment into oval shapes, each one measuring about 30 x 37 cm (12 x 15 in). Put the ovals together in pairs to make a double thickness.

2 Melt 30 g (1 oz) of the butter. Brush the butter over the top oval of each pair, and over two large baking trays.

3 Place a fish fillet on the buttered side of one of the oval pairs, positioning it on one side. Top with ginger, spring onions, and garlic, and dot with one-quarter of the remaining butter.

4 Whisk together the soy sauce, mirin, and sugar, and drizzle one-quarter of this mixture over the fish. Fold the paper over the fish, and fold and pleat the edges together like a Cornish pasty to seal in the fish and juices. Repeat to make four parcels altogether.

5 Put the paper cases on to the prepared baking trays and bake the fish in a preheated oven at 230°C (210°C fan, Gas 8) for 8–10 minutes until the paper has turned brown and the cases have puffed up. Serve at once, on individual plates.

Cheese-topped baked bream

SERVES 4 **CALS PER SERVING** 401

2 x 560 g (1 lb 2 oz) sea bream, filleted and skinned
grated zest and juice of ½ lemon
salt and black pepper
150 ml (¼ pint) water
butter, for greasing
30 g (1 oz) mature Cheddar cheese, grated
lemon zest and chopped parsley, to garnish

White sauce

30 g (1 oz) butter
1 tbsp plain flour
150 ml (¼ pint) milk

1 Cut the sea bream fillets in half lengthways, and arrange them in a single layer in a large ovenproof dish.

2 Sprinkle the fish evenly with the grated lemon zest and season with salt and pepper. Pour the lemon juice and measured water over the fish fillets. Cover the dish with buttered greaseproof paper.

3 Bake in a preheated oven at 160°C (140°C fan, Gas 3) for about 20 minutes until the flesh flakes easily.

4 Transfer the bream to a warmed flameproof platter, cover, and keep hot. Strain the cooking liquid and reserve. Increase the oven temperature to 220°C (200°C fan, Gas 7).

5 Make the white sauce: melt the butter in a small saucepan, add the flour, and cook, stirring, for 1 minute. Remove from the heat, and gradually blend in the milk and the reserved cooking liquid. Bring to a boil, stirring constantly until the mixture thickens. Simmer for 2–3 minutes. Taste for seasoning.

6 Pour the white sauce over the fish, sprinkle with the cheese, and bake in the oven for 3–5 minutes until bubbling and golden. Serve hot, garnished with lemon zest and chopped parsley.

Sea bream niçoise

SERVES 4 **CALS PER SERVING** 356

2 x 560 g (1 lb 2 oz) sea bream, cleaned (page 104), with heads removed
salt and black pepper
3 tbsp olive oil
1 large onion, sliced
1 small fennel bulb, sliced
1 garlic clove, crushed
12 pitted black olives
2 tbsp chopped parsley
juice of 1 lemon
lemon segments and parsley sprigs, to garnish

1 Prepare the bream (see box, below).

2 Heat 2 tbsp of the oil in a frying pan, add the onion, fennel, and garlic, and cook gently, stirring occasionally, for 5–8 minutes until the vegetables are soft but not coloured.

3 Spoon the vegetables into an ovenproof dish, and place the bream on top. Scatter the olives and parsley over the fish, sprinkle with the lemon juice, and drizzle with the remaining olive oil.

4 Cover the fish loosely with foil, and bake in a preheated oven at 200°C (180°C fan, Gas 6) for 15 minutes.

5 Remove the foil and bake for 10 minutes or until the fish is cooked. Garnish with lemon segments and parsley sprigs before serving.

Preparing the bream

Make two deep diagonal cuts in the flesh on both sides of each bream, using a sharp knife. Put salt and pepper into a bowl and combine. Sprinkle on the inside and outside of the bream.

Koulibiac

This is a type of salmon kedgeree enclosed in crisp puff pastry, which makes an impressive dish for a dinner party or other special occasion. In Russia, its country of origin, there is a saying, "Houses make a fine street, pies make a fine table".

SERVES 8–10 **CALS PER SERVING** 518–414

75 g (2½ oz) long grain rice
salt and black pepper
60 g (2 oz) butter, plus extra for greasing
1 large onion, chopped
1 x 400 g can chopped tomatoes, drained
500 g (1 lb) fresh salmon fillets, cooked and flaked
2 tbsp chopped parsley
grated zest and juice of 1 lemon
500 g (1 lb) puff pastry
1 egg, beaten
60 g (2 oz) butter, melted, and juice of ½ lemon, to serve
lemon twists and watercress sprigs, to garnish

1 Cook the rice in boiling salted water for 12 minutes or until just tender.

2 Meanwhile, melt the butter in a saucepan, add the onion, and cook very gently for about 10 minutes until soft but not coloured. Add the tomatoes and cook for 15 minutes. Leave to cool.

3 Drain the rice thoroughly, and combine with the onion and tomato mixture, the flaked salmon, parsley, and lemon zest and juice. Season with salt and pepper.

4 Roll out 425 g (14 oz) of the puff pastry into a 28 x 40 cm (11 x 16 in) rectangle.

5 Arrange the salmon mixture down the middle of the rectangle, leaving a 7 cm (3 in) border on each side. Brush the border with a little of the beaten egg, and wrap and decorate the koulibiac (see box, left).

6 Bake the koulibiac in a preheated oven at 220°C (200°C fan, Gas 7) for 30–45 minutes until golden.

7 Transfer to a warmed serving dish, and pour the melted butter and lemon juice into the cuts. Serve in thick slices, garnished with lemon twists and watercress.

Wrapping and decorating the koulibiac

Fold the shortest ends of pastry over the salmon filling and brush the top of the folded pastry with beaten egg.

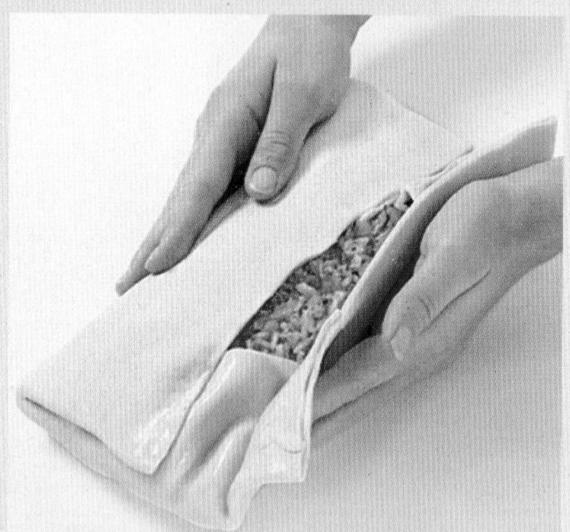

Fold the longest sides over the filling to make a long parcel. Turn the parcel over and place on a lightly buttered baking tray. Brush all over with beaten egg.

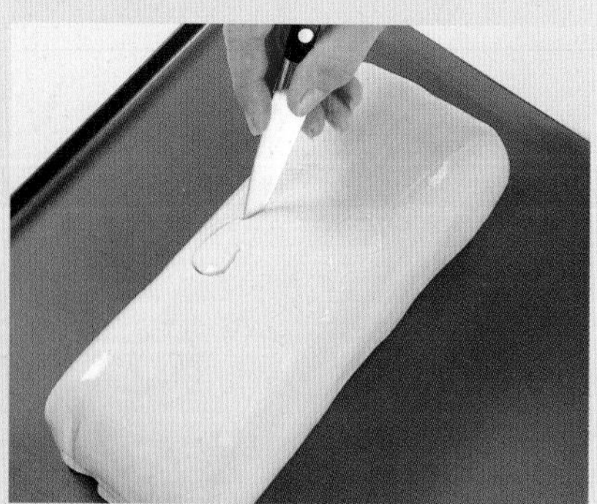

Make two decorative cuts in the top of the pastry. Roll the remaining pastry into a 5 x 30 cm (2 x 12 in) piece, trim, then cut into three equal strips. Press the ends together and plait the strips. Lay the plait down the middle of the parcel, and glaze with beaten egg.

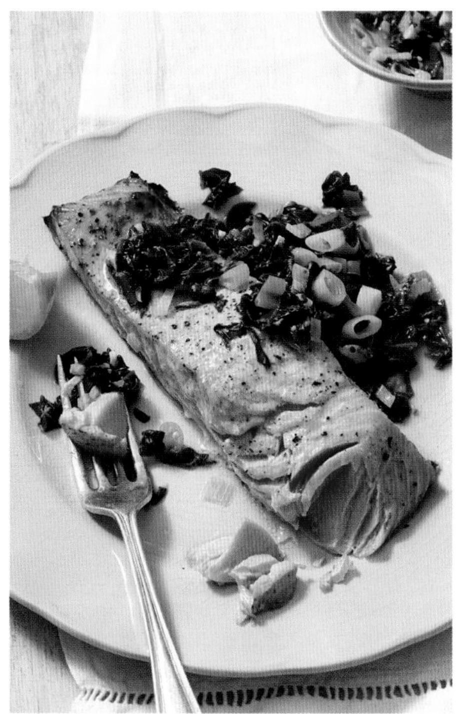

Salmon with spinach salsa

SERVES 4 **CALS PER SERVING** 454

4 x 175 g (6 oz) salmon steaks
salt and black pepper
15 g (½ oz) butter
lemon twists and watercress, to garnish

Spinach salsa

2 tbsp olive oil
8 spring onions, finely sliced
1 garlic clove, crushed
4 tbsp lemon juice
1 tsp wholegrain mustard
500 g (1 lb) spinach leaves, finely chopped

1 Season the salmon steaks with black pepper and dot with the butter.

2 Cook the salmon steaks under a hot grill, 7 cm (3 in) from the heat, for 2–3 minutes on each side until the fish is opaque and the flesh flakes easily. Leave to rest.

3 Make the spinach salsa: heat the oil in a frying pan, add the spring onions and garlic, and cook, stirring, for about 1 minute. Stir in the lemon juice, mustard, and spinach, and cook, stirring, for about 2 minutes. Transfer to a bowl, and season with salt and pepper.

4 Garnish the salmon with lemon twists and serve at once, with the salsa.

Golden fish cakes

SERVES 4 **CALS PER SERVING** 613

500 g (1 lb) potatoes, cut into chunks
salt and black pepper
500 g (1 lb) cod, haddock or salmon fillets (or a mixture of white fish and salmon)
300 ml (½ pint) milk
1 bay leaf
9 black peppercorns
60 g (2 oz) butter
4 tbsp chopped parsley
finely grated zest of 1 lemon
a dash of Tabasco (optional)
1 egg, beaten
175 g (6 oz) fresh breadcrumbs
sunflower oil, for frying
tartare sauce (page 110), to serve

1 Cook the potatoes in boiling salted water for 15–20 minutes until tender.

2 Meanwhile, put the fish into a pan with the milk, bay leaf, and peppercorns. Bring slowly to a boil, and simmer for 10 minutes or until the fish is just opaque.

3 Drain the fish, reserving the liquid. Cool the fish, then flake the flesh, discarding the skin and bones.

4 Drain the potatoes, put them in a bowl, and mash with the butter and 3 tbsp of the fish cooking liquid. Add the fish, parsley, lemon zest, Tabasco if using, and salt and pepper to taste, and mix well.

5 Shape the mixture into eight flat cakes, 7 cm (3 in) in diameter. Coat with beaten egg, then with breadcrumbs.

6 Heat a little oil in a frying pan and fry the fish cakes, a few at a time, for 5 minutes on each side or until golden. Serve hot, with the tartare sauce.

Salmon en croûte

SERVES 8 **CALS PER SERVING** 745

1.7–2 kg (3½–4 lb) salmon, cleaned and filleted (page 104), then cut lengthways in half and skinned
1 tbsp chopped fresh dill
grated zest and juice of 1 lemon
salt and black pepper
30 g (1 oz) butter
8 spring onions, sliced
250 g (8 oz) spinach leaves, coarsely shredded
250 g (8 oz) low-fat soft cheese
plain flour for dusting
750 g (1½ lb) puff pastry
1 egg, beaten
lemon slices, cherry tomatoes, and parsley sprigs, to garnish

1 Put the two pieces of salmon into a shallow non-metallic dish and sprinkle with the dill, lemon zest and juice, and salt and pepper. Cover and leave to marinate in the refrigerator for about 1 hour.

2 Melt the butter in a small pan, add the onions, and cook gently for 2–3 minutes until soft but not coloured. Remove from the heat.

3 Add the spinach, toss in the butter, then leave to cool. Drain any excess water from the pan. Stir in the cheese, and season with salt and pepper.

4 Roll out half of the pastry on a lightly floured surface to a 20 x 38 cm (8 x 15 in) rectangle. Put the pastry on a baking tray, and place one salmon fillet, skinned side down, on top. Spread with the spinach mixture, then put the second salmon fillet on top, skinned side up. Brush the pastry border with a little beaten egg.

5 Roll out the remaining pastry to a slightly larger rectangle, cover the salmon completely, then trim and seal the edges. Make "scales" on the top with the edge of a spoon, then make two small holes to let steam escape during baking.

6 Brush with beaten egg and bake in a preheated oven at 200°C (180°C fan, Gas 6) for 40–45 minutes until the pastry is risen and golden brown. Serve hot, garnished with lemon, tomatoes, and parsley.

Severn salmon

SERVES 6 **CALS PER SERVING** 414

6 x 175 g (6 oz) salmon fillets or steaks
butter for greasing
salt and black pepper
watercress sprigs, to garnish

Watercress sauce

300 ml (½ pint) single cream
60 g (2 oz) watercress, trimmed
90 g (3 oz) butter, melted
1 tsp plain flour
juice of 1 lemon
1 egg yolk

1 Arrange the salmon fillets or steaks in a single layer in a buttered roasting tin, and sprinkle with black pepper.

2 Cover tightly with foil, and bake in a preheated oven at 180°C (160°C fan, Gas 4) for 15 minutes or until the fish is opaque and flakes easily.

3 Meanwhile, make the watercress sauce: put the cream, watercress, butter, flour, lemon juice, and egg yolk into a food processor, season with salt and pepper, and purée until smooth.

4 Transfer the cream and watercress mixture to a small saucepan, and cook over a gentle heat, stirring, until the sauce thickens. Taste for seasoning.

5 Serve the salmon hot with the watercress sauce, herby new potatoes, fresh sprigs of watercress, and lemon wedges.

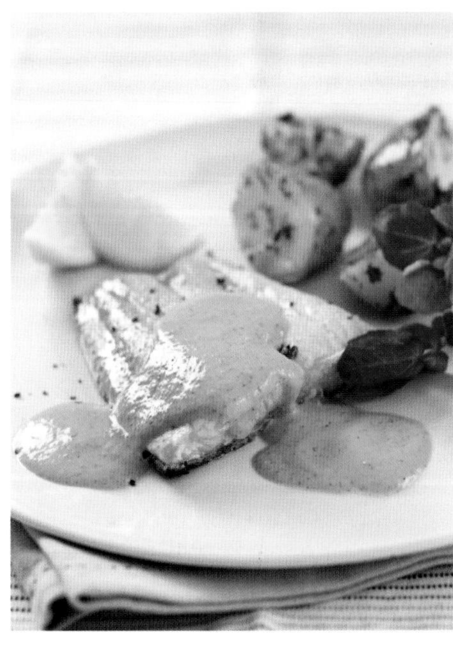

Warm honeyed salmon salad

SERVES 4 **CALS PER SERVING** 455

4 x 150–175 g (5–6 oz) middle-cut salmon fillets, skinned
3 tbsp clear honey
1 tbsp olive oil
juice of 1 lemon
about 2 tbsp chopped fresh thyme
new potatoes, to serve

For the salad

1 fennel bulb, thinly sliced
6 spring onions, thinly sliced
3 tbsp extra virgin olive oil
1 tbsp lemon juice
1 tbsp clear honey
4 tbsp Greek yogurt
salt and black pepper
1 romaine lettuce, shredded
2 tbsp chopped parsley
2 tbsp snipped fresh chives

1 Make the salad. Mix the fennel and spring onions in a bowl with the olive oil, lemon juice, honey, yogurt, and seasoning. Toss the lettuce in a separate large salad bowl with the chopped fresh herbs and seasoning. Cover both bowls and refrigerate for about 1 hour.

2 Cut each salmon fillet into four lengthways – they will look like flat sausages. Toss in the honey and season well. Heat the oil in a large non-stick frying pan and pan-fry the salmon over a high heat for 2–3 minutes on each side or until just opaque. Take care when turning the salmon as it breaks up quite easily. Add the lemon juice and thyme to the pan and heat until bubbling.

3 Toss the fennel salad through the lettuce, then spoon the honeyed salmon on top. Serve warm.

Salmon with avocado

SERVES 4 **CALS PER SERVING** 543

30 g (1 oz) butter, melted
4 x 175 g (6 oz) salmon steaks
salt and black pepper
4 tarragon sprigs
4 slices of lime

Avocado sauce

2 avocados, halved, stoned (page 395), and peeled
150 ml (¼ pint) plain yogurt
grated zest and juice of 1 lime

1 Brush four large squares of foil with melted butter. Put a salmon steak on each square, season, and top with a tarragon sprig and a slice of lime. Wrap the foil around the salmon. Put on a baking tray, and bake in a preheated oven at 150°C (130°C fan, Gas 2) for 25 minutes or until the fish is opaque and the flesh flakes easily.

2 Meanwhile, make the avocado sauce: put the flesh of one avocado into a food processor with the yogurt, and lime zest and juice. Season with salt and pepper and purée until smooth. Transfer to a serving bowl. Dice the remaining avocado, and stir into the sauce.

3 Unwrap the salmon, transfer to warmed serving plates, and serve with the avocado sauce.

Classic buffet party salmon

This is the perfect dish for a buffet party. The salmon is gently poached, with the skin and head for added flavour, and left to cool in the cooking liquid to keep it moist. Fish kettles can be hired from some fishmongers or the fish counters of some supermarkets.

SERVES 10 **CALS PER SERVING** 410

salt and black peppercorns
4 bay leaves
1 onion, sliced
4 tbsp white wine vinegar
2.75 kg (5½ lb) salmon, cleaned (page 104)
3 tbsp chopped fresh dill
about 200 ml (7 fl oz) mayonnaise (page 397)

To serve

8–10 cooked jumbo prawns, tail shells taken off but heads left on
1–2 bunches of fresh dill
lemon wedges

FISH KETTLE

1 Lift out the rack from the fish kettle and set aside. Half fill the kettle with water and add 2 tbsp salt, 12 black peppercorns, the bay leaves, onion, and vinegar.

2 Put the salmon on to the rack, and lower into the kettle. Bring to a boil, then simmer for 1 minute only. Remove from the heat, cover, and leave to stand for about 2 hours, until the fish is just warm.

3 Lift the rack and salmon out of the fish kettle. Cover the salmon with a large piece of cling film and flip the fish over on to the cling film. Bone and skin the salmon (see box, below). Cover and chill in the refrigerator for at least 1 hour.

4 Mix the dill into the mayonnaise, then taste for seasoning. Spoon into a serving bowl, and chill until ready to serve.

5 Arrange the salmon on the serving plate. Scatter the prawns over the salmon and around the plate, along with the dill and lemon wedges. Serve with the dill mayonnaise.

Boning and skinning a salmon

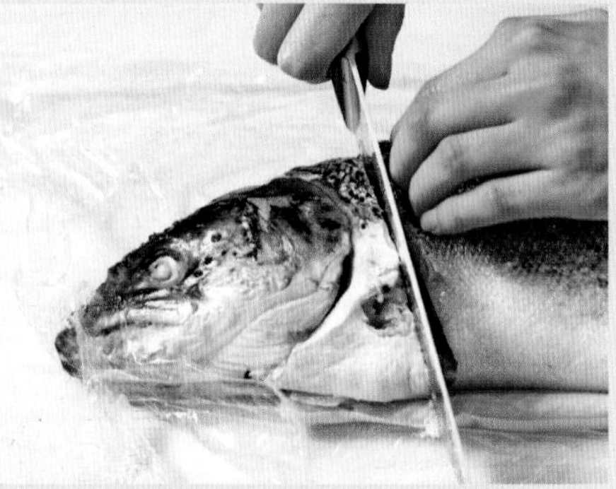

1 Using a chef's knife, neatly remove the head from the salmon.

2 Run the knife along the backbone of the fish to loosen the top fillet.

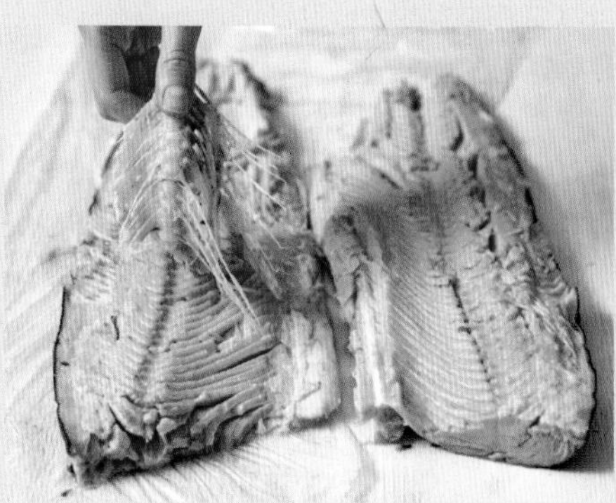

3 Flip the top fillet over and remove the bones from the fish.

4 Use the cling film to flip the bottom fillet back on to the top and remove the skin and any dark flesh.

5 Use the cling film to flip the fish on to a large serving plate, and remove the remaining skin.

6 With a small knife, gently scrape away the brownish flesh, leaving behind only the pink flesh.

Griddled salmon tranches

SERVES 4 **CALS PER SERVING** 367

a little olive oil
4 x 150–175 g (5–6 oz) middle-cut salmon fillets, skinned
salt and black pepper

Sauce

200 ml (7 fl oz) crème fraîche
about 5 cm (2 in) cucumber, peeled, deseeded, and finely diced
4 tbsp chopped fresh dill
pinch of caster sugar
1 tbsp capers
a good squeeze of lemon juice

1 Heat a griddle pan until piping hot, and lightly oil a sheet of foil on a baking sheet. Lightly oil and season the salmon.

2 Cook the salmon in the hot pan on one side only for 1½ minutes until golden underneath. Transfer, cooked side up, to the foil and finish cooking in a preheated oven at 190°C (170°C fan, Gas 5) for about 10 minutes or until the salmon is opaque and the flesh flakes easily. Leave to cool.

3 Mix the sauce ingredients in a bowl with salt and pepper to taste. Cover and refrigerate. When the salmon is cold, cover and refrigerate too – for up to 12 hours.

4 To serve, let the salmon come to room temperature and serve with a babyleaf salad, with the chilled sauce spooned alongside.

Herb-roasted salmon

SERVES 4 **CALS PER SERVING** 396

4 x 150 g (5 oz) salmon tail fillets, skinned
salt and black pepper
a little vegetable oil
125 g (4 oz) full-fat garlic and herb soft cheese

Topping

30 g (1 oz) fresh white breadcrumbs
30 g (1 oz) mature Cheddar cheese, grated
2 tbsp chopped fresh flat-leaf parsley
finely grated zest of 1 lime

To serve

lemon wedges
flat-leaf parsley sprigs

1 Season the salmon on both sides with salt and pepper. Place on lightly oiled baking parchment and spread with the soft cheese, not going quite to the edges.

2 Mix the topping ingredients together, adding seasoning to taste, then sprinkle over the salmon. (You can prepare ahead to this stage, cover the salmon, and keep it in the refrigerator for up to 12 hours.)

3 Cook in a preheated oven at 220°C (200°C fan, Gas 7) for 15 minutes or until the salmon is opaque and the flesh flakes easily. Serve with lemon and parsley.

Thai chilli salmon

SERVES 4 **CALS PER SERVING** 274

4 x 150–175 g (5–6 oz) middle-cut salmon fillets, skinned

Marinade

2 tbsp fish sauce
finely grated zest and juice of 1 lime
1 large fresh red chilli, halved, seeded, and finely chopped
2.5 cm (1 in) piece of fresh root ginger, peeled and finely grated
a few fresh coriander stems, finely chopped

To serve

fresh coriander leaves
1 lime, cut into wedges

1 Put the salmon fillets in a single layer in a shallow non-metallic dish, add the marinade ingredients and turn to coat. Cover and marinate in the refrigerator for 2–3 hours, turning the salmon once.

2 Lift the salmon from the marinade and cook under a preheated hot grill, 7.5 cm (3 in) away from the heat, for 5–6 minutes on each side until the salmon is opaque and the flesh flakes easily. Serve hot, with coriander and lime, and boiled rice noodles.

Baked trout with orange

SERVES 4 **CALS PER SERVING** 378

4 x 375–425 g (12–14 oz) trout, cleaned (page 104)
4 large thyme sprigs
4 large parsley sprigs
125 g (4 oz) button mushrooms, sliced
2 shallots, chopped
4 tbsp white wine vinegar
grated zest and juice of 1 orange
salt and black pepper
orange zest and thyme, to garnish

1 With a sharp knife, make two diagonal cuts through the skin and into the flesh on both sides of each trout.

2 Strip the thyme and parsley leaves from their stalks. In a bowl, combine the mushrooms, shallots, white wine vinegar, orange zest and juice, thyme and parsley leaves, and salt and pepper to taste.

3 Reserve one-quarter of the mushroom and herb mixture to spoon over the stuffed trout.

4 Stuff the trout with the remaining mushroom and herb mixture (see box, right).

5 Arrange the trout in a non-metallic baking dish and spoon over the reserved mushroom mixture. Cover and marinate in the refrigerator for up to 4 hours.

6 Bake in a preheated oven at 180°C (160°C fan, Gas 4) for 20–25 minutes until the fish is opaque and the flesh flakes easily. Garnish with orange zest and thyme before serving.

Stuffing the trout

Hold the fish open, spoon in one-quarter of the mushroom and herb mixture, then press firmly to close.

Smoked trout bake

SERVES 6 **CALS PER SERVING** 550

350 g (12 oz) floury potatoes, peeled and cut into 2 cm (3/4 in) cubes
salt and black pepper
500 g (1 lb 2 oz) baby spinach
1 tbsp olive oil
250 g (9 oz) button mushrooms, sliced in half
knob of butter
3 eggs, hard-boiled, peeled, and sliced into quarters
500 g (1 lb 2oz) smoked trout fillets, skinned
300 ml (10 fl oz) double cream
2 tsp Dijon mustard
75 g (2½ oz) Parmesan cheese, grated

2 LITRE (3½ PINT) WIDE-BASED OVENPROOF DISH

1 Preheat the oven to 200°C (180°C fan, Gas 6). Meanwhile, put the potatoes into a pan of cold salted water, cover with a lid, bring to the boil, and cook for 10–15 minutes or until just cooked. Drain well and set aside.

2 Heat a large frying pan, add the spinach, and cook for a few minutes or until just wilted but still holding its shape. Drain well in a colander, squeezing to remove excess liquid, then set aside. You may need to do this in batches.

3 Heat the oil in the frying pan, add the mushrooms, and fry for 3 minutes or until just cooked.

4 Grease the ovenproof dish with the butter, then arrange the potatoes, spinach, and mushrooms in the base. Scatter over the eggs, flake the trout fillets over the top, and season with salt and freshly ground black pepper.

5 Mix the cream and mustard in a bowl with some salt and freshly ground black pepper, then pour over the fish mixture, and sprinkle with the cheese.

6 Bake for 20–25 minutes or until golden on top and cooked through.

Mackerel with gooseberry sauce

SERVES 4 **CALS PER SERVING** 489

4 x 250 g (8 oz) mackerel, cleaned, with heads removed (page 104)
salt and black pepper

Gooseberry sauce
375 g (12 oz) gooseberries
2 tbsp water
30 g (1 oz) caster sugar, more if needed
30 g (1 oz) butter
½ tsp ground ginger

1 Cut the fins off the mackerel, and make 3–4 diagonal cuts on both sides of each fish. Season the mackerel inside and out with salt and pepper.

2 Make the gooseberry sauce: top and tail the gooseberries, and put them into a pan with the water and sugar. Cover tightly and simmer very gently, shaking the pan occasionally, for 5 minutes or until tender.

3 Reserve 12 of the cooked gooseberries for garnish, then work the remainder through a nylon sieve. Beat in the butter and ginger, and add more sugar if necessary. Return the sauce to the pan and keep warm.

4 Cook the mackerel under a hot grill, 10 cm (4 in) from the heat, for 7–8 minutes on each side until the fish is opaque and the flesh flakes easily.

5 Serve the mackerel hot, garnished with the reserved gooseberries. Hand the sauce separately.

MACKEREL WITH CRANBERRY SAUCE
Substitute 375 g (12 oz) cranberries for the gooseberries. You can use frozen cranberries, but they will take slightly longer to cook – simmer them until they pop open.

Grilled trout with cucumber and dill

SERVES 4 **CALS PER SERVING** 435

1 cucumber, peeled
30 g (1 oz) butter
small bunch of fresh dill, chopped, plus extra to garnish
salt and black pepper
juice of 1 lemon
4 x 375–425 g (12–14 oz) trout, cleaned (page 104)
new potatoes, to serve
dill cream sauce (page 110), to serve

1 Cut the cucumber in half lengthways and scoop out the seeds, then cut the flesh across into 5 mm (¼ in) slices. Melt the butter in a saucepan, add the cucumber, and cook gently for 2 minutes.

2 In a bowl, combine two-thirds of the cooked cucumber with the chopped dill, season with salt and pepper, and sprinkle with the lemon juice. Stuff the trout with the mixture.

3 Line a grill pan with foil. Arrange the trout on the foil, and put the remaining cucumber around them. Grill the trout under a hot grill, 10 cm (4 in) from the heat, for 4–7 minutes on each side until the flesh flakes easily.

4 Garnish with dill sprigs, and serve at once with new potatoes, and the dill cream sauce handed separately.

TROUT WITH ALMONDS
Dip the trout in seasoned flour. Melt 60 g (2 oz) butter in a large frying pan, and cook the trout in batches for 6–8 minutes on each side until the fish is opaque and the flesh flakes easily. Drain on paper towels, and keep warm. Wipe the pan, melt 15 g (½ oz) butter, and fry 60 g (2 oz) flaked almonds until lightly browned. Add a squeeze of lemon juice, then pour the lemon and almonds over the trout. Serve at once.

Hot and sour mackerel

SERVES 4 **CALS PER SERVING** 539

2 carrots
1 red pepper, cored and deseeded
1 fresh green chilli, halved and deseeded
6 garlic cloves
8 spring onions
4 x 175 g (6 oz) mackerel fillets
2 tbsp sunflower oil
1 lemongrass stalk, slit lengthways and bruised
coriander sprigs, to garnish

Hot and sour sauce

4 tbsp Thai fish sauce or light soy sauce
4 tbsp cider vinegar, white wine vinegar, or rice vinegar
2 tbsp lime juice
2 tbsp sugar

1 Make the hot and sour sauce: in a small bowl, combine the fish sauce or soy sauce, vinegar, lime juice, and sugar.

2 Cut the carrots, red pepper, green chilli, and garlic into matchstick-thin strips. Slice the spring onions.

3 Line a grill pan with foil. Arrange the mackerel on the foil, and cook under a hot grill, 10 cm (4 in) from the heat, for 3 minutes on each side. Continue to grill until the fish is opaque and the flesh flakes easily.

4 Meanwhile, stir-fry the vegetables. Heat the sunflower oil in a wok or large frying pan. Add the carrots, red pepper, chilli, garlic, spring onions, and lemongrass, and stir-fry over a high heat for 3 minutes or until the vegetables are just tender.

5 Remove and discard the lemongrass. Arrange the vegetable mixture on top of the fish, pour the sauce over, garnish with the coriander sprigs, and serve at once.

Herrings with mustard sauce

SERVES 4 **CALS PER SERVING** 479

4 x 175–250 g (6–8 oz) herrings, cleaned (page 104), heads removed, and filleted
salt and black pepper
butter, for greasing
lemon wedges and parsley sprigs, to garnish

Mustard sauce

30 g (1 oz) butter
30 g (1 oz) plain flour
300 ml (½ pint) milk
2 tsp mustard powder
1 tsp caster sugar
2 tsp white wine vinegar

1 Season the herrings inside and out with salt and black pepper, fold the fish over, and place in a single layer in a buttered ovenproof dish.

2 Cover and bake in a preheated oven at 200°C (180°C fan, Gas 6) for 12 minutes or until the fish is opaque and the flesh flakes easily.

3 Meanwhile, make the mustard sauce: melt the butter in a saucepan, add the flour, and cook, stirring, for 1 minute. Remove from the heat and gradually blend in the milk. Bring to a boil, stirring constantly until the mixture thickens. Simmer for 2–3 minutes. Blend the mustard powder, sugar, and vinegar together in a bowl, then add to the saucepan and cook for a further minute.

4 Garnish the herrings with lemon wedges and parsley sprigs, and a spoonful of mustard sauce. Serve with lightly sautéed potatoes and rocket leaves, if wished.

Herrings with oatmeal

SERVES 4 **CALS PER SERVING** 461

125 g (4 oz) medium oatmeal
2 tsp mustard powder
salt and black pepper
4 x 175–250 g (6–8 oz) herrings, cleaned (page 104), heads removed, and butterflied
8 parsley sprigs
parsley and lemon wedges, to garnish

1 In a shallow dish, combine the oatmeal and mustard powder, and season with salt and pepper.

2 Open out the herrings and press them into the oatmeal mixture to coat well on both sides.

3 Grill the herrings under a hot grill, 10 cm (4 in) from the heat, for about 4 minutes on each side or until the fish is opaque and the flesh flakes easily.

4 Arrange the grilled herrings on a warmed serving platter, and garnish with parsley and lemon wedges.

Tuna with fennel and tomato relish

SERVES 4 **CALS PER SERVING** 467

4 tbsp olive oil
juice of ½ lemon
3 garlic cloves, crushed
4 x 175 g (6 oz) tuna steaks, about 2.5 cm (1 in) thick
salt and black pepper
lime wedges and fennel tops, to garnish
salad leaves, to serve

Fennel and tomato relish

1 small fennel bulb, chopped
2 ripe but firm tomatoes, finely chopped
2 tbsp olive oil
1 tbsp lemon juice
1 tbsp tapenade (see Cook's know-how, right)
1 garlic clove, chopped

1 Combine the olive oil, lemon juice, and garlic in a large non-metallic dish. Add the tuna steaks and turn to coat. Cover dish and leave to marinate in the refrigerator, turning occasionally, for about 1 hour.

2 Meanwhile, make the relish: put the fennel, tomatoes, olive oil, lemon juice, tapenade, and garlic into a bowl, and stir well to combine.

3 Remove the tuna from the marinade, reserving the marinade. Cook the tuna under a hot grill, 7 cm (3 in) from the heat, basting once or twice with the reserved marinade, for 3–4 minutes on each side.

4 Season the tuna with salt and pepper, and top with the fennel and tomato relish. Garnish with lime wedges and fennel tops before serving with a simple salad.

Cook's know-how

Tapenade comes from Provence in the south of France. It is a tangy paste made of typical Provençal ingredients – black olives, capers, anchovies, and fruity olive oil. It is sold in tubes, jars, and tubs at supermarkets.

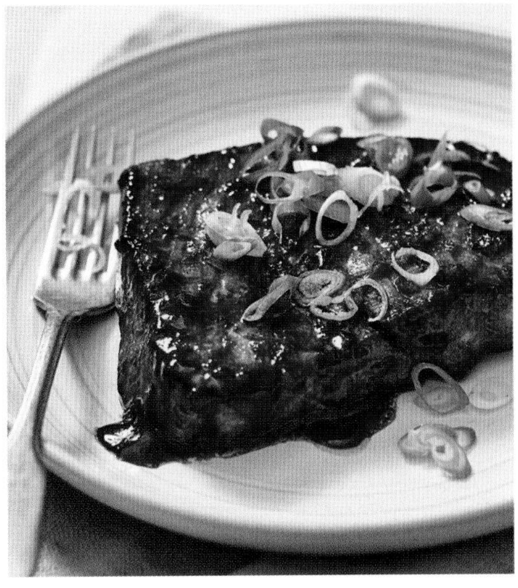

Tuna teriyaki

SERVES 4 **CALS PER SERVING** 339

4 x 175 g (6 oz) tuna steaks, about 2.5 cm (1 in) thick
2 spring onions, thinly sliced, to garnish

Marinade

3 tbsp dark soy sauce
2 tbsp sesame oil
1 tbsp rice wine vinegar
3 garlic cloves, chopped
1 tbsp caster sugar
1 cm (½ in) piece of fresh root ginger, peeled and grated

1 Make the marinade: put the soy sauce, sesame oil, rice wine vinegar, garlic, sugar, and ginger into a non-metallic dish. Add the tuna steaks to the marinade and turn to coat. Cover the dish and marinate in the refrigerator for up to 4 hours.

2 Reserve the marinade. Cook the steaks under a hot grill, 7 cm (3 in) from the heat, brushing with the marinade, for 3–4 minutes on each side. Serve at once, garnished with spring onions.

BARBECUED SALMON TERIYAKI

Cut 4 salmon fillets into 2.5 cm (1 in) cubes and marinate in the refrigerator for up to 4 hours, as in step 1, then thread on to kebab skewers. Cook over a hot barbecue, turning and brushing frequently with the marinade, for 6–8 minutes.

Simple sushi rice

500 g (1 lb) sushi rice
4 tbsp rice wine vinegar
50 ml (2 fl oz) Japanese rice wine (mirin or sake)
¼ tsp salt

1 Put the rice into a sieve and rinse under cold running water, then tip it into a saucepan and pour in 750 ml (1¼ pints) cold water. Bring to a boil, lower the heat, and simmer, covered, for 15 minutes or until all the water has been absorbed.

2 Remove the pan from the heat and cover it immediately with a tea towel and lid (this is to make sure no steam can escape). Leave for about 10 minutes.

3 Mix together the vinegar, rice wine, and salt in a small bowl and fold gently into the rice. Continue to cut and fold through the rice while cooling with a fan or a firm piece of card (it is important to cool the rice down quickly so that it remains sticky).

Cook's **know-how**

The secret of good sushi is to make a good sticky rice, which is very simple. Instructions are usually on the packet, but the recipe here includes a little rice wine for sweetness, and a little salt. To stop the rice sticking to your hand you will need a bowl of vinegar water (water with a little vinegar added). Always use sushi rice on the day it is made. After you have made all the sushi, you can refrigerate them for up to 24 hours until ready to serve.

Sushi squares with smoked salmon

MAKES 40 **CALS EACH** 49

a bowl of vinegar water
(see Cook's know-how, above right)
prepared Simple sushi rice
(see above)
4 thin slices of smoked salmon
a few strips of sushi pickled ginger (gari), from a jar

32.5 X 23 CM (13 X 9 IN) SWISS ROLL TIN

1 Line the Swiss roll tin with cling film (if you don't have a tin, cover a chopping board with cling film). Dip your hand in vinegar water, take a handful of the sushi rice, and press it into the tin, patting it level with your hand. Repeat with more handfuls of rice until the tin is full. Refrigerate for about 15 minutes until firm.

2 Turn the tin upside down on to a board and remove the cling film. Cut into about 40 small squares with a very sharp, wet knife. Cut the smoked salmon into little strips to fit on each square and top with a little pickled ginger.

Hoso maki

MAKES 20 **CALS EACH** 94

2 sheets of nori (dried Japanese seaweed)
a bowl of vinegar water
(see Cook's know-how, above right)
prepared Simple sushi rice
(see above)
a little wasabi
175 g (6 oz) canned white crabmeat, drained and flaked
½ cucumber, halved lengthways, deseeded, and cut into long thin strips

BAMBOO ROLLING MAT

1 Lay the rolling mat on a flat surface with one of the longest edges facing towards you. Lay one sheet of nori shiny-side down on the mat.

2 Dip your hand in vinegar water, take a handful of the sushi rice, and spread it over the nori, leaving a 2.5 cm (1 in) gap along the edge furthest away from you.

3 Spread a thin layer of wasabi – about 1 cm (½ in) wide – lengthways along the middle of the rice (from left to right). Cover the wasabi with half the crab, then put a strip of cucumber on either side of the crab.

4 Moisten the uncovered edge of the nori with a little cold water. Using the mat and starting from the edge nearest to you, roll the rice in the nori, squeezing it to make a tight roll. Seal the moistened edge around the roll, then wrap in cling film. Now make a second roll in the same way.

5 To serve, unwrap the rolls and cut each one into 10 pieces with a very sharp knife that has been dipped in cold water (trim off the ends first so you get neat slices).

Nigiri sushi

MAKES 10 **CALS EACH** 182

10 raw tiger prawns, shells and tails on
salt
a little wasabi (Japanese horseradish paste)
a bowl of vinegar water
(see Cook's know-how, above)
prepared Simple sushi rice
(see above left)

10 SMALL METAL SKEWERS

1 Push a skewer lengthways through each prawn so the prawn becomes straight. Boil for 1–2 minutes in salted water until pink and cooked, drain, and cool. Remove the skewers and gently shell the prawns, leaving the tails intact.

2 Make a slit down the length of the belly of each prawn (without cutting right through), and gently open the prawn out. Remove the black vein from the back.

3 Using your finger, spread a little wasabi along the middle of the slit in the belly. Dip your hand in vinegar water and take a small amount of rice, about the size of a small walnut. Shape the rice with your hand (it will be very sticky) so that it fills the slit on top of the wasabi, then reshape the prawn around the rice by squeezing. Turn the right way up to serve.

Opposite, clockwise from top:
Sushi squares with smoked salmon, Hoso maki, Nigiri sushi

Seafood and avocado salad

SERVES 4 **CALS PER SERVING** 396

500 g (1 lb) monkfish, trimmed and skinned
150 ml (¼ pint) fish stock
1 slice of onion
6 black peppercorns
squeeze of lemon juice
1 bay leaf
mixed salad leaves, such as frisée, radicchio, and rocket
2 avocados
lemon juice, for brushing
2 large tomatoes, peeled (page 32), deseeded, and cut into strips
125 g (4 oz) cooked peeled prawns
90 g (3 oz) white crabmeat
flat-leaf parsley, to garnish

Crème fraîche dressing

125 ml (4 fl oz) crème fraîche
3 tbsp lemon juice
salt and black pepper

1 Put the monkfish into a saucepan with the stock, onion, peppercorns, lemon juice, and bay leaf. Bring to a gentle simmer, cover, and poach very gently, turning once, for 10 minutes until opaque throughout and firm.

2 Remove the pan from the heat and leave the fish to cool in the liquid, then lift it out and cut into bite-sized pieces.

3 Make the crème fraîche dressing: put the crème fraîche and lemon juice into a bowl, add salt and pepper to taste, and stir to mix.

4 To serve, arrange the salad leaves in individual bowls. Halve, stone, and peel the avocados (page 395), and brush with lemon juice. Slice lengthways and arrange in a fan shape on the leaves. Add the strips of tomato, the monkfish, prawns, and crabmeat. Spoon the crème fraîche dressing over the salad, garnish with the parsley, and serve at once.

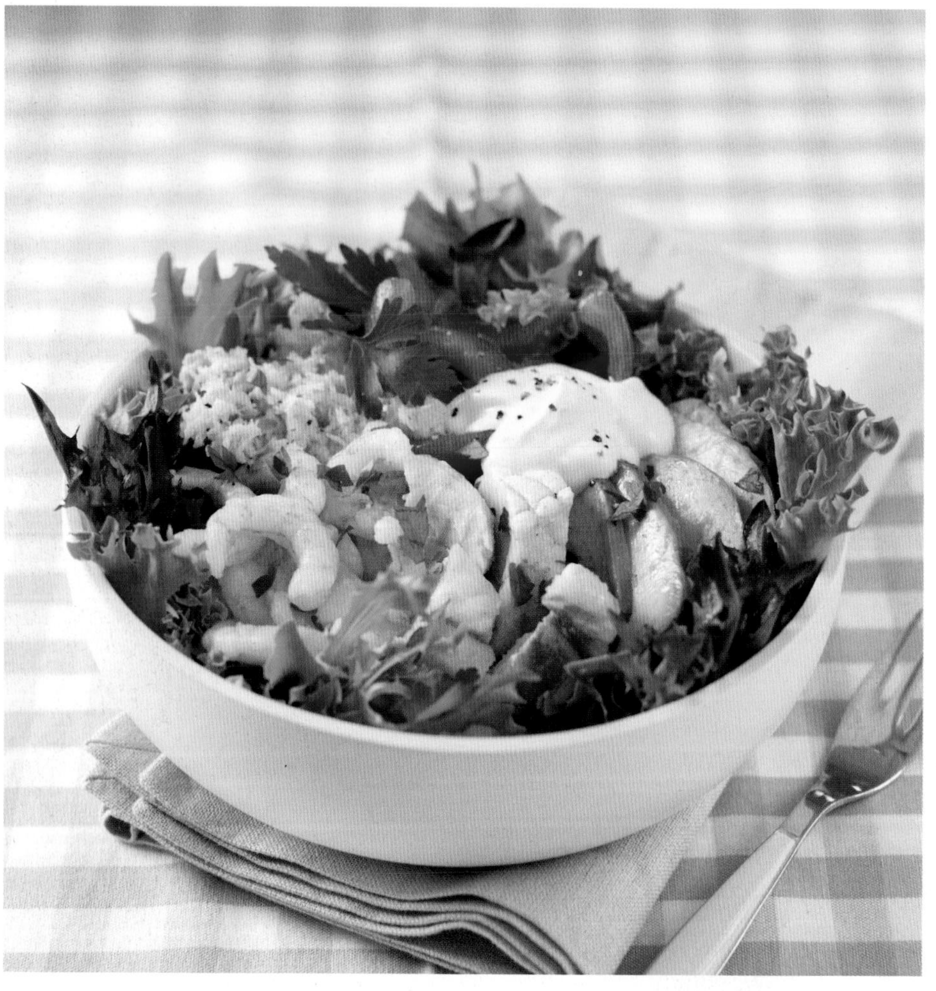

Crispy-topped seafood pie

SERVES 4 **CALS PER SERVING** 575

500 g (1 lb) cod fillet
300 ml (½ pint) milk
1 bay leaf
2 leeks, trimmed and sliced
175 g (6 oz) broccoli, cut into florets
175 g (6 oz) cooked peeled prawns
15 g (½ oz) butter
15 g (½ oz) plain flour
salt and black pepper
250 g (8 oz) ready-made shortcrust pastry, well chilled
30 g (1 oz) Gruyère cheese, grated

2.4 LITRE (4 PINT) PIE DISH

1 Put the cod into a saucepan with the milk and bay leaf, bring slowly to a boil, and poach gently for about 5 minutes until the fish flakes easily.

2 Meanwhile, blanch the leeks and broccoli for 3 minutes in a saucepan of boiling salted water. Drain.

3 Lift out the fish, remove and discard the skin and bones, and flake the fish. Strain and reserve the milk.

4 Put the blanched leeks and broccoli into the pie dish, and add the cod and prawns.

5 Melt the butter in a small saucepan, add the flour, and cook, stirring, for 1 minute. Remove from the heat and gradually blend in the reserved milk. Bring to a boil, stirring constantly until thickened. Simmer for 2–3 minutes. Season to taste and pour over the pie filling.

6 Grate the pastry, and sprinkle over the sauce. Sprinkle with the grated cheese. Bake in a preheated oven at 200°C (180°C fan, Gas 6) for 25–30 minutes. Serve at once.

Prawn tacos

SERVES 4 **CALS PER SERVING** 414

2 tbsp sunflower oil
2 onions, chopped
3 garlic cloves, crushed
1 green pepper, halved, deseeded, and diced
1 tbsp paprika
2 tsp mild chilli powder
½ tsp ground cumin
4 ripe firm tomatoes, chopped
500 g (1 lb) cooked peeled prawns
2 tbsp chopped fresh coriander
salt and black pepper
12 taco shells
1 round lettuce, shredded
sliced pickled chillies, large cooked peeled prawns, and coriander leaves, to garnish

1 Heat the oil in a large frying pan, add the onions, and cook gently, stirring occasionally, for 3–5 minutes until softened but not coloured. Add the garlic and diced green pepper, and cook, stirring occasionally, for 3 minutes or until the pepper is soft.

2 Stir in the paprika, chilli powder, and cumin, and cook, stirring, for 1 minute. Add the tomatoes and cook for 3–5 minutes until soft.

3 Lower the heat and stir in the prawns and chopped coriander, and season with salt and pepper.

4 Meanwhile, heat the taco shells in a preheated oven at 180°C (160°C fan, Gas 4) for 3 minutes or according to packet instructions.

5 Spoon the prawn mixture into the taco shells, top with the shredded lettuce, and garnish with chillies, prawns, and coriander. Serve at once.

Tiger prawns with tarragon sauce

SERVES 4 **CALS PER SERVING** 252

12 uncooked tiger prawns in their shells
olive oil, for brushing
300 ml (½ pint) dry white wine
1 garlic clove, crushed
4 tbsp chopped fresh parsley
lemon and tarragon, to garnish

Tarragon sauce

150 ml (¼ pint) soured cream
4 tbsp chopped fresh tarragon
1 tsp Dijon mustard
squeeze of lemon juice
salt and black pepper

1 Make the tarragon sauce: combine the soured cream, tarragon, mustard, and lemon juice, and season with salt and pepper.

2 Heat a heavy frying pan. Brush the prawns with oil, add to the pan, and cook the prawns over a high heat for 2 minutes or until pink.

3 Keeping the heat high, add 150 ml (¼ pint) of the wine and the garlic. Boil rapidly for 2–3 minutes, then stir in 2 tbsp of the parsley.

4 When the wine has reduced slightly, lower the heat, and add the remaining wine, and season with salt and pepper. Simmer for 5 minutes or until the prawns have released their juices into the wine.

5 Spoon the cooking juices over the prawns, sprinkle with the remaining parsley, and garnish with lemon and sprigs of fresh tarragon. Serve hot, with the tarragon sauce.

Thai prawn stir-fry

SERVES 4 **CALS PER SERVING** 522

250 g (8 oz) rice noodles
salt
3 tbsp sunflower oil
1 red pepper, halved, deseeded, and cut into thin strips
1 carrot, cut into thin strips
1 fresh green chilli, halved, deseeded, and cut into thin strips
2.5 cm (1 in) piece of fresh root ginger, peeled and cut into thin strips
1 garlic clove, crushed
8 spring onions, sliced
2 lemongrass stalks, trimmed and sliced
500 g (1 lb) cooked peeled tiger prawns
2 tbsp white wine vinegar
2 tbsp soy sauce
juice of ½ lime
1 tbsp sesame oil
3 tbsp chopped fresh coriander, to garnish

1 Put the rice noodles into a large saucepan of boiling salted water and stir to separate the noodles. Turn off the heat, cover, and leave to stand for 4 minutes. Drain well and set aside.

2 Heat 1 tbsp of the sunflower oil in a wok or large frying pan. Add the red pepper, carrot, chilli, ginger, garlic, spring onions, and lemongrass, and stir-fry over a high heat for 2 minutes.

3 Add the prawns, and stir-fry for 1 minute, then stir in the noodles.

4 Add the remaining sunflower oil, the vinegar, soy sauce, lime juice, and sesame oil, and stir-fry for 1 minute.

5 Sprinkle with the chopped fresh coriander, and serve at once.

SCALLOP STIR-FRY

Substitute 500 g (1 lb) shelled scallops for the tiger prawns, cutting each scallop into two or three pieces if they are large. Stir-fry for about 2 minutes, then add the red pepper, carrot, chilli, fresh root ginger, garlic, spring onions, and lemongrass, and stir-fry for a further 2 minutes. Add the soaked and drained noodles, then continue with the recipe from the beginning of step 4.

Devilled crab

SERVES 4 **CALS PER SERVING** 502

75 g (2½ oz) butter
1½ tbsp plain flour
175 ml (6 fl oz) milk
¼ tsp mustard powder
¼ tsp grated nutmeg
1 egg yolk
1½ tbsp dry sherry
1 tsp Worcestershire sauce
2–3 dashes of Tabasco sauce
4 small dressed crabs with their claws (page 106), or 500 g (1 lb) white and dark crabmeat
1 spring onion, thinly sliced
salt and black pepper
125 g (4 oz) fresh breadcrumbs
paprika and finely chopped spring onions, to garnish

1 Melt 45 g (1½ oz) of the butter in a saucepan, add the flour, and cook, stirring, for 1 minute. Remove from the heat, and gradually blend in the milk. Bring to a boil, stirring constantly until the mixture thickens. Simmer for 2–3 minutes. Remove from the heat, and stir in the mustard and nutmeg.

2 Put the egg yolk into a small bowl, and whisk in a little of the sauce. Stir this mixture back into the sauce.

3 Add the dry sherry, Worcestershire sauce, Tabasco sauce, crabmeat, spring onion, and salt and pepper to taste, and stir to mix. Spoon the mixture into the crab shells, or into ramekins, and stand them on a baking sheet.

4 Melt the remaining butter in a saucepan, add the breadcrumbs, and cook, stirring, for 5 minutes or until golden brown.

5 Spoon the breadcrumbs over the crabmeat mixture, replace the claws if you have them, and bake in a preheated oven at 200°C (180°C fan, Gas 6) for 10 minutes or until the tops are browned and bubbling. Sprinkle with paprika and chopped spring onions before serving.

Spicy clams with coriander dressing

SERVES 4–6 **CALS PER SERVING** 349–233

4 tbsp olive oil
6 ripe firm tomatoes, diced
4 garlic cloves, crushed
1 tbsp mild chilli powder
about 4 dozen baby clams, cleaned (page 105)
600 ml (1 pint) fish stock, or 300 ml (½ pint) each dry white wine and fish stock
juice of ½ lime
lime wedges, to serve

Coriander dressing

12 coriander sprigs
2 tbsp olive oil
1 large garlic clove, roughly chopped
1 mild fresh green chilli, halved, deseeded, and roughly chopped
salt and black pepper

1 Make the coriander dressing: strip the coriander leaves from the stalks. Purée the coriander leaves, olive oil, garlic, and green chilli in a food processor or blender until smooth. Season with salt and pepper, and set aside.

2 Heat the oil in a large saucepan, add the tomatoes, garlic, and chilli powder, and cook gently, stirring occasionally, for 8 minutes or until slightly thickened.

3 Add the clams and stir for about 1 minute, then pour in the stock. Cover the pan tightly, and cook the clams over a medium heat, shaking the pan frequently, for about 5–8 minutes until the clams open. Discard any that have not opened; do not try to force them open.

4 Using a slotted spoon, transfer the clams to a warmed bowl.

5 Pour the cooking juices into a small pan, and boil until reduced by about half. Add the lime juice, and season to taste, then pour the sauce over the clams.

6 Serve the clams at once, with lime wedges and the coriander dressing.

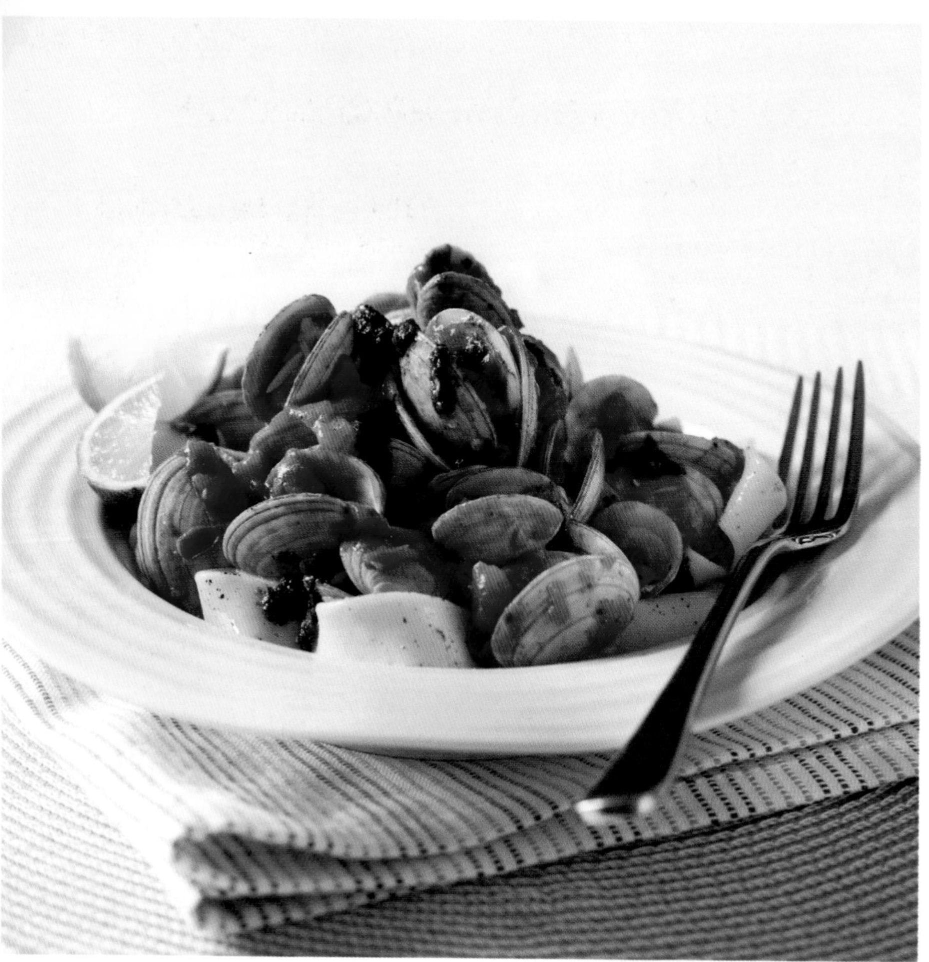

Classic steamed clams with parsley

SERVES 4 **CALS PER SERVING** 207

45 g (1½ oz) butter
2 onions, coarsely chopped
2 garlic cloves, crushed
300 ml (½ pint) dry white wine
150 ml (¼ pint) water
about 6 tbsp chopped fresh parsley
about 3 dozen clams, cleaned (page 105)

1 Melt 15g (½ oz) of the butter in a large, deep saucepan. Add the onions and garlic, and fry for 2–3 minutes.

2 Pour in the wine and water, and add 2 tbsp of the parsley. Add the clams, cover the pan, and bring to a boil. Cook, shaking the pan, for about 12 minutes until the clams open. Discard any that have not opened; do not force them open.

3 Using a slotted spoon, transfer the clams to a warmed bowl or serving dish.

4 Bring the sauce to a boil, and whisk in the remaining butter and parsley. Pour the sauce over the clams, and serve immediately.

Cook's **know-how**

Hard-shell clams come in different sizes. The smallest are called littlenecks, the next size up are cherrystones, and the largest are chowder clams, although your fishmonger may use other names. Buy whatever you can get for this recipe, bearing in mind that the smaller they are the more fiddly they will be to prepare and eat.

Lobster tails with black-eyed bean salsa

SERVES 4 **CALS PER SERVING** 531

4 cooked lobster tails
lime twists and coriander sprigs, to garnish

Black-eyed bean salsa

4 ripe but firm tomatoes, finely chopped
1 small onion, chopped
1 garlic clove, crushed
2 tbsp chopped fresh coriander
1 mild fresh green chilli, halved, deseeded, and chopped
1 x 375 g can black-eyed beans, drained
salt and black pepper

Garlic butter

150 g (5 oz) butter
5 garlic cloves, crushed
2 tsp finely chopped fresh oregano

1 Make the black-eyed bean salsa: in a bowl, combine the tomatoes, onion, garlic, coriander, and chilli. Add the beans, and salt and pepper to taste.

2 With a sharp knife, cut each lobster tail in half lengthways and loosen the flesh, keeping it in the shell.

3 Make the garlic butter: cream the butter in a bowl, add the garlic, oregano, and salt and pepper to taste, and mix well. Spread half of the butter mixture over the lobster flesh.

4 Place the lobster under a hot grill, 10 cm (4 in) from the heat, and grill for 5 minutes or until slightly browned in patches and heated through.

5 Spread the lobster with the remaining garlic butter, and then garnish with lime twists and coriander sprigs. Serve hot, with the black-eyed bean salsa.

Lobster tails with mango and lime

SERVES 4 **CALS PER SERVING** 442

4 cooked lobster tails
90 ml (3 fl oz) dry white wine
250 ml (8 fl oz) double cream
1 small mango, peeled, stoned, and cut into cubes (page 518)
grated zest and juice of 1 lime
30 g (1 oz) Parmesan cheese, grated

1 Remove the flesh from the lobster tails (see box, right), then cut each piece of lobster flesh in half lengthways. Arrange the pieces of lobster flesh, cut side-side up, in a large, shallow ovenproof dish.

2 Pour the white wine into a small saucepan and boil rapidly until it has reduced to about 2 tbsp.

3 Add the cream to the saucepan and boil until the mixture has reduced to a coating consistency. Stir in the mango cubes and grated lime zest and juice.

4 Spoon the mixture over the lobster in the dish. Sprinkle with the Parmesan cheese and bake in a preheated oven at 220°C (200°C fan, Gas 7) for about 20 minutes, until hot and bubbling. Serve hot.

Removing the flesh from a lobster tail

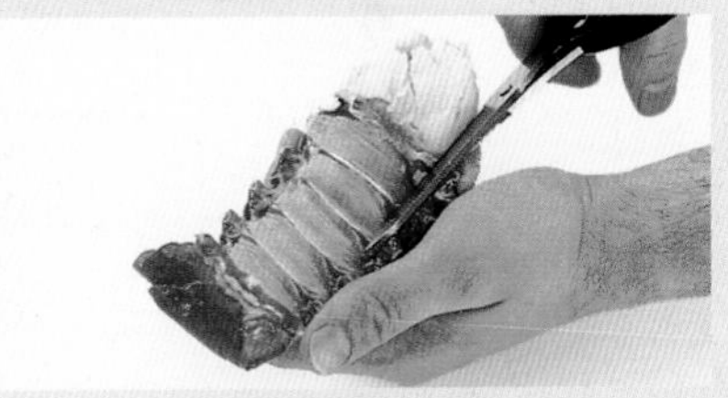

Hold the tail in one hand. With a pair of scissors, cut along both sides of the underside of the shell, towards the end, without damaging the flesh.

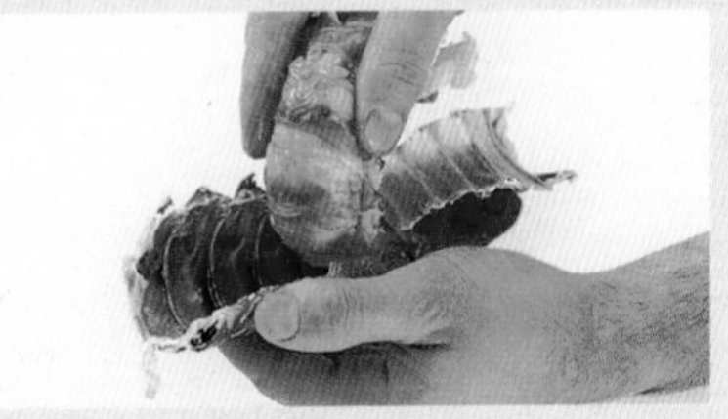

Pull back the underside of the shell, and lift out the lobster flesh, making sure it is all in one piece.

Mediterranean stuffed squid

SERVES 4 **CALS PER SERVING** 224

8 small whole squid, cleaned (page 107)
30 g (1 oz) butter, plus a little extra for frying
1 large onion, finely chopped
2 garlic cloves, crushed
60 g (2 oz) fine fresh breadcrumbs
1 tbsp chopped fresh dill
1 tbsp chopped parsley
salt and black pepper
lemon slices and chopped fresh parsley, to serve
salad leaves, to serve

1 Chop the squid tentacles roughly and set aside.

2 Make the stuffing: melt the butter in a frying pan, add the onion and garlic, cover, and sauté over a low heat for about 15–20 minutes until very soft.

3 Add the chopped squid tentacles, breadcrumbs, dill, and parsley to the onion and garlic, and fry over a high heat for 2–3 minutes. Season with salt and pepper, and leave to cool.

4 Fill the squid bodies with the cold stuffing, and secure the tops (see box, right).

5 Heat a little butter in a clean frying pan, and fry the stuffed squid for about 4–5 minutes until golden brown and firm to the touch, and the filling is heated through.

6 Garnish the squid with the lemon slices and parsley, and serve at once with mixed salad leaves.

Securing the squid

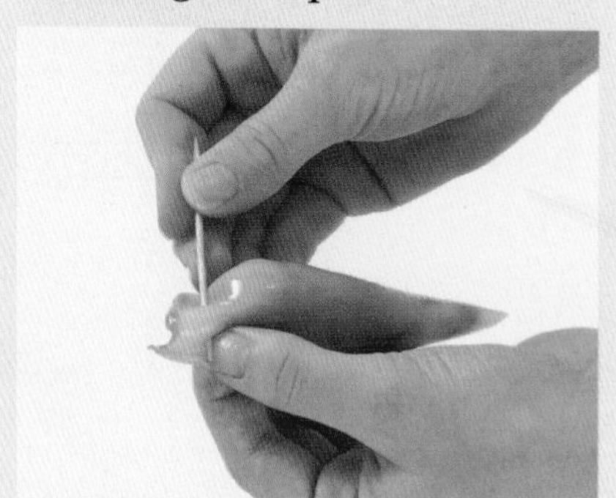

Thread a cocktail stick through the top of each stuffed squid to secure the opening.

Chinese-style oysters

SERVES 4 **CALS PER SERVING** 248

8 streaky bacon rashers, rinds removed, cut in half
1 x 100 g can smoked oysters, drained
1 small green pepper, halved, deseeded, and cut into bite-sized pieces
1 garlic clove, crushed
250 g (8 oz) canned water chestnuts, drained
1 spring onion, thinly sliced
lemon wedges and Tabasco sauce, to serve

1 Wrap half a bacon rasher around each oyster, and fasten securely with wooden cocktail sticks.

2 Heat a frying pan, add the bacon-wrapped oysters, and cook gently for 6–8 minutes until browned and crisp. Add the green pepper, garlic, and water chestnuts, and stir-fry over a high heat for 2 minutes.

3 Sprinkle with the spring onion slices, and serve with lemon wedges and Tabasco.

Mussel gratin

Serves 4 **CALS PER SERVING** 448

150 ml (¼ pint) dry white wine
1 shallot, finely chopped
1 garlic clove, crushed
3 kg (6 lb) large mussels, cleaned (page 105)
300 ml (½ pint) single cream
3 tbsp chopped parsley
salt and black pepper
30 g (1 oz) fresh white breadcrumbs
30 g (1 oz) butter, melted

1 Pour the wine into a large saucepan, add the chopped shallot and crushed garlic, and bring to a boil. Simmer for 2 minutes.

2 Add the mussels, cover tightly, and return to a boil. Cook, shaking the pan frequently, for 5–6 minutes until the mussels open.

3 Using a slotted spoon, transfer the mussels to a large bowl. Discard any that have not opened; do not try to force them open.

4 Strain the cooking liquid into a saucepan, bring to a boil, and simmer until reduced to about 3 tbsp. Add the cream and heat through. Stir in half of the parsley, and season with salt and pepper.

5 Remove the top shell of each mussel and discard. Arrange the mussels, in their bottom shells, on a large flameproof serving dish.

6 Spoon the sauce over the mussels, and sprinkle with the breadcrumbs and melted butter. Cook under a hot grill, 10 cm (4 in) from the heat, for 3–5 minutes until golden. Garnish with the remaining parsley and serve at once.

Cook's know-how

Mussels are often sold by volume: 900 ml (1½ pints) is equivalent to 750 g (1½ lb), which will yield about 375 g (12 oz) shelled mussels.

Scallops with asparagus and lemon

SERVES 6 **CALS PER SERVING** 159

500 g (1 lb) fresh asparagus tips, chopped into 2 cm (1 in) lengths
60 g (2 oz) butter
500 g (1 lb) queen scallops
3 garlic cloves, crushed
juice of 1 lemon
2 tbsp finely chopped fresh parsley
1 tbsp chopped fresh tarragon
salt and black pepper

1 Blanch the asparagus in boiling salted water for about 2 minutes, then drain and refresh in cold water to stop the cooking and set the bright green colour.

2 Melt half the butter in a frying pan, and fry the scallops for about 30 seconds on each side until just opaque and firm to the touch (you may need to do this in batches). Remove the scallops with a slotted spoon, and keep warm.

3 Heat the remaining butter in the frying pan. Add the garlic, lemon juice, parsley, and tarragon, and season with salt and pepper.

4 Return the scallops and asparagus to the pan and heat them through very gently, shaking the pan to coat them in the sauce. Serve hot.

Cook's know-how

Scallops are sweet and succulent to taste. Care must be taken as they can easily overcook and become rubbery and tough.

Poultry and game

In this chapter...

Chicken Marengo
page 175

Yogurt and mint barbecued chicken
page 176

Fruity coriander barbecued chicken
page 176

Orange and rosemary barbecued chicken
page 176

Chicken kebabs
page 178

Herb-grilled chicken
page 178

Provençal-style roast chicken
page 180

Roast chicken with orange and peppers
page 180

Sunday roast chicken
page 182

French roast chicken
page 183

Chicken satay
page 184

Chicken tikka
page 184

Fragrant chicken curry with almonds
page 186

Sweet and sour Chinese chicken
page 187

Chicken stir-fry
page 187

Stir-fried chicken with crisp vegetables
page 188

Chinese chicken with mango
page 189

Tarragon chicken with avocado
page 190

Vietnamese turkey salad
page 190

Thai chicken with water chestnuts
page 190

In this chapter... *continued*

Warm chicken salad with mango and avocado
page 192

Coronation chicken
page 192

Greek chicken salad
page 193

Red pepper herbed chicken salad
page 193

Poussins with romesco sauce
page 194

Lemon poussins with artichoke hearts
page 194

Moroccan poussins
page 196

Oriental poussins
page 196

Roast turkey with garlic and tarragon
page 197

Turkey with soured cream and chives
page 197

Christmas roast turkey
page 198

Turkey mole
page 200

Turkey and lemon stir-fry
page 200

Stir-fried turkey meatballs
page 201

Turkey casserole with peppers and cider
page 202

Turkey schnitzel
page 202

Turkey salad with mango and grapes
page 204

Turkey to go
page 204

Roast duck with cranberries
page 206

Duck breasts with raspberry sauce
page 207

Duck breasts with red wine sauce
page 208

Oriental duck with ginger
page 208

Peking duck
page 210

Hot and spicy stir-fried duck
page 211

Lacquered duck
page 211

Christmas roast goose
page 213

Pheasant stew
page 213

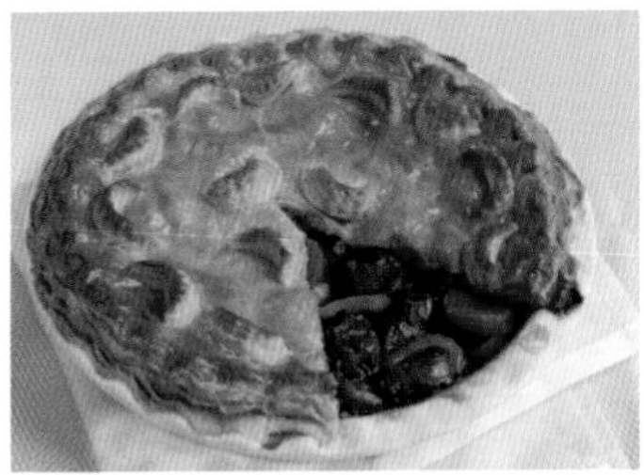
Game pie with fennel and carrots
page 214

Normandy pheasant
page 215

Mushroom-stuffed quail
page 216

Traditional roast pheasant
page 216

Rather special game pie
page 218

Guinea fowl Madeira
page 220

Pot roast venison
page 220

Braised rabbit with mushrooms and cider
page 222

Rabbit with mustard and marjoram
page 222

Venison casserole
page 224

Ruby hare casserole
page 224

Poultry and game know-how

Poultry is the term for all domesticated birds reared for the table – the most familiar being chicken, turkey, goose, and duck – but the classification "poultry" can also be applied to game birds that once lived in the wild and are now farmed, such as guinea fowl, pigeon, and quail. Pheasant and partridge are also often intensively reared, to be released into the so-called "wild" for the shooting season. Truly wild game birds taste quite different from their farmed or semi-wild counterparts; they are left to hang to enhance their "gamey" flavour and tenderize their flesh.

Buying and storing

There is a great variety of poultry available, produced by different farming methods. Free-range birds, which have been allowed access to the open air, cost more than intensively reared birds but they tend to have a superior flavour as they are slaughtered when they are older. Corn-fed chickens, which may or may not be free-range, are another option. Their diet does include maize (corn), but it is an artificial dye in their food that gives their flesh its yellow colour. The more expensive organically reared birds are not routinely given antibiotics nor artificial growth-promoting hormones in their feed.

Poultry can be bought fresh or frozen as whole birds – ranging in size from tiny quail and poussins to huge turkeys – as well as in pieces. Game birds are generally sold whole. Poultry and game birds should have a plump breast and moist, unblemished skin, and poultry should smell fresh and sweet, never "off".

All poultry and game birds are very perishable so they must be kept cool. As soon as you can, remove any tight plastic wrapping and giblets, then put the bird on a plate to collect any drips, cover it loosely, and store in the refrigerator. Check the use-by date – most poultry should be cooked within 2 days of purchase.

Types of birds

Poussins are small single-serving-size chickens; spring chickens or poulets are a little bigger. Roasters are the most widely available, either whole or in joints. The largest chickens are boiling fowl, which are old laying hens, and capons, which are neutered male birds. Turkey is sold whole as well as in escalopes, breast steaks, and large thigh, leg, or breast joints, boned or on the bone. Duck is sold whole and in legs or boneless breasts.

Other poultry (eg goose, guinea fowl, pigeon, and quail) and game birds (eg wild duck such as mallard, widgeon and teal, grouse, partridge, and pheasant) are sold whole, sometimes boned.

Freezing

Frozen poultry and game, particularly "fresh-frozen" (quickly air-cooled before freezing), is very good and a useful standby. When buying frozen poultry and game, check it is completely frozen and get it home as quickly as possible. Chicken, turkey, and wild game birds can be stored for up to 6 months; duck, goose, and guinea fowl for 4 months.

Poultry and game must be thoroughly thawed before cooking. This can take time – a 4.5 kg (10 lb) turkey needs 22–24 hours. Unwrap the bird, cover loosely with fresh wrapping, and set on a plate to thaw in the refrigerator. Remove any giblets as soon as possible. Raw poultry or game should never be re-frozen once thawed.

Microwaving

Casseroles and stews made with poultry and game can be cooked quite easily in the microwave oven. They are quick to prepare and the meat stays tender and juicy. You may choose to brown the poultry or game and any vegetables on the hob first, then transfer to a dish to finish cooking in the microwave. Be sure to transfer the flavoursome pan drippings to the microwave dish as well.

The microwave is also really good for reheating cooked poultry and game dishes, particularly when the meat is off the bone.

Poultry or game stock

To make 2.5 litres (4 pints) stock, use 1.5 kg (3 lb) raw poultry or game pieces or bones, or the carcass and trimmings from a roast bird. Don't mix raw and cooked bones.

1 Crush or break up bones and carcasses, and put them into a stockpot or large pan. Add 2–3 halved, unpeeled onions. Cook until browned.

2 Add 4 litres (7 pints) water. Bring to a boil, skimming off any scum from the surface. Add 3 chopped carrots, 3 chopped celery stalks, 1 large bouquet garni, and a few black peppercorns.

3 Half cover the pan and simmer for 2½–3 hours. Strain the stock into a bowl. Leave to cool, then remove the solidified fat from the surface and discard. Cover and keep in the refrigerator for up to 3 days, or freeze for 3 months. (You can keep raw or cooked bones in the freezer too, for making stock at a later date.)

Stock know-how

If you do not have a carcass from a whole bird, chicken wings make a good base for a stock.

Peppercorns, instead of ground black pepper, are used in stock: prolonged cooking can turn ground black pepper bitter.

Skim off fat with a large spoon, soak it up with paper towels, or cool and lift it off.

Jellied stock

This stock is used in cold dishes such as Rather special game pie (page 218), where it forms a jelly around the meat. Make it in the same way as other stocks, but use bones only, because they contain a high level of gelatine. Crack the bones before adding them to the pot. The stock will set when cool.

Giblet stock

Giblets are not often found in birds, but they make a really good stock.

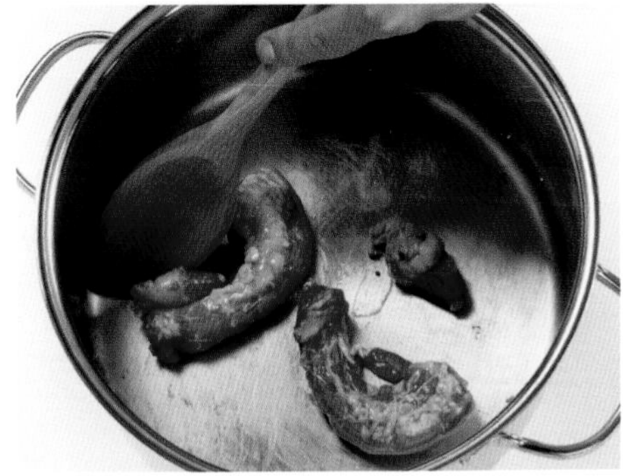

1 Put the giblets (the neck, heart, and gizzard but not the liver) in a stockpot or large saucepan and cook until lightly browned. Stir in 1 litre (1¾ pints) water (or previously made stock). Bring to a boil, skimming off any scum that forms on the surface.

2 Add 1–2 quartered, unpeeled onions, 1 chopped celery stalk, 1 chopped carrot, 1 bouquet garni, and a few black peppercorns. Simmer for about 1 hour. Strain, then cool, cover, and keep in the refrigerator for up to 3 days, or freeze for 3 months.

Poultry portions

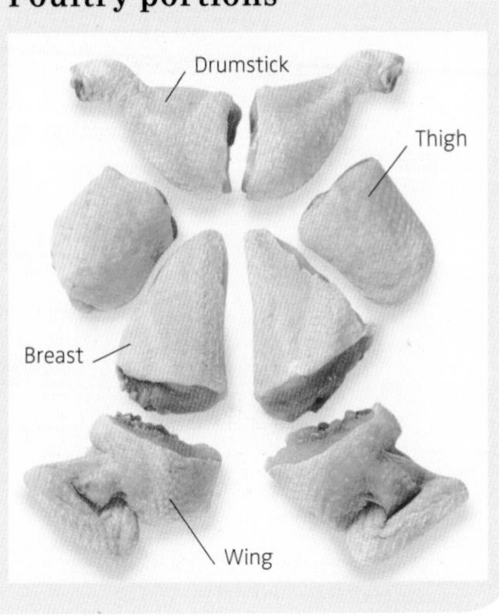

Spatchcocking

This method of splitting and flattening a bird makes it quicker to cook and suitable for grilling or cooking over a barbecue. Poussins, chickens, guinea fowl, and game birds can all be spatchcocked.

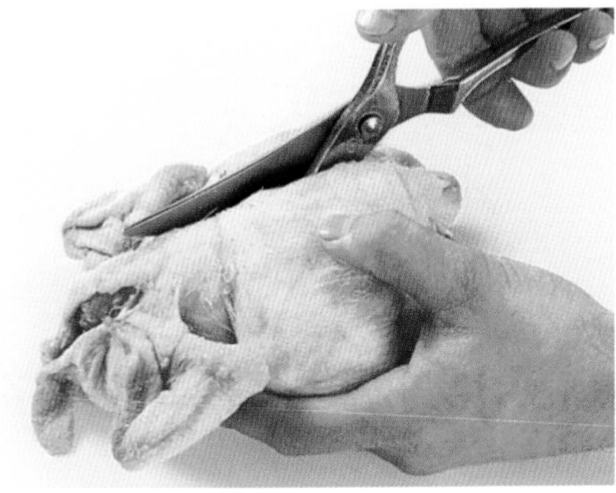

1 With poultry shears or a knife, cut along both sides of the backbone and discard. Cut off the wing tips and the ends of the legs. Remove the wishbone.

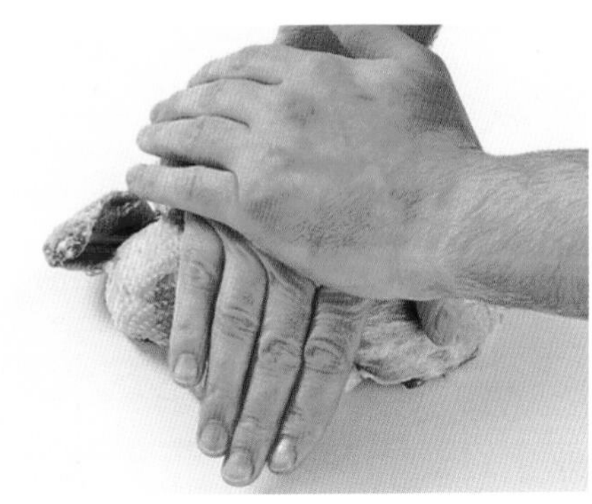

2 Turn the bird over. Put your hands on top of the breast and press down firmly with the heels of your hands to break the breastbone and flatten the bird.

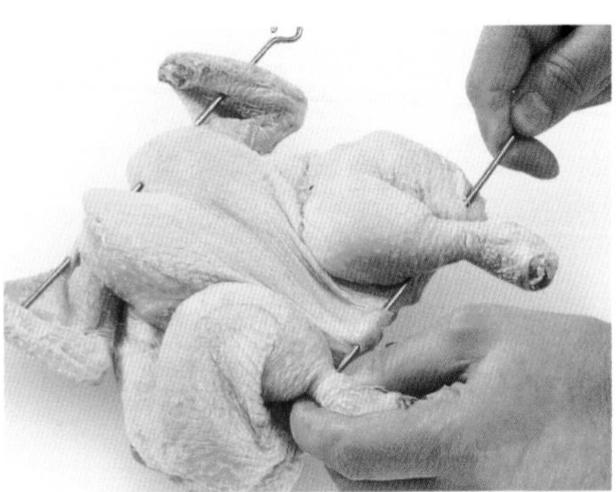

3 Thread a long metal skewer through the bird at the neck end, passing through the wings. Thread another skewer below the breast, passing through the legs. If small birds are spatchcocked, two or three can be threaded on the same skewers.

Jointing a bird

Chicken portions are widely available, but cutting a bird into four or eight serving pieces is not at all difficult to do yourself, and it can be done before or after cooking. A pair of special poultry shears makes the job particularly easy; otherwise, use good, strong scissors or a sharp chef's knife.

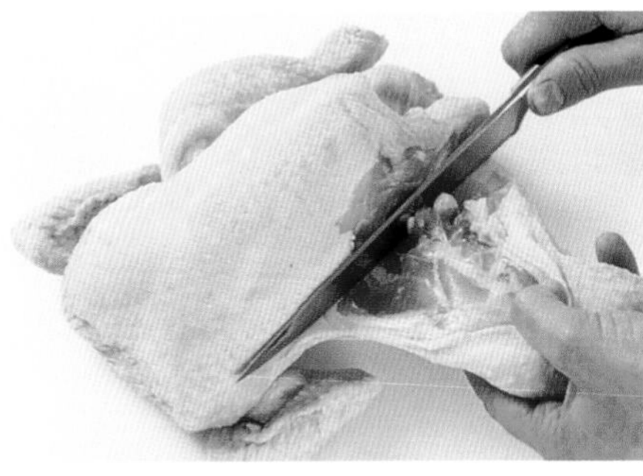

1 Cut through to the joint between one of the legs and the body. Twist the leg out and away from the body to pop the ball and socket joint, then cut through the joint to remove the leg. Remove the other leg.

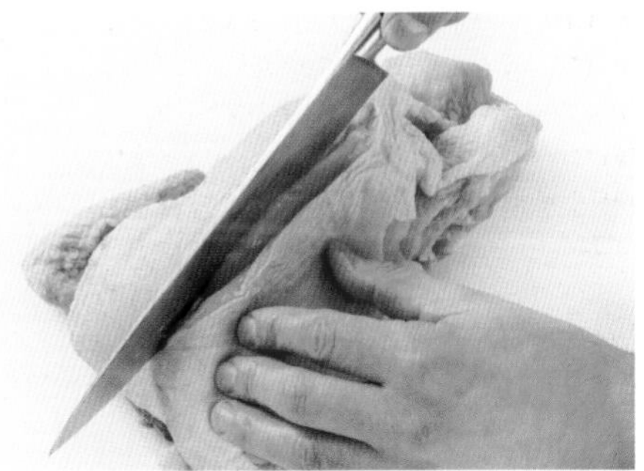

2 To remove the breasts, cut through the skin and flesh along both sides of the breastbone. Cut through the bones of the ribcage where it joins the sides of the breastbone, then remove the breastbone.

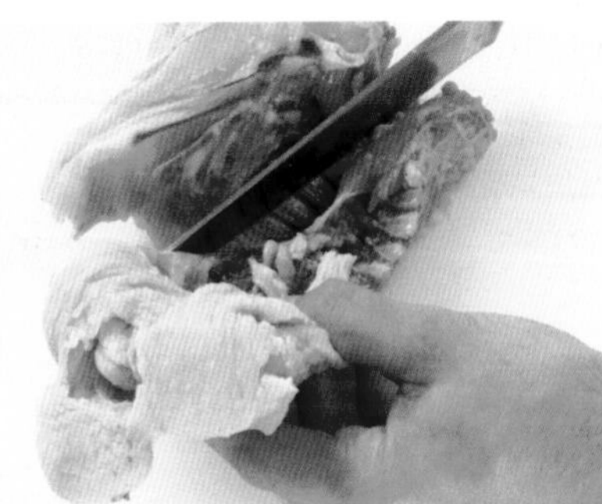

3 Turn over and cut along the backbone, to give two breasts with wings attached. For eight pieces, cut each breast diagonally in two: the wing half should be slightly smaller. Cut each leg through the joint into thigh and drumstick.

Boning a whole chicken

Although boning a chicken requires a little time and effort, the result is impressive. Stuffed and rolled into a ballotine, it is ideal for entertaining because it is so easy to carve. Other birds can be boned in the same way.

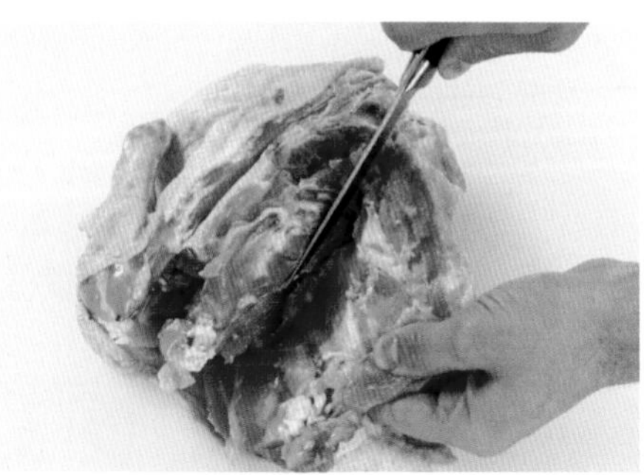

1 Set the bird breast-side down and slit the skin along the backbone. Remove the wishbone (see box, opposite). Slide the knife into the cut and gently pull and scrape the flesh away from the ribcage. Continue cutting away the flesh until you reach the leg and wing joints. Repeat on the other side.

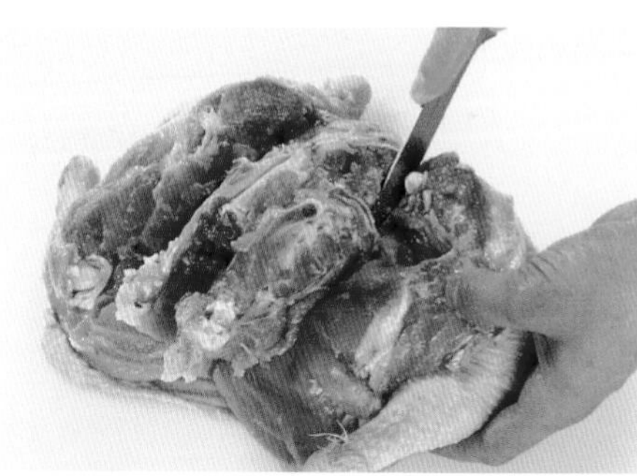

2 Scrape away the flesh from the ribcage, working on one side at a time. Take care not to make any holes in the skin as you are doing this. Cut through the ball and socket joints connecting the legs to the carcass (they will still be attached to the skin).

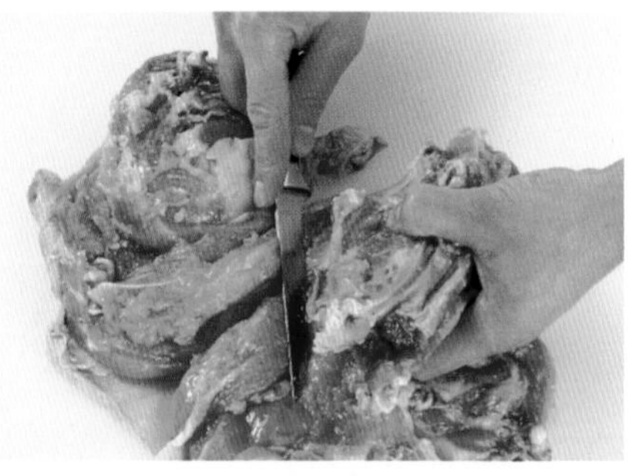

3 Keep cutting the flesh from the bone on both sides until you reach the ridge of the breastbone in the middle. Cut the breastbone free, without cutting through the skin, and lift it away with the carcass.

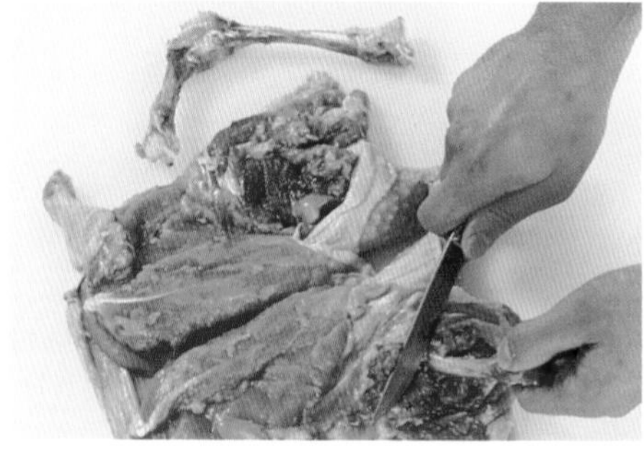

4 Cut through the tendons in the legs that join the flesh to the bone. Scrape back the flesh until the bones of each leg have been exposed, then pull out the bones, cutting them free of the skin.

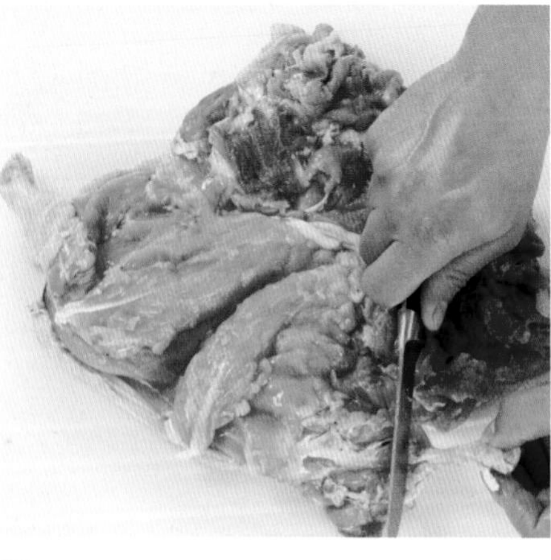

5 Bone the wings in the same way as the legs. Push the legs and wings skin-side out. The chicken is now ready for stuffing and rolling. Keep the carcass and bones for making chicken stock.

Removing the wishbone

A bird is easier to carve if the wishbone is removed before cooking.

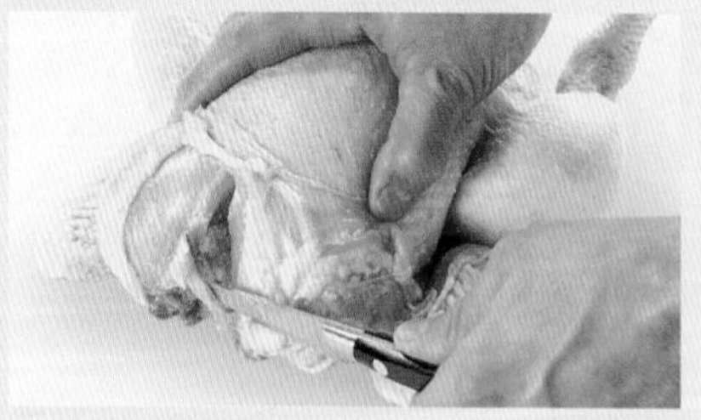

With your fingers, loosen the skin from the flesh at the neck end. Fold back the skin to expose the breastbone. Use a small, sharp knife to cut the wishbone free, taking any fat with it.

Boning a quail

For a special occasion, tiny quail can be boned but left whole. It is then quite simple to fill them with a savoury stuffing and secure with a cocktail stick ready for roasting. Make sure you use a very small knife and be careful not to pierce the skin.

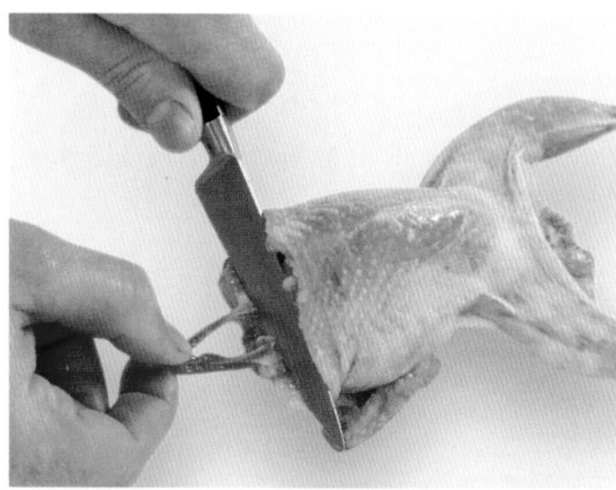

1 With your fingers, carefully loosen the skin at the neck of the quail, and push it back to reveal the wishbone. With a small, sharp knife, cut the flesh from around the wishbone and remove it.

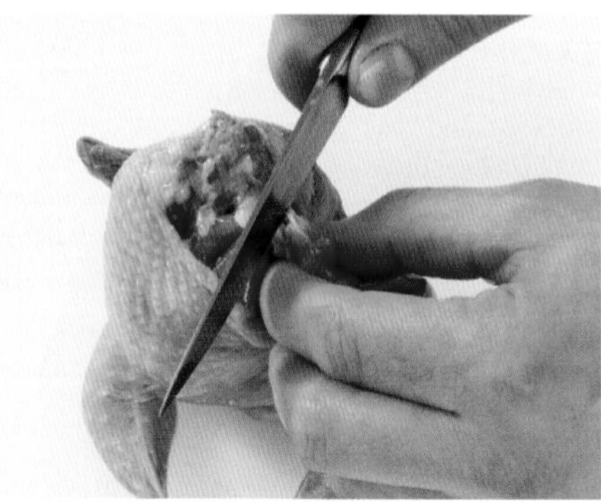

2 Loosen one wing by carefully cutting through the tendon at the base. Repeat with the other wing.

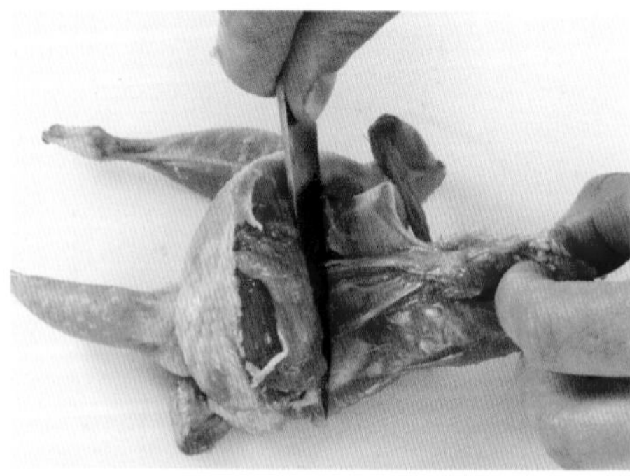

3 Insert the knife between the ribcage and the flesh and, working all around the bird, scrape the flesh from the bones, pushing it back as you go. Remove the ribcage. The bird is now ready to stuff.

Preparing poultry for roasting

Tying or skewering a bird before roasting holds it together so that it keeps a neat shape during cooking. It will also prevent any stuffing from falling out. To be sure that heat can penetrate into the centre of the bird and cook it thoroughly, it is best to put stuffing into the neck end and not into the large body cavity.

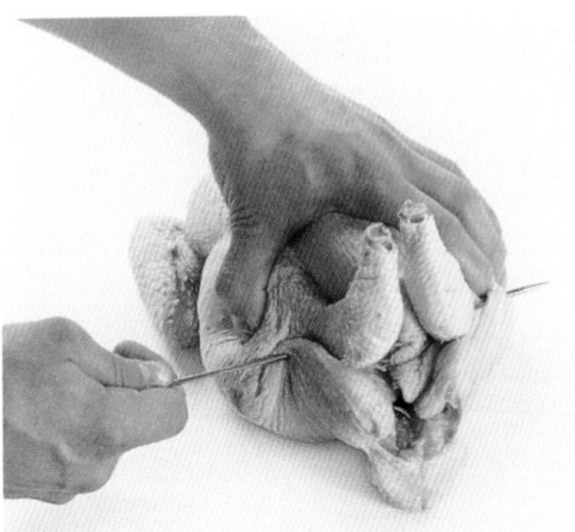

Simple trussing

1 Put the bird breast-side up and push the legs back and down. Holding the legs with one hand, insert a skewer below the knee joint and push it through the bird.

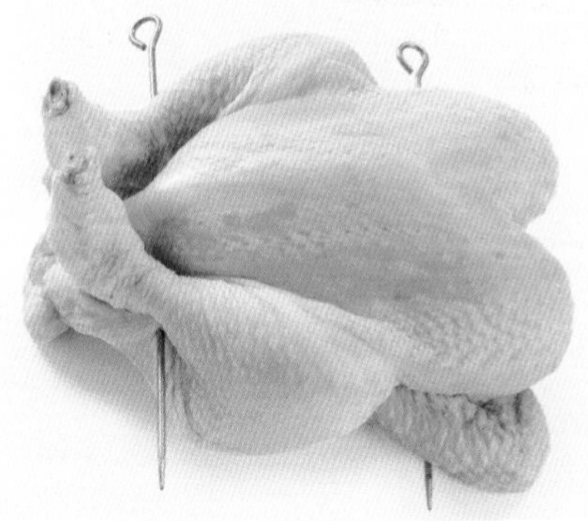

2 Turn the bird over. Pull the neck skin over the end and tuck the wing tips over it. Push a skewer through one wing, the neck skin, and out through the other wing.

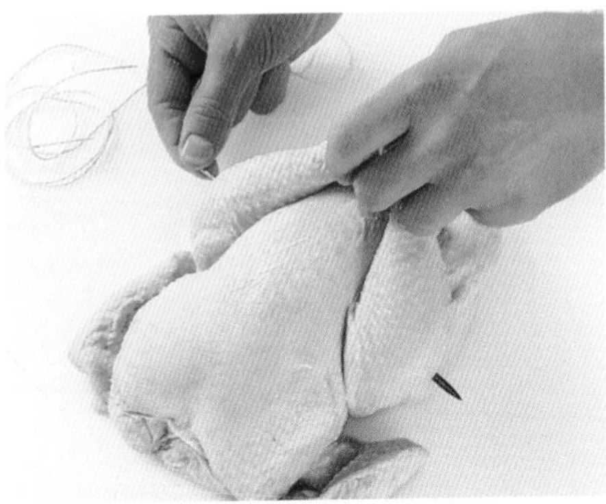

Trussing with string

1 Thread a trussing needle with string. Put the bird breast-side up. Push the legs back and down. Insert the needle into a knee joint. Pass through the bird and then out through the other knee.

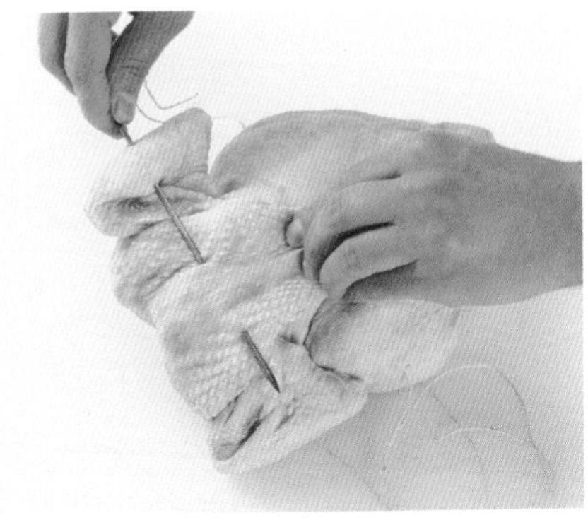

2 Pull the neck skin over the end of the bird and tuck the wing tips over it. Push the needle through both sections of one wing, through the neck skin and beneath the backbone, and out the other wing.

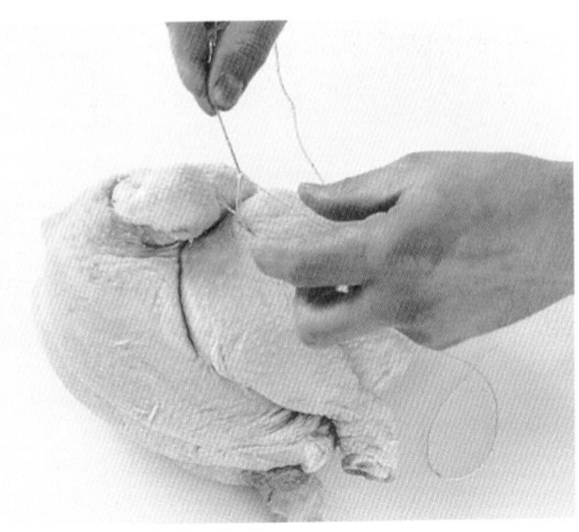

3 With the bird on its side, pull the string tightly, tie the ends together, and trim. Tuck the tail into the cavity and fold the top skin over it.

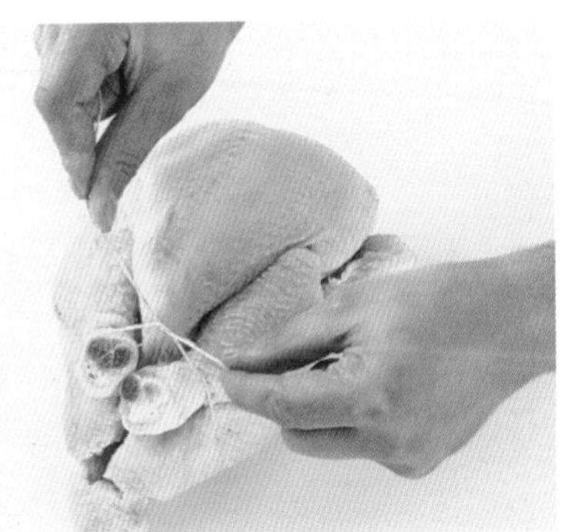

4 Push the needle through the top skin. Loop the string around one of the drumsticks, under the breastbone, and then around the other drumstick. Pull the string tight and tie the ends.

Roasting times

These times are a guide only; always test a bird to make sure it is thoroughly cooked (page 158).

Bird	Oven temperature	Time
Poussin	190°C (170°C fan, Gas 5)	40–45 minutes total cooking, depending on size
Chicken	190°C (170°C fan, Gas 5)	20 minutes per 500 g (1 lb) plus 20 minutes
Duck	200°C (180°C fan, Gas 6)	25 minutes per 500 g (1 lb) for "just cooked"
Goose	180°C (160°C fan, Gas 4)	20 minutes per 500 g (1 lb) plus 20 minutes
Pheasant	200°C (180°C fan, Gas 6)	50 minutes total cooking
Turkey	190°C (170°C fan, Gas 5)	2½–3 hours total cooking 3.5–4.5 kg (7–9 lb) turkey; 3½–4 hours total cooking for 5–6 kg (10–12 lb); 4½–5 hours total cooking for 6.5–8.5 kg (13–17 lb)

Carving poultry

After roasting, wrap the bird in foil and leave to rest before carving – at least 15 minutes and up to 45 minutes for a large bird – to allow the juices to settle. Remove any trussing first.

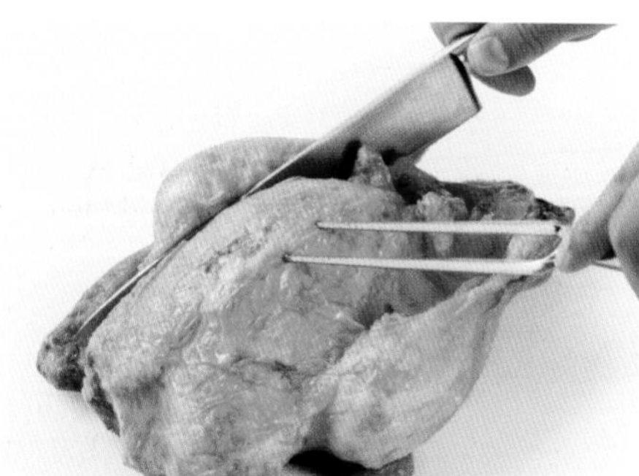

1 Put the bird breast-side up on a carving board (ideally one with a well to catch all the juices). Insert a carving fork into one breast to keep the bird steady, then cut into the joint between the far leg and body.

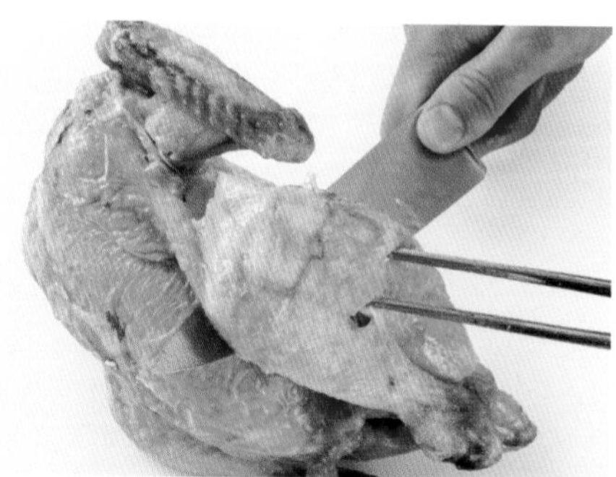

2 Turn the bird on its side and cut away the meat close to the backbone, cutting around the "oyster" meat on the back so that it remains attached to the thigh. Turn the bird over.

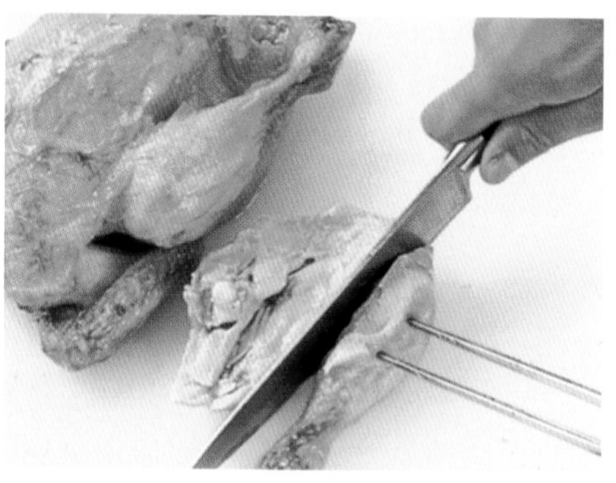

3 Twist the leg outwards to break the joint, then cut it to remove the leg. If preferred, divide into thigh and drumstick, cutting through the ball and socket joint. Remove the other leg.

4 Make a horizontal cut into the breast above the wing joint on one side, cutting all the way to the bone. Carve neat slices from the breast, holding the knife blade parallel to the ribcage. Repeat on the other side.

Roasting know-how

Calculate the roasting time by weighing the bird after you have added any stuffing.

Cover large birds loosely with foil if the skin is becoming too browned.

Place fatty birds, such as duck and goose, on a rack, to allow the fat to drain away and keep the skin crisp.

Thorough cooking

Cook all poultry and game thoroughly to kill any bacteria.

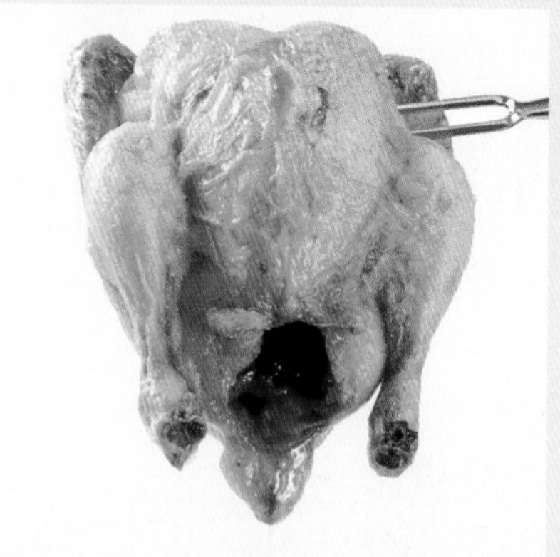

To test a whole roasted bird, lift it on a long fork – the juices that run out should be clear. For joints, insert a skewer into the thickest part of the meat and check the colour of the juices. Alternatively, use an instant-read thermometer: the thigh meat should register 75°C (170°F), breast 70°C (160°F).

Carving ducks and geese

Once cooked, small ducks need simply to be cut into quarters or even halves for serving. Larger ducks and geese can be carved as for other poultry (see above).

1 Remove any trussing. Cut through the joints between legs and body to remove the legs. (Cook them further if necessary.) Cut off the wings in the same way.

2 Slit the skin along both sides of the breastbone. Slide the knife blade into the cut on one side to free the breast meat in a single piece. Repeat on the other side.

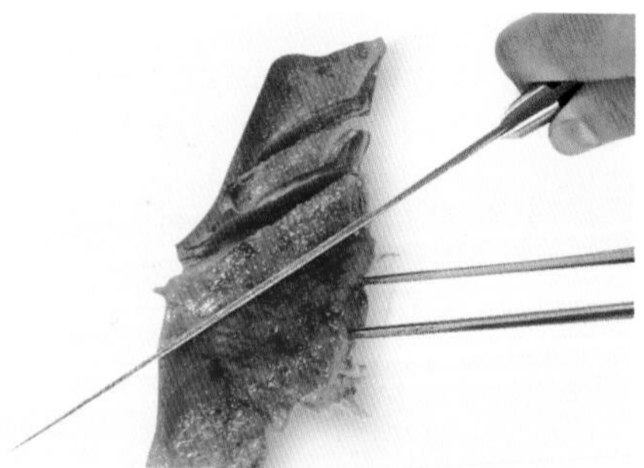

3 Carve the breast meat in diagonal slices. For a larger bird, carve the breast meat without removing it first, as for a chicken (see above).

Chicken thighs Normande

SERVES 4 **CALS PER SERVING** 599

3 leeks, trimmed and thinly sliced
4 lean back bacon rashers, rinds removed, diced
2 garlic cloves, crushed
350 ml (12 fl oz) strong dry cider
8 chicken thighs, with the bone in and skin left on
½ tsp chopped fresh thyme
salt and black pepper
125 ml (4 fl oz) full-fat crème fraîche

1 Put the leeks, bacon, and garlic into a roasting tin. Pour in the cider, and put the chicken on top. Sprinkle with the thyme, and season.

2 Roast in a preheated oven at 190°C (170°C fan, Gas 5) for 20–25 minutes until the chicken is tender and cooked through. Remove the chicken thighs, bacon, and vegetables, and keep warm.

3 Spoon off any excess fat from the roasting tin. Put the tin on the hob, and boil the cooking juices until reduced by half. Stir in the crème fraîche, and heat gently. Pour the sauce on to serving plates, arrange the bacon, vegetables, and chicken on top, and serve hot.

Cheese and garlic stuffed chicken

SERVES 6 **CALS PER SERVING** 628

6 boneless chicken breasts, with the skin on
melted butter, for brushing

Stuffing
30 g (1 oz) butter
1 onion, finely chopped
2 large garlic cloves, crushed
250 g (8 oz) full-fat soft cheese
1 tbsp chopped fresh tarragon
1 egg yolk
pinch of grated nutmeg
salt and black pepper

1 Make the stuffing: melt the butter in a small saucepan, add the onion and garlic, and cook gently, stirring occasionally, for a few minutes until soft but not coloured. Turn the onion mixture into a bowl, and leave to cool slightly.

2 Add the soft cheese to the onion mixture with the tarragon, egg yolk, and nutmeg. Season with salt and pepper and mix well.

3 Stuff the chicken breasts: lift up the skin along one side of each breast, spread the cheese mixture over the chicken, and then gently press the skin back on top. Put the chicken breasts into an ovenproof dish and brush with the melted butter.

4 Roast the chicken in a preheated oven at 190°C (170°C fan, Gas 5) for 25–30 minutes until the chicken is cooked through. Cut each breast into diagonal slices, and serve hot.

Tarragon chicken with lime

SERVES 4 **CALS PER SERVING** 428

60 g (2 oz) butter, softened
grated zest of 1 lime and juice of 2 limes
4 skinless, boneless chicken breasts
1 tbsp chopped fresh tarragon
salt and black pepper
150 ml (¼ pint) full-fat crème fraîche
lime wedges and fresh tarragon, to garnish

1 Put the butter into a bowl, and beat in the lime zest. Prepare the chicken breasts (see box, right).

2 Put the chicken breasts into a roasting tin. Sprinkle with the lime juice, tarragon, and salt and pepper, and roast in a preheated oven at 200°C (180°C fan, Gas 6) for 20 minutes or until the chicken is cooked through.

3 Transfer the chicken breasts to warmed serving plates and keep warm.

4 Put the tin on the hob, add 1 tbsp water to the cooking juices, stirring to dissolve the sediment, and bring to a boil, stirring. Cook, stirring, for 1–2 minutes. Stir in the crème fraîche and heat gently until warmed through.

5 Serve the chicken with the sauce, and garnish each serving with the lime wedges and fresh tarragon.

Preparing the chicken

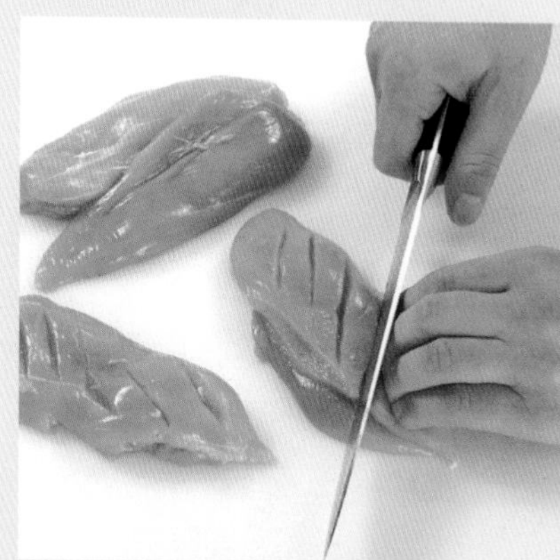

Make 3–4 deep diagonal cuts in each chicken breast with a sharp knife. Spread the top of each breast with one-quarter of the lime butter.

Marinated chicken with peppers

SERVES 6 **CALS PER SERVING** 376

1.7 kg (3½ lb) chicken
2 tbsp olive oil
1 large red pepper, halved, deseeded, and cut into thin strips
1 large yellow pepper, halved, deseeded, and cut into thin strips
125 g (4 oz) pitted black olives

Marinade

4 tbsp olive oil
2 tbsp clear honey
juice of ½ lemon
1 tbsp chopped mixed fresh herbs, such as parsley, thyme, and basil
salt and black pepper

1 Put the chicken into a roasting tin, rub the breast with oil, and roast in a preheated oven at 190°C (170°C fan, Gas 5) for 20 minutes per 500 g (1 lb). Twenty minutes before the end of the roasting time, remove from the oven, and spoon off the fat. Add the peppers and return to the oven for 20 minutes.

2 Remove the chicken and peppers from the tin with a slotted spoon, and leave to stand until cool.

3 Meanwhile, make the marinade: in a large bowl, combine the olive oil, honey, lemon juice, and herbs, and season with salt and pepper.

4 Strip the chicken flesh from the carcass, and cut it into small bite-sized strips. Toss the strips in the marinade, cover, and leave to cool completely.

5 Spoon the chicken and peppers on to a platter, arrange the olives around the edge, and serve at room temperature.

Cook's know-how

If time is short, use a ready-cooked chicken and toss with roasted peppers from a jar. If the peppers are packed in oil they will be very moist, so you will only need half the amount of marinade.

Chicken pinwheels

This is an elegant dinner party dish that is simple and economical to make, yet it looks stunning. An accompaniment of fresh tagliatelle goes well with the tomato and herb sauce.

SERVES 4 **CALS PER SERVING** 423

4 skinless, boneless chicken breasts
melted butter, for greasing
basil sprigs, to garnish

Filling

125 g (4 oz) full-fat garlic and herb soft cheese
2 tbsp sun-dried tomatoes in oil, drained and chopped
4 tbsp shredded fresh basil
salt and black pepper

Tomato and herb sauce

1 tbsp olive oil
1 small onion, chopped
1 x 400 g can chopped tomatoes
1 tbsp chopped fresh herbs, such as parsley, chives, and thyme

1 Make the filling: combine the cheese, sun-dried tomatoes, and basil. Season with salt and pepper, and mix well to combine.

2 Put the chicken breasts between sheets of cling film, and pound with a rolling pin until 5 mm (¼ in) thick. Spread one-quarter of the filling over each breast, and tightly roll up each one.

3 Brush four squares of foil with melted butter, and wrap each chicken roll in a square, twisting the ends to seal them tightly. Put the rolls into a shallow pan of gently simmering water, cover, and poach for 15 minutes.

4 Meanwhile, make the tomato and herb sauce: heat the oil in a pan, add the onion, and cook, stirring often, for a few minutes until soft. Stir in the tomatoes with half of their juice, bring to a boil, and simmer for 3 minutes.

5 Purée the tomato mixture in a food processor until smooth. Work the purée through a sieve, and add more tomato juice if the sauce is too thick. Stir in the chopped fresh herbs, and season with salt and pepper.

6 Unwrap the chicken, and slice on the diagonal. Serve with the tomato and herb sauce, and garnish with basil.

Bacon-wrapped chicken breasts

SERVES 6 **CALS PER SERVING** 528

6 skinless, boneless chicken breasts
4 tbsp coarse-grain mustard
black pepper
18 streaky bacon rashers, rinds removed
snipped fresh chives, to garnish

1 Spread both sides of the chicken breasts with the mustard, and season with pepper.

2 Take three bacon rashers, stretch them with the back of a knife, and arrange them side by side and slightly overlapping. Wrap a chicken breast with the bacon (see box, right). Repeat with the remaining bacon and chicken.

3 Place the chicken breasts with the bacon seam-side down in a roasting tin, and roast in a preheated oven at 190°C (170°C fan, Gas 5) for 25–30 minutes until the bacon is crisp and brown and the chicken cooked through. Serve at once, garnished with snipped chives.

Wrapping a chicken breast in bacon

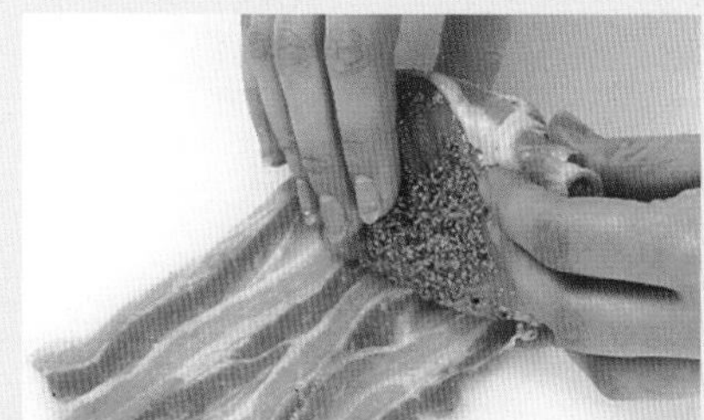

Place a chicken breast at one end of the overlapped bacon rashers, and then wrap the rashers diagonally (working from side to side) around the chicken to make a neat parcel.

Ballotine of chicken

A ballotine is a bird or cut of meat that has been boned, stuffed, and rolled. It is slowly cooked in the oven, allowed to cool, then chilled for several hours or overnight until firm. With its colourful, pistachio-studded filling, this ballotine makes an excellent centrepiece for a buffet party, and is easy to slice and serve.

SERVES 10 **CALS PER SERVING** 494

2 kg (4 lb) chicken, boned (page 156)
4 thin slices of cooked ham
125 g (4 oz) pistachio nuts, shelled
60 g (2 oz) butter, softened
600 ml (1 pint) chicken stock

Stuffing

500 g (1 lb) belly pork
375 g (12 oz) chicken livers, trimmed
250 g (8 oz) streaky bacon rashers, rinds removed, coarsely chopped
2 shallots, quartered
2 garlic cloves
4 tbsp brandy
2 tsp chopped fresh thyme
1 tsp chopped fresh sage
½ tsp ground ginger
½ tsp ground cinnamon
salt and black pepper

1 Make the stuffing: chop the pork into 5 mm (¼ in) pieces, and place in a bowl.

2 Purée the chicken livers, bacon, shallots, garlic, and brandy in a food processor until smooth. Add to the pork in the bowl with the thyme, sage, ginger, and cinnamon, and season generously with salt and pepper. Stir well to combine.

3 Place the boned chicken, skin-side down, between two pieces of cling film and pound to an even thickness with a rolling pin.

4 Remove the cling film from the chicken, and assemble the ballotine (see box, opposite). Tie several pieces of string around the chicken to keep it in shape.

5 Spread the softened butter over the chicken skin, and season generously with salt and pepper. Place the chicken roll on a wire rack in a roasting tin.

6 Bring the stock to a boil, and pour over the chicken in the roasting tin. Cook in a preheated oven at 160°C (140°C fan, Gas 3), basting occasionally and adding more stock if necessary, for 2 hours or until the juices run clear when the chicken is pierced.

7 Transfer the ballotine to a plate, and leave to cool. Cover and chill overnight. Cut into thin slices to serve.

Cook's know-how

Classic French ballotine recipes wrap the chicken roll in muslin before cooking, but this is not necessary.

Assembling the ballotine

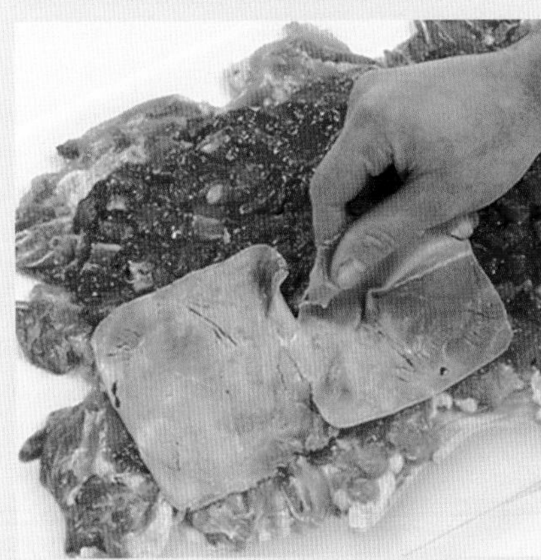

Spread half of the stuffing over the chicken, to within 2.5 cm (1 in) of the edges. Arrange the ham slices on top. Scatter the pistachio nuts on top of the ham.

Spoon on and spread the remaining stuffing over the pistachio nuts.

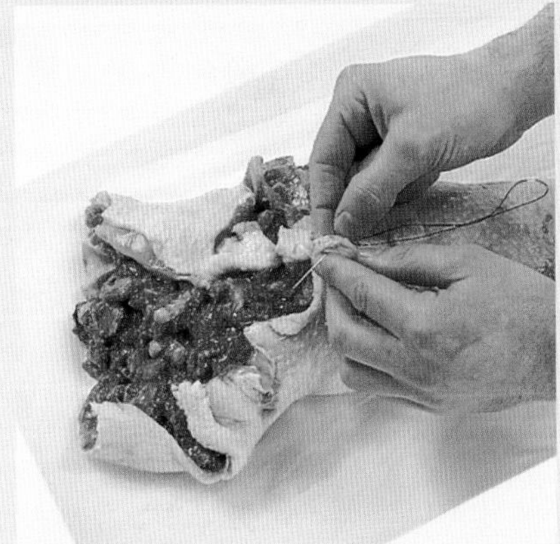

Fold the chicken over the stuffing to form a sausage shape, and sew the edges together with thin string or fasten them with small metal skewers.

Mustard chicken

SERVES 4 **CALS PER SERVING** 380

1 tbsp olive oil
4 skinless, boneless chicken breasts, cut diagonally into 2.5 cm (1 in) strips
1 garlic clove, crushed
250 ml (8 fl oz) single cream
1 tbsp plain flour
1 tbsp coarse-grain mustard
salt and black pepper
flat-leaf parsley sprigs, to garnish

1 Heat the oil in a frying pan until hot. Add the chicken strips and garlic, in batches if necessary, and cook over a moderate heat, stirring frequently, for 3–4 minutes.

2 With a slotted spoon, lift the chicken and garlic out of the frying pan, and keep them warm.

3 In a small bowl, mix a little of the cream with the flour to make a smooth paste, then mix in the remaining cream.

4 Lower the heat and pour the cream into the pan. Cook gently for 2 minutes, stirring constantly until the sauce has thickened. Stir in the mustard and heat through gently, then season with salt and pepper.

5 Return the chicken to the pan, coat with the sauce, and cook gently for a few minutes more until the chicken is tender when pierced with a fork. Serve hot, garnished with parsley sprigs.

Cook's know-how

Do not let the sauce boil once you have added the mustard or it may taste bitter. Coarse-grain mustard gives an interesting texture to this dish; if you prefer a smooth sauce, use Dijon mustard.

Chicken cordon bleu

SERVES 4 **CALS PER SERVING** 602

4 skinless, boneless chicken breasts
4 thin slices of Gruyère cheese
4 thin slices of cooked ham
salt and black pepper
1 egg, beaten
125 g (4 oz) fresh white breadcrumbs
30 g (1 oz) butter
3 tbsp sunflower oil

1 With a sharp knife, cut each chicken breast horizontally, leaving it attached at one side.

2 Open out each chicken breast, place between two sheets of greaseproof paper, and pound to a 3 mm (⅛ in) thickness with a rolling pin. Fill and fold the chicken breasts (see box, right).

3 Dip each folded chicken breast into the beaten egg, then dip each breast into the breadcrumbs, making sure each one is evenly coated. Cover and chill for 15 minutes.

4 Melt the butter with the sunflower oil in a large frying pan. When the butter is foaming, add the chicken breasts, and cook for 10 minutes on each side or until the breadcrumb coating is crisp and golden and the chicken is cooked through. Remove the chicken breasts with a slotted spoon and drain thoroughly on paper towels. Serve at once.

Folding the chicken

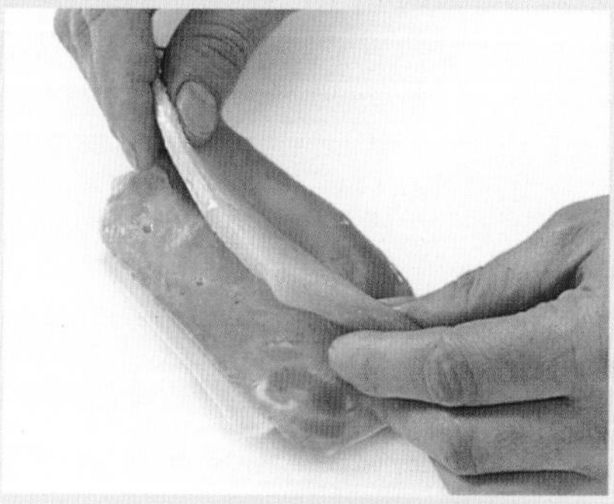

Place 1 slice of cheese and 1 slice of ham on half of each chicken breast, season with salt and pepper, and fold the breast over to cover the filling.

Lemon and herb drumsticks

MAKES 12 **CALS EACH** 200

12 chicken drumsticks

Marinade

150 ml (¼ pint) olive oil
grated zest and juice of 1 lemon
6 large parsley sprigs, chopped, plus extra to garnish
1 onion, thinly sliced
2 large garlic cloves, crushed
salt and black pepper

1 Make the marinade: in a bowl, combine the olive oil, lemon zest and juice, parsley sprigs, onion, and garlic. Season with salt and pepper.

2 Turn the drumsticks in the marinade. Cover and leave to marinate in the refrigerator for at least 30 minutes.

3 Place the drumsticks under a hot grill, 10 cm (4 in) from the heat, and grill, turning frequently and basting with the marinade, for 20 minutes until crisp, brown, and cooked through. Serve the drumsticks hot or cold, garnished with parsley sprigs.

STICKY HONEYED DRUMSTICKS

Use a different marinade: combine 250 g (8 oz) plain yogurt, 2 tbsp clear honey, and 1 tsp ground coriander, and season with salt and black pepper.

Devilled chicken drumsticks

MAKES 12 **CALS EACH** 138

12 chicken drumsticks
2 tbsp sesame seeds
tortilla chips, to serve (optional)

Spicy coating

2 tbsp olive oil
2 tbsp white wine vinegar
2 tbsp tomato ketchup
1 tbsp Dijon mustard
1 small onion, quartered
2 tbsp dark muscovado sugar
1 large garlic clove, coarsely crushed
¼ tsp chilli powder
salt and black pepper

1 Make the spicy coating: put the oil, vinegar, ketchup, mustard, onion, sugar, garlic, and chilli powder in a food processor. Season with salt and pepper, and purée until fairly smooth.

2 Make three deep cuts in each chicken drumstick, arrange in a single layer in a shallow ovenproof dish, and spoon the coating over them. Sprinkle with half of the sesame seeds.

3 Roast in a preheated oven at 190°C (170°C fan, Gas 5) for 30 minutes or until the drumsticks are cooked through. Turn and baste halfway through cooking, and sprinkle with the remaining sesame seeds. Serve hot or cold, with tortilla chips if you wish.

CHILLI-ROASTED DRUMSTICKS WITH BACON

Use a different spicy coating: combine 3 tbsp lemon juice, 4 crushed garlic cloves, 1½ tbsp paprika, 1 tbsp mild chilli powder, 1 tsp ground cumin, and ¼ tsp oregano. Coat the drumsticks with the mixture, then wrap each one in a streaky bacon rasher.

Chicken thighs with chestnut stuffing

You do not need to roast a whole bird to enjoy the classic combination of chicken with a savoury stuffing. In this recipe, chicken thighs are wrapped around a nutty filling of chestnuts and bacon, and served with cranberry sauce.

SERVES 4 **CALS PER SERVING** 598

8 boneless chicken thighs, with the skin left on
150 ml (1/4 pint) chicken stock
1 tbsp cranberry or redcurrant jelly

Stuffing

15 g (1/2 oz) butter
2 streaky bacon rashers, rinds removed, diced
1 small onion, finely chopped
125 g (4 oz) frozen chestnuts, thawed and finely chopped
30 g (1 oz) fresh brown breadcrumbs
1 tbsp chopped parsley
salt and black pepper
1 egg yolk

1 Make the stuffing: melt the butter in a frying pan, add the bacon and onion, and cook over a medium heat for 3–5 minutes until the bacon is crisp and the onion soft but not coloured.

2 Add the chestnuts, and cook, stirring occasionally, for 5 minutes. Remove from the heat, add the breadcrumbs, and parsley, and season with salt and pepper, then bind with the egg yolk.

3 Place the chicken thighs, skin-side down, on a chopping board, and divide the stuffing among them. Roll up each thigh to enclose the stuffing.

4 Arrange the chicken thighs in a single layer in a roasting tin, and cook in a preheated oven at 190°C (170°C fan, Gas 5) for 20–25 minutes until the chicken is lightly browned and cooked through. Lift the chicken thighs out of the roasting tin, and keep hot.

5 Spoon off any excess fat, put the tin on the hob, and pour in the stock. Bring to a boil, and boil for 3–5 minutes until syrupy, stirring to dissolve any sediment and cooking juices.

6 Stir in the cranberry or redcurrant jelly, and cook for 1 minute to melt the jelly. Taste for seasoning. Strain the sauce, and serve at once, with the chicken thighs.

Filling, covering, and decorating the pie

Invert the pie dish on to the pastry, and use a small knife to cut around the edge, keeping the blade close to the dish. Reserve all trimmings. Transfer the cold filling to the pie dish, and top with the pastry.

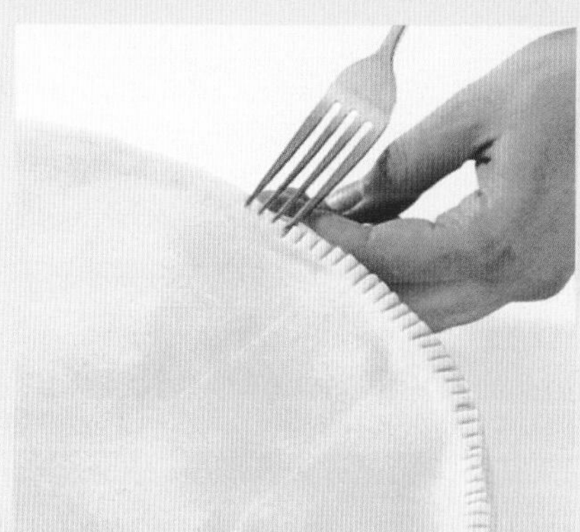

Press the pastry with your fingertips on to the rim of the pie dish. Crimp the edge of the pastry with a fork. Brush the pastry with the beaten egg yolk, making a lattice pattern.

Cut decorative shapes from the reserved pastry trimmings with a pastry cutter. Arrange on top of the pie, and glaze the shapes with the beaten egg yolk.

Chicken pot pie

This recipe makes a great family dish, packed with tender chicken and colourful vegetables. You can vary the vegetables according to season and availability. The pie will be a great success any time of the year.

SERVES 6 **CALS PER SERVING** 508

1 kg (2 lb) chicken
1.25 litres (2 pints) chicken stock
1 onion, quartered
1 celery stalk, thickly sliced
pared zest and juice of 1 lemon
2 carrots
2 waxy potatoes, peeled and cut into quarters
45 g (1½ oz) butter
45 g (1½ oz) plain flour, plus extra for dusting
salt and black pepper
125 g (4 oz) frozen peas
175 g (6 oz) shortcrust pastry
beaten egg yolk, for glazing

2 LITRE (3½ PINT) PIE DISH

1 Put the chicken, stock, onion, celery, and lemon zest into a large saucepan. Bring to a boil, cover, and simmer for 30 minutes.

2 Add the carrots and potatoes, cover, and simmer for about 20 minutes or until the vegetables are cooked and the chicken is just tender. Remove the vegetables from the liquid and set aside. Leave the chicken to cool in the liquid.

3 Remove the meat from the chicken, and cut into bite-sized pieces, discarding the skin and bones. Dice the vegetables.

4 Skim the fat from the cooking liquid, then bring 600 ml (1 pint) of the liquid to a boil. Melt the butter in another pan, add the flour, and cook, stirring occasionally, for 1 minute. Stir in the hot stock, whisking until it comes to a boil and thickens. Add the lemon juice and season with salt and pepper.

5 Stir the chicken, diced vegetables, and peas into the sauce, then leave to cool.

6 On a lightly floured work surface, roll out the pastry, then cut out the lid, and fill, cover, and decorate the pie (see box, opposite).

7 Bake in a preheated oven at 190°C (170°C fan, Gas 5) for 30 minutes or until the top is crisp and golden brown. Serve hot.

Saffron chicken

SERVES 6 **CALS PER SERVING** 527

6 boneless chicken breasts, with the skin left on
1 tbsp vegetable oil
200 ml (7 fl oz) full-fat crème fraîche
salt and black pepper
chopped coriander, to garnish

Marinade

2 pinches of saffron threads
2.5 cm (1 in) piece of fresh root ginger, peeled and grated
juice of 1 lemon
1 tsp ground cardamom
1 tsp ground coriander
1 tsp ground cinnamon

1 Make the marinade: put the saffron and the ginger into a mortar and grind with a pestle. Add the lemon juice, cardamom, coriander, and cinnamon, and mix well.

2 Put the chicken into a non-metallic dish, and brush the marinade over it. Cover and marinate in the refrigerator for at least 20 minutes.

3 Pour the oil into a small roasting tin. Turn the chicken breasts in the oil, and put them, skin-side up, in the roasting tin. Cook in a preheated oven at 190°C (170°C fan, Gas 5) for 15–20 minutes or until the juices run clear when the chicken is pierced with a fork. Remove from the tin and keep warm.

4 Put the tin on the hob, pour in the crème fraîche, and stir to combine with the juices. Season with salt and pepper, and heat through. Sprinkle with coriander and serve.

Herb-marinated chicken breasts

SERVES 4 **CALS PER SERVING** 641

4 boneless chicken breasts, with the skin left on
30 g (1 oz) butter
2 tbsp sunflower oil
150 ml (¼ pint) chicken stock
1 bunch of watercress, tough stalks removed, to serve
chopped parsley, to garnish

Marinade

2 tbsp olive oil
1 tbsp lemon juice
3 garlic cloves, crushed
3 tbsp chopped parsley
2 tbsp chopped mixed fresh herbs, e.g. parsley, chives, tarragon, or thyme
salt and black pepper

1 Make the marinade: combine the oil, lemon juice, garlic, parsley, and herbs, and season with salt and pepper. Turn the chicken in the marinade, cover, and marinate in the refrigerator for at least 30 minutes.

2 Remove the chicken from the marinade, and dry on paper towels.

3 Melt the butter with the oil in a large frying pan. When the butter is foaming, add the chicken breasts, skin-side down, and cook for 10 minutes. Turn the chicken, and cook for a further 5 minutes or until golden and cooked through.

4 Using a slotted spoon, remove the chicken breasts, and keep hot.

5 Pour the chicken stock into the pan, and boil until reduced to about 8 tbsp.

6 Arrange the chicken breasts on beds of watercress, and strain over the hot sauce. Serve hot, garnished with chopped parsley.

SPICY CHICKEN BREASTS

Substitute 1 tsp paprika and ¼ tsp crushed dried red chillies (chilli flakes) for the herbs in the marinade.

Jerk chicken

SERVES 4 **CALS PER SERVING** 304

4 chicken legs or drumsticks

Jerk paste

3 tbsp lime juice
2 tbsp dark rum
2 tbsp sunflower oil
4 spring onions, roughly chopped
1–2 fresh green chillies, halved, deseeded, and roughly chopped
2 garlic cloves, roughly chopped
1 tbsp ground allspice
2 tsp fresh thyme leaves
salt and black pepper

To serve

chopped fresh thyme
grilled pineapple rings (optional)

1 Make the jerk paste: purée the ingredients in a food processor with a pinch each of salt and pepper.

2 Put the chicken pieces in a non-metallic dish and brush them all over with the jerk paste. Cover and marinate in the refrigerator for at least 30 minutes, or overnight.

3 Put the chicken over a hot barbecue, or under a hot grill, 10 cm (4 in) from the heat. Cook for 10 minutes on each side or until the juices run clear when the chicken is pierced.

4 Serve the chicken hot or cold, sprinkled with thyme, and accompanied by grilled pineapple rings, if you like.

Cook's know-how

Garlic is an essential ingredient in classic jerk paste and you can use as many as 6–8 cloves if you like. The purple-skinned varieties have the best flavour.

Tex-mex chicken

SERVES 4 **CALS PER SERVING** 659

4 skinless, boneless chicken breasts
2 avocados
2 tbsp lime juice
1 red onion, finely chopped

Marinade

4 tbsp olive oil
4 tbsp orange juice
1 tsp ground cumin

Salsa

500 g (1 lb) tomatoes, chopped
1 small red onion, finely chopped
3 tbsp olive oil
2 tbsp lime juice
3 tbsp chopped fresh coriander
2 garlic cloves, crushed
1 fresh green chilli, halved, deseeded, and chopped
salt

1 Make several diagonal slashes in each chicken breast, then put the chicken in a non-metallic dish. Mix the marinade ingredients together, and pour over the chicken. Cover and marinate in the refrigerator for at least 30 minutes, or overnight.

2 Make the salsa: combine the tomatoes, onion, oil, lime juice, coriander, garlic, chilli, and salt to taste. Cover and chill until ready to serve.

3 Remove the chicken from the marinade, and put under a hot grill, 10 cm (4 in) from the heat. Grill for 3–5 minutes on each side, depending on the size of the chicken, until the juices run clear when the chicken is pierced.

4 Meanwhile, halve, stone, and peel the avocados (page 395). Slice lengthways, and brush with lime juice.

5 Thinly slice the chicken breasts, following the slashes made before marinating. Arrange the avocado and chicken slices on plates and add some salsa. Serve the salsa and chopped spring onion alongside.

Chicken cacciatore

SERVES 4 **CALS PER SERVING** 540

8 small chicken portions (4 legs and 4 breasts or 8 thighs)
plain flour, for dusting
salt and black pepper
3–4 tbsp olive oil
90 g (3 oz) streaky bacon rashers or pancetta, cut into strips
1 large onion, chopped
1 small green pepper, halved, deseeded, and diced
2 garlic cloves, crushed
250 g (8 oz) mushrooms, quartered
125 ml (4 fl oz) red or white wine
1 x 400 g can chopped tomatoes
75 ml (2½ fl oz) tomato purée
2 tsp chopped fresh sage
4 tbsp chopped parsley
grated zest of 1 lemon
2 tbsp capers, chopped
fresh sage leaves, to garnish

1 Lightly dust the chicken pieces with flour seasoned with salt and pepper, and shake off any excess.

2 Heat half of the oil in a large frying pan, add the chicken and the bacon or pancetta, and cook for 10–12 minutes until browned all over. Transfer to a casserole with a slotted spoon, then pour off the fat from the frying pan.

3 Heat the remaining oil in the frying pan, add the onion, green pepper, and half of the garlic, and cook gently, stirring, for 5 minutes until soft but not coloured. Transfer to the casserole with a slotted spoon. Add the mushrooms, and cook for 2 minutes. Add to the casserole.

4 Pour the wine into the frying pan, and boil until reduced to about 4 tbsp. Add to the casserole with the tomatoes, tomato purée, and the sage. Cover and cook in a preheated oven at 180°C (160°C fan, Gas 4) for 45 minutes or until the chicken is tender when pierced with a fork.

5 Combine the remaining garlic with the chopped parsley, lemon zest, and capers. Stir into the casserole, and taste for seasoning. Serve hot, with mashed potatoes and garnished with sage leaves.

Chicken casserole

SERVES 4 **CALS PER SERVING** 659

2 tbsp sunflower oil
4 chicken portions (legs or thighs)
125 g (4 oz) streaky bacon rashers, cut into strips
250 g (8 oz) carrots, thickly sliced
2 celery stalks, thickly sliced
1 large onion, sliced
30 g (1 oz) plain flour
600 ml (1 pint) chicken stock
1 bouquet garni
salt and black pepper
4 potatoes, peeled and cut into large chunks
chopped parsley, to garnish

1 Heat the oil in a large flameproof casserole. Add the chicken, skin-side down, and cook for 10–12 minutes until browned all over. Lift out and drain on paper towels. Add the bacon, carrots, celery, and onion, and cook over a high heat, stirring, until golden. Lift out with a slotted spoon, and drain on paper towels.

2 Spoon off all but 1 tbsp fat from the casserole. Add the flour, and cook, stirring constantly, for 3–5 minutes until lightly browned. Gradually pour in the chicken stock, stirring until smooth. Add the bouquet garni, and season with salt and pepper.

3 Return the chicken, bacon, carrots, celery, and onion to the casserole, add the potatoes, and bring to a boil. Cover and cook in a preheated oven at 160°C (140°C fan, Gas 3) for 1–1¼ hours or until the chicken is tender when pierced with a fork. Serve hot, garnished with parsley.

ITALIAN CHICKEN CASSEROLE

Substitute 250 g (8 oz) sliced courgettes for the carrots, and 1 x 400 g can chopped tomatoes and 1 tbsp tomato purée for the chicken stock. If the mixture is too thick, add a splash of water, chicken stock, or wine.

Coq au vin

SERVES 4 **CALS PER SERVING** 531

30 g (1 oz) butter
1 tbsp sunflower oil
1.5 kg (3 lb) chicken, cut into 8 serving pieces (page 155)
125 g (4 oz) streaky bacon rashers, cut into strips
8 small shallots or pickling onions
250 g (8 oz) button mushrooms
30 g (1 oz) plain flour
300 ml (½ pint) chicken stock
600 ml (1 pint) red wine
1 bouquet garni
1 large garlic clove, crushed
salt and black pepper
2 tbsp chopped parsley, to garnish

1 Melt the butter with the oil in a large flameproof casserole. Add the chicken, and cook for 10–12 minutes until browned all over. Lift out and leave to drain on paper towels.

2 Spoon off any excess fat, then add the bacon, shallots or onions, and mushrooms, and cook over a high heat, stirring, until golden brown.

3 Using a slotted spoon, remove the mixture, and leave to drain on paper towels.

4 Add the flour to the pan, and cook for 3–5 minutes, stirring constantly until lightly browned. Reduce the wine in a separate pan until it reduces to 300 ml (½ pint). Gradually pour in the stock, then the wine, stirring until smooth.

5 Return the chicken, bacon, shallots or onions, and mushrooms to the casserole. Add the bouquet garni and garlic, and season. Bring to a boil, cover, and cook in a preheated oven at 180°C (160°C fan, Gas 4) for 45 minutes or until the chicken is tender when pierced with a fork.

6 Sprinkle the chicken with the chopped parsley, and serve hot.

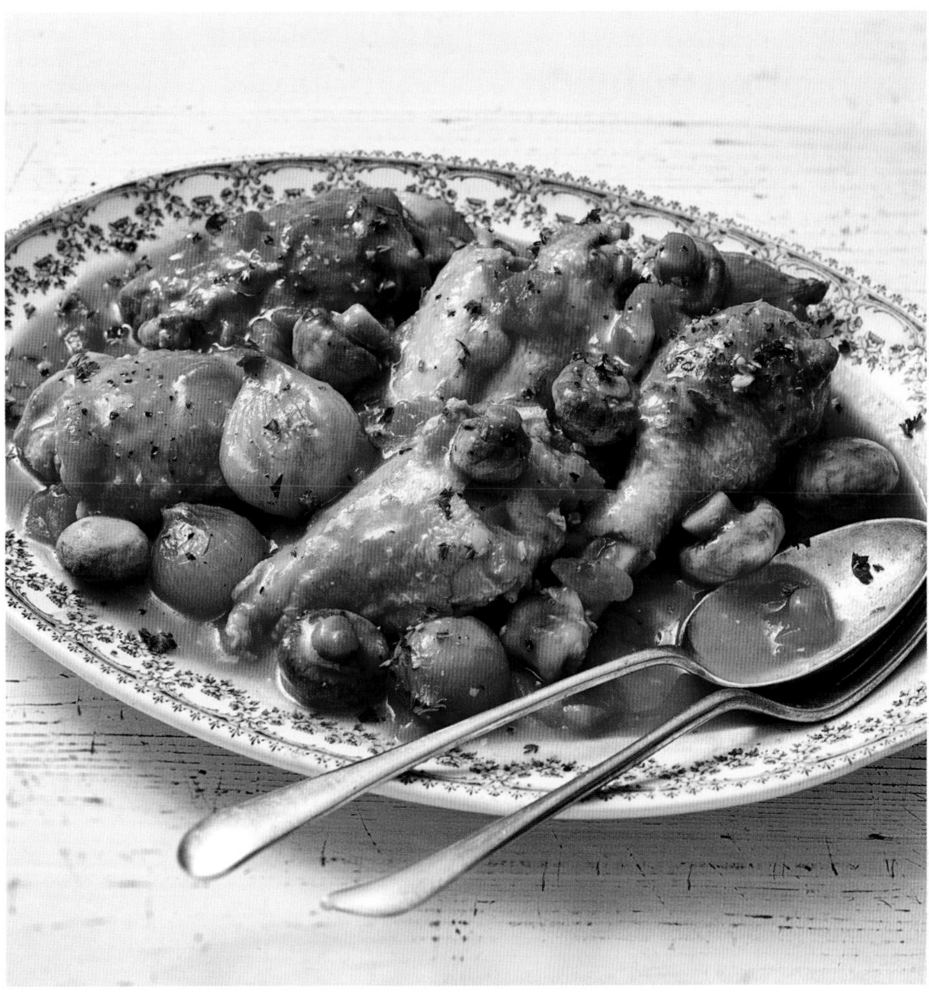

Chicken Marengo

SERVES 4 **CALS PER SERVING** 479

30 g (1 oz) butter
1 tbsp sunflower oil
1.5 kg (3 lb) chicken, cut into 8 serving pieces (page 155)
8 small shallots or pickling onions
30 g (1 oz) plain flour
300 ml (½ pint) dry white wine
150 ml (¼ pint) chicken stock
1 x 400 g can chopped tomatoes
250 g (8 oz) button mushrooms
1 tbsp tomato purée
2 garlic cloves, crushed
1 bouquet garni
salt and black pepper
chopped parsley, to garnish

1 Melt the butter with the oil in a large flameproof casserole. Add the chicken pieces, and cook for 10–12 minutes until browned all over. Lift out and leave to drain on paper towels.

2 Add the shallots or onions, and cook over a high heat for about 8 minutes or until golden brown.

3 Lift out the shallots or onions and leave to drain on paper towels. Spoon off all but 1 tbsp of the fat from the casserole, add the flour, and cook, stirring, for 3–5 minutes until lightly browned.

4 Lower the heat and stir in the wine and stock until combined. Add the tomatoes, mushrooms, tomato purée, garlic, and bouquet garni. Season with salt and pepper.

5 Return the shallots or onions and the chicken to the casserole, and bring to a boil. Cover and cook in a preheated oven at 180°C (160°C fan, Gas 4) for 45 minutes, or until the chicken is tender when pierced with a fork. To serve, garnish each portion with chopped parsley.

Yogurt and mint barbecued chicken

SERVES 4 **CALS PER SERVING** 279

8 chicken thighs on the bone, with the skin left on
couscous salad (page 432), to serve

Marinade

4 tbsp olive oil
juice of ½ lemon
3 garlic cloves, crushed
30 g (1 oz) fresh mint, chopped
150 g (5 oz) plain yogurt
¼ tsp each ground cumin and turmeric
salt and black pepper

1 Combine the marinade ingredients in a shallow non-metallic dish. Add the chicken and turn to coat, then cover and leave to marinate in the refrigerator for up to 24 hours.

2 Barbecue the chicken, turning and basting or brushing with the marinade, for 15–20 minutes or until the juices run clear.

3 Serve the chicken thighs hot or cold, on a bed of couscous salad, or with couscous salad served separately in a bowl.

Successful marinating

A marinade will give poultry or meat extra flavour before it is cooked over a barbecue, and it may help tenderize it at the same time.

- A marinade is a mixture of liquids and seasonings. There is always an acid such as lemon juice, wine, or vinegar, which helps make poultry or meat more tender.
- An oil, such as olive, sesame, or sunflower, keeps the meat or poultry moist and carries the flavours of the seasonings into the food.
- Seasonings usually include salt and pepper, but all kinds of spices and herbs can be used as well.
- Marinades often include garlic, onions, and fresh root ginger, which also add flavour.
- Allow enough time for any large pieces of poultry or meat to pick up the flavour of the marinade. Smaller pieces will pick up the flavour more quickly.
- Turn the food in the marinade occasionally to ensure an even coating, and baste or brush with the marinade when barbecuing.

Fruity coriander barbecued chicken

SERVES 4 **CALS PER SERVING** 312

8 chicken drumsticks, with the skin left on

Marinade

75 ml (2½ fl oz) olive oil
juice of 1 lime
2 tbsp mango chutney
2.5 cm (1 in) piece of fresh root ginger, peeled and grated
30 g (1 oz) fresh coriander, chopped
salt and black pepper

Mango salsa

1 ripe large mango, diced (page 519)
1 cm (½ in) piece of fresh root ginger, peeled and grated
3 spring onions, finely chopped
1 tbsp mango chutney
1 tbsp lime juice

1 Combine the marinade ingredients in a shallow non-metallic dish. With a sharp knife, score the skin of the drumsticks, then add to the marinade, and turn to coat. Cover and leave to marinate in the refrigerator for up to 24 hours.

2 Barbecue the drumsticks, turning and basting or brushing with the marinade, for 15–20 minutes or until the juices run clear.

3 Mix together the ingredients for the salsa. Serve the drumsticks hot, with the mango salsa alongside.

Orange and rosemary barbecued chicken

SERVES 4 **CALS PER SERVING** 330

4 chicken breasts, with the skin left on
a few rosemary sprigs

Marinade

75 ml (2½ fl oz) olive oil
75 ml (2½ fl oz) white wine vinegar
juice of 1 orange
2 tbsp clear honey
4 garlic cloves, crushed
salt and black pepper

Orange salsa

2 oranges, peeled, segmented, and diced
1 red pepper, halved, deseeded, and diced
¼ tsp crushed dried red chillies (chilli flakes)
1 tbsp clear honey

1 Combine the marinade ingredients in a shallow non-metallic dish. Add the chicken and turn to coat, then cover and leave to marinate in the refrigerator for up to 24 hours.

2 Lay the rosemary sprigs on the barbecue rack, put the chicken on top, and barbecue for 15–20 minutes until the juices run clear. Turn the chicken over several times during cooking, and baste or brush with the marinade.

3 Mix together the ingredients for the salsa, and serve alongside the barbecued chicken breasts.

Opposite, clockwise from top:
Yogurt and mint barbecued chicken,
Fruity coriander barbecued chicken,
Orange and rosemary barbecued chicken

Chicken kebabs

SERVES 6 **CALS PER SERVING** 441

4 skinless, boneless chicken breasts, cut into 2.5 cm (1 in) pieces
2 green peppers, halved, deseeded, and cut into 2.5 cm (1 in) pieces
500 g (1 lb) cherry tomatoes
375 g (12 oz) button mushrooms

Marinade
175 ml (6 fl oz) olive oil
125 ml (4 fl oz) dark soy sauce
4 tbsp red wine vinegar
freshly ground black pepper

12 METAL SKEWERS

1 Make the marinade: in a large bowl, combine the oil, soy sauce, and wine vinegar. Season with pepper, add the chicken, and mix well. Cover and marinate for 5–10 minutes.

2 Lift the chicken out of the marinade, reserving the marinade. Thread the skewers, alternating green peppers, tomatoes, chicken, and mushrooms.

3 Place the kebabs under a hot grill, 10 cm (4 in) from the heat. Grill the kebabs, basting with the marinade, for 3–5 minutes on each side or until the chicken is tender and cooked through. Serve hot.

Herb-grilled chicken

SERVES 8 **CALS PER SERVING** 297

8 chicken portions (legs or breasts)

Herb butter
90 g (3 oz) butter, softened
3 tbsp chopped parsley
3 tbsp snipped fresh chives
2 garlic cloves, crushed (optional)
salt and black pepper

1 Mix the butter with the parsley, chives, and garlic, if using, and a good pinch each of salt and pepper.

2 Score the skin of the chicken portions. Spread the butter over the skin, and put the chicken portions either skin-side down over a hot barbecue or skin-side up under a hot grill, 10 cm (4 in) from the heat. Cook for 10 minutes on each side or until the juices run clear when the chicken is pierced.

HOT PAPRIKA CHICKEN

Substitute 2 tsp paprika and 2 tsp mustard powder for the parsley and chives.

JAMAICAN CHICKEN

Substitute ½ tsp crushed peppercorns (red, green, and black), 1 tsp chopped fresh thyme, and 3 chopped spring onions for the parsley and chives.

THAI CORIANDER CHICKEN

Substitute 1–2 tbsp chopped fresh coriander and 2 tbsp Thai green curry paste for the parsley and chives.

Provençal-style roast chicken

SERVES 6 **CALS PER SERVING** 547

1 large onion, cut into wedges
2 large carrots, peeled and sliced
125 g (4 oz) whole button mushrooms
3 garlic cloves, peeled
250 ml (8 fl oz) dry white wine
375 ml (12 fl oz) chicken stock
1.7 kg (3½ lb) chicken, giblets removed
1 x 400 g can chopped tomatoes
1 tbsp tomato purée
salt and black pepper
chopped parsley, to garnish
green beans and buttered new potatoes, to serve (optional)

1 Arrange the onion wedges, carrot slices, whole mushrooms, and garlic cloves in a single layer in a roasting tin, and pour over the wine and stock.

2 Place the chicken breast-side up on a small roasting rack, and place in the middle of the roasting tin on top of the vegetables. Roast in a preheated oven at 200°C (180°C fan, Gas 6) for 1½ hours or until the chicken is tender and done (page 158).

3 Remove the chicken from the tin, transfer to a large warmed serving dish, and keep warm.

4 Make the sauce: add the chopped tomatoes and tomato purée to the vegetables in the tin, stir well, and return to the oven for 5 minutes or until hot.

5 Carefully pour the contents of the tin into a food processor or blender, and purée until smooth. Season with salt and pepper.

6 Pour the sauce over the roast chicken, garnish with chopped parsley, and serve at once, with green beans and buttered new potatoes, if you like.

Roast chicken with orange and peppers

SERVES 4 **CALS PER SERVING** 411

3 oranges
a few parsley sprigs
1 head of garlic, separated into cloves
1.7–2 kg (3½–4 lb) chicken
salt and black pepper
1 tsp paprika
pinch of cayenne pepper
15 g (½ oz) butter, softened
1 red pepper, halved, deseeded, and diced
90 ml (3 fl oz) orange juice
75 ml (2½ fl oz) brandy
fresh basil, to garnish

1 Cut two of the oranges lengthways into quarters, leaving them unpeeled. Peel the remaining orange and separate into segments, removing the tough membranes.

2 Put the parsley, orange quarters, and half of the garlic cloves into the cavity of the chicken.

3 Weigh the chicken, and calculate the roasting time at 20 minutes per 500 g (1 lb), plus an extra 20 minutes.

4 Rub the chicken with salt and pepper, and the paprika, cayenne, and butter. Place the chicken, breast-side down, in a roasting tin. Add the red pepper and the remaining garlic cloves.

5 Roast in a preheated oven at 190°C (170°C fan, Gas 5) for the calculated time, turning the chicken breast-side up halfway through cooking.

6 Check that the chicken is done (page 158), then remove it from the tin with the red pepper and garlic. Carve the chicken, and arrange on a warmed serving platter with the red pepper and garlic. Keep hot.

7 Spoon off all but 1 tbsp fat from the roasting tin, leaving behind the cooking juices. Add the orange juice and brandy and boil on the hob until reduced. Add the orange segments and heat through.

8 Spoon the orange segments and sauce over the chicken, sprinkle with the basil, and serve at once.

Sunday roast chicken

Traditional roast chicken is very much a family favourite at weekends. With its crisp skin, and light, juicy stuffing of apple, herbs, onion, and lemon zest, accompanied by rich homemade gravy, it is hard to beat.

SERVES 4 **CALS PER SERVING** 534

- a few parsley and thyme sprigs
- 1.7–2 kg ($3\frac{1}{2}$–4 lb) chicken
- ½ lemon, sliced
- ½ onion, sliced
- 60 g (2 oz) butter, softened

Apple and herb stuffing

- 30 g (1 oz) butter
- 1 small onion, finely chopped
- 1 cooking apple, peeled, cored, and grated
- 60 g (2 oz) fresh white breadcrumbs
- 1 small egg, beaten
- 1 tbsp chopped parsley
- 1 tbsp chopped fresh thyme
- grated zest of 1 lemon
- salt and black pepper

Gravy

- 2 tsp plain flour
- 300 ml (½ pint) chicken stock or giblet stock (page 155)
- splash of red wine or sherry and a spoonful of redcurrant jelly or cranberry sauce (optional)

1 Make the apple and herb stuffing: melt the butter in a saucepan, add the onion, and cook gently for a few minutes until softened. Remove from the heat, cool slightly, then stir in the apple, breadcrumbs, egg, parsley, thyme, and lemon zest. Season with salt and pepper, then leave until cold.

2 Put the parsley and thyme sprigs into the cavity of the chicken, add the lemon and onion, and season well with black pepper. Tie the legs together with string.

3 Spoon the stuffing into the neck end of the chicken, secure the skin flap over the stuffing with a small skewer, and pat into a rounded shape. Put any remaining stuffing into a baking dish.

4 Weigh the stuffed chicken, and calculate the roasting time at 20 minutes per 500 g (1 lb), plus an extra 20 minutes. Rub the butter over the breast, and season with salt and pepper.

5 Place the chicken, breast-side down, in a roasting tin. Roast in a preheated oven at 190°C (170°C fan, Gas 5) for the calculated time, turning the bird over when lightly browned and basting it every 20 minutes. Put any stuffing in the oven for the last 40 minutes.

6 Check that the chicken is done (page 158), then transfer to a warmed serving platter, and cover with foil. Make the gravy (see box, right).

7 Carve the chicken (page 158). Remove the stuffing from the neck cavity and transfer to a serving dish. Serve hot, with the gravy and roast potatoes (page 406).

Making gravy

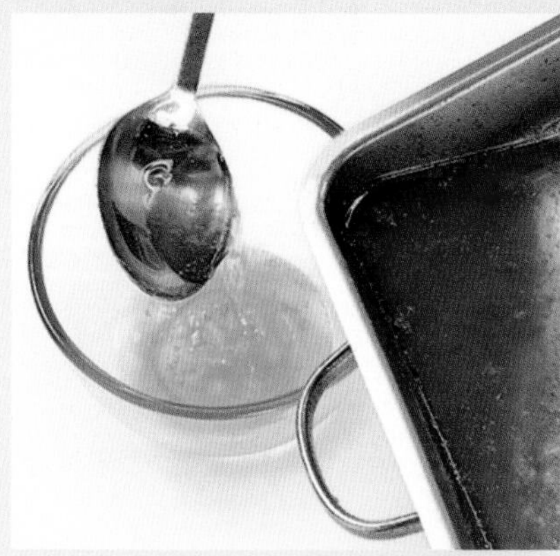

Tilt the roasting tin, and spoon off all but 1 tbsp of the fat that is on the surface, leaving behind the cooking juices and sediment. Put the roasting tin on the hob.

Add the flour, and cook over a medium heat for 1–2 minutes, stirring constantly with a whisk or metal spoon to dissolve any sediment from the bottom of the tin.

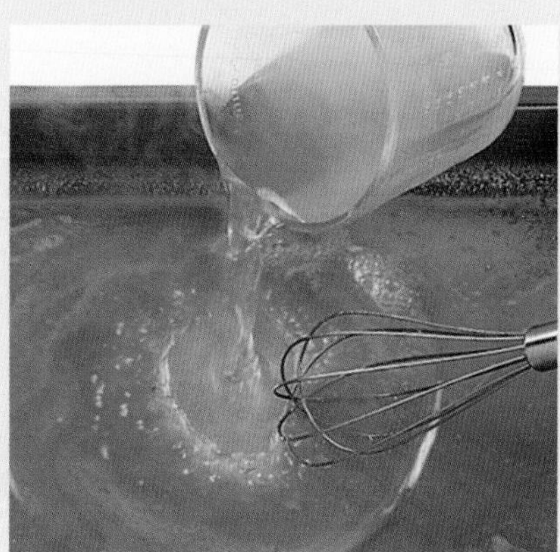

Pour in the stock, and bring to a boil, stirring. Simmer for 2 minutes, then add wine or sherry, redcurrant jelly or cranberry sauce, and salt and pepper to taste. Strain.

French roast chicken

Chicken roasted in the traditional French style is particularly moist and succulent because of the stock added to the roasting tin. In France, the chicken liver is often cooked in a little butter, then sliced and added to the gravy, but this is optional.

SERVES 4 **CALS PER SERVING** 433

a small bunch of tarragon or rosemary
90 g (3 oz) butter, softened, plus extra for greasing
1.7–2 kg (3½–4 lb) chicken
salt and black pepper
300 ml (½ pint) chicken stock or giblet stock (page 155)
4 heads of roast garlic (see box, right), to serve
a good splash of red or white wine

1 Put the bunch of herbs and 30 g (1 oz) of the butter into the cavity of the chicken. Tie the legs together with string. Weigh the chicken and calculate the roasting time at 20 minutes per 500 g (1 lb), plus an extra 20 minutes.

2 Rub the remaining butter all over the chicken and sprinkle with salt and pepper.

3 Put the chicken, breast-side down, into a small roasting tin. Pour the stock into the bottom of the tin, and cover the chicken with buttered greaseproof paper or foil. Roast in a preheated oven at 190°C (170°C fan, Gas 5) for the calculated time. At regular intervals, baste the chicken and turn it first on to one side, then on to the other, and finally on to its back.

4 Check that the chicken is done (page 158), then transfer to a warmed serving platter, and cover with foil.

5 Leave the chicken to rest for about 15 minutes, then carve and serve with the cooking juices, boiled in the roasting tin with some red or white wine, and the roasted garlic.

Roasting garlic

Cut the stalk ends off 4 heads of garlic, arrange in an oiled baking dish, and drizzle a little olive oil over the tops. Cook in a preheated oven at 190°C (170°C fan, Gas 5) for 45–60 minutes. To eat, squeeze the soft cloves of garlic from the papery skins.

Chicken satay

In this traditional Indonesian speciality, the rich satay sauce made from peanuts and coconut complements the pieces of chicken tenderized by a tangy marinade. Serve as a starter or a buffet party dish.

SERVES 4 **CALS PER SERVING** 815

4 skinless, boneless chicken breasts, cut into 2 cm (¾ in) pieces
chopped flat-leaf parsley and coarsely chopped peanuts, to garnish

Marinade

90 ml (3 fl oz) dark soy sauce
juice of 1 lemon
3 tbsp sunflower oil
2 tbsp dark brown sugar
3 garlic cloves, crushed
3 spring onions, thinly sliced

Satay sauce

250 g (8 oz) peanut butter
2 garlic cloves, crushed
175 ml (6 fl oz) water
30 g (1 oz) creamed coconut, coarsely chopped
1 tbsp dark soy sauce
1 tbsp dark brown sugar
1 cm (½ in) piece of fresh root ginger, peeled and grated
1 tbsp lemon juice
cayenne pepper
salt and black pepper

12 BAMBOO SKEWERS

1 Make the marinade: in a bowl, combine the soy sauce, lemon juice, oil, sugar, garlic, and spring onions.

2 Toss the chicken in the marinade. Cover and leave to marinate in the refrigerator for 30 minutes.

3 Meanwhile, soak the skewers in warm water for 30 minutes.

4 Make the satay sauce: heat the peanut butter with half of the garlic for 2 minutes. Add the water, creamed coconut, soy sauce, sugar, and ginger, and cook, stirring, for about 2 minutes or until the sauce is smooth.

5 Add the lemon juice and remaining garlic, and season with cayenne pepper, salt, and black pepper. Keep warm.

6 Thread the chicken pieces on to the skewers. Place under a hot grill, 10 cm (4 in) from the heat, and grill for 2–3 minutes on each side until cooked through.

7 Serve the chicken satay at once, garnishing the sauce with chopped parsley and peanuts.

Chicken tikka

SERVES 4–6 **CALS PER SERVING** 266–177

750 g (1½ lb) skinless, boneless chicken breasts, cut into 2.5 cm (1 in) cubes
cucumber raita (see box, below), to serve

Marinade

2 tbsp full-fat yogurt
2 tbsp tomato purée
1 small onion, finely chopped
2.5 cm (1 in) piece of fresh root ginger, peeled and grated
3 garlic cloves, crushed
1 tbsp tamarind paste (optional)
1 tbsp paprika
1 tsp ground cumin
large pinch of cayenne pepper

4–6 METAL SKEWERS

1 Make the marinade: in a large bowl, combine the yogurt, tomato purée, onion, ginger, garlic, tamarind paste (if using), paprika, cumin, and cayenne pepper.

2 Toss the chicken in the marinade. Cover and marinate in the refrigerator for at least 2 hours (or overnight), stirring occasionally.

3 Thread the chicken on to skewers, put under a hot grill, 10 cm (4 in) from the heat, and grill for 3–5 minutes on each side or until cooked through. Serve hot, with raita.

Cucumber raita

Cut half a cucumber in half lengthways. Scoop out the seeds, then coarsely grate the flesh into a sieve set over a bowl. Sprinkle with salt, and leave to drain for 10 minutes. Press hard to extract the juices.

Tip the cucumber into a bowl and add 1 x 150 g carton plain yogurt, 3 thinly sliced spring onions, 3 heaped tbsp chopped fresh mint, and pepper to taste. Stir well to combine. Serve chilled.

Fragrant chicken curry with almonds

The spices in this recipe are among those used in ready-made curry powders, but using your own individual blend of spices gives a truly authentic flavour to a curry. This is a creamy, mild dish – not too hot or spicy.

SERVES 4 **CALS PER SERVING** 527

2 cloves
2 tsp cumin seeds
seeds of 4 cardamom pods
1 tsp garam masala
pinch of cayenne pepper
2 tbsp sunflower oil
4 skinless, boneless chicken breasts
1 large onion, finely chopped
2 garlic cloves, crushed
2.5 cm (1 in) piece of fresh root ginger, peeled and finely grated
salt and black pepper
300 ml (½ pint) chicken stock
150 ml (¼ pint) single cream
1 x 150 g carton full-fat yogurt
whole almonds, blanched, shredded, and toasted (see box, right), sultanas, and coriander, to garnish

1 Crush the cloves in a mortar and pestle with the cumin and cardamom seeds. Mix in the garam masala and cayenne.

2 Heat the oil in a flameproof casserole. Add the chicken breasts, and cook for 2–3 minutes on each side until golden. Remove with a slotted spoon and leave to drain on paper towels.

3 Add the onion, garlic, and ginger to the pan, and cook gently, stirring occasionally, for a few minutes until just beginning to soften. Add the spice mixture, and season with salt and pepper, then stir over a high heat for 1 minute.

4 Return the chicken to the casserole. Pour in the stock, and bring to a boil. Cover and simmer gently for 15 minutes or until the chicken is tender.

5 Stir in the cream and yogurt, heat through very gently, then taste for seasoning.

6 Serve hot with boiled rice (page 354). Sprinkle with the toasted shredded almonds, sultanas, and a few torn coriander leaves.

Almonds

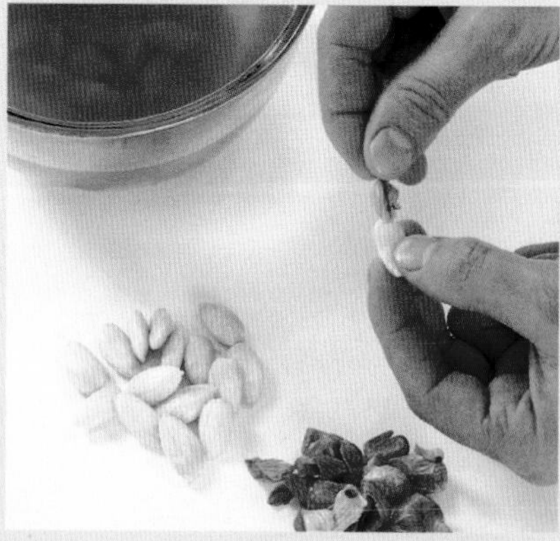

Blanch the almonds and loosen the skins: immerse in a bowl of boiling water. When cool enough to handle, squeeze the almonds between your fingers to slide and pull off the skins.

Slice the almonds in half lengthways. Cut the halves into shreds.

Place the shredded almonds on a baking tray, and toast in a preheated oven at 180°C (160°C fan, Gas 4), stirring the almonds occasionally to ensure that they colour evenly, for 8–10 minutes until lightly browned.

Sweet and sour Chinese chicken

SERVES 4–6 **CALS PER SERVING** 458–305

- 500 g (1 lb) skinless, boneless chicken breasts, cut into 2.5 cm (1 in) pieces
- 2 tbsp dark soy sauce
- 1 tbsp Chinese rice wine or dry sherry
- 1 x 250 g can pineapple chunks in natural juice, drained and juice reserved
- 2 tbsp cornflour
- 3 tbsp sunflower oil
- 1 green pepper, halved, deseeded, and cut into bite-sized pieces
- 1 red pepper, halved, deseeded, and cut into bite-sized pieces
- 1 celery stalk, thickly sliced
- 1 onion, cut into bite-sized chunks
- 4 tbsp tomato ketchup
- 250 g (8 oz) canned lychees, drained and juice reserved
- salt and black pepper
- chopped fresh coriander, to garnish (optional)

1 Toss the chicken pieces in a large bowl with the soy sauce and rice wine or sherry. Cover, and marinate in the refrigerator for at least 30 minutes.

2 Meanwhile, make the reserved pineapple juice up to 250 ml (8 fl oz) with water and blend with the cornflour. Set aside.

3 Heat the oil in a wok or large frying pan, add the chicken, in batches if necessary, and stir-fry for 3–4 minutes until golden all over. Lift out with a slotted spoon.

4 Add the green and red peppers, celery, and onion to the wok, and stir-fry for about 5 minutes.

5 Add the cornflour and pineapple juice mixture, ketchup, and reserved lychee juice to the wok, and cook for 3–5 minutes until thickened.

6 Return the chicken to the wok with the lychees and pineapple chunks, and heat through. Season with salt and pepper, and serve at once.

Chicken stir-fry

SERVES 4 **CALS PER SERVING** 381

- 3 tbsp sunflower oil
- 4 spring onions, sliced
- 2.5 cm (1 in) piece of fresh root ginger, peeled and grated
- 1 tsp Chinese five-spice powder
- ½ tsp crushed dried red chillies
- 3 carrots, thinly sliced
- 1 red pepper halved, deseeded, and cut into thin strips
- 1 yellow pepper halved, deseeded, and cut into thin strips
- 4 tbsp dark soy sauce
- 2 tbsp dry sherry mixed with 2 tsp cornflour
- 4 skinless, boneless chicken breasts, cut into 1 cm (½ in) strips

1 Heat 1 tbsp of the oil in a wok or large frying pan, add the spring onions, ginger, five-spice powder, and chillies, and stir-fry for 1 minute.

2 Add the remaining oil, then add the carrots and peppers, and stir-fry over a high heat for 2–3 minutes. Add the soy sauce, sherry mixture, and chicken strips, and stir-fry for 3–4 minutes.

3 Add 125 ml (4 fl oz) water and stir-fry for 1–2 minutes until the liquid boils and thickens slightly. Serve at once.

Stir-fried chicken with crisp vegetables

SERVES 4 **CALS PER SERVING** 405

4 skinless, boneless chicken breasts, cut diagonally into 5 mm (¼ in) strips
2 tbsp mild curry powder
salt and black pepper
8 spring onions
250 g (8 oz) carrots
3 tbsp sunflower oil
175 g (6 oz) baby sweetcorn
175 g (6 oz) sugarsnap peas, strings removed
2–3 tbsp lemon juice
2 tbsp clear honey
2.5 cm (1 in) piece of fresh root ginger, peeled and finely grated
125 g (4 oz) bean sprouts
noodles, to serve

1 Put the chicken strips in a bowl with the curry powder and season with black pepper. Toss until the chicken is coated, then set aside while you prepare the vegetables.

2 Finely slice the white parts of the spring onions, reserving the green tops to garnish the finished dish.

3 Peel the carrots and cut them into matchstick-thin strips.

4 Heat 2 tbsp of the oil in a wok or large frying pan. Add the chicken strips and stir-fry over a high heat for 3–4 minutes until golden brown.

5 Add the sliced spring onions, the carrot matchsticks, the whole baby sweetcorn, and the sugarsnap peas, then add the lemon juice, honey, ginger, and a pinch of salt. Stir-fry over a high heat for 4 minutes or until the vegetables are tender-crisp and the chicken is cooked through.

6 Toss in the bean sprouts, and stir-fry over a high heat for 1–2 minutes until heated through. Taste for seasoning. Serve on a bed of noodles, and garnish with the reserved sliced green spring onions.

Chinese chicken with mango

SERVES 6 **CALS PER SERVING** 251

- 3 skinless, boneless chicken breasts (about 125 g/4 oz each), cut into thin strips
- about 2 tbsp sunflower oil
- 1 large red pepper, halved, deseeded, and cut into strips
- 250 g (8 oz) button chestnut mushrooms, halved
- 2 tsp cornflour blended with 5 tbsp cold chicken stock or water
- salt and black pepper
- 250 g (8 oz) bean sprouts
- about 200 g (7 oz) pak choi, coarsely sliced
- 60 g (2 oz) roasted cashew nuts, salted or unsalted
- 1 large ripe mango, peeled and sliced lengthways (see page 519)
- chopped fresh coriander, to serve (optional)

Marinade

- 1 tbsp soy sauce
- 3 tbsp rice wine vinegar or white wine vinegar
- 3 tbsp clear honey

1 Put the chicken in a bowl with the marinade ingredients and mix well. Cover and marinate in the refrigerator for about 2 hours, more if time allows.

2 Heat 1 tbsp oil over a high heat in a wok or large frying pan. Lift half the chicken from the marinade (reserving it), and stir-fry for 1–2 minutes until golden all over and nearly cooked. Remove the chicken and set aside, then repeat with the remainder.

3 Heat the remaining oil in the pan, add the red pepper and mushrooms, and stir-fry for 1–2 minutes.

4 Return the chicken to the wok. Stir the cornflour mixture and pour it into the wok, then add the reserved marinade. Season with salt and pepper and bring to a boil. Add the bean sprouts and pak choi, and stir-fry until the pak choi has just wilted, about 2 minutes. Stir in the cashew nuts and mango slices, and serve at once, sprinkled with chopped coriander if you like.

Tarragon chicken with avocado

SERVES 6 **CALS PER SERVING** 382

500 g (1 lb) skinless, boneless cooked chicken
3 spring onions, finely sliced

Sauce

5 tbsp sunflower oil
3 tbsp white wine vinegar
2 tsp Dijon mustard
2–3 tsp caster sugar, to taste
2 canned anchovy fillets, finely chopped
200 ml (7 fl oz) half-fat crème fraîche
1 tbsp chopped fresh tarragon
1 tbsp chopped parsley
salt and black pepper

To serve

2 perfectly ripe avocados
juice of ½ lemon
1 bunch of watercress
2 spring onions, trimmed and cut lengthways into fine slices

1 Cut the chicken into bite-sized pieces and mix with the spring onions in a bowl. Whisk all the sauce ingredients together in another bowl, adding salt and pepper to taste. Mix the sauce with the chicken, cover, and marinate in the refrigerator for at least 2 hours, or overnight if possible.

2 Just before serving, halve, stone, and peel the avocados, slice the flesh into 1 cm (½ in) strips, and toss in the lemon juice. The lemon juice stops it from discolouring. Gently mix the avocado into the salad, and spoon into a serving dish. Garnish with watercress and spring onions, and serve.

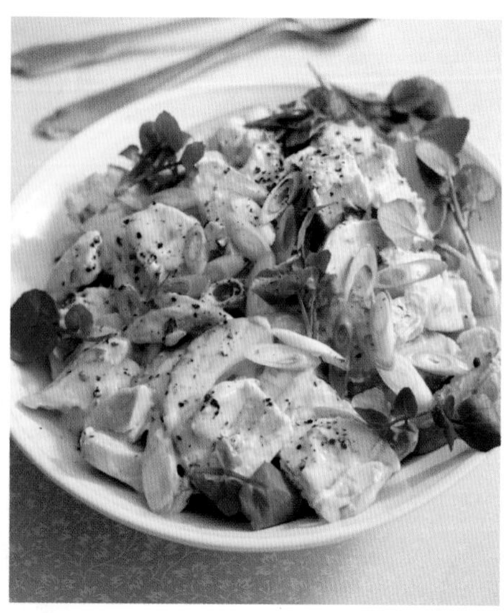

Vietnamese turkey salad

SERVES 4 **CALS PER SERVING** 199

4 tbsp fish sauce (nam pla)
500 g (1 lb) turkey breast steaks
4 tbsp lime juice
1 tbsp sugar, or more to taste
¼ tsp ground black pepper
1 small fresh red chilli, halved, deseeded, and finely chopped
250 g (8 oz) hard white cabbage, finely shredded
2 medium carrots, finely shredded
1 small onion, finely sliced
1 large bunch of fresh mint

1 Half fill a medium wok or deep frying pan with water, sprinkle in half the fish sauce and bring to a boil. Turn the heat down to a simmer, lower in the turkey breast steaks, and cover the pan with a lid. Simmer for 10 minutes or until the turkey is cooked through. Lift the turkey out of the water, and leave until cool enough to handle.

2 Meanwhile, mix the remaining fish sauce in a large bowl with the lime juice, 1 tbsp sugar, black pepper, and chilli. Add the cabbage, carrots, and onion, and mix well.

3 Cut the turkey into bite-sized strips and roughly chop 2 tbsp mint. Toss the turkey and chopped mint into the salad, and mix again. Cover and marinate in the refrigerator for 2–4 hours.

4 To serve, toss the salad again, then taste for seasoning and add more sugar if you like. Serve on a bed of the remaining mint leaves.

Thai chicken with water chestnuts

SERVES 4 **CALS PER SERVING** 272

4 skinless, boneless chicken breasts, cut into 2.5 cm (1 in) pieces
3 tbsp sunflower oil
2 garlic cloves, crushed
2.5 cm (1 in) piece of fresh root ginger, peeled and grated
½–1 fresh green chilli, halved, deseeded, and chopped
1 tsp light soy sauce, or more to taste
½ tsp sugar
black pepper
600 ml (1 pint) chicken stock
1 stem of lemongrass, bruised
grated zest of 1 lime
1 x 200 g can water chestnuts, drained, rinsed, and sliced
1 small bunch of fresh coriander, coarsely chopped
lime wedges, sliced spring onions, and peanuts, to garnish

1 Put the chicken into a dish, and add the oil, garlic, ginger, chilli, soy sauce, and sugar. Season with black pepper, stir well, then leave to stand for a few minutes.

2 Heat a non-stick wok or frying pan, add the chicken mixture, in batches if necessary, and stir-fry for 2–3 minutes or until lightly browned.

3 Pour in the stock, add any marinade left in the dish, then add the lemongrass, lime zest, water chestnuts, and coriander. Continue stir-frying for a few minutes more until the chicken is tender.

4 Taste the stir-fry and add more soy sauce, if you like. Serve at once, garnished with lime wedges, spring onion slices, and peanuts.

Warm chicken salad with mango and avocado

This unusual salad combines refreshing slices of mango and avocado with spicy chicken breast and a warm, rum-flavoured dressing. The combination of flavours makes a truly tropical dish.

SERVES 4 **CALS PER SERVING** 411

3 skinless, boneless chicken breasts, cut into 2.5 cm (1 in) strips
1 round lettuce, leaves separated
1 bunch of watercress, trimmed
1 avocado, peeled, stoned (page 395), and sliced lengthways
1 mango, peeled, stoned (page 519), and sliced lengthways
4 tbsp dark rum
paprika, to garnish

Marinade

2 tbsp olive oil
2 tbsp lemon juice
2 tsp balsamic vinegar
2 garlic cloves, crushed
1 tbsp paprika
1 mild fresh red chilli, halved, deseeded, and finely chopped
½ tsp ground cumin
salt

1 Make the marinade: combine the oil, lemon juice, vinegar, garlic, paprika, chilli, and cumin, and season with salt. Toss in the chicken strips, cover, and leave to marinate for a few minutes.

2 Arrange beds of lettuce and watercress on four serving plates. Arrange the avocado and mango slices on top.

3 Heat a large frying pan, and add the chicken strips with the marinade. Cook over a high heat, stirring, for 5–6 minutes until cooked through and golden brown on all sides.

4 Using a slotted spoon, remove the chicken strips from the pan, and arrange on top of the avocado and mango.

5 Return the frying pan to the heat, and pour in the rum. Let it bubble, stirring constantly to dissolve any sediment in the frying pan and incorporate the cooking juices, for about 1 minute. Pour the hot rum mixture over the salads, sprinkle with a little paprika, and serve at once.

Coronation chicken

SERVES 6 **CALS PER SERVING** 580

1 tbsp sunflower oil
125 g (4 oz) spring onions, chopped
4 tsp mild curry paste
150 ml (¼ pint) red wine
pared zest and juice of 1 lemon
1 tbsp tomato purée
2 tbsp apricot jam
300 ml (½ pint) mayonnaise
150 g (5 oz) plain yogurt
salt and pepper
500 g (1 lb) cooked chicken, cut into bite-sized pieces
watercress sprigs, to garnish

1 Heat the oil in a small saucepan, add the spring onions, and cook for about 2 minutes until beginning to soften but not colour. Stir in the curry paste, and cook, stirring, for 1 minute.

2 Add the red wine, lemon zest and juice, and tomato purée. Simmer, stirring, for 5 minutes or until reduced to 4 tbsp. Strain into a bowl, cover, and leave to cool.

3 Work the apricot jam through the sieve, then stir it into the curry paste and wine mixture. Add the mayonnaise and yogurt, season with salt and pepper, then stir well to blend evenly. The mixture should have a coating consistency, and be the colour of pale straw.

4 Add the chicken pieces to the mayonnaise mixture, and stir to coat evenly. Garnish with watercress sprigs before serving with boiled rice (page 354) dressed with chopped flat-leaf parsley.

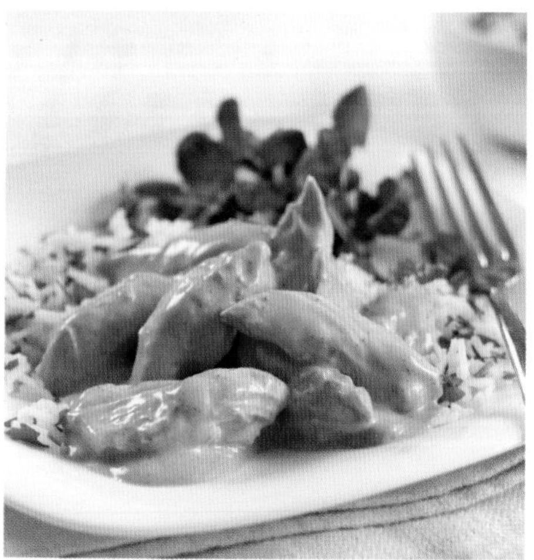

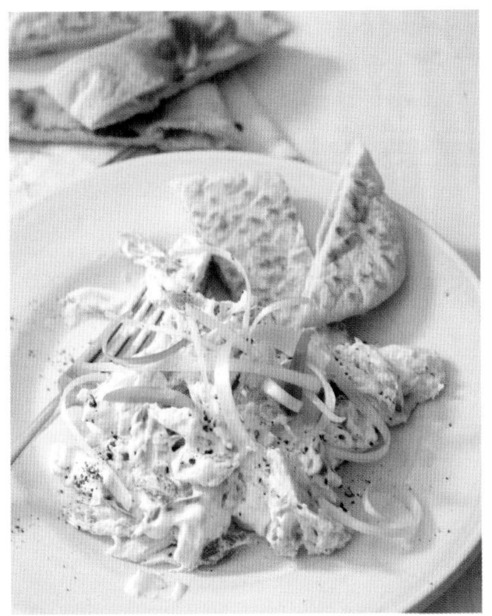

Greek chicken salad

SERVES 6 **CALS PER SERVING** 264

500 g (1 lb) cooked chicken, cut into bite-sized pieces
1 spring onion, cut into strips, to garnish
pitta bread, to serve

Sauce

150 g (5 oz) Greek-style yogurt
150 ml (¼ pint) crème fraîche
8 spring onions, thinly sliced
2 tbsp chopped fresh mint
1 tbsp chopped flat-leaf parsley
2 tbsp lemon juice
a pinch of sugar
salt and black pepper

1 Make the sauce: in a large bowl, combine the yogurt, crème fraîche, spring onions, mint, parsley, lemon juice, and sugar, and season with salt and pepper.

2 Add the chicken pieces to the bowl and toss to coat in the sauce.

3 Sprinkle the bread with a little water and cook under a hot grill for 1 minute on each side. Garnish the chicken with the spring onion strips, and serve with the pitta bread.

Red pepper herbed chicken salad

SERVES 6 **CALS PER SERVING** 224

500 g (1 lb) skinless, boneless cooked chicken
fresh basil, to garnish
tossed salad leaves, to serve

Sauce

1 bunch of fresh parsley
1 bunch of fresh basil
60 g (2 oz) red pepper in oil or brine (from a jar), drained and cut into strips, plus extra to serve
juice of 1 small lemon
2 tsp caster sugar, plus extra to taste
90 g (3 oz) low-fat Greek-style yogurt
4 tbsp low-fat mayonnaise
90 g (3 oz) half-fat soft cheese
salt and black pepper

1 Make the sauce. Put the parsley, basil, red pepper, lemon juice, and 2 tsp sugar in a food processor and pulse for about 30 seconds until quite coarsely chopped. Add the yogurt, mayonnaise, soft cheese, and seasoning and pulse again for about 30 seconds. The sauce should be mixed but not finely chopped – it should have texture and flecks of herbs. Taste and add more sugar and seasoning if you like. (If you haven't got a food processor, coarsely chop the parsley, basil, and red pepper. Mix the other ingredients together, then mix in the chopped herbs and red pepper.)

2 Cut the chicken into strips, mix into the sauce, and turn into a shallow serving dish. Cover and leave in the refrigerator for at least 4 hours, or overnight, for the flavours to infuse.

3 Before serving, check the seasoning, and garnish with basil and strips of roasted red pepper. Serve with tossed salad leaves.

Poussins with romesco sauce

SERVES 2 **CALS PER SERVING** 845

2 x 375 g (12 oz) poussins, spatchcocked (page 155)
8 spring onions, trimmed (optional)
coriander sprigs, to garnish

Marinade

2 tbsp olive oil
1 tbsp balsamic vinegar
4 garlic cloves, crushed
½ tsp ground cinnamon
salt and black pepper

Romesco sauce

1 x 225 g can chopped tomatoes
90 g (3 oz) blanched almonds
1 slice of stale bread, broken into pieces
2 tbsp olive oil
1 tbsp balsamic vinegar
1 garlic clove
1 small dried red chilli, crumbled
a few parsley sprigs
½ tsp ground cinnamon

1 Make the marinade: combine the oil, vinegar, garlic, and cinnamon, and season with salt and pepper. Brush over the poussins and spring onions (if using), cover, and marinate in the refrigerator for 1 hour, or overnight.

2 Place the poussins skin-side down under a hot grill, 15 cm (6 in) from the heat, and grill for 15–20 minutes on each side. Grill the spring onions, if using, close to the heat for 5–8 minutes on each side until the onions are slightly charred.

3 Meanwhile, make the romesco sauce: put all the ingredients in a food processor with a pinch of salt and purée until smooth.

4 Check the poussins are done by pricking with a fork – the juices should run clear, not pink or red. Serve hot, with the romesco sauce and the spring onions, if using. Garnish each serving with a coriander sprig.

Lemon poussins with artichoke hearts

SERVES 4 **CALS PER SERVING** 555

salt and black pepper
4 x 375 g (12 oz) poussins
4 garlic cloves
1 lemon, cut into quarters lengthwise
4 rosemary sprigs
60 g (2 oz) butter, softened
1 x 300 g jar artichoke hearts in oil
175 ml (6 fl oz) dry white wine
fresh rosemary and lemon wedges, to garnish

1 Season the poussins inside and out, and put a garlic clove, lemon quarter, and rosemary sprig into each one. Tie the legs together with string, then rub the birds with the softened butter.

2 Put the poussins upside down on a rack in a roasting tin. Roast in a preheated oven at 190°C (170°C fan, Gas 5) for 40–45 minutes, turning them the right way up halfway through.

3 While the poussins are roasting, drain the artichoke hearts, reserving 2–3 tbsp of the oil, and cut each artichoke heart in half.

4 Check the poussins are done by pricking with a fork – the juices should run clear, not pink or red. Remove them from the tin, and keep warm. Spoon off all but 1 tbsp fat from the tin, leaving behind the cooking juices.

5 Add the wine to the tin, mix with the juices, then boil on the hob until reduced to about 90 ml (3 fl oz).

6 Stir in the artichokes and the reserved oil, and heat through gently. Serve the poussins with the artichokes and sauce, garnished with rosemary and lemon wedges.

Moroccan poussins

SERVES 2 **CALS PER SERVING** 467

2 x 375 g (12 oz) poussins, spatchcocked (page 155)

Marinade

3 tbsp olive oil
grated zest of 1 lime and juice of 2 limes
1 small onion, finely chopped
2–3 garlic cloves, crushed
2 tbsp chopped fresh coriander
1 tbsp paprika
2 tsp curry powder
pinch of cayenne pepper
salt

1 Mix all the marinade ingredients, except the salt, in a non-metallic dish. Turn the poussins in the marinade, cover, and marinate in the refrigerator for at least 3 hours (or overnight), turning occasionally.

2 When ready to cook, preheat the grill to hot, and sprinkle the poussins with a little salt.

3 Put the poussins, skin-side down, on a rack under the grill, 15 cm (6 in) from the heat, and grill for 15–20 minutes on each side, turning once and brushing with the marinade. Check the poussins are done by pricking with a fork – the juices should run clear, not pink or red. Serve hot or cold.

Cook's **know-how**

It is quick and easy to spatchcock poussins, but you can buy them ready spatchcocked at most supermarkets, especially during the barbecue season.

Oriental poussins

SERVES 4 **CALS PER SERVING** 395

2 x 625 g ($1\frac{1}{4}$ lb) poussins
4 tbsp dark soy sauce
3 tbsp dry sherry
3 tbsp hoisin sauce
3 tbsp sunflower oil
3 garlic cloves, crushed
2 tbsp brown sugar
1 tsp five-spice powder
2.5 cm (1 in) piece of fresh root ginger, peeled and grated
boiled rice, to serve (see page 354)
spring onions and sliced red and green peppers, to garnish

1 Halve the poussins, and remove the backbones (see box, right).

2 Combine the soy sauce, sherry, hoisin sauce, oil, garlic, sugar, five-spice powder, and ginger. Brush this mixture on both sides of the poussins.

3 Put the poussins, skin-side up, into a roasting tin, and roast in a preheated oven at 190°C (170°C fan, Gas 5) for 30 minutes. Check the poussins by pricking with a fork – the juices should run clear.

4 With a sharp knife, finely shred the green tops of the spring onions, working on the diagonal. Serve the poussins hot, with boiled rice and garnished with the spring onion and pepper slices.

Halving a poussin

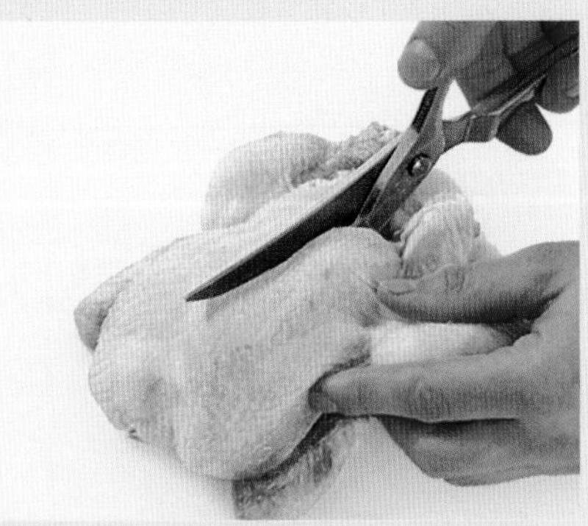

Cut along the middle of the breast with poultry shears or sturdy kitchen scissors. Take the two sides and open out slightly.

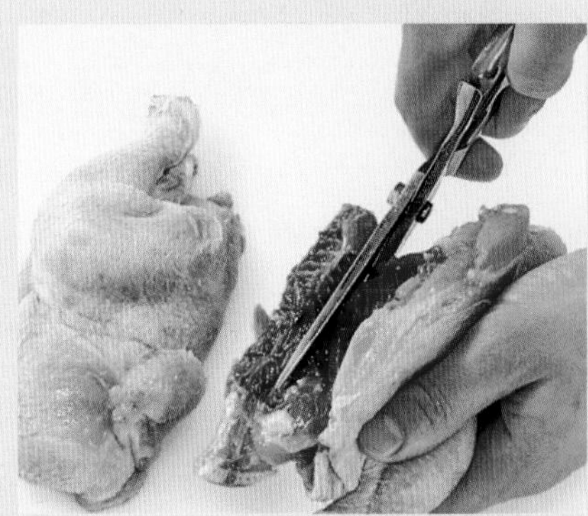

Turn the poussin over and cut in half, along one side of the backbone. Remove and discard the backbone.

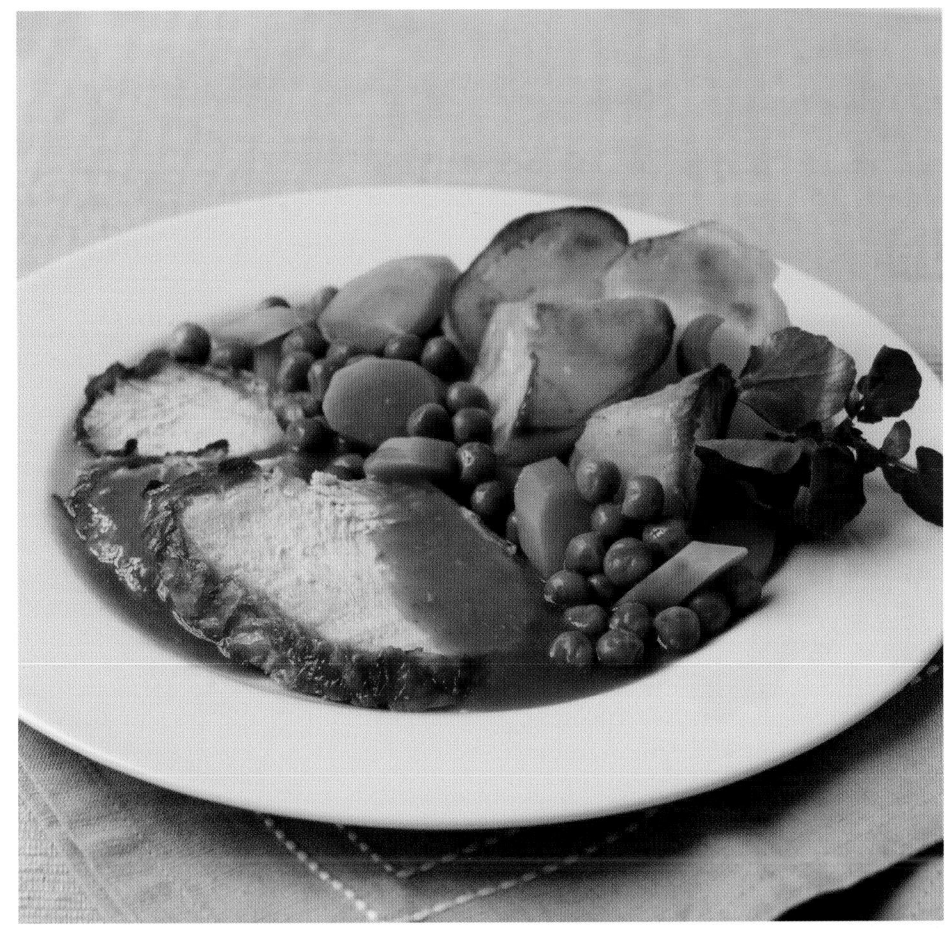

Roast turkey with garlic and tarragon

SERVES 4 **CALS PER SERVING** 296

1.25 kg (2½ lb) turkey breast joint
1 tsp plain flour
300 ml (½ pint) chicken stock
salt and black pepper
watercress sprigs, to garnish
boiled carrots and peas, to serve

Marinade

3 tbsp sunflower oil
grated zest and juice of 1 lemon
1 small onion, sliced
1 garlic clove, crushed
1 large tarragon sprig
1 large lemon thyme sprig

1 Make the marinade: combine the oil, lemon zest and juice, onion, garlic, tarragon, and thyme. Spoon the marinade over the turkey, cover, and leave to marinate in the refrigerator, turning occasionally, for 8 hours.

2 Put the turkey into a roasting tin. Strain the marinade, and pour around the turkey. Cover with foil, and cook in a preheated oven at 190°C (170°C fan, Gas 5) for 20 minutes per 500 g (1 lb). Remove the foil after 20 minutes of cooking to brown the turkey.

3 Test whether the turkey is done by inserting a fine skewer into the thickest part: the juices will run clear when it is cooked. Remove the turkey from the roasting tin, and keep warm while you make the gravy.

4 Put the tin on the hob, add the flour to the juices in the tin, and cook, stirring, for 1 minute until lightly browned. Add the stock, and bring to a boil, stirring until thickened slightly. Simmer for 2–3 minutes, season, and strain into a warm gravy boat.

5 Garnish the turkey with watercress, and serve with roast potatoes, boiled carrots and peas, and the hot gravy.

Turkey with soured cream and chives

SERVES 4 **CALS PER SERVING** 542

30 g (1 oz) butter
2 tbsp sunflower oil
600 g (1¼ lb) turkey breast fillets, cut diagonally into 1 cm (½ in) strips
4 streaky bacon rashers, rinds removed, diced
1 large onion, sliced
250 g (8 oz) button mushrooms, halved
30 g (1 oz) plain flour
150 ml (¼ pint) turkey or chicken stock
salt and black pepper
150 g (5 oz) full-fat soured cream
2 tbsp snipped fresh chives

1 Melt the butter with the oil in a large frying pan until foaming. Add the turkey, and cook over a high heat, stirring, for 8 minutes. Remove the turkey from the pan with a slotted spoon, and keep warm.

2 Lower the heat and add the bacon, onion, and mushrooms. Cook gently, stirring occasionally, for 3–5 minutes until the onion is soft but not coloured. Sprinkle in the flour and cook, stirring, for about 1 minute.

3 Pour in the stock, and bring to a boil, stirring until thickened. Add the turkey, and season with salt and pepper. Cover and simmer for about 5 minutes or until the turkey is tender.

4 Stir in the soured cream, and heat gently without boiling. Serve at once, sprinkled with the chives.

Christmas roast turkey

If you have a large number to cater for at Christmas, be sure to order a fresh turkey well in advance from your butcher. You can collect it on Christmas Eve or store it for up to 2 days in the refrigerator. If you buy a frozen turkey, make sure that it is thoroughly thawed before cooking – see page 154 for thawing times.

SERVES 12 **CALS PER SERVING** 675

pared zest of 1 lemon
a few parsley stalks
a few thyme sprigs
2 celery stalks, roughly sliced
5 kg (10 lb) oven-ready turkey, with giblets
75 g (3 oz) butter, softened
salt and black pepper
250 g (8 oz) streaky bacon rashers (optional)

Chestnut stuffing

30 g (1 oz) butter
1 onion, finely chopped
90 g (3 oz) streaky bacon, finely chopped
375 g (12 oz) frozen chestnuts, thawed, or 175 g (6 oz) dried chestnuts, soaked, finely chopped
175 g (6 oz) pork sausagemeat
3 tbsp chopped parsley
1 tbsp chopped fresh thyme
salt and black pepper
1 small egg, beaten

Gravy

30 g (1 oz) plain flour
600 ml (1 pint) giblet stock (page 155) or chicken stock
about 2 tbsp port, Madeira, or sherry
redcurrant jelly, to taste (optional)

To serve (see box, right)

bread sauce
cranberry sauce
bacon rolls
chipolatas

1 Prepare the stuffing: melt the butter in a frying pan, add the onion and bacon, and cook until the onion is soft and both the onion and bacon are golden. Transfer to a large bowl, mix in the remaining stuffing ingredients, and leave until cold.

2 Place the lemon zest, parsley stalks, thyme, and celery into the cavity of the turkey. Fill the neck end with stuffing. Put the leftover stuffing into an ovenproof dish and set aside.

3 Shape the stuffed end of the turkey into a neat round and secure the loose skin with fine skewers. Tie the legs with string to give a neat shape.

4 Weigh the turkey and calculate the cooking time, allowing 20 minutes per 500 g (1 lb). Arrange two large sheets of foil across a large roasting tin. Place the turkey on top and spread the butter over the bird, concentrating on the breast in particular.

5 Season with a little salt and plenty of pepper. If you are using the bacon rashers, overlap them across the turkey, again concentrating on the breast.

6 Fold the sheets of foil loosely over the turkey, leaving a large air gap between the foil and the turkey. Cook the turkey in a preheated oven at 220°C (200°C fan, Gas 7) for 30 minutes.

7 Reduce the oven temperature to 160°C (140°C fan, Gas 3) and cook for the remainder of the calculated cooking time.

8 Thirty minutes before the end of the cooking time, fold back the foil and remove the bacon (if used), to allow the breast to brown, then baste with the cooking juices. To check if the turkey is thoroughly cooked, pierce the thickest part of the thigh with a fine skewer: the juices should run clear, not pink or red.

9 Lift the turkey on to a warmed serving platter, cover with fresh foil, and leave to stand in a warm place for 30 minutes before carving.

10 Meanwhile, put the dish of stuffing in the oven and cook for 25–30 minutes. Now make the gravy: spoon all but 2 tbsp of fat from the roasting tin, leaving behind the cooking juices. Place the tin over a low heat on the hob, add the flour, and cook, stirring, for 1 minute. Add the stock and port, Madeira, or sherry to taste, then cook, stirring, until thickened. Season to taste, and add some redcurrant jelly if you think the gravy is too sharp.

11 Carve the turkey and serve with the extra stuffing, gravy, bread sauce, cranberry sauce, bacon rolls, and chipolatas.

Classic accompaniments

Bread sauce

Insert 8 whole cloves into 1 onion. Put it into a pan with 900 ml ($1\frac{1}{2}$ pints) milk, 1 bay leaf, and 6 whole black peppercorns. Bring to a boil, remove from the heat, cover, and leave to infuse for 1 hour. Strain the milk and return to the pan. Gradually add about 175 g (6 oz) fresh white breadcrumbs, then bring to a boil, stirring. Simmer for 2–3 minutes. Season with salt and black pepper, and stir in 60 g (2 oz) butter. If liked, stir in 4 tbsp double cream before serving. Serve hot.

Cranberry sauce

Put 500 g (1 lb) fresh cranberries into a saucepan with 125 ml (4 fl oz) water. Bring to a boil and simmer for about 5 minutes, until the cranberries have begun to break down. Stir in 125 g (4 oz) caster sugar and simmer until the sugar has dissolved. Stir in 2 tbsp port before serving. Serve hot or cold.

Bacon rolls

With the back of a knife, stretch 6 streaky bacon rashers until twice their original size. Cut in half and roll up loosely. Thread on to skewers and cook under a hot grill, turning, for 6 minutes or until browned.

Chipolatas

Twist 6 chipolata sausages in the centre and cut in half, to make 12 small sausages. Cook under a hot grill for 10–15 minutes until cooked through and browned all over.

Turkey mole

SERVES 6 **CALS PER SERVING** 334

2 tbsp sunflower oil
750 g (1½ lb) turkey pieces
300 ml (½ pint) turkey or chicken stock
salt and black pepper

Mole sauce

1 x 400 g can chopped tomatoes
1 small onion, coarsely chopped
90 g (3 oz) blanched almonds
30 g (1 oz) raisins (optional)
20 g (¾ oz) plain chocolate, coarsely chopped
1 garlic clove
1 tbsp sesame seeds
1 tbsp hot chilli powder
1 tsp ground cinnamon
½ tsp ground cloves
½ tsp ground coriander
½ tsp ground cumin
¼ tsp ground aniseed (optional)

1 Make the mole sauce: put the tomatoes, onion, almonds, raisins (if using), chocolate, garlic, sesame seeds, chilli powder, cinnamon, cloves, coriander, cumin, aniseed (if using), and 4 tbsp water into a food processor and process briefly.

2 Heat the sunflower oil in a large saucepan, add the turkey pieces, and cook over a high heat for about 5 minutes until golden on all sides.

3 Add the mole sauce mixture, and cook, stirring, for 2 minutes. Pour in the stock, and bring to a boil. Cover and simmer very gently for 40 minutes or until the turkey is tender. Season with salt and pepper before serving.

If you would rather not use the almonds, you can use 15 g (½ oz) plain flour to thicken the sauce instead.

Turkey and lemon stir-fry

SERVES 4 **CALS PER SERVING** 342

600 g (1¼ lb) turkey breast fillets, cut diagonally into 2.5 cm (1 in) strips
375 g (12 oz) courgettes
1 large green pepper
1 tbsp olive oil
250 g (8 oz) baby sweetcorn
salt
chopped parsley and lemon slices, to garnish

Marinade

125 ml (4 fl oz) dry white wine
grated zest and juice of 1 large lemon
2 tbsp olive oil
black pepper

1 Make the marinade: combine the wine, lemon zest and juice, oil, and season with pepper. Toss the turkey strips in the marinade, cover, and marinate in the refrigerator for at least 30 minutes.

2 Slice the courgettes thickly on the diagonal. Halve the green pepper and remove the seeds, then cut the pepper halves into long thin strips.

3 Heat the oil in a wok, add the courgettes, sweetcorn, and green pepper, and stir-fry over a high heat for 2 minutes. Remove with a slotted spoon, and keep warm.

4 Remove the turkey strips from the marinade, reserving the marinade. Add the turkey to the wok, and stir-fry over a high heat for 5 minutes or until golden.

5 Pour the reserved marinade over the turkey and cook for 3 minutes or until tender. Return the vegetables to the wok, and heat through. Taste for seasoning. Serve at once, garnished with parsley and lemon slices.

Stir-fried turkey meatballs

SERVES 4 **CALS PER SERVING** 232

3 tsp sunflower oil
1 onion, thinly sliced
1 green pepper, halved, deseeded, and cut into bite-sized pieces
1 courgette, sliced
4–6 mushrooms, thinly sliced
125 g (4 oz) bean sprouts

Meatballs

375 g (12 oz) minced turkey
45 g (1½ oz) parsley stuffing mix or breadcrumbs
1 onion, finely chopped
4 garlic cloves, crushed
3 tbsp soy sauce
1 cm (½ in) piece of fresh root ginger, peeled and grated
salt and black pepper

1 Make the meatballs: in a bowl, combine the turkey, stuffing or breadcrumbs, onion, garlic, 1 tbsp of the soy sauce, and the ginger. Season with salt and pepper, then shape into meatballs (see box, right).

2 Heat 1 tsp of the oil in a wok, add the onion, green pepper, and courgette, and stir-fry for 2–3 minutes.

3 Remove the vegetables with a slotted spoon. Heat another 1 tsp of the oil, add the mushrooms, and stir-fry for 2–3 minutes. Remove with a slotted spoon.

4 Heat the remaining oil in the wok, add the meatballs, and cook gently, turning, for 6–7 minutes or until cooked through. Return the vegetables to the wok, add the bean sprouts and the remaining soy sauce, and heat through for 1 minute. Serve hot.

Shaping meatballs

Break off pieces of the turkey mixture and, with dampened hands to prevent the mixture sticking, roll into 5 cm (2 in) meatballs.

Turkey casserole with peppers and cider

SERVES 6 **CALS PER SERVING** 234

30 g (1 oz) butter
1 tbsp sunflower oil
750 g (½ lb) turkey pieces
1 onion, sliced
1 garlic clove, crushed
1 red pepper, halved, deseeded, and thinly sliced
1 yellow pepper, halved, deseeded, and thinly sliced
300 ml (½ pint) dry cider
salt and black pepper
chopped parsley, to garnish

1 Melt the butter with the oil in a flameproof casserole. When the butter is foaming, add the turkey pieces, and cook over a high heat for 5 minutes or until golden on all sides. Lift out with a slotted spoon, and drain on paper towels.

2 Lower the heat, add the onion, garlic, and red and yellow pepper slices to the casserole, and cook for 5 minutes or until the vegetables are just beginning to soften.

3 Return the turkey to the casserole, pour in the cider, and bring to a boil. Season with salt and pepper, cover, and cook in a preheated oven at 160°C (140°C fan, Gas 3) for 1 hour or until the turkey is tender.

4 Using a slotted spoon, transfer the turkey and vegetables to a warmed platter. Put the casserole on the hob and boil, stirring, until the cooking juices are thickened slightly. Taste for seasoning.

5 Spoon the sauce over the turkey and vegetables, garnish with chopped parsley, and serve at once.

TURKEY AND APPLE CASSEROLE
Substitute 2 cored, halved, and sliced eating apples for the red and yellow peppers, and add them 20 minutes before the end of the cooking time.

Turkey schnitzel

SERVES 4 **CALS PER SERVING** 394

3 tbsp plain flour
salt and black pepper
1 large egg, beaten
60 g (2 oz) fresh breadcrumbs
4 x 175 g (6 oz) turkey breast escalopes
15 g (½ oz) butter
2 tbsp sunflower oil
lemon slices and chopped parsley, to garnish

1 Sprinkle the flour on to a plate, and season generously with salt and pepper. Pour the beaten egg on to another plate, and sprinkle the breadcrumbs on to a third plate.

2 Coat each escalope with the seasoned flour, shaking off any excess. Dip each floured escalope into the beaten egg, then dip into the breadcrumbs.

3 With a sharp knife, score the escalopes in a criss-cross pattern. Cover and chill in the refrigerator for 30 minutes.

4 Heat the butter with the oil in a large frying pan. When the butter is foaming, add the escalopes, and cook over a high heat until golden on both sides.

5 Lower the heat and cook for 10 minutes or until the escalopes are tender. Test the escalopes by piercing with a fine skewer: the juices should run clear.

6 Lift the escalopes out of the pan, and drain on paper towels. Garnish with lemon slices and chopped parsley, and serve at once.

Cook's know-how

If you can't find turkey breast escalopes, buy breast fillets. Put them between two sheets of cling film, and pound with the bottom of a saucepan until they are about 5 mm (¼ in) thick.

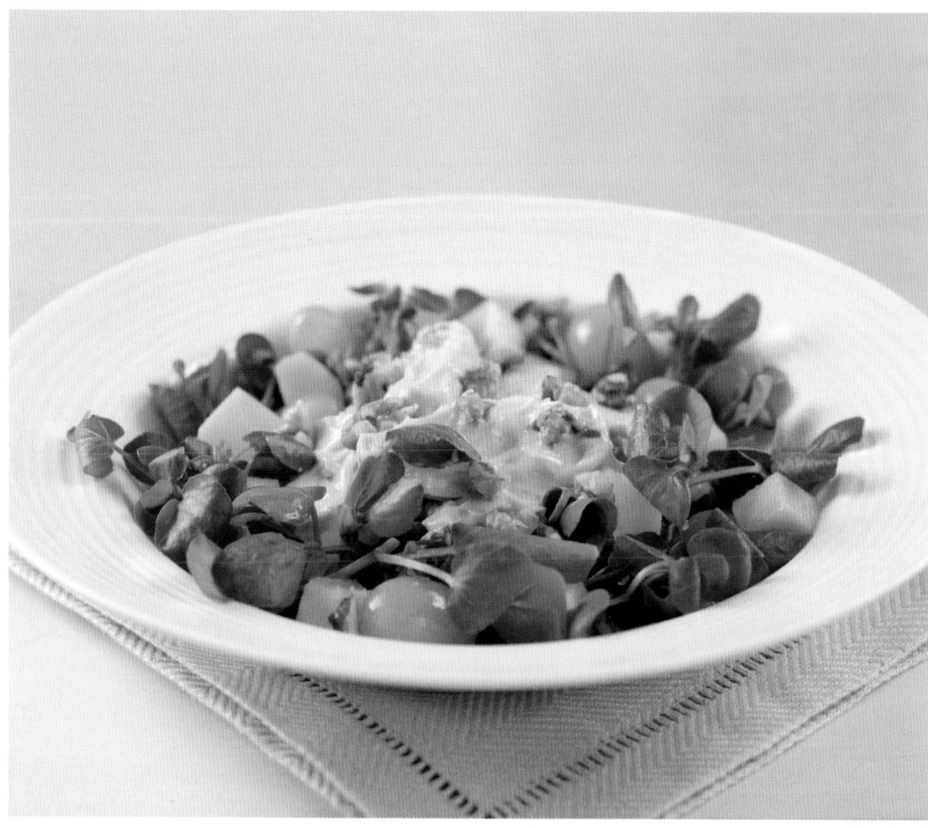

Turkey salad with mango and grapes

SERVES 4 **CALS PER SERVING** 734

1.25 kg (2½ lb) turkey breast joint
1 onion, quartered
1 carrot, sliced
a few parsley sprigs
pared zest of 1 lemon
6 black peppercorns
1 bay leaf
200 ml (7 fl oz) lemon mayonnaise
1 bunch of watercress, tough stalks removed
1 ripe mango, peeled, stoned, and cut into cubes (page 519)
125 g (4 oz) seedless green grapes
90 g (3 oz) walnut pieces

1 Put the turkey joint into a large saucepan, and cover with cold water. Add the onion, carrot, parsley, lemon zest, peppercorns, and bay leaf, and bring to a boil. Cover and simmer very gently for 1 hour or until the turkey is tender. Remove from the heat, and leave the turkey to cool completely in the poaching liquid.

2 Lift the turkey out of the poaching liquid, and remove the flesh from the carcass. Discard the skin and bones, then cut the meat into bite-sized pieces.

3 Put the turkey pieces into a large bowl, and add the lemon mayonnaise. Stir well to coat the turkey pieces thoroughly and evenly.

4 Arrange the watercress on individual serving plates, and pile the turkey mixture on top. Arrange the mango cubes and grapes around the edge, sprinkle with the walnut pieces, and serve at room temperature.

WALDORF TURKEY SALAD

Substitute 2 cored and cubed red eating apples, and 2 sliced celery stalks for the mango and grapes, and then add to the turkey and lemon mayonnaise mixture.

Turkey to go

SERVES 6 **CALS PER SERVING** 439

about 750 g (1½ lb) turkey breast fillets, cut into thin strips
1 tsp ground coriander
1 tsp ground cumin
salt and black pepper
12 soft tortilla wraps
about 2 tbsp sunflower oil
1 large red pepper, halved, deseeded, and thinly sliced

To serve

tomato salsa or mango chutney
shredded romaine lettuce

1 Put the turkey strips in a bowl with the coriander and cumin. Season with salt and pepper, then mix well to coat the turkey in the spices. Cover and marinate in the refrigerator for about 30 minutes, more if time allows.

2 When you are ready to cook the turkey, warm the tortillas (see page 264). Heat the oil in a wok or large frying pan and fry the turkey in batches with the red pepper strips until golden brown and cooked through, for about 4 minutes. You may need to add more oil with each batch.

3 Arrange the tortillas, turkey and pepper mixture, salsa or chutney, and lettuce together on a serving tray. Let each person spread their tortillas with the salsa or chutney, and add turkey, peppers, and lettuce as desired, then roll each one into a fat cigar shape. The filled tortillas are easy to eat if they are sliced in half on the diagonal.

Cook's know-how

Soft tortillas are flat Mexican breads that can be made from wheat or corn (both are suitable for this recipe). They are widely available at supermarkets, and some are flavoured with tomato, garlic, or herbs.

Roast duck with cranberries

Many people like the flesh of roast duck breast a little pink, but the legs need to be well cooked, or they may be tough. To accommodate the difference, serve the breast meat first, and return the duck to the oven for 15 minutes to finish cooking the legs.

SERVES 4 **CALS PER SERVING** 580

2.5 kg (5 lb) duck, with any giblets reserved for stock
cranberry sauce, to serve (page 198)
watercress sprigs, to garnish

Cranberry stuffing

30 g (1 oz) butter
1 small onion, finely chopped
175 g (6 oz) fresh brown breadcrumbs
125 g (4 oz) cranberries
1 tbsp chopped parsley
¼ tsp ground mixed spice
salt and black pepper
1 egg, beaten

Gravy

1 tsp plain flour
300 ml (½ pint) duck giblet stock (page 155)

1 Make the cranberry stuffing: melt the butter in a pan, add the onion, and cook gently for 3–5 minutes until softened.

2 Stir in the breadcrumbs, cranberries, parsley, and mixed spice, and season with salt and pepper. Bind with the egg, and leave to cool.

3 Remove any fat from the cavity of the duck. Spoon the stuffing into the neck end of the duck, secure the skin flap over the stuffing with a small skewer, and pat into a rounded shape. Put any leftover stuffing into an ovenproof dish and set aside.

4 Prick the skin of the duck all over with a fork, and rub salt and pepper into the skin. Place the duck, breast-side down, on a wire rack in a deep roasting tin, and roast in a preheated oven at 200°C (180°C fan, Gas 6) for 25 minutes or until golden brown.

5 Pour off some of the fat from the tin to reduce splashing. Turn the duck breast-side up, and roast for another 20 minutes or until brown.

6 Reduce the oven temperature to 180°C (160°C fan, Gas 4), and roast the duck, without basting, for 1–1¼ hours. Cook any leftover stuffing with the duck for the last 40 minutes.

7 Test the duck by inserting a fine skewer into the thickest part of a thigh: the juices will run clear when it is cooked. Keep warm, uncovered, while you make the gravy.

8 Pour off all but 1 tbsp of the fat from the roasting tin. Set the tin on the hob, add the flour, and cook, stirring, for 2 minutes. Pour in the stock, and bring to a boil, stirring until lightly thickened. Taste for seasoning, and strain into a warmed gravy boat.

9 Put the stuffing into a serving dish, carve the duck (page 158), and garnish with watercress. Serve with the gravy and cranberry sauce (page 198).

Other sauces for duck

Orange sauce
Put 2 finely chopped shallots, 300 ml (½ pint) chicken stock, and the juice of 2 oranges into a pan, and bring to a boil. Simmer until reduced by half, then season with salt and pepper. Push through a sieve, add the pared zest of 1 large orange, cut into fine strips, and reheat gently. Serve hot.

Honey sauce
Cook 2 finely chopped shallots in 30 g (1 oz) butter until soft. Add 1 tbsp plain flour, and cook, stirring, for 1 minute. Blend in 300 ml (½ pint) chicken stock and 75 ml (2½ fl oz) dry white wine. Boil, stirring, until thick. Add 3 tbsp clear honey, 1 tbsp white wine vinegar, and a pinch each of salt and pepper, and cook for 1 minute. Push through a sieve, and add 3 tbsp finely chopped parsley. Serve hot.

Blackcurrant sauce
Put 250 g (8 oz) blackcurrants and 300 ml (½ pint) water into a saucepan, and bring slowly to a boil. Simmer for 10 minutes until tender. Add 250 g (8 oz) caster sugar and 1 tbsp port, and cook gently until the sugar has dissolved. Serve hot or cold.

Duck breasts with raspberry sauce

SERVES 4 **CALS PER SERVING** 975

4 x 250–300 g (8–10 oz) duck breasts, with the skin left on
salt and black pepper

Raspberry sauce
150 ml (1/4 pint) port
75 ml (2 1/2 fl oz) water
45 g (1 1/2 oz) caster sugar
250 g (8 oz) raspberries
1 tsp cornflour
juice of 2 oranges
salt and black pepper

1 Make the raspberry sauce: pour the port and measured water into a small saucepan. Add the sugar, and bring to a boil, stirring until the sugar has dissolved. Add the raspberries, bring back to a boil, then cover and simmer very gently for 5 minutes.

2 With a wooden spoon, push the raspberry mixture through a sieve to extract the seeds. Return the raspberry purée to the saucepan, and bring back to a boil.

3 Mix the cornflour with the orange juice. Add a little of the raspberry purée to the cornflour mixture, and blend together. Return to the saucepan, and bring back to a boil, stirring constantly until thickened. Season with salt and pepper, and set aside.

4 Score and season each duck breast (see box on page 208).

5 Place the duck breasts under a hot grill, 10 cm (4 in) from the heat, and cook for 8 minutes on each side or until the skin is crisp and the duck is tender but still slightly pink inside.

6 Slice the duck breasts, skin-side up, and arrange on warmed plates. Spoon raspberry sauce around each of the servings, and serve at once.

Duck breasts with red wine sauce

SERVES 4 **CALS PER SERVING** 906

4 x 250–300 g (8–10 oz) duck breasts, with the skin left on
125 ml (4 fl oz) beef stock
125 ml (4 fl oz) red wine
1 tsp tomato purée
1 tsp lemon juice
15 g (½ oz) butter
salt and black pepper
1 tbsp chopped fresh rosemary, to garnish
boiled potatoes and green beans, to serve

Marinade

5 garlic cloves, sliced
2 tbsp balsamic vinegar
1 tbsp chopped fresh rosemary

1 Make the marinade: in a bowl, combine the garlic, vinegar, and rosemary. Score the duck breasts (see box, right), and put them, skin-side down, in a shallow dish. Spoon the marinade over the top. Chill for 30 minutes.

2 Put the duck breasts, skin-side down, with the marinade, in a frying pan and cook for 5–7 minutes. Turn, and cook for a further 5 minutes. Remove from the pan, and keep warm.

3 Spoon any excess fat from the frying pan. Add the stock and wine, and boil over a high heat until reduced to a dark glaze, then add the tomato purée and lemon juice.

4 Remove from heat, and whisk in the butter, letting it thicken the sauce as it melts. Taste for seasoning.

5 Slice the duck, and arrange on warmed plates. Spoon the sauce around the duck, sprinkle with the chopped rosemary, and serve with boiled potatoes and green beans.

Scoring and seasoning the duck

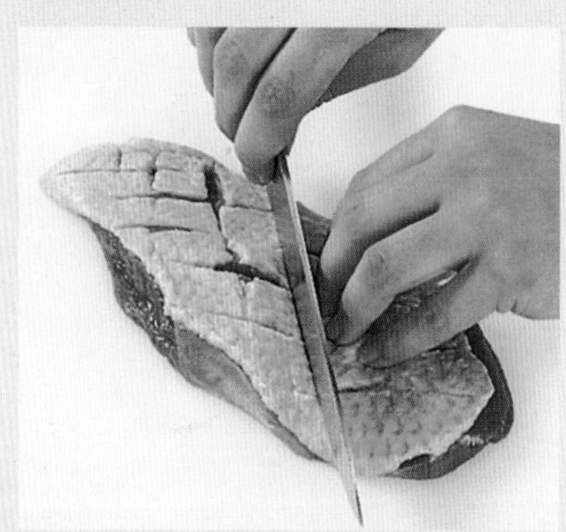

With a sharp knife, score the skin of each duck breast with criss-cross lines. Season both sides with salt and pepper.

Oriental duck with ginger

SERVES 4 **CALS PER SERVING** 445

salt and black pepper
4 x 250–300 g (8–10 oz) skinless duck breasts
1 tbsp sunflower oil
8 baby sweetcorn
bean sprouts and 1 tbsp toasted sesame seeds, to garnish

Marinade

200 ml (7 fl oz) orange juice
3 tbsp dark soy sauce
1 tbsp sesame oil
1 tbsp Chinese rice wine or dry sherry
1 tbsp clear honey
5 cm (2 in) piece of fresh root ginger, peeled and grated
1 garlic clove, crushed

1 Make the marinade: in a large bowl, combine the orange juice, soy sauce, sesame oil, rice wine or sherry, honey, fresh root ginger, and garlic, then season with salt and pepper.

2 With a sharp knife, make several diagonal slashes in each duck breast. Pour the marinade over the duck breasts, turn them over, then cover and marinate in the refrigerator for about 30 minutes.

3 Lift the duck breasts out of the marinade, reserving the marinade. Heat the oil in a large frying pan, add the duck breasts, and cook over a high heat, turning frequently, for 10–12 minutes until tender. Add the marinade and simmer for 2–3 minutes until slightly reduced.

4 Meanwhile, blanch the baby sweetcorn in boiling salted water for 1 minute. Drain, then make lengthways cuts in each one, leaving them attached at the stem.

5 To serve, slice each duck breast, and arrange on four individual plates. Spoon the hot sauce over the duck, add the sweetcorn, then garnish with bean sprouts and the toasted sesame seeds. Serve hot.

Peking duck

This Chinese dish is great fun to make, but you can buy the pancakes if you are short of time – they are sold at most large supermarkets. Let everyone help themselves to some crisp-skinned duck, spring onions, cucumber, and hoisin sauce, so they can assemble their own pancakes.

SERVES 6 **CALS PER SERVING** 848

2.5 kg (5 lb) duck, with any giblets removed
3 tbsp dry sherry
3 tbsp clear honey
3 tbsp soy sauce

Chinese pancakes

275 g (9 oz) plain flour
200 ml (7 fl oz) boiling water
2 tbsp sesame oil

To serve

6 spring onions, cut into matchstick-thin strips
½ cucumber, peeled and cut into matchstick-thin strips
90 ml (3 fl oz) hoisin sauce, sprinkled with sesame seeds
spring onions, to garnish (optional)

1 Remove any fat from the cavity of the duck. Put the duck into a bowl, pour boiling water over it, then remove and dry inside and out.

2 Mix together the sherry, honey, and soy sauce, and brush over the duck. Leave to stand, uncovered and at room temperature, for 4 hours or until the skin is dry.

3 Put the duck, breast-side down, on a wire rack in a roasting tin, and roast in a preheated oven at 200°C (180°C fan, Gas 6) for 25 minutes or until browned. Turn over and roast for a further 1–1¼ hours or until tender.

4 Meanwhile, make the pancake dough: sift the flour into a large bowl, add the boiling water, and stir to form a soft dough. Knead until smooth. Cover and leave to stand for about 30 minutes.

5 Knead the dough for 5 minutes. Shape into a roll about 2.5 cm (1 in) in diameter. Cut into 18 pieces, then roll into balls. Shape and cook the pancakes (see box, right).

6 When the duck is cooked, leave it to stand for about 15 minutes. Meanwhile, stack the pancakes on a plate in a steamer, cover, and steam for 10 minutes. Cut the duck into small pieces. Serve with the pancakes, spring onions, cucumber, and hoisin sauce, and garnish with spring onions, if you like.

Shaping and cooking Chinese pancakes

Pour the sesame oil into a bowl. Take two balls of dough, dip half of one ball into the oil, then press the oiled half on to the second ball.

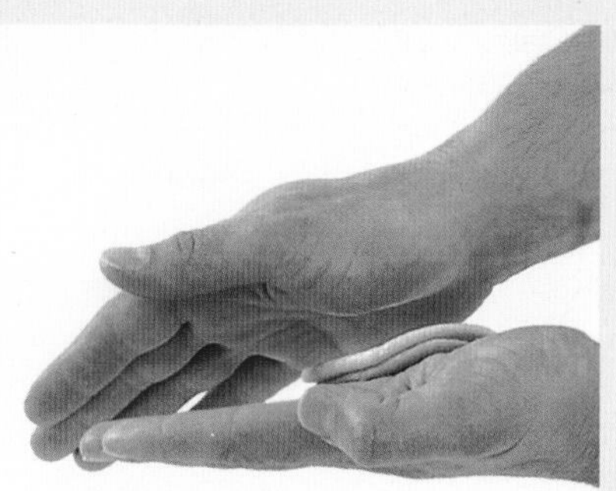

Flatten the dough balls with the palms of your hands and roll out to a pancake about 15 cm (6 in) in diameter. Heat a frying pan. Put the double pancake into the pan and cook for 1 minute. Flip over and cook the other side for 1 minute.

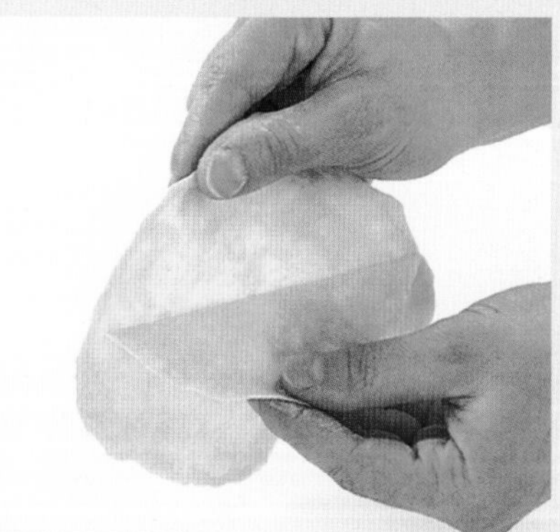

Remove from the pan, and peel the two pancakes apart. Repeat with the remaining dough, to make 18 pancakes in all. Cover the pancakes with a damp tea towel to stop them drying out.

Hot and spicy stir-fried duck

SERVES 4 **CALS PER SERVING** 453

4 x 250–300 g (8–10 oz) skinless duck breasts, cut diagonally into 1 cm (½ in) strips
2 tbsp sunflower oil
8 spring onions, cut into 2.5 cm (1 in) lengths
125 g (4 oz) carrots, cut into matchstick-thin strips
250 g (8 oz) mangetout
1 x 200 g can water chestnuts, drained, rinsed, and sliced

Marinade

2 tsp dark soy sauce
2 tsp red wine vinegar
2.5 cm (1 in) piece of fresh root ginger, peeled and grated
2 fresh red chillies, halved, deseeded, and coarsely chopped
grated zest and juice of 1 orange
1 tsp sesame oil
1 tsp cornflour
1 tsp caster sugar
salt and black pepper

1 Make the marinade: in a large bowl, combine the soy sauce, vinegar, ginger, chillies, orange zest and juice, sesame oil, cornflour, and sugar, then season with salt and pepper.

2 Toss the duck strips in the marinade, cover, and leave to stand for 10 minutes.

3 Lift the duck strips out of the marinade, reserve the marinade, and drain the duck on paper towels.

4 Heat the oil in a wok or large frying pan, add the duck, and stir-fry over a high heat for 5 minutes or until browned all over. Add the spring onions and carrots, and stir-fry for 2–3 minutes. Add the mangetout, and stir-fry for 1 minute.

5 Pour the marinade into the wok, and stir-fry for about 2 minutes or until the duck is just tender. Stir in the water chestnuts, heat through, and taste for seasoning. Serve hot.

Lacquered duck

SERVES 4 **CALS PER SERVING** 269

4 skinless duck breasts, 150–175 g (5–6 oz) each, cut diagonally into 1 cm (½ in) strips
2 tbsp sunflower oil
8 spring onions, trimmed and cut into 2.5 cm (1 in) lengths
salt and black pepper
1 tbsp sesame seeds, toasted
egg noodles (p353), to serve

Marinade

2 large garlic cloves, crushed
1 tbsp soy sauce
1 tbsp olive oil
2 tbsp clear honey

1 Put the duck in a bowl with the marinade ingredients and mix well. Cover and marinate in the refrigerator for about 2 hours, or overnight if time allows.

2 Heat the sunflower oil in a wok or large frying pan. Lift the duck from the marinade (reserving it), and stir-fry over a high heat for about 3–4 minutes or until browned all over. Add the spring onions, and stir-fry for a further 2–3 minutes or until the duck is cooked.

3 Pour the marinade and 5 tbsp water into the pan, bring quickly to a boil, and simmer for a few moments until the sauce has a syrupy consistency – take care not to overcook or the marinade may burn. Season with salt and pepper, scatter over the sesame seeds, and serve immediately with boiled egg noodles.

Christmas roast goose

Goose is a traditional Christmas bird in Britain and northern Europe, and it is a favourite festive alternative to turkey when a small group of people is to be served. It is simple to cook and tastes delicious with a fruit stuffing and spicy accompaniments.

SERVES 6–8 **CALS PER SERVING** 1228–921

5–6 kg (10–12 lb) goose, with giblets reserved for stock
1 onion, quartered
1 cooking apple, quartered
a few sage sprigs
salt and black pepper
30 g (1 oz) plain flour
450 ml (¾ pint) goose giblet stock (page 155)
150 ml (¼ pint) dry white wine
spiced stuffed apples (see box, right), to serve
watercress sprigs, to garnish

Pork and apple stuffing

300 g (10 oz) pork sausagemeat
60 g (2 oz) fresh breadcrumbs
2 tsp dried sage
30 g (1 oz) butter
1 onion, finely chopped
1 large cooking apple, peeled, cored, and finely chopped

1 Make the pork and apple stuffing: in a bowl, combine the sausagemeat, breadcrumbs, and sage.

2 Melt the butter in a pan, add the onion, and cook gently, stirring occasionally, for 3–5 minutes until soft but not coloured.

3 Add the cooking apple, and cook for 5 minutes. Stir the onion and apple into the sausagemeat mixture, season with salt and pepper, and leave to cool.

4 Remove any fat from the cavity of the goose. Put the onion and apple quarters into the cavity together with the sage. Spoon the stuffing into the neck end of the goose, pat it into a rounded shape, and secure the skin flap with a small skewer. Weigh the goose.

5 Prick the skin of the goose all over with a fork, and rub with salt and pepper. Place the goose, breast-side down, on a wire rack in a large roasting tin, and cook in a preheated oven at 220°C (200°C fan, Gas 7) for 30 minutes.

6 Turn the goose breast-side up, and cook for 20 minutes. Reduce the oven temperature to 180°C (160°C fan, Gas 4) and cook for 20 minutes per 500 g (1 lb).

7 Test the goose by inserting a fine skewer into the thickest part of a thigh: the juices should run clear when the meat is thoroughly cooked.

8 Lift the goose on to a warmed serving platter, and then leave to rest, covered with foil, for about 20 minutes.

9 Make the gravy while the goose is resting: pour off all but 2 tbsp of the fat from the roasting tin. Put the tin on the hob, add the flour, and cook, stirring, for 1 minute. Add the stock and wine, and bring to a boil, stirring constantly. Simmer for 2–3 minutes, then taste for seasoning. Strain into a warmed gravy boat.

10 To serve, arrange the spiced stuffed apples around the goose, and garnish with watercress. Hand the gravy separately.

Spiced stuffed apples

Core 8 eating apples, keeping them whole. For the stuffing, combine 2 tbsp Calvados in a small bowl with 1 tsp ground cinnamon, ½ tsp ground allspice, and 8 finely chopped ready-to-eat prunes.

Place the apples in a buttered ovenproof dish, and spoon the stuffing into the centres. Melt 60 g (2 oz) butter, pour over the apples, and cover with foil. Bake in a preheated oven at 180°C (160°C fan, Gas 4) for 1 hour or until tender.

Cook's know-how

Goose is even richer and fattier than duck. Putting it on a wire rack in the roasting tin ensures it does not sit in the fat during cooking and this gives it a good, crisp skin.

Pheasant stew

SERVES 6-8 **CALS PER SERVING** 633–475

2 tbsp sunflower oil
2 pheasants, cut into serving pieces (page 155)
375 g (12 oz) shallots, chopped
125 g (4 oz) piece of smoked streaky bacon, cut into strips
3 garlic cloves, crushed
1 tbsp plain flour
600 ml (1 pint) game stock or chicken stock (page 154)
300 ml (½ pint) red wine
1 head of celery, separated into stalks, sliced
250 g (8 oz) button mushrooms
1 tbsp tomato purée
salt and black pepper
chopped parsley, to garnish

1 Heat the oil in a large flameproof casserole. Add the pheasant pieces and cook over a high heat until browned. Lift out and drain.

2 Add the shallots and bacon and cook for 5 minutes. Add the garlic and flour and cook, stirring, for 1 minute. Add the stock and wine and bring to a boil. Add the celery, mushrooms, tomato purée, and season. Simmer for 5 minutes.

3 Add the pheasant, bring back to a boil, cover, and cook in a preheated oven at 160°C (140°C fan, Gas 3) for 2 hours. Garnish with parsley.

Game pie with fennel and carrots

SERVES 6 **CALS PER SERVING** 672

- 2 tbsp sunflower oil
- 750 g (1½ lb) boneless game meat, cut into strips or dice
- 2 large carrots, sliced
- 1 large onion, chopped
- 1 fennel bulb, sliced
- 2 tsp plain flour, plus extra for dusting
- 300 ml (½ pint) game stock or chicken stock (page 154)
- 150 ml (¼ pint) red wine
- 1 tbsp redcurrant jelly
- salt and black pepper
- 250 g (8 oz) ready-made puff pastry
- beaten egg, for glazing

2 LITRE (3½ PINT) PIE DISH

1 Heat the oil in a large flameproof casserole. Add the game in batches and cook over a high heat until browned all over. Lift out and drain on paper towels.

2 Lower the heat, add the carrots, onion, and fennel, and cook, stirring occasionally, for 5 minutes or until softened. Add the flour and cook, stirring, for about 1 minute.

3 Gradually pour in the stock and bring to a boil, stirring until thickened slightly. Add the game, wine, and redcurrant jelly, and season with salt and pepper. Cover tightly and simmer very gently for 1 hour. Leave to cool.

4 Lightly flour a work surface. Roll out the puff pastry until 2.5 cm (1 in) larger than the pie dish. Invert the dish on to the dough and cut around the edge. Cut a long strip of pastry from the trimmings and press on to the rim of the pie dish. Reserve the remaining trimmings. Spoon in the game and vegetable mixture. Brush the pastry strip with water, top with the pastry lid, and crimp the edge with a fork.

5 Make a hole in the top of the pie to let the steam escape. Roll out the reserved pastry and cut decorative shapes with a pastry cutter. Brush the beaten egg over the bottoms of the shapes, and arrange on the pie. Glaze with beaten egg.

6 Bake the pie in a preheated oven at 200°C (180°C fan, Gas 6) for 25–30 minutes until the pastry is well risen and golden.

Apple rings

Core 2 cooking apples, leaving them whole, and slice crosswise into 5 mm (¼ in) rings. Melt 30 g (1 oz) butter in a frying pan, add the apple rings, and sprinkle with a little caster sugar. Cook over a high heat for 3 minutes, turning once, until caramelized and golden.

Extras for game

These traditional accompaniments can be served with roast pheasant and many other game dishes, including grouse and partridge.

Fried breadcrumbs
Melt 30 g (1 oz) butter with 1 tbsp sunflower oil. When the butter is foaming, add 90 g (3 oz) fresh white breadcrumbs and cook, stirring, for 3–5 minutes until golden.

Stuffing balls
Combine 60 g (2 oz) grated cold butter, 125 g (4 oz) fresh white breadcrumbs, 1 beaten egg, 2 tbsp chopped parsley, and the finely grated zest of 1 lemon. Season with salt and pepper, stir to mix well, then roll into 12 small balls. Melt 30 g (1 oz) butter with 1 tbsp olive oil in a frying pan. When the butter is foaming, add the stuffing balls, and cook for 5 minutes or until golden all over. Drain thoroughly.

Normandy pheasant

Apples and cream are traditional ingredients in the cuisine of Normandy. Here, apples and a rich sauce perfectly complement the pheasant, which is cooked slowly and gently in wine and stock to keep it moist and tender.

SERVES 6–8 **CALS PER SERVING** 751–563

30 g (1 oz) butter
1 tbsp sunflower oil
2 pheasants, cut into serving pieces (page 155)
2 cooking apples, quartered, cored, and sliced
4 celery stalks, sliced
1 onion, sliced
1 tbsp plain flour
300 ml (½ pint) chicken or game stock (page 154)
150 ml (¼ pint) dry white wine
salt and black pepper
150 ml (¼ pint) double cream
apple rings, to serve (see box, opposite)
chopped parsley, to garnish

1 Melt the butter with the oil in a flameproof casserole. When the butter is foaming, add the pheasant pieces, and cook for about 5 minutes until browned. Lift out and drain.

2 Lower the heat, add the apples, celery, and onion, and cook for 5–6 minutes until soft.

3 Add the flour and cook, stirring, for 1 minute. Pour in the stock and wine, season with salt and pepper, and bring to a boil, stirring until lightly thickened.

4 Return the pheasant to the casserole and spoon the sauce over the top. Bring back to a boil, cover with greaseproof paper and the casserole lid, and cook in a preheated oven at 180°C (160°C fan, Gas 4) for 1–1½ hours until tender. Remove the pheasant from the casserole with a slotted spoon and keep warm.

5 Strain the sauce into a saucepan. Whisk in the cream, taste for seasoning, then reheat gently. Arrange the pheasant on serving plates with the apple rings. Spoon the sauce over the pheasant and serve at once, garnished with parsley.

Mushroom-stuffed quail

SERVES 6 **CALS PER SERVING** 651

12 quail, boned (page 156)
30 g (1 oz) butter, plus extra for greasing
3 tbsp lime marmalade
steamed vegetables, to serve

Mushroom stuffing

60 g (2 oz) butter
3 shallots, finely chopped
375 g (12 oz) button mushrooms, coarsely chopped
60 g (2 oz) fresh white breadcrumbs
salt and black pepper
1 egg, beaten

Lime sauce

150 ml (¼ pint) chicken stock
juice of 1 lime and lime wedges, to garnish
200 ml (7 fl oz) full-fat crème fraîche
4 tbsp chopped parsley

1 Make the mushroom stuffing: melt the butter in a saucepan, add the shallots, and cook gently, stirring occasionally, for 3–5 minutes until soft but not coloured.

2 Add the mushrooms and cook for 2 minutes, then remove from the heat. Stir in the breadcrumbs, season with salt and pepper, then stir in the egg and leave to cool. Stuff the quail (see box, right).

3 Put the quail into a buttered roasting tin. Melt the butter gently in a saucepan, add the lime marmalade, and heat gently, stirring, until combined. Brush over the quail, and cook in a preheated oven at 200°C (180°C fan, Gas 6) for 15–20 minutes until golden brown and tender. Remove from the tin and keep warm.

4 Make the lime sauce: put the roasting tin on the hob. Add the stock, and bring to a boil, then stir for 5 minutes or until reduced a little.

5 Stir in the lime juice and crème fraîche, and heat gently, stirring constantly, until the sauce has a smooth, creamy consistency.

6 Add half of the parsley and season. Serve the quail with a selection of steamed vegetables, the lime sauce, and garnish with the remaining parsley and lime wedges.

Stuffing the quail

Spoon some of the stuffing into the cavity of each quail, then secure the skin with a wooden cocktail stick.

Traditional roast pheasant

Pheasants are often sold in pairs (a cock and a hen) known as a brace. Make sure you get young pheasants for this recipe; old ones are not suitable for roasting and can be very tough unless they are cooked slowly in a casserole.

SERVES 4 **CALS PER SERVING** 660

2 pheasants, any giblets reserved
90 g (3 oz) butter, softened
salt and black pepper
4 streaky bacon rashers
1 tsp plain flour
300 ml (½ pint) pheasant giblet stock or chicken stock (page 155)
1 tsp redcurrant jelly
watercress sprigs, to garnish

To serve

fried breadcrumbs (page 214)
bread sauce (page 198)

1 Coat the pheasants with the butter, then season with salt and pepper. Lay two bacon rashers crosswise over each breast.

2 Put the pheasants into a roasting tin, and cook in a preheated oven at 200°C (180°C fan, Gas 6), basting once, for 1 hour or until tender.

3 Test the pheasants by inserting a fine skewer in the thickest part of a thigh: the juices should run clear when they are cooked.

4 Lift the pheasants on to a warmed serving platter, cover with foil, and keep warm.

5 To make the gravy, pour off all but 1 tbsp of the fat from the roasting tin, reserving any juices. Put the tin on the hob, add the flour, and cook, stirring, for 1 minute.

6 Add the stock and redcurrant jelly, and bring to a boil, stirring until lightly thickened. Simmer for 2–3 minutes, then taste for seasoning. Strain into a warmed gravy boat.

7 To serve, garnish the pheasants with the watercress sprigs, and serve with fried breadcrumbs, bread sauce, and the gravy.

Rather special game pie

This raised game pie follows a classic recipe that takes about 6 hours to make, over 3 days, but it is well worth the effort. Boned mixed game meats – usually pheasant, hare, and venison – are available in large supermarkets and food halls. There is chicken in the pie too, which goes very well with game, but you could use turkey instead.

SERVES 20 **CALS PER SERVING** 507

- 2 kg (4 lb) chicken, boned and skinned
- 1 kg (2 lb) boneless mixed game meats, cut into 1 cm (½ in) pieces
- 375 g (12 oz) belly pork, coarsely chopped
- 500 g (1 lb) piece of streaky bacon, cut into small pieces
- butter, for greasing
- hot-water crust pastry (see box, below)
- about 2 tsp salt
- black pepper
- 1 egg, beaten
- 450 ml (¾ pint) jellied stock (page 155)

Marinade

- 150 ml (¼ pint) port
- 1 small onion, finely chopped
- 3 garlic cloves, crushed
- leaves of 4 thyme sprigs, chopped
- 1 tsp grated nutmeg

30 CM (12 IN) SPRINGFORM OR LOOSE-BOTTOMED CAKE TIN

1 Make the marinade: in a bowl, combine the port, onion, garlic, thyme, and grated nutmeg.

2 Cut the chicken breast into long strips, about 1 cm (½ in) wide, and set aside. Cut the rest of the chicken into 1 cm (½ in) chunks. Add the chunks to the marinade with the game meats, belly pork, and bacon. Cover and leave to marinate in the refrigerator for 8 hours.

3 Lightly butter the tin. Take two-thirds of the hot-water crust pastry, pat it out over the bottom of the tin, and push it up the side, until it stands 1 cm (½ in) above the rim.

4 Season the meat mixture with plenty of salt and pepper, and spoon half into the pastry shell. Smooth the surface evenly.

5 Arrange the reserved chicken breast strips on top of the meat, radiating from the middle. Season with salt and pepper.

6 Top with the remaining meat mixture. Brush the top edge of the pastry with beaten egg. Roll out the remaining pastry and cover the pie, reserving the trimmings. Pinch around the edge to seal, then crimp.

7 Decorate the pie with the pastry trimmings, attaching them with beaten egg. Make three steam holes in the pastry lid, and glaze the pie with beaten egg.

8 Bake in a preheated oven at 220°C (200°C fan, Gas 7) for 1 hour. If the pastry browns too quickly, cover it with foil. Reduce the heat to 160°C (140°C fan, Gas 3) and cook for 2–2¼ hours.

9 Test the pie by piercing the centre with a skewer: the juices will run clear and the meat will feel tender when it is done. Leave the pie to cool in the tin for 8 hours.

10 Put the jellied stock into a saucepan and heat until melted. Using a funnel, slowly pour the stock through the holes in the pie. Cover and chill for 6 hours or until the stock has set. Unmould the pie and cut into wedges to serve.

Hot-water crust pastry

Sift 750 g (1½ lb) plain flour and 1 tsp salt into a large bowl. Put 400 ml (14 fl oz) water and 300 g (10 oz) white vegetable fat into a saucepan and heat until the water is boiling and the fat has melted.

Pour on to the flour and mix quickly with a wooden spoon until the mixture holds together.

Turn the dough on to a floured surface, invert the bowl over the top to keep the dough moist, and leave to cool until lukewarm.

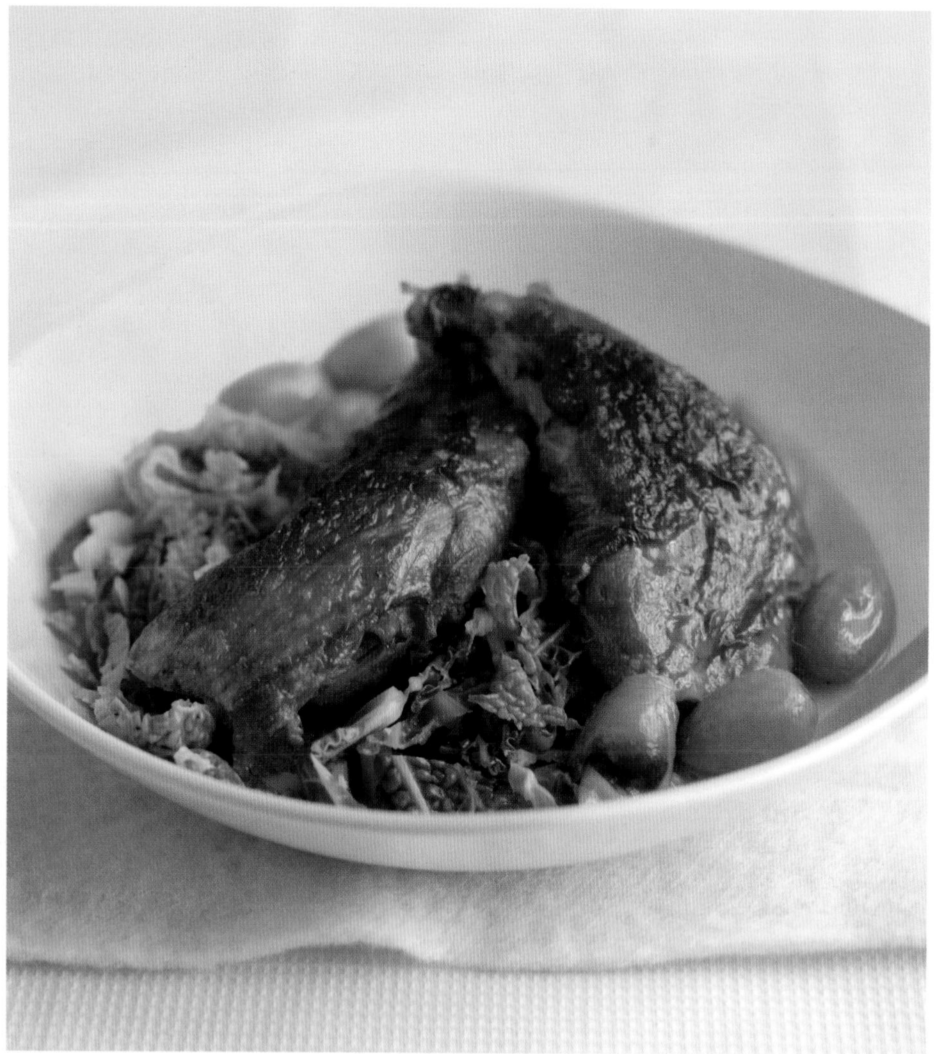

Guinea fowl Madeira

SERVES 6 **CALS PER SERVING** 613

2 tbsp sunflower oil
2 x 1.25 kg (2½ lb) guinea fowl, cut into serving pieces (page 155)
4 shallots, halved
1 tbsp plain flour
600 ml (1 pint) chicken stock
150 ml (¼ pint) dry white wine
4 tbsp Madeira
salt and black pepper
375 g (12 oz) seedless green grapes
150 ml (¼ pint) double cream
chopped parsley, to garnish
Savoy cabbage, to serve

1 Heat the oil in a flameproof casserole, and cook the guinea fowl pieces in batches for a few minutes until browned all over. Lift out and drain. Lower the heat, add the shallots, and cook, stirring, for 5 minutes or until softened. Lift out and drain.

2 Add the flour, and cook, stirring, for 1 minute. Pour in the stock, and bring to a boil, stirring. Add the wine and Madeira, and season with salt and pepper. Add the guinea fowl and shallots, and bring to a boil. Cook in a preheated oven at 160°C (140°C fan, Gas 3) for 1 hour or until just tender.

3 Transfer the casserole to the hob, add the grapes, and cook for 15 minutes. Add the cream, and heat gently. Garnish with parsley and serve hot, with boiled Savoy cabbage.

Pot roast venison

SERVES 6 **CALS PER SERVING** 454

1.25–1.5 kg (2½–3 lb) boned venison shoulder, rolled and tied
30 g (1 oz) butter
2 tbsp sunflower oil
1 large onion, chopped
2 large carrots, sliced
2 celery stalks, sliced
300 ml (½ pint) beef stock
salt and black pepper
1 tbsp redcurrant jelly
thyme sprigs, to garnish (optional)

Marinade

300 ml (½ pint) red wine
2 tbsp olive oil
pared zest of 1 orange
pared zest of 1 lemon
2 tsp crushed juniper berries
6 black peppercorns
1 garlic clove, crushed
1 large thyme sprig
1 large parsley sprig

1 Make the marinade: in a large bowl, combine the wine, oil, orange and lemon zests, juniper berries, black peppercorns, garlic, thyme, and parsley. Turn the venison in the marinade, cover, and marinate in the refrigerator, turning occasionally, for 2–3 days.

2 Lift the venison out of the marinade, straining and reserving the marinade, and pat dry. Melt the butter with the oil in a large flameproof casserole. When the butter is foaming, add the venison and cook over a high heat for 5 minutes or until well browned all over. Remove the venison from the casserole.

3 Lower the heat and add the onion, carrots, and celery to the casserole. Cover and cook very gently for 10 minutes. Place the venison on top of the vegetables, add the stock and the strained marinade, then season with salt and pepper and bring to a boil. Cover with a piece of greaseproof paper and the casserole lid, and cook in a preheated oven at 160°C (140°C fan, Gas 3) for 2½–3 hours until tender.

4 Lift out the venison and keep warm. Strain the liquid in the casserole, spoon off the fat, then return the liquid to the casserole. Add the redcurrant jelly, and boil for a few minutes until syrupy. Slice the venison, and arrange on a warmed platter. Pour over the sauce and serve hot, garnished with thyme sprigs (if wished).

Braised rabbit with mushrooms and cider

SERVES 4 **CALS PER SERVING** 506

30 g (1 oz) butter
1 tbsp sunflower oil
4 rabbit portions
2 red dessert apples, cored and quartered
8 small shallots
375 g (12 oz) mushrooms, quartered
300 ml (½ pint) dry cider
a few parsley sprigs
3–4 tarragon sprigs
salt and black pepper
300 ml (½ pint) single cream
2 tbsp roughly chopped parsley, to garnish

1 Melt the butter and oil in a flameproof casserole. When the butter is foaming, add the rabbit, and cook for 5 minutes or until browned. Remove the rabbit.

2 Add the apple quarters and lightly brown, then remove and set aside. Add the shallots to the casserole and cook over a high heat, stirring, for about 3 minutes until golden. Add the mushrooms, and cook, stirring occasionally, for 3–4 minutes until softened.

3 Return the rabbit to the casserole, and add the cider, parsley sprigs, and tarragon. Season with salt and pepper, and bring to a boil. Cover and cook in a preheated oven at 160°C (140°C fan, Gas 3) for 1½ hours or until the rabbit is tender.

4 Transfer the rabbit to a warmed platter and keep warm. Remove and discard the parsley and tarragon. Bring the sauce in the casserole to a boil on the hob, then boil until slightly reduced. Stir in the cream, taste for seasoning, and reheat gently.

5 Pour the sauce over the rabbit, and serve at once, garnished with the apple quarters and parsley.

BRAISED RABBIT WITH PRUNES

Substitute 125 g (4 oz) ready-to-eat pitted prunes for the mushrooms. Add to the casserole 30 minutes before the end of the cooking time.

Rabbit with mustard and marjoram

SERVES 4 **CALS PER SERVING** 548

4 tbsp Dijon mustard
1 tsp chopped fresh marjoram
4 rabbit portions
30 g (1 oz) butter
2 tbsp olive oil
1 large onion, chopped
2 garlic cloves, crushed
90 g (3 oz) piece of smoked streaky bacon, cut into pieces
1 tsp plain flour
450 ml (¾ pint) chicken stock
salt and black pepper
150 ml (¼ pint) single cream
2 tbsp chopped parsley, to garnish

1 Mix the mustard and marjoram and spread over the rabbit pieces. Place in a shallow dish, cover, and leave to marinate in the refrigerator for 8 hours.

2 Melt the butter with the oil in a large flameproof casserole. When the butter is foaming, add the rabbit, and cook for about 5 minutes until browned all over. Lift out and drain on paper towels.

3 Add the onion, garlic, and bacon to the casserole and cook for 3–5 minutes. Add the flour and cook, stirring, for 1 minute. Gradually blend in the stock and bring to a boil, stirring until thickened.

4 Return the rabbit to the casserole, season with salt and pepper, and bring back to a boil. Cover and cook in a preheated oven at 160°C (140°C fan, Gas 3) for 1½ hours or until the rabbit is tender.

5 Transfer the rabbit to a warmed platter and keep hot. Boil the sauce for 2 minutes until reduced. Stir in the cream, taste for seasoning, and spoon over the rabbit. Garnish with parsley.

Venison casserole

SERVES 6 **CALS PER SERVING** 466

1 kg (2 lb) stewing venison, cut into 2.5 cm (1 in) cubes
2 tbsp olive oil
6 celery stalks, thickly sliced on the diagonal
150 g (5 oz) chestnut mushrooms, quartered
30 g (1 oz) plain flour
salt and black pepper
125 g (4 oz) small carrots
roast potatoes, to serve
parsley sprigs, for garnish

Marinade

450 ml (3/4 pint) red wine
3 tbsp sunflower oil
1 onion, sliced
1 tsp ground allspice
a few parsley sprigs
1 bay leaf

1 Make the marinade: in a large bowl, combine the red wine, oil, onion, allspice, parsley sprigs, and bay leaf. Toss the venison cubes in the marinade to coat them thoroughly, cover, and leave to marinate in the refrigerator, turning occasionally, for 2 days.

2 Lift the venison and onion out of the marinade and pat dry. Strain and reserve the marinade.

3 Heat the oil in a large flameproof casserole, add the venison and onion, and cook for 3–5 minutes until well browned. Lift out and drain on paper towels.

4 Lower the heat, add the celery and mushrooms, and cook for 2–3 minutes until softened. Remove with a slotted spoon. Add the flour and cook, stirring, for 1 minute. Gradually blend in the marinade and bring to a boil, stirring until thickened.

5 Return the venison, onion, celery, and mushrooms to the casserole, and season with salt and pepper. Bring to a boil, cover, and cook in a preheated oven at 160°C (140°C fan, Gas 3) for 1½ hours.

6 Add the carrots, and return to the oven for 30 minutes or until the venison is tender. Serve hot with roast potatoes, and garnish with parsley.

Ruby hare casserole

SERVES 4 **CALS PER SERVING** 1068

1 hare, cut into serving pieces
30 g (1 oz) butter
2 tbsp olive oil
125 g (4 oz) piece of streaky bacon, cut into strips
16 small shallots
250 g (8 oz) chestnut mushrooms, halved
30 g (1 oz) plain flour
900 ml (1½ pints) game stock or chicken stock (page 154)
2 large thyme sprigs
2 large parsley sprigs
salt and black pepper
stuffing balls (page 214)
fresh thyme, to garnish

Marinade

300 ml (½ pint) ruby port
4 tbsp olive oil
1 large onion, sliced
2 bay leaves

1 Make the marinade: in a large bowl, combine the port, oil, onion, and bay leaves. Add the hare pieces, turn in the marinade, cover, and leave to marinate in the refrigerator for 8 hours.

2 Remove the hare from the marinade, reserving the marinade. Melt the butter with the oil in a large flameproof casserole. When the butter is foaming, add the hare pieces and cook over a high heat until browned all over. Lift out and drain on paper towels.

3 Lower the heat, add the bacon and shallots, and cook for 5 minutes or until lightly browned. Add the mushrooms and cook for 2–3 minutes. Remove and drain on paper towels. Add the flour and cook, stirring, for 1 minute. Gradually add the stock and bring to a boil, stirring until thickened.

4 Return the hare, bacon, shallots, and mushrooms to the casserole with the strained marinade. Add the thyme and parsley, season with salt and pepper, and bring to a boil. Cover and cook in a preheated oven at 160°C (140°C fan, Gas 3) for 2 hours.

5 Taste for seasoning. Place the stuffing balls on top, garnish with fresh thyme, and serve hot.

Meat dishes

In this chapter...

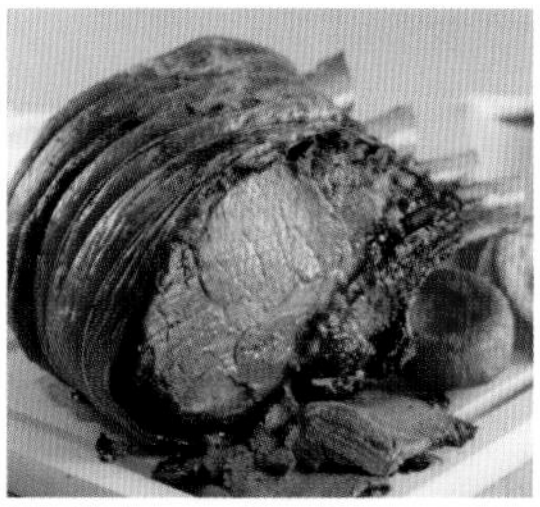
English roast beef
page 238

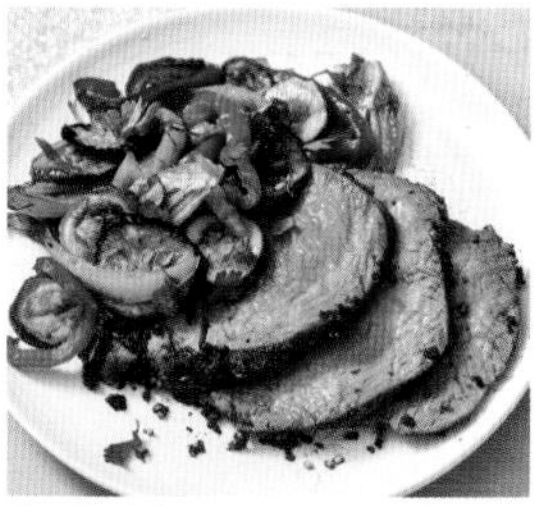
Beef with roast vegetable salad
page 239

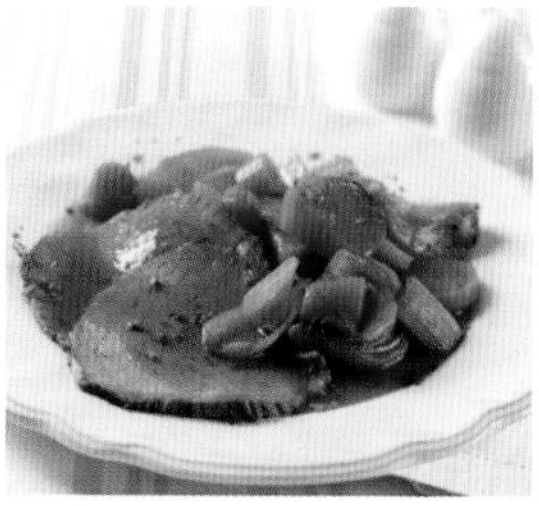
Beef pot roast with winter vegetables
page 240

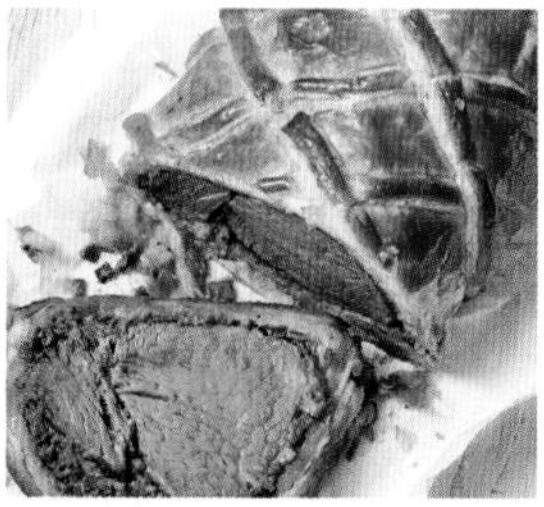
Beef Wellington
page 240

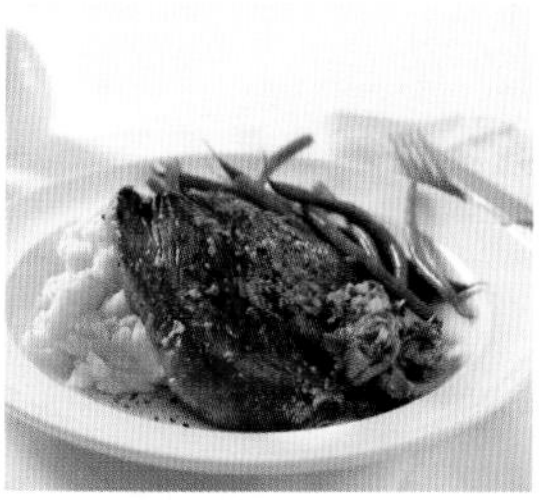
Steaks with smoked oyster relish
page 242

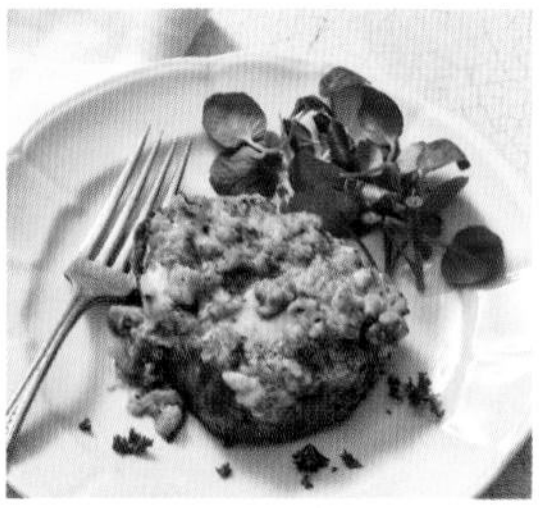
Tournedos Roquefort
page 242

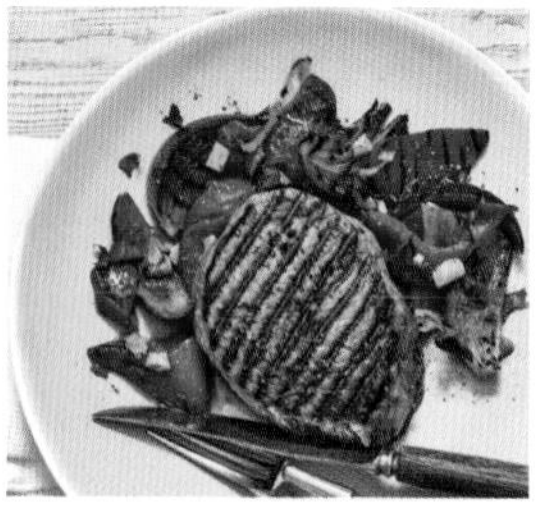
Chargrilled steaks with red vegetables
page 243

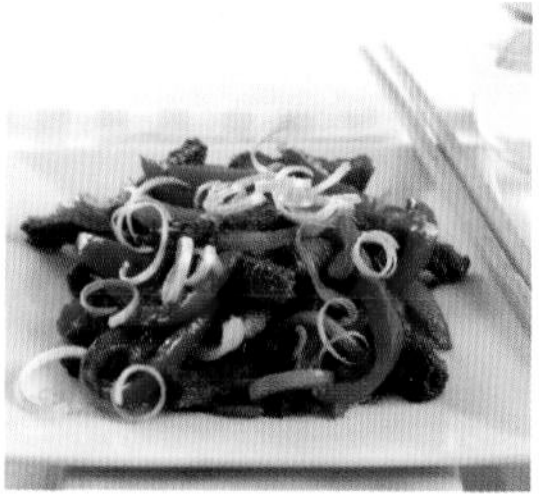
Teriyaki beef
page 244

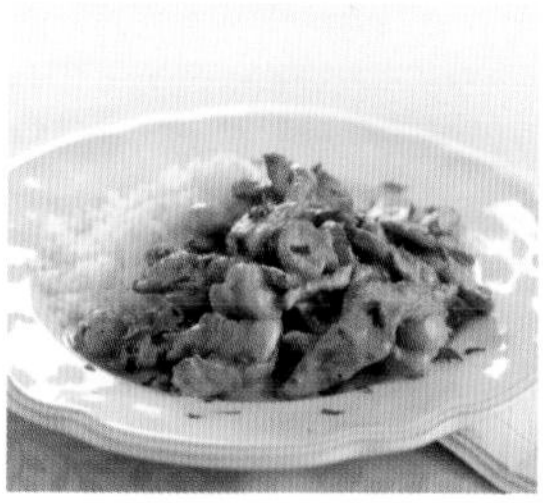
Beef Stroganoff
page 244

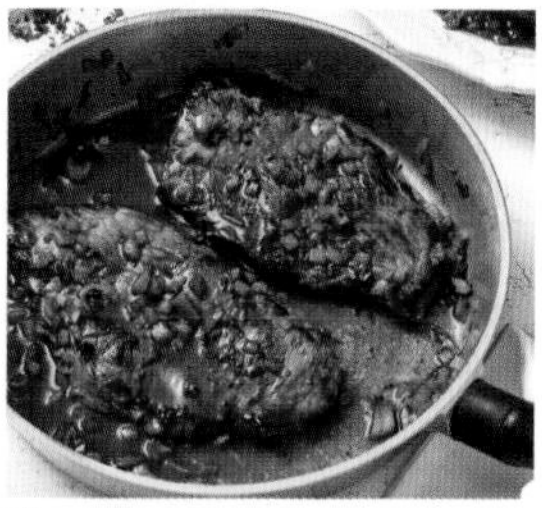
Steak Diane
page 245

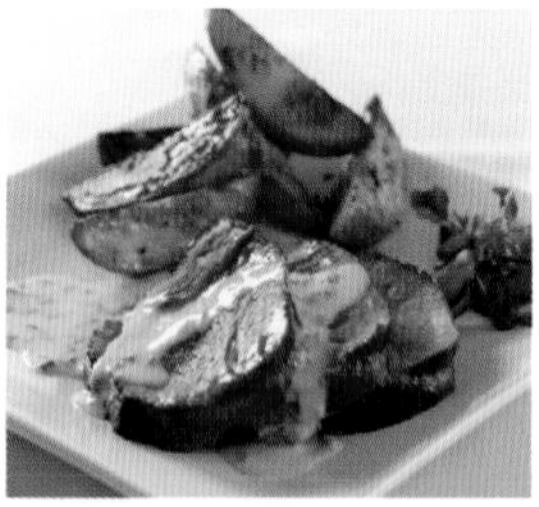
Chateaubriand with béarnaise sauce
page 246

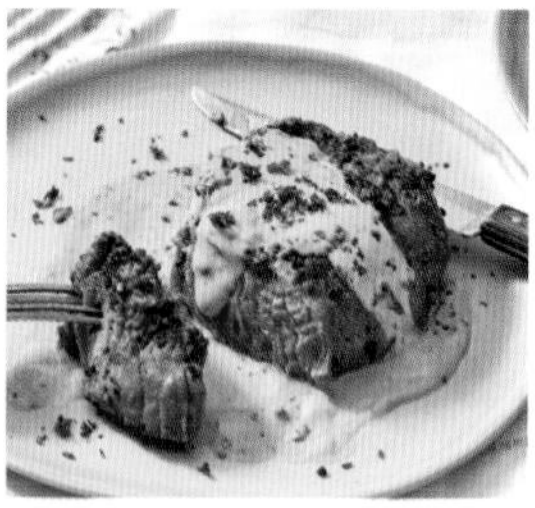
Pepper steaks
page 247

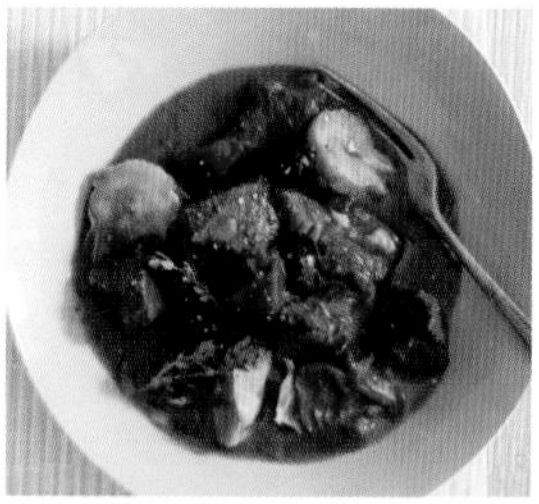
Chianti beef casserole
page 248

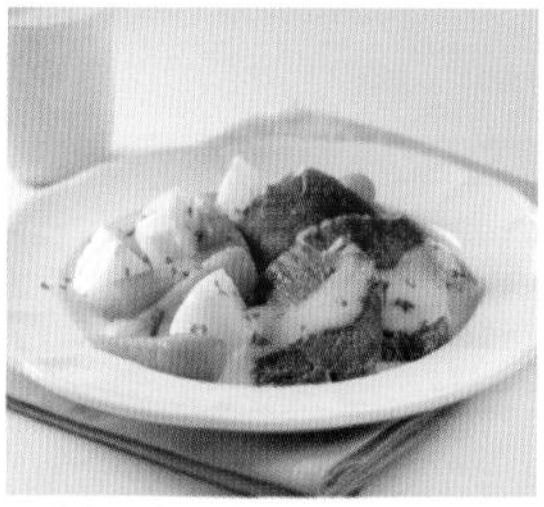
Salt beef with mustard sauce
page 248

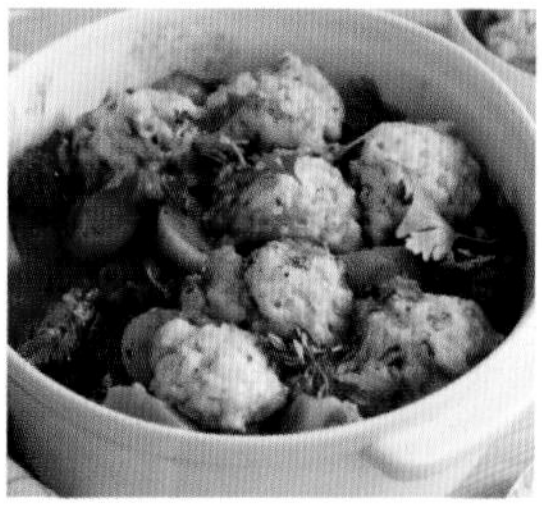
Country beef casserole
page 249

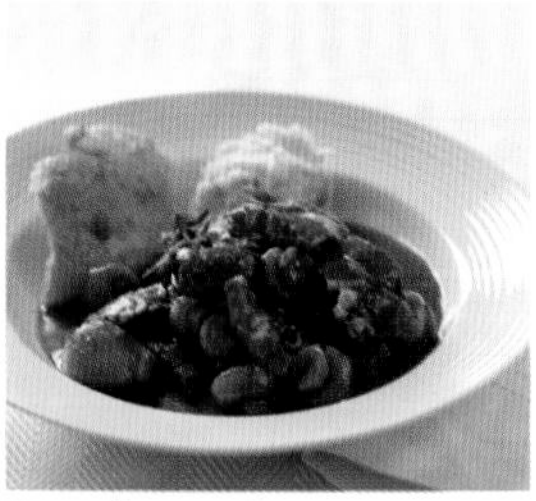
Boeuf bourguignon
page 250

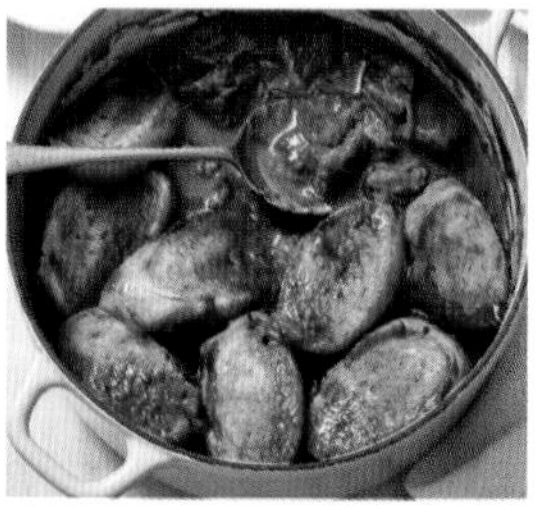
Carbonnade of beef
page 251

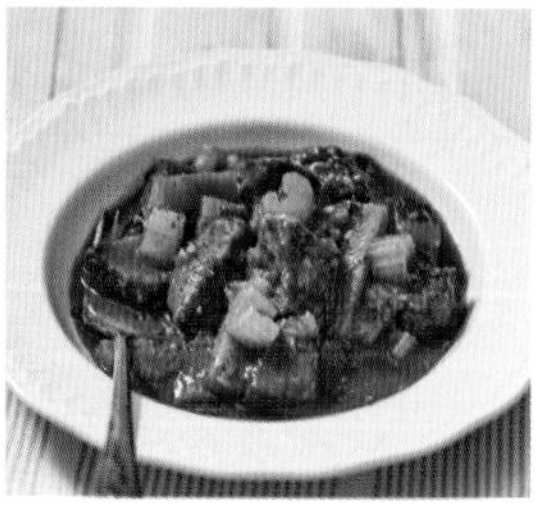
Winter beef casserole
page 252

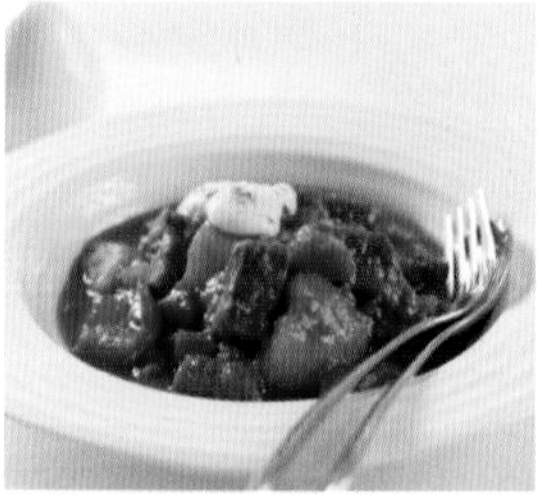
Hungarian goulash
page 252

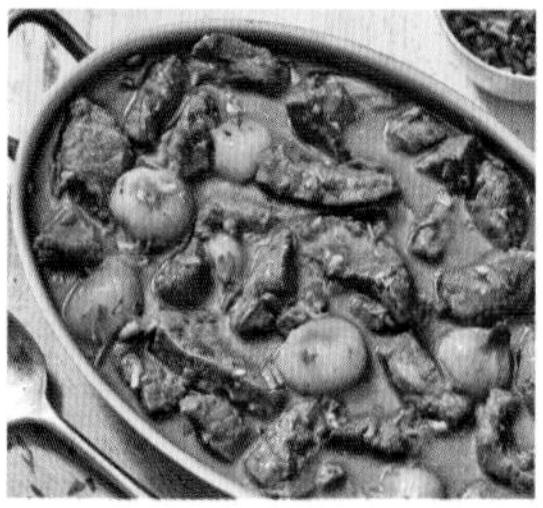
Latimer beef with horseradish
page 253

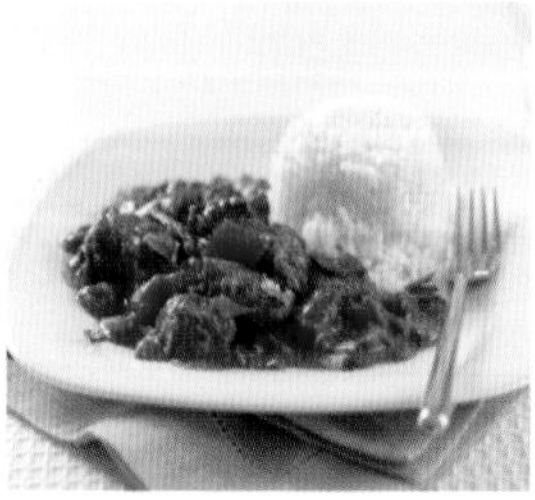
Thai red beef curry
page 254

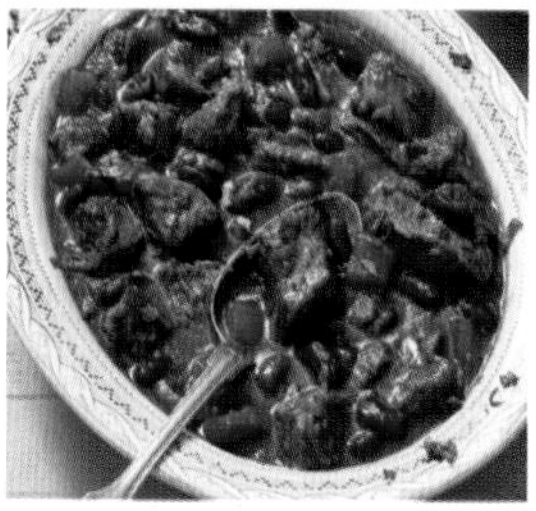
Chilli con carne
page 254

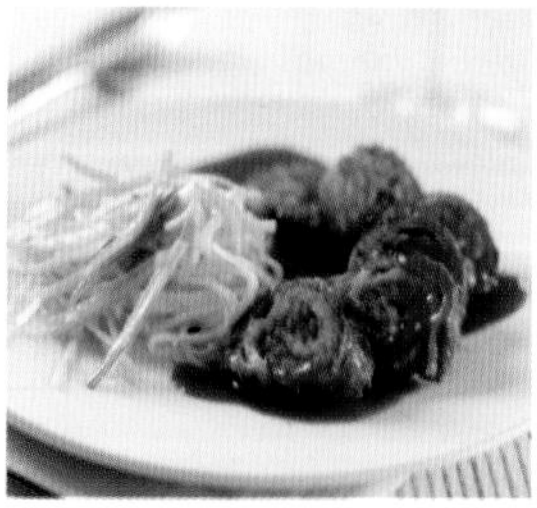
Beef olives with vegetable julienne
page 256

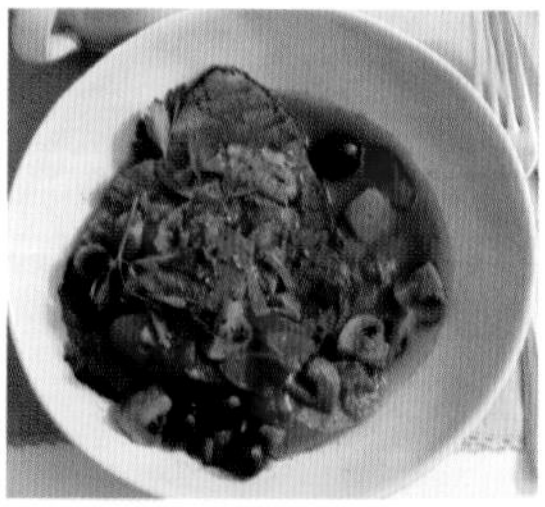
French-style braised beef
page 256

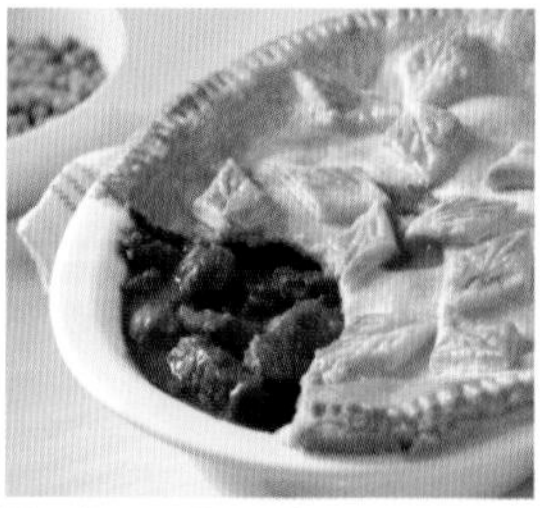
Traditional steak and kidney pie
page 258

Oxtail stew
page 259

Bobotie
page 260

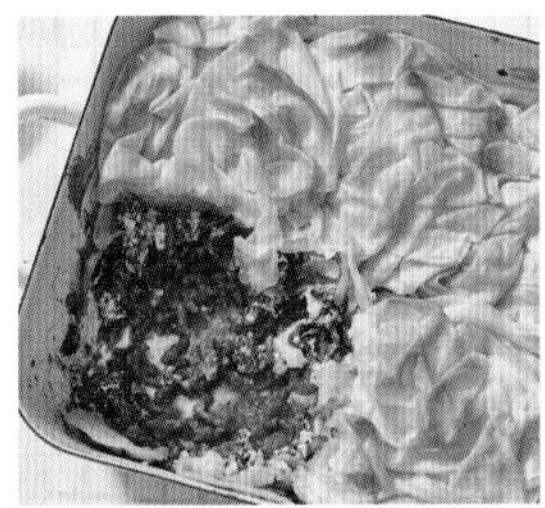
Beef Florentine
page 260

Cottage pies with cheesy potato topping
page 262

Beef tacos
page 263

Beef and bean burritos
page 263

Fajitas
page 264

Corned beef hash
page 265

Meat loaf
page 265

Thai beef burgers
page 265

Meatballs in cider
page 266

Pressed tongue
page 266

Veal Marsala
page 267

Veal with tuna mayonnaise
page 267

Saltimbocca
page 268

Lemon roast veal with spinach stuffing
page 269

Calf's liver with sage
page 270

Veal schnitzels
page 270

Veal stew with olives and peppers
page 271

Osso buco
page 272

Veal chops with mushrooms and cream
page 273

Liver and bacon with onion sauce
page 274

Creamed sweetbreads
page 274

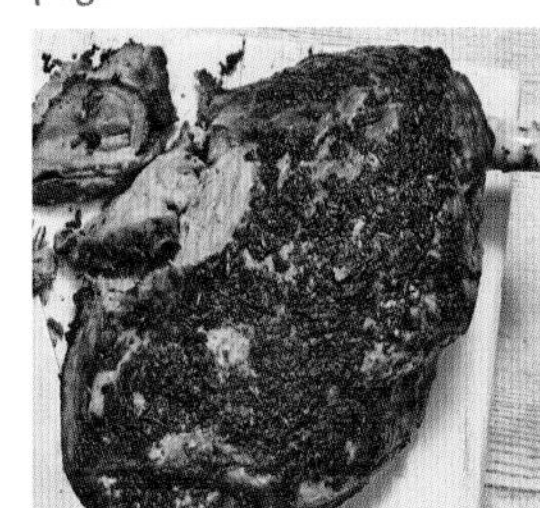
Shoulder of lamb with garlic and herbs
page 275

Slow-roast shoulder of lamb
page 276

In this chapter... *continued*

Beef and onion kebabs
page 292

Shepherd's pie
page 294

Lamb burgers
page 294

Moussaka
page 296

Kidneys turbigo
page 297

Marinated loin of pork with pineapple
page 297

Roast leg of pork
page 298

Slow-roast belly of pork
page 299

Boston baked beans
page 299

Boned loin of pork with apricot stuffing
page 301

Sweet and sour Chinese spare ribs
page 301

Madeira pork with paprika
page 302

Grilled pork chops with mango sauce
page 302

Pork with chilli and coconut
page 304

Pork steaks with mixed peppercorns
page 304

Danish meatballs
page 305

Toad in the hole with onion sauce
page 306

Wiltshire pork casserole
page 306

Sausage cassoulet
page 307

Mustard-glazed ham
page 308

Bacon-wrapped pork in vermouth sauce
page 309

Farmer's bacon bake
page 310

Sausage bake
page 310

Meat know-how

For centuries, meat has been the protein food around which the majority of meals have been planned. Today that tradition has been turned on its head, with healthy eating advice to make meat and other protein foods just one part of a healthy diet, not the major part. Nevertheless, meat is enjoyed by most families several times a week, and it still forms the traditional centrepiece for many celebration meals. By making sure the cooking method suits the cut of meat you are preparing – quick cooking for lean meats, long, slow cooking for tougher cuts – you will always have perfectly moist and tender results.

Buying and storing

If possible, buy your meat from a good local butcher, or the butcher in a supermarket. Your butcher is most likely to have just the cut you want (or will be prepared to cut it for you), and will also advise you how to cook it. Wherever you shop, choose meat that looks fresh and moist (not wet), with a good colour and no greyish tinge. Check that pieces are neatly trimmed, without excess fat and splinters of bone. If the meat is packaged, check the use-by date. Appetites vary, but as a general guide, allow 125–175 g (4–6 oz) of lean boneless meat per person, and about 250 g (8 oz) each if the meat has a reasonable amount of bone.

Store all meat in the refrigerator, with raw kept separate from cooked and on a lower shelf (also below any food that will not be cooked before eating). Mince and offal are more perishable than other kinds of meat, so cook them within 1 day of purchase. Chops, steaks, and joints can be kept for about 3 days: remove the wrapping and replace with fresh. Eat cooked meat within 2–3 days.

Preparing meat for cooking

Trim off excess fat before cooking and remove any visible gristle, sinew, and tough connective tissue. If grilling or frying steaks, chops, or bacon rashers, slash or snip any fat at intervals to prevent the meat from curling up during cooking.

Marinate very lean joints to be roasted or lean cuts to be grilled or barbecued to keep them moist during cooking.

Freezing

Meat to be frozen must be very fresh. Wrap it tightly and thoroughly so that all the air is excluded. Pad any sharp bones so that they don't pierce the wrapping. If packing chops, cutlets, steaks, or hamburgers, separate them with cling film or freezer wrap. The larger the piece of meat the longer it will keep. Mince and sausages can be stored in a freezer for 3 months; offal, chops, and cutlets for 4 months; joints and steaks for 6 months. Thaw frozen meat, in its wrapping and on a plate to catch any juices, at the bottom of the refrigerator.

Microwaving

Because microwave cooking is so fast, meat does not have time to brown and become crisp. This can be overcome by using a special browning dish, which sears meat in the way a frying pan does.

The microwave is very useful for thawing frozen meat. This must be done evenly at the manufacturer's recommended setting to prevent some parts of the meat beginning to cook before others are totally thawed. All wrapping should be removed from the meat before thawing to ensure that the meat does not start to cook.

Meat stock

Ask your butcher to saw 2 kg (4 lb) bones into 6 cm (2½ in) pieces. Beef and veal bones are best.

1 Roast the bones in a preheated oven at 230°C (210°C fan, Gas 8) for 30 minutes. If you have time, add 2–3 roughly chopped onions, carrots, and celery stalks and roast for another 30 minutes.

2 Transfer the bones and vegetables to a large stockpot. Add 4 litres (7 pints) water, a bouquet garni made of 1–2 bay leaves, a few parsley stalks, 1–2 sprigs of thyme, and a few black peppercorns.

3 Bring to a boil. Skim off scum, then cover and simmer for 4–6 hours. Ladle into a sieve to strain. Skim off fat, or let cool and lift off solidified fat.

Basic cooking techniques

Tougher pieces of meat should be cooked slowly by stewing or braising to make them beautifully tender. Those cuts that are naturally tender can be cooked quickly by frying or grilling or by roasting.

Braising

1 Brown the meat on all sides in a flameproof casserole, to add flavour and a rich colour. Remove the meat from the casserole.

2 Add chopped vegetables and cook until they are beginning to brown. Return the meat and add liquid and any flavourings. Bring to a boil, then cover and cook gently on the hob or in the oven, as instructed in the recipe.

Stir-frying

1 Cut the meat into uniform pieces for even cooking. Heat a wok or heavy frying pan, then add a little oil.

2 When the oil is hot, start adding the meat, a little at a time – adding too much at once will lower the temperature of the oil. Using a slotted spoon or a spatula, stir and toss the meat constantly until it is evenly browned.

3 If some of the pieces of meat are cooked before others, they can be pushed up the side of the wok or to the side of the pan where they will keep warm but not overcook.

Grilling and barbecuing

1 Preheat the grill to hot, or light the barbecue (it will take 20–30 minutes to reach cooking temperature unless it is gas, which will heat up immediately).

2 Put the meat on the grill rack and put under the hot grill, or arrange on the grid over charcoal. Brush with oil or a marinade, and cook the meat until it is browned on both sides, turning and re-brushing as necessary.

3 For sausages or thicker pieces of meat that need to be well cooked, reduce the heat or move the meat further away from the heat, and complete cooking.

Stewing

Cut the meat into even cubes. Put into a flameproof casserole with any vegetables and liquid to cover plus any flavourings. Bring to a boil, then cover and simmer on the hob, or cook in the oven. Alternatively, heat some oil in the casserole and brown the cubes of meat, then brown the vegetables. Add the liquid and any flavourings. Bring to a boil, cover, and simmer as above.

Frying and sautéing

1 Dry the meat with paper towels (if too moist it will not brown quickly and evenly). Heat oil or a mixture of oil and butter in a heavy frying pan until it is very hot, then add the meat, taking care not to crowd the pan.

2 Cook until well browned on both sides. Reduce the heat and continue cooking until the meat is done to your taste. When turning meat, use tongs rather than a fork, as a fork pierces the meat and allows the juices to run out.

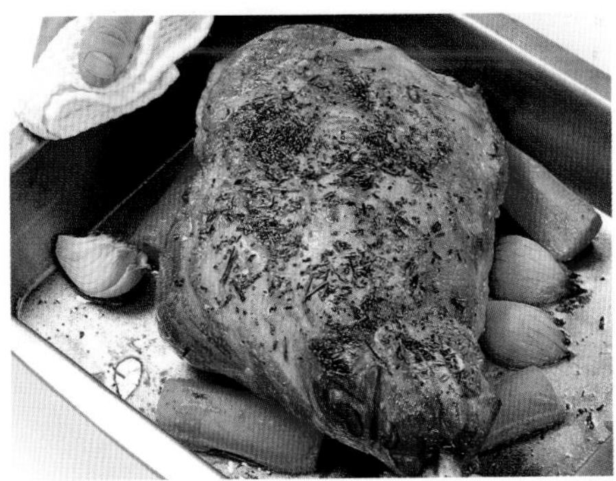

Roasting

1 Take the joint from the refrigerator and allow it to come to room temperature.

2 Preheat the oven. Rub the meat with fat or oil and seasonings, or make incisions all over and insert herbs or slivers of garlic. Insert a meat thermometer, if using.

3 Put the joint and any vegetables in a roasting tin. Roast, basting with the fat and juices in the tin, until cooked to your taste (page 237). If not using a meat thermometer (or an instant-read thermometer), test whether the meat is cooked by inserting a skewer into the centre. If the juices that run out are bloody, the meat is rare; if pink, medium; if clear, well-done.

4 Transfer the joint to a carving board and leave to rest for 10–15 minutes while making gravy. Carve the joint (page 236) and serve.

Boning and butterflying a leg of lamb

A boned leg of lamb is much easier to carve than meat still on the bone. Tunnel boning leaves a pocket that can be filled with a savoury stuffing. If the leg is cut open to lie flat, this is known as butterflying.

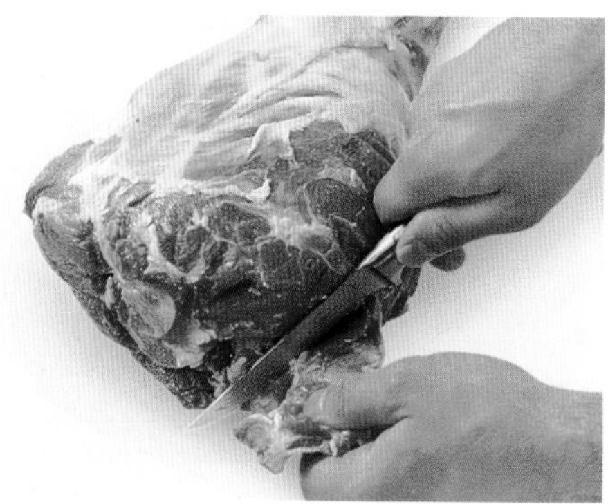

1 To tunnel bone, trim the skin and most or all of the fat from the lamb. Cut around the pelvic bone, at the wide end of the leg, to separate it from the meat. Sever the tendons that connect it to the leg bone. Remove the pelvic bone.

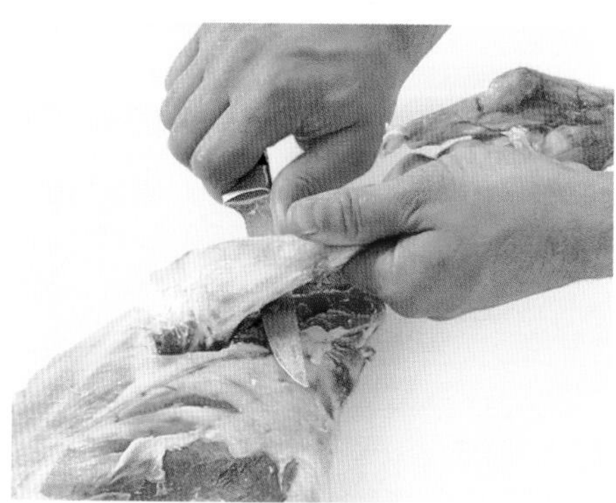

2 At the narrow end of the leg, cut around the shank bone and then scrape the meat away from the whole length of the bone using short strokes.

3 Cut away the meat to expose the joint that joins the shank bone to the leg bone. Sever the tendons and then remove the shank bone.

4 Cut around each end of the leg bone. Ease the leg bone out, cutting and scraping away the meat as you twist and pull the bone out. Trim off the tendons.

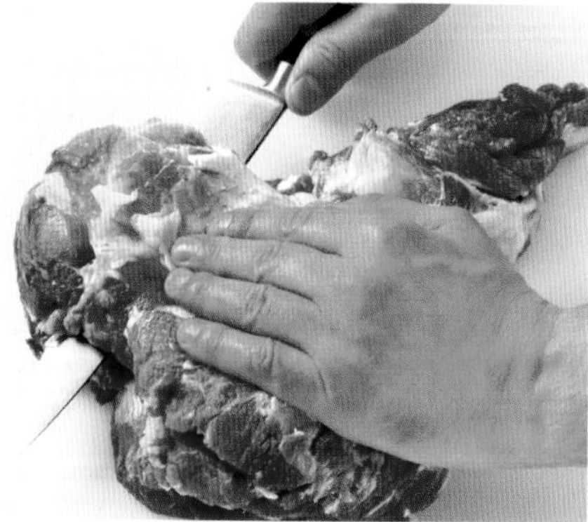

5 If you want to butterfly the boned leg, carefully insert a large chef's knife into the cavity left by the leg bone and cut to one side to slit open the meat.

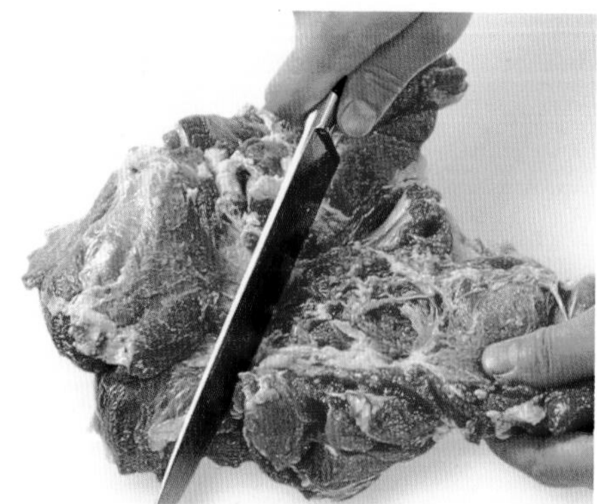

6 Open out the boned leg into a "butterfly" shape. Cut through any thick portions of meat so that the whole leg can be opened out flat and is roughly even in thickness. Trim off excess fat and any remaining tendons.

Boning a shoulder of lamb

A special boning knife, with a narrow, pointed blade, is useful for preparing shoulders of lamb, pork, and veal. If you don't have such a knife, a small, sharp chef's knife can be used instead.

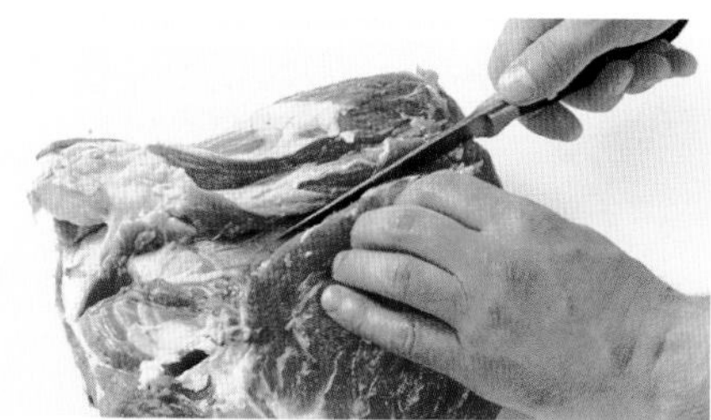

1 Remove the skin and fat. Set the shoulder meat-side up. Cut through the meat to the blade bone, and then cut away the meat on either side, keeping the knife as close to the bone as possible, until the bone is revealed.

2 Cut through the ball and socket joint that lies between the blade bone and the central shoulder bone. This will separate the two bones.

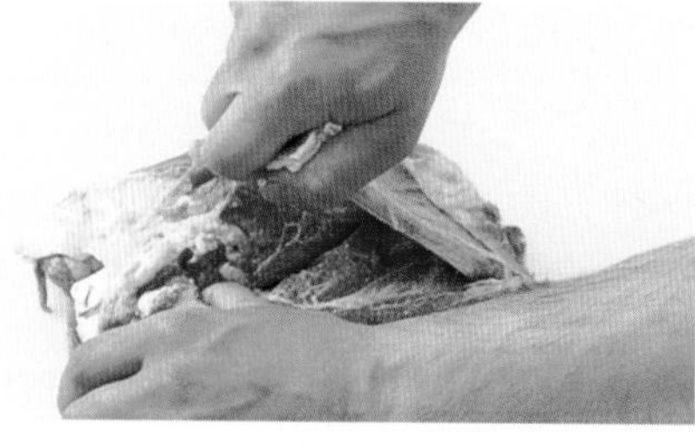

3 Cut beneath the ball and socket joint to free the end. Hold it firmly in one hand and pull the blade bone away from the meat.

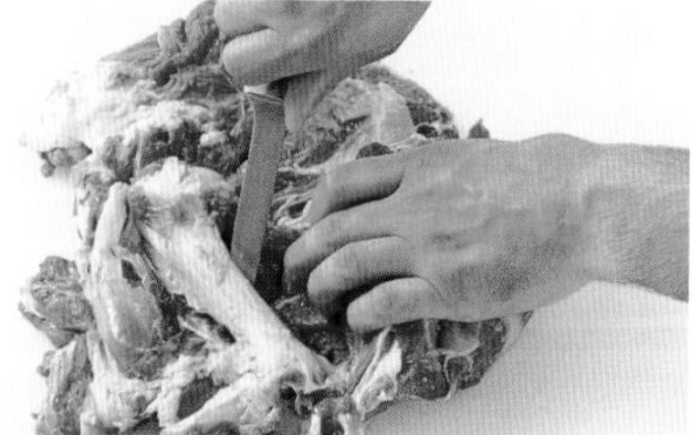

4 Cut around the central shoulder bone, severing the tendons, and cutting and scraping away the meat. Pull out the bone. If necessary, enlarge the pocket left by the bone so that it will accommodate a stuffing.

Stuffing, rolling, and tying a joint

Joints that have been boned and opened out can be rolled around a savoury stuffing, which adds moisture and flavour to the meat during cooking.

1 Open out the meat and spread with an even layer of stuffing, leaving a small border clear around the edge.

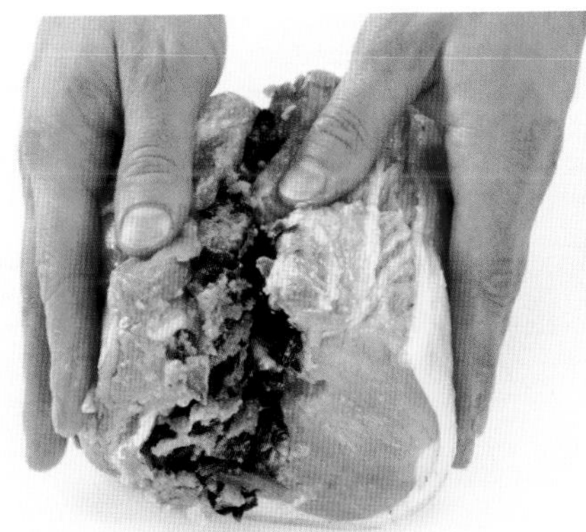

2 Roll up or fold the joint around the stuffing, to make a compact bolster shape. Turn it so that the joint is underneath.

3 Tie string around the meat at regular intervals, to hold it in shape during cooking. Remove the string before carving.

Preparing a best end of neck or rack of lamb

Best end of neck, or rack of lamb, is a tender joint for roasting or grilling. A single rack, which is one side of the upper ribcage, comprises 6–9 cutlets and serves 2–3 people. Two racks can be used to make impressive joints such as a guard of honour or crown roast.

Rack of lamb

1 If the butcher hasn't done so, remove the backbone (chine) from the meaty end. Pull off the skin. Score through the fat and meat 5 cm (2 in) from the ends of the rib bones.

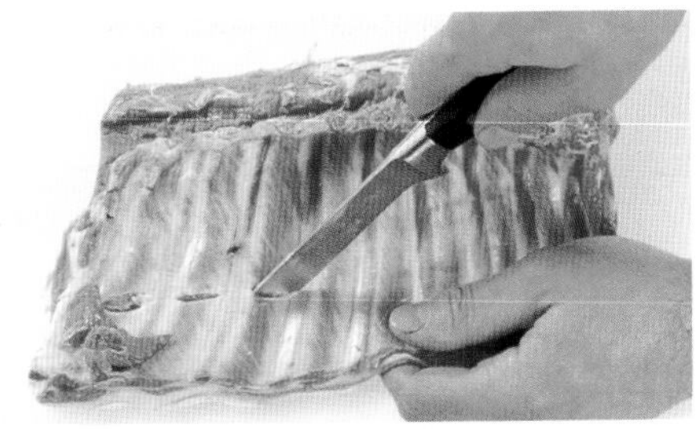

2 Turn the rack over and set it at the edge of the chopping board, so the ends of the rib bones are suspended. Score the meat along the rack, about 5 cm (2 in) from the ends of the rib bones, cutting through the meat to the bones.

3 Cut out the meat from between the bones, cutting from the crosswise cuts to the ends. Scrape the ends of the bones clean.

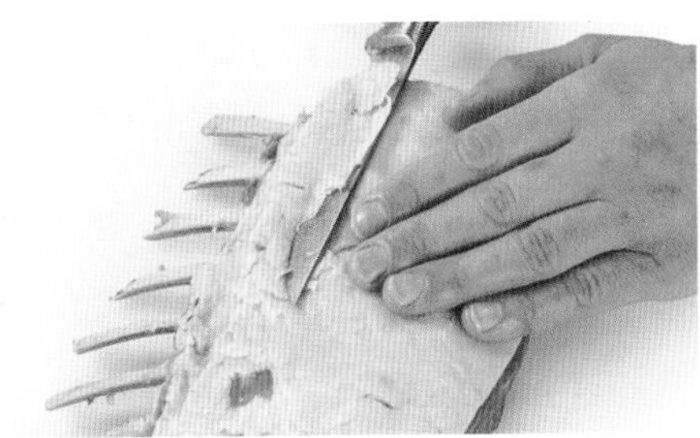

4 Turn the rack over and trim away most of the fat from the meat.

Guard of honour

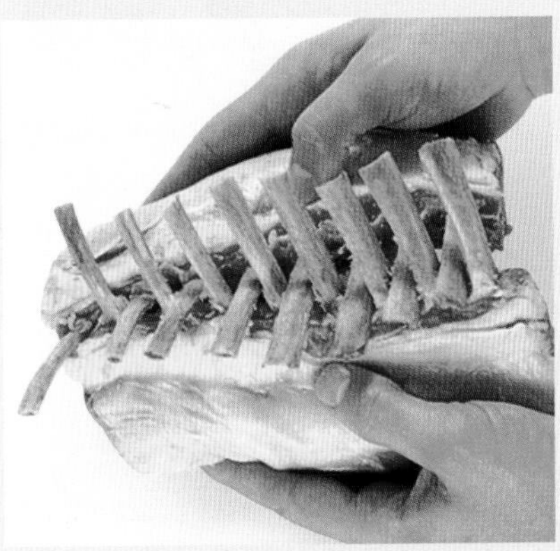

Hold one rack in each hand, meat-side out, and push them together, interlocking the rib bones. Cover the exposed bones with foil, if desired, to prevent them from charring during cooking, then cook as directed in the recipe.

Crown roast

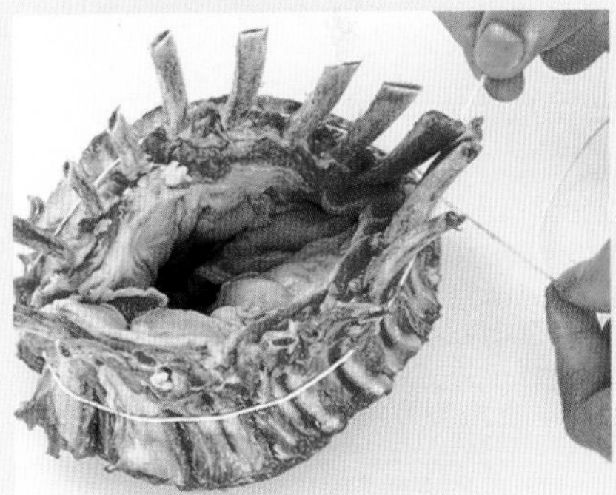

Two racks of lamb are tied together in the shape of a crown.

Prepare two racks as above. Slit the membrane between the rib bones at the meaty end so that the racks can be bent.

Stand the racks, meat-side in, on a work surface and curve to form a crown shape. Bend the bones so that the crown will stand upright.

Tie string around the middle of the two racks, to hold them in place.

Fill the centre of the roast with a stuffing, then roast (or add a filling just before serving). Carve the roast by cutting down between the rib bones.

Carving a joint on the bone

Once a joint of meat has finished cooking, transfer it to a carving board, cover with foil, and let it "rest" in a warm place for 10–15 minutes. During this time, the temperature of the joint will even out, and the flesh will reabsorb most of the juices. To carve, use a very sharp, long carving knife and a two-pronged carving fork.

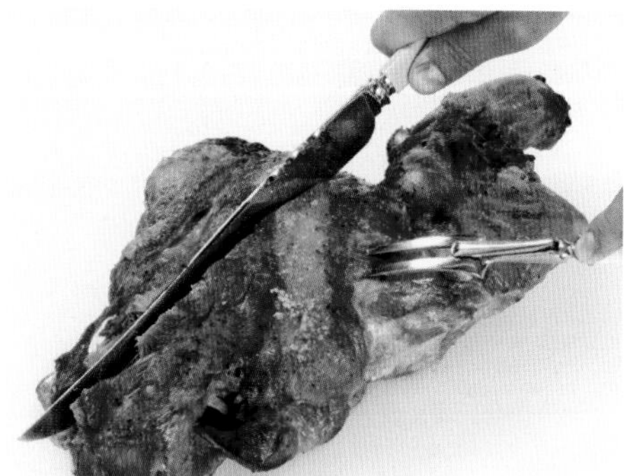

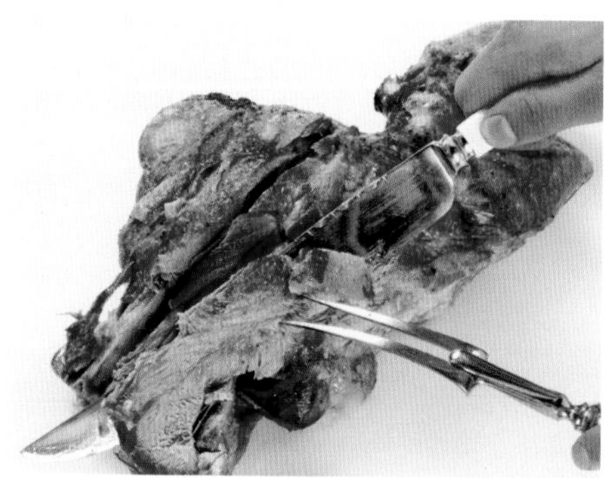

Shoulder of lamb

1 Insert the fork into the shank end. Cut a narrow, wedge-shaped piece from the centre, in the meatiest part between the angle formed by the blade bone and the shoulder bone.

2 Carve neat slices from either side of this wedge-shaped cut until the blade and central shoulder bones are reached. Turn the shoulder over and cut horizontal slices lengthways.

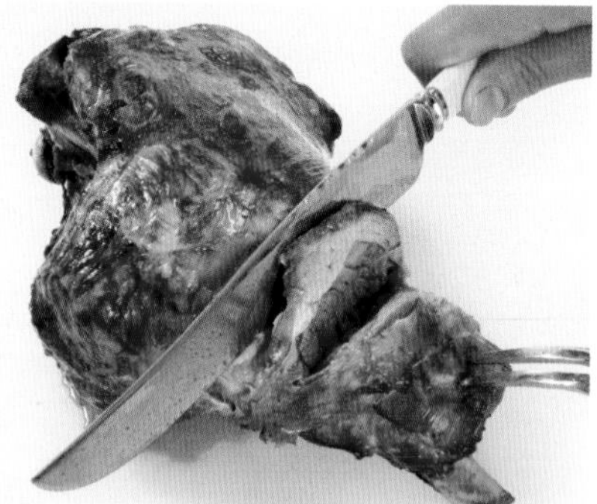

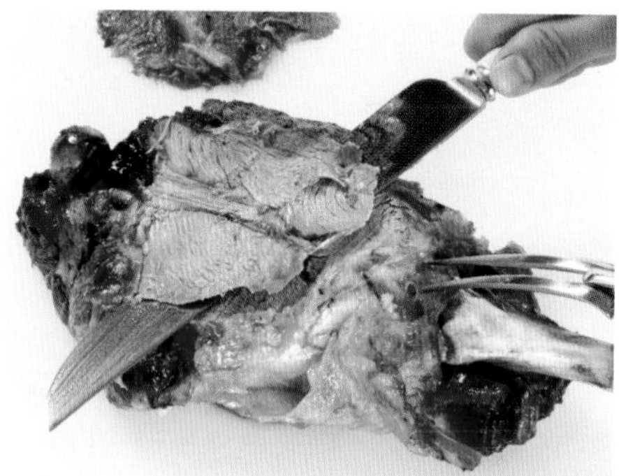

Leg of lamb

1 Set the joint with the meaty side up, and insert the carving fork firmly into the meat at the knuckle end. Cut a narrow, wedge-shaped piece from the centre of the meaty portion, cutting all the way to the bone.

2 Carve neat slices from either side of this wedge-shaped cut, gradually changing the angle of the knife to make the slices larger. Turn the leg over. Trim off the fat, then carve off horizontal slices.

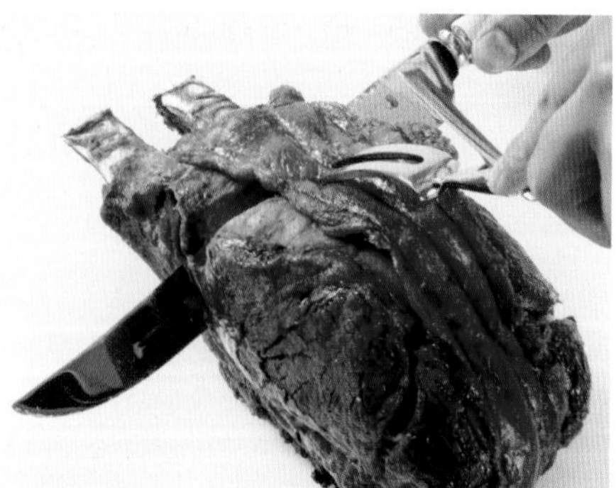

Rib of beef

1 Set the roast upright on a carving board, insert the carving fork into the meaty side, to steady the joint, and cut close to the large rib bones at the base of the meat, to remove them.

2 Hold the now boneless roast upright on the board. With the knife at a slight angle, carve the meat into slices that are about 2 cm (¾ in) thick.

Whole ham

1 Cut a few horizontal slices from one side of the ham, to make a flat surface. Turn the ham over on to this surface. Insert the carving fork into the meat at the shank end. Make three or four cuts through to the bone at the shank end.

2 Insert the knife into the last cut and slide it along the bone, to detach the slices. Make a few more cuts in the ham and continue to remove the slices in the same way. Turn over and carve off horizontal slices.

Using a meat thermometer

The most accurate way to test if a large piece of meat is cooked is to use a meat thermometer, which registers the internal temperature. Before cooking, insert the spike of the thermometer into the middle or thickest part of the joint. Make sure that the thermometer does not touch a bone as bones become hotter than meat and will therefore give a false reading. Start checking the temperature reading towards the end of the suggested cooking time. Alternatively, use an instant-read thermometer, which is inserted near the end of the calculated cooking time. A joint will continue to cook by retained heat for 5–10 minutes after it is removed from the oven.

Making gravy

A delicious gravy can be made from the richly flavoured sediment and juices from roasting meat. Boost flavour with a splash of red or fortified wine, redcurrant jelly, Worcestershire sauce, or lemon juice, to taste.

1 Pour all but about 2 tbsp fat from the roasting tin, leaving the juices and sediments. Set the tin on the hob and heat until sizzling. Stir in 2 tbsp plain flour. Whisk briskly to mix the flour with the juices, and scrape the bottom and sides of the tin to dislodge any sediment and make a well-browned paste.

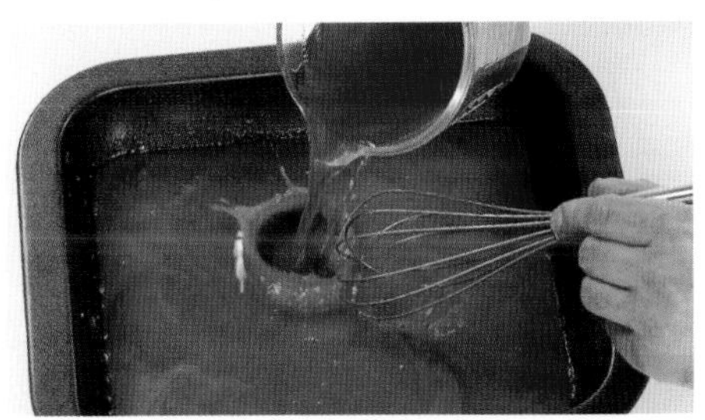

2 Gradually add 1 litre (1¾ pints) stock or vegetable cooking water, whisking constantly to combine with the flour paste. Whisk until smooth. Simmer, stirring frequently, until the gravy reaches the desired consistency. Season and flavour to taste, then strain if wished. Serve piping hot, in a warmed gravy boat.

Preparing offal

Although not as popular as it used to be, offal, which includes liver, kidneys, sweetbreads, and tongue, is both nutritious and delicious. Flavour and texture vary according to the animal from which the offal comes – offal from veal has the most delicate flavour and texture; offal from pork has the strongest and toughest.

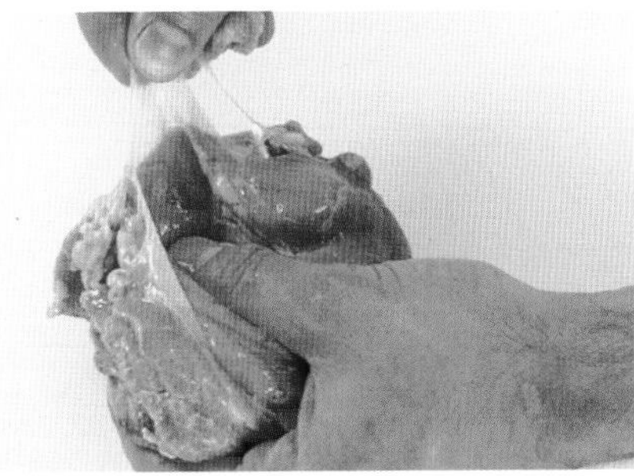

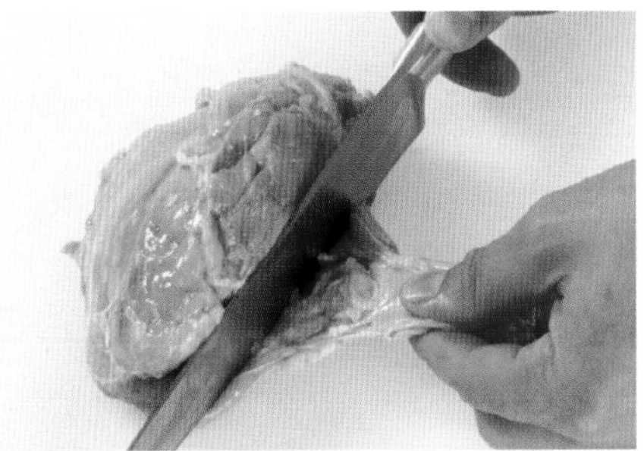

Sweetbreads

1 Soak the sweetbreads in cold water with 1 tbsp lemon juice for 2–3 hours to clean them. Drain, and rinse well. Cut away any discoloured parts. Use your fingers to carefully peel off the thin membrane surrounding the sweetbreads.

2 Cut 1away the ducts and any fat and discard. Don't remove too much or the sweetbreads will break up. Put into a saucepan of cold water and bring to a boil. Blanch calf's sweetbreads for 5 minutes, and lamb's sweetbreads for 3 minutes.

Lamb's kidneys

1 (If using beef or veal kidneys, first separate them.) Carefully cut through any fine membrane around each kidney and use your fingers to peel it off (cut the ducts from beef or veal kidneys).

2 Set each kidney round-side up and slice lengthways in half (or leave attached at the base, according to recipe directions). With a sharp pair of scissors, snip out the small fatty, white core and the tubes.

Roasting meat

As all ovens are different, these times are intended as a general guide only. When calculating timings, add an extra 500 g (1 lb) on the weight of your joint if it weighs less than 1.5 kg (3 lb). Be sure to preheat the oven before putting the meat in to cook.

Meat		Oven temperature	Time	Internal temperature
Beef	Rare	180°C (160°C fan, Gas 4)	15 mins per 500 g (1 lb)	60°C (140°F)
	Medium	180°C (160°C fan, Gas 4)	20 mins per 500 g (1 lb)	70°C (160°F)
	Well-done	180°C (160°C fan, Gas 4)	25 mins per 500 g (1 lb)	80°C (175°F)
Veal	Well-done	180°C (160°C fan, Gas 4)	25 mins per 500 g (1 lb)	80°C (175°F)
Lamb	Medium rare	180°C (160°C fan, Gas 4)	20 mins per 500 g (1 lb)	75°C (170°F)
	Well-done	180°C (160°C fan, Gas 4)	25 mins per 500 g (1 lb)	80°C (175°F)
Pork	Medium	180°C (160°C fan, Gas 4)	25 mins per 500 g (1 lb)	80°C (175°F)
	Well-done	180°C (160°C fan, Gas 4)	30 mins per 500 g (1 lb)	85°C (180°F)

English roast beef

SERVES 8 **CALS PER SERVING** 394

3.25 kg (6½ lb) prime rib of beef on the bone
vegetable oil, for brushing
salt and black pepper
1 onion, quartered

To serve

Yorkshire puddings (see box, opposite)
gravy of your choice (page 268)
horseradish sauce (see box, right)

1 Insert a meat thermometer, if using, into the middle of the meat. Put the beef into a roasting tin, brush all over the meat with oil, and season with salt and pepper. Add the onion quarters to the tin and roast with the beef in a preheated oven at 200°C (180°C fan, Gas 6) for 20 minutes.

2 Meanwhile, make the Yorkshire pudding batter and set aside.

3 After the beef has been roasting for 20 minutes, baste it with the juices from the tin, and lower the oven temperature to 180°C (160°C fan, Gas 4).

4 Roast, basting frequently, for a further 1½ hours for rare beef, 1¾ hours for medium, and 2 hours for well-done, or until the meat thermometer registers 60°C (140°F), 70°C (160°F), or 80°C (175°F).

5 Transfer the beef to a carving board, cover with foil, and leave to stand in a warm place. Increase the oven temperature to 220°C (200°C fan, Gas 7) and bake the Yorkshire puddings.

6 While the puddings are in the oven and the meat is resting, make the gravy in the roasting tin according to the instructions on page 268.

7 Serve the beef with the Yorkshire puddings, gravy, and horseradish sauce.

Horseradish sauce

Mix 2–3 tbsp grated fresh horseradish with 1 tbsp white wine vinegar in a bowl. In another bowl, whisk 150 ml (¼ pint) whipping cream until thick. Fold the cream into the horseradish mixture, and add salt, black pepper, and caster sugar to taste. Cover and leave to chill until ready to serve.

Yorkshire puddings

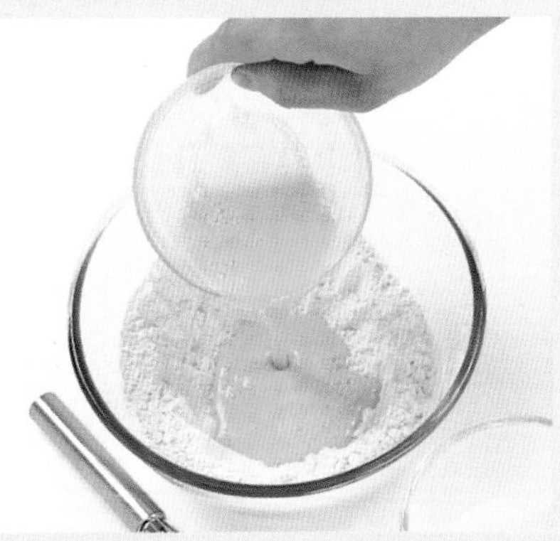

Sift 125 g (4 oz) plain flour and a pinch of salt into a bowl. Make a well, and add 3 beaten eggs and a little milk taken from 200 ml (7 fl oz).

Whisk the milk and egg together in the well with a little of the flour from the sides, then whisk in the remaining milk, gradually drawing in all of the flour to make a smooth batter.

Put some white vegetable fat into each cup of a 12-hole bun tin and heat in a preheated oven at 220°C (200°C fan, Gas 7) until very hot. Remove the tin from the oven. Whisk the batter and pour into the cups in the tin. Bake the Yorkshire puddings in the oven for 15 minutes or until well risen, golden, and crisp. Serve immediately.

Beef with roast vegetable salad

SERVES 4–6 **CALS PER SERVING** 522–348

1 kg (2 lb) beef fillet cut from the centre, trimmed
2 tbsp tapenade (black olive paste)
1 tbsp black peppercorns, coarsely crushed
2 tbsp olive oil
chopped parsley, to garnish

Roast vegetable salad

1 tbsp olive oil
1 aubergine, cut into 5 mm (¼ in) slices
3 courgettes, cut into 5 mm (¼ in) slices
1 fennel bulb, cut lengthways into 5 mm (¼ in) pieces
1 red pepper, halved, deseeded, and cut into 5 mm (¼ in) strips
1 yellow pepper, halved, deseeded, and cut into 5 mm (¼ in) strips
salt and black pepper
2 tsp balsamic vinegar

1 Tie the beef to retain its shape, if necessary. Spread the tapenade all over the beef, then press on the peppercorns.

2 Pour the oil into a deep roasting tin and heat in a preheated oven at 220°C (200°C fan, Gas 7).

3 Insert a meat thermometer, if using, into the middle of the beef.

4 Put the beef into the hot oil, and roast for 25 minutes for rare beef, 35 minutes for medium, or 40 minutes for well-done, or until the meat thermometer registers 60°C (140°F), 70°C (160°F), or 75°C (170°F).

5 Meanwhile, put the olive oil for the roast vegetable salad into a large bowl. Add the aubergine, courgettes, fennel, and red and yellow peppers, and toss in the oil.

6 When the beef is cooked to your liking, remove it from the roasting tin and leave until cold. Meanwhile, put the vegetables into the hot tin and sprinkle with salt and pepper. Cook in the oven, turning the vegetables once, for 30 minutes or until tender. Leave to cool, then sprinkle with the balsamic vinegar and toss to coat.

7 When the beef is cold, slice very thinly and serve with the roast vegetable salad. Garnish with parsley.

Beef pot roast with winter vegetables

SERVES 6 **CALS PER SERVING** 360

2 tbsp sunflower oil
1.15 kg (2½ lb) beef, topside or silverside
4 onions, quartered
1 large swede, cut into thick chunks
2 celery stalks, thickly sliced
2 large carrots, thickly sliced
150 ml (¼ pint) dry white wine
150 ml (¼ pint) hot water
1 bouquet garni
salt and black pepper
chopped parsley, to garnish

1 Heat the sunflower oil in a large flameproof casserole. Add the beef and cook over a high heat, turning occasionally, for about 10 minutes until browned all over.

2 Lift the beef out of the casserole and put in the onions, swede, celery, and carrots. Stir well to coat the vegetables in the oil, then cook, stirring occasionally, for about 5 minutes.

3 Push the vegetables to the side of the casserole, and place the meat in the middle, with the vegetables around it.

4 Add the wine, measured water, and bouquet garni, and season with salt and pepper. Bring to a boil, then cover tightly, and cook in a preheated oven at 150°C (130°C fan, Gas 2) for 2½–3 hours until the meat is tender.

5 Transfer the meat and vegetables to a warmed platter, cover, and keep warm.

6 Spoon the fat from the surface of the cooking liquid, then boil over a high heat until the liquid is reduced by half. Taste for seasoning, and strain into a warmed gravy boat. Carve the meat into thin slices, serve with the vegetables and gravy, and garnish with parsley.

Wrapping the beef in pastry

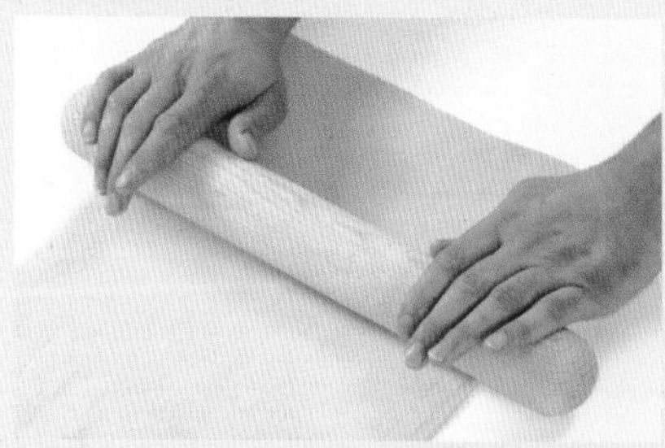

Roll out 300 g (10 oz) of the pastry to a 30 x 40 cm (12 x 16 in) rectangle. Spread half of the pâté mixture down the middle, leaving a 10 cm (4 in) border on each side.

Remove the string from the beef and place the beef on the pâté mixture. Cover with remaining pâté mixture.

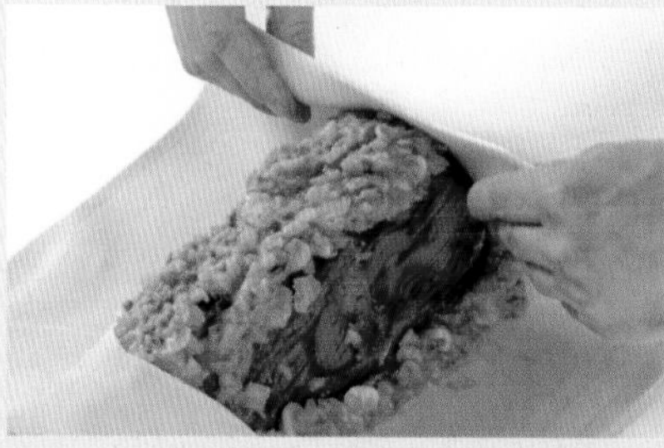

Brush the pastry border with beaten egg. Fold the short sides of the pastry over the beef.

Fold over the long ends and turn the parcel over. Brush with beaten egg. Roll out the remaining pastry, and cut into strips, 5 mm (¼ in) wide. Arrange in a lattice pattern on top of the pastry, then glaze the strips with beaten egg.

Beef Wellington

Inside a puff pastry case is a succulent piece of prime beef and a rich stuffing of liver pâté and mushrooms. The pastry locks in all the juices and ensures none of the wonderful flavours are lost. Serve with a mushroom and red wine gravy.

SERVES 8 **CALS PER SERVING** 580

1.5 kg (3 lb) beef fillet, trimmed and tied
salt and black pepper
2 tbsp sunflower oil
45 g (1½ oz) butter
1 small onion, finely chopped
250 g (8 oz) flat mushrooms, finely chopped
175 g (6 oz) smooth liver pâté
400 g (13 oz) ready-made puff pastry
1 egg, beaten
thin mushroom gravy, to serve (page 268)

1 Season the beef with black pepper. Heat the oil in a large frying pan, add the beef, and cook over a high heat until browned all over.

2 Put the beef fillet in a roasting tin and cook in a preheated oven at 220°C (200°C fan, Gas 7) for 25 minutes for rare beef, 35 minutes for medium, or 40 minutes for well-done. Leave to cool completely.

3 Meanwhile, melt the butter in the frying pan, add the onion and mushrooms, and cook, stirring, for 3 minutes or until softened. Increase the heat to high, and cook until the excess moisture has evaporated. Turn into a bowl and leave to cool completely.

4 Add the liver pâté to the mushroom and onion mixture, season with salt and pepper, and stir well to combine.

5 Wrap the beef and pâté mixture in the pastry (see box, left).

6 Bake at 220°C (200°C fan, Gas 7) for 45 minutes or until the pastry is crisp and golden. Cover with foil after 30 minutes to prevent the pastry becoming too brown. Leave to stand for about 10 minutes, then slice and serve with the gravy.

INDIVIDUAL BEEF WELLINGTONS

Cut the raw beef into eight slices. Brown the slices in a frying pan, cool, then wrap each one in pastry with a little of the pâté mixture. Bake for 25–30 minutes.

Steaks with smoked oyster relish

SERVES 4 **CALS PER SERVING** 278

4 x 175 g (6 oz) rump steaks
salt and black pepper
2 garlic cloves, crushed
1 tbsp olive oil
smoked oyster relish (see box, right) and lemon wedges, to serve

1 Season the steaks with salt and pepper, rub with the garlic, and brush with the oil.

2 Heat a frying pan over a high heat, add the steaks, and cook for 3–4 minutes on each side for rare steaks, 4–5 minutes for medium steaks, or 7–8 minutes for well-done steaks. Transfer the steaks to warmed serving plates.

3 Generously spoon the smoked oyster relish over the steaks, and serve at once, accompanied by mashed potatoes and green beans.

CLASSIC CARPETBAG STEAKS

Melt 15 g (½ oz) butter and cook 2 chopped shallots until softened. Remove from the heat and add 6 chopped fresh oysters, 125 g (4 oz) fresh breadcrumbs, 1 tbsp chopped parsley, and salt and pepper. Cut a pocket in each steak and fill with the stuffing.

Smoked oyster relish

Drain 1 x 100 g can smoked oysters. Finely chop 1 small onion and 1 handful of parsley sprigs.

Chop the drained smoked oysters with a large, sharp chef's knife.

Put the oysters, onion, and parsley into a small bowl and mix well. Chill until needed.

Tournedos Roquefort

SERVES 4 **CALS PER SERVING** 430

125 g (4 oz) Roquefort cheese, crumbled
60 g (2 oz) walnut pieces, roughly chopped
30 g (1 oz) butter, softened
salt and black pepper
4 x 125 g (4 oz) tournedos (small fillet steaks), 2.5 cm (1 in) thick
chopped parsley, to garnish

1 In a small bowl, combine the Roquefort, walnuts, butter, and pepper to taste.

2 Season the tournedo steaks on both sides with salt and pepper, and place them under a hot grill, 7–10 cm (3–4 ins) from the heat. Grill for 3–4 minutes on each side for rare steaks, 4–5 minutes for medium steaks, or 7–8 minutes for well-done steaks.

3 Two minutes before the steaks are ready, sprinkle with the Roquefort mixture, and return to the hot grill until the cheese has melted. Serve hot, garnished with chopped parsley.

Chargrilled steaks with red vegetables

SERVES 6 **CALS PER SERVING** 258

6 x 150 g (5 oz) fillet steaks
2 roasted red peppers in olive oil (from a jar), cut into strips, with oil reserved
salt and black pepper
2 red onions, cut into chunky wedges
2 garlic cloves, coarsely chopped
2 tbsp lime juice
fresh coriander, to garnish

1 Heat a ridged cast iron chargrill pan over a medium heat until very hot. Brush the fillet steaks with a little of the reserved oil from the peppers, and season with salt and pepper. When the pan is hot, chargrill the steaks for about 3–4 minutes on each side for rare meat, 4–5 minutes on each side for medium, and 7–8 minutes on each side for well-done. Remove the steaks from the pan and leave to rest.

2 Turn down the heat under the pan to low, add the red onion wedges, and cook for about 5–8 minutes, turning them occasionally, until they are charred and softened. Add the red pepper strips, the garlic and lime juice, and stir-fry for 1–2 minutes until hot and sizzling. Season with salt and pepper.

3 Serve the steaks whole or sliced thickly on the diagonal, with a garnish of fresh coriander and the red peppers and onions spooned alongside.

Teriyaki beef

SERVES 4 **CALS PER SERVING** 329

500 g (1 lb) rump steak, trimmed and cut into thin strips
2 tbsp sunflower oil
1 large onion, thinly sliced
1 red pepper, halved, deseeded, and cut into strips
2 spring onions, sliced lengthways, to garnish

Marinade

125 ml (4 fl oz) dark soy sauce
90 ml (3 fl oz) Japanese rice wine or dry sherry
2 tbsp caster sugar

1 Make the marinade: in a bowl, combine the soy sauce, rice wine or sherry, and sugar. Toss the steak strips in the marinade, cover, and leave in the refrigerator overnight.

2 Remove the steak strips from the marinade, reserving the marinade. Heat 1 tbsp of the oil in a wok, add the onion and red pepper, and stir-fry for about 2 minutes. Remove from the wok with a slotted spoon and set aside. Heat the remaining oil, and stir-fry the steak strips for 5 minutes or until just cooked through.

3 Return the onion and red pepper to the wok with the marinade and cook for 2 minutes or until heated through. Garnish with the spring onions before serving.

Beef Stroganoff

SERVES 6 **CALS PER SERVING** 329

30 g (1 oz) butter
1 tbsp sunflower oil
750 g (1½ lb) rump steak, trimmed and cut into strips (see box, right)
8 shallots, quartered
300 g (10 oz) button mushrooms, halved
salt and black pepper
300 ml (½ pint) soured cream
chopped parsley, to garnish

1 Melt the butter with the oil in a large frying pan. When the butter is foaming, add the steak strips, in batches if necessary, and cook over a high heat for 5 minutes or until browned all over. Remove from the pan with a slotted spoon.

2 Add the shallots and mushrooms and cook for about 5 minutes until browned.

3 Return the steak strips to the pan, and season with salt and pepper. Stir in the soured cream and heat gently. Garnish with the chopped parsley, and serve at once with boiled rice (page 354).

Cutting the beef

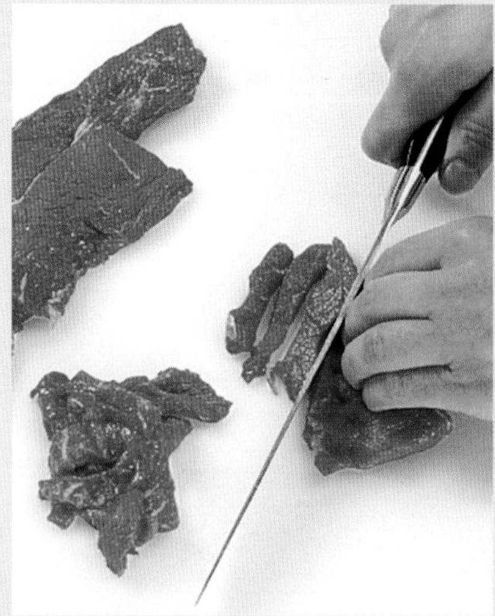

Slice the beef at an angle into thin strips, 5 mm (¼ in) wide and 5 cm (2 in) long, using a sharp chef's knife.

Steak Diane

SERVES 4 **CALS PER SERVING** 373

4 x 150–175 g (5–6 oz) rump steaks, trimmed
30 g (1 oz) butter
2 tbsp sunflower oil
3 tbsp brandy
1 small onion, finely chopped
300 ml (½ pint) beef stock
2 tbsp Worcestershire sauce
1 tbsp lemon juice
1 tbsp chopped parsley
salt and black pepper

1 Place the steaks between two sheets of greaseproof paper and pound with a rolling pin until 5 mm (¼ in) thick.

2 Melt the butter with the sunflower oil in a large frying pan. When the butter is foaming, add the pounded steaks and cook over a high heat for about 3 minutes on each side until browned. Lift the steaks out of the frying pan and cover with foil to keep warm.

3 Pour the brandy into the pan, and add the onion. Cook over a high heat, stirring occasionally, for a few minutes until the onion has softened and absorbed most of the brandy. Stir in the stock, Worcestershire sauce, lemon juice, and parsley, season with salt and pepper, and cook for about 2 minutes.

4 Return the steaks to the pan and spoon over the sauce. Reheat quickly and briefly, and serve hot.

Chateaubriand with béarnaise sauce

SERVES 2 **CALS PER SERVING** 761

400 g (13 oz) Chateaubriand steak (a thick piece of fillet from the middle of the tenderloin)
30 g (1 oz) butter, melted
black pepper
béarnaise sauce (see box, right)

1 Cut the steak crosswise in half. Brush one side of each half with melted butter and season with pepper.

2 Put the steaks, buttered-side up, under a hot grill, 7 cm (3 in) from the heat, and cook for 2 minutes or until browned. Turn the steaks over, brush with melted butter, and season with pepper. Grill for about 2 minutes until browned.

3 Lower the heat and cook, turning once and brushing with the butter, for 4–5 minutes. Cover and leave to stand for 5 minutes. Slice the steaks, and serve with the béarnaise sauce.

Béarnaise sauce

Put 4 tbsp tarragon vinegar, 1 finely chopped shallot, and 1 tbsp chopped tarragon into a pan and boil for a few minutes until reduced by one-third. Leave to cool. Pour 2 egg yolks into a bowl over a saucepan of simmering water, add the vinegar mixture, and whisk over a gentle heat until thick and fluffy.

Melt 90 g (3 oz) butter and gradually add to the sauce, whisking constantly until thick. Season with salt and white pepper.

Savoury butters

These simple butters are quickly made, and ideal for adding an elegant touch to plain grilled meats such as steaks, chops, and noisettes.

Anchovy butter
Soften 125 g (4 oz) butter and blend in 2 tbsp finely chopped anchovies, 1 tbsp lemon juice, 1 tsp ground coriander, and season with black pepper. Chill. Garnish with anchovy fillets.

Parsley butter
Soften 125 g (4 oz) butter and blend in 2 tbsp chopped parsley, 1 tbsp lemon juice, and season with salt and black pepper. Chill. Garnish with a lemon twist and a parsley sprig.

Coriander butter
Soften 125 g (4 oz) butter and blend in 2 tbsp chopped fresh coriander, 1 tbsp lemon juice, 1 tsp ground coriander, and season with salt and black pepper. Chill. Garnish with a coriander sprig and a sprinkling of ground coriander.

Mustard butter
Soften 125 g (4 oz) butter and blend in 2 tbsp Dijon mustard, 2 tbsp chopped fresh tarragon, and season with salt and black pepper. Chill. Garnish with a tarragon sprig.

Coating steaks

Press each steak firmly on to the peppercorns, until both sides are well coated.

Pepper steaks

SERVES 4 **CALS PER SERVING** 489

4 x 150–175 g (5–6 oz) fillet steaks, about 2.5 cm (1 in) thick, trimmed
salt and black pepper
2 tbsp black peppercorns
30 g (1 oz) butter
1 tbsp sunflower oil
2 tbsp brandy
150 ml (1/4 pint) double cream
chopped parsley, to garnish

1 Season the steaks on both sides with salt. Crush the peppercorns and spread them on a plate. Coat the steaks with the peppercorns (see box, opposite).

2 Melt the butter with the oil in a frying pan. When the butter is foaming, add the steaks, and cook over a high heat for 2 minutes on each side.

3 Lower the heat and continue cooking until the steaks are to your liking: rare steaks need 1–2 minutes on each side, medium steaks 3 minutes on each side, and well-done steaks 4–5 minutes on each side. Lift out of the pan and keep warm.

4 Pour the brandy into the frying pan, and boil rapidly to drive off the alcohol. When the brandy has almost disappeared, stir in the cream, and add salt and pepper to taste. Gently reheat the sauce, pour it over the steaks, and garnish with parsley. Serve hot.

Chianti beef casserole

SERVES 4–6 **CALS PER SERVING** 512–342

60 g (2 oz) sun-dried tomatoes in oil, roughly chopped, with oil reserved
1 kg (2 lb) braising steak, trimmed and cut into 5 cm (2 in) cubes
2 large onions, roughly chopped
2 large garlic cloves, crushed
45 g (1½ oz) plain flour
150 ml (¼ pint) Chianti or any good red wine
300 ml (½ pint) beef stock
a few fresh thyme sprigs
salt and black pepper
1 x 400 g can artichoke hearts, drained and halved
12 pitted black olives
1 heaped tbsp mango chutney

1 Heat 2 tbsp of the reserved oil from the sun-dried tomatoes in a large frying pan, and brown the beef on all sides (you may need to do this in batches). Remove with a slotted spoon and keep warm.

2 Heat another 2 tbsp sun-dried tomato oil in a large flameproof casserole, add the onions and garlic, and cook for 2–3 minutes.

3 Add the flour and cook, stirring, for 1 minute. Blend in the wine and stock, bring to a boil, and add the tomatoes and thyme (reserving a sprig for garnish). Season with salt and pepper.

4 Return the beef to the casserole, cover, and reduce the heat. Simmer for 1½–2 hours or until the meat is tender.

5 Add the artichokes, olives, and mango chutney, and simmer for 10 minutes. Taste for seasoning and garnish with thyme before serving.

Salt beef with mustard sauce

SERVES 6–8 **CALS PER SERVING** 575–431

1 kg (2 lb) salted silverside
500 g (1 lb) baby carrots
8 potatoes, halved
8 celery stalks, cut into chunks
250 g (8 oz) turnips, cut into chunks
chopped parsley, to garnish

Mustard sauce

30 g (1 oz) butter
30 g (1 oz) plain flour
150 ml (¼ pint) milk
4 tsp white wine vinegar
2 tsp mustard powder
2 heaped tsp caster sugar
salt and black pepper

1 Put the salt beef into a large bowl. Cover with cold water and leave to soak overnight to remove any excess salt.

2 Rinse the beef under cold running water, place in a large saucepan, and cover with cold water. Cover the pan with its lid, bring to a boil, and simmer very gently, topping up the water in the pan when necessary, for about 1 hour.

3 Add the carrots, potatoes, celery, and turnips and cook for 40 minutes or until the beef and vegetables are tender.

4 Transfer the meat to a warmed platter. Lift out the vegetables with a slotted spoon, reserving the liquid, and arrange around the meat. Cover and keep warm.

5 Make the sauce: melt the butter in a saucepan, add the flour, and cook, stirring, for 1 minute. Remove from the heat and gradually blend in the milk and 150 ml (¼ pint) of the cooking liquid from the beef. Bring to a boil, stirring constantly, until the sauce thickens. Simmer for 2 minutes.

6 In a jug, combine the vinegar, mustard powder, and sugar, and stir into the sauce. Cook for 1 minute, then season with salt and pepper. (Be careful not to add too much salt because the liquid from the beef is salty.)

7 Slice the beef and arrange on warmed serving plates with the vegetables. Pour the mustard sauce over the beef, and sprinkle with parsley.

Country beef casserole

SERVES 8 **CALS PER SERVING** 405

3 tbsp sunflower oil
1 kg (2 lb) braising steak, trimmed and cut into 5 cm (2 in) cubes
500 g (1 lb) carrots, thickly sliced
250 g (8 oz) turnips, cut into large chunks
250 g (8 oz) parsnips, thickly sliced
2 onions, sliced
1 large leek, sliced
1 tbsp plain flour
600 ml (1 pint) beef stock
1 x 400 g can chopped tomatoes
2 tbsp chopped fresh herbs, such as parsley and thyme
1 large bay leaf
salt and black pepper
herb dumplings (see box, right)

1 Heat the oil in a large flameproof casserole, add the beef in batches, and cook over a high heat until browned. Lift out the beef with a slotted spoon.

2 Add the carrots, turnips, parsnips, onions, and leek, and cook over a high heat, stirring occasionally, for 5 minutes or until the vegetables are softened.

3 Add the flour and cook, stirring, for 1 minute. Add the stock and tomatoes, and 1 tbsp of the herbs, and season with salt and pepper. Bring to a boil, then return the meat to the casserole. Cover and cook in a preheated oven at 160°C (140°C fan, Gas 3) for 2 hours.

4 Place the dumplings on top of the meat. Increase the oven temperature to 190°C (170°C fan, Gas 5) and cook for 20–25 minutes until the dumplings are firm. Serve hot, sprinkled with the remaining chopped herbs.

Herb dumplings

Sift 125 g (4 oz) self-raising flour into a bowl, and add 60 g (2 oz) shredded vegetable suet, 1 tbsp chopped fresh thyme or parsley, and salt and pepper. Add 4–5 tbsp water to make a soft dough. Shape into 12–16 balls with your hands.

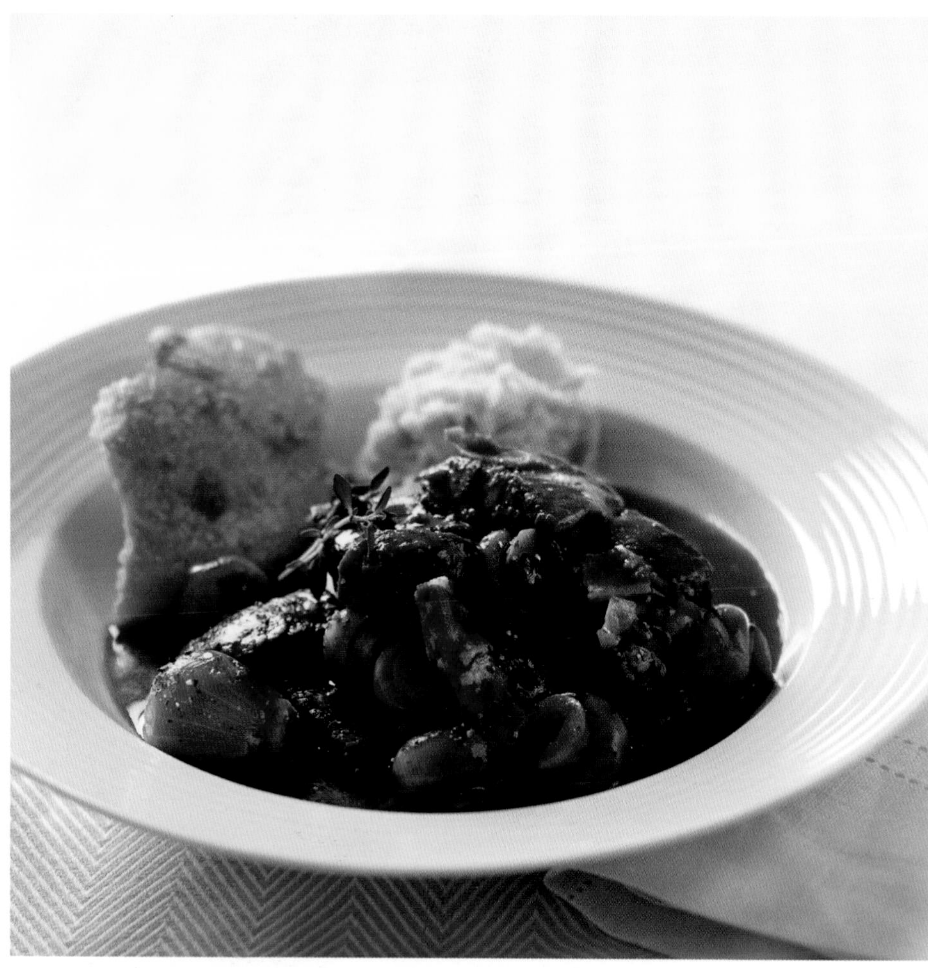

Boeuf bourguignon

SERVES 6 **CALS PER SERVING** 490

2 tbsp sunflower oil
1 kg (2 lb) braising steak, trimmed and cut into 5 cm (2 in) cubes
250 g (8 oz) thickly sliced smoked bacon, rinds removed, cut into strips
12 shallots
30 g (1 oz) plain flour
300 ml (½ pint) red Burgundy or any good red wine
150 ml (¼ pint) beef stock
1 bouquet garni
1 garlic clove, crushed
salt and black pepper
250 g (8 oz) button mushrooms

1 Heat the oil in a large flameproof casserole. Add the beef in batches, and cook over a high heat, turning occasionally, until browned on all sides. Remove with a slotted spoon and set aside to drain on paper towels.

2 Add the bacon and shallots and cook gently, stirring occasionally, for 3 minutes or until the bacon is crisp and the shallots are softened. Lift out and drain on paper towels.

3 Add the flour and cook, stirring, for 1 minute. Gradually blend in the wine and stock and bring to a boil, stirring until thickened.

4 Return the beef and bacon to the casserole, add the bouquet garni and garlic, and season with salt and pepper. Cover and cook in a preheated oven at 160°C (140°C fan, Gas 3) for 1½ hours.

5 Return the shallots to the casserole, add the whole button mushrooms, and cook for 1 hour or until the beef is very tender.

6 Remove the bouquet garni and discard. Taste the sauce for seasoning before serving with warm, crusty bread.

Carbonnade of beef

SERVES 6 **CALS PER SERVING** 465

2 tbsp sunflower oil
1 kg (2 lb) braising steak, trimmed and cut into 5 cm (2 in) cubes
2 large onions, sliced
1 garlic clove, crushed
2 tsp light muscovado sugar
1 tbsp plain flour
150 ml (¼ pint) beef stock
450 ml (¾ pint) beer or lager
1 tbsp red wine vinegar
1 bouquet garni
salt and black pepper
½ baguette, cut into 1.25 cm (½ in) slices
Dijon mustard, for spreading

1 Heat the oil in a large flameproof casserole, add the beef in batches, and cook over a high heat for a few minutes until browned. Lift out with a slotted spoon.

2 Lower the heat and add the onions, garlic, and sugar. Cook, stirring, for 4 minutes or until browned. Add the flour and cook, stirring, for 1 minute. Add the stock and beer or lager, and bring to a boil, stirring until thickened.

3 Return the meat to the casserole, add the vinegar and bouquet garni, and season with salt and pepper. Bring back to a boil, cover, and cook in a preheated oven at 150°C (130°C fan, Gas 2) for 2½ hours or until the meat is really tender. Remove from the oven, lift out the bouquet garni, and discard. Taste for seasoning.

4 Increase the oven temperature to 190°C (170°C fan, Gas 5). Toast the baguette slices, and spread with mustard on one side. Put them, mustard-side up, in the casserole, and baste with sauce.

5 Return the casserole to the oven, uncovered, for 10 minutes or until the croûtes are just crisp. Divide the beef between six serving bowls, topped with the croûtes.

Winter beef casserole

SERVES 4–6 **CALS PER SERVING** 680–454

2 tbsp sunflower oil
1 kg (2 lb) braising steak, trimmed and cut into 2.5 cm (1 in) cubes
3 streaky bacon rashers, rinds removed, cut into strips
1 large onion, chopped
45 g (1½ oz) plain flour
500 g (1 lb) passata (sieved tomatoes)
450 ml (¾ pint) beef stock
150 ml (¼ pint) red wine
6 celery stalks, sliced
250 g (8 oz) carrots, cut into thin strips
1 garlic clove, crushed
1 tsp chopped fresh marjoram or oregano
salt and black pepper
chopped parsley, to garnish

1 Heat the oil in a large flameproof casserole, add the beef and bacon, and cook over a moderately high heat for 2–3 minutes until browned. Remove with a slotted spoon, and drain on paper towels.

2 Add the onion and cook, stirring occasionally, for a few minutes until soft but not coloured.

3 Add the flour and cook, stirring, for 1 minute. Add the passata, stock, and wine and bring to a boil, stirring until smooth and thickened. Return the meat to the pan, add the celery, carrots, garlic, and marjoram or oregano, and season with salt and pepper.

4 Bring to a boil, cover and cook in a preheated oven at 160°C (140°C fan, Gas 3) for 2 hours or until the beef is tender. Taste for seasoning and garnish with chopped parsley before serving.

Hungarian goulash

SERVES 6 **CALS PER SERVING** 474

2 tbsp sunflower oil
1 kg (2 lb) braising steak, trimmed and cut into 5 cm (2 in) cubes
2 large onions, sliced
1 garlic clove, crushed
1 tbsp plain flour
1 tbsp paprika, plus extra to garnish
600 ml (1 pint) beef stock
1 x 400 g can tomatoes
2 tbsp tomato purée
salt and black pepper
2 large red peppers, halved, deseeded, and cut into 2.5 cm (1 in) pieces
4 potatoes, peeled and quartered
150 ml (¼ pint) soured cream

1 Heat the sunflower oil in a large flameproof casserole, add the beef in batches, and cook over a high heat until browned.

2 Lift out the beef with a slotted spoon. Lower the heat slightly, add the onions and garlic, and cook gently, stirring occasionally, for a few minutes until soft but not coloured.

3 Add the flour and paprika and cook, stirring, for 1 minute. Pour in the stock and bring to a boil, stirring.

4 Return the meat to the casserole, add the tomatoes and tomato purée, and season with salt and pepper. Bring back to a boil, cover, and cook in a preheated oven at 160°C (140°C fan, Gas 3) for 1 hour.

5 Add the red peppers and potatoes and continue cooking for 1 hour or until the potatoes and meat are tender.

6 Taste for seasoning, and serve with a tablespoonful of soured cream, sprinkled with a little paprika.

Latimer beef with horseradish

SERVES 6 **CALS PER SERVING** 298

2 tbsp sunflower oil
1 kg (2 lb) braising steak, trimmed and cut into strips
12 shallots or button onions
30 g (1 oz) plain flour
2 tsp mild curry powder
2 tsp light muscovado sugar
1 tsp ground ginger
600 ml (1 pint) beef stock
2 tbsp Worcestershire sauce
salt and black pepper
3 tbsp chopped parsley, plus extra to garnish
4 tbsp creamed horseradish

1 Heat the sunflower oil in a large flameproof casserole, and cook the beef strips over a high heat until browned all over. Lift out with a slotted spoon and drain on paper towels.

2 Lower the heat, add the shallots or button onions, and cook gently, stirring occasionally, for a few minutes until softened. Lift out with a slotted spoon and drain on paper towels.

3 Add the flour, curry powder, sugar, and ginger to the casserole and cook, stirring, for 1 minute. Pour in the stock and bring to a boil, stirring until smooth and thickened. Add the Worcestershire sauce, season with salt and pepper, and return to a boil.

4 Return the beef and shallots to the casserole and stir in the parsley. Bring back to a boil, cover, and cook in a preheated oven at 160°C (140°C fan, Gas 3) for 2–2½ hours until the meat is tender.

5 Stir in the creamed horseradish, taste for seasoning, and garnish with parsley.

Thai red beef curry

SERVES 6 **CALS PER SERVING** 327

3 tbsp sunflower oil
8 cardamom pods, split
2.5 cm (1 in) piece of cinnamon stick
6 cloves
8 black peppercorns
1 kg (2 lb) braising steak, trimmed and cut into 2.5 cm (1 in) cubes
1 large onion, chopped
5 cm (2 in) piece of fresh root ginger, peeled and grated
4 garlic cloves, crushed
4 tsp paprika
2 tsp ground cumin
1 tsp ground coriander
1 tsp salt
¼ tsp cayenne pepper or ½ tsp chilli powder
600 ml (1 pint) water
90 g (3 oz) full-fat plain yogurt
1 x 400 g can chopped tomatoes
1 large red pepper, halved, deseeded, and cut into chunks
2 tbsp torn fresh coriander leaves, to garnish

1 Heat the oil in a large flameproof casserole, add the cardamom pods, cinnamon stick, cloves, and peppercorns, and cook over a moderate heat, stirring, for 1 minute. Lift out with a slotted spoon and set aside on a plate.

2 Add the beef in batches, and cook over a high heat until browned all over. Lift out the beef with a slotted spoon and drain on paper towels.

3 Add the onion to the pan and cook over a high heat, stirring, for about 3 minutes until beginning to brown. Add the ginger, garlic, paprika, cumin, coriander, salt, cayenne or chilli, and 4 tbsp of the measured water. Cook, stirring, for about 1 minute.

4 Return the beef and spices to the casserole, then gradually add the yogurt, stirring. Stir in the remaining water. Add the tomatoes and red pepper, and bring to a boil. Cover and cook in a preheated oven at 160°C (140°C fan, Gas 3) for 2 hours or until the beef is tender. Taste for seasoning, before serving with boiled rice (page 334) and garnished with the coriander leaves.

Cook's know-how

If you are short of time, use 3–4 tbsp ready-made Thai red curry paste instead of the whole and ground spices in this recipe. If you prefer, you can use coconut milk instead of the yogurt.

Chilli con carne

SERVES 6 **CALS PER SERVING** 362

250 g (8 oz) dried red kidney beans
2 tbsp sunflower oil
750 g (1½ lb) braising steak, trimmed and cut into large cubes
2 onions, chopped
2 fresh red chillies, halved, deseeded, and finely chopped
1 garlic clove, crushed
1 tbsp plain flour
900 ml (1½ pints) beef stock
2 tbsp tomato purée
1 square of plain chocolate, grated
salt and black pepper
1 large red pepper, halved, deseeded, and cut into chunks
chopped coriander, to garnish

1 Put the red kidney beans into a large bowl, cover generously with cold water, and leave to soak overnight.

2 Drain the beans, rinse under cold running water, and drain again. Put the beans into a large saucepan. Cover with cold water, bring to a boil, and boil rapidly for 10 minutes. Lower the heat and simmer, partially covered, for 50 minutes or until the beans are just tender. Drain.

3 Heat the oil in a large flameproof casserole. Add the beef and cook in batches over a high heat for 5–7 minutes until browned. Lift out with a slotted spoon.

4 Lower the heat, add the onions, chillies, and garlic, and cook, stirring occasionally, for a few minutes until softened.

5 Add the flour and cook, stirring, for 1 minute. Add the stock, tomato purée, and chocolate, and season with salt and pepper. Return the beef to the casserole, add the beans, and bring to a boil. Cover and cook in a preheated oven at 150°C (130°C fan, Gas 2) for 1½ hours.

6 Add the red pepper to the casserole and cook for 30 minutes. Taste for seasoning and serve, garnished with coriander.

QUICK CHILLI CON CARNE

Substitute 1 x 400 g can red kidney beans for the dried beans, and minced beef for the braising steak. Simmer gently on the hob for 45 minutes.

Beef olives with vegetable julienne

SERVES 6 **CALS PER SERVING** 257

8 thin slices of beef topside, total weight about 750 g (1½ lb)
2 tbsp sunflower oil
375 g (12 oz) piece of celeriac, peeled and cut into matchstick-thin strips
250 g (8 oz) carrots, peeled and cut into matchstick-thin strips
2 small leeks, cut into matchstick-thin strips
salt and black pepper
30 g (1 oz) plain flour
1 onion, sliced
1 garlic clove, sliced
450 ml (¾ pint) beef stock

1 Pound each slice of topside between two sheets of cling film with a rolling pin until 3 mm (⅛ in) thick.

2 Heat 1 tbsp of the oil in a large frying pan, add the celeriac, carrots, and leeks, and stir-fry over a high heat for 1 minute. Season with salt and pepper, then lift out and drain. Leave to cool.

3 Divide the vegetables among the beef slices. Roll up and secure with wooden cocktail sticks.

4 Lightly coat the beef olives in half of the flour, shaking off any excess. Heat the remaining oil in a flameproof casserole, add the beef olives, and cook over a high heat for 5–7 minutes until browned. Lift out with a slotted spoon.

5 Add the onion and garlic and cook gently until softened. Add the remaining flour and cook, stirring, for 1 minute. Gradually blend in the stock, season with salt and pepper, and bring to a boil, stirring until thick.

6 Return the beef olives to the casserole, bring to a boil, cover, and cook in a preheated oven at 180°C (160°C fan, Gas 4) for 1½ hours. Lift out the beef and set aside. Sieve the sauce, then reheat. Thinly slice the beef, removing the cocktail sticks. Pour over the sauce and serve hot, with fresh julienne vegetables if wished.

French-style braised beef

SERVES 4–6 **CALS PER SERVING** 604–402

1 kg (2 lb) piece of lean braising steak (e.g. chuck steak)
2 tbsp olive oil
125 g (4 oz) piece of lean bacon, cut into strips
1 onion, sliced
250 g (8 oz) carrots, thickly sliced
250 g (8 oz) mushrooms, quartered
500 g (1 lb) tomatoes, chopped
125 g (4 oz) pitted black olives
600 ml (1 pint) beef stock
salt and black pepper
parsley, to garnish

Marinade

500 ml (16 fl oz) red wine
3 tbsp red wine vinegar
2 large garlic cloves
1 strip of orange zest
1 bouquet garni

1 Make the marinade: combine the wine, vinegar, garlic, orange zest, and bouquet garni. Add the beef, cover, and leave to marinate in the refrigerator overnight.

2 Remove the beef from the marinade and pat dry with paper towels. Strain the marinade and reserve. Heat the oil in a large flameproof casserole, add the beef and bacon, and brown all over. Lift out and drain on paper towels.

3 Add the onion, carrots, and mushrooms and cook, stirring, for 5 minutes or until lightly browned.

4 Add the beef, bacon, tomatoes, olives, and reserved marinade. Pour in sufficient stock to cover the meat and season with salt and pepper.

5 Bring to a boil, cover tightly, and cook in a preheated oven at 180°C (160°C fan, Gas 4) for 1½–2 hours or until the meat is very tender.

6 Slice the meat and arrange on a warmed platter with the vegetables. Skim the sauce and pour over the meat. Garnish with parsley before serving.

Traditional steak and kidney pie

This pie is a classic, but for those who do not like kidneys you can omit them and use double the amount of mushrooms. For convenience, the meat can be cooked a day in advance, then all you have to do on the day of serving is make the pastry and bake the pie in the oven.

SERVES 6 **CALS PER SERVING** 577

2 tbsp sunflower oil
1 large onion, chopped
750 g (1½ lb) stewing steak, cut into 2.5 cm (1 in) cubes
250 g (8 oz) beef or lamb's kidney, trimmed (page 237), and cut into 2.5 cm (1 in) cubes
30 g (1 oz) plain flour
300 ml (½ pint) beef stock
2 tbsp Worcestershire sauce
salt and black pepper
250 g (8 oz) button mushrooms
beaten egg, for glazing

Shortcrust pastry

250 g (8 oz) plain flour
125 g (4 oz) butter
about 3 tbsp cold water

PIE FUNNEL

1 Heat the oil in a large saucepan, add the onion, and cook, stirring from time to time, for a few minutes until soft but not coloured.

2 Add the beef and kidney and cook until browned. Add the flour and cook, stirring, for 1 minute. Add the stock and Worcestershire sauce, season with salt and pepper, and bring to a boil, stirring. Partially cover, and simmer gently for 2 hours.

3 Add the mushrooms and cook for 30 minutes or until the meat is tender. Taste for seasoning, then leave to cool completely.

4 Make the pastry: sift the flour into a bowl. Add the butter and rub in lightly with your fingertips until the mixture looks like fine breadcrumbs. Add the water and mix with a flat-bladed knife until the dough comes together to form a ball.

5 Roll out the pastry on a floured work surface until 2.5 cm (1 in) larger than the pie dish. Invert the dish over the pastry and cut around the dish. Brush the rim of the dish with water and press on a strip of pastry cut from the trimmings.

6 Put a pie funnel into the middle of the dish then spoon in the meat mixture.

7 Lightly brush the pastry strip with water and top with the pastry lid, making a hole in the middle so the steam can escape through the pie funnel. Seal the pastry edges and crimp with a fork, then decorate the top of the pie with pastry trimmings, attaching them with beaten egg.

8 Brush the pastry all over with the beaten egg, and bake in a preheated oven at 200°C (180°C fan, Gas 6) for 25–30 minutes until the pastry is crisp and golden. Serve hot.

STEAK AND KIDNEY PUDDING

Mix 300 g (10 oz) self-raising flour, 150 g (5 oz) shredded suet, salt and pepper, and 200 ml (7 fl oz) water. Use ¾ pastry to line a 1.7 litre (3 pint) bowl. Add the uncooked filling, top with pastry, and steam for 5 hours.

Oxtail stew

SERVES 6 **CALS PER SERVING** 337

1 tbsp sunflower oil
1.25 kg (2½ lb) oxtail, cut into 5 cm (2 in) slices and trimmed
30 g (1 oz) plain flour
900 ml (1½ pints) beef stock
2 large onions, sliced
1 tbsp tomato purée
1 tbsp chopped parsley
1 tbsp chopped fresh thyme
1 bay leaf
salt and black pepper
8 celery stalks, thickly sliced
chopped parsley, to garnish

1 Heat the oil in a large flameproof casserole, add the oxtail, and cook over a high heat for 10 minutes or until browned all over. Remove the oxtail and drain on paper towels.

2 Add the flour and cook, stirring occasionally, for about 1 minute. Blend in the beef stock and bring to a boil, stirring until the sauce has thickened.

3 Return the oxtail to the casserole, and add the onions, tomato purée, parsley, thyme, and bay leaf. Season with salt and pepper, and bring to a boil. Cover and simmer gently for 2 hours.

4 Add the celery and cook for a further 1½–2 hours or until the meat can be removed from the bones easily. Skim off any fat, then taste the sauce for seasoning. Sprinkle with parsley before serving.

Cook's know-how

Oxtail stew needs long, slow cooking to develop its rich brown gravy and to make the meat so soft that it falls off the bone. If possible, make the stew the day before serving; the excess fat can then be easily lifted from the surface of the cooled stew before reheating.

Bobotie

SERVES 6–8 **CALS PER SERVING** 656–492

1 slice of white bread, crusts removed
300 ml (½ pint) milk
30 g (1 oz) butter
1 large onion, chopped
2 garlic cloves, crushed
1 kg (2 lb) minced beef
1 tbsp medium–hot curry powder
90 g (3 oz) ready-to-eat dried apricots, coarsely chopped
90 g (3 oz) blanched almonds, coarsely chopped
2 tbsp fruit chutney
1 tbsp lemon juice
salt and black pepper
2 eggs
30 g (1 oz) flaked almonds

1 Put the bread into a shallow dish. Sprinkle over 2 tbsp of the milk and leave to soak for 5 minutes.

2 Meanwhile, melt the butter in a large frying pan, add the onion and garlic, and cook gently, stirring occasionally, for a few minutes until soft.

3 Increase the heat, add the beef, and cook, stirring, for 5 minutes or until browned. Spoon off any excess fat.

4 Add the curry powder and cook, stirring, for 2 minutes. Add the chopped apricots and almonds, the chutney, lemon juice, and salt and pepper to taste.

5 Mash the bread and milk in the dish, then stir into the minced beef. Turn into an ovenproof dish and bake in a preheated oven at 180°C (160°C fan, Gas 4) for 35 minutes.

6 Break the eggs into a bowl, and whisk in the remaining milk, and salt and pepper to taste. Pour over the minced beef mixture, sprinkle with the flaked almonds, and bake for 25–30 minutes until the topping is set.

Beef Florentine

SERVES 8 **CALS PER SERVING** 576

11 sheets of filo pastry
60 g (2 oz) butter, melted

Beef layer

30 g (1 oz) butter
1 kg (2 lb) lean minced beef
1 tbsp plain flour
1 x 400 g can chopped tomatoes
2 tbsp tomato purée
2 garlic cloves, crushed
1 tsp caster sugar
salt and black pepper

Spinach and cheese layer

625 g (1 ¼ lb) spinach leaves, tough stalks removed, roughly chopped
90 g (3 oz) mature Cheddar cheese, grated
90 g (3 oz) Gruyère or Emmental cheese, grated
125 g (4 oz) full-fat soft cheese
2 eggs, lightly beaten

1 Prepare the beef layer: melt the butter in a large saucepan, add the minced beef, and cook, stirring, for 10–15 minutes or until the meat is browned all over.

2 Add the flour and cook, stirring, for 1 minute. Add the tomatoes, tomato purée, garlic, and sugar, season with salt and pepper, and bring to a boil. Cover and simmer, stirring occasionally, for 35 minutes. Taste for seasoning.

3 Meanwhile, prepare the spinach and cheese layer: wash the spinach and put it into a large saucepan. Cook over a gentle heat until the spinach wilts. Drain thoroughly, squeezing to remove excess water. Mix the spinach with the Cheddar, Gruyère or Emmental, soft cheese, and eggs, and season with salt and pepper.

4 Spoon the beef mixture into a shallow ovenproof dish, then spoon the spinach mixture over the top.

5 Prepare the filo topping for the dish (see box, opposite).

6 Bake in a preheated oven at 200°C (180°C fan, Gas 6) for 20–25 minutes until the filo pastry is crisp and golden. Serve hot.

Preparing the filo topping

Brush three of the filo pastry sheets with a little of the melted butter and layer them on top of the spinach mixture, trimming to fit the dish if necessary.

Arrange the remaining eight filo pastry sheets over the dish, lightly brushing with a little butter and scrunching each one up, in order to completely cover the lower layer of filo pastry.

Covering the pies

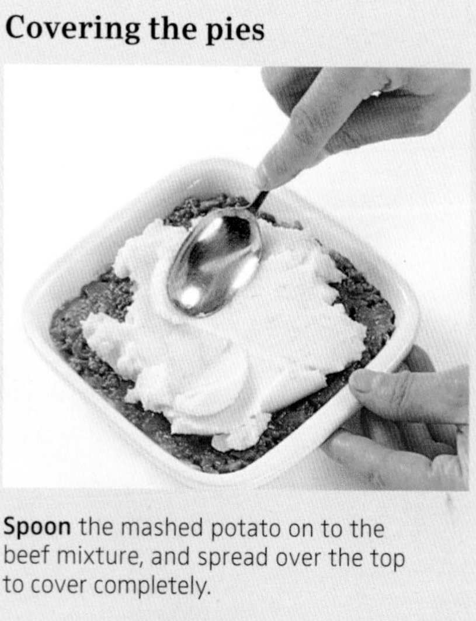

Spoon the mashed potato on to the beef mixture, and spread over the top to cover completely.

Score the surface of the mashed potato, using a fork, to make a decorative topping.

Cottage pies with cheesy potato topping

The minced beef mixture can be made a day ahead of serving, and kept in the refrigerator overnight. If you prefer you can omit the cheese in the potato topping, and use olive oil instead of butter.

SERVES 6 **CALS PER SERVING** 576

2 tbsp sunflower oil
1 large onion, finely chopped
1 celery stalk, finely chopped
1 large carrot, finely chopped
750 g (1½ lb) minced beef
2 tsp plain flour
300 ml (½ pint) beef stock
1 tbsp tomato purée
2 tbsp Worcestershire sauce
salt and black pepper

Topping

750 g (1½ lb) potatoes, cut into chunks
30 g (1 oz) butter
2–3 tbsp hot milk
125 g (4 oz) mature Cheddar cheese, grated

1 Heat the oil in a large saucepan, add the onion, celery, and carrot, and cook for 3 minutes. Add the minced beef, and cook for 5 minutes or until browned.

2 Add the flour and cook, stirring, for 1 minute. Add the stock, tomato purée, and Worcestershire sauce, season with salt and pepper, and bring to a boil. Cover and simmer, stirring occasionally, for 45 minutes. Remove from the heat and spoon into six individual ovenproof dishes, or one large dish. Leave to cool.

3 Prepare the potato topping: cook the potatoes in boiling salted water for 20 minutes or until tender. Drain. Add the butter and hot milk to the potatoes and mash until soft, then stir in the cheese and season with salt and pepper.

4 Cover the minced beef mixture with the mashed potato (see box, above). Cook in a preheated oven at 200°C (180°C fan, Gas 6), allowing 20–25 minutes for small pies or 35–40 minutes for a large one, until the potato topping is golden brown and the meat mixture is bubbling. Serve hot, accompanied by fresh rocket, or other salad leaves.

Beef tacos

SERVES 4 **CALS PER SERVING** 407

1 tbsp sunflower oil
375 g (12 oz) minced beef
1 onion, chopped
3 garlic cloves, crushed
½ tsp chilli powder
1 tsp paprika
½ tsp ground cumin (optional)
1 x 225 g can chopped tomatoes
salt and black pepper
1 fresh green chilli, halved, deseeded, and thinly sliced
2 tbsp chopped fresh coriander
8 taco shells
8 lettuce leaves, finely shredded
4 tbsp soured cream
chopped coriander, to garnish

1 Heat the oil in a large frying pan, add the minced beef, onion, and garlic, and cook, stirring, for 5 minutes or until the beef is browned and the onion and garlic are softened.

2 Add the chilli powder, paprika, and cumin (if using), and cook, stirring, for 2 minutes.

3 Stir in the tomatoes, cover, and cook over a medium heat for 5 minutes. Add salt and pepper to taste, remove from the heat, and stir in the chilli and coriander.

4 Warm the taco shells in a preheated oven at 180°C (160°C fan, Gas 4) for 2–3 minutes, or according to packet instructions. Fill the taco shells (see box, below), and serve hot.

Filling taco shells

Hold each shell in one hand and put a layer of shredded lettuce into the bottom. Add a generous spoonful of the meat mixture and top with soured cream and a sprinkling of chopped coriander.

Beef and bean burritos

SERVES 4 **CALS PER SERVING** 471

375 g (12 oz) rump steak, trimmed of fat and cut into thin strips
salt and black pepper
2 tbsp olive oil
1 garlic clove, crushed
½–1 fresh red chilli, halved, deseeded, and chopped
½ tsp cumin seeds
1 x 400 g can tomatoes, drained, juice reserved
1 x 400 g can pinto or black beans, drained
8 flour tortillas
4 tbsp soured cream or crème fraîche
chopped fresh coriander, to garnish

1 Season the steak strips with salt and pepper. Heat the olive oil in a large frying pan, add the steak, crushed garlic, chopped chilli, and cumin seeds, and cook, stirring, for 5 minutes or until lightly browned.

2 Add the tomatoes to the pan and cook for about 3 minutes. Pour in the reserved tomato juice and boil for 8–10 minutes until the liquid is reduced.

3 Add the beans and cook until heated through. Taste for seasoning, cover, and keep hot. Warm the tortillas (page 264).

4 Divide the steak and tomato mixture among the tortillas and roll them up. Serve with soured cream and garnished with coriander.

Fajitas

This Mexican speciality features slices of steak marinated in spices and fruit juice. Serve with tortillas, avocado, soured cream, and *pico de gallo* relish.

SERVES 4 **CALS PER SERVING** 543

500 g (1 lb) piece of rump steak
8 tortilla wraps
chopped coriander, to garnish
1 avocado, stoned, peeled (page 395), and diced
soured cream

Marinade

juice of 1 orange and 1 lime
3 garlic cloves, crushed
2 tbsp chopped fresh coriander
a few drops of Tabasco sauce
salt and black pepper

***Pico de gallo* relish**

6 tomatoes, diced
10 radishes, coarsely chopped
5 spring onions, thinly sliced
1–2 green chillies, halved, deseeded, and chopped
4 tbsp chopped fresh coriander
juice of ½ lime

1 Make the marinade: in a large bowl, combine the orange and lime juice, garlic, coriander, and Tabasco, and season with salt and pepper. Turn the steak in the marinade, cover, and leave to marinate in the refrigerator overnight.

2 Make the *pico de gallo* relish: in a bowl, combine the tomatoes, radishes, spring onions, chillies, coriander, lime juice, and salt to taste. Cover and chill until ready to serve.

3 Remove the steak from the marinade and pat dry. Put the steak under a hot grill, 7–10 cm (3–4 in) from the heat, and grill for 3 minutes on each side for rare steak, 4 minutes for medium steak, or 5–6 minutes for well-done steak. Cover with foil and leave to stand for 5 minutes.

4 Meanwhile, warm the tortillas (see box, right).

5 Slice the steak, arrange on serving plates, and sprinkle with coriander. Serve with the tortillas, *pico de gallo* relish, diced avocado, and soured cream.

Warming tortillas

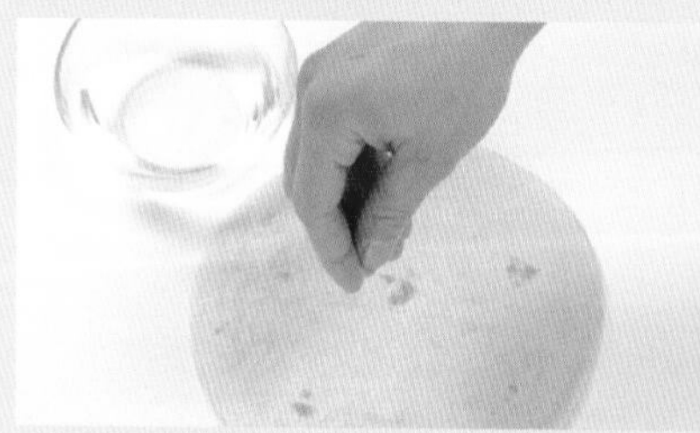

Sprinkle each tortilla with a little water, and stack the tortillas in a pile.

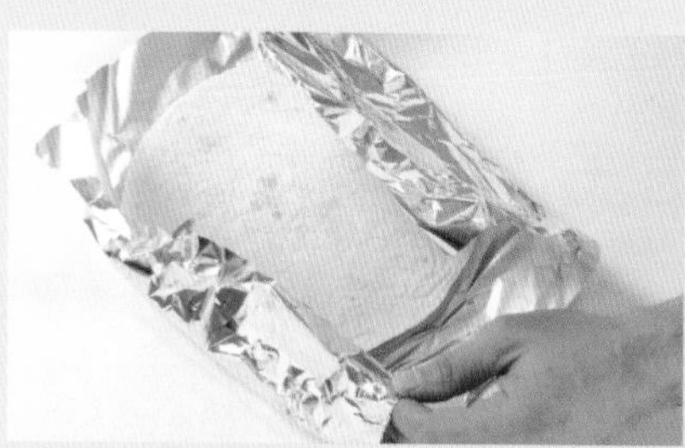

Wrap the tortillas in foil and warm in a preheated oven at 140°C (120°C fan, Gas 1) for 10 minutes.

Corned beef hash

SERVES 4 **CALS PER SERVING** 444

60 g (2 oz) butter
1 large onion, chopped
750 g (1½ lb) potatoes, cut into small chunks
300 ml (½ pint) beef stock
salt and black pepper
1 x 325 g can corned beef, cut into chunks
chopped parsley, to garnish

1 Melt the butter in a large ovenproof frying pan, add the onion, and cook gently, stirring occasionally, for a few minutes until softened.

2 Add the potatoes and stir to coat in the butter. Pour in the stock, and season with salt and pepper. Simmer for 10–15 minutes until the potatoes are tender and the stock absorbed.

3 Stir in the corned beef and heat to warm through. Put the pan under a hot grill, 7 cm (3 in) from the heat, to brown the top. Garnish with parsley.

Meat loaf

SERVES 6 **CALS PER SERVING** 478

750 g (1½ lb) minced beef
1 x 400 g can chopped tomatoes
90 g (3 oz) herby stuffing mix
1 onion, chopped
1 carrot, coarsely shredded
3 garlic cloves, crushed
2 tbsp chopped parsley
1 egg, beaten
1 tbsp Worcestershire sauce
salt and black pepper
4–5 streaky bacon rashers, rinds removed

1 KG (2 LB) LOAF TIN

1 Combine the minced beef, tomatoes, stuffing mix, onion, carrot, garlic, parsley, beaten egg, and Worcestershire sauce, and season with salt and pepper.

2 Arrange bacon rashers crosswise in the loaf tin, letting them hang over the sides. Put the beef mixture into the tin and fold over the bacon. Turn the loaf out into a roasting tin and bake in a preheated oven at 190°C (170°C fan, Gas 5), basting once or twice, for 1 hour.

3 Increase the heat to 230°C (210°C fan, Gas 8) and bake for 15 minutes or until the meat loaf is firm. Spoon off any fat, slice the loaf, and serve hot (or leave whole and serve cold).

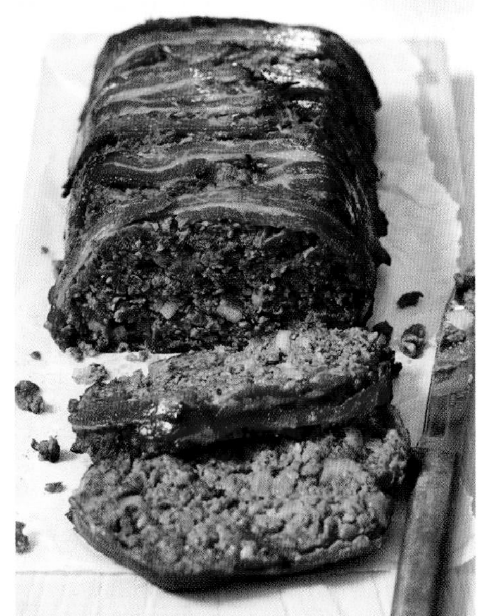

Thai beef burgers

SERVES 6 **CALS PER SERVING** 160

500 g (1 lb) best-quality minced beef
1 tbsp red Thai curry paste
2 tbsp chopped fresh coriander
2.5 cm (1 in) piece of fresh root ginger, peeled and finely grated
salt and black pepper
1 tbsp olive oil

1 Put the beef in a bowl with the curry paste, fresh coriander, grated ginger, and salt and pepper. Mix together thoroughly.

2 Shape the mixture into six even-sized burgers. Put on a large plate, cover and refrigerate for about 30 minutes (they will keep for up to 24 hours).

3 Heat the oil in a large non-stick frying pan or lightly coat a preheated ridged griddle pan with a little oil. Cook the burgers over a medium heat for about 3–4 minutes on each side until they are brown. They are best eaten just pink in the middle, but they can be cooked another minute or two on each side if you prefer them more done than this. Serve with a julienne of raw carrot and cucumber, and a small bowl of unsweetened natural yogurt.

Meatballs in cider

SERVES 4 **CALS PER SERVING** 416

250 g (8 oz) minced beef
125 g (4 oz) minced pork
salt and black pepper
plain flour, for dusting
2 tbsp sunflower oil
2 large onions, sliced
1 garlic clove, crushed
300 ml (½ pint) dry cider
3 tbsp tomato purée
4 celery stalks, thickly sliced
1 large red pepper, halved, deseeded, and cut into strips
125 g (4 oz) mushrooms, sliced
2 tsp caster sugar

1 Mix together the beef and pork, and season with salt and pepper. On a floured work surface, shape the mixture into 16 even-sized balls.

2 Heat the oil in a flameproof casserole, add the meatballs, and cook over a high heat until browned. Remove and drain on paper towels. Lower the heat, add the onions and garlic, and cook, stirring occasionally, for a few minutes until softened.

3 Return the meatballs to the casserole and add the cider, tomato purée, celery, red pepper, mushrooms, and sugar. Season with salt and pepper, and bring to a boil. Cover and simmer for 20 minutes or until the meatballs are cooked through. Serve hot.

Pressed tongue

SERVES 10 **CALS PER SERVING** 392

2–2.5 kg (4–5 lb) salted ox tongue, trimmed
1 onion, quartered
1 bay leaf
1 tbsp gelatine powder
3 tbsp cold water

15 CM (6 IN) ROUND CAKE TIN OR STAINLESS STEEL SAUCEPAN

1 Put the ox tongue, onion, and bay leaf into a large saucepan, cover with cold water, and bring to a boil. Simmer very gently for 3–4 hours until tender. Test the water after 2 hours; if it is very salty, replace it with fresh water.

2 Lift the tongue out of the saucepan, reserving the cooking liquid, and leave to cool slightly. Remove and discard the skin, then cut the tongue in half lengthways.

3 Sprinkle the gelatine over the measured water in a small bowl. Leave to stand for 3 minutes or until the gelatine is spongy. Put the bowl into a saucepan of gently simmering water and leave for 3 minutes or until the gelatine has dissolved.

4 Add 150 ml (¼ pint) of the cooking liquid to the gelatine and mix well.

5 Squash one half of the tongue, cut-side down, into the cake tin or saucepan, and put in the other half, cut-side up. Pour in the gelatine mixture, cover with a small plate, and weigh down with weights or heavy cans. Chill in the refrigerator overnight.

6 Dip the base of the tin or saucepan into a bowl of hot water, just long enough to melt the jelly slightly so that it comes away from the bottom. Serve the tongue chilled, and very thinly sliced.

Veal Marsala

SERVES 4 **CALS PER SERVING** 239

4 x 60–90 g (2–3 oz) veal escalopes
1 tbsp plain flour
salt and black pepper
45 g (1½ oz) butter
1 large onion, finely chopped
125 ml (4 fl oz) Marsala
125 ml (4 fl oz) chicken stock
chopped parsley, to garnish

1 Put each veal escalope between two sheets of cling film and pound until 3 mm (⅛ in) thick with a rolling pin.

2 Season the flour with salt and pepper and use lightly to coat the escalopes.

3 Melt 30 g (1 oz) of the butter in a frying pan, and cook the escalopes, in batches if necessary, for 2 minutes on each side or until golden. Remove from the pan and keep hot.

4 Melt the remaining butter, add the onion, and cook gently for about 5 minutes until soft and lightly browned. Pour in the Marsala and boil, stirring, until reduced to 2 tbsp. Add the stock and boil until reduced to 90 ml (3 fl oz).

5 Return the escalopes to the pan, spoon over the sauce, and warm the escalopes through. Sprinkle with chopped parsley.

Veal with tuna mayonnaise

SERVES 8 **CALS PER SERVING** 636

1.5 kg (3 lb) boned and rolled veal roasting joint, such as loin
2 large rosemary sprigs
2 garlic cloves, cut into slivers
salt and black pepper
250 ml (8 fl oz) dry white wine

Tuna mayonnaise

1 x 200 g can tuna in oil, drained
2 tbsp lemon juice
1 garlic clove, crushed
2 tbsp capers
1 tsp chopped fresh thyme
a dash of Tabasco sauce
125 ml (4 fl oz) olive oil
250 ml (8 fl oz) mayonnaise

To garnish

black olives
1 red pepper, halved, deseeded, and cut into strips
fresh basil (optional)

1 Make incisions in the veal and push one or two rosemary leaves and a sliver of garlic into each incision. Season, and rub with any remaining rosemary and garlic.

2 Place the veal in a large roasting tin and pour the wine around it. Cover with foil and roast in a preheated oven at 160°C (140°C fan, Gas 3) for 2–2½ hours or until tender.

3 Remove the veal from the oven, and leave to cool completely in the cooking liquid. Remove any fat that solidifies on the surface. Slice the veal thinly and arrange the slices on a serving platter.

4 Make the tuna mayonnaise: purée the tuna, reserving a little for the garnish, with the lemon juice, garlic, capers, thyme, and Tabasco sauce in a food processor until smooth. Gradually blend in the oil, then add the mayonnaise, and season with salt and pepper. Pour over the veal. At this stage you can garnish and serve, or cover and refrigerate overnight to serve the next day.

5 To serve, garnish with the reserved tuna, the black olives, red pepper, and basil. Serve at room temperature (if refrigerated overnight, take it out for about 1 hour before serving).

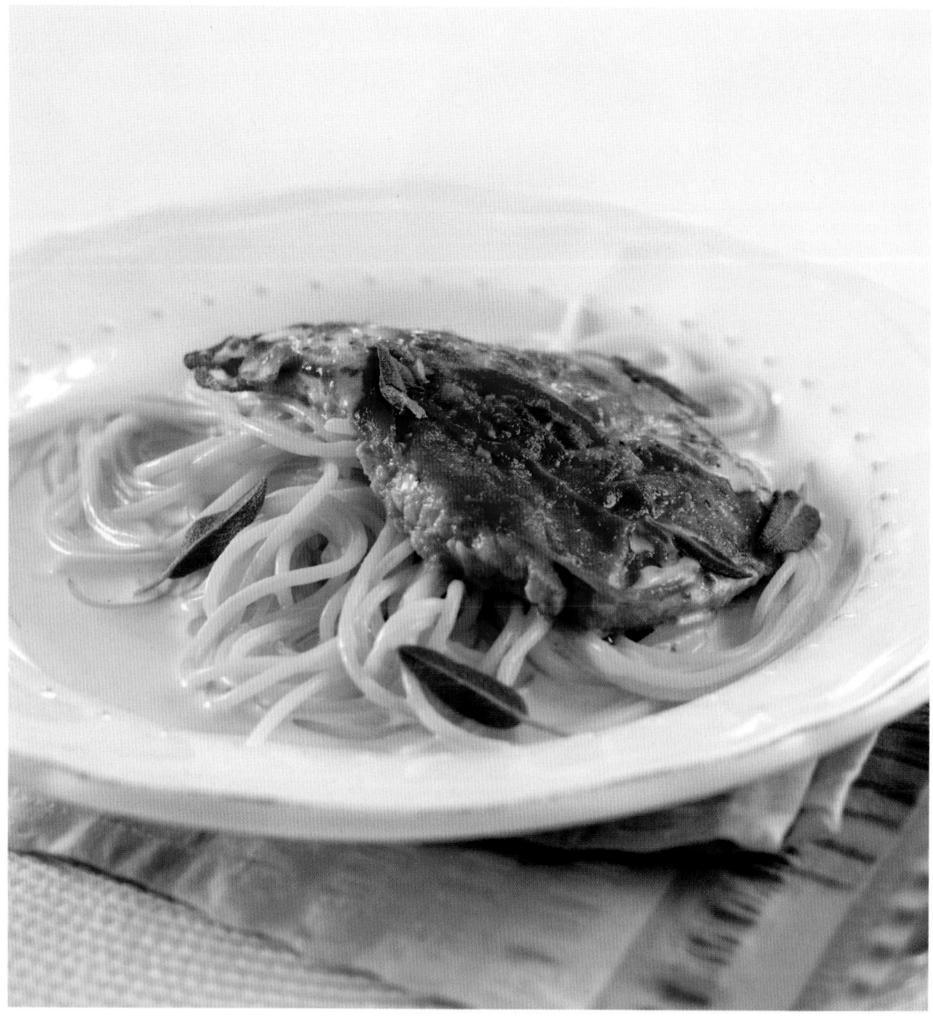

Saltimbocca

SERVES 4 **CALS PER SERVING** 342

4 x 60–90 g (2–3 oz) veal escalopes
8–12 fresh sage leaves, plus extra to garnish
4 thin slices of Parma ham, trimmed of fat
2 tbsp plain flour
salt and black pepper
30 g (1 oz) butter
1 garlic clove, crushed
125 ml (4 fl oz) dry white wine
4 tbsp double cream
spaghetti (page 353), to serve

1 Put each veal escalope between two sheets of cling film and pound until 3 mm (⅛ in) thick with a rolling pin.

2 Lay 2 or 3 sage leaves on each escalope, and press a slice of Parma ham firmly on top. Sprinkle the flour on to a plate and season with salt and pepper. Lightly coat both sides of the escalopes with the flour, shaking off any excess.

3 Melt half of the butter in a large frying pan until foaming. Add half of the escalopes and cook for 2 minutes on each side, sprinkling them with half of the garlic as they cook. Lift out and keep warm while you cook the remaining escalopes in the same way, with the remaining butter and garlic.

4 Pour the white wine into the empty pan and boil for a few minutes until it is reduced to about 2 tbsp.

5 Stir in the cream and heat gently, then taste for seasoning. Place the escalopes on a bed of cooked spaghetti, pour the sauce over, and serve at once, garnished with a few fresh sage leaves.

Rolling up the veal

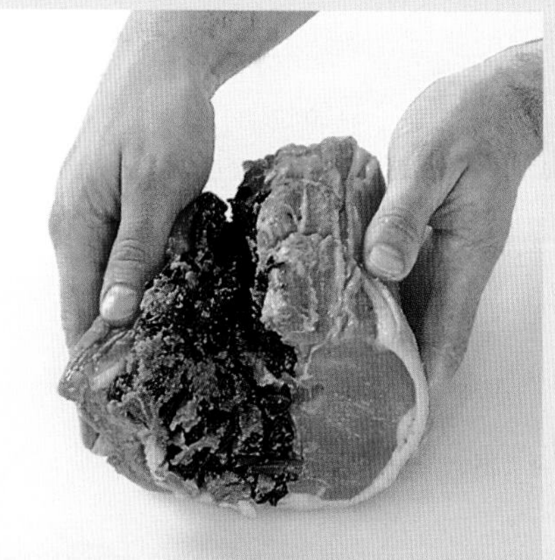

Bring the two sides of the veal together, enclosing the stuffing. Tie fine string around the veal at regular intervals.

Gravies for meat

Mushroom gravy
Melt 30 g (1 oz) butter in a saucepan. Add 1 finely chopped shallot and cook for 2 minutes until softened. Add 250 g (8 oz) sliced mushrooms and cook gently for 5 minutes. Pour in 300 ml (½ pint) beef stock, and simmer for about 5 minutes. Add 1 tbsp chopped parsley, 1 tsp chopped fresh thyme, and salt and black pepper to taste.

Onion gravy
Heat 1 tbsp sunflower oil and 30 g (1 oz) butter in a saucepan. Add 1 sliced onion and cook for 5–7 minutes until golden. Add 1 tbsp plain flour and cook, stirring, for 1 minute. Add 300 ml (½ pint) chicken stock. Simmer for about 5 minutes. Add salt and pepper to taste.

Red wine gravy
Melt 30 g (1 oz) butter in a saucepan. Add 1 sliced small onion and cook for 5 minutes or until beginning to brown. Add 1 tbsp plain flour and cook, stirring, for 1 minute. Add 100 ml (3½ fl oz) red wine and 300 ml (½ pint) beef stock. Simmer for about 5 minutes. Pour in any juices from the meat, and add salt and pepper to taste.

Lemon roast veal with spinach stuffing

Loin of veal is a lean cut, so it has a tendency to be dry. Marinating for 2 days before roasting makes it more succulent. Loin of pork can be marinated and cooked in the same way.

SERVES 6–8 **CALS PER SERVING** 444–333

- 1.25 kg (2½ lb) boned veal roasting joint, such as loin
- 150 ml (¼ pint) dry white wine
- 150 ml (¼ pint) chicken stock

Marinade

- 3 tbsp olive oil
- grated zest and juice of 1 lemon
- 4 thyme sprigs
- black pepper

Stuffing

- 30 g (1 oz) butter
- 1 shallot, finely chopped
- 2 streaky bacon rashers, rinds removed, finely chopped
- 175 g (6 oz) spinach leaves, coarsely shredded
- grated zest of 1 lemon
- 60 g (2 oz) fresh brown breadcrumbs
- salt and black pepper
- 1 small egg, lightly beaten

1 Combine the marinade ingredients in a non-metallic dish. Turn the veal in the marinade, cover, and leave to marinate in the refrigerator for 2 days.

2 Make the stuffing: melt the butter in a saucepan, add the shallot and bacon, and cook for 5 minutes or until the shallot is softened. Stir in the spinach and cook for 1 minute. Remove from the heat, add the lemon zest and breadcrumbs, and season with salt and pepper. Mix well, then bind with the egg. Leave to cool completely.

3 Remove the veal from the marinade, reserving the marinade. Spread the stuffing over the veal and roll up (see box, opposite).

4 Weigh the veal, insert a meat thermometer, if using, into the middle of the meat, and place in a roasting tin. Pour the marinade around the meat. Roast in a preheated oven at 180°C (160°C fan, Gas 4) for 25 minutes per 500 g (1 lb), until the juices run clear or until the thermometer registers 80°C (175°F). Transfer to a platter, cover loosely with foil, and leave to stand in a warm place for 10 minutes.

5 Meanwhile make the gravy: spoon the fat from the tin and remove the thyme sprigs. Put the tin on the hob, add the wine and stock, and bring to a boil, stirring to dissolve the sediment from the bottom of the tin. Boil for 5 minutes or until thickened and reduced by about half.

6 Taste the gravy for seasoning, and pour into a warmed gravy boat. Carve the veal, and serve hot.

Calf's liver with sage

SERVES 4 **CALS PER SERVING** 364

2 tbsp plain flour
salt and black pepper
500 g (1 lb) calf's liver, sliced
60 g (2 oz) butter
1 tbsp sunflower oil
juice of 1 lemon
3 tbsp roughly chopped fresh sage
sage leaves and lemon slices, to garnish

1 Sprinkle the flour on to a plate and season with salt and pepper. Coat the liver slices in the seasoned flour, shaking off any excess.

2 Melt half of the butter with the oil in a large frying pan. When the butter is foaming, add half of the liver slices and cook over a high heat for about 1 minute on each side until browned all over. Lift out with a slotted spoon and keep warm. Repeat with the remaining liver slices.

3 Melt the remaining butter in the pan, and add the lemon juice and sage, stirring to dissolve any sediment from the bottom of the pan. Pour the pan juices over the liver, garnish with sage leaves and lemon slices, and serve at once.

CALF'S LIVER WITH APPLE

Halve and slice 1 eating apple and add to the pan with the lemon juice and sage. Cook, stirring, for 3 minutes, and serve with the liver.

Cook's know-how

Overcooking liver will toughen it, so make sure that the butter and oil are really hot. This will ensure that the liver cooks quickly.

Veal schnitzels

SERVES 4 **CALS PER SERVING** 373

4 x 60–90 g (2–3 oz) veal escalopes
salt and black pepper
1 egg, beaten
125 g (4 oz) fresh white breadcrumbs
60 g (2 oz) butter
1 tbsp sunflower oil

To serve

8 anchovy fillets, drained and halved lengthways
2 tbsp coarsely chopped capers
lemon wedges
parsley

1 Put each veal escalope between two sheets of cling film and pound to a 3 mm (⅛ in) thickness with a rolling pin. Season with salt and pepper.

2 Spread the beaten egg over a plate, and sprinkle the breadcrumbs over another plate. Dip each escalope into the beaten egg, then into the breadcrumbs, to coat evenly. Chill in the refrigerator for about 30 minutes.

3 Melt the butter with the oil in a large frying pan until foaming, add two of the escalopes, and cook for 2 minutes on each side until golden. Drain on paper towels and keep warm while cooking the remaining escalopes. Serve the veal escalopes hot, with anchovy fillets, capers, lemon wedges, and parsley.

Veal stew with olives and peppers

SERVES 8 **CALS PER SERVING** 355

2 tbsp plain flour
salt and black pepper
1.5 kg (3 lb) stewing veal, cut into 3.5 cm (1½ in) cubes
2–3 tbsp olive oil
2 garlic cloves, crushed
1 red, 1 green, and 1 yellow pepper, halved, deseeded, and cut into strips
250 ml (8 fl oz) dry white wine
2 x 400 g cans chopped tomatoes
4 tbsp tomato purée
1 tsp chopped rosemary
250 g (8 oz) pitted black olives
1 tbsp chopped fresh rosemary, to garnish
1 tbsp chopped parsley, to garnish

1 Put the flour into a plastic bag and season with salt and pepper. Toss the veal in the seasoned flour to coat lightly.

2 Heat the oil in a large flameproof casserole. Add the veal and sprinkle with half of the garlic, then cook for 5–7 minutes until browned all over. Lift out the veal and set aside.

3 Add the peppers and cook, stirring, for 3 minutes, until almost soft. Remove from the casserole and set aside.

4 Return the veal to the casserole, and add the wine, tomatoes, tomato purée, remaining garlic, and rosemary. Cover and simmer for 1 hour.

5 Return the peppers to the casserole and cook for a further 30 minutes or until the meat is very tender.

6 Stir the olives into the casserole and heat through. Serve hot, lightly sprinkled with rosemary and parsley.

Osso buco

Originally from Milan, the name of this Italian classic means "bone with a hole", as it is made from thick slices of veal shin that have the central bone in – they are called shanks by some butchers. For authenticity, serve with gremolata and a creamy Risotto Milanese (page 377).

SERVES 6 **CALS PER SERVING** 354

30 g (1 oz) plain flour
salt and black pepper
6 veal shanks (bone-in), cut about 3.5–5 cm (1½–2 in) thick
30 g (1 oz) butter
2 tbsp olive oil
2 onions, finely chopped
175 g (6 oz) carrots, finely chopped
2 celery stalks, finely chopped
2 garlic cloves, crushed
300 ml (½ pint) dry white wine
300 ml (½ pint) chicken stock
1 x 400 g can chopped tomatoes
2 tsp chopped fresh oregano
1 bay leaf
risotto Milanese and gremolata (see box, right), to serve

1 Put the flour into a large plastic bag and season with salt and pepper. Put the veal shanks into the bag and shake until all the meat is evenly coated with flour.

2 Melt the butter with the oil in a large flameproof casserole. When the butter is foaming, add the veal and cook in batches, for 10 minutes or until golden all over. Lift out and drain on paper towels. Lower the heat, add the onions, carrots, celery, and garlic, and cook for 5 minutes.

3 Pour in the wine and boil until reduced by half. Add the stock, tomatoes, oregano, and bay leaf, and bring to a boil. Return the veal to the casserole, bring back to a boil, cover, and cook in a preheated oven at 160°C (140°C fan, Gas 3) for 1½–2 hours until very tender.

4 If the sauce in the casserole is too thin, lift out the veal and keep hot, then boil the sauce until reduced to a thicker consistency. Taste for seasoning. Serve the veal on a bed of risotto, and sprinkle over the gremolata.

Cook's know-how

In Italy, the veal is sold with the marrow in the middle of the bone because it is a traditional custom to scoop it out of the bone after finishing the meat. It tastes really good spread on fresh crusty bread.

Gremolata

Put 2 tbsp chopped parsley, the finely grated zest of 1 lemon, and 1 finely chopped garlic clove into a small bowl and stir to mix thoroughly.

Veal chops with mushrooms and cream

SERVES 4 **CALS PER SERVING** 604

15 g (½ oz) dried porcini mushrooms
250 ml (8 fl oz) warm water
2 tbsp plain flour
salt and black pepper
4 x 250 g (8 oz) veal loin chops
45 g (1½ oz) butter
8 shallots, chopped
3 garlic cloves, crushed
250 g (8 oz) button mushrooms, thinly sliced
250 ml (8 fl oz) dry white wine
300 ml (½ pint) single cream
1 tbsp chopped fresh tarragon, plus extra to garnish

1 Put the dried mushrooms into a bowl, pour over the warm water, and leave to soak for 30 minutes or until soft.

2 Sprinkle the flour on to a plate, and season with salt and pepper. Lightly coat the chops with the flour.

3 Melt half of the butter in a frying pan, add the veal chops, and cook for about 4 minutes on each side.

4 Remove the chops and keep warm. Melt the remaining butter in the pan, add the shallots and garlic, and cook gently, stirring occasionally, for a few minutes until softened.

5 Drain the dried mushrooms, reserving the soaking liquid. Add the dried and button mushrooms to the pan and cook for 3 minutes or until tender. Remove the shallots and mushrooms from the pan and keep warm.

6 Pour in the wine and boil until reduced to about 3 tbsp. Add the mushroom liquid and boil until reduced to about 125 ml (4 fl oz).

7 Stir in the cream and heat gently. Add the tarragon, and season with salt and pepper. Return the chops, shallots, and mushrooms to the pan and heat through gently. Transfer to serving plates, sprinkle with the extra chopped tarragon, and serve hot.

Liver and bacon with onion sauce

SERVES 4 **CALS PER SERVING** 441

2 tbsp sunflower oil
1 large onion, thinly sliced
125 g (4 oz) streaky bacon rashers, rinds removed, cut into strips
500 g (1 lb) calf's liver, trimmed and cut into 1 cm (½ in) strips
2 tbsp plain flour
600 ml (1 pint) beef stock
3 tbsp tomato ketchup
a dash of Worcestershire sauce
salt and black pepper
chopped fresh tarragon, to garnish

1 Heat the oil in a large frying pan, add the onion and bacon, and cook gently, stirring occasionally, for a few minutes until the onion is soft and the bacon crisp. Add the liver and cook, stirring, for 2 minutes. Remove with a slotted spoon and keep warm.

2 Add the flour to the pan and cook, stirring, for 1 minute. Pour in the stock and bring to a boil, stirring until thickened.

3 Add the ketchup and Worcestershire sauce, and season. Return the onion, bacon, and liver to the pan, cover, and simmer for 5 minutes. Sprinkle with tarragon and serve with boiled potatoes and peas.

LIVER STROGANOFF

Use 150 ml (¼ pint) chicken stock instead of the beef stock and omit the ketchup and Worcestershire sauce. Stir in 150 ml (¼ pint) soured cream.

Creamed sweetbreads

SERVES 6 **CALS PER SERVING** 230

500 g (1 lb) calf's sweetbreads
2 tbsp lemon juice
1 small onion, chopped
a few parsley sprigs
1 bay leaf
salt and black pepper
45 g (1½ oz) butter
45 g (1½ oz) plain flour
300 ml (½ pint) milk
chopped parsley, to garnish

1 Put the sweetbreads into a bowl, cover with cold water, add 1 tbsp of the lemon juice. Leave to soak for 2–3 hours.

2 Drain, rinse, and trim the sweetbreads (page 237).

3 Put the sweetbreads into a large saucepan with the onion, parsley, bay leaf, and a sprinkling of salt and pepper. Cover with cold water and bring slowly to a boil. Simmer gently for 5 minutes or until just tender, skimming off any scum as it rises to the surface.

4 Drain the sweetbreads, and reserve 300 ml (½ pint) of the cooking liquid. Cut the sweetbreads into bite-sized pieces.

5 Melt the butter in a saucepan, add the flour, and cook, stirring, for 1 minute. Remove the pan from the heat, and gradually blend in the milk and reserved cooking liquid. Bring to a boil, stirring constantly, and boil for 2–3 minutes until the mixture thickens. Add the remaining lemon juice and season with salt and pepper.

6 Add the sweetbreads to the sauce and simmer gently for about 5 minutes to warm through. Transfer to warmed plates and garnish with chopped parsley before serving.

Shoulder of lamb with garlic and herbs

SERVES 6 **CALS PER SERVING** 464

2 kg (4 lb) shoulder of lamb, trimmed of excess fat
haricot bean cassoulet (page 405), to serve

Herb butter

90 g (3 oz) butter, softened
2 garlic cloves, crushed
1 tbsp chopped fresh thyme
1 tbsp chopped fresh rosemary
1 tbsp chopped fresh mint
2 tbsp chopped parsley
salt and black pepper

Gravy

1 tbsp plain flour
150 ml (1/4 pint) red wine
150 ml (1/4 pint) lamb or chicken stock

1 Make the herb butter: mix the butter, garlic, thyme, rosemary, mint, and parsley, and season with salt and pepper.

2 Slash the lamb at regular intervals with a sharp knife, then push the herb butter into the cuts. Rub any remaining butter over the lamb. Weigh the lamb.

3 Put the lamb on a rack in a roasting tin and insert a meat thermometer, if using, into the middle of the meat. Cook in a preheated oven at 200°C (180°C fan, Gas 6) for 30 minutes.

4 Lower the temperature to 180°C (160°C fan, Gas 4) and cook for 20 minutes per 500 g (1 lb). The thermometer should register 75–80°C (170–175°F).

5 Remove the lamb. Cover loosely with foil and leave to stand in a warm place for about 10 minutes.

6 Make the gravy: drain all but 1 tbsp of the fat from the tin. Set the tin on the hob, add the flour, and cook, stirring, for 1 minute. Pour in the wine and stock, bring to a boil, and simmer for 2–3 minutes. Taste for seasoning, and strain into a warmed gravy boat. Serve with the lamb and haricot bean cassoulet.

Slow-roast shoulder of lamb

SERVES 4–6 **CALS PER SERVING** 656–437

1.35 kg (3 lb) shoulder of lamb, bone in
2 large garlic cloves, sliced
3 rosemary sprigs, snipped into pieces
1 onion, cut into quarters
finely grated zest and juice of 1 lemon
2 tbsp olive oil
salt and black pepper
600 ml (1 pint) beef stock
1 tbsp plain flour
3 tbsp port
new potatoes, to serve

1 With the tip of a small pointed knife, make incisions through the skin of the lamb and into the meat. Push the garlic and rosemary into the slits.

2 Scatter the onion quarters over the bottom of a roasting tin, and sit the lamb skin-side up on top. Sprinkle over the lemon zest and juice and the olive oil, and season with salt and pepper. Pour the stock into the tin around the lamb.

3 Roast in a preheated oven at 220°C (200°C fan, Gas 7) for 30–40 minutes until the lamb is brown on top. Lower the oven temperature to 150°C (130°C fan, Gas 2), and roast for a further 3–3½ hours until the lamb is completely tender, basting from time to time.

4 Transfer the lamb to a board, and cover with foil. Leave to stand in a warm place for about 15 minutes.

5 Meanwhile, skim off the fat from the roasting tin, then put 3 tbsp of the fat into a saucepan. Tip the stock and onions into a sieve held over a bowl, and strain the liquid through, pressing on the onions to extract their juices. Measure 600 ml (1 pint) liquid, making it up with a little stock or water if necessary. Heat the fat in the saucepan, sprinkle in the flour, and whisk over a high heat to combine. Gradually blend in the measured stock, whisk until boiling and smooth, then stir in the port and continue boiling until the gravy has reduced by half. Serve the lamb with herby new potatoes and the hot gravy.

Greek roast lamb

SERVES 6 **CALS PER SERVING** 328

2 kg (4 lb) leg of lamb
4 garlic cloves, cut into slivers
2 large rosemary sprigs, chopped
1 tbsp olive oil
salt and black pepper
chopped fresh rosemary, to garnish

1 With a sharp knife, make small incisions in the lamb and insert a sliver of garlic into each incision.

2 Rub the lamb with the rosemary, olive oil, and salt and pepper, then put it in a roasting tin.

3 Roast in a preheated oven at 220°C (200°C fan, Gas 7) for 30 minutes or until the lamb is browned. Lower the oven temperature to 140°C (120°C fan, Gas 1), cover, and cook for a further 3½ hours or until the lamb is very tender.

4 Cover the lamb with foil and leave to rest in a warm place for 10 minutes. Carve the lamb and serve hot, garnished with rosemary. Any cooking juices can be served with the meat, if you like.

Other sauces for lamb

Mint sauce
In a small bowl, combine 3 tbsp finely chopped fresh mint with 1–2 tbsp caster sugar, to taste. Add 3 tbsp white wine vinegar or cider vinegar and stir well to mix.

Cumberland sauce
Put 4 tbsp redcurrant jelly into a small saucepan and heat gently until melted. Add 125 ml (4 fl oz) red wine and the grated zest of 1 orange. Bring to simmering point, and simmer, whisking constantly, for 5 minutes. Add the juices of 1 orange and ½ lemon and simmer for a further 5 minutes. Strain, then add salt and pepper. Serve hot.

Tzatziki sauce
Put 150 g (5 oz) Greek-style yogurt, the grated zest and juice of 1 lemon, 1 crushed garlic clove, 1 tbsp chopped fresh mint, and salt and pepper into a small bowl. Mix well to combine, then taste for seasoning. Cover and chill until required.

Roast leg of lamb with red wine gravy

A rich gravy that incorporates all the flavoursome juices from the meat is traditional with roast lamb. Red wine boosts the gravy's flavour, and you can add a spoonful of redcurrant jelly too, plus a squeeze of lemon juice and a dash of Worcestershire sauce if you like.

SERVES 4–6 **CALS PER SERVING** 517–344

2 kg (4 lb) leg of lamb
salt and black pepper
2 tbsp chopped fresh rosemary
1 tbsp plain flour
300 ml (½ pint) lamb or chicken stock
90 ml (3 fl oz) red wine
mint sauce (see box, page 276), to serve
thyme, to garnish

1 Trim the skin and excess fat from the lamb. Score the fat (see box, right).

2 Insert a meat thermometer, if using, into the middle of the meat. Put the lamb, fat-side up, on a rack in a roasting tin, and rub with salt and pepper and the rosemary.

3 Roast the lamb in a preheated oven at 200°C (180°C fan, Gas 6) for 20 minutes. Lower the oven temperature to 180°C (160°C fan, Gas 4) and roast for 20 minutes per 500 g (1 lb) for medium-done meat, or 25 minutes per 500 g (1 lb) for well-done meat, until the meat thermometer registers 75–80°C (170–175°F), and the fat is crisp and golden.

4 Remove the lamb, cover with foil, and leave to stand for 10 minutes.

5 Meanwhile, make the gravy: spoon all but 1 tbsp fat from the tin. Put the tin on the hob, add the flour, and cook, stirring, for 1 minute. Pour in the stock and wine, and bring to a boil, stirring to dissolve any sediment.

6 Simmer the gravy for about 3 minutes, season with salt and pepper, then strain if you like. Serve the lamb garnished with thyme, and accompanied by the gravy and mint sauce.

Scoring the fat

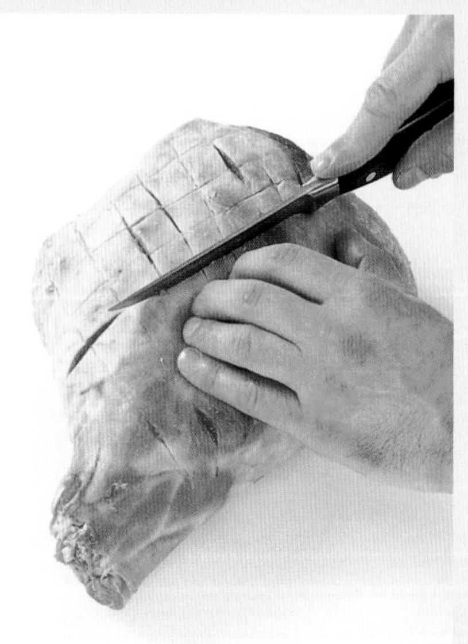

Score the fat in a criss-cross pattern using a small, sharp knife, making sure that only the fat is cut, and that the meat underneath remains completely untouched.

Spinach-stuffed lamb

The lamb in this recipe is distinctively flavoured with spinach, wine, and anchovies. Stuffed mushrooms are a perfect accompaniment.

SERVES 6–8 **CALS PER SERVING** 459–344

2 kg (4 lb) leg of lamb, boned but left whole (page 234)
150 ml (¼ pint) dry white wine
4 canned anchovy fillets, chopped
about 150 ml (¼ pint) lamb or chicken stock
salt and black pepper

Spinach stuffing

30 g (1 oz) butter
3–4 garlic cloves, crushed
250 g (8 oz) spinach leaves, coarsely shredded
60 g (2 oz) fresh brown breadcrumbs
1 egg, beaten

1 Make the stuffing: melt the butter in a pan. Add the garlic and cook, stirring, for 2–3 minutes until soft. Stir in the spinach, season with salt and pepper, and cook for 1 minute. Add the breadcrumbs, cool, then mix in the egg.

2 Stuff the lamb (see box, right). Secure with fine skewers or thin string.

3 Put the lamb on a rack in a roasting tin and roast in a preheated oven at 200°C (180°C fan, Gas 6) for 15 minutes. Turn, insert a meat thermometer, if using, and cook for 15 minutes.

4 Drain the fat from the tin, then add the wine and anchovies. Cover the lamb loosely with foil, lower the oven temperature to 180°C (160°C fan, Gas 4), and cook for 1½ hours or until the juices run slightly pink. The thermometer should register 75–80°C (170–175°F).

5 Remove the lamb from the tin. Leave to stand, covered with the foil, in a warm place for about 10 minutes.

6 Pour the cooking liquid into a measuring jug and make up to 300 ml (½ pint) with stock.

7 Return the cooking liquid to the tin. Bring to a boil, stirring to dissolve the sediment. Season, and strain into a warmed gravy boat. Serve the lamb, and hand the gravy separately.

Stuffing the lamb

Season the cavity of the lamb with salt and pepper, then spoon in the cold spinach stuffing, packing it in tightly.

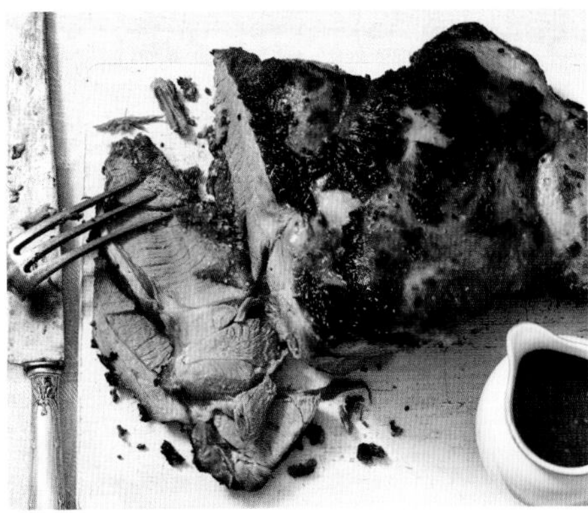

Lemon-grilled lamb

SERVES 6–8 **CALS PER SERVING** 425–318

2–2.5 kg (4–5 lb) leg of lamb, butterflied (page 234)

Marinade

juice of 3 lemons
4 tbsp clear honey
3 large garlic cloves, quartered
2 tbsp coarse-grain mustard

1 Make the marinade: in a non-metallic dish, mix together the lemon juice, honey, garlic, and mustard. Turn the lamb in the marinade, cover, and leave to marinate in the refrigerator, turning the lamb occasionally, for 1–2 days.

2 Remove the lamb from the marinade. Strain and reserve the marinade. Cook the lamb under a hot grill, 15 cm (6 in) from the heat, for 20–25 minutes on each side, basting with the marinade from time to time.

3 Test the lamb: insert a skewer into the thickest part – the juices will run clear when it is cooked.

4 Leave the lamb to stand, covered with foil, in a warm place for 5–10 minutes. Spoon the fat from the grill pan, strain the juices into a gravy boat, and serve with the lamb.

Cook's know-how

Butterflied leg of lamb is a good cut for cooking on the barbecue as well as under the grill because the meat is thin enough to cook quickly without becoming too charred on the outside.

Shoulder of lamb with lemon and olives

SERVES 6–8 **CALS PER SERVING** 460–345

2 kg (4 lb) shoulder of lamb, boned
2 garlic cloves, cut into slivers
150 ml (¼ pint) dry white wine
150 ml (¼ pint) lamb or chicken stock

Lemon and olive stuffing

1 tbsp olive oil
1 shallot, finely chopped
125 g (4 oz) fresh breadcrumbs
30 g (1 oz) pitted black olives, roughly chopped
finely grated zest of 1 lemon
1 tbsp chopped fresh thyme
1 tbsp chopped fresh rosemary
1 small egg, beaten
salt and black pepper

1 Make the stuffing: heat the olive oil in a small pan, add the shallot, and cook for about 5 minutes. Remove from the heat and add the breadcrumbs, olives, lemon zest, herbs, and egg. Season with salt and pepper, stir, and leave to cool.

2 Make incisions in the meat side of the lamb, insert the garlic slivers into them, then sprinkle with salt and pepper and spread with the stuffing. Roll up and secure with skewers, then weigh the lamb.

3 Put the lamb into a roasting tin and insert a meat thermometer, if using, into the middle of the meat. Pour over the wine and stock and cook in a preheated oven at 200°C (180°C fan, Gas 6) for 20–25 minutes. Lower the temperature to 180°C (160°C fan, Gas 4) and cook for 20 minutes per 500 g (1 lb) or until the juices run clear. The meat thermometer should register 75–80°C (170–175°F).

4 Remove the lamb, cover loosely with foil, and leave to stand for 10 minutes. Put the tin on the hob and spoon off any fat. Bring to a boil, and boil for 5 minutes, stirring to dissolve any sediment from the tin. Season, strain, and serve.

Indian spiced lamb

SERVES 6 **CALS PER SERVING** 379

1.5 kg (3 lb) shoulder or leg of lamb
1 tsp lemon juice
salt and black pepper
cashew nuts and chopped coriander, to garnish

Spiced yogurt marinade

4 garlic cloves, coarsely chopped 7 cm (3 in) piece of fresh root ginger, peeled and grated
2 tbsp clear honey
1 tbsp lemon juice
seeds of 5 cardamom pods
1 tsp ground cumin
1 tsp turmeric
¼ tsp cayenne pepper
1 tsp salt
½ tsp ground cinnamon
¼ tsp ground cloves (optional)
150 g (5 oz) Greek yogurt

1 Make the spiced yogurt marinade: purée the garlic, ginger, honey, lemon juice, cardamom, cumin, turmeric, cayenne, salt, cinnamon, cloves (if using), and yogurt in a blender or food processor.

2 Spread the mixture over the lamb (see box, below). Cover and leave to marinate in the refrigerator for at least 2 hours, or overnight.

3 Put the lamb on a rack in a roasting tin and cook in a preheated oven at 160°C (140°C fan, Gas 3) for 3½ hours or until the meat is tender.

4 Remove the lamb and keep hot. Spoon the fat from the tin. Set the tin on the hob and stir in the lemon juice and enough water to make a sauce. Bring to a boil, stirring, and season with salt and pepper.

5 Cut the lamb from the bone, then cut the meat into chunks and mix with the sauce on the hob. Serve hot, garnished with cashew nuts and chopped coriander.

Coating the lamb

Make incisions in the lamb, then spread the marinade over the whole joint, making sure it goes into the incisions.

Irish stew

SERVES 4 **CALS PER SERVING** 539

1 kg (2 lb) main-crop potatoes, cut into 5 mm (¼ in) slices
2 large onions, sliced
1 kg (2 lb) middle neck lamb chops, trimmed
a few parsley stalks, plus extra to garnish (optional)
1 thyme sprig
1 bay leaf
salt and black pepper
300–500 ml (10–16 fl oz) water

1 Put half of the potatoes into a flameproof casserole, cover with half of the onions, then add the chops, parsley, thyme, and bay leaf, and season with salt and pepper. Add the remaining onions, then the remaining potatoes, seasoning each layer with salt and pepper.

2 Pour in enough water to half-fill the casserole, and then bring to a boil. Cover tightly and cook in a preheated oven at 160°C (140°C fan, Gas 3) for 2–2½ hours until the lamb and potatoes are just tender.

3 Remove the lid, increase the oven temperature to 220°C (200°C fan, Gas 7), and cook for 20–30 minutes to brown the topping. Sprinkle with chopped parsley if you wish, and serve.

Blanquette of lamb

SERVES 6 **CALS PER SERVING** 439

1 kg (2 lb) boneless shoulder of lamb, trimmed and cut into chunks
1.25 litres (2 pints) water
8 button onions
2 large carrots, thickly sliced
2 bay leaves
juice of ½ lemon
salt and black pepper
250 g (8 oz) button mushrooms
45 g (1½ oz) butter
45 g (1½ oz) plain flour
150 ml (¼ pint) single cream
1 egg yolk
chopped parsley, to garnish

1 Put the chunks of lamb into a large saucepan, cover with cold water, and bring to a boil. Drain, then rinse the meat thoroughly to remove the scum.

2 Return the meat to the saucepan and pour in the measured water. Add the button onions, carrots, bay leaves, and lemon juice, and season with salt and pepper. Bring to a boil, cover, and simmer gently for 1 hour.

3 Add the mushrooms and simmer for 30 minutes. Lift out the lamb and vegetables, reserving the liquid, and keep hot.

4 Melt the butter in a small pan. Add the flour and cook, stirring occasionally, for 1 minute. Gradually blend in the reserved cooking liquid, stirring constantly. Bring to a boil, stirring, then simmer until the sauce thickens.

5 In a bowl, whisk together the cream and egg yolk. Blend in 2 tbsp of the hot sauce. Take the saucepan off the heat, stir the cream mixture into the sauce, then reheat very gently. Taste for seasoning. Pour the sauce over the lamb and garnish with parsley before serving.

Lancashire hot pot

SERVES 4 **CALS PER SERVING** 689

2 tbsp sunflower oil
1 kg (2 lb) middle neck lamb chops, trimmed
3 lamb's kidneys, trimmed (page 237) and halved
1 kg (2 lb) potatoes, cut into 5 mm (¼ in) slices
500 g (1 lb) carrots, sliced
2 large onions, chopped
1 tsp caster sugar
salt and black pepper
1 bay leaf
1 rosemary sprig
a few parsley sprigs, plus extra to garnish
600–750 ml (1–1¼ pints) lamb or chicken stock, or water

1 Heat the oil in a flameproof casserole, add the lamb in batches, and brown over a medium heat for 5 minutes. Remove and set aside. Add the kidneys and cook for 3–5 minutes. Remove and set aside.

2 Add the potatoes, carrots, and onions, and cook for 5 minutes. Remove from the casserole.

3 Make layers of lamb chops, kidneys, and vegetables in the casserole, sprinkling with the sugar and a little salt and pepper, and putting the herbs in the middle.

4 Top with a neat layer of potatoes. Pour in enough stock or water to come up to the potato layer. Cover tightly and cook in a preheated oven at 160°C (140°C fan, Gas 3) for 2 hours or until the meat and vegetables are tender.

5 Remove the casserole lid, increase the oven temperature to 220°C (200°C fan, Gas 7), and cook for 20–30 minutes to brown the potato topping. Sprinkle with chopped parsley before serving.

COUNTRY HOT POT

Omit the kidneys, and substitute 250 g (8 oz) swede for half of the carrots. Layer the meat and vegetables with 60 g (2 oz) pearl barley.

Spiced lamb shanks

SERVES 4 **CALS PER SERVING** 869

2 tbsp sunflower oil
4 small lamb shanks
2 carrots, diced
2 onions, coarsely chopped
2 garlic cloves, crushed
45 g (1½ oz) plain flour
2 tsp five-spice powder
500 ml (16 fl oz) lager
200 ml (7 fl oz) beef stock
3 tbsp soy sauce
2 tsp tomato purée
1 tbsp brown sugar
salt and black pepper

1 Heat 1 tbsp of the oil in a large flameproof casserole, and brown the lamb shanks over a high heat until golden on all sides. Remove the lamb from the pan, and set aside.

2 Heat the remaining oil in the pan, add the vegetables and garlic, and fry over a medium heat for about 5 minutes. Sprinkle in the flour and five-spice powder, and fry for 1 minute. Gradually blend in the lager and stock, whisk over a high heat until boiling and smooth, then add the soy sauce, tomato purée, and sugar, and season with salt and pepper. Return the lamb to the pan, cover, and bring to a boil.

3 Cook in a preheated oven at 160°C (140°C fan, Gas 3) for 2–2½ hours until the lamb is tender and just falling off the bones. Check the seasoning before serving the lamb hot, with mashed potato and the gravy poured over.

Lamb tagine

SERVES 8 **CALS PER SERVING** 412

¼ tsp saffron threads
150 ml (¼ pint) hot water
3 tbsp olive oil
1.5 kg (3 lb) boneless shoulder of lamb, well trimmed and cut into 2.5 cm (1 in) cubes
1 fennel bulb or 4 celery stalks, trimmed and sliced crosswise
2 green peppers, halved, deseeded, and cut into strips
1 large onion, sliced
30 g (1 oz) plain flour
½ tsp ground ginger
450 ml (¾ pint) lamb or chicken stock
grated zest and juice of 1 orange
125 g (4 oz) ready-to-eat dried apricots
salt and black pepper
mint sprigs, to garnish
couscous, to serve (page 432)

1 Prepare the saffron (see box, right). Heat the oil in a flameproof casserole, add the lamb in batches, and cook over a high heat for 5 minutes or until browned. Lift out and drain on paper towels.

2 Lower the heat, add the fennel or celery, peppers, and onion, and cook gently, stirring, for 5 minutes.

3 Sprinkle the flour and ginger into the vegetables and cook, stirring occasionally, for 1 minute. Add the saffron liquid to the casserole, return the cubes of lamb, then add the stock and orange zest (retaining a pinch for garnish), and season with salt and pepper. Bring to a boil, cover, and cook in a preheated oven at 160°C (140°C fan, Gas 3) for 1 hour.

4 Add the orange juice and apricots and cook for about 30 minutes until the lamb is very tender. Taste for seasoning and garnish with mint sprigs and reserved orange zest before serving with couscous.

Preparing saffron

Put the saffron threads into a small bowl, add the measured hot water, and leave to soak for 10 minutes.

Spiced lamb with coconut

SERVES 6 **CALS PER SERVING** 496

1 kg (2 lb) lamb neck fillet, trimmed and cut into 2.5 cm (1 in) cubes
30 g (1 oz) butter
1 tbsp sunflower oil
1 large Spanish onion, sliced
2 large garlic cloves, crushed
1 tbsp plain flour
1 x 400 g can chopped tomatoes
150 ml (¼ pint) lamb or chicken stock
grated zest and juice of 1 lime
2 tbsp mango chutney
60 g (2 oz) creamed coconut, chopped
250 g (8 oz) Greek yogurt
coriander sprigs, to garnish
salt and black pepper

Spice mix

2.5 cm (1 in) piece of fresh root ginger, peeled and grated
1 tbsp ground cumin
1 tbsp ground coriander
1 tbsp mild curry powder

1 Toss the meat in the spice mix, and season with salt and pepper.

2 Melt the butter with the oil in a large flameproof casserole. When the butter is foaming, add the lamb in batches, and cook over a high heat for about 5 minutes until browned all over.

3 Lift out with a slotted spoon and set aside. Lower the heat, add the onion and garlic, and cook gently, stirring occasionally, for a few minutes until soft but not coloured.

4 Sprinkle in the flour and cook, stirring, for 1 minute. Add the tomatoes, stock, lime zest and juice, and chutney, and season with salt and pepper. Bring to a boil, stirring.

5 Return the lamb to the casserole, add the coconut, and bring back to a boil. Cover and cook in a preheated oven at 160°C (140°C fan, Gas 3) for 2 hours or until the lamb is tender.

6 Stir in the yogurt and taste for seasoning. Garnish with coriander before serving.

Aromatic lamb with lentils

SERVES 8 **CALS PER SERVING** 475

1.5 kg (3 lb) lamb neck fillet, trimmed and cut into chunks
2 tbsp olive oil
2 onions, chopped
125 g (4 oz) brown or green Puy lentils, rinsed
175 g (6 oz) ready-to-eat dried apricots
salt and black pepper
600 ml (1 pint) lamb or chicken stock

Marinade

175 ml (6 fl oz) orange juice
2 tbsp olive oil
3 garlic cloves, crushed
1 tsp ground ginger
1 tsp ground coriander
½ tsp ground cinnamon

1 Make the marinade: in a large bowl, combine the orange juice, oil, garlic, ginger, coriander, and cinnamon.

2 Turn the chunks of lamb in the marinade, cover loosely, and then leave to marinate in the refrigerator overnight.

3 Remove the lamb from the marinade, reserving the marinade. Heat the olive oil in a large flameproof casserole, add the lamb in batches, and cook over a high heat for 5 minutes or until browned all over. Lift out the lamb chunks with a slotted spoon.

4 Lower the heat slightly, add the onions, and cook gently, stirring occasionally, for a few minutes until just soft but not coloured. Lift out of the casserole.

5 Make layers of lamb, onions, lentils, and apricots in the casserole, sprinkling each layer with salt and pepper. Pour in the stock and the reserved marinade and bring to a boil. Cover and cook in a preheated oven at 160°C (140°C fan, Gas 3) for 2 hours or until the meat is tender. Taste for seasoning before serving.

Fragrant lamb korma

This aromatic lamb dish is enriched with yogurt instead of cream, which makes it healthier than a traditional korma. The fresh mint and paprika garnish adds to both flavour and presentation. For an authentic accompaniment, serve with spiced red lentils.

SERVES 6 **CALS PER SERVING** 508

5 cm (2 in) piece of fresh root ginger, peeled and grated
3 large garlic cloves, peeled
2 large green chillies, halved and deseeded
60 g (2 oz) salted cashew nuts (optional)
2 tsp ground cumin
2 tsp ground cardamom
2 tsp turmeric
6 tbsp water
3 tbsp sunflower oil
1 kg (2 lb) lamb neck fillet, trimmed and cut into 4 cm (1½ in) cubes
2 large onions, roughly chopped
300 ml (¼ pint) full-fat Greek-style yogurt
salt and black pepper
about 1 tbsp lemon juice
fresh mint and paprika, to garnish

1 Place the ginger, garlic, chillies, cashew nuts (if using), cumin, cardamom, turmeric, and measured water in a food processor or blender, and purée until smooth.

2 Heat 2 tbsp of the oil in a large flameproof casserole, and brown the lamb on all sides (you may need to do this in batches). Remove with a slotted spoon and set aside to drain on kitchen paper.

3 Heat the remaining oil in the same pan, and fry the onions over a high heat for 2–3 minutes. Return the lamb to the pan, add the puréed spice blend, and stir in the yogurt. Season with salt and pepper, cover, and simmer gently for about 1½–2 hours until the lamb is tender.

4 Just before serving, add the lemon juice, and check the seasoning. Garnish with a sprinkling of mint and paprika, and serve hot.

Lamb noisettes with orange and honey

SERVES 4 **CALS PER SERVING** 457

8 lamb noisettes
2 lamb's kidneys, trimmed (page 237) and quartered (optional)
chopped fresh thyme and rosemary, to garnish

Marinade

grated zest and juice of 1 orange
4 tbsp clear honey
3 tbsp olive oil
2 garlic cloves, crushed
1 tbsp chopped fresh thyme
1 tbsp chopped fresh rosemary
salt and black pepper

1 Make the marinade: in a shallow, non-metallic dish, combine the orange zest and juice, honey, oil, garlic, thyme, and rosemary, and season with salt and pepper. Add the lamb noisettes to the marinade, turn them, then cover, and leave to marinate in the refrigerator overnight.

2 Lift the lamb noisettes out of the marinade, reserving the marinade. Place a piece of kidney, if using, in the middle of each lamb noisette.

3 Put under a hot grill, 10 cm (4 in) from the heat, and cook for 7 minutes on each side until the lamb is tender.

4 Meanwhile, strain the marinade into a small saucepan, bring to a boil, and simmer for a few minutes until it reaches a syrupy consistency. Taste for seasoning, spoon over the lamb noisettes, and garnish with thyme and rosemary.

Cook's know-how

Noisettes are taken from the loin of the lamb. The eye of meat is cut away, then rolled, tied, and cut into thick slices. It is an expensive cut but gives neat portions of tender, lean meat, with no waste.

Lamb chops with minted hollandaise sauce

Instead of the traditional mint sauce, lamb chops are served here with a creamy hollandaise sauce flavoured with fresh mint. The sauce is easy to make, as long as you take care not to get the melted butter too hot.

SERVES 4 **CALS PER SERVING** 611

4 chump lamb chops
a little olive oil
salt and black pepper
minted hollandaise sauce, to serve (see box, right)

1 Brush the chops on both sides with a little oil, and season with salt and pepper.

2 Put the chops under a hot grill, 10 cm (4 in) from the heat, and cook for 3–4 minutes on each side for medium–rare chops, slightly longer for well-done.

3 Arrange the lamb chops on warmed serving plates and serve at once with the warm minted hollandaise sauce.

Minted hollandaise sauce

Whisk together 2 tsp lemon juice, 2 tsp white wine vinegar, and 3 egg yolks at room temperature. Put over a pan of simmering water and whisk until thick. In another pan, gently melt 125 g (4 oz) unsalted butter (do not let it get too hot). Pour into a jug. Pour the melted butter, a little at a time, into the egg-yolk mixture, whisking constantly until the sauce thickens. Remove from the heat, stir in 2 tbsp chopped fresh mint, and season with salt and pepper. Pour into a sauce boat and serve at once.

Herbed butterfly chops

SERVES 4 **CALS PER SERVING** 320

4 butterfly lamb chops
1 tbsp olive oil
black pepper
4 rosemary sprigs
4 mint sprigs
4 thyme sprigs

1 Place the lamb chops on a grill rack and brush each one with half of the oil. Sprinkle with black pepper and scatter with the herb sprigs.

2 Place the chops under a hot grill, 10 cm (4 in) from the heat, and cook for 4–6 minutes. Remove from the heat, lift off the herbs, and turn the chops over. Brush the chops with the remaining oil, replace the herbs, and grill for 4–6 minutes until done to your liking. Serve hot.

Rack of lamb with a walnut and herb crust

Also called best end of neck, a rack of lamb usually has 6–8 bones, which are called cutlets. The bones should be scraped clean of all fat – this is called "French trimmed" by some butchers.

SERVES 4–6 **CALS PER SERVING** 626–417

2 prepared racks of lamb (page 235)
1 egg, beaten

Walnut and herb crust

30 g (1 oz) fresh wholemeal breadcrumbs
30 g (1 oz) parsley, chopped
2 tbsp coarsely chopped walnut pieces
2 large garlic cloves, crushed
finely grated zest of 1 lemon
1 tbsp walnut oil
salt and black pepper

Wine and grape sauce

150 ml (¼ pint) dry white wine
150 ml (¼ pint) lamb or chicken stock
125 g (4 oz) seedless green grapes, halved

1 Brush the outsides of the racks of lamb with some of the beaten egg.

2 Prepare the walnut and herb crust: combine the breadcrumbs, parsley, walnuts, garlic, lemon zest, and oil, season with salt and pepper, and bind with the remaining egg. Chill for 30 minutes.

3 Coat the racks with the walnut and herb crust (see box, right), and put them crust-side up into a roasting tin. Cook in a preheated oven at 200°C (180°C fan, Gas 6) for 30 minutes.

4 Remove the lamb, cover with foil, and leave to stand in a warm place for 10 minutes.

5 Meanwhile, make the sauce: spoon all but 1 tbsp of the fat from the roasting tin. Set the tin on the hob, pour in the wine, and bring to a boil, stirring to dissolve any sediment from the bottom of the tin.

6 Add the stock and boil, stirring occasionally, for 2–3 minutes. Taste the sauce for seasoning, strain into a warmed sauce boat, and stir in the grapes. Serve the lamb with sautéed potatoes, purple-sprouting broccoli, and the sauce.

Coating the lamb

Press half of the walnut and herb crust mixture on to the meaty side of each rack of lamb, using a palette knife.

Lamb with mint glaze

SERVES 4 **CALS PER SERVING** 304

8 best end lamb chops, well-trimmed

Mint glaze

3 tbsp dry white wine
1 tbsp white wine vinegar
4 mint sprigs, leaves stripped and chopped
1 tbsp clear honey
1 tsp Dijon mustard
salt and black pepper

1 Make the mint glaze: combine the wine, vinegar, mint, honey, and mustard, and season with salt and pepper. Brush the glaze over the chops, and leave to marinate for about 30 minutes.

2 Place the chops over a barbecue or under a hot grill, 7 cm (3 in) from the heat, and cook, brushing often with the glaze, for 4–6 minutes on each side, until done to your liking.

LAMB WITH ORANGE GLAZE

Instead of the mint glaze, combine 3 tbsp orange juice with 1 tbsp each white wine vinegar, orange marmalade, and chopped fresh thyme, and 1 tsp Dijon mustard. Season with salt and pepper.

Curried lamb kebabs

SERVES 4 **CALS PER SERVING** 203

500 g (1 lb) boneless loin or leg of lamb, trimmed and cut into chunks
lime wedges, to serve

Marinade

3 tbsp plain yogurt
juice of ½ lime
4 garlic cloves, crushed
3 tbsp chopped fresh coriander
1 tbsp chopped fresh mint
2 tsp curry powder

4 METAL SKEWERS

1 Combine the marinade ingredients in a large bowl. Stir in the lamb, cover, and marinate in the refrigerator for at least 2 hours, turning the meat occasionally.

2 Thread the lamb on to the skewers. Barbecue for 4 minutes on each side for medium lamb, or 5 minutes for well-done, basting with the marinade a few times. Serve with lime wedges.

Oriental pork kebabs

SERVES 4 **CALS PER SERVING** 378

500 g (1 lb) pork fillet (tenderloin), cut into chunks
1 red pepper, halved, deseeded, and cut into chunks
1 green pepper, halved, deseeded, and cut into chunks
1 onion, cut into chunks
¼ fresh pineapple, peeled and cut into chunks

Marinade

90 ml (3 fl oz) sunflower oil
90 ml (3 fl oz) soy sauce
juice of 1 lime
3 garlic cloves, crushed
3 tbsp sugar
¼ tsp ground ginger

4 BAMBOO SKEWERS

1 Combine the marinade ingredients in a bowl. Add the pork, peppers, onion, and pineapple, and stir well. Cover and chill for at least 2 hours.

2 Thread the meat on to the skewers, alternating with peppers, onions, and pineapple. Baste with any remaining marinade. Barbecue for 4–5 minutes on each side, basting, until the pork is cooked.

Sausage and sesame kebabs

SERVES 4 **CALS PER SERVING** 225

16 cocktail sausages
8 button mushrooms
8 cherry tomatoes
2 courgettes, each cut into 4 thick slices on the diagonal
salt and black pepper
olive oil, for brushing
about 2 tbsp mango chutney
about 2 tbsp toasted sesame seeds

8 METAL SKEWERS

1 Thread the sausages lengthways on to four of the skewers, putting four sausages on each skewer. Thread the vegetables on to the four remaining skewers, alternating the mushrooms, tomatoes, and courgettes. Season and brush with olive oil.

2 Barbecue for 4–5 minutes on each side, until cooked through. While the sausages are still hot, brush them with mango chutney and sprinkle with toasted sesame seeds.

Beef and red onion kebabs

SERVES 4 **CALS PER SERVING** 263

500 g (1 lb) rump steak, cut into chunks
2 red onions, cut into wedges
salt and black pepper
olive oil, for brushing

Marinade

50 ml (2 fl oz) olive oil
50 ml (2 fl oz) port, sherry, or Marsala
2 tbsp Dijon mustard

4 BAMBOO SKEWERS

1 Combine the marinade ingredients in a bowl, add the beef, and stir well. Cover and leave to marinate in the refrigerator for at least 2 hours, turning the meat occasionally.

2 Thread the beef and onions on to the skewers, season, and brush with olive oil. Barbecue for 2–3 minutes on each side for rare beef, 3–4 minutes for medium, and 4–5 minutes for well-done.

Successful barbecues

Cooking over charcoal requires no special skills, but it helps to know a few simple rules before you start.

Marinate meat before cooking over a barbecue. For best results, a marinade should contain an oil to keep the food moist, an acid such as lemon or lime juice to help tenderize the meat, and herbs, spices, or other seasonings to add flavour.

Baste or brush the meat with the marinade as it cooks, to help keep it moist.

Light the barbecue well before you want to start cooking – the coals should have stopped glowing and be covered in grey ash or the food may singe and burn on the outside before it is cooked inside. It takes about 30 minutes to get to this stage.

Soak bamboo skewers, if using, in warm water for 30 minutes before use so that they don't burn.

Opposite, left to right: Curried lamb kebabs, Oriental pork kebabs, Sausage and sesame kebabs, Beef and onion kebabs

Shepherd's pie

SERVES 6 **CALS PER SERVING** 383

750 g (1½ lb) minced lamb
125 g (4 oz) mushrooms, sliced
2 carrots, diced
1 large onion, chopped
1 garlic clove, crushed
30 g (1 oz) plain flour
150 ml (¼ pint) beef stock
2 tbsp Worcestershire sauce
salt and black pepper
750 g (1½ lb) potatoes
about 4 tbsp hot milk
30 g (1 oz) butter

1 Put the minced lamb into a large frying pan and heat gently until the fat runs. Increase the heat and cook, turning and mashing the meat, until it browns. Using a slotted spoon, lift the lamb out of the pan and spoon off the excess fat.

2 Add the mushrooms, carrots, onion, and garlic to the pan, and cook gently, stirring occasionally, for a few minutes until just beginning to soften.

3 Return the lamb to the frying pan. Sprinkle in the flour and cook, stirring, for about 1 minute.

4 Add the stock and the Worcestershire sauce, and season with salt and pepper. Bring to a boil, cover, and simmer gently for 30 minutes.

5 Preheat the oven to 200°C (180°C fan, Gas 6). Meanwhile, cook the potatoes in boiling salted water for 15–20 minutes until tender. Drain. Add the milk and butter to the potatoes and mash until soft, then season with salt and pepper.

6 Taste the lamb mixture for seasoning. Turn into an ovenproof dish, then spread the potato on top. With a fork, score the potato in a decorative pattern. Cook in the oven for about 20 minutes until the potato topping is golden and the meat mixture bubbling.

Lamb burgers

SERVES 8 **CALS PER SERVING** 270

1–2 tbsp olive oil
1 small onion, finely chopped
1 garlic clove, crushed
500 g (1 lb) best-quality minced lamb
1 tsp ground cumin
2 tbsp chopped fresh mint
salt and black pepper

To serve

4 warm pitta breads, halved
about 8 tbsp tzatziki
(ready-made or see page 276)

1 Heat 1 tbsp oil in a frying pan and cook the onion and garlic until completely softened – this can take up to 10 minutes. Allow to cool completely.

2 Mix the cooled onion and garlic with the remaining ingredients, then shape into eight small burgers. Put on a large plate, cover, and refrigerate for about 30 minutes (they will keep for up to 24 hours).

3 Heat a large non-stick frying pan or lightly coat a preheated ridged griddle pan with a little oil. Cook the burgers over a medium heat until browned and cooked through, about 3–4 minutes on each side. Serve in warm pitta pockets, with tzatziki.

Toppings for burgers

Chilli aïoli
In a small bowl, combine 2 egg yolks, 1 tbsp lemon juice, 1 tsp Dijon mustard, and salt and pepper to taste, and whisk until thick. Gradually add 250 ml (8 fl oz) olive oil, whisking constantly until the mixture is very thick. Stir in 1 crushed garlic clove, ½ tsp chilli powder, and ¼ tsp ground cumin. Taste for seasoning. Cover and refrigerate until ready to serve. Use on the day of making.

Barbecue sauce
Heat 1 tbsp sunflower oil in a saucepan and cook 1 finely chopped onion and 1 crushed garlic clove until soft but not coloured. Add 1 x 400 g can chopped tomatoes, 2 tbsp water, 2 tbsp lemon juice, 1 tbsp brown sugar, 1 tbsp Worcestershire sauce, 2 tsp Dijon mustard, ½ tsp each paprika and chilli powder, and salt and pepper. Bring to a boil, and simmer for 20 minutes. Serve warm or cold.

Moussaka

SERVES 8 **CALS PER SERVING** 724

750 g (1½ lb) lean minced lamb
2 large onions, finely chopped
2 garlic cloves, crushed
2 tbsp plain flour
2 x 400 g cans chopped tomatoes
4 tbsp tomato purée
salt and black pepper
3 large aubergines, cut into 1 cm (½ in) slices
olive oil, for shallow-frying

Topping

60 g (2 oz) butter
60 g (2 oz) plain flour
150 ml (¼ pint) milk
1 x 500 g carton full-fat crème fraîche
125 g (4 oz) Parmesan cheese, grated
2 tsp ready-made English mustard
1 large egg, beaten

WIDE-BASED 2.2 LITRE (4 PINT) OVENPROOF DISH

1 Heat a large, deep non-stick frying pan until hot, and fry the lamb until browned, breaking up any lumps with a wooden spoon. Stir in the onions and garlic, and fry for 5 minutes more. Sprinkle in the flour, blend in the tomatoes and tomato purée, and season with salt and pepper. Bring to a boil, then cover and lower the heat. Simmer gently for 45 minutes, stirring occasionally.

2 Meanwhile, bring a saucepan of salted water to a boil. Add the aubergine slices, and bring back to a boil, then blanch for 2 minutes until they are just starting to cook but are still firm. Drain, and dry well with paper towels.

3 Heat 2 tbsp olive oil in a large frying pan, and fry a single layer of aubergine slices until light golden on each side. Do this in batches, using more oil as necessary. As each batch is done, remove from the pan with a fish slice, and set aside.

4 Make the topping: melt the butter in a saucepan, sprinkle in the flour, and cook, stirring, for 1 minute. Remove from the heat, and gradually blend in the milk followed by the crème fraîche. Bring to a boil, stirring constantly until thickened. Simmer for 2–3 minutes, remove from the heat, and stir in half of the Parmesan. Add the mustard, season with salt and pepper, and stir until combined. Leave to cool for 5 minutes, then add the egg and stir well to mix.

5 Spoon the lamb into the ovenproof dish, and level the surface. Arrange the aubergine slices over the lamb, cover with the topping, and sprinkle with the remaining Parmesan. Bake in a preheated oven at 200°C (180°C fan, Gas 6) for 40–45 minutes until golden and bubbling. Leave to stand for a few minutes before serving.

Kidneys turbigo

SERVES 4 **CALS PER SERVING** 455

6 lamb's kidneys
60 g (2 oz) butter
250 g (8 oz) thin chipolata sausages
250 g (8 oz) button mushrooms
12 button onions, peeled, with roots left intact
1 tbsp plain flour
300 ml (½ pint) lamb or chicken stock
3 tbsp medium sherry
2 tsp tomato purée
1 bay leaf
salt and black pepper
2 tbsp chopped parsley, to garnish
croûtes (page 28), to serve (optional)

1 Prepare the kidneys (page 237). Melt the butter in a large frying pan, add the kidneys, and cook, stirring, over a high heat for about 3 minutes until browned.

2 Lift the kidneys out and drain on paper towels. Add the sausages and cook for 3 minutes or until browned. Lift out and drain on paper towels.

3 Add the mushrooms and onions to the pan and cook for 3–5 minutes until browned.

4 Sprinkle in the flour and cook, stirring, for 1 minute. Add the stock, sherry, and tomato purée, and bring to a boil, stirring constantly. Add the bay leaf, and season with salt and pepper.

5 Slice the sausages thickly. Return to the pan with the kidneys, cover and simmer for 20–25 minutes until tender.

6 Spoon the kidney mixture on to a warmed platter, garnish with parsley, and serve with croûtes, if you like.

Marinated loin of pork with pineapple

SERVES 8 **CALS PER SERVING** 320

1.5 kg (3 lb) boned loin of pork, skin removed
grilled pineapple rings and parsley sprigs (optional) to serve

Marinade

250 ml (8 fl oz) pineapple juice
2 tbsp maple syrup
2 tbsp soy sauce
2 garlic cloves, crushed
2 tbsp chopped fresh thyme
1 tsp ground coriander

1 Make the marinade: in a large non-metallic bowl, combine the pineapple juice, maple syrup, soy sauce, garlic, thyme, and coriander. Add the pork, cover, and marinate in the refrigerator, turning occasionally, for 8 hours.

2 Remove the pork from the marinade, reserving the marinade. Put the pork flat, fat-side up, in a small roasting tin. Insert a meat thermometer, if using, into the middle of the pork. Cover loosely with foil and cook in a preheated oven at 220°C (200°C fan, Gas 7) for 1 hour.

3 Remove the foil and pour the marinade over the pork. Return to the oven and cook for 20–30 minutes or until the marinade has darkened and the juices run clear when the meat is pierced with a fine skewer. The meat thermometer should register 80°C (175°F).

4 Transfer the pork to a carving board, cover with foil, and leave to stand for 10 minutes. Strain the cooking juices and remove the fat (see box, below), then reheat. Serve the pork sliced, with the juices poured over, garnished with pineapple and parsley, if you wish.

Removing the fat

Skim the layer of fat from the surface of the juices, using a skimmer or spoon.

Roast leg of pork

SERVES 6-8 **CALS PER SERVING** 338–254

2 kg (4 lb) leg of pork, skin removed and scored at 1 cm (½ in) intervals
sunflower oil for brushing
salt and black pepper
1 carrot, thickly sliced
1 onion, thickly sliced
1 tbsp plain flour
300 ml (½ pint) chicken stock
apple sauce, to serve (see box, right)

1 Brush the scored side of the pork skin with a little oil, and sprinkle generously with salt and black pepper. Place on a rack in a small roasting tin.

2 Remove as much fat as possible from the pork, especially on top where the skin has been removed. Put the pork into another roasting tin, and arrange the carrot and onion around it. Brush the meat with a little oil, season well, and insert a meat thermometer, if using, into the middle of the pork.

3 Put both roasting tins in a preheated oven at 180°C (160°C fan, Gas 4), with the pork skin at the top.

4 Roast for 2½ hours or until the thermometer registers 80°C (175°F). Transfer the pork to a carving board, cover with foil, and leave to stand for 10 minutes. If the crackling is not really crisp, increase the oven temperature to 200°C (180°C fan, Gas 6) and let it continue to cook while making the gravy.

5 Put the roasting tin on the hob. Remove the carrot and onion and spoon off all but 1 tbsp of the fat from the tin.

6 Add the flour and cook, stirring to dissolve any sediment from the bottom of the tin, for 1 minute. Pour in the stock and bring to a boil. Simmer for 3 minutes, then season, and strain into a gravy boat. Serve the pork with the gravy, roast potatoes, tenderstem broccoli, and apple sauce.

Cook's know-how

The high oven temperature needed for crisp crackling can make meat tough and dry. Removing the skin and cooking it separately, above the pork, avoids this problem.

Sauces for pork

Apricot sauce
Melt 30 g (1 oz) butter, and cook 1 thinly sliced small onion until soft. Add 125 g (4 oz) chopped ready-to-eat dried apricots, 150 ml (¼ pint) each chicken stock and dry white wine, and ¼ tsp ground cinnamon. Season with salt and pepper, and simmer for about 20 minutes until pulpy.

Apple sauce
Peel, core, and slice 500 g (1 lb) cooking apples and put into a saucepan with the finely grated zest of 1 lemon and 2–3 tbsp water. Cover tightly and cook gently for about 10 minutes until soft. Stir in 30 g (1 oz) caster sugar. Beat the sauce until smooth, then stir in 15 g (½ oz) butter if you like.

Sweet and sour sauce
Finely slice 1 onion, 1 leek, and 2 celery stalks. Cut 2 carrots into matchstick-thin strips. Heat 2 tbsp sunflower oil in a pan and cook the vegetables for 3 minutes or until softened. Blend 2 tbsp tomato ketchup, 1 tbsp soy sauce, 1 tbsp white wine vinegar, 4 tsp cornflour, and 2 tsp caster sugar, then blend in 300 ml (½ pint) water. Add to the pan and bring to a boil, stirring until thickened.

Slow-roast belly of pork

SERVES 6 **CALS PER SERVING** 558

1.35 kg (3 lb) boned belly of pork, skin scored at 1 cm (½ in) intervals
1 tbsp sunflower oil
salt and black pepper
apple sauce or fruit jelly (e.g. apple, medlar, gooseberry), to serve

Gravy
a large knob of butter
3 tbsp plain flour
600 ml (1 pint) beef stock
3 tbsp port
a few drops of Worcestershire sauce
a dash of gravy browning

1 Brush the skin of the pork with the oil. Season with salt and pepper, and rub well into the skin. Sit the pork skin-side up in a small roasting tin, and pour 1.3 litres (2¼ pints) cold water around the meat.

2 Roast the pork in a preheated oven at 150°C (130°C fan, Gas 2) for 4–5 hours until the meat feels very soft and tender.

3 Increase the oven temperature to 220°C (200°C fan, Gas 7), and roast the pork for another 30 minutes or until the skin is crisp and golden.

4 Transfer the pork to a board, and pour any juices from the roasting tin into a jug. Tent the pork loosely with foil (do not cover closely or the crackling will soften), and leave to stand in a warm place for about 15 minutes.

5 Meanwhile, make the gravy: melt the butter in a saucepan, sprinkle in the flour, and stir over a high heat to combine. Gradually blend in the stock, and whisk over a high heat until boiling and smooth. Stir in the port and any pork juices, then lower the heat and add the Worcestershire sauce and gravy browning. Season with a little salt and pepper, and stir well to combine.

6 Carve the pork into 6 slices. Serve hot, with the gravy and apple sauce or fruit jelly.

Cook's know-how

The pork can be cooked the day before. Cool after the long, slow cooking in step 2, and keep covered in the refrigerator overnight. Bring back to room temperature, then roast in a preheated oven at 220°C (200°C fan, Gas 7) for about 30 minutes until the crackling is crisp and the meat is hot.

Boston baked beans

SERVES 6–8 **CALS PER SERVING** 433–325

375 g (12 oz) dried haricot beans
60 g (2 oz) dark muscovado sugar
2 tbsp tomato purée
2 tsp black treacle
2 tsp golden syrup
2 tsp mustard powder
2 tsp salt
black pepper
250 g (8 oz) piece of streaky bacon, cut into 2.5 cm (1 in) cubes
3 onions, quartered
600 ml (1 pint) water

1 Put the haricot beans into a large bowl, cover with plenty of cold water, and leave to soak overnight.

2 Drain the beans, and rinse under cold running water. Put the beans into a saucepan, cover with cold water, and bring to a boil. Boil rapidly for 10 minutes, then partially cover the pan and simmer for 30 minutes. Drain and set aside.

3 Put the sugar, tomato purée, black treacle, golden syrup, and mustard into a large flameproof casserole. Season with salt and pepper and heat gently, stirring constantly.

4 Add the bacon and onions to the casserole with the drained beans and measured water. Bring to a boil, cover tightly, and cook in a preheated oven at 140°C (120°C fan, Gas 1), stirring occasionally, for 4½–5 hours. Taste for seasoning before serving.

Boned loin of pork with apricot stuffing

Succulent boned loin of pork, with an apricot stuffing flavoured with lemon juice and lemon thyme, is served here with a white wine gravy. The crackling is cooked separately, in the top half of the oven, to ensure that it is deliciously crisp.

SERVES 8 **CALS PER SERVING** 428

1.5 kg (3 lb) boned loin of pork, skin removed and scored at 1 cm (½ in) intervals
sunflower oil, for brushing

Apricot stuffing

30 g (1 oz) butter
1 small onion, finely chopped
90 g (3 oz) fresh brown breadcrumbs
90 g (3 oz) ready-to-eat dried apricots, coarsely chopped
1 tbsp chopped parsley
1 tbsp lemon juice
2 tsp chopped fresh lemon thyme
1 egg, beaten
salt and black pepper

Gravy

1 tbsp plain flour
150 ml (¼ pint) chicken stock
150 ml (¼ pint) dry white wine

1 Make the stuffing: melt the butter in a saucepan and cook the onion gently until soft.

2 Remove from the heat and add the breadcrumbs, apricots, parsley, lemon juice, lemon thyme, and egg. Season with salt and pepper, mix well, and leave until cold.

3 Brush the scored side of the pork skin with a little oil, and sprinkle generously with salt and pepper. Place the skin on a rack in a roasting tin.

4 Remove as much fat as possible from the pork, expecially on the top where the skin has been removed. Season the meat well, then stuff and roll (see box, below).

5 Place the pork skin in the top of a preheated oven at 180°C (160°C fan, Gas 4). Put the pork into another roasting tin, brush with oil, and season generously. Insert a meat thermometer, if using, into the middle of the loin, and cook the pork in the oven for 2 hours or until the thermometer registers 80°C (175°F).

6 Transfer the pork to a carving board, cover with foil, and leave to stand for 10 minutes. If the crackling is not really crisp, increase the oven temperature to 200°C (180°C fan, Gas 6) and let it continue to cook while making the gravy.

7 Put the roasting tin on the hob and spoon off all but 1 tbsp of the fat. Sprinkle in the flour, and cook, stirring to dissolve any sediment from the bottom of the tin, for 1 minute. Pour in the stock and wine, and bring to a boil, stirring constantly. Simmer for 3 minutes. Season to taste and strain into a gravy boat. Serve with the pork.

Stuffing and rolling a loin of pork

Open out the loin of pork and spread the stuffing over the meat.

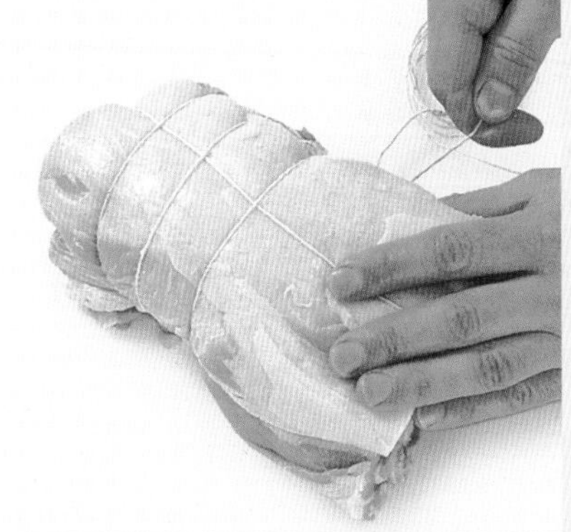

Roll the pork around the stuffing and tie at intervals with fine string, or use skewers.

Sweet and sour Chinese spare ribs

SERVES 4 **CALS PER SERVING** 491

1.25 kg (2½ lb) pork spare ribs
salt and black pepper
spring onions, to garnish (optional)

Sweet and sour sauce

2.5 cm (1 in) piece of fresh root ginger, peeled and grated
2 garlic cloves, crushed
2 tbsp soy sauce
2 tbsp rice wine vinegar
2 tbsp hoisin sauce
2 tbsp tomato purée
1 tbsp sesame oil (optional)
1 tbsp caster sugar

1 Lay the ribs in one layer in a roasting tin, season with salt and pepper, and cook in a preheated oven at 140°C (120°C fan, Gas 1) for 1½ hours.

2 Make the sauce: combine all the ingredients in a small pan and heat gently.

3 Spoon the sauce over the ribs, turning them to coat. Increase the oven temperature to 180°C (160°C fan, Gas 4), and cook for 25–30 minutes. Serve hot, garnished with spring onions if you like.

SPICY SPARE RIBS

Add 1 tbsp brown sugar, ½ tsp grated nutmeg, and ¼ tsp each of ground cloves and ground cinnamon to the sauce.

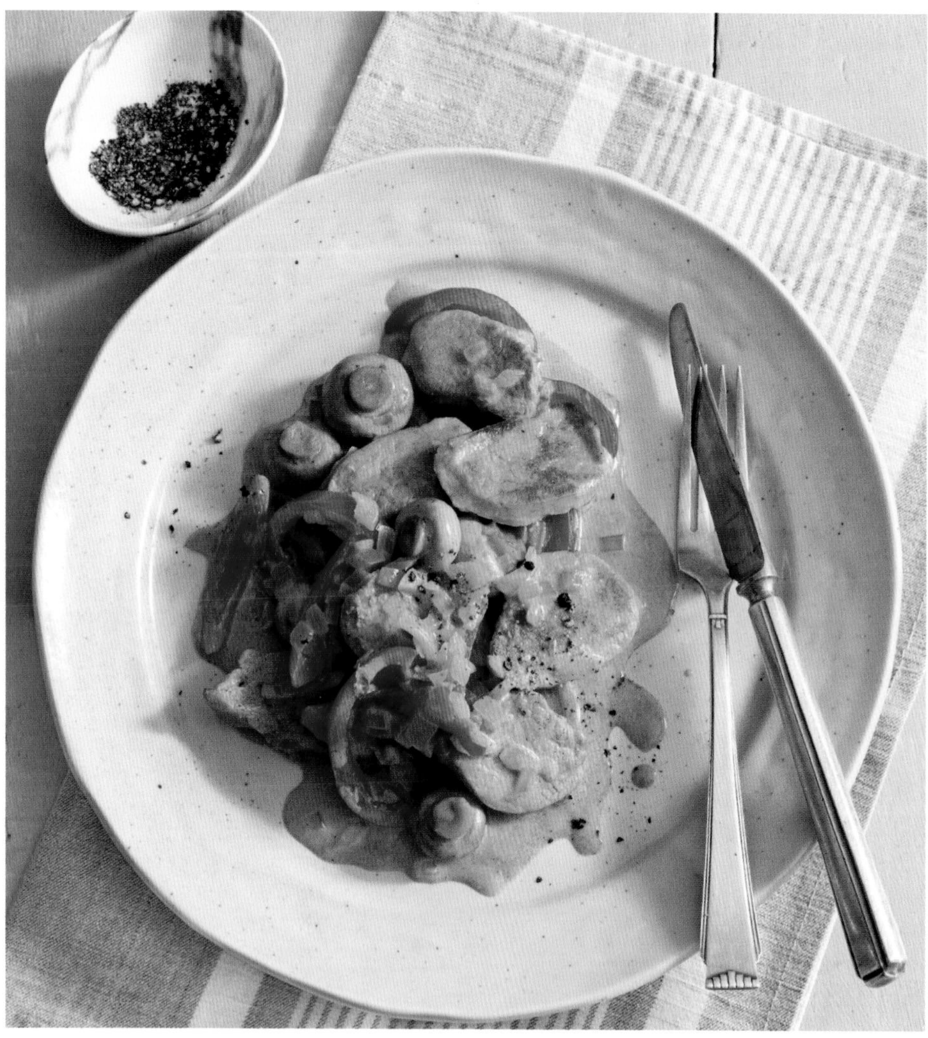

Madeira pork with paprika

SERVES 4 **CALS PER SERVING** 560

30 g (1 oz) butter
2 tbsp sunflower oil
750 g (1½ lb) pork fillet (tenderloin), trimmed and cut diagonally into 1 cm (½ in) slices
1 onion, chopped
1 large red pepper, halved, deseeded, and cut into strips
1 tbsp paprika
1 tbsp plain flour
300 ml (½ pint) chicken stock
75 ml (2½ fl oz) Madeira
175 g (6 oz) button mushrooms
1 tsp tomato purée
150 ml (¼ pint) single cream
salt and black pepper

1 Melt the butter with the oil in a large frying pan. When the butter is foaming, add the pork slices, in batches if necessary, and cook over a high heat for about 3 minutes until just beginning to brown. Lift out with a slotted spoon and drain on paper towels.

2 Add the onion and red pepper and cook, stirring, for 2 minutes. Add the paprika and flour, and cook, stirring, for 1 minute. Remove the pan from the heat and blend in the stock. Return to the heat and add the Madeira, mushrooms, and tomato purée. Simmer for 2–3 minutes.

3 Return the pork to the pan and season with salt and pepper. Cover and simmer very gently for 20 minutes or until the pork is tender. Stir in the cream, taste for seasoning, and heat through gently. Serve hot.

Grilled pork chops with mango sauce

SERVES 4 **CALS PER SERVING** 347

4 pork loin chops, on the bone
sunflower oil, for brushing
salt and black pepper
1 ripe mango
flat-leaf parsley, to garnish

Mango sauce

1 ripe mango
150 ml (¼ pint) chicken stock
1 tbsp mango chutney

1 Cut through the fat at regular intervals on the edge of each pork chop (this will help prevent the chops from curling up during cooking).

2 Brush the chops on each side with oil and sprinkle with black pepper. Put under a hot grill, 10 cm (4 in) from the heat, and grill for 6 minutes on each side or until cooked through (timing depends on size of chops).

3 Meanwhile, make the mango sauce: peel, stone, and cube the mango (page 519), then purée in a food processor until smooth.

4 Put into a small saucepan with the stock, mango chutney, and salt and pepper. Bring to a boil and simmer for about 3 minutes until heated through. Taste for seasoning.

5 Peel the remaining mango and cut it into two pieces lengthways, slightly off-centre to miss the stone. Cut the flesh from around the stone and slice into thin strips.

6 Arrange the mango strips beside the chops, garnish with flat-leaf parsley, and serve with the mango sauce.

Pork with chilli and coconut

SERVES 6 **CALS PER SERVING** 332

750 g (1½ lb) pork fillet (tenderloin), trimmed and cut into 5 mm (¼ in) strips
2 tbsp sunflower oil
8 spring onions, cut into 2.5 cm (1 in) pieces
1 large red pepper, halved, deseeded, and cut into thin strips
1 x 400 g can chopped tomatoes
60 g (2 oz) creamed coconut, coarsely chopped
4 tbsp water
2 tbsp chopped fresh coriander
1 tbsp lemon juice
salt and black pepper
coriander sprigs, to garnish
boiled rice, to serve (page 354)

Spice mix

2.5 cm (1 in) piece of fresh root ginger, peeled and grated
2 fresh red chillies, halved, deseeded, and finely chopped
1 garlic clove, crushed
1 tbsp mild curry powder

1 Make the spice mix: in a bowl, combine the ginger, chillies, garlic, and curry powder, and season with salt and pepper. Turn the pork in the mix, cover, and leave to marinate in the refrigerator for 2 hours.

2 Heat a wok or large frying pan, add the oil, and heat until hot. Add the strips of pork in batches, and stir-fry over a high heat for 5 minutes or until browned all over.

3 Add the spring onions and stir-fry for 1 minute. Add the red pepper and stir-fry for 1 minute, then add the tomatoes, coconut, and measured water. Bring to a boil, cover, and simmer very gently for 15 minutes or until the pork is tender.

4 Add the chopped coriander, lemon juice, and salt and pepper to taste. Garnish with coriander sprigs before serving with boiled rice.

Pork steaks with mixed peppercorns

SERVES 4 **CALS PER SERVING** 567

4 lean boneless pork steaks
salt
3–4 tbsp mixed or black peppercorns
30 g (1 oz) butter
350 ml (12 fl oz) dry white wine
350 ml (12 fl oz) chicken stock
175 ml (6 fl oz) double cream
potato wedges and grilled mushrooms, to serve

1 Season the steaks on each side with salt. Coarsely crush the peppercorns, spread them on a plate, and press the steaks into them to encrust the surface of the meat. Turn the steaks over and repeat on the other side. Cover and set aside for about 30 minutes, if you have the time.

2 Melt the butter in a large frying pan, add the steaks, and cook over a medium heat for 5 minutes on each side or until the meat is just cooked through but still juicy. Lift the steaks out, and keep hot.

3 Pour the wine into the pan and boil until it has reduced by half, stirring to mix in the peppercorns and the sediment from the bottom of the pan.

4 Pour in the stock and cook for 5 minutes. Strain the sauce to remove the peppercorns, then return to the pan and boil for 3 minutes or until the sauce is reduced but not too thick.

5 Add the cream and cook, stirring, over a high heat until the sauce is reduced and thickened. Return the pork steaks to the pan, heat through, and serve at once with a little of the sauce poured over, accompanied by potato wedges and grilled mushrooms.

Danish meatballs

SERVES 4–6 **CALS PER SERVING** 586–391

500 g (1 lb) minced pork
1 small onion, very finely chopped
30 g (1 oz) plain flour, plus extra for coating
1 tsp chopped fresh thyme, plus extra to garnish
¼ tsp paprika
1 egg, beaten
salt and black pepper
a little milk
30 g (1 oz) butter
1 tbsp sunflower oil
boiled rice (page 354)
Greek-style yogurt or soured cream, to garnish
chopped fresh thyme, to garnish

Tomato sauce

30 g (1 oz) butter
30 g (1 oz) plain flour
450 ml (¾ pint) chicken stock
1 x 400 g can chopped tomatoes
1 tbsp tomato purée
1 garlic clove, crushed
1 bay leaf

1 Mix the pork, onion, flour, thyme, paprika, and egg. Season, and add enough milk to give a soft, not sticky, texture.

2 Shape the mixture into 20 ovals, using two dessert spoons or your hands. Roll lightly in flour, then chill in the refrigerator.

3 Make the tomato sauce: melt the butter in a pan, sprinkle in the flour, and cook, stirring, for 1 minute.

4 Blend in the stock, then add the tomatoes, tomato purée, garlic, and bay leaf, and season with salt and pepper. Bring to a boil, stirring until thickened. Cover and simmer for 20–25 minutes.

5 Meanwhile, melt the butter with the oil in a flameproof casserole. Cook the meatballs in batches, for 5 minutes or until browned all over. Lift out and drain on paper towels.

6 Pour the fat out of the casserole. Return the meatballs, add the sauce, and bring to a boil. Cover and cook in a preheated oven at 180°C (160°C fan, Gas 4) for 30 minutes. Serve hot with boiled rice. Spoon over a little yogurt or soured cream, and garnish with thyme.

Toad in the hole with onion sauce

SERVES 4 **CALS PER SERVING** 802

400 g (13 oz) pork sausagemeat
1 leek, finely chopped
2 tbsp chopped fresh sage
1 tbsp chopped parsley, plus extra to garnish
3 tbsp sunflower oil
3 onions, chopped
2 tbsp plain flour
300 ml (½ pint) milk
250 ml (8 fl oz) chicken stock

Batter

125 g (4 oz) self-raising flour
3 eggs, beaten
300 ml (½ pint) milk
1 tbsp chopped parsley
salt and black pepper

1 Make the batter: sift the flour into a bowl. Make a well in the middle and add the eggs and a little milk. Blend to a smooth paste, then gradually whisk in the remaining milk until the batter has the pouring consistency of cream.

2 Add the chopped parsley, season with salt and pepper, and whisk again.

3 In another bowl, combine the sausagemeat, leek, sage, and parsley, and season with salt and pepper. Shape into 12 balls and set aside.

4 Heat the oil in a saucepan, add the onions, and cook for a few minutes until soft but not coloured. Transfer one-third of the onions to one large ovenproof dish or four small dishes. Set aside the remainder.

5 Add the sausage balls and bake in a preheated oven at 220°C (200°C fan, Gas 7) for about 10 minutes until brown.

6 Add the batter mixture, and return at once to the oven. Bake for 20–25 minutes until the batter is risen and golden.

7 Meanwhile, add the plain flour to the onions in the pan and cook, stirring, for 1 minute. Remove from the heat and gradually blend in the milk and stock. Bring to a boil, stirring constantly, and simmer for 2–3 minutes until the mixture thickens. Serve the toad in the hole hot, sprinkled with parsley, with the sauce handed separately.

Wiltshire pork casserole

SERVES 8 **CALS PER SERVING** 402

2 tbsp sunflower oil
1.5 kg (3 lb) shoulder of pork, trimmed and cut into 3.5 cm (1½ in) cubes
40 g (1½ oz) plain flour
450 ml (¾ pint) chicken stock
4 tbsp white wine vinegar
3 tbsp clear honey
2 tbsp soy sauce
salt and black pepper
250 g (8 oz) large mushrooms, quartered
250 g (8 oz) ready-to-eat pitted prunes
chopped parsley, to garnish

1 Heat the oil in a large flameproof casserole. Add the pork in batches and cook over a medium to high heat for 5 minutes or until golden brown all over.

2 Return all of the meat to the casserole, sprinkle in the flour, and cook, stirring, for 1 minute.

3 Stir in the chicken stock, white wine vinegar, honey, and soy sauce, season with salt and pepper, and bring to a boil. Cover and cook in a preheated oven at 160°C (140°C fan, Gas 3) for 2 hours.

4 Stir the mushrooms and prunes into the casserole and cook for 1 hour or until the pork is tender. Taste for seasoning and garnish with parsley before serving.

Sausage cassoulet

Cassoulet is a hearty dish from Languedoc in the south-west of France. This is a simple and satisfying version. The types of meat used in more traditional recipes may include duck, goose, or lamb.

SERVES 8 **CALS PER SERVING** 619

375 g (12 oz) dried haricot beans
2 tbsp olive oil
500 g (1 lb) coarse pork sausages, such as Toulouse
250 g (8 oz) piece of smoked bacon, cut into strips
2 large onions, sliced
250 g (8 oz) piece of garlic sausage, cut into 2.5 cm (1 in) chunks
2 x 400 g cans chopped tomatoes
300 ml (½ pint) chicken stock
150 ml (¼ pint) dry white wine
2 tbsp tomato purée
2 garlic cloves, crushed
1 bouquet garni
salt and black pepper
125–175 g (4–6 oz) fresh white breadcrumbs
chopped parsley, to garnish

1 Put the haricot beans into a large bowl, cover with plenty of cold water, and leave to soak overnight.

2 Drain the beans, and rinse under cold running water. Put the beans into a saucepan, cover with fresh cold water, and bring to a boil. Boil rapidly for 10 minutes, then simmer for 30 minutes or until just tender. Drain.

3 Heat the olive oil in a large flameproof casserole, add the sausages and bacon, and cook for 5 minutes or until browned all over. Lift out and drain on paper towels. Thickly slice the sausages.

4 Pour off all but 1 tbsp of the fat from the casserole. Add the onions and cook gently, stirring occasionally, for a few minutes until soft but not coloured.

5 Return the bacon and sausages to the casserole, add the beans, the garlic sausage, tomatoes, stock, wine, tomato purée, garlic, and bouquet garni. Season with salt and pepper and bring to a boil.

6 Cover and cook in a preheated oven at 160°C (140°C fan, Gas 3) for 1 hour, then sprinkle the breadcrumbs over the top and continue cooking, uncovered, for 30 minutes or until the topping is golden brown. Garnish with chopped parsley before serving.

Mustard-glazed ham

Gammon tastes best when it is cooked on the bone, especially if it is home-baked. Here, gammon slowly steam-roasts in its own juices, spiked with cider, and it is coated with a tangy glaze. Watercress and orange slices are the perfect finishing touch. Once gammon is cooked it is properly called ham.

SERVES 16–20 **CALS PER SERVING** 477–382

4–5 kg (8–10 lb) smoked gammon
400 ml (14 fl oz) cider or apple juice
3 tbsp English mustard
90 g (3 oz) demerara sugar

Lemon mustard sauce

4 tbsp olive oil
juice of 1 lemon
1 tbsp caster sugar
2 tsp coarse-grain mustard
salt and black pepper
150 ml (¼ pint) crème fraîche

1 Put the gammon into a large container, cover with cold water, and leave to soak for at least 12 hours.

2 Drain and rinse the gammon. Arrange two pieces of foil, long enough to cover the gammon, across a large roasting tin.

3 Pour the cider or apple juice into the foil. Stand a wire rack on the foil and stand the gammon on the rack. Insert a meat thermometer, if using, into the thickest part of the meat.

4 Wrap the foil loosely over the gammon, leaving plenty of space for air to circulate. Place the gammon just below the middle of a preheated oven and cook at 160°C (140°C fan, Gas 3) for 20 minutes per 500 g (1 lb). The meat thermometer should register 75°C (170°F). Remove the ham from the oven and leave to cool for a few minutes.

5 Increase the oven temperature to 230°C (210°C fan, Gas 8). Transfer the ham to a board, drain the cooking juices from the foil, and discard. Glaze the gammon with the mustard and sugar (see box, opposite).

6 Return the ham to the rack in the roasting tin. Cover any lean parts with foil, return to the oven, and cook, turning the roasting tin if necessary, for 15–20 minutes until the glaze is golden brown all over.

7 Meanwhile, make the lemon mustard sauce: put the olive oil, lemon juice, caster sugar, and mustard into a screw-top jar, season with salt and pepper, and shake vigorously to mix the ingredients together.

8 Put the crème fraîche into a bowl and stir in the lemon and mustard mixture. Taste for seasoning and leave to chill in the refrigerator until needed.

9 Carve the ham into slices and serve either warm or cold, with the lemon mustard sauce.

Glazing ham

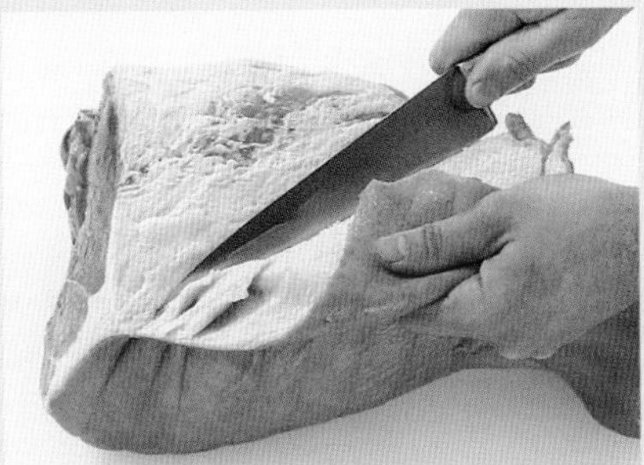

Cut away the skin with a sharp knife, leaving behind a thin layer of fat. Discard the skin.

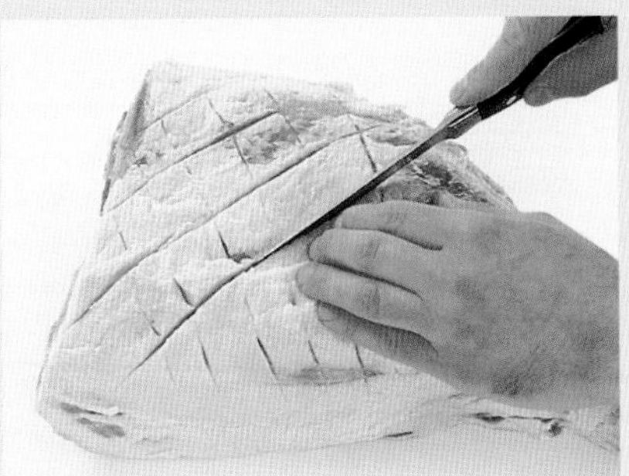

Score the fat all over in a diamond pattern, so that the glaze penetrates the fat.

Spread a generous layer of mustard over the fat, using a palette knife or your hands.

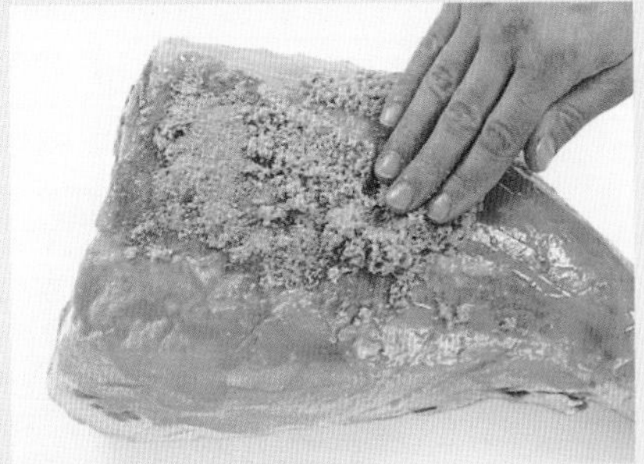

Press the demerara sugar on to the layer of mustard, making sure it is evenly coated all over.

Bacon-wrapped pork in vermouth sauce

SERVES 6 **CALS PER SERVING** 547

2 pork fillets (tenderloins), about 375 g (12 oz) each, trimmed
2 tbsp Dijon mustard
salt and black pepper
375 g (12 oz) streaky bacon rashers, rinds removed

Vermouth sauce

30 g (1 oz) butter
1 tbsp olive oil
1 shallot, finely chopped
1 tbsp plain flour
200 ml (7 fl oz) chicken stock
90 ml (3 fl oz) dry vermouth
125 g (4 oz) button or chestnut mushrooms, sliced

1 Spread the pork fillets with the mustard and season with salt and pepper. Stretch the bacon rashers with the back of a knife and wrap around the fillets (see box, right).

2 Place the fillets in a roasting tin and cook in a preheated oven at 220°C (200°C fan, Gas 7), turning the fillets halfway through cooking, for 30–35 minutes until the juices from the pork run clear and the bacon is crisp and golden.

3 Meanwhile, make the sauce: melt the butter with the oil in a small pan. When the butter is foaming, add the shallot, and cook gently until softened.

4 Add the flour and cook, stirring, for 1 minute. Gradually blend in the stock and vermouth. Bring to a boil, add the mushrooms, and simmer for 15 minutes.

5 Transfer the pork to a warmed platter. Spoon off the fat from the roasting tin and strain the juices into the sauce. Heat through and taste for seasoning. Serve with the pork.

Wrapping pork fillets

Overlap half of the bacon rashers on a work surface. Lay 1 pork fillet across the bacon and plait the rashers around the meat. Secure with a fine skewer. Repeat with the second pork fillet.

Farmer's bacon bake

SERVES 6–8 **CALS PER SERVING** 510–383

1 x 750 g (1½ lb) bacon joint
a few parsley stalks, plus extra to garnish (optional)
6 black peppercorns
1 bay leaf
4 potatoes, cut into large chunks
4 carrots, thickly sliced
4 celery stalks, thickly sliced

Cheese sauce

45 g (1½ oz) butter
45 g (1½ oz) plain flour
200 ml (7 fl oz) milk
90 g (3 oz) mature Cheddar cheese, grated
salt and black pepper

1 Put the bacon joint into a large pan, cover with cold water, and bring to a boil. Drain, rinse, and cover with fresh cold water. Add the parsley stalks, peppercorns, and bay leaf, and bring to a boil. Cover and simmer very gently for 45 minutes.

2 Add the potatoes, carrots, and celery and bring back to a boil. Cover and simmer very gently for 20 minutes or until the meat and vegetables are tender. Drain, reserving the cooking liquid, and allow the bacon to cool slightly.

3 Remove the rind and fat from the bacon, cut the meat into bite-sized pieces, and place in a shallow baking dish with the vegetables. Keep hot.

4 Make the cheese sauce: melt the butter in a saucepan, sprinkle in the flour, and cook, stirring, for 1 minute. Remove from the heat and gradually blend in the milk and 250 ml (8 fl oz) of the reserved cooking liquid. Bring to a boil, stirring constantly until the mixture thickens. Simmer for 2–3 minutes. Add three-quarters of the cheese, and season with salt and pepper.

5 Pour the sauce over the meat and vegetables and sprinkle with the remaining cheese. Bake in a preheated oven at 180°C (160°C fan, Gas 4) for 30 minutes or until the cheese topping is bubbling. Garnish with chopped parsley before serving, if you wish.

Sausage bake

SERVES 6 **CALS PER SERVING** 712

1 tbsp sunflower oil
1 kg (2 lb) coarse-cut pork sausages
500 g (1 lb) leeks, thickly sliced
750 g (1½ lb) potatoes, cut into 5 mm (¼ in) slices
90 g (3 oz) red lentils
salt and black pepper
2 bay leaves
2 cloves
1 garlic clove, crushed
900 ml (1½ pints) chicken stock
chopped parsley, to garnish

1 Heat the oil in a large flameproof casserole and brown the sausages. Lift out, then cut into thick slices.

2 Layer the leeks, potatoes, sausages, and lentils in the casserole, adding seasoning and placing the bay leaves, cloves, and garlic among the layers. Top with a layer of potatoes.

3 Pour in the stock and bring to a boil. Cover tightly and cook in a preheated oven at 160°C (140°C fan, Gas 3) for 2½ hours, checking the liquid level occasionally.

4 Remove the lid, increase the oven temperature to 200°C (180°C fan, Gas 6), and cook for 20–25 minutes until the potato is browned. Garnish with parsley and serve hot.

Vegetarian dishes

In this chapter...

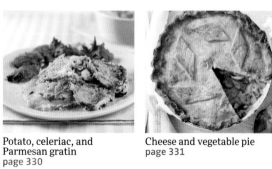

Mushroom lasagne
page 334

Chestnut loaf
page 335

Red bean and tomato curry
page 336

Christmas nut loaf
page 336

Red lentil and coconut curry
page 337

Veggie burgers
page 337

Saag aloo
page 338

Dhal
page 338

Niramish tarkari
page 338

Thai curry
page 340

Peking tofu with plum sauce
page 340

Firecracker stir-fry
page 341

Vegetable stir-fry with tofu
page 342

Japanese noodle soup
page 342

Mexican bean salad
page 343

Halloumi and vegetable kebabs
page 346

Mexican chilli with tofu
page 343

Vegetarian enchiladas
page 344

Spinach and ricotta samosas
page 344

Falafel with sesame yogurt sauce
page 346

Vegetarian know-how

There are two basic types of vegetarian diet. A vegan diet is the strictest – vegans do not eat any meat, poultry, fish, eggs, or dairy products – while a vegetarian diet excludes meat, poultry, and fish, but may include eggs and dairy products. In addition, there is the "demi-vegetarian" diet, which can include fish and even poultry. With such a great variety of foods from which to choose, vegetarian diets, based largely on complex carbohydrates, pulses, vegetables, fruits, nuts, and seeds, can be imaginative and nutritious.

Maintaining a balanced diet

Fish, meat, poultry, dairy products, and eggs are high-quality protein foods – they contain all the essential dietary amino acids (the building blocks of protein) that the body needs. Many vegetarians replace fish, meat, and poultry with eggs, cheese, and other dairy products, but this is not the ideal solution as many dairy foods are high in saturated fats and calories.

A healthy alternative in a vegetarian diet is to focus on protein-rich pulses, nuts, and seeds. The protein these foods offer does not contain all eight of the essential amino acids (with the exception of that from soya beans, which is "complete"), but it is easy to enhance their nutritional value – simply eat them with bread, pasta, and rice or other grains. Examples of vegetarian protein combinations drawn from cuisines around the world are beans or dhal (lentils) and rice, hummus and pitta bread, or a mixed nut, lentil, and vegetable salad.

Another dietary interaction that vegetarians should be aware of is that between iron and vitamin C. The form of iron found in meat is easily absorbed by the body, whereas the iron in vegetables, nuts, grains, pulses, and eggs needs a helping hand. This is provided by vitamin C, which enhances iron uptake. So, when planning meals, include vitamin C-rich foods such as fresh fruit (in particular citrus, berries, and kiwi fruit) and vegetables (peppers, tomatoes, broccoli, mangetout, and cabbages are all good sources).

A gelatine substitute

Gelatine is a natural protein found in the bones, skin, and connective tissues of animals. Commercial powdered gelatine is derived from pig skin, and is thus unacceptable in a vegetarian diet. The most common substitutes are agar-agar (or kanten) and carrageen (or Irish moss), both of which are derived from seaweeds. They have stronger setting properties than gelatine, so less is needed. Follow the packet instructions for amounts to use.

Tofu

Tofu is a high-protein food manufactured from soya beans. It is low in fat and calories, so can make a healthy basis for many vegetarian dishes. It is very bland (unless it is smoked), but easily absorbs flavours from marinades and sauces. Silken tofu has a soft, creamy texture: use it in sauces, dips, and puddings. Firm tofu, which has a texture similar to feta cheese, can be stir-fried, grilled, or casseroled. Other vegetarian meat substitutes include TVP (textured vegetable protein), which is also made from soya beans, and Quorn.

Pulses know-how

Pulses are usually soaked for at least 8 hours, but you can speed up the process: boil for 3 minutes, then cover and soak for 1–2 hours.

Add salt towards the end of cooking: if it is added at the beginning, it could toughen the skins of the pulse.

Pulses double in size and weight when cooked, so if a recipe calls for 250 g (8 oz) cooked pulses, you will need 125 g (4 oz) dried weight.

Adding bicarbonate of soda to the cooking water can adversely affect the nutritional value of pulses.

Grains

Whole grains are first-class sources of carbohydrate, fibre, vitamins, and minerals.

Bulgur wheat

Also known as burghul wheat, this is made from steamed, dried, and crushed wheat kernels. It cooks very quickly, or can just be soaked and used in salads. Cracked wheat is similar, but is not pre-cooked and so takes longer to cook than bulgur wheat.

Couscous

Made from semolina, the wheat flour also used for pasta, couscous only needs to be soaked to allow the grains to swell and soften. For extra flavour, steam the couscous over a vegetable stew in a colander set over a large pot.

Pearl barley

The nutty flavour and chewy texture of this grain is delicious in vegetable soups and stews. The starch in the grain acts as a thickener too.

Polenta

Made from ground maize or corn, and also known as cornmeal, polenta is added to simmering water and stirred constantly until it is very thick. Instant polenta takes only about 8 minutes to cook. Serve warm, or leave to cool and set, then slice and grill.

Millet

Available as flakes or whole grains, millet has a delicate, slightly nutty flavour. Add a small handful to soups to thicken them.

Oats

Oatflakes, also called rolled oats, are the basis of porridge and muesli. Fine oatmeal can be used to make biscuits, bread, and oatcakes – and to thicken soups; coarser varieties can be cooked into porridge.

Quinoa

A tiny grain from South America with a slightly sweet taste, quinoa can be used like brown rice and other whole grains. Rinse it well before cooking.

Cooking pulses

Pulses are the dried, edible seeds of the legume family – beans, peas, and lentils. Stored in a cool, dark place, they will keep for up to 6 months. They're easy to prepare, but if you want to save time you can use canned pulses, which are already cooked.

1 Put the pulses into a large bowl and cover with plenty of cold water. Leave to soak for the recommended time (see below). Drain and rinse in cold water.

2 Put into a saucepan and add cold water – about twice their volume. Bring to a boil and fast boil for 10–15 minutes. Cover and simmer until tender (see below).

Soaking and cooking times of pulses

Cooking times depend on the variety of pulse and whether it is recently dried or has been stored a long time and thus is very dry. The cooking times given below are therefore only a guide.

Pulse	Soaking	Cooking
Aduki beans	8–12 hours	45 minutes
Black-eyed beans	8–12 hours	1 hour
Butter beans	8–12 hours	1–1½ hours
Chick peas	8–12 hours	2 hours
Flageolet beans	8–12 hours	1–1½ hours
Haricot beans	8–12 hours	1–1½ hours
Red lentils	not required	20–30 minutes
Green lentils	not required	30–45 minutes
Mung beans (whole)	8–12 hours	45 minutes
Red kidney beans	8–12 hours	1¾ hours
Soya beans	10–12 hours	2½–4 hours
Split peas	not required	2 hours

Warning Most pulses contain toxins that we cannot digest, and these can cause symptoms of severe food poisoning. To destroy the toxins, boil the pulses rapidly for 10–15 minutes at the start of cooking, then reduce the heat to carry on cooking at a simmer. Chick peas, lentils, and split peas do not need this fast boil.

Vegetable stock

Add any vegetable trimmings you have (celery tops or tomato skins, for example), or vary the ingredients to emphasize the flavour of the dish in which you want to use the stock.

1 Coarsely chop 2 onions, 1 leek, 3 celery stalks, and 2–3 carrots. Put into a large saucepan or stockpot and add 1 large bouquet garni, plus 1 crushed garlic clove, if wished.

2 Add 1.25 litres (2 pints) water and bring to a boil. Skim off any scum that rises to the surface, then lower the heat and simmer for 30 minutes.

3 Strain the stock through a sieve. If not using immediately, leave to cool, then cover and store in the refrigerator for up to 5 days or in the freezer for up to 1 month.

Stuffed red peppers

SERVES 4 **CALS PER SERVING** 622

8 small red peppers
4 tbsp water

Stuffing
4 tbsp olive oil
1 large onion, finely chopped
1 garlic clove, crushed
175 g (6 oz) button mushrooms, chopped
250 g (8 oz) long grain rice
90 g (3 oz) dried red lentils
450 ml (¾ pint) vegetable stock
salt and black pepper
60 g (2 oz) pine nuts, toasted
4 tbsp chopped parsley
fresh coriander, to garnish (optional)

1 Slice the tops off the red peppers and reserve. Cut out and discard the cores, seeds, and white ribs, and set the peppers aside.

2 Make the stuffing: heat the oil in a pan. Add the onion and garlic and cook gently, stirring occasionally, for 3–5 minutes until soft but not coloured. Add the mushrooms and cook for 10 minutes.

3 Add the rice and lentils and stir to coat in the oil. Pour in the stock, season with salt and pepper, and bring to a boil. Cover and simmer very gently for 15–20 minutes until the rice is tender and the liquid has been absorbed. Stir in the pine nuts and parsley, then taste for seasoning.

4 Divide the stuffing among the peppers, stand them upright in a casserole dish that just contains them, and replace the tops.

5 Pour the measured water into the bottom of the casserole, cover, and bake in a preheated oven at 180°C (160°C fan, Gas 4) for about 40 minutes until the peppers are tender. Serve at once, garnished with coriander if you wish.

Cheese-topped baked aubergines

SERVES 4 **CALS PER SERVING** 447

3 tbsp chopped parsley
2 tbsp chopped fresh basil
2 tbsp olive oil
1 tsp salt
4 medium aubergines
6 garlic cloves, cut into thin slivers
175 g (6 oz) Gorgonzola or Danish blue cheese, crumbled
175 g (6 oz) Cheddar or mozzarella cheese, grated

1 In a small bowl, combine the parsley, half of the basil, the olive oil, and salt.

2 Prepare the aubergines (see box, below). Put the aubergines into an ovenproof dish and bake in a preheated oven at 180°C (160°C fan, Gas 4) for 40–50 minutes until they are very tender and soft to the touch.

3 Remove the aubergines from the oven, sprinkle with the Gorgonzola and Cheddar cheeses, and bake for 5 minutes or until the cheese is melted. Serve at once, sprinkled with the remaining basil.

Preparing the aubergines

Cut diagonal slits one-third of the way into each aubergine. Stuff the garlic slivers and then the chopped herb mixture into each slit.

Roast vegetables niçoise

SERVES 4 **CALS PER SERVING** 237

750 g (1½ lb) courgettes, sliced
1 large red onion, thinly sliced
3 garlic cloves, crushed
4 tbsp olive oil, more if needed
125 g (4 oz) black olives, pitted
2 tsp fresh mixed herbs
1 tbsp capers
black pepper
250 g (8 oz) cherry tomatoes, halved
1 tbsp shredded fresh basil

1 Put the courgettes, red onion, and garlic in an ovenproof dish, drizzle with 4 tbsp oil, and toss to mix.

2 Arrange the black olives on top of the vegetables, then sprinkle with the herbs and capers, and plenty of pepper.

3 Roast in a preheated oven at 190°C (170°C fan, Gas 5) for 25 minutes, then add the tomatoes and roast for a further 20 minutes, checking occasionally to see if the surface is getting too dry. If it is, drizzle a little more olive oil over the vegetables.

4 Sprinkle the dish with the shredded fresh basil. Serve hot or cold.

Couscous with roasted peppers

SERVES 4–6 **CALS PER SERVING** 418–279

1 large red pepper
1 large yellow pepper
175 g (6 oz) couscous
600 ml (1 pint) hot vegetable stock
2 tbsp olive oil
60 g (2 oz) blanched almonds
2 courgettes, sliced
1 large red onion, chopped
1 large carrot, thinly sliced
1–2 garlic cloves, crushed
1 x 400 g can chick peas, drained and rinsed
1 tsp ground cumin
½ tsp curry powder
¼–½ tsp crushed dried red chillies
salt and black pepper
chopped coriander, to garnish

1 Halve the red and yellow peppers, and remove the cores and seeds. Roast and peel the peppers (page 426), and set aside to cool.

2 Put the couscous into a bowl and stir in the hot stock. Cover and leave to stand for 10 minutes.

3 Meanwhile, heat the oil in a large frying pan, add the almonds, and cook gently, stirring, for 3 minutes or until lightly browned. Lift out with a slotted spoon and drain on paper towels.

4 Add the courgettes, onion, carrot, and garlic to the pan, and cook, stirring, for about 5 minutes.

5 Stir in the chick peas, cumin, curry powder, and crushed chillies, and cook, stirring occasionally, for a further 5 minutes. Stir in the couscous, and cook for 3–4 minutes until heated through. Season to taste.

6 Cut the flesh of the cooled roasted peppers into thin strips.

7 Divide the couscous among warmed serving plates and arrange the pepper strips on top. Serve at once, sprinkled with the almonds and chopped coriander.

Polenta with grilled vegetables

SERVES 6 **CALS PER SERVING** 319

175 g (6 oz) polenta
150 ml (¼ pint) cold water
600 ml (1 pint) boiling salted water
30 g (1 oz) butter
2 courgettes, halved and thickly sliced lengthways
2 tomatoes, cored and sliced
1 fennel bulb, trimmed and quartered lengthways
1 red onion, thickly sliced
melted butter, for brushing

Marinade

4 tbsp olive oil
2 tbsp red wine vinegar
3 garlic cloves, chopped
2–3 tbsp chopped parsley
salt and black pepper

1 Put the polenta into a saucepan, cover with the measured cold water, and leave to stand for 5 minutes.

2 Add the boiling salted water to the pan, return to a boil, and stir for 10–15 minutes, until smooth and thickened.

3 Sprinkle a baking tray with water. Stir the butter into the polenta, then spread the mixture over the tray in a 1 cm (½ in) layer. Leave to cool.

4 Combine the marinade ingredients in a bowl. Add the courgettes, tomatoes, fennel, and onion. Cover and marinate in the refrigerator for 30 minutes.

5 Lift the vegetables out of the marinade and cook over a hot barbecue for 2–3 minutes on each side. Cut the polenta into triangles and cook over a hot barbecue, brushing with melted butter, for 1–2 minutes on each side until golden. Serve hot.

Cook's know-how

Instead of barbecuing the polenta and vegetables, you can cook them on a ridged cast-iron chargrill pan, or under a preheated grill, for the same length of time.

Italian stuffed courgettes

SERVES 4 **CALS PER SERVING** 437

4 large courgettes
30 g (1 oz) butter
2 tbsp olive oil, plus extra for greasing
1 small onion, finely chopped
4 ripe tomatoes, finely chopped
4 tbsp chopped fresh basil
salt and black pepper
2 tbsp capers, drained and coarsely chopped
250 g (8 oz) fontina cheese, grated

1 Cut the courgettes in half lengthways. Scoop out the flesh and chop finely.

2 Melt the butter with 1 tbsp of the olive oil in a saucepan.

3 When the butter is foaming, add the onion and cook gently, stirring occasionally, for 3–5 minutes until softened but not coloured.

4 Add the courgette flesh, tomatoes, and basil, and season with salt and pepper. Cook, stirring, for 5 minutes.

5 Brush the insides of the courgette shells with the remaining oil and arrange in a lightly oiled shallow ovenproof dish. Bake the shells in a preheated oven at 180°C (160°C fan, Gas 4) for 5–10 minutes.

6 Divide half of the tomato mixture among the courgette shells. Cover with the chopped capers and a thin layer of cheese. Spoon over the remaining tomato mixture and top with the remaining cheese. Return to the oven and bake for 10–15 minutes until the cheese topping is bubbling.

Spiced aubergines with filo crust

SERVES 6 **CALS PER SERVING** 569

2 tbsp olive oil
2 large onions, chopped
2 tbsp mild curry paste
2 aubergines, cut into 1 cm (½ in) dice
2 red peppers, halved, deseeded, and diced
salt and black pepper
175 g (6 oz) dried red lentils
250 g (8 oz) Caerphilly cheese, diced
300 g (10 oz) filo pastry
60 g (2 oz) melted butter

26 CM (10½ IN) SPRINGFORM CAKE TIN

1 Heat the oil in a large saucepan or deep frying pan. Cook the onions over a low heat, stirring occasionally, for 3–5 minutes until softened. Stir in the curry paste, and cook for 2 minutes.

2 Add the aubergines and the red peppers and cook for 10–15 minutes until soft. Season with salt and pepper and leave to cool.

3 Meanwhile, put the lentils into a pan, cover with water, and bring to a boil. Simmer for 15 minutes or until just soft. Drain and cool.

4 Stir the lentils and diced cheese into the aubergine mixture. Taste for seasoning.

5 Using two-thirds of the filo, line the bottom and side of the cake tin, brushing each sheet with melted butter, and letting them overhang the rim of the tin. Spoon in the aubergine mixture and fold the filo over the top. Brush the remaining filo with butter, crumple, and arrange on top.

6 Bake in a preheated oven at 190°C (170°C fan, Gas 5) for 40 minutes or until the pastry is golden. Serve hot accompanied by a mixed leaf salad.

Cook's know-how

If you are short of time, omit the filo. Spread the aubergine, pepper, and lentil mixture in a baking dish and grate the cheese over the top.

Aubergine parmigiana

SERVES 6 **CALS PER SERVING** 516

1.5 kg (3 lb) aubergines
2 eggs, lightly beaten
60 g (2 oz) plain flour
3 tbsp olive oil, more if needed
2 onions, chopped
3 x 400 g cans chopped tomatoes, drained
1 x 140 g can tomato purée
2 garlic cloves, crushed
2 tbsp chopped fresh basil
¼ tsp caster sugar
salt and black pepper
350 g (11 oz) mozzarella cheese, sliced
125 g (4 oz) Parmesan cheese, grated

1 Cut the aubergines into 1 cm (½ in) slices. Dip into the beaten eggs, then into the flour, shaking off any excess.

2 Heat 1 tbsp olive oil in a large frying pan, add the aubergine slices in batches, and cook for 3–4 minutes on each side until golden, adding more oil between batches if necessary. Lift out with a slotted spoon and drain on paper towels.

3 Heat another tablespoon of olive oil in a saucepan, add the onions, and cook gently until soft. Stir in the tomatoes, tomato purée, garlic, and basil. Bring to a boil, then simmer for 10–15 minutes until thickened. Add the sugar and season with salt and pepper.

4 Spoon some of the tomato mixture into a shallow ovenproof dish and cover with a layer of aubergine slices, then with a layer each of mozzarella and Parmesan. Continue layering, finishing with tomato mixture, mozzarella, and Parmesan.

5 Bake in a preheated oven at 190°C (170°C fan, Gas 5) for 15–20 minutes until the cheese is lightly browned.

Country vegetable pies

SERVES 6 **CALS PER SERVING** 428

8 carrots, diced
8 parsnips, diced
300 ml (½ pint) vegetable stock
2 tbsp olive oil
1 onion, chopped
1 head of garlic, separated into cloves and peeled
750 g (1½ lb) potatoes, diced
salt and black pepper
4 tbsp hot milk
45 g (1½ oz) butter
paprika, to garnish

Parsley sauce

45 g (1½ oz) butter
45 g (1½ oz) plain flour
150 ml (¼ pint) milk
4 tbsp chopped parsley

1 Blanch the carrots and parsnips in the stock for 1 minute. Drain, reserving the stock. Put the oil into an ovenproof dish, add the vegetables and half of the garlic, and stir well. Roast in a preheated oven at 200°C (180°C fan, Gas 6) for 30 minutes.

2 Meanwhile, cook the potatoes and the remaining garlic in boiling salted water for 15–20 minutes until tender. Drain, return to the pan, and add the hot milk and 30 g (1 oz) of the butter. Mash, and season with salt and pepper.

3 Remove the roasted vegetables with a slotted spoon, and place in six small ovenproof dishes or one large dish, and season.

4 Make the parsley sauce: melt the butter in a small pan, add the flour, and cook, stirring, for 1 minute. Remove from the heat and blend in the milk and stock. Bring to a boil, stirring, until thick. Simmer for 2–3 minutes, then stir in the parsley and season.

5 Pour the sauce over the vegetables, top with the potato, and dot with the remaining butter. Bake for 20 minutes. Serve hot, with paprika sprinkled on top, accompanied by a mixed leaf salad.

Tomato and olive tart

SERVES 8 **CALS PER SERVING** 377

3 tbsp olive oil
2 large onions, coarsely chopped
3 garlic cloves, crushed
1 x 400 g can chopped tomatoes
1 x 140 g can tomato purée
2 tsp chopped fresh basil
1 tsp caster sugar
125 g (4 oz) vignotte or mozzarella cheese, grated
90 g (3 oz) pitted black olives
shredded fresh basil, to garnish

Poppyseed base

250 g (8 oz) plain flour
125 g (4 oz) butter
90 g (3 oz) poppyseeds
1 tbsp light muscovado sugar
salt and black pepper
about 4 tbsp cold water

1 Make the base: put the flour, butter, poppyseeds, and sugar in a food processor, season with salt and pepper, and pulse until the mixture resembles fine breadcrumbs.

2 Add the water and process until the mixture forms a ball. Turn out and knead lightly, then roll out to a 30 cm (12 in) round on a baking sheet and pinch the edge to form a rim. Prick the base all over with a fork and chill for 30 minutes.

3 Heat the oil in a pan, add the onions and garlic, and cook gently for 3–5 minutes until soft. Add the tomatoes, tomato purée, basil, and sugar. Season and bring to a boil. Boil for 5–7 minutes until thick. Leave to cool slightly.

4 Bake the poppyseed base in a preheated oven at 220°C (200°C fan, Gas 7) for 15 minutes. Spread the tomato mixture over the base, sprinkle with the cheese and olives, and bake for 15–20 minutes. Serve hot or cold, sprinkled with basil.

Cook's know-how

If you are short of time, use ready-made shortcrust pastry instead of the poppyseed base. You will need a 500 g (1 lb) packet.

Mixed bean bake

SERVES 6 **CALS PER SERVING** 376

2 tbsp olive oil
3 large leeks, trimmed and sliced
1 garlic clove, crushed
250 g (8 oz) mushrooms, sliced
1 x 400 g can aduki or red kidney beans, drained and rinsed
1 x 400 g can butter beans, drained and rinsed
1 x 400 g can chopped tomatoes
3 tbsp tomato purée
3 tbsp chopped parsley, plus extra to garnish
salt and black pepper

Cheese sauce

30 g (1 oz) butter
30 g (1 oz) plain flour
300 ml (½ pint) milk
1 egg, beaten
125 g (4 oz) Cheddar cheese, grated

1 Heat the olive oil in a large saucepan. Add the leeks and cook gently, stirring, for a few minutes until softened but not coloured. Lift out with a slotted spoon and set aside.

2 Add the garlic and mushrooms and cook, stirring occasionally, for about 5 minutes. Add the canned beans, tomatoes, tomato purée, and 3 tbsp of the parsley. Season with salt and pepper. Bring to a boil, cover, and simmer very gently for about 20 minutes.

3 Meanwhile, make the cheese sauce: melt the butter in a small saucepan, add the flour, and cook, stirring, for 1 minute. Remove the pan from the heat and gradually blend in the milk. Bring to a boil, stirring constantly until the mixture thickens. Simmer for 2–3 minutes, then leave to cool slightly. Stir in the egg and cheese, and season with salt and black pepper.

4 Transfer the bean mixture to an ovenproof dish and arrange the leeks on top. Pour the cheese sauce over the leeks, and bake in a preheated oven at 190°C (170°C fan, Gas 5) for 30 minutes or until golden. Serve hot.

Roasted vegetable medley

SERVES 4 **CALS PER SERVING** 245

175 g (6 oz) small new potatoes, scrubbed and halved
8 baby carrots, scrubbed and trimmed
2 red onions, cut into wedges
2 garlic cloves, sliced
salt and black pepper
about 2 tbsp olive oil
a few rosemary sprigs
250 g (8 oz) cherry tomatoes
125 g (4 oz) French beans
1 small cauliflower, broken into florets
1 x 400 g can butter beans, drained
2 tbsp balsamic vinegar
2 tbsp coarse-grain mustard
a handful of chopped fresh herbs (e.g. parsley, chives, basil, chervil)

1 Put the potatoes, carrots, onions, and garlic in a roasting tin. Season and add the olive oil, then turn to coat. Tuck in the rosemary sprigs, and roast in a preheated oven at 190°C (170°C fan, Gas 5) for 40–45 minutes or until the vegetables are tender, stirring in the tomatoes about 15–20 minutes before the end.

2 Meanwhile, cook the French beans and cauliflower in boiling salted water for 4 minutes. Drain and set aside.

3 Mix the roasted vegetables with the French beans, cauliflower, and butter beans, then gently mix in the balsamic vinegar, mustard, and herbs. Serve hot.

ROASTED VEGETABLE GRATIN

Transfer the vegetables to an ovenproof dish. Sprinkle with 90 g (3 oz) grated Cheddar cheese mixed with 60 g (2 oz) fresh breadcrumbs. Return to the oven for about 10–15 minutes until golden.

Kilkerry pie

SERVES 6 **CALS PER SERVING** 494

90 g (3 oz) butter
500 g (1 lb) leeks, trimmed and thickly sliced
60 g (2 oz) plain flour
300 ml (½ pint) apple juice
300 ml (½ pint) milk
1 tsp coarse-grain mustard
salt and black pepper
4 hard-boiled eggs, roughly chopped
150 g (5 oz) mature Cheddar cheese, grated
500 g (1 lb) potatoes, cut into 5 mm (¼ in) slices (not peeled)
5 sheets of filo pastry, each about 25 x 38 cm (10 x 15 in)

SHALLOW OVENPROOF DISH, ABOUT 25 CM (10 IN) SQUARE

1 Melt 60 g (2 oz) of the butter in a large frying pan, and cook the leeks for about 8–10 minutes until softened. Stir in the flour and cook for 1 minute, then gradually add the apple juice and milk, stirring constantly until boiling. It may look slightly curdled at this stage, but don't worry, it will come together. Reduce the heat, and simmer gently for 2–3 minutes. Add the mustard and season well.

2 Remove the sauce from the heat and stir in the roughly chopped eggs and the cheese. Now cook the potatoes in boiling salted water for 4–5 minutes until just tender. Drain, and mix into the sauce, then season, and pour into the dish.

3 Melt the remaining butter. Brush one of the filo sheets with butter and put it over the mixture in the dish, scrunching up the edges to fit. Repeat with the remaining filo sheets, scrunching up the last sheet before putting it on top of the pie. (You can leave the pie for up to 6 hours at this stage, then bake it when you need it.)

4 Bake in a preheated oven at 200°C (180°C fan, Gas 6) for 30–40 minutes until the filo is crisp and golden and the pie is hot right through.

Spicy pumpkin casserole

SERVES 4 **CALS PER SERVING** 196

2 tbsp olive oil
2 onions, cut into wedges
2 potatoes, cut into 2.5 cm (1 in) cubes
2 parsnips, cut into 2.5 cm (1 in) cubes
500 g (1 lb) pumpkin, peeled and cut into 2.5 cm (1 in) cubes
1–2 tbsp curry paste
375 ml (13 fl oz) vegetable stock
salt and black pepper
chopped fresh coriander, to garnish

1 Heat the olive oil in a flameproof casserole. Add the onions and cook gently for 3–5 minutes or until softened.

2 Add the cubed vegetables, curry paste, and stock. Season and bring to a boil. Cover and simmer, stirring, for 20 minutes.

3 Remove the vegetables with a slotted spoon and transfer to a warmed serving dish. Bring the sauce to a boil, and continue to boil until reduced and thickened. Spoon the sauce over the vegetables, garnish with coriander, and serve hot.

SPICY PUMPKIN IN A PIE

Cool the vegetables and sauce, transfer to a pie dish, and top with ready-rolled pastry. Bake at 190°C (170°C fan, Gas 5) for 15 minutes or until the pastry is cooked and the filling is hot.

Majorcan tumbet casserole

SERVES 6 **CALS PER SERVING** 188

625 g (1¼ lb) baby new potatoes
salt and black pepper
500 g (1 lb) courgettes, thickly sliced
500 g (1 lb) Spanish onions, thickly sliced
500 g (1 lb) tomatoes, halved
3 fat garlic cloves, peeled and left whole
olive oil
3 tsp chopped fresh rosemary
400 ml (14 fl oz) passata (sieved tomatoes)
Tabasco sauce
3 fresh thyme sprigs, plus extra to garnish

1.8 LITRE (3 PINT) OVENPROOF DISH, ABOUT 20 X 28 X 5 CM (8 X 11 X 2 IN)

1 Boil the potatoes in salted water for about 15–20 minutes until not quite done. Drain and leave until cool enough to handle, then peel and cut in half.

2 Toss the courgettes, onions, tomatoes, and garlic cloves in a couple of tablespoons of olive oil and season well. Arrange cut-side down on a large baking sheet or in a shallow roasting tin. Roast in a preheated oven at 220°C (200°C fan, Gas 7) for about 30–40 minutes, turning once, until the vegetables are charred and soft.

3 Pick out the garlic, squash it with the back of a knife, and return it to the other vegetables. Layer the vegetables in an ovenproof dish – first the potatoes with some seasoning and rosemary, about 6 tbsp passata, and a good dash of Tabasco, then the onions, tomatoes, and courgettes with seasoning, rosemary, passata, and Tabasco as before. Push 3 sprigs of thyme in near the top.

4 Bake in a preheated oven at 200°C (180°C fan, Gas 6) for about 15–20 minutes, or at 170°C (150°C fan, Gas 3) for 30–40 minutes, until hot and bubbling. Before serving, replace the cooked thyme with fresh thyme.

Mushroom Stroganoff

SERVES 4 **CALS PER SERVING** 177

20 g (¾ oz) dried mushrooms (porcini)
2 tbsp olive oil
1 onion, chopped
1 garlic clove, crushed
500 g (1 lb) chestnut mushrooms
2 red peppers, halved, deseeded, and sliced
2 tsp paprika
salt and black pepper
30 g (1 oz) cornflour
300 ml (½ pint) cold vegetable stock
1 x 400 g can artichoke hearts, drained
2 tbsp dry white or red wine
1 tbsp tomato purée
low-fat crème fraîche or plain yogurt, to serve

1 Soak the dried mushrooms in 150 ml (¼ pint) warm water for 20 minutes, then drain and reserve the soaking water.

2 Heat the oil in a flameproof casserole, add the onion and garlic, and cook for 3–5 minutes until softened.

3 Add the mushrooms, peppers, and paprika, and season with salt and pepper. Cook, stirring, for 5 minutes. Mix the cornflour and stock, add to the pan with the artichokes, wine, mushroom soaking water, and tomato purée, and bring to a boil. Simmer gently for 10–15 minutes. Taste for seasoning. Serve hot, with crème fraîche or yogurt.

MUSHROOM VOL-AU-VENT

When cooking the mushrooms, increase the heat to reduce and thicken the sauce. Warm through a ready-made large vol-au-vent shell, and fill with the hot Mushroom Stroganoff.

Tuscan cannelloni

SERVES 4 **CALS PER SERVING** 482

8 sheets of fresh lasagne, or dried lasagne cooked according to packet instructions
500 g (1 lb) passata (sieved tomatoes) or ready-made fresh tomato and basil pasta sauce
2–3 tbsp grated fresh Parmesan cheese
a small handful of chopped fresh basil

Filling

a little olive oil
2 shallots, finely chopped
1 garlic clove, crushed
2 x 300 g cans cannellini beans, drained
60 g (2 oz) SunBlush or sun-dried tomatoes, snipped into pieces
150 g (5 oz) Dolcelatte cheese, roughly chopped
2 heaped tbsp chopped fresh basil
salt and black pepper

SHALLOW OVENPROOF DISH, ABOUT 28 X 20 CM (11 X 8 IN)

1 Make the filling: heat the oil in a small pan, and cook the shallots and garlic until soft. Allow to cool. Crush the beans with a fork so that most are mashed but a few still retain some shape, then mix them with the shallots and garlic, tomatoes, Dolcelatte, and basil. Season well, taste, and add more seasoning if necessary.

2 Lay the lasagne sheets flat, divide the filling among them, and roll up from the short ends to enclose the filling. Put the cannelloni seam-side down into an oiled or buttered ovenproof dish – they should fit snugly. Season, then pour over the passata or pasta sauce.

3 Cover and cook in a preheated oven at 190°C (170°C fan, Gas 5) for 45–50 minutes until the pasta is cooked and the filling piping hot. (If pre-cooked pasta was used, bake for 25–30 minutes.) Scatter the Parmesan and basil over the top before serving.

Potato, celeriac, and Parmesan gratin

SERVES 6 **CALS PER SERVING** 451

60 g (2 oz) butter, plus extra for greasing
1 onion, sliced
2 garlic cloves, crushed
1 kg (2 lb) floury potatoes, thinly sliced
375 g (12 oz) celeriac, peeled and thinly sliced
300 ml (½ pint) single cream
150 ml (¼ pint) milk
250 g (8 oz) ricotta cheese
3 tbsp snipped fresh chives
salt and black pepper
2 tbsp fresh breadcrumbs
3 tbsp grated Parmesan cheese, plus extra to serve

1 Melt the butter in a frying pan, add the sliced onion and crushed garlic, and cook gently, stirring occasionally, for 3–5 minutes until softened but not coloured. Lightly butter a large gratin dish.

2 Arrange the potatoes, celeriac, and the onion mixture in layers in the prepared gratin dish, finishing with a neat layer of potatoes.

3 In a large bowl, combine the cream, milk, ricotta cheese, and chives, and season with salt and pepper. Beat well together, then pour over the vegetables.

4 In a small bowl, combine the breadcrumbs and 3 tbsp grated Parmesan cheese, and then sprinkle evenly over the potatoes.

5 Bake in a preheated oven at 180°C (160°C fan, Gas 4) for about 1 hour or until the potatoes and celeriac are tender and the top is golden brown.

6 Serve the gratin hot with a simple, mixed salad, and sprinkled with extra grated Parmesan cheese.

Cheese and vegetable pie

SERVES 4–5 **CALS PER SERVING** 216

30 g (1 oz) butter
1 onion, chopped
2 carrots, sliced
500 g (1 lb) courgettes, sliced
2 large tomatoes, chopped
125 g (4 oz) mushrooms, sliced
2 tbsp chopped parsley
½ tsp fresh marjoram or oregano
salt and black pepper

Cheese sauce

30 g (1 oz) butter
30 g (1 oz) plain flour
300 ml (½ pint) milk
60 g (2 oz) mature Cheddar cheese, grated
1 tsp English mustard
pinch of cayenne pepper

Cheese pastry

125 g (4 oz) plain flour, plus extra for rolling
60 g (2 oz) butter
60 g (2 oz) mature Cheddar cheese, grated
1 small egg, beaten

1 Make the cheese pastry: sift the flour into a bowl, add the butter, and rub in lightly until the mixture resembles fine breadcrumbs. Stir in the cheese, then bind to a soft but not sticky dough with 1 tbsp of the beaten egg and 1 tbsp cold water. Chill for 30 minutes.

2 Melt the butter in a large pan, add the onion, and cook gently for 3–5 minutes until softened. Add the carrots and cook for about 5 minutes.

3 Add the courgettes, tomatoes, mushrooms, and herbs, and season with salt and pepper. Cook over a low heat, stirring occasionally, for 10–15 minutes until softened. Remove from the heat.

4 Make the cheese sauce: melt the butter in a saucepan, add the flour, and cook, stirring, for 1 minute. Remove from the heat and gradually blend in the milk.

5 Bring to a boil, stirring until the mixture thickens. Simmer for 2–3 minutes, then stir in the cheese, mustard, and cayenne, and season with salt and pepper. Stir the vegetables into the sauce, remove from the heat, and leave to cool.

6 Roll out the pastry on a floured work surface. Invert a pie dish on to the pastry and cut around the edge. Reserve the trimmings.

7 Transfer the vegetable and sauce mixture to the pie dish and top with the pastry. Crimp the edges and make a hole in the top of the pastry to allow steam to escape.

8 Decorate the pie with the pastry trimmings, attaching them with beaten egg. Brush the pastry all over with the remaining beaten egg. Bake in a preheated oven at 200°C (180°C fan, Gas 6) for 30 minutes or until the pastry is crisp and golden all over. Serve hot.

Dairy-free lasagne

SERVES 4–6 **CALS PER SERVING** 364–243

2–3 tbsp olive oil, more if needed
2 courgettes, sliced
salt and black pepper
1 aubergine, cut into 5 mm (1/4 in) slices
2 onions, chopped
1 red pepper, halved, deseeded, and diced
2 garlic cloves, crushed
2 x 400 g cans chopped tomatoes
1 x 140 g can tomato purée
1/4 tsp caster sugar
3 tbsp chopped fresh basil
150 g (5 oz) pre-cooked lasagne sheets
250 g (8 oz) frozen chopped spinach, thawed, drained, and seasoned well

1 Heat 1 tbsp olive oil in a large non-stick frying pan, add the courgettes, and cook for 3 minutes. Turn into a bowl, and sprinkle with salt.

2 Heat another tablespoon of oil in the pan, and cook the aubergine slices for about 3–5 minutes on each side until golden. Remove and set aside.

3 Add the onions, red pepper, and garlic to the pan, with more oil if needed, and soften gently for 3–5 minutes. Add the tomatoes, tomato purée, and sugar and bring to a boil. Simmer for 10 minutes until thickened, stir in the basil, and season with salt and pepper.

4 Spoon one-third of the tomato sauce into a large ovenproof dish and cover with one-third of the lasagne. Add the aubergine, then half of the remaining tomato sauce. Add half of the remaining lasagne, then the spinach. Add the remaining lasagne and tomato sauce, and finish with an overlapping layer of courgettes.

5 Bake in a preheated oven at 190°C (170°C fan, Gas 5) for 35 minutes or until the pasta is tender and the top is golden.

Spinach gnocchi with tomato sauce

SERVES 4 **CALS PER SERVING** 738

1 kg (2 lb) spinach leaves
375 g (12 oz) ricotta cheese
3 eggs
4 tbsp grated Parmesan cheese
pinch of grated nutmeg
salt and black pepper
60–75 g (2–2½ oz) plain flour

Tomato sauce

30 g (1 oz) butter
1 small onion, chopped
1 small carrot, chopped
30 g (1 oz) plain flour
1 x 400 g can chopped tomatoes
300 ml (1/2 pint) vegetable stock
1 bay leaf
1 tsp caster sugar

To serve

125 g (4 oz) butter
grated Parmesan cheese and Parmesan shavings

1 Wash the spinach and put into a saucepan with only the water remaining on the leaves. Cook over a gentle heat until just wilted. Drain the spinach throughly, squeezing to remove any excess water.

2 Put the spinach, ricotta, eggs, Parmesan, and nutmeg into a food processor, season with salt and pepper and purée until smooth. Turn into a bowl and gradually add flour until the mixture just holds its shape.

3 Using two dessertspoons, form the mixture into 20 oval shapes. Cover and chill in the refrigerator for 1 hour.

4 Make the tomato sauce: melt the butter in a pan, add the onion and carrot, and cook for 10 minutes or until softened. Sprinkle in the flour and cook, stirring, for 1 minute. Add the tomatoes, stock, bay leaf, and sugar, season with salt and pepper, and bring to a boil. Cover and simmer for 30 minutes. Purée in a food processor until smooth. Keep hot.

5 Cook the gnocchi in batches in boiling salted water for about 5 minutes or until they float to the surface. Lift out and keep hot. Melt the butter and pour over the gnocchi. Serve the gnocchi hot, with the tomato sauce, grated Parmesan, and Parmesan shavings.

Spinach roulade

SERVES 6–8 **CALS PER SERVING** 250–187

560 g (1 lb 2 oz) spinach leaves
30 g (1 oz) butter, plus extra for greasing
4 eggs, separated
¼ tsp grated nutmeg
1 tbsp finely grated Parmesan cheese

Filling

15 g (½ oz) butter
250 g (8 oz) button mushrooms, sliced
juice of ½ lemon
salt and black pepper
200 ml (7 fl oz) crème fraîche
2 tbsp chopped parsley

33 X 23 CM (13 X 9 IN) SWISS ROLL TIN

1 Make the filling: melt the butter in a pan, add the mushrooms and lemon juice, and season with salt and pepper. Cook for 3 minutes until just softened, then leave to cool.

2 Wash the spinach and put into a pan with only the water remaining on the leaves. Cook over a gentle heat for 1–2 minutes until the spinach has just wilted. Drain well, and squeeze out the excess water.

3 Butter the tin and line with baking parchment. Butter the parchment.

4 Coarsely chop the spinach, turn into a large bowl, and beat in the butter, egg yolks, and nutmeg. Season with salt and pepper. In another bowl, whisk the egg whites until firm but not dry, then fold gently into the spinach mixture.

5 Pour the spinach mixture into the Swiss roll tin and bake in a preheated oven at 220°C (200°C fan, Gas 7) for 10–12 minutes until firm.

6 Sprinkle the Parmesan cheese on to a sheet of baking parchment. Turn the roulade out on to the cheese, leave to cool for 5–10 minutes, then peel off the lining paper. Trim the edges of the roulade.

7 Drain the mushrooms, reserving some of the cooking liquid. Put them into a bowl, add the crème fraîche, parsley, and season to taste. Add a little of the reserved liquid if too thick. Spread the filling over the roulade, leaving a 2.5 cm (1 in) border. Roll up from one long side. Cover and chill for 30 minutes. Cut into slices to serve.

Mushroom lasagne

SERVES 6 **CALS PER SERVING** 684

2 tbsp olive oil
1 large onion, finely chopped
500 g (1 lb) mushrooms, sliced
2 large garlic cloves, crushed
30 g (1 oz) plain flour
2 x 400 g cans chopped tomatoes
1 tbsp chopped fresh basil
1 tsp caster sugar
salt and black pepper
500 g (1 lb) frozen whole leaf spinach, thawed and drained
white sauce made with 90 g (3 oz) each butter and plain flour, 900 ml (1½ pints) milk, and 1 tsp Dijon mustard
300 g (10 oz) mature Cheddar cheese, grated
150 g (5 oz) pre-cooked lasagne sheets

1 Heat the oil in a saucepan, add the onion, mushrooms, and garlic, and cook for 10 minutes or until soft. Sprinkle in the flour and cook, stirring, for 1 minute.

2 Add the tomatoes, basil, and sugar, and season with salt and pepper. Cover and simmer for 20 minutes.

3 Season the spinach with salt and pepper. Taking 1 teaspoonful at a time, shape it loosely into 24 balls.

4 Spoon one-third of the mushroom mixture into a large ovenproof dish, and place eight of the spinach balls on top. Cover with one-third of the white sauce and one-third of the cheese. Arrange half of the lasagne on top. Repeat the layers, finishing with cheese.

5 Bake in a preheated oven at 190°C (170°C fan, Gas 5) for 35 minutes or until the pasta is tender. Serve hot, accompanied by a mixed leaf salad.

Chestnut loaf

SERVES 6 **CALS PER SERVING** 226

250 g (8 oz) chestnuts
1 tbsp olive oil, plus extra for greasing
1 onion, coarsely chopped
2 celery stalks, chopped
2 garlic cloves, crushed
250 g (8 oz) potatoes, boiled and mashed
125 g (4 oz) fresh wholemeal breadcrumbs
1 egg, beaten
2 tbsp chopped parsley
1 tbsp soy sauce
1 tbsp tomato purée
salt and black pepper
red pepper strips and watercress sprigs, to garnish
spicy tomato salsa (see box, right), to serve

1 KG (2 LB) LOAF TIN

1 Coarsely chop half of the chestnuts, and finely chop the remainder.

2 Heat the oil in a pan, add the onion, celery, and garlic, and cook, stirring, for 3–5 minutes until soft. Remove from the heat.

3 Stir in the chestnuts, potatoes, breadcrumbs, egg, parsley, soy sauce, and tomato purée, and season with salt and pepper.

4 Spoon the mixture into the greased loaf tin, and level the top. Cover with foil and cook in a preheated oven at 180°C (160°C fan, Gas 4) for 1 hour or until firm. Turn out, cut into slices, and garnish. Serve hot or cold, accompanied by the salsa.

Spicy tomato salsa

Dice 8 large tomatoes, and put into a bowl. Stir in 2 chopped spring onions, 1 deseeded and finely chopped fresh green chilli, the zest and juice of 2 limes, 3 tbsp chopped fresh coriander, and 1 tsp caster sugar. Season with salt and pepper, and chill.

Red bean and tomato curry

SERVES 4 **CALS PER SERVING** 218

2 tbsp sunflower oil
1 large onion, sliced
3 garlic cloves, crushed
1–2 fresh green chillies, halved, deseeded, and sliced
2.5 cm (1 in) piece of fresh root ginger, peeled and grated
1 tbsp Madras or other hot curry powder
salt
1 x 400 g can chopped tomatoes
2 x 400 g cans red kidney beans, drained and rinsed
1 tbsp lemon juice
fresh coriander leaves, to garnish

1 Heat the oil in a large frying pan, add the onion, garlic, chillies, and ginger, and cook, stirring occasionally, for a few minutes until all the aromas are released, and the onion is softened but not coloured.

2 Add the curry powder and season with salt, then cook, stirring, for 2 minutes.

3 Add the tomatoes with most of their juice and cook for about 3 minutes. Add the beans and cook for a further 5 minutes or until the beans are warmed through and the sauce is thickened. Add the lemon juice and serve hot, garnished with coriander.

Christmas nut loaf

SERVES 6–8 **CALS PER SERVING** 600–450

75 g (2½ oz) brown rice
salt and black pepper
15 g (½ oz) dried porcini mushrooms
30 g (1 oz) butter
2 carrots, grated
1 small onion, finely chopped
1 garlic clove, crushed
250 g (8 oz) button mushrooms, chopped
2 tbsp chopped parsley
1 tbsp chopped fresh rosemary
125 g (4 oz) walnuts, toasted and chopped
125 g (4 oz) Brazil nuts, toasted and chopped
60 g (2 oz) pine nuts, toasted
175 g (6 oz) Cheddar cheese, grated
1 egg, beaten
sunflower oil, for greasing
rosemary sprigs, to garnish
cranberry sauce (page 198), to serve

1 KG (2 LB) LOAF TIN

1 Cook the rice in boiling salted water for 30–35 minutes until tender.

2 Meanwhile, soak the porcini mushrooms in a bowl of warm water for about 20–30 minutes.

3 Drain the rice when it is ready. Drain the mushrooms, pat dry, and chop finely.

4 Melt the butter in a frying pan, add the carrots, onion, and garlic, and cook gently, stirring occasionally, for 5 minutes. Stir in the chopped button mushrooms, rice, porcini mushrooms, parsley, and rosemary, and cook until softened.

5 Purée the mixture in a food processor. Stir in the walnuts, Brazil nuts, pine nuts, cheese, and egg. Season with salt and pepper.

6 Line and lightly grease the loaf tin, spoon in the mixture, and level the top. Cover with foil and bake in a preheated oven at 190°C (170°C fan, Gas 5) for 1½ hours or until firm. Turn out, cut into slices, and garnish. Serve hot, with cranberry sauce.

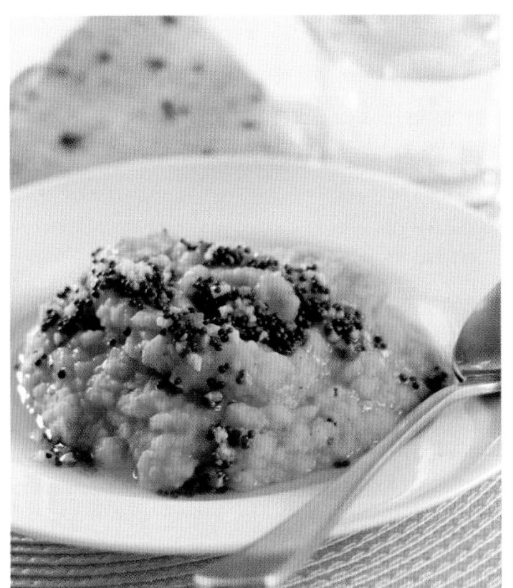

Red lentil and coconut curry

SERVES 6 **CALS PER SERVING** 481

300 g (10 oz) red lentils
900 ml (1½ pints) water
2.5 cm (1 in) piece of fresh root ginger, peeled and grated
1½ fresh green chillies, halved, deseeded, and finely chopped
4 garlic cloves
90 g (3 oz) creamed coconut, grated
½ tsp turmeric
1 tbsp lemon juice
salt
30 g (1 oz) butter
4 tsp black mustard seeds

1 Put the lentils into a pan and add the water. Bring to a boil and simmer for about 20 minutes or until tender.

2 Using a pestle and mortar, crush the ginger, two-thirds of the chillies, and 2 garlic cloves until smooth. Add to the lentils.

3 Add the creamed coconut, turmeric, lemon juice, and a pinch of salt. Cook gently, stirring, until the coconut dissolves, then increase the heat and cook for 5 minutes or until any excess liquid has evaporated. Taste for seasoning.

4 Crush the remaining garlic and set aside. Melt the butter in a frying pan and add the mustard seeds. As soon as they begin to pop, remove the frying pan from the heat and stir in the crushed garlic and the chopped chilli. Serve the lentils with the mustard seeds, grated coconut, and chopped chillies on top.

Veggie burgers

SERVES 6 **CALS PER SERVING** 216

1 small red onion, finely chopped
3 tbsp chopped parsley
1 x 400 g can cannellini beans, drained
1 x 300 g can red kidney beans, drained
60 g (2 oz) ready-to-eat dried apricots, snipped into pieces
175 g (6 oz) carrots, grated
60 g (2 oz) Cheddar cheese, grated
salt and black pepper
30 g (1 oz) pine nuts, toasted
about 2–3 tbsp olive oil

1 Purée the onion and parsley in a food processor until fairly smooth. Add the remaining ingredients, except the pine nuts and oil, and blitz until smooth. (If you haven't got a processor, mash the beans and mix with the other ingredients except the pine nuts and oil.) Season really well.

2 Add the toasted pine nuts and pulse the machine to mix them in. Shape the mixture into 12 small burgers. Put on a large plate, cover, and refrigerate for about 1 hour (they will keep for up to 24 hours).

3 Place the burgers on a grill tray lined with foil, under a hot grill 7 cm (3 in) from the heat. Brush the burgers frequently with oil, for 4 minutes each side until they are hot right through. Serve with spicy tomato salsa (page 96).

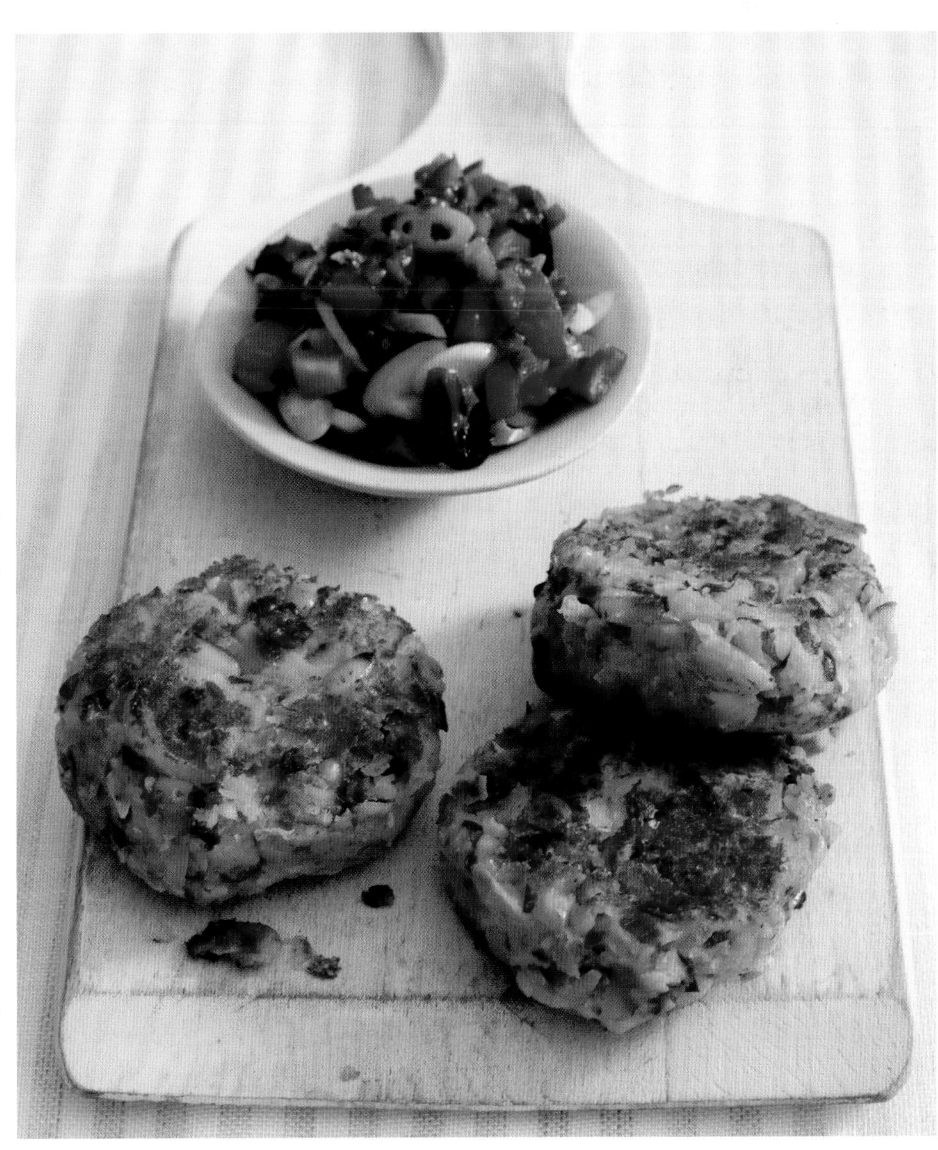

Saag aloo

SERVES 6 **CALS PER SERVING** 143

500 g (1 lb) new potatoes
salt
2 tbsp sunflower oil
1 tsp mustard seeds
1 tsp cumin seeds
2 onions, sliced
3 garlic cloves, chopped
2.5 cm (1 in) piece of fresh root ginger, peeled and grated
1 small fresh green chilli, halved, deseeded, and finely chopped
2 tsp ground coriander
½ tsp turmeric
250 ml (8 fl oz) water
500 g (1 lb) fresh baby leaf spinach
2 tbsp lime or lemon juice
plain yogurt, to serve

1 Cook the potatoes in a saucepan of boiling salted water for 10 minutes. Drain and leave to cool. Cut into bite-sized pieces and set aside.

2 Heat the oil in a large, heavy frying pan. Add the mustard and cumin seeds and cook, stirring, for a few seconds until they pop. Add the onions, garlic, ginger, and chilli and cook for about 5 minutes until soft.

3 Add 1 tsp salt, the ground coriander, and the turmeric. Cook, stirring, for 1 minute. Add the potatoes and turn to coat in the spices, then pour in the water and bring to a boil. Cover and cook over a gentle heat for 15 minutes or until the potatoes are tender.

4 Remove the lid and stir in the spinach. Increase the heat and cook, stirring occasionally, for about 10 minutes or until the spinach wilts right down into the sauce. Stir in the lime or lemon juice and taste for seasoning. Serve hot, with yogurt.

Dhal

SERVES 6 **CALS PER SERVING** 275

225 g (8 oz) green lentils
1 bay leaf
2 tbsp vegetable oil
1 large carrot, chopped
1 large green pepper, halved, deseeded, and chopped
1 large onion, chopped
1 garlic clove, crushed
1 cm (½ in) piece of fresh root ginger, peeled and finely grated
½ tsp each ground cinnamon, cumin, and coriander
1 x 400 g can chopped tomatoes
salt and black pepper

1 Rinse and drain the lentils, put them into a large saucepan, and pour in enough cold water to cover. Bring to a boil and add the bay leaf, then cover and simmer for 30 minutes or until the lentils are tender. Drain the lentils and set aside. Discard the bay leaf.

2 Heat the oil in the saucepan, add the vegetables, garlic, and ginger, and fry for 10 minutes, stirring occasionally. Add the lentils, ground spices, and tomatoes and cook gently for 10 minutes or until the carrot is soft.

3 Purée the mixture in three batches in a blender or food processor. Do not purée for longer than about 30 seconds for each batch because the dhal should not be too smooth – it should retain some of the texture of the lentils. Reheat in the rinsed-out pan, and add salt and pepper to taste. Serve hot.

Accompaniments

- tomato and coriander relish
- cucumber raita
- grated carrot salad
- mango chutney
- poppadoms
- basmati rice
- naan bread

Niramish tarkari

SERVES 6 **CALS PER SERVING** 303

2 tbsp sunflower oil
3 tbsp curry paste
½ tsp chilli powder
2.5 cm (1 in) piece of fresh root ginger, peeled and grated
1 large onion, chopped
2 garlic cloves, crushed
3 tbsp mango chutney
1 small cauliflower, cut into florets
2 potatoes, cut into chunks
2 large carrots, sliced
2 red peppers, halved, deseeded, and cut into chunks
1 x 400 g can chopped tomatoes
1 x 400 g can coconut milk
250 g (8 oz) green beans, chopped into short lengths
salt and black pepper
juice of 1 lime
fresh coriander leaves, to garnish

1 Heat the oil in a large saucepan, add the curry paste and chilli powder, and cook, stirring constantly, for 1 minute. Add the ginger, onion, garlic, and mango chutney, and cook, stirring, for 3–5 minutes until the onion is softened but not coloured.

2 Add the cauliflower, potatoes, and carrots to the pan, and stir well to coat in the spices. Cook, stirring occasionally, for 5 minutes.

3 Add the red peppers, tomatoes, and coconut milk to the pan and bring to a boil, then add the beans and season with salt and pepper. Stir well.

4 Cover and simmer gently for 25–30 minutes or until all the vegetables are tender. Stir in the lime juice and taste for seasoning. Serve hot, garnished with coriander leaves.

Opposite, clockwise from top:
Saag aloo, Dhal, Niramish tarkari

Peking tofu with plum sauce

SERVES 6 **CALS PER SERVING** 269

sunflower oil, for frying
250 g (8 oz) tofu, cut into 1.5 cm (just over ½ in) cubes
18 Chinese pancakes (ready-made or see page 210)
6 spring onions, trimmed and cut into matchsticks
¼ cucumber, peeled, deseeded, and cut into matchsticks

Plum sauce

250 g (8 oz) dark red plums, halved and stoned
1 small cooking apple, peeled, cored, and sliced
1 fresh red chilli, halved, deseeded, and finely chopped
90 g (3 oz) caster sugar
50 ml (2 fl oz) white wine vinegar

1 Make the plum sauce: put the plums, apple, chilli, sugar, vinegar, and 25 ml (1 fl oz) water into a pan. Heat gently to dissolve the sugar, then bring to a boil. Partially cover and simmer gently for about 30–40 minutes until the fruits have cooked down and only a little liquid remains. Remove from the heat and allow to cool.

2 Pour enough oil into a non-stick frying pan to cover the base. Heat until hot, then fry the tofu for 3–4 minutes until golden all over, turning carefully. Remove and drain on kitchen paper.

3 To serve, spread a pancake with a little plum sauce, top with a little crispy fried tofu, spring onions, and cucumber, and roll up to eat.

Thai curry

SERVES 4 **CALS PER SERVING** 296

1 tbsp sunflower or sesame oil
1 fresh green chilli, halved, deseeded, and finely chopped
2.5 cm (1 in) piece of fresh root ginger, peeled and grated
1 tbsp Thai green curry paste
1 large cauliflower, cut into bite-sized florets
375 g (12 oz) fine green beans, halved
1 x 400 g can coconut milk
150 ml (¼ pint) vegetable stock
1 fresh lemongrass stalk, bruised by bashing with a rolling pin
salt and black pepper
1 x 200 g can water chestnuts
3 tbsp chopped fresh coriander, to garnish
boiled or steamed Thai jasmine rice, to serve

1 Heat the oil in a wok or large non-stick frying pan and stir-fry the chilli and ginger for 2 minutes. Add the curry paste and stir-fry for a further minute.

2 Add the cauliflower and beans and stir evenly to coat the vegetables in the spices. Pour in the coconut milk and stock, then add the lemongrass and seasoning. Bring to a boil and simmer gently for about 20–30 minutes until the beans and cauliflower are just cooked (take care not to overcook them). Add the water chestnuts for the last 5 minutes. Remove and discard the lemongrass, scatter over the coriander, and serve with rice.

Firecracker stir-fry

SERVES 4 **CALS PER SERVING** 129

250 g (8 oz) pak choi
2–3 tbsp sunflower or sesame oil
250 g (8 oz) sugarsnap peas, trimmed
1 red pepper, halved, deseeded, and cut into strips
1 yellow pepper, halved, deseeded, and cut into strips
2–3 hot fresh red chillies, halved, deseeded, and sliced
300 g (10 oz) shiitake mushrooms, sliced
2–3 tbsp soy sauce
salt and black pepper

1 Cut the leafy tops off the pak choi, shred the leaves coarsely, and reserve. Slice the stems in half, or into quarters if they are large.

2 Heat the oil in a wok or large frying pan. Add the peas, peppers, and chilli, and stir-fry over a high heat for about 3–4 minutes. Add the mushrooms and pak choi stems and continue to stir-fry for another 2–3 minutes.

3 When the vegetables are just about tender, add the shredded pak choi leaves with a dash of soy sauce. Taste and add salt and pepper if needed, plus more soy sauce if you like. Serve immediately.

Vegetable stir-fry with tofu

SERVES 4 **CALS PER SERVING** 335

250 g (8 oz) firm tofu, cut into bite-sized pieces
2 tbsp sesame oil
1 tbsp sunflower oil
1 head of chicory, halved lengthways
4 carrots, thinly sliced diagonally
5 cm (2 in) piece of fresh root ginger, peeled and grated
250 g (8 oz) shiitake mushrooms, sliced
8 spring onions, sliced into 2.5 cm (1 in) pieces
250 g (8 oz) bean sprouts
3 tbsp toasted sesame seeds

Marinade

3 tbsp soy sauce
3 tbsp dry sherry
1 garlic clove, crushed
salt and black pepper

1 Make the marinade: in a bowl, combine the soy sauce, sherry, and garlic, and season with salt and pepper. Turn the tofu in the marinade, cover, and leave to marinate at room temperature for at least 15 minutes.

2 Drain the tofu, reserving the marinade. Heat the sesame and sunflower oils in a wok or large frying pan, add the tofu, and carefully stir-fry over a high heat for 2–3 minutes, being careful not to break up the tofu. Remove from the wok with a slotted spoon and drain on paper towels.

3 Separate the chicory halves into leaves. Add the carrots and ginger to the wok and stir-fry for about 2 minutes. Add the mushrooms and spring onions and stir-fry for a further 2 minutes, then add the bean sprouts and chicory leaves and stir-fry for 1 minute.

4 Return the tofu to the wok, pour the reserved marinade over the top, and boil quickly until almost all of the marinade has evaporated and the tofu has warmed through. Taste for seasoning, generously sprinkle with the toasted sesame seeds, and serve at once.

Japanese noodle soup

SERVES 6 **CALS PER SERVING** 213

1.5 litres (2½ pints) miso soup (3 sachets)
1 tsp five-spice paste or 1 tsp five-spice powder mixed to a paste with a little water
300 g (10 oz) udon noodles (made from wheat flour)
250 g (8 oz) tofu, cut into 1 cm (½ in) cubes
3 spring onions, trimmed and shredded

1 Make the miso soup, bring to a boil and add the five-spice paste. Simmer for 5 minutes, then add the noodles and simmer for 2 minutes, gently separating them with chopsticks or a fork.

2 Add the tofu and heat through for 1 minute. Ladle into soup bowls and scatter over the shredded spring onions before serving.

Mexican bean salad

SERVES 6 **CALS PER SERVING** 245

350 g (12 oz) mixed dried beans, e.g. red kidney, haricot, black eye, and aduki, soaked in cold water overnight, or 2 x 400 g cans beans
3 celery stalks, finely chopped
1 red onion, finely chopped
2 garlic cloves, crushed

Dressing
4 tbsp olive oil
2 tbsp lime juice
2 tbsp chopped fresh coriander
1 tsp Dijon mustard
1 tsp clear honey
salt and black pepper

1 Drain the soaked dried beans into a colander and rinse well under cold running water. Tip them into a large saucepan, cover with cold water, and bring to a boil. Half cover the pan and simmer for 1 hour or until all the beans are tender.

2 Drain the beans, rinse under hot water, and tip into a large bowl. If using canned beans, drain and rinse them before putting them in the bowl.

3 Whisk together all the dressing ingredients with plenty of salt and pepper, pour over the beans, and add the celery, red onion, and garlic. Toss well, cover the bowl, and leave to marinate until cold, or overnight.

REFRIED BEANS

Heat 1–2 tbsp sunflower oil in a frying pan. Add ½ finely chopped onion, and cook for 8 minutes, until lightly browned. Add 1 crushed garlic clove, and cook for 2 minutes. Drain and rinse 1 x 400 g can red kidney beans, and add to the pan. Cook over a gentle heat until warmed through, mashing the beans with a potato masher or fork and adding 1–2 tbsp water if necessary, to prevent sticking.

Mexican chilli with tofu

SERVES 6 **CALS PER SERVING** 257

3 onions, chopped
3 garlic cloves, roughly chopped
1 fresh green chilli, halved, deseeded, and roughly chopped
2 tsp paprika
1 tbsp mild chilli powder
4 tbsp sunflower oil
1 x 400 g can chopped tomatoes, drained and juice reserved
500 ml (16 fl oz) hot vegetable stock
625 g (1¼ lb) firm tofu, cut into bite-sized pieces
1 x 400 g can red kidney beans, drained
salt and black pepper
chopped fresh coriander, to garnish

1 Put the onions, garlic, green chilli, and spices into a food processor and process until fairly chunky.

2 Heat the oil in a large frying pan. Add the onion mixture and cook for a few minutes, stirring occasionally, until softened and fragrant.

3 Add the tomatoes to the pan and cook, stirring occasionally, until reduced and thickened. Pour in the stock and cook for 5–10 minutes more until thickened again.

4 Add the tofu, kidney beans, and the reserved tomato juice, and cook, spooning the sauce over the tofu pieces, for 5–8 minutes until heated through. Do not stir the tofu as it may break up. Season, and serve hot, sprinkled with coriander.

Cook's know-how

Reducing a sauce involves cooking it over a high heat to allow the moisture to evaporate and the flavours to become concentrated.

Vegetarian enchiladas

SERVES 6 **CALS PER SERVING** 242

4 large tortilla wraps, about 23 cm (9 in) in diameter
1 x 175 g can red kidney beans, drained
60 g (2 oz) feta cheese, grated
60 g (2 oz) Cheddar cheese, grated
1 tbsp olive oil

Mexican tomato sauce

1 tbsp olive oil
½ small onion, finely chopped
1 green chilli, halved, deseeded, and finely chopped
1 garlic clove, crushed
1 x 400 g can chopped tomatoes
grated zest of ½ lime
2 tbsp chopped fresh coriander
salt and black pepper

1 Make the tomato sauce: heat the oil in a pan, add the onion, chilli, and garlic, and fry over a high heat for a few minutes. Add the tomatoes and simmer without a lid over a low heat, stirring from time to time, for about 10 minutes until the mixture is fairly thick (the consistency of chutney). If it is still a little runny, reduce it by boiling over a high heat, stirring continuously. Add the lime zest and coriander, and season with salt and pepper.

2 Take one tortilla and spread half of the tomato sauce over it to within 2.5 cm (1 in) of the edge. Top with half of the red kidney beans, and sprinkle over half of both the cheeses. Put another tortilla on top and press down a little with your hand so the two tortillas are sandwiched together. Make a separate tortilla sandwich (enchilada) with the remaining ingredients.

3 Heat the oil in a frying pan with a wide base, so the tortillas can fit in flat. Fry each enchilada for 3–4 minutes on each side or until the tortillas are golden brown and crisp, the filling is hot, and the cheese melted. Slice each enchilada into six wedges to serve with guacamole (see box, below).

Guacamole

Mash the flesh of 1 large ripe avocado in a bowl with a fork. Add ½ finely chopped onion, 1 tbsp chopped fresh coriander, and the juice of 1 lime. Mix well and season to taste. Chill for no more than 30 minutes before serving, or the avocado will discolour.

Spinach and ricotta samosas

SERVES 4 **CALS PER SERVING** 307

4 sheets of filo pastry
60 g (2 oz) melted butter, plus extra for greasing

Filling

30 g (1 oz) butter
1 small onion, finely chopped
300 g (10 oz) spinach leaves, shredded
125 g (4 oz) ricotta cheese
pinch of grated nutmeg
salt and black pepper
tomato sauce (page 333), to serve

1 Make the filling: melt the butter in a saucepan, add the onion, and cook gently for 3–5 minutes until softened.

2 Add the spinach to the onion and cook for 1–2 minutes. Leave to cool. Add the ricotta and nutmeg, season with salt and pepper, and mix well. Divide into eight portions.

3 Lightly butter a baking tray. Cut each sheet of filo pastry lengthways into two long strips. Brush one strip with melted butter, covering the remaining strips with a damp tea towel. Fill and fold the parcels (see box, below).

4 Bake in a preheated oven at 200°C (180°C fan, Gas 6) for 20 minutes or until the pastry is crisp and golden. Serve with the tomato sauce.

Filling and folding the parcels

Spoon one portion of filling on to a corner of the filo strip. Fold over opposite corner to form a triangle.

Fold the filled triangle until you reach the end of the strip. Brush with melted butter and put on to the baking tray. Butter, fill, and fold the remaining filo strips.

Falafel with sesame yogurt sauce

SERVES 6 **CALS PER SERVING** 326

1 x 400 g can chick peas, drained and rinsed
6 spring onions, chopped
30 g (1 oz) fresh white bread
1 egg
grated zest and juice of ½ lemon
1 garlic clove, roughly chopped
2 tbsp roughly chopped fresh coriander
2 tbsp roughly chopped parsley
1 tbsp tahini paste
1 tsp ground coriander
1 tsp ground cumin
½ tsp ground cinnamon
pinch of cayenne pepper
salt and black pepper
sunflower oil, for shallow-frying
chopped fresh coriander, to garnish
warmed mini pitta breads, to serve

Sesame yogurt sauce

4 tbsp plain yogurt
2 tbsp olive oil
1 tbsp lemon juice
1 tbsp tahini paste

1 Put the chick peas into a food processor, add the onions, bread, egg, lemon zest and juice, garlic, coriander, parsley, tahini, ground coriander, cumin, cinnamon, and cayenne pepper, and season with salt and pepper. Purée until smooth.

2 Turn into a bowl, cover, and leave to stand for at least 30 minutes.

3 Meanwhile, make the sesame yogurt sauce: in a bowl, combine the yogurt, oil, lemon juice, tahini, and salt and pepper to taste.

4 With dampened hands, shape the falafel mixture into balls about the size of a walnut, then flatten them into patties.

5 Pour enough oil into a non-stick frying pan just to cover the base, and heat until hot. Shallow-fry the falafel in batches for 2–3 minutes on each side until golden. Lift out and drain on paper towels. Garnish with coriander and serve warm, with mini pitta breads and sesame yogurt sauce.

Halloumi and vegetable kebabs

SERVES 4 **CALS PER SERVING** 722

1 small baguette
250 g (8 oz) halloumi cheese
1 large red pepper, halved and deseeded
150 ml (¼ pint) olive oil, plus extra for greasing
16 large cherry tomatoes
grated zest and juice of 1 lemon
1 garlic clove, crushed
2 tbsp chopped fresh basil
1 tbsp snipped fresh chives
salt and black pepper

8 METAL SKEWERS

1 Cut the bread into eight thick slices and cut each slice in half. Cut the halloumi into 16 cubes and cut the red pepper into eight pieces.

2 Oil the skewers and thread alternately with the tomatoes, bread, cheese, and red pepper. Place in a shallow flameproof dish.

3 Mix the oil, lemon zest and juice, garlic, and herbs, and season with salt and pepper. Drizzle over the kebabs.

4 Cook the kebabs under a hot grill, 10 cm (4 in) from the heat, turning once and basting with the marinade, for 3–4 minutes until the cheese is lightly browned.

TOFU AND VEGETABLE KEBABS

Substitute smoked tofu for the halloumi cheese, and 8 button mushrooms for the red pepper.

Cook's know-how

Halloumi is a semi-hard Greek cheese, which is usually made from ewe's milk. It is best eaten hot, straight from the grill, as it becomes rubbery when it cools down.

Pasta, rice, and noodles

In this chapter...

Pasta alla marinara
page 371

Tuna and fennel pasta bake
page 372

Pasta shells with scallops
page 372

Pad Thai with tiger prawns
page 374

Szechuan noodles with water chestnuts
page 375

Singapore noodles
page 375

Risi e bisi
page 376

Stir-fried Chinese noodles
page 376

Risotto Milanese
page 377

Chicken liver risotto
page 378

Risotto al verde
page 378

Quick nasi goreng
page 380

Vegetarian nasi goreng
page 380

Chicken nasi goreng
page 381

Kedgeree
page 382

Paella
page 382

Portuguese rice with tuna
page 384

Caribbean rice and peas
page 385

Egg-fried rice
page 386

Persian pilaf
page 386

Savoury rice
page 387

Wild rice gratin
page 387

Pasta, rice, and noodles know-how

Both pasta and rice are natural convenience foods: they are so quick to cook and they do not need any elaborate preparation. They are also endlessly versatile, working well with almost every ingredient imaginable to make starters, soups, main dishes, side dishes, salads, snacks, and even a few desserts.

Pasta and rice are very nutritious, being high in starchy carbohydrates, and in their wholegrain forms also offering vitamins, minerals, and fibre. As long as rich ingredients such as butter, cream, and cheese are kept to a minimum, pasta and rice dishes can be very low in fat and calories.

Buying and storing

Pasta is available both fresh and dried as well as vacuum-packed, in a huge variety of shapes, both plain and stuffed. The best commercial dried pasta is made from durum wheat. Egg is sometimes added to dried pasta, while the fresh pasta sold in packets in supermarkets is most often enriched with eggs. Pasta is also coloured and flavoured – with spinach or tomato, for example. Fresh pasta is convenient because it cooks quickly, but its texture is not necessarily as good as some dried pasta. A good Italian brand of dried pasta, made from 100% durum wheat (*semola di grano duro*), is often of superior quality.

Dried pasta, in a tightly closed packet, will keep almost indefinitely in the store cupboard (up to 2 years); fresh pasta must be refrigerated and can only be kept for 2–3 days (check the use-by date). For longer storage, freeze it (see below).

Rice is another good store cupboard stand-by. As long as it is stored in an airtight container in a cool, dry, dark place, it will keep for up to a year. But make sure that the container is tightly closed to prevent moisture or insects from getting in.

Store any leftover cooked pasta or rice in a tightly closed container in the refrigerator. Use pasta within 2 days. Rice should be eaten on the day it is cooked as it is susceptible to toxins that cause food poisoning.

Freezing

Fresh uncooked pasta can be frozen for up to 3 months and then cooked from frozen. Layered or filled pasta dishes such as cannelloni, lasagne, and macaroni cheese freeze very well and can also be stored for up to 3 months. Put them in foil or other freezerproof containers that can go straight from the freezer into the oven.

There is no advantage to freezing cooked rice as it takes a long time to thaw – longer than it would take to cook a fresh batch.

It is not advisable to freeze pasta and rice in soups and other dishes that contain a lot of liquid because the pasta and rice become mushy when thawed. Instead, add when reheating the soup or casserole.

Microwaving

There is no advantage to cooking pasta in a microwave because it takes just as long as conventional cooking. However, many pasta sauces can be microwaved quickly and successfully, dishes containing layered or filled pasta cook really well in the microwave, and it is also an excellent way to reheat cooked pasta (be careful not to overcook it). The microwave is excellent for cooking rice, plain or turned into a pilaf or risotto, and the liquid does not have to be brought to a boil before the rice is added. Risotto turns out as tender and creamy as one made by the classic method that involves constant stirring, and yet it can be left totally unattended in the microwave.

Cooking times and quantities for pasta

These times can only be a guide because they depend on the freshness of fresh pasta and the age of dried pasta, as well as shape and thickness. Start timing as soon as the water returns to a boil, and for fresh pasta, start testing three-quarters of the way through the suggested cooking time. If using dried pasta, start testing as soon as the minimum time given on the packet is reached. Fresh, store-bought pasta takes 2–4 minutes, 7–10 minutes if filled. Most dried pastas cook in 8–12 minutes (less for fine pasta such as capelli d'angelo and vermicelli).

In Italy, pasta is usually eaten as a first course. Use 500 g (1 lb) fresh or dried pasta (uncooked weight) to serve six people as a first course and four people as a main dish. If the dish has a rich sauce or filling it will stretch even further. As an accompaniment to another dish, this amount would serve 6–8 people.

Pre-cooked lasagne

The sheets of dried lasagne that are labelled "pre-cooked" or "no pre-cooking required" are a great boon to the busy, time-stretched cook because they can be taken straight from the packet and layered with the other ingredients. However, this lasagne needs to absorb liquid during cooking, so if you are using it in a recipe that calls for fresh pasta or for ordinary dried lasagne, increase the quantity of sauce and make it thinner and runnier. Or briefly soak the sheets in a dish of hot water for about 5 minutes to moisten and soften them before layering in the baking dish.

Coloured and flavoured pasta

Not only does pasta come in a vast range of shapes, you can also choose from a variety of colours and flavours. Green is the most common colour, and is derived from spinach. Other colours include red, from tomato purée, pink, coloured with beetroot, yellow, from saffron, and even black pasta, coloured with squid ink. These colourings affect the taste very little. Flavoured pasta usually has ingredients such as herbs, garlic, or black pepper added to the dough. Serve with a complementary sauce.

Pasta shapes

Of the many pasta shapes available there are some that are traditionally served with certain sauces – spaghetti with bolognese sauce, for example. But you can mix and match as you wish.

Long, thin varieties

Capelli d'angelo or angel hair, vermicelli, spaghettini, spaghetti, and bucatini are best served with a thin oily sauce that clings without making the strands stick together.

Long flat ribbons

Pasta such as linguine, fettuccine, and tagliatelle is usually served with a creamy sauce such as alfredo.

Tubular pasta

Macaroni, penne (quills), and rigatoni are best with rich sauces that will run inside their tubes.

Interesting shapes

There is a vast range of small pasta shapes, and more are being created every day. The most common include ditali (thimbles), fusilli (spirals), conchiglie (shells), farfalle (bows), gnocchi (fluted shells), lumache (snails), orecchiette (ears), and radiatori (grills). Sauce them like tubular pasta.

Soup pasta

Very small pasta shapes, such as conchigliette, ditalini, farfallette, and orzo, are used in soup.

Filled pastas

Agnolotti, capelletti, ravioli, and tortellini are some of the shapes stuffed with ground meats or mixtures such as spinach and ricotta, and served with a simple sauce.

Sheet pasta

Flat sheets of lasagne are layered with sauce and baked. Fresh lasagne, and cooked dried lasagne, can be rolled around a filling to make cannelloni.

Pasta know-how

To test pasta, lift out a piece and bite it – it should be tender but still a little firm. The Italians call this *al dente*; literally "to the tooth".

If you are going to use cooked pasta in a baked dish, undercook it slightly before mixing it with sauce. This will help prevent it from being overcooked when it comes out of the oven.

Cooking pasta

There is one golden rule when cooking pasta: use plenty of water and salt – at least 2 litres (3½ pints) water and 2 tsp salt for every 250 g (8 oz) of pasta.

1 Bring the salted water to a boil. Add the pasta and stir to separate. If cooking spaghetti, let the ends soften before stirring. Return the water to a boil as quickly as possible. Reduce the heat so that the water is bubbling briskly and cook, uncovered.

2 When the pasta is al dente (see box, left), immediately tip it into a large colander, and shake to drain the pasta thoroughly.

3 Return the pasta to the pan or transfer to a warmed bowl. Toss with olive oil or butter, add plenty of ground black pepper and chopped fresh herbs, if liked, and serve immediately.

Noodles

Noodles are made from a variety of flours. The most popular types are available in supermarkets and delicatessens; others can be found in Chinese or Japanese shops.

Wheat noodles

The most common of noodles, these are made from wheat flour usually enriched with egg. They are available both flat and round and in a variety of widths.

Cellophane noodles

Sometimes referred to as transparent noodles or bean thread noodles, these are very fine and white. They are made from ground mung beans.

Rice noodles

Rice vermicelli are long, thin, white strands made from rice flour. Sold dried or fresh in bundles, they are used in soups and are also deep-fried.

Rice sticks

Made from the same dough as rice noodles, rice sticks are broad ribbons. They are usually served in a broth or sauce.

Soba

These thin, brownish Japanese noodles are made from buckwheat flour. They are often served with a dipping sauce.

Udon

Made from white wheat flour, these are also from Japan.

Noodles know-how

Store noodles in the same way as pasta. Most noodles need only be soaked or briefly cooked in boiling water before being added to soups and broths, vegetable dishes, and stir-fries.

Cooking with rice

The length of the rice grain determines how it should be cooked and used. Short grain rice is almost round in shape and very starchy. It is best cooked by absorption, so that it remains moist and sticky, and used for puddings, risottos, paella, stir-fried rice, and croquettes. The grains of long grain rice are separate, dry, and fluffy after cooking so it can be boiled and then used in pilafs, salads, and other savoury dishes.

White rice has been milled to remove the husk, bran, and germ, whereas for brown rice only the tough outer husk has been removed, leaving the nutritious bran layer. This gives it its distinctive colour and nutty flavour.

Cooking rice by absorption

Cook the rice very gently in simmering salted water. Use two parts water to one part rice.

1 Bring the salted water to a boil and add the rice. Return to a boil and stir once. Cover, reduce the heat, and cook gently until the water is absorbed.

2 Remove the pan from the heat and leave to stand, covered, for at least 5 minutes. Fluff up the rice with chopsticks or a fork just before serving.

Cooking risotto rice

An authentic risotto requires constant attention as the hot liquid (usually stock) must be stirred into the rice very gradually. This basic technique can be varied in many ways by adding shellfish, mushrooms, herbs, ham, and so on.

1 Heat butter or oil in a large saucepan and soften the onion, garlic, or other flavourings as specified in the recipe.

2 Add the rice and stir to coat the grains with the fat (this will keep them separate during cooking). Cook, stirring, for 1–2 minutes or until the rice grains look translucent.

3 Add a ladleful, about 150 ml (¼ pint), of the hot stock. Stir and cook until absorbed. Add another ladleful and cook until absorbed.

4 Continue adding stock, stirring, for 25–30 minutes. When the rice is tender but still firm to the bite, you have added enough stock.

Rice varieties

There are many varieties of rice, each with a distinct flavour and aroma. Here are the most common.

Camargue red
Similar to brown rice in texture, flavour, and cooking time.

Basmati
Available in brown or white varieties. Used mainly in Indian dishes. Cook for 10–15 minutes.

Brown
Has a slightly chewy texture with a mild nutty flavour. Cook for 30–35 minutes.

Easy-cook
Part-cooked so the grains stay separate. Cook for 10–12 minutes.

Long grain
Mild in flavour. The most widely used type of white rice. Cook for 12–15 minutes.

Short grain
Italian short grain (e.g. arborio, carnaroli) is used for risotto; Spanish paella rice is similar but less creamy (the best is said to come from Valencia). Short grain rice is also used for rice pudding. Cook for 20–25 minutes.

Wild
Not a true rice, but an aquatic grass from North America. Cook for 35–40 minutes.

Boiling rice

Long grain rice should be rinsed well before and after boiling, to remove starch that would cause stickiness.

Pour the rice into a large bowl of cold water. Swirl it around with your fingertips until the water becomes milky. Drain and repeat until the water stays clear. Drain again. Bring a large pan of salted water to a boil and add the rice.

Bring the water back to a boil. Reduce the heat so that the water is simmering quite vigorously. Cook until the rice is just tender. Drain well and rinse with boiling water to remove any excess starch.

Fettuccine primavera

SERVES 6 **CALS PER SERVING** 554

125 g (4 oz) asparagus, trimmed and cut into bite-sized pieces
125 g (4 oz) broccoli florets
1 courgette, sliced
salt and black pepper
3 tbsp olive oil
½ red and ½ yellow pepper, halved, deseeded, and diced
3 garlic cloves, crushed
1 x 200 g can chopped tomatoes
90 g (3 oz) frozen petits pois
125 ml (4 fl oz) double cream
500 g (1 lb) fettuccine
4 tbsp shredded fresh basil
90 g (3 oz) Parmesan cheese, grated, to serve

1 Cook the asparagus, broccoli, and courgette in boiling salted water for 3 minutes or until just tender. Drain, rinse under cold running water, and set aside.

2 Heat the oil in a large, deep frying pan, add the peppers and garlic, and cook, stirring, for 4 minutes or until the peppers are softened.

3 Add the tomatoes and the petits pois, and cook for 5 minutes or until the liquid in the pan is reduced by half.

4 Add the asparagus, broccoli, and courgette, stir in the cream, and boil for 1–2 minutes to reduce the liquid and concentrate the flavour. Add salt and pepper to taste, and remove from the heat.

5 Meanwhile, cook the fettuccine in a large saucepan of boiling salted water for 8–10 minutes until just tender.

6 Drain the fettuccine thoroughly, add to the sauce, and toss over a high heat. Stir in the shredded basil and serve at once, sprinkled with Parmesan cheese.

Tagliatelle with vegetable ribbons

SERVES 4 **CALS PER SERVING** 294

375 g (12 oz) courgettes
250 g (8 oz) carrots, peeled
salt
375 g (12 oz) fresh tagliatelle
scant 1 tbsp olive oil
1 garlic clove, crushed
200 ml (7 fl oz) full-fat crème fraîche
2 tbsp pesto (page 428)
60 g (2 oz) Dolcelatte cheese
chopped parsley, to garnish

1 Thinly slice the courgettes and carrots into wide, thin ribbons (page 394).

2 Bring a large pan of salted water to a boil, add the tagliatelle, courgettes, and carrots, and cook for 3 minutes. Drain and refresh under cold running water.

3 Heat the oil in a large frying pan, add the garlic, and stir-fry for about 1 minute.

4 Add the crème fraîche and pesto, then crumble in the cheese. Simmer and stir the sauce for 2–3 minutes, then add the tagliatelle and vegetables. Mix gently, turn into a warmed serving dish, and sprinkle with chopped parsley. Serve immediately.

Penne with spinach and Stilton

SERVES 6 976 CALS PER SERVING

500 g (1 lb) penne
salt and black pepper
45 g (1½ oz) butter
2 large garlic cloves, crushed
250 g (8 oz) chestnut mushrooms, sliced
300 ml (½ pint) double cream
1 egg, lightly beaten (optional)
90 g (3 oz) spinach leaves, coarsely shredded
90 g (3 oz) blue Stilton cheese, coarsely grated
juice of ½ lemon
pinch of grated nutmeg

1 Cook the pasta in boiling salted water for 8–10 minutes until just tender.

2 Meanwhile, melt the butter in a large pan, add the garlic, and cook, stirring, for 1 minute. Add the mushrooms and cook, stirring occasionally, for 2 minutes. Stir in the cream and boil for 2–3 minutes until the mixture reaches a coating consistency.

3 Drain the pasta, add to the mushroom and cream mixture with the egg (if using), stir well, and heat through. Add the spinach, Stilton cheese, lemon juice, nutmeg, and pepper to taste, and stir well to coat the pasta. Serve at once.

PENNE WITH BROCCOLI AND STILTON

Substitute 125 g (4 oz) small broccoli florets for the spinach. Cook in boiling salted water for 3–4 minutes or until just tender. Add to the pasta with the cheese, lemon juice, nutmeg, and pepper, omitting the egg. Stir well, and serve at once.

Penne with asparagus

SERVES 6 **CALS PER SERVING** 462

125 g (4 oz) goat's cheese, cut into small pieces
3 tbsp olive oil
3 garlic cloves, crushed
3 tbsp shredded fresh basil
500 g (1 lb) penne or spaghetti
salt and black pepper
500 g (1 lb) asparagus

1 In a small bowl, combine the goat's cheese, olive oil, garlic, and shredded fresh basil.

2 Cook the pasta in a large saucepan of boiling salted water for 8–10 minutes until just tender.

3 Meanwhile, trim any woody ends from the asparagus and peel the spears if they are not young. Cut the asparagus into bite-sized pieces and cook in boiling salted water for about 3 minutes until just tender.

4 Drain the pasta thoroughly, add the goat's cheese mixture, and toss together. Drain the asparagus and add to the pasta mixture. Toss lightly together, season with salt and black pepper, and serve at once.

Spaghetti all'Amatriciana

A speciality of Amatrice, near Rome, this tomato-based sauce is spiked with chilli and garlic, and richly flavoured with diced bacon and roast peppers.

SERVES 6 **CALS PER SERVING** 431

1 red pepper
1 green pepper
4 tbsp olive oil
5 unsmoked bacon or pancetta rashers, any rinds removed, diced
½–1 fresh green chilli, halved, deseeded, and thinly sliced
3 garlic cloves, crushed
2 ripe tomatoes, finely chopped
2 tbsp chopped flat-leaf parsley
salt and black pepper
500 g (1 lb) spaghetti
shavings of Parmesan cheese, to serve

1 Halve the red and green peppers, and remove the cores and seeds. Roast and peel the peppers (page 426). Cut the flesh into thin strips.

2 Heat the oil in a frying pan, add the bacon, and cook over a high heat for 5 minutes or until crisp. Add the roasted pepper strips and the chilli, and cook for 2 minutes. Stir in the garlic and cook for about 1 minute.

3 Add the tomatoes and parsley and cook for 3 minutes or until thickened. Remove from the heat and season with salt and pepper.

4 Cook the spaghetti in a large saucepan of boiling salted water for 8–10 minutes until just tender.

5 Drain the spaghetti thoroughly. Add the sauce and toss with the spaghetti. Serve at once, topped with Parmesan cheese shavings.

SPAGHETTI ALL'ARRABBIATA

Melt 30 g (1 oz) butter with 2 tbsp olive oil in a frying pan, add 3 crushed garlic cloves and ½–1 tsp crushed dried red chillies (chilli flakes), and cook gently. Drain 1 x 400 g can chopped tomatoes, stir the tomatoes into the pan, and bring slowly to a boil. Simmer until reduced and thickened, add ¼ tsp fresh oregano, and season with salt and black pepper. Toss with the spaghetti, and serve at once.

Red hot ragù

SERVES 6 **CALS PER SERVING** 517

375 g (12 oz) rigatoni or other tubular pasta
60 g (2 oz) Parmesan cheese, coarsely grated
3 tbsp chopped parsley, or 175 g (6 oz) young spinach leaves, shredded

Sauce

500 g (1 lb) good-quality pork sausages with herbs
a little olive oil
3 garlic cloves, crushed
2 small red chillies, halved, cored, and finely chopped
2 x 400 g cans chopped tomatoes
1 large onion, finely chopped
1 good tbsp sun-dried tomato purée
1 tbsp chopped fresh basil
½–1 tsp caster or granulated sugar, to taste
salt and black pepper

1 Make the sauce: cut long slits in each sausage and remove the skins. Heat a little oil in a non-stick frying pan and add the garlic and sausagemeat. Fry over a medium heat for about 4–5 minutes, breaking the meat up with a wooden spatula until it is brown, with a minced pork consistency. Stir in the remaining sauce ingredients. Bring to a boil, cover, and simmer gently for 40–50 minutes or until the sausagemeat is cooked. Check the seasoning.

2 Meanwhile, cook the pasta in boiling salted water according to packet instructions until just tender.

3 Drain the pasta and mix it into the sauce in the pan with half the Parmesan, then check the seasoning again. Scatter the parsley and remaining Parmesan over individual servings.

Cook's know-how

If using spinach, stir it into the bubbling sauce and cook for a couple of minutes until it wilts before adding the pasta and half the Parmesan.

Fusilli with double tomatoes

SERVES 4 **CALS PER SERVING** 464

375 g (12 oz) fusilli tricolore
salt and black pepper
250 g (8 oz) asparagus tips, cut into 5 cm (2 in) lengths
3 tbsp olive oil
2 garlic cloves, crushed
90 g (3 oz) chestnut mushrooms, sliced
500 g (1 lb) ripe cherry tomatoes, halved
60 g (2 oz) SunBlush or sun-dried tomatoes, each piece snipped into three

To serve

30 g (1 oz) pine nuts, toasted
a small handful of fresh basil leaves, shredded

1 Cook the pasta in boiling salted water according to packet instructions until just tender, adding the asparagus 2 minutes before the end of cooking. Drain the pasta and asparagus together and refresh under cold running water. Drain well.

2 Heat the oil in a large frying pan, add the garlic and mushrooms, and fry over a high heat for a couple of minutes. Add both kinds of tomatoes and continue to stir-fry over a high heat until they are just heated through. Season well.

3 Quickly toss the pasta and asparagus through the tomato mixture in the pan until everything is hot, then scatter over the pine nuts and basil. Serve at once.

Rigatoni with mushrooms and rocket

SERVES 6 **CALS PER SERVING** 355

375 g (12 oz) rigatoni or other tubular pasta
150 ml (5 fl oz) dry white wine
1 small onion, finely chopped
500 g (1 lb) mixed cultivated or wild mushrooms, such as shiitake, oyster, or porcini, coarsely sliced
salt and black pepper
6 tbsp double cream
4 tbsp good-quality pesto (ready-made or see page 428)
60 g (2 oz) rocket leaves
coarsely grated Parmesan cheese, to serve

1 Cook the pasta in boiling salted water according to packet instructions until just tender.

2 Meanwhile, pour the wine into a large frying pan, add the onion and cook over a low heat until the onion has softened, about 10–15 minutes. Add the mushrooms and stir over a high heat for a few minutes until the mushrooms are cooked and the liquid has reduced (there should be about 2 tbsp left). Season with salt and pepper, add the cream, and pesto, and stir to mix.

3 Drain the pasta and add to the mushroom mixture in the pan. Check the seasoning. At the last moment, stir in the rocket leaves, and allow to wilt for about 2 minutes. Serve immediately, scattered with Parmesan.

Cook's know-how

The warm, peppery, pungent taste of rocket is one people love or hate. If you love it and you're making your own pesto for this dish, try substituting rocket for basil in the pesto recipe on page 428.

Fusilli alla napoletana

SERVES 4 **CALS PER SERVING** 713

250 g (8 oz) fusilli
salt and black pepper
250 g (8 oz) broccoli
15 g (½ oz) butter
1 tbsp olive oil
1 large onion, chopped
2 large garlic cloves, crushed
150 g (5 oz) shiitake mushrooms, coarsely chopped
1 red pepper, halved, deseeded, and sliced
250 g (8 oz) courgettes, sliced
75 g (3 oz) Cheddar cheese, grated

Sauce

60 g (2 oz) butter
60 g (2 oz) plain flour
600 ml (1 pint) milk
1 tsp Dijon mustard

1 Cook the pasta in a large pan of boiling salted water for 8–10 minutes until just tender. Drain thoroughly.

2 Cook the broccoli stalks in boiling salted water for 3 minutes, then add the florets, and cook for 2 minutes longer. Drain and rinse in cold water.

3 Melt the butter with the oil in a large frying pan. Add the onion and garlic and cook gently, stirring occasionally, for 3–5 minutes, until softened.

4 Add the mushrooms, red pepper, and courgette slices, and cook, stirring occasionally, for 3 minutes. Remove from the heat and stir in the broccoli.

5 Make the sauce: melt the butter in a large saucepan, sprinkle in the flour and cook, stirring, for 1 minute. Remove from the heat and gradually blend in the milk. Bring to a boil, stirring constantly until thickened. Simmer for 2–3 minutes. Add the mustard, and season with salt and pepper.

6 Remove the sauce from the heat, add the vegetables and pasta, and stir well to coat.

7 Divide the mixture among four individual gratin dishes, sprinkle with the Cheddar cheese, and bake in a preheated oven at 200°C (180°C fan, Gas 6) for 20–25 minutes until golden. Serve hot.

Spaghetti bolognese

SERVES 4 **CALS PER SERVING** 904

3 tbsp olive oil
500 g (1 lb) minced beef
1 large onion, finely chopped
2 celery stalks, sliced
1 tbsp plain flour
2 garlic cloves, crushed
90 g (3 oz) tomato purée
150 ml (¼ pint) beef stock
150 ml (¼ pint) red wine
1 x 400 g can chopped tomatoes
1 tbsp redcurrant jelly
salt and black pepper
500 g (1 lb) spaghetti
grated Parmesan cheese, to serve

1 Heat 2 tbsp of the oil in a saucepan. Add the minced beef, onion, and celery, and cook, stirring, for 5 minutes or until the beef is browned. Add the flour, garlic, and tomato purée, and cook, stirring, for about 1 minute.

2 Pour in the stock and wine. Add the tomatoes and redcurrant jelly, season with salt and pepper, and bring to a boil. Cook, stirring, until the mixture has thickened.

3 Lower the heat, partially cover the pan, and simmer very gently, stirring occasionally, for about 1 hour.

4 Meanwhile, cook the spaghetti in boiling salted water for 8–10 minutes until just tender. Drain thoroughly.

5 Return the spaghetti to the saucepan, add the remaining oil, and toss gently to coat.

6 Divide the spaghetti among warmed serving plates and ladle some of the sauce on top of each serving. Sprinkle with a little Parmesan cheese and hand around the remainder separately.

Pasta spirals with herby meatballs

SERVES 8 **CALS PER SERVING** 384

500 g (1 lb) pasta spirals (fusilli)
salt and black pepper
shredded fresh basil, to garnish
grated Parmesan cheese, to garnish

Tomato–basil sauce

1 tbsp olive oil
1 onion, coarsely chopped
2 garlic cloves, crushed
2 x 400 g cans chopped tomatoes
1 tsp caster sugar
1 tbsp chopped fresh basil

Meatballs

500 g (1 lb) minced turkey or chicken
2 tbsp chopped parsley
1 tsp chopped fresh thyme
60 g (2 oz) Parmesan cheese, grated
60 g (2 oz) fresh breadcrumbs
1 egg, beaten
a little olive oil, for frying

1 Make the tomato–basil sauce: heat the oil in a deep frying pan, add the onion and garlic, and cook gently, stirring occasionally, for 3–4 minutes.

2 Add the tomatoes, sugar, and basil, season with salt and pepper, and stir well. Simmer, uncovered, for about 20 minutes, stirring occasionally, until the onion is soft and the sauce reduced.

3 Make the meatballs: in a large bowl, combine the minced turkey or chicken, parsley, thyme, Parmesan cheese, breadcrumbs, and egg, then season with salt and pepper. With dampened hands, shape the mixture into balls about the size of large walnuts.

4 Heat a little oil in a large frying pan, add the meatballs, and cook for about 8 minutes until browned and cooked through. Lift out with a slotted spoon and drain on paper towels. Add to the tomato sauce and heat gently for about 5 minutes.

5 Meanwhile, cook the pasta in a large pan of boiling salted water for 8–10 minutes until tender. Drain thoroughly, and top with the meatballs and sauce. Serve, garnished with shredded basil and grated Parmesan.

Tortellini with peas and bacon

SERVES 6 **CALS PER SERVING** 643

500 g (1 lb) tortellini
salt and black pepper
1 tbsp sunflower oil
250 g (8 oz) bacon or pancetta rashers, any rinds removed, diced
175 g (6 oz) frozen petits pois
300 ml (½ pint) double cream
grated Parmesan cheese, to serve

1 Cook the tortellini in boiling salted water for about 10–12 minutes, or according to packet instructions, until tender.

2 Meanwhile, heat the oil in a frying pan, add the bacon, and cook over a high heat, stirring, for 3 minutes or until crisp.

3 Cook the petits pois in boiling salted water for about 2 minutes until just tender. Drain.

4 Drain the tortellini thoroughly and return to the saucepan. Add the bacon, petits pois, and cream, and season with salt and pepper. Heat gently for 1–2 minutes to warm through. Serve at once, sprinkled with grated Parmesan cheese.

Three-cheese macaroni

SERVES 8 **CALS PER SERVING** 436

375 g (12 oz) short-cut macaroni
salt and black pepper
45 g (1½ oz) butter, plus extra for greasing
45 g (1½ oz) plain flour
900 ml (1½ pints) milk
2 tsp Dijon mustard
175 g (6 oz) smoked Cheddar cheese, grated
60 g (2 oz) light mozzarella cheese, shredded
90 g (3 oz) mature Cheddar cheese, grated
60 g (2 oz) fresh white breadcrumbs

1 Cook the macaroni in boiling salted water for 8–10 minutes until just tender. Drain and set aside.

2 Melt the butter in a large saucepan. Add the flour and cook, stirring, for 1 minute. Remove the pan from the heat and gradually blend in the milk. Bring to a boil, stirring constantly until the mixture thickens. Simmer for about 5 minutes, stirring.

3 Stir in the mustard, smoked Cheddar and mozzarella cheeses, 60 g (2 oz) of the mature Cheddar cheese, and the cooked macaroni. Season with salt and pepper.

4 Lightly butter a large shallow ovenproof dish and spoon in the macaroni mixture. Sprinkle with the breadcrumbs and the remaining Cheddar cheese and bake in a preheated oven at 200°C (180°C fan, Gas 6) for about 15–20 minutes until golden and bubbling.

CHEESE AND LEEK MACARONI

Omit the mozzarella cheese. Melt 30 g (1 oz) butter in a saucepan, add 2–3 trimmed and finely sliced leeks, and cook gently for 3–5 minutes until softened. Add the leeks to the sauce with the two Cheddar cheeses and the cooked and drained macaroni.

Cannelloni with ricotta and spinach

SERVES 4 **CALS PER SERVING** 462

butter, for greasing
18 cannelloni tubes
30 g (1 oz) Parmesan cheese, grated

Tomato sauce

1 tbsp olive oil
2 celery stalks, chopped
1 small onion, chopped
1 carrot, chopped
1 garlic clove, crushed
300 ml (½ pint) chicken or vegetable stock
2 x 400 g cans chopped tomatoes
2 tbsp tomato purée
salt and black pepper
60 g (2 oz) sun-dried tomatoes in oil, drained and chopped

Filling

2 tbsp olive oil
1 small onion, chopped
1 garlic clove, crushed
500 g (1 lb) spinach leaves, chopped
500 g (1 lb) ricotta cheese
¼ tsp grated nutmeg

1 Make the tomato sauce: heat the oil in a saucepan, add the celery, onion, carrot, and garlic, and cook gently for 3–5 minutes until softened. Stir in the stock, tomatoes, and tomato purée, season with salt and pepper, and bring to a boil. Cover and simmer, stirring occasionally, for 30 minutes.

2 Meanwhile, make the filling: heat the oil in a large pan, add the onion and garlic, and cook for 3–5 minutes until softened. Add the spinach and cook over a high heat for 1–2 minutes. Cool slightly, add the ricotta and nutmeg, and season with salt and pepper.

3 Purée the tomato sauce in a food processor, then stir in the chopped sun-dried tomatoes.

4 Grease an ovenproof dish. Spoon the spinach filling into the cannelloni. Arrange in the dish, cover with the sauce, and sprinkle with Parmesan. Bake in a preheated oven at 200°C (180°C fan, Gas 6) for 30 minutes. Serve hot, with a little extra Parmesan cheese grated over the top.

Spaghetti alla carbonara

SERVES 4 **CALS PER SERVING** 906

500 g (1 lb) spaghetti
salt and black pepper
175 g (6 oz) diced pancetta or streaky bacon, any rinds removed
1 garlic clove, crushed
4 eggs
125 g (4 oz) Parmesan cheese, grated
150 ml (¼ pint) single cream
chopped parsley, to garnish

1 Cook the spaghetti in a large saucepan of boiling salted water for 8–10 minutes until just tender.

2 Meanwhile, put the pancetta or bacon into a frying pan and heat gently for 7 minutes until the fat runs. Increase the heat and add the garlic. Cook for 2–3 minutes or until the bacon is crisp.

3 Break the eggs into a bowl. Add the bacon and garlic mixture, using a slotted spoon. Add the Parmesan cheese, season generously with salt and pepper, and whisk until well blended.

4 Drain the spaghetti and return to the hot pan. Stir in the bacon and egg mixture and toss quickly until the egg just begins to set. Stir in the cream and heat gently. Serve at once, sprinkled with parsley.

SPAGHETTI ALFREDO

Heat 150 ml (¼ pint) double cream with 30 g (1 oz) butter until the mixture has thickened. Set aside. Cook the pasta, drain, then add to the cream mixture. Add 90 ml (3 fl oz) more cream, 90 g (3 oz) Parmesan cheese, a pinch of grated nutmeg, and season with salt and pepper. Heat gently until thickened, and serve.

Cook's know-how

It is best to buy a whole piece of Parmesan cheese and grate the quantity you need for a given dish. Ready grated Parmesan in packets is less economical and lacks the flavour of freshly grated Parmesan.

Basic pasta dough

SERVES 3 **CALS PER SERVING** 322

300 g (10 oz) "00" flour or strong plain white flour
3 eggs
1 tsp salt
1 tbsp olive oil

1 Sift the flour into a mound on a work surface. Make a well in the middle of the flour and add the eggs, salt, and oil. Using your fingertips, gradually draw the flour into the egg mixture until a sticky ball of dough is formed.

2 Knead the dough on a floured work surface for 10 minutes or until the pasta dough is smooth and no longer sticks to the work surface.

3 Shape the dough into a ball, put into an oiled plastic bag, and leave to rest at room temperature for about 30 minutes.

4 Roll out the dough very thinly on a lightly floured work surface into a 37 cm (15 in) square. Leave the pasta uncovered for about 20 minutes to dry out slightly. Cut the pasta in half, and use it to make one of the ravioli recipes on this page.

Filling and cooking the ravioli

1 Place 18 spoonfuls of filling at regular intervals on to one half of the pasta. Lightly brush the pasta between the filling with water.

2 Roll the remaining pasta around a rolling pin and unroll over the filling. Press the pasta around the edges and the filling.

3 With a knife, pastry wheel, or pastry cutter, cut into round or square ravioli. Leave for about 30 minutes, turning once, until dried out.

4 Add a little oil to a large saucepan of boiling salted water, add the ravioli, and cook for 4–5 minutes until just tender. Drain and serve immediately.

Crab and prawn ravioli

SERVES 3 **CALS PER SERVING** 322

90 g (3 oz) cooked white crabmeat, flaked
90 g (3 oz) cooked peeled prawns, chopped
60 g (2 oz) full-fat soft cheese
1 spring onion, very finely chopped
salt and black pepper
1 quantity Basic pasta dough (see above)
coriander dressing (page 142), to serve

1 Make the filling: combine the crabmeat and prawns with the cheese and spring onion, and season with salt and pepper.

2 Fill, cook, and drain the ravioli (see box, above right). Toss with the coriander dressing and serve at once.

Chicken and prosciutto ravioli

SERVES 3 **CALS PER SERVING** 464

15 g (½ oz) butter
90 g (3 oz) cooked chicken, minced
75 g (2½ oz) prosciutto, finely chopped
1 tbsp fresh white breadcrumbs
1 tbsp chopped fresh flat-leaf parsley
2 tsp each water and tomato purée
1 egg
salt and black pepper
1 quantity Basic pasta dough (see above left)
tomato–basil sauce (page 362), to serve
basil sprigs, to garnish

1 Make the filling: melt the butter in a saucepan, add the chicken and fry for 5 minutes. Stir in the prosciutto, breadcrumbs, parsley, water, tomato purée, and egg. Season.

2 Fill, cook, and drain the ravioli (see box, above). Toss in the tomato basil sauce, and serve at once, garnished with basil sprigs.

Ricotta and spinach ravioli

SERVES 3 **CALS PER SERVING** 341

125 g (4 oz) ricotta cheese
60 g (2 oz) Parmesan cheese, grated
1 egg, beaten
¼ tsp grated nutmeg
250 g (8 oz) spinach leaves, cooked, squeezed dry, and chopped
salt and black pepper
1 quantity Basic pasta dough (see above left)
30 g (1 oz) butter, to serve

1 Make the filling: beat together the ricotta, half of the Parmesan, the egg, nutmeg, and spinach. Season with salt and pepper.

2 Fill, cook, and drain the ravioli (see box, above). Serve with butter, the remaining Parmesan, and black pepper.

Opposite, clockwise from top:
Crab and prawn ravioli, Chicken and prosciutto ravioli, Ricotta and spinach ravioli

Classic lasagne

SERVES 8 **CALS PER SERVING** 641

125 g (4 oz) mature Cheddar cheese, grated
30 g (1 oz) Parmesan cheese, grated
175 g (6 oz) pre-cooked lasagne sheets
chopped parsley, to garnish

Meat sauce

2 tbsp olive oil
1 kg (2 lb) minced beef
45 g (1½ oz) plain flour
300 ml (½ pint) beef stock
1 x 400 g can chopped tomatoes
6 celery stalks, sliced
2 onions, chopped
2 large garlic cloves, crushed
4 tbsp tomato purée
1 tsp sugar
salt and black pepper

White sauce

60 g (2 oz) butter
45 g (1½ oz) plain flour
600 ml (1 pint) milk
1 tsp Dijon mustard
¼ tsp grated nutmeg

1 Make the meat sauce: heat the oil in a saucepan, add the beef, and cook, stirring, until browned.

2 Sprinkle in the flour and stir for 1 minute, then add the stock, tomatoes, celery, onions, garlic, tomato purée, and sugar. Season with salt and pepper and bring to a boil. Cover and simmer for 1 hour.

3 Meanwhile, make the white sauce: melt the butter in a saucepan, sprinkle in the flour and cook, stirring, for 1 minute. Remove from the heat and gradually blend in the milk. Bring to a boil, stirring until the mixture thickens. Simmer for 2–3 minutes. Stir in the mustard and nutmeg, and season with salt and pepper.

4 Spoon one-third of the meat sauce into a large shallow ovenproof dish, cover with one-third of the white sauce, and one-third of the Cheddar and Parmesan cheeses. Arrange half of the lasagne in a single layer. Repeat the layers, finishing with the Cheddar and Parmesan cheeses.

5 Bake in a preheated oven at 190°C (170°C fan, Gas 5) for 45–60 minutes until the pasta is tender and the topping is a golden brown colour. Serve at once, sprinkled with parsley.

Smoked haddock lasagne

SERVES 8 **CALS PER SERVING** 473

6 fresh lasagne sheets
knob of butter
250 g (8 oz) button mushrooms, sliced
750 g (1½ lb) undyed smoked haddock fillets, skinned and cut into large pieces
60 g (2 oz) mature Cheddar cheese, grated

Sauce

90 g (3 oz) butter
1 large onion, chopped
90 g (3 oz) plain flour
600 ml (1 pint) milk
1 x 200 g carton crème fraîche
60 g (2 oz) mature Cheddar cheese, grated
1 tbsp Dijon mustard
20 g (¾ oz) fresh dill, finely chopped
juice of ½ lemon
salt and black pepper

1.8 LITRE (3 PINT) OVENPROOF DISH, ABOUT 15 X 25 X 5 CM (6 X 10 X 2 IN)

1 Immerse the sheets of lasagne in a dish of hot water, and leave to stand until ready to use. This will soften them before baking, and ensure they cook properly when layered with the fish and sauce.

2 Make the sauce: melt the butter in a large saucepan, add the onion, and fry over a high heat for 1 minute. Turn the heat down to low, cover the pan, and cook for about 10 minutes until the onion has softened. Remove the lid, increase the heat to medium, and sprinkle in the flour. Cook, stirring, for 1 minute, then remove from the heat, and gradually blend in the milk followed by the crème fraîche. Bring to a boil, stirring constantly until thickened. Simmer for 2–3 minutes, remove from the heat, and stir in the cheese. Add the mustard, dill, and lemon juice, season with salt and pepper, and stir until combined. Set aside.

3 Melt the knob of butter in a frying pan, and fry the mushrooms over a medium heat for a few minutes until tender. Increase the heat to high, and continue frying for 1–2 minutes to drive off any liquid, stirring constantly. Tip the mushrooms into the sauce, and stir well to combine.

4 Scatter one-third of the haddock pieces over the bottom of the ovenproof dish, and pour over one-third of the sauce. Drain the lasagne sheets, and dry with paper towels. Arrange three sheets of lasagne over the sauce, without overlapping the edges (you may have to trim the pasta to fit neatly). Repeat the layers, then top with the remaining haddock and sauce, and cover with the cheese.

5 Bake in a preheated oven at 200°C (180°C fan, Gas 6) for 25–30 minutes until bubbling, cooked through, and golden on top. Leave to stand for about 5 minutes before serving.

Spaghetti alle vongole

SERVES 4 **CALS PER SERVING** 626

- about 3 dozen fresh clams in their shells, cleaned (page 105)
- 2 tbsp olive oil, plus extra for tossing
- 1 onion, chopped
- 1 garlic clove, crushed
- 1/4 tsp chilli powder
- 1 x 400 g can chopped tomatoes
- 4 tbsp dry white wine
- salt and black pepper
- 500 g (1 lb) spaghetti
- 2 tbsp chopped parsley

1 Holding each clam in a tea towel, insert a thin knife blade between the shells and twist the knife to open the shells. Reserve 4 clams for garnish. Remove the remaining clams from their shells, cut them into bite-sized pieces, and set aside with any juices.

2 Heat the olive oil in a large pan, add the onion and garlic, and cook gently, stirring occasionally, for 3–5 minutes until softened but not coloured. Add the chilli powder and cook gently, stirring, for 1 minute.

3 Add the tomatoes and wine, season with salt and pepper, and bring to a boil. Simmer, uncovered, for about 15 minutes or until the mixture has thickened.

4 Meanwhile, cook the spaghetti in a large saucepan of boiling salted water for 8–10 minutes until just tender. Drain, then toss the spaghetti in a little olive oil to prevent sticking. Transfer to warmed serving bowls.

5 Add the parsley, and the clams and their juices to the tomato mixture, and cook for 2 minutes. Do not cook longer or the clams will toughen.

6 Transfer the spaghetti to warmed serving bowls. Taste the sauce for seasoning, then spoon over the spaghetti. Serve at once, garnished with the reserved clams in their shells.

Cook's **know-how**

Live clams should be tightly closed in their shells. If any are open, give them a sharp tap on the work surface, then discard any that do not close.

Tagliatelle with prawns

SERVES 4 **CALS PER SERVING** 294

2 tbsp olive oil
1 large onion, chopped
1 garlic clove, crushed
375 g (12 oz) button mushrooms, halved
500 g (1 lb) tomatoes, chopped into small pieces, cores removed
salt and black pepper
500 g (1 lb) tagliatelle
375 g (12 oz) cooked peeled prawns
125 ml (4 fl oz) full-fat crème fraîche
4 tbsp chopped parsley, to garnish

1 Heat the oil in a large pan, add the onion and garlic, and cook gently, stirring, for 3–5 minutes until softened but not coloured. Add the mushrooms and cook over a high heat, stirring, for about 5 minutes.

2 Add the tomatoes, season with salt and pepper, and simmer gently, uncovered, for about 20 minutes or until the mixture has thickened.

3 Meanwhile, cook the tagliatelle in a large saucepan of boiling salted water for 8–10 minutes until just tender.

4 Add the prawns and crème fraîche to the tomato mixture and cook gently for about 2 minutes until the prawns are heated through. Taste for seasoning.

5 Drain the tagliatelle thoroughly and pile on to warmed serving plates. Spoon the prawn mixture on top, sprinkle with parsley, and serve at once.

PASTA WITH SMOKED SALMON AND PRAWNS

Substitute 125 g (4 oz) smoked salmon, cut into bite-sized pieces, for 125 g (4 oz) of the prawns. Add the smoked salmon after the prawns have been heated through in step 4.

Pasta alla marinara

SERVES 6 CALS PER SERVING 531

500 g (1 lb) pasta bows
salt and black pepper
2 tbsp olive oil
1 large onion, finely chopped
1 large garlic clove, crushed
125 ml (4 fl oz) dry white wine
125 g (4 oz) squid, cut into strips or rings
60 g (2 oz) button mushrooms, sliced
125 g (4 oz) scallops, halved
125 g (4 oz) cooked peeled prawns
150 ml (1/4 pint) double cream or full-fat crème fraîche
4 tbsp chopped parsley

1 Cook the pasta bows in a large saucepan of boiling salted water for 8–10 minutes until just tender.

2 Meanwhile, heat the oil in a large pan, add the onion and garlic, and cook gently, stirring occasionally, for 3–5 minutes until softened but not coloured.

3 Pour in the white wine and boil to reduce the liquid in the saucepan to about 2 tbsp, stirring constantly. Add the squid and cook for 1 minute, then add the mushrooms and scallops, and cook, stirring, for a further 2 minutes. Add the prawns, cream, and half of the parsley, and heat through.

4 Drain the pasta bows thoroughly, and add to the seafood mixture, stirring well to combine. Season with salt and black pepper, and serve at once, garnished with the remaining chopped parsley.

Tuna and fennel pasta bake

SERVES 6 **CALS PER SERVING** 512

250 g (8 oz) pasta shells (conchiglie)
salt and black pepper
1 tbsp sunflower oil
1 fennel bulb, trimmed and finely sliced
1 onion, finely sliced
60 g (2 oz) butter
60 g (2 oz) plain flour
600 ml (1 pint) milk
1 x 200 g can tuna in brine, drained and flaked
3 hard-boiled eggs, coarsely chopped
125 g (4 oz) mature Cheddar cheese, grated
2 tbsp chopped parsley, to garnish

1 Cook the pasta shells in boiling salted water for 8–10 minutes until just tender. Drain thoroughly and set aside.

2 Heat the sunflower oil in a large frying pan, add the fennel and onion, and cook for 3–5 minutes until softened but not coloured. Set aside.

3 Melt the butter in a large saucepan, sprinkle in the flour, and cook, stirring, for 1 minute. Remove from the heat and gradually blend in the milk. Bring to a boil, stirring until the mixture thickens. Simmer for 2–3 minutes.

4 Stir in the pasta, the fennel and onion, tuna, eggs, and cheese. Season with salt and pepper, then turn the mixture into a shallow ovenproof dish.

5 Bake in a preheated oven at 200°C (180°C fan, Gas 6) for about 30 minutes or until heated through and golden brown on top. Serve hot, sprinkled with chopped parsley.

Pasta shells with scallops

SERVES 4 **CALS PER SERVING** 753

8 large scallops, each cut into 3 slices
75 ml (2½ fl oz) water
juice of 1 lemon
1 slice of onion
6 black peppercorns
1 small bay leaf
500 g (1 lb) pasta shells
15 g (½ oz) butter
chopped parsley and lemon slices, to garnish

Sauce

45 g (1½ oz) butter
125 g (4 oz) button mushrooms, sliced
30 g (1 oz) plain flour
150 ml (¼ pint) double cream or full-fat crème fraîche
1 tbsp tomato purée
salt and black pepper

1 Put the scallops into a pan with the measured water, half the lemon juice, the onion, peppercorns, and bay leaf.

2 Bring to a gentle simmer, cover, and poach very gently for 2–3 minutes or until the scallops are opaque.

3 Remove the scallops with a slotted spoon, strain the liquid, and reserve.

4 Make the sauce: melt the butter in a saucepan, add the mushrooms, and cook gently, stirring occasionally, for 2 minutes. Sprinkle in the flour and cook, stirring, for 1 minute. Remove from the heat and blend in the strained poaching liquid. Cook, stirring, for 1 minute until thickened.

5 Add the cream and tomato purée and bring to a boil, stirring constantly until the mixture thickens. Simmer for 2 minutes, then add salt and pepper to taste.

6 Cook the pasta shells in a large saucepan of boiling salted water for 8–10 minutes or until tender. Drain, then toss with the butter and the remaining lemon juice. Add the scallops to the sauce, and heat through very gently.

7 Pile the pasta on warmed serving plates, and spoon the sauce on top. Serve at once, garnished with the parsley and lemon slices.

Pad Thai with tiger prawns

SERVES 6 **CALS PER SERVING** 245

- 250 g (8 oz) thick rice noodles
- 2 tbsp olive oil
- 2 skinless, boneless chicken breasts (about 125 g/4 oz each), cut into thin strips
- 1 small fresh red chilli, halved, deseeded, and finely chopped
- 2.5 cm (1 in) piece of fresh root ginger, peeled and finely grated
- 2.5 cm (1 in) piece of fresh lemongrass from the lower part of the stalk, very finely chopped
- 125 g (4 oz) peeled raw tiger prawns
- 90 g (3 oz) oyster mushrooms, thinly sliced
- 125 g (4 oz) sugarsnap peas, trimmed and sliced on the diagonal
- 3 tbsp soy sauce
- 2 tbsp lime juice
- 1 tbsp fish sauce
- salt and black pepper

To serve

- 30 g (1 oz) salted or unsalted peanuts, coarsely chopped
- a handful of fresh coriander, chopped

1 Cook the noodles according to packet instructions. Drain, refresh under cold running water, and set aside.

2 Heat 1 tbsp of the oil in a wok or large non-stick frying pan, and stir-fry the chicken over a high heat for 2 minutes or until golden brown and cooked through. Remove with a slotted spoon and set aside.

3 Heat the remaining oil in the pan, add the chilli, ginger, lemongrass, prawns, mushrooms, and peas and stir-fry for 1 minute. Add the soy sauce, lime juice, and fish sauce and season with salt and pepper. Return the chicken to the pan and add the noodles. Stir-fry until the prawns are pink and everything is piping hot, for 2–3 minutes. Serve hot, with peanuts and coriander scattered on top.

Szechuan noodles with water chestnuts

SERVES 6 **CALS PER SERVING** 367

375 g (12 oz) medium egg noodles
1 tbsp olive oil
250 g (8 oz) minced pork
2.5 cm (1 in) piece of fresh root ginger, peeled and finely grated
2 garlic cloves, crushed
2 spring onions, trimmed and sliced on the diagonal, keeping white and green parts separate
1 red pepper, halved, deseeded, and finely sliced
3 tbsp soy sauce, or more, to taste
3 tbsp black bean sauce
2 tsp caster or granulated sugar
90 g (3 oz) bean sprouts
1 x 220 g can water chestnuts, drained and halved
salt and black pepper

1 Cook the noodles according to packet instructions. Drain, refresh under cold running water, and set aside.

2 Heat the oil in a wok or large non-stick frying pan and stir-fry the pork for about 2 minutes until brown. Add the ginger, garlic, white parts of the spring onions, and the red pepper, and stir-fry for a few minutes more.

3 Stir in the 3 tbsp soy sauce, the black bean sauce, sugar, and 5 tbsp water, and boil for few minutes. Add the bean sprouts and water chestnuts, and the noodles to the pan, then toss over a high heat for about 2 minutes until everything is hot. Check the seasoning, and add more soy sauce if you like. Serve immediately, with the green spring onions scattered on top.

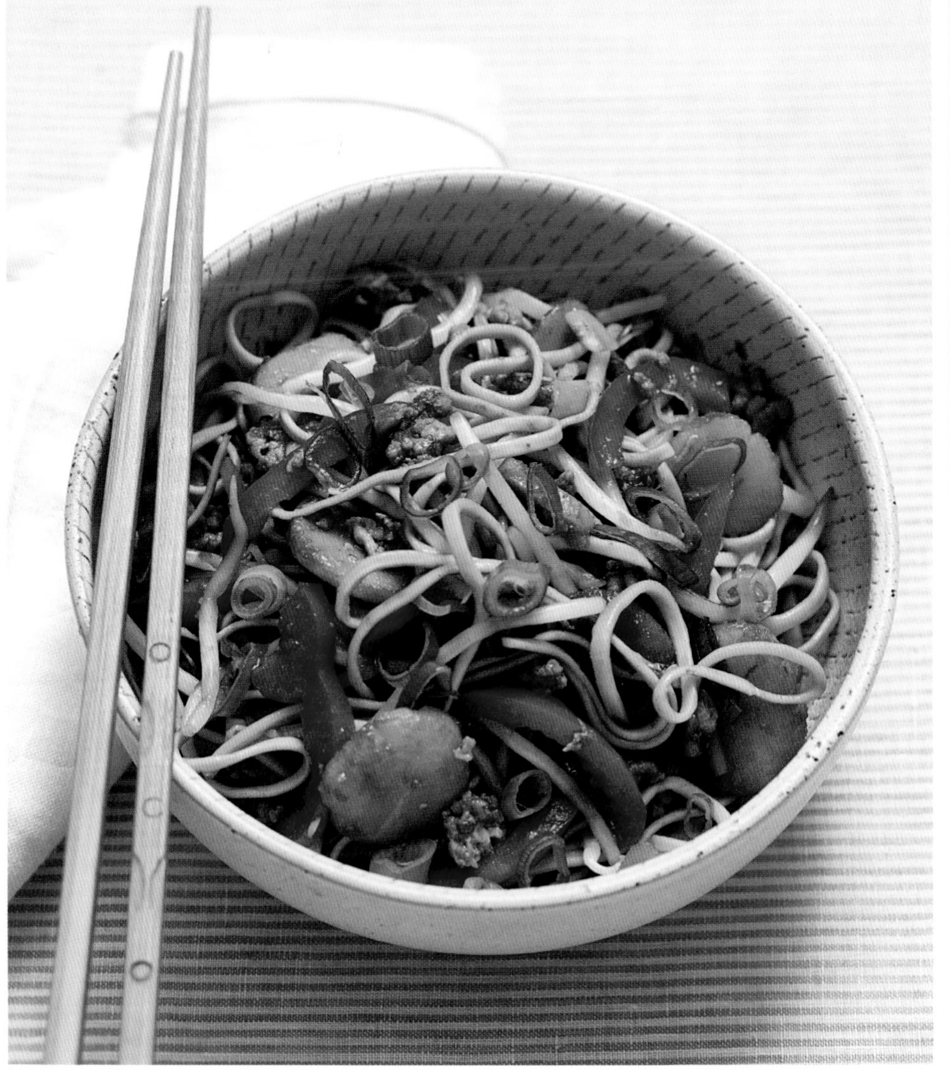

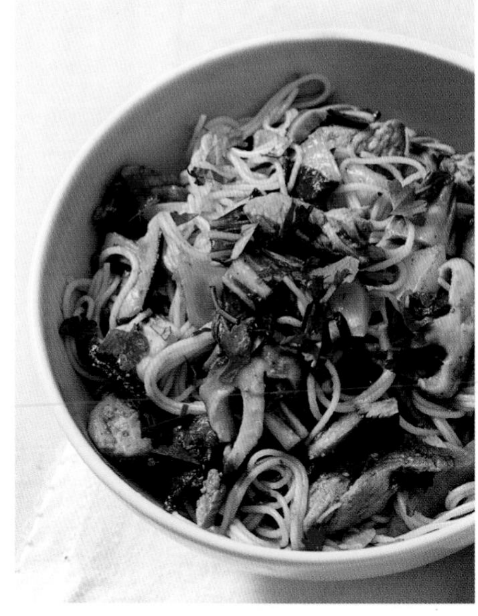

Singapore noodles

SERVES 6 **CALS PER SERVING** 324

250 g (8 oz) rice noodles
2 tbsp sunflower oil
375 g (12 oz) pork fillet or tenderloin, cut into thin strips
1 tsp crushed dried red chillies (chilli flakes)
90 g (3 oz) shiitake mushrooms, sliced
200 g (7 oz) pak choi, coarsely chopped, keeping white and green parts separate
2 tbsp mild curry powder
2 tbsp soy sauce
2 tbsp oyster sauce
juice of ½ lime
4 tbsp coconut cream
chopped fresh coriander, to garnish

1 Cook the noodles according to packet instructions. Drain, refresh under cold running water, and set aside.

2 Heat 1 tbsp oil in a large wok or non-stick frying pan and stir-fry the pork over a high heat for about 2 minutes until brown and cooked through. Remove from the pan with a slotted spoon and set aside.

3 Heat the remaining oil in the pan. Add the chilli flakes, mushrooms, and the white parts of the pak choi, and stir-fry for 1–2 minutes. Add the curry powder, soy sauce, oyster sauce, lime juice, and coconut cream, and stir-fry for a further few minutes.

4 Add the green parts of the pak choi, then return the pork and add noodles to the pan. Stir-fry for a few minutes until piping hot, then scatter over the coriander.

Risi e bisi

SERVES 6 **CALS PER SERVING** 390

60 g (2 oz) butter
1 onion, finely chopped
60 g (2 oz) Parma ham, diced, or 90 g (3 oz) unsmoked lean bacon rashers, rinds removed, diced
2 garlic cloves, crushed
300 g (10 oz) risotto rice
300 g (10 oz) frozen peas
salt and black pepper
1 litre (1¾ pints) hot chicken or vegetable stock
60 g (2 oz) Parmesan cheese, grated, and 2 tbsp chopped parsley, to garnish

1 Melt the butter in a large pan. When it is foaming, add the onion, Parma ham, and garlic, and cook gently, stirring occasionally, for 3–5 minutes until the onion is soft but not coloured.

2 Add the rice and stir to coat in the butter. Then add the frozen peas and seasoning.

3 Pour in half of the stock and cook, stirring constantly, over a low heat until it is absorbed. Add a little more stock and cook, stirring, until it has been absorbed.

4 Continue adding the stock in this way until the rice is just tender and the mixture is thick and creamy. It should take about 25 minutes.

5 Serve hot, sprinkled with the grated Parmesan cheese and chopped parsley.

Stir-fried Chinese noodles

SERVES 4 **CALS PER SERVING** 476

5 dried shiitake mushrooms
250 ml (8 fl oz) hot vegetable stock
375 g (12 oz) Chinese egg noodles
salt
about 2 tsp soy sauce
1 tbsp sunflower oil
250 g (8 oz) mangetout
3 garlic cloves, crushed
5 mm (¼ in) piece of fresh root ginger, peeled and grated
¼ tsp sugar (optional)
125 g (4 oz) bean sprouts
about ½ tsp crushed dried red chillies (chilli flakes)

To serve

3 spring onions, sliced
2 tsp sesame oil
1 tbsp chopped fresh coriander

1 Put the mushrooms into a bowl, pour over the hot vegetable stock, and leave to soak for about 30 minutes.

2 Drain the mushrooms, reserving the liquid. Squeeze the mushrooms dry, then cut into thin strips.

3 Cook the noodles in a large saucepan of boiling salted water for 3 minutes or according to packet instructions. Drain the noodles, toss with soy sauce to taste, and set aside.

4 Heat the sunflower oil in a wok or large frying pan, add the mushrooms, mangetout, garlic, and ginger, and stir-fry for 2 minutes. Add the sugar, if using, bean sprouts, crushed chillies to taste, and 3 tbsp of the reserved mushroom soaking liquid. Stir-fry for 2 minutes.

5 Add the egg noodles and stir-fry for 2 minutes or until heated through. Serve at once, sprinkled with the spring onions, sesame oil, and coriander.

Risotto Milanese

SERVES 6 **CALS PER SERVING** 403

90 g (3 oz) butter
1 onion, chopped
375 g (12 oz) risotto rice
1.25 litres (2 pints) hot vegetable or chicken stock
a few pinches of saffron strands
salt and black pepper
60 g (2 oz) Parmesan cheese, grated
Parmesan shavings, to serve

1 Melt 30 g (1 oz) of the butter in a large saucepan, add the chopped onion, and cook gently, stirring occasionally, for 3–5 minutes until softened but not coloured.

2 Add the rice, stirring to coat the grains in the butter, and cook for 1 minute. Add a ladleful of hot stock to the pan, and cook gently, stirring constantly, until all the stock has been absorbed.

3 Sprinkle in the saffron strands and season with salt and pepper. Continue to add the stock, a ladleful at a time, stirring constantly, until the risotto is thick and creamy and the rice tender. This will take 20–25 minutes.

4 Stir in the remaining butter and the Parmesan cheese, and season to taste with salt and pepper. Serve at once, topped with Parmesan shavings.

Cook's **know-how**

Risotto Milanese is the traditional accompaniment to osso buco (page 272), but you can serve it with any other dish of meat or poultry, or as a first course on its own. In the past, it was traditionally cooked with the marrow from the veal shanks used for the osso buco, but nowadays the finished risotto is sometimes topped with a few spoonfuls of the juices from a veal roast to give it a more traditional and authentic flavour.

Chicken liver risotto

SERVES 4–6 **CALS PER SERVING** 619–413

75 g (2½ oz) butter
1 tbsp sunflower oil
125 g (4 oz) smoked bacon rashers, rinds removed, diced
1 onion, chopped
1 garlic clove, crushed
175 g (6 oz) risotto rice
60 g (2 oz) wild rice
600 ml (1 pint) hot chicken stock
250 g (8 oz) chicken livers, sliced
125 g (4 oz) wild mushrooms, sliced
60 g (2 oz) sun-dried tomatoes in oil, drained and chopped
salt and black pepper
30 g (1 oz) Parmesan cheese, grated
1 tbsp chopped fresh rosemary

1 Melt 60 g (2 oz) of the butter with the oil in a large frying pan. When the butter is foaming, add the bacon, onion, and garlic, and cook gently, stirring occasionally, for 3–5 minutes until the onion is soft but not coloured.

2 Add the risotto rice and wild rice, stirring to coat the grains in the oil, then pour in the hot chicken stock. Cover and simmer for 25 minutes.

3 Meanwhile, melt the remaining butter in a saucepan. Add the chicken livers, and cook, stirring, for 2–3 minutes until a rich brown colour. Add the mushrooms, and cook, stirring occasionally, for 5–7 minutes.

4 Stir the chicken livers into the rice. Add the sun-dried tomatoes, season with salt and pepper, and cook for 5 minutes or until all the liquid has been absorbed. Serve hot, garnished with Parmesan and rosemary.

Risotto al verde

SERVES 4 **CALS PER SERVING** 734

15 g (½ oz) butter
3 garlic cloves, crushed
250 g (8 oz) risotto rice
1 litre (1¾ pints) hot vegetable stock
175 ml (6 fl oz) single cream
90 g (3 oz) blue cheese, crumbled
4 tbsp ready-made pesto
90 g (3 oz) Parmesan cheese, grated
4 tbsp pine nuts, lightly toasted
4 tbsp shredded fresh basil

1 Melt the butter in a large saucepan. When it is foaming, add the garlic and cook gently for 1 minute.

2 Add the risotto rice, stirring to coat the grains in the butter, and cook for 2 minutes. Add a ladleful of the hot vegetable stock, and cook gently, stirring constantly, until the stock has been absorbed. Continue to add the stock, a ladleful at a time, and cook for 20–25 minutes or until the rice is just tender.

3 Add the cream, and cook gently, stirring, until it has been absorbed. Stir in the blue cheese, then the pesto, Parmesan, and pine nuts. Garnish with shredded fresh basil, and serve.

CHICKEN AND MUSHROOM RISOTTO

Add 125 g (4 oz) sliced mushrooms to the saucepan with the garlic in step 1 and cook for 3–5 minutes until the mushrooms are soft. Substitute chicken stock for the vegetable stock, omit the blue cheese and pesto, then add 250 g (8 oz) cooked diced chicken with the cream in step 3.

ASPARAGUS RISOTTO

Add 1 finely chopped onion to the pan with the garlic in step 1 and cook for 3–5 minutes until soft. Omit the blue cheese and pesto, and add 375 g (12 oz) trimmed and chopped asparagus in step 2, about 5 minutes before the end of the cooking time.

Quick nasi goreng

SERVES 6 **CALS PER SERVING** 296

375 g (12 oz) long grain rice
salt
2 tbsp vegetable oil
1 onion, chopped
½ tsp paprika
1 tsp ground ginger
125 g (4 oz) button mushrooms, sliced
60 g (2 oz) bean sprouts
1 tsp soy sauce
125 g (4 oz) cooked peeled prawns
2 spring onions, finely sliced
chopped coriander, to garnish

1 Cook the rice in boiling salted water for 12–15 minutes until tender. Drain, rinse with boiling water, drain again, and set aside.

2 Heat 1 tbsp of the oil in a frying pan or wok, add the onion, and cook for 3–5 minutes until soft. Add the paprika and ginger, and cook over a low heat for 1 minute. Add the mushrooms and bean sprouts and cook for 2–3 minutes until softened. Remove from the pan.

3 Heat the remaining oil in the pan, add the rice, and cook over a gentle heat, stirring, for 7–8 minutes to warm through. Stir in the soy sauce. Return the onions and vegetables to the pan and add the prawns. Serve hot, garnished with coriander.

Vegetarian nasi goreng

SERVES 6 **CALS PER SERVING** 379

375 g (12 oz) long grain rice
salt
2 tbsp tamarind paste (optional)
2 tbsp vegetable oil
1 red pepper, halved, deseeded, and thinly sliced
1 large onion, chopped
3 garlic cloves, crushed
1 cm (½ in) piece of fresh root ginger, peeled and grated
2 tsp curry powder
¼ tsp crushed dried red chillies (chilli flakes)
¼ tsp turmeric
½ small hard white cabbage, thinly sliced
1 x 200 g can chopped tomatoes
3 tbsp soy sauce

To serve

3 tomatoes, cut into strips
½ cucumber, cut into strips
omelette strips (see box, right)

1 Cook the rice in boiling salted water for 12–15 minutes until tender. Drain, rinse with boiling water, and drain again. Stir in the tamarind paste (if using) and set aside.

2 Heat 1 tbsp of the oil in a large frying pan or wok, add the red pepper and onion, and cook for 3–5 minutes until softened. Add the garlic, ginger, curry powder, crushed chillies, and turmeric, and cook gently, stirring, for 1 minute.

3 Add the cabbage and cook for 3–5 minutes. Add the tomatoes and cook for 2–3 minutes. Remove from the pan.

4 Heat the remaining oil in the pan, add the rice, and cook gently until lightly browned. Return the vegetables to the pan. Add the soy sauce and heat gently to warm through.

5 Serve hot, garnished with tomato, cucumber, and omelette strips.

Omelette garnish

Whisk 2 eggs with plenty of salt and pepper. Melt 30 g (1 oz) butter in an omelette pan or small frying pan. Add the eggs to the pan and cook until set. Slide the omelette out of the pan and roll it up, then leave to cool before slicing across into fine strips..

Chicken nasi goreng

SERVES 6 **CALS PER SERVING** 622

375 g (12 oz) long grain rice
salt and black pepper
90 ml (3 fl oz) olive oil
6 streaky bacon rashers, chopped
2 large onions, chopped
3 garlic cloves, crushed
¼ tsp chilli powder
2 tsp mild curry powder
2 cooked chicken breasts, skinned and cubed
90 ml (3 fl oz) soy sauce
6 spring onions, chopped
60 g (2 oz) cooked peeled prawns
60 g (2 oz) almonds, halved, and toasted (page 186)

To serve
coriander sprigs
6 fried eggs (optional)
prawn crackers

1 Cook the rice in boiling salted water for 12–15 minutes until tender. Drain, rinse with boiling water, drain again, and set aside.

2 Heat 1 tbsp of the oil in a large frying pan or wok, add the bacon, and cook for 3–5 minutes until browned. Add the remaining oil, the onions, and garlic, and cook over a gentle heat for 3–5 minutes until the onions are soft but not coloured.

3 Add the chilli and curry powders and cook, stirring, for 1 minute or until fragrant. Add the chicken and cook for 5–6 minutes until just beginning to brown.

4 Add the soy sauce and half of the rice and stir well. Add the remaining rice, and season with salt and pepper. Cook over a gentle heat, stirring, for 7–8 minutes until the rice is heated through. Stir in the spring onions, prawns, and almonds, and heat through.

5 Serve hot, garnished with coriander sprigs, and fried eggs if you like. Serve prawn crackers in a separate bowl.

Kedgeree

SERVES 4 **CALS PER SERVING** 470

175 g (6 oz) long grain rice
¼ tsp turmeric
375 g (12 oz) smoked haddock fillet
2 hard-boiled eggs
60 g (2 oz) butter, plus extra for greasing
juice of ½ lemon
150 ml (¼ pint) single cream
salt
cayenne pepper
2 tbsp finely chopped parsley

1 Simmer the rice and turmeric, covered, in boiling salted water for 12–15 minutes until tender. Rinse with boiling water, drain, and keep warm.

2 Meanwhile, put the haddock, skin-side down, in a frying pan, cover with cold water, and poach for 8–10 minutes.

3 Cut one egg lengthways into quarters and reserve for garnish. Coarsely chop the second egg.

4 Drain the haddock, remove the skin and bones, then flake the fish. Put the fish into a large bowl, add the rice, chopped egg, butter, lemon juice, and cream, and season with salt and cayenne pepper. Stir gently to mix.

5 Butter an ovenproof dish, add the kedgeree, and bake in a preheated oven at 180°C (160°C fan, Gas 4), stirring occasionally, for 10–15 minutes.

6 To serve, stir in the parsley and garnish with the reserved egg quarters.

Cook's know-how

Some smoked haddock is dyed bright yellow, so look out for smoked haddock that is pale in colour and labelled "undyed" if you want to avoid artificial colourings.

Paella

SERVES 6 **CALS PER SERVING** 718

3 tbsp olive oil
6 chicken thighs
250 g (8 oz) smoked bacon, rind removed, cut into strips
1 large onion, chopped
1 litre (1¾ pints) chicken stock
250 g (8 oz) tomatoes, chopped
2 garlic cloves, crushed
a few pinches of saffron threads, soaked in a little hot water
500 g (1 lb) short grain rice
1 red and 1 green pepper, halved, deseeded, and sliced
125 g (4 oz) frozen peas
salt and black pepper
500 g (1 lb) mussels, cleaned (page 105)
125 g (4 oz) cooked peeled prawns

To serve

12 black olives, pitted
6 large cooked prawns, unpeeled
lemon wedges
2 tbsp chopped parsley

1 Heat the oil in a paella pan or a large, deep, ovenproof frying pan or sauté pan. Add the chicken and cook over a medium heat for 10 minutes until browned all over. Add the bacon and onion and cook for 5 minutes.

2 Stir in the stock, tomatoes, garlic, and the saffron with its soaking liquid, and bring to a boil. Add the rice, red and green peppers, and peas, and season with salt and pepper. Cover and bake in a preheated oven at 180°C (160°C fan, Gas 4) for 35–40 minutes until the rice is nearly tender and the stock has been absorbed.

3 Meanwhile, put the mussels into a large pan with about 1 cm (½ in) water. Cover tightly, and cook, shaking the pan occasionally, for 5 minutes or until the shells open. Drain the mussels, and throw away any that have not opened: do not try to force them open.

4 Stir the peeled prawns into the paella, cover, and cook gently on the hob for about 5 minutes. Taste for seasoning. Arrange the mussels around the pan, and the olives, large prawns, and lemon wedges on top. Serve hot, sprinkled with parsley.

Portuguese rice with tuna

SERVES 4 **CALS PER SERVING** 603

- 3 streaky bacon rashers, rinds removed, cut into strips
- 3 tbsp olive oil
- 1 small onion, thinly sliced
- 250 g (8 oz) long grain brown rice
- 600 ml (1 pint) hot chicken stock
- salt and black pepper
- 375 g (12 oz) fresh tuna, cut into chunks
- 1 x 400 g jar pimientos, drained and cut into strips
- 16 black olives
- dill sprigs and lemon slices, to garnish

1 Put the bacon into a large, heavy saucepan and heat until it begins to sizzle. Add the olive oil, and onion, and cook gently, stirring occasionally, for 3–5 minutes until soft but not coloured. Add the rice and stir to coat the grains in the oil.

2 Pour the stock into the pan, season with salt and pepper, and bring to a boil. Cover and simmer for 25–30 minutes.

3 Add the tuna, pimientos, and olives, and cook for 5 minutes or until all the liquid has been absorbed and the rice and tuna are tender. Season, garnish with dill sprigs and lemon slices, and serve at once.

PORTUGUESE RICE WITH CANNED TUNA

Substitute 2 x 200 g cans tuna in brine for the fresh tuna. Drain the tuna well, and flake it roughly with a fork.

Cook's know-how

If you prefer, use 1 x 300 g jar roasted peppers instead of the pimientos.

Caribbean rice and peas

SERVES 4–6 **CALS PER SERVING** 435–290

2 tbsp olive oil
8 spring onions, sliced
3 smoked bacon rashers, rinds removed, diced
2 garlic cloves, crushed
250 g (8 oz) long grain rice
1 x 200 g can tomatoes
3 tbsp chopped parsley
2 bay leaves
1 small green chilli, halved, deseeded, and thinly sliced
½ tsp turmeric
½ tsp cumin seeds
1 tsp fresh thyme leaves
1 x 400 g can red kidney beans or black-eyed beans, drained and rinsed
375 ml (13 fl oz) chicken stock
1 lime, cut into wedges, to serve

1 Heat the oil in a pan, add the spring onions and bacon, and cook for about 5 minutes or until the bacon is crisp. Add the garlic and cook for 2 minutes.

2 Add the rice and stir to coat the grains in the oil. Add the tomatoes with their juice, 2 tbsp of the parsley, the bay leaves, chilli, turmeric, cumin, and thyme, and cook for 2 minutes.

3 Add the beans and stock and bring to a boil. Cover and cook over a low heat for 15 minutes until the rice is tender and the liquid has been absorbed.

4 Sprinkle with remaining parsley, and serve at once, with lime wedges.

Cook's **know-how**

Don't be misled by the name of this dish – there are no peas in it, but this is not a mistake. In the Caribbean the dish is traditionally made with small round beans known as pigeon peas, hence the name of the dish. As pigeon peas are not widely available in the UK, red kidney beans have been used in this recipe instead.

Egg-fried rice

SERVES 4 **CALS PER SERVING** 441

250 g (8 oz) long grain rice
salt and black pepper
3 tbsp sunflower oil
60 g (2 oz) bacon rashers, rinds removed, diced
125 g (4 oz) frozen peas
2 eggs, beaten
125 g (4 oz) bean sprouts
6 spring onions, sliced

1 Cook the rice in boiling salted water for 12–15 minutes until tender. Drain.

2 Heat the oil in a wok or large frying pan, add the bacon, and cook over a high heat, stirring, for 2 minutes. Add the rice and peas and cook, stirring, for 5 minutes.

3 Add the eggs and bean sprouts, and stir-fry for 2 minutes until the eggs have just set. Taste for seasoning, sprinkle with the sliced spring onions, and serve at once.

SPECIAL EGG-FRIED RICE

Add 125 g (4 oz) cooked peeled prawns with the rice and peas in step 2, and sprinkle with 60 g (2 oz) toasted cashew nuts just before serving.

Cook's know-how

Bean sprouts are nutritious and crunchy, making them ideal for stir-fries. They do not keep well, so use as soon as possible after purchase.

Persian pilaf

SERVES 4 **CALS PER SERVING** 426

1 small cinnamon stick
2 tsp cumin seeds
6 black peppercorns
seeds of 4 cardamom pods, crushed
3 cloves
2 tbsp sunflower oil
1 small onion, chopped
1 tsp turmeric
250 g (8 oz) long grain rice
1.25 litres (2 pints) hot vegetable or chicken stock
2 bay leaves, torn into pieces
salt and black pepper
60 g (2 oz) shelled pistachio nuts, coarsely chopped
30 g (1 oz) raisins
fresh coriander, to garnish

1 Heat a heavy pan and add the cinnamon stick, cumin seeds, peppercorns, cardamom seeds, and cloves.

2 Dry-fry the spices over a medium heat for 2–3 minutes until they begin to release their aromas.

3 Add the oil to the pan and, when it is hot, add the onion and turmeric. Cook gently, stirring occasionally, for about 10 minutes until the onion is softened.

4 Add the rice and stir to coat the grains in the oil. Slowly pour in the hot stock, add the bay leaves, season with salt and pepper, and bring to a boil. Lower the heat, cover, and cook very gently for about 10 minutes without lifting the lid.

5 Remove the saucepan from the heat and leave to stand, still covered, for about 5 minutes.

6 Add the pistachio nuts and raisins to the pilaf, and fork them in gently to fluff up the rice. Garnish with fresh coriander, and serve at once.

Savoury rice

SERVES 4 **CALS PER SERVING** 356

2 tbsp olive oil
1 onion, chopped
1 carrot, diced
200 g (7 oz) long grain rice
250 g (8 oz) tomatoes, finely chopped
500 ml (16 fl oz) hot chicken or vegetable stock
150 g (5 oz) sweetcorn kernels
90 g (3 oz) frozen peas
2 tbsp tomato purée
salt and black pepper
1 garlic clove, crushed
chopped parsley, to garnish (optional)

1 Heat the oil in a frying pan, add the onion and carrot, and cook gently, stirring, for 3–5 minutes until the onion is softened but not coloured.

2 Add the rice, and stir to coat the grains in the oil. Add the tomatoes and stock.

3 Add the sweetcorn, peas, and tomato purée, and bring to a boil. Simmer, stirring occasionally, for 12–15 minutes or until the rice is tender and the liquid has been absorbed.

4 Add salt and pepper to taste, and stir in the garlic. Serve at once, sprinkled with parsley if you like.

Wild rice gratin

SERVES 6 **CALS PER SERVING** 446

375 g (12 oz) mixed basmati and wild rice
salt and black pepper
250–375 g (8–12 oz) broccoli
15 g (½ oz) butter
2 onions, chopped
3 garlic cloves, crushed
125 ml (4 fl oz) full-fat soured cream or crème fraîche
125 g (4 oz) mozzarella cheese, grated
60 g (2 oz) Parmesan cheese, grated
1 tbsp chopped fresh rosemary

1 Cook the rice in boiling salted water for about 35 minutes, or according to packet instructions. Drain thoroughly and rinse with cold water. Drain again.

2 Meanwhile, cut the stalks off the broccoli and cook them in boiling salted water for 8–10 minutes until almost tender, then add the florets, and cook for 2 minutes longer. Drain and rinse in cold water. Drain again and set aside.

3 Melt the butter in a frying pan, add the onions, and cook gently, stirring occasionally, for 3–5 minutes until softened. Add the garlic, and cook, stirring occasionally, for 3–5 minutes until the onions are lightly browned.

4 Coarsely chop the broccoli, then stir into the rice with the onion and garlic mixture, soured cream or crème fraîche, three-quarters of the mozzarella and Parmesan cheeses, and the rosemary. Season with salt and pepper.

5 Turn the mixture into an ovenproof dish and sprinkle with the remaining mozzarella and Parmesan cheeses. Bake in a preheated oven at 180°C (160°C fan, Gas 4) for about 20 minutes until the cheese has melted. Serve hot.

Vegetables and salads

In this chapter...

Potatoes lyonnaise
page 407

Garlic creamed potatoes
page 408

Hasselback potatoes
page 408

Swiss rösti
page 409

Gratin dauphinois
page 410

Spinach and cheese baked potatoes
page 411

Spiced yams
page 411

Roasted fennel and sweet potato gratin
page 412

Glazed carrots and turnips
page 412

Italian fennel
page 412

Ginger parsnips
page 414

Mixed vegetable stir-fry
page 414

Ratatouille
page 415

Okra with chilli
page 415

Sweet and sour beetroot
page 416

Glazed shallots
page 416

Herbed roasted tomatoes
page 416

In this chapter... *continued*

Mushroom salad
page 426

Waldorf salad
page 427

Potato, apple, and celery salad
page 427

Aubergine with fresh pesto
page 428

Salade niçoise
page 429

Three-bean salad
page 429

Puy lentil salad
page 430

Italian pesto salad
page 430

Tabbouleh
page 431

Rice salad
page 432

Bulgur wheat salad
page 434

Wild rice salad
page 432

Couscous salad
page 433

Pasta and mackerel salad
page 434

Pasta salad with peppers
page 435

Vegetables and salads know-how

On every shopping trip there seem to be more new vegetables to try – strangely shaped squashes and roots like kohlrabi, tomatoes and peppers of all colours, exotic mushrooms, Chinese cabbages, and salad greens such as wild rocket, mizuna, and red chard – as well as different varieties of familiar vegetables like potatoes, each suitable for particular cooking methods. Imported produce adds to the bounty of our own seasonal vegetables. And for added convenience, chilled ready-prepared vegetables and salads are widely available. This wonderful variety enables a cook to be innovative, creating nutritious, appetizing dishes with minimum effort.

Buying and storing

When choosing vegetables and salad leaves, look for the freshest available. Their colour should be bright and their texture firm and crisp. Any vegetables that are bruised or show signs of age – those that are discoloured, shrivelled, or flabby – are past their best. In general, small, young vegetables are more tender than large, older ones, although very small baby vegetables can be quite tasteless.

Some vegetables, including onions, garlic, roots such as potatoes, parsnips and swede, and pumpkin, can be stored in a cool, dark, well-ventilated place. More perishable vegetables, such as peas, sweetcorn, celery, salad leaves, spinach, and ripe tomatoes, should be chilled. Keep them in the special salad drawer in the refrigerator, unwrapping them or piercing their bags to prevent moisture build-up.

Many vegetables can be prepared ahead of time and kept in sealed plastic bags in the fridge. The exceptions to this are vegetables such as celeriac and Jerusalem artichokes that discolour when cut and exposed to the air. Salad leaves can also be prepared in advance, but do not dress until ready to serve or they will wilt.

Nutrition

A healthy, well-balanced diet should include plenty of vegetables, because they supply essential vitamins, minerals, fibre, and disease-fighting compounds. And vegetables are low in calories and fat. To get the maximum benefit from the vegetables you eat:

- choose the freshest produce
- keep it in the fridge, or in a cool, dark place, and do not store for too long
- prepare as close to cooking or eating as possible
- leave on the peel or skin as it provides fibre, and nutrients are often concentrated just under the skin
- rinse thoroughly but don't soak before cooking, particularly if the vegetable is peeled or cut
- cut large pieces if boiling or steaming
- use the cooking liquid in a sauce or soup

Freezing

Most vegetables freeze very well, whether plain, in a sauce, or in a prepared dish. The exceptions are potatoes and watery vegetables like cucumber and tomatoes. Vegetables that are to be frozen plain should be very fresh. Before freezing blanch them in boiling water, then cool quickly in iced water; this will set the fresh colour. Vegetables can be kept in the freezer for 6–12 months, and can be cooked directly from frozen.

Microwaving

The microwave is ideal for cooking small quantities of vegetables: little water is used so they retain their nutrients as well as colours and flavours. Cut vegetables into uniform pieces, or pierce skins of those that are left whole. Arrange them so that the tender parts are in the centre of the dish, to prevent overcooking. Add salt when serving. Keep the dish tightly covered during cooking, and turn or stir once or twice if necessary.

Cutting vegetables

Keep pieces to a uniform size and shape to ensure they cook evenly.

Julienne
Cut into 5 mm (¼ in) slices. Stack the slices then cut into sticks, 5 mm (¼ in) thick.

Dice
Cut into 1 cm (½ in) strips, then cut across the strips to form neat dice.

Ribbons
Using a vegetable peeler, carefully shave off thin, wide ribbons.

Preparing vegetables

Knowing the most efficient way to prepare vegetables will save you time and effort in the kitchen. For most tasks, a chopping board and a sharp chef's knife, small knife, or vegetable peeler are all you'll need. Here's how the professionals deal with some vegetables.

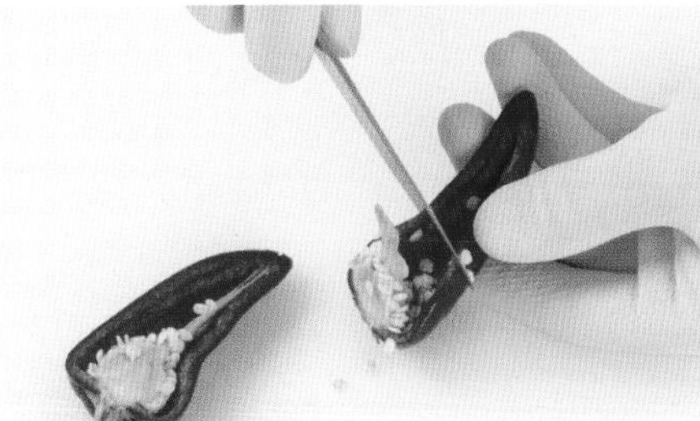

Dicing fresh chillies

1 Cut the chilli in half lengthways. Remove the stalk and core and scrape out the fleshy white ribs and seeds.

2 Set the chilli cut-side up and cut into thin strips. Hold the strips together and cut across to make dice. (See Cutting vegetables, opposite.)

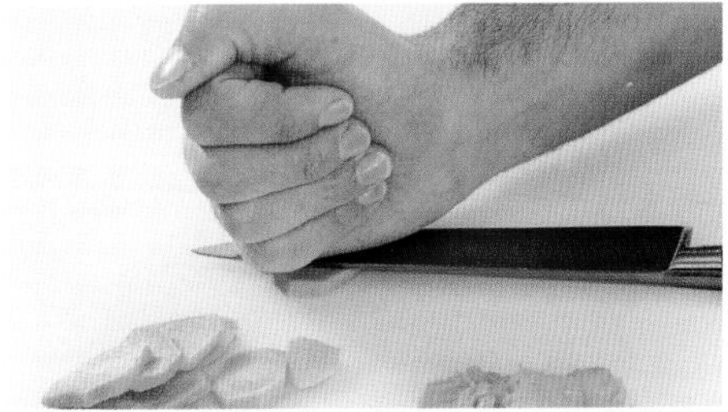

Chopping fresh root ginger

1 With a small knife, peel off the skin. Slice the ginger across the fibrous grain.

2 Set the flat of a knife on top of the slices and crush. Chop the crushed slices.

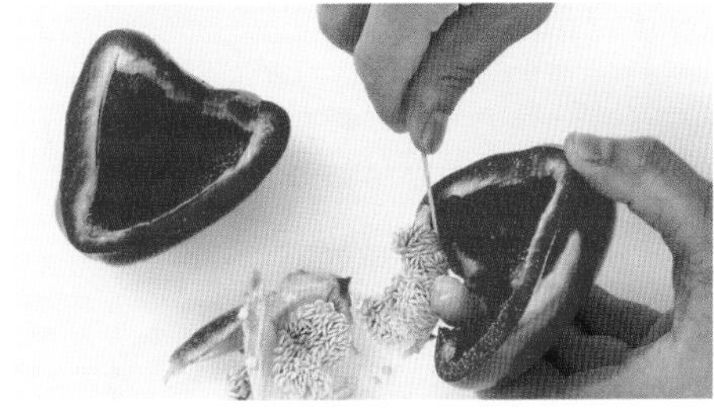

Preparing peppers

1 Cut around the stalk and the core. Twist and pull them out in one piece.

2 Cut the pepper in half. Scrape out the fleshy white ribs and the seeds.

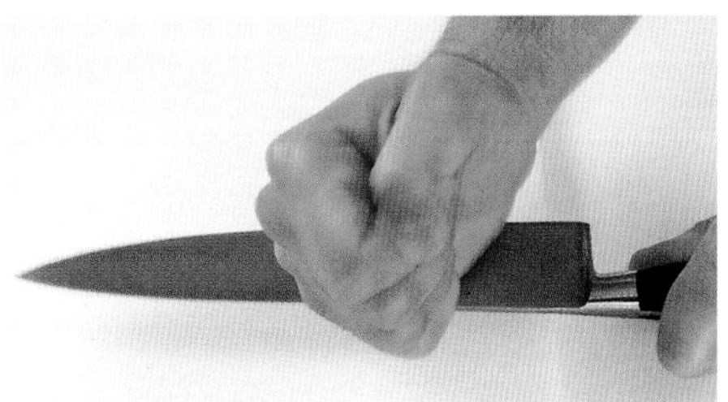

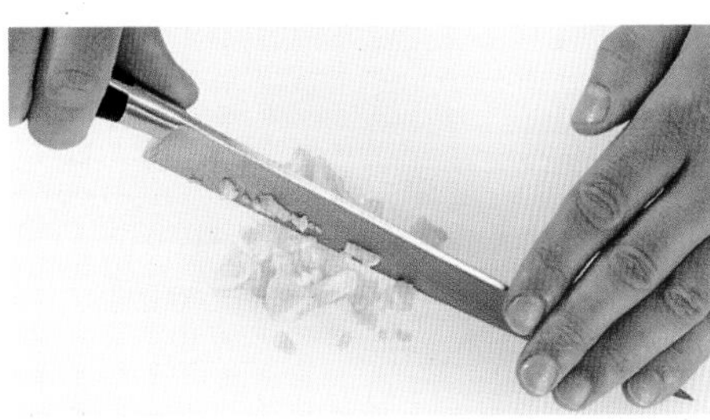

Chopping garlic

1 Set the flat side of a knife on top of the clove and crush it lightly. Peel off the skin.

2 With a sharp chef's knife, chop the crushed garlic clove finely.

Preparing vegetables know-how

The juices produced by fresh chillies can burn the skin, so it's best to wear rubber gloves when cutting them and to avoid touching your eyes or lips.

The more finely you chop garlic, the stronger the flavour. Garlic crushed in a press will have the strongest flavour of all.

Avocados discolour quickly, so brush cut surfaces with lemon juice, and use as soon as possible.

Other vegetables that discolour when cut and exposed to the air include globe artichokes, celeriac and Jerusalem artichokes.

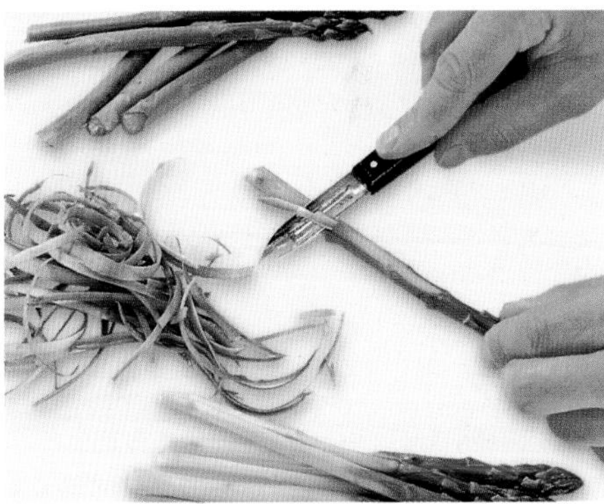

Preparing asparagus

Cut off any woody ends from the asparagus and make the spears uniform in length. If you like, peel them: using a vegetable peeler, and working down towards the end of the spear, shave off the tough layer of skin from all sides.

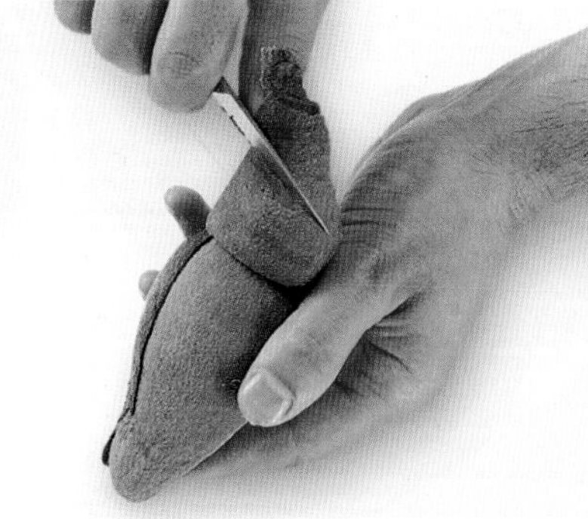

Preparing avocado

Cut the avocado in half lengthways around the stone and twist the two halves to separate them. Remove the stone. If the avocado is to be mashed, the flesh can simply be scooped out of the skin with a teaspoon. To serve in slices, lightly score the skin into two or three strips, then peel off the strips of skin and slice the flesh.

Cooking vegetables

Choose the right cooking method to bring out the best in vegetables and create exciting accompaniments or main dishes. If cooking a variety of vegetables at the same time, remember that some take longer to cook than others, so you may have to add them in stages.

Steaming

This method is ideal for delicate vegetables such as cauliflower, broccoli, and asparagus. Bring water to the boil in a steamer base. Put the vegetables in a single layer on the rack, cover, and steam until just tender. If you don't have a steamer, use a large saucepan with a steamer basket, or a wok and a bamboo steamer.

Stir-frying

Cut the vegetables into small, even-sized pieces. Heat a little oil in a wok. When it is hot, add the vegetables, starting with those that need the longest cooking time. Keep the heat high, and toss and stir the vegetables constantly. Cook for just a few minutes until the vegetables are tender but still crisp.

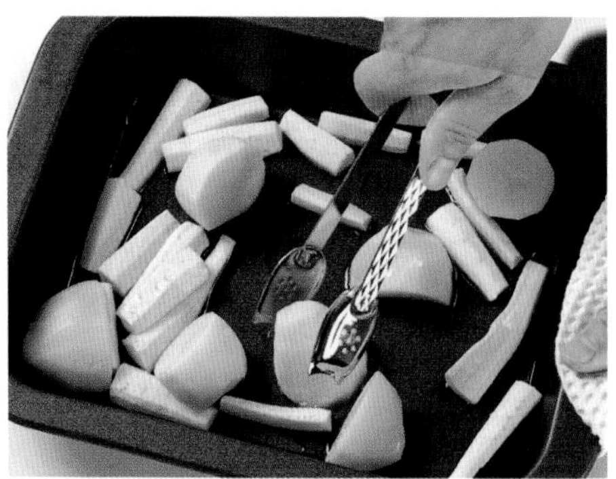

Roasting

Cut any root vegetables into large chunks and parboil them. Drain well. Put olive oil or duck fat into a roasting tin and heat in a preheated 180°C (160°C fan, Gas 4) oven. Add the vegetables to the tin and turn to coat with the fat. Roast, turning occasionally, until well browned.

Boiling

Drop vegetables (both greens and roots) into a large pan of boiling salted water and bring back to the boil as quickly as possible. Simmer until just tender, then drain. To stop further cooking and set the colour of green vegetables, rinse briefly under cold running water.

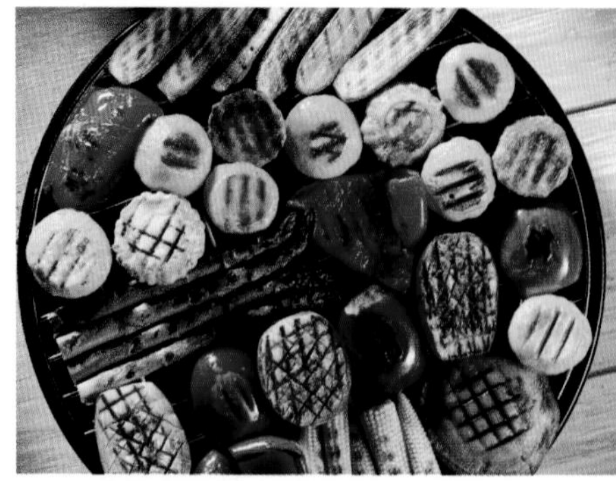

Chargrilling

Many types of quick-cooking vegetables can be cooked on a chargrill, as well as under a grill or on a barbecue. Halve the vegetables or cut into thick slices. Brush with oil and chargrill, turning at least once, until tender. For extra flavour, marinate vegetables first (page 415).

Baking

Potatoes, sweet potatoes, aubergines, and pumpkin are all delicious baked. Prick the skins of whole vegetables or, if cut, moisten cut surfaces with oil or butter. Push a skewer through the centres of large vegetables to conduct heat and speed up cooking time.

Braising

Carrots, celery, and other root vegetables are ideal for braising. Put the vegetables into a heavy pan or flameproof casserole, add a small amount of water or stock, and bring to the boil. Cover tightly and cook over a gentle heat until just tender. Boil to evaporate the liquid or drain.

Sautéing

Vegetables can be sautéed in oil or a mixture of oil and butter (butter alone burns if it becomes too hot). Cook the vegetables over a high heat, stirring and turning constantly, until they start to brown. Reduce the heat and continue cooking, stirring occasionally, until tender.

Salad dressings

Most salad dressings can be made in a matter of seconds. Vinaigrette ingredients only need to be shaken together in a screw-topped jar. Other dressings are simply made by whisking flavourings into a creamy mayonnaise-based mixture.

Vinaigrette dressing

Put 6 tbsp olive oil, 2 tbsp white wine vinegar, 1 tbsp lemon juice, 1 tbsp Dijon mustard, ¼ tsp caster sugar, and salt and pepper to taste into a screw-topped jar. Shake until combined. This makes 150 ml (¼ pint).

Nutty vinaigrette

Use red wine vinegar instead of the white wine vinegar and lemon juice in the recipe above, and replace 2 tbsp of the olive oil with walnut or hazelnut oil.

Easy coleslaw dressing

Whisk 5 tbsp cider vinegar and 1 tbsp caster sugar into 150 ml (¼ pint) mayonnaise. Season with salt and pepper to taste. If liked, stir in a pinch of caraway seeds.

Blue cheese dressing

Put 150 ml (¼ pint) each of mayonnaise and soured cream into a bowl with 90 g (3 oz) mashed blue cheese, 1 tsp white wine vinegar, 1 crushed garlic clove, and black pepper to taste. Whisk until smooth.

Green mayonnaise dressing

Put 50 g (2 oz) each watercress sprigs and flat-leaf parsley in a blender or food processor with 4 chopped spring onions and 1 garlic clove. Process until finely chopped. Whisk into a mixture of 150 ml (¼ pint) each mayonnaise and soured cream or Greek-style yogurt.

Herb vinaigrette

Add 2 tbsp chopped fresh herbs (e.g. dill, tarragon, chervil, or flat-leaf parsley) to the vinaigrette just before serving.

Salad dressings know-how

If mayonnaise curdles, add 1 tbsp hot water and beat well, or start again with fresh egg yolks and oil and slowly add the curdled mixture once the eggs and oil thicken. For best results, use eggs at room temperature. Keep mayonnaise, tightly covered, in the refrigerator for no more than 1–2 days (remember that it contains raw eggs).

Vinaigrette dressing can be kept in its screw-topped jar in the fridge for up to 1 week. Shake well before serving.

Mayonnaise

This always useful sauce is the base for many others – add crushed garlic and you have aïoli – and for salad dressings. It can be made by hand, with a balloon whisk, or more quickly in a food processor or blender. For a lighter result use 1 whole egg rather than 2 egg yolks, and sunflower oil alone.

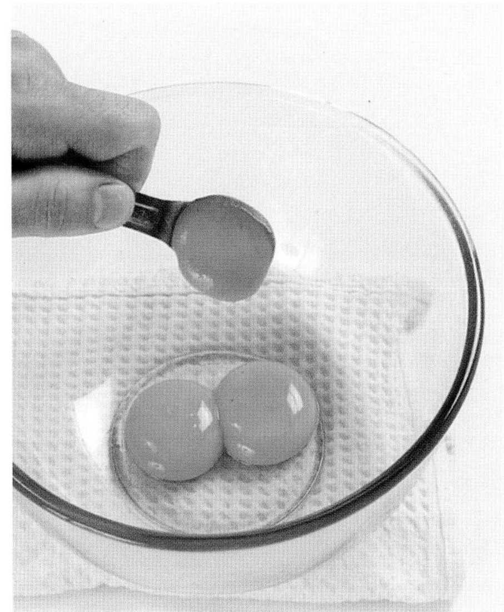

Traditional mayonnaise

1 Put a bowl on a tea towel to steady it. Add 2 egg yolks, 1 tsp Dijon mustard, and salt and pepper to taste, and beat together with a balloon whisk until the egg yolks have thickened slightly.

2 Whisk in 150 ml (¼ pint) olive or sunflower oil, or a mixture of the two, just a drop at a time at first, whisking until the mixture is thick. Stir in 2 tsp white wine vinegar or lemon juice. Check the seasoning, adding sugar to taste if liked. Serve at once, or chill. This makes 200 ml (7 fl oz).

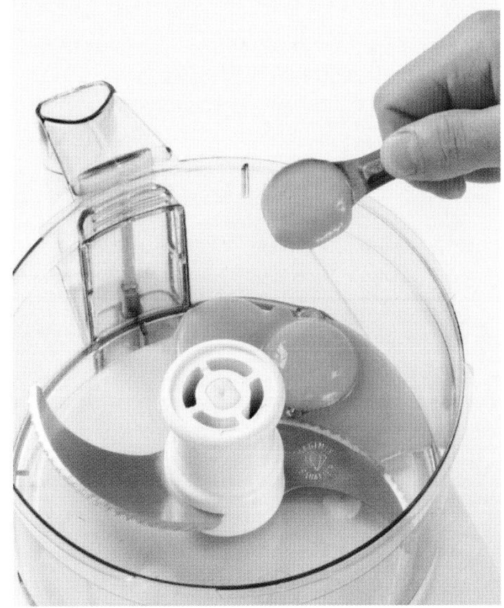

Food-processor mayonnaise

1 Put 2 whole eggs, 2 tsp Dijon mustard, and salt and pepper to taste in the bowl of a food processor or blender. Process briefly to combine.

2 With blades turning, slowly add 300 ml (½ pint) olive or sunflower oil, or a mixture of the two. Finish as for traditional mayonnaise above.

Aromatic Brussels sprouts

SERVES 6–8 **CALS PER SERVING** 125–94

1 kg (2 lb) Brussels sprouts
salt and black pepper
45 g (1½ oz) butter
2 tsp mustard seeds
1 tbsp lemon juice

1 Cut a cross in the base of each sprout, and simmer the sprouts in boiling salted water for 5–10 minutes until just tender. Drain.

2 Melt the butter in a large saucepan, add the mustard seeds, cover, and cook over a low heat for 1–2 minutes until the mustard seeds have stopped popping and the butter is lightly browned. Do not let the butter burn.

3 Add the sprouts to the pan, tossing to heat them through and coat them in the mustard-seed butter. Add the lemon juice, season with salt and pepper, and serve at once.

Cauliflower and broccoli cheese

SERVES 4 **CALS PER SERVING** 513

1 head of cauliflower, weighing about 500 g (1 lb)
1 head of broccoli, weighing about 500 g (1 lb)
salt and black pepper
butter, for greasing
60 g (2 oz) mature Cheddar cheese, grated

Cheese sauce
60 g (2 oz) butter
60 g (2 oz) plain flour
600 ml (1 pint) milk
60 g (2 oz) Parmesan cheese, grated
60 g (2 oz) mature Cheddar cheese, grated
2 tsp Dijon mustard

1 Trim off and discard any thick, woody cauliflower and broccoli stalks. Break the heads into large florets, then cut off the thin, tender stalks and reserve.

2 Bring a saucepan of salted water to a boil. Add the cauliflower florets with all of the reserved stalks, and bring back to a boil. Boil for 2 minutes, then add the broccoli florets and boil for a further 2 minutes, or until the vegetables are just cooked but still have bite (they should not be soft). Drain and rinse under cold running water. Drain again, then spread out in a buttered, shallow ovenproof dish with the florets facing upwards.

3 Make the cheese sauce: melt the butter in a saucepan, sprinkle in the flour, and cook, stirring, for 1 minute. Remove from the heat, and gradually blend in the milk. Bring to a boil, stirring constantly until thickened. Simmer for 2–3 minutes, remove from the heat, and stir in the Parmesan and Cheddar cheeses. Add the mustard, season with salt and pepper, and stir until combined.

4 Pour the sauce over the vegetables, and sprinkle with the Cheddar cheese. Bake in a preheated oven at 200°C (180°C fan, Gas 6) for 20 minutes or until golden and bubbling. Serve hot.

Garlic spring greens

SERVES 6 **CALS PER SERVING** 103

1 kg (2 lb) spring greens, tough stalks removed
salt
2 tbsp olive oil
3 garlic cloves, coarsely chopped

1 Roll up the spring greens, a few leaves at a time, and cut across into thin strips. Blanch in boiling salted water for 2 minutes.

2 Drain and rinse in iced water to cool. Drain thoroughly, squeezing to remove excess water.

3 Heat the olive oil in a large saucepan, add the garlic, and cook gently for 1 minute or until lightly browned. Add the spring greens, toss to coat thoroughly in the garlic and oil, and cook for 2–3 minutes until the spring greens are heated through.

4 Season with salt to taste. Serve hot or cold.

Platter of vegetables

SERVES 6 **CALS PER SERVING** 190

750 g (1½ lb) celeriac, peeled and cut into 3.5 cm (1½ in) pieces
salt and black pepper
3 tbsp full-fat crème fraîche
500 g (1 lb) baby new potatoes, scrubbed
500 g (1 lb) small Chantenay carrots, trimmed
1 large pointed cabbage, core removed and leaves finely shredded
30 g (1 oz) butter
1 garlic clove, crushed

1 Put the celeriac pieces into a large saucepan. Cover with cold water, add a little salt, and bring to a boil. Cover, and simmer for 15–20 minutes or until tender. Lift out the celeriac with a slotted spoon, and purée in a food processor or blender until smooth. Stir in the crème fraîche, and season with salt and pepper.

2 Bring the water in the pan back to a boil. Add the potatoes, cover, and simmer for 10–12 minutes or until tender. Remove from the pan with a slotted spoon, rinse under cold running water, and set aside to drain.

3 Add the carrots to the boiling water in the pan, and boil for 8 minutes or until tender. Remove from the pan with the slotted spoon, rinse under cold running water, and set aside to drain.

4 Add the cabbage to the boiling water in the pan, and simmer for 3 minutes or until tender. Drain in a colander, rinse under cold running water, and squeeze to remove as much water as possible.

5 Melt the butter in the pan. Brush a large ovenproof platter with some of the butter, then add the garlic to the butter in the pan and heat for a minute. Toss in the potatoes, and season with salt and pepper.

6 Put the potatoes, cabbage, celeriac purée, and carrots in rows on the platter, and season with salt and pepper. Cover with foil, and refrigerate until needed.

7 To serve, reheat the vegetables on the foil-covered platter in a preheated oven at 220°C (200°C fan, Gas 7) for about 25 minutes until hot and steaming. Serve immediately, or the cabbage will lose its colour.

Cook's **know-how**

This is an excellent vegetable dish for entertaining, and it goes especially well with a Sunday roast. It can be prepared up to the end of step 6 as long as 24 hours ahead, then all you have to do before the meal is reheat it in the oven.

Chargrilled vegetable platter

SERVES 4 **CALS PER SERVING** 194

4 baby aubergines
4 baby courgettes
1 red pepper
1 yellow pepper
1 large red onion
500 g (1 lb) asparagus
4 large mushrooms
175 g (6 oz) pattypan squash
olive oil or flavoured oils (see box, right), for brushing
salt and black pepper

8–10 WOODEN COCKTAIL STICKS

1 Prepare the vegetables. Trim the aubergines, cut in half lengthways, and score a criss-cross pattern on the cut surfaces.

2 Cut the courgettes in half lengthways. Cut the red and yellow peppers in half lengthways and cut out the fleshy ribs and seeds. Peel the red onion and cut lengthways into 4–6 wedges. Trim the woody ends from the asparagus and cut the spears to an even length.

3 Gently wipe the mushrooms with damp paper towels and remove the stalks. Trim the squash if necessary.

4 Place the asparagus spears side by side in groups of three or four (depending on thickness). Gently push a cocktail stick through the asparagus, about 1 cm (½ in) from the tips, until they are all skewered. Insert a second cocktail stick at the bases of the spears. Repeat for the remaining groups of asparagus spears.

5 Brush all of the vegetables generously with olive oil and season with salt and pepper to taste.

6 Place a batch at a time over a hot barbecue or on a preheated ridged griddle pan, and cook for 10–15 minutes, turning occasionally, until the vegetables are lightly charred. Keep each batch warm while you cook the remaining vegetables.

Adding extra flavour

If you are cooking the vegetables over a barbecue, lay some woody herbs such as thyme or rosemary over the rack before you put the vegetables on.

Another way of injecting flavour into the vegetables is to soak them in a well-flavoured marinade for about an hour before cooking – you can leave them overnight if this suits you better.

Herb and garlic marinade
Put 250 ml (8 fl oz) olive oil, 2 finely chopped garlic cloves, 1 tbsp chopped fresh rosemary, oregano, or thyme, and salt and pepper to taste into a bowl and whisk to mix thoroughly.

Honey and mustard marinade
Put 250 ml (8 fl oz) sunflower oil, 2 tbsp soy sauce, 1 tbsp clear honey, 2 tsp Dijon mustard, and salt and pepper to taste into a small bowl and whisk to mix.

Flavoured oils

Instead of olive oil, you can use flavoured oils to baste the vegetables during chargrilling. These oils are easy to make and add an individual touch to any barbecue.

Thai perfumed oil
Lightly bruise 2–3 sprigs of coriander and 3 x 5 cm (2 in) pieces of fresh lemongrass. Put the coriander, lemongrass, and 2 dried chillies into a clean jar or bottle. Pour in 500 ml (16 fl oz) groundnut oil or corn oil and seal the bottle. Leave in a cool, dark place for 2 weeks, remove the coriander and lemongrass, and use to baste as directed.

Paprika oil
Spoon 2 tbsp paprika into a clean jar or bottle. Pour in 500 ml (16 fl oz) extra-virgin olive oil and seal the bottle. Leave in a cool, dark place, shaking the bottle from time to time, for 1 week. Line a funnel with a double layer of muslin and then strain the oil into another bottle. Use the oil to baste as directed.

Mixed herb oil
Lightly bruise 1 rosemary sprig and 1 thyme sprig. Put the herbs, 1 bay leaf, and 6 black peppercorns into a clean jar or bottle. Pour in 500 ml (16 fl oz) extra-virgin olive oil and seal the bottle. Leave in a cool, dark place for about 2 weeks. Use to baste as directed.

Asparagus with Parmesan

SERVES 4 **CALS PER SERVING** 215

625 g (1¼ lb) asparagus
90 g (3 oz) Parmesan cheese, grated
lemon wedges and flat-leaf parsley sprigs, to garnish

Marinade
2 tbsp olive oil
2 tsp white wine vinegar
3 garlic cloves, crushed
salt and black pepper

1 Trim the woody ends from the asparagus. Make the marinade: in a shallow non-metallic dish, combine the oil, vinegar, garlic, a pinch of salt, and plenty of pepper.

2 Roll the asparagus in the marinade, cover, and leave to marinate for 15 minutes.

3 Sprinkle the Parmesan on to a plate. Roll the asparagus in the Parmesan, then arrange in a single layer in a large lined ovenproof dish.

4 Pour any remaining marinade over the asparagus, and roast in a preheated oven at 200°C (180°C fan, Gas 6) for 10–15 minutes until lightly browned and sizzling hot. Garnish with the lemon wedges and parsley sprigs, and serve hot.

Cook's know-how

To save time, you can omit the marinating and cook the asparagus on a ridged cast-iron chargrill pan. The charred stripes from the pan will boost the flavour of the asparagus and make it look attractive too.

Golden roasted pumpkin

SERVES 6–8 **CALS PER SERVING** 93–70

1 kg (2 lb) piece of pumpkin, skinned, deseeded, and cut into large chunks
2–3 tbsp olive oil
1 tsp balsamic or red wine vinegar
3 garlic cloves, crushed
1 tsp chopped fresh thyme
1 tsp paprika
salt and black pepper
fresh thyme, to garnish

1 Put the pumpkin chunks on a baking tray. Mix the oil, vinegar, garlic, thyme, and paprika, season with salt and pepper, and pour over the pumpkin.

2 Roast in a preheated oven at 190°C (170°C fan, Gas 5) for 15–20 minutes until the pumpkin is tender and lightly browned on top. Garnish with thyme, and serve at once. If preferred, leave to cool and serve with a vinaigrette dressing (page 397).

Creamed spinach

SERVES 4 **CALS PER SERVING** 250

750 g (1½ lb) fresh spinach leaves
45 g (1½ oz) butter
125 ml (4 fl oz) full-fat crème fraîche
¼ tsp grated nutmeg
salt and black pepper
1–2 tbsp grated Parmesan cheese

1 Cut any coarse outer leaves and stalks off the spinach and discard, then wash thoroughly in plenty of cold water.

2 Melt the butter in a saucepan, add the spinach, and stir until it has absorbed the butter.

3 Add half of the crème fraîche, season with the nutmeg and salt and pepper, and heat through.

4 Transfer to a shallow flameproof dish, pour the remaining crème fraîche on top, and sprinkle with grated Parmesan. Put under a hot grill for a few minutes until lightly browned. Serve hot.

Yankee succotash

SERVES 6 **CALS PER SERVING** 491

2 tbsp sunflower oil
1 large onion, chopped
8 thick streaky bacon rashers, rinds removed, diced
500 g (1 lb) sweetcorn kernels
250 ml (8 fl oz) single cream
1 x 400 g can beans, such as borlotti or broad beans, drained
salt
Tabasco sauce
3–4 tbsp snipped fresh chives, plus extra to garnish

1 Heat the sunflower oil in a large frying pan, add the onion and bacon, and cook gently, stirring occasionally, for 7 minutes or until lightly browned.

2 Stir in the sweetcorn and cream and simmer for 2 minutes. Purée 3–4 tbsp of the sweetcorn mixture in a food processor until quite smooth, then stir back into the frying pan.

3 Add the beans and return to a boil. Simmer, stirring occasionally, for 5–10 minutes until the mixture is thickened.

4 Add salt and Tabasco sauce to taste, and stir in the snipped chives. Serve at once, garnished with fresh chives.

Celery and leek stir-fry

SERVES 6 **CALS PER SERVING** 235

30 g (1 oz) butter
2 tbsp olive oil
500 g (1 lb) young leeks, trimmed and thinly sliced
12 celery stalks, thinly sliced on the diagonal
salt and black pepper
2 tbsp snipped fresh chives
125 g (4 oz) salted cashew nuts, to garnish

1 Melt the butter with the olive oil in a wok or large frying pan.

2 When the butter is foaming, add the leeks, and cook over a high heat, stirring occasionally, for 5 minutes.

3 Add the celery, and cook for 3–5 minutes. Season with salt and pepper, then stir in the snipped fresh chives. Garnish with the salted cashew nuts, and serve at once.

Cabbage and mixed pepper stir-fry

SERVES 6–8 **CALS PER SERVING** 128–96

2–3 tbsp olive oil
1 large onion, finely sliced
6 celery stalks, sliced diagonally
2 red peppers, halved, deseeded, and cut into thin strips
1 yellow pepper, halved, deseeded, and cut into thin strips
175 g (6 oz) mushrooms, quartered
salt and black pepper
1 small white cabbage, finely shredded

1 Heat 1 tbsp olive oil in a wok or large frying pan, add the sliced onion, and stir-fry over a high heat for about 2 minutes until beginning to brown.

2 Add the sliced celery and stir-fry for about 1 minute, then lower the heat and stir-fry for 2 minutes.

3 Add another tablespoon of olive oil to the wok. When it is hot, add the peppers and mushrooms, season with salt and pepper, and stir-fry for 3 minutes.

4 Add the cabbage, with the remaining oil if needed, and stir-fry for 2 minutes or until tender–crisp. Taste for seasoning.

SAVOY CABBAGE STIR-FRY

Heat 1 tbsp sunflower oil in a wok and stir-fry 1 finely sliced large onion, and 2 crushed garlic cloves for a few minutes. Add a further 1 tbsp sunflower oil, then 1 shredded small Savoy cabbage, and stir-fry for 2 minutes. Sprinkle with 2 tbsp soy sauce and 1 tsp sesame oil.

Cook's know-how

This is a good vegetable dish to serve when entertaining. Prepare and stir-fry the vegetables up to the end of step 3. The final cooking of the cabbage can be done just before serving.

Sweet and sour red cabbage

SERVES 8 **CALS PER SERVING** 225

1 tbsp sunflower oil
4 streaky bacon rashers, rinds removed, diced
125 g (4 oz) light soft brown sugar
1 red cabbage, weighing about 1 kg (2 lb), shredded
2 onions, chopped
1 tart apple, cored and diced
250 ml (8 fl oz) red wine
4 tbsp red wine vinegar
60 g (2 oz) sultanas
2 tsp caraway seeds
¼ tsp ground cinnamon
pinch of grated nutmeg (optional)
salt and black pepper

1 Heat the oil in a large saucepan, add the diced bacon, and cook for about 5 minutes until crisp and browned.

2 Stir in 90 g (3 oz) of the sugar and cook gently, stirring constantly, for 1–2 minutes, taking care that it does not burn.

3 Add the cabbage, onions, and apple, and cook, stirring occasionally, for about 5 minutes.

4 Pour in the wine and half of the wine vinegar, then add the sultanas, caraway seeds, cinnamon, and nutmeg (if using). Season with salt and pepper. Cover and cook over a low heat for 30 minutes or until the cabbage is tender but still firm. If there is too much liquid, uncover, and boil rapidly until the liquid evaporates completely.

5 Stir in the remaining sugar and wine vinegar, heat through, and taste for seasoning. Serve hot.

VEGETARIAN RED CABBAGE WITH CHESTNUTS

Omit the bacon. Add 125 g (4 oz) coarsely chopped peeled chestnuts in step 3, with the cabbage, onions, and diced apple.

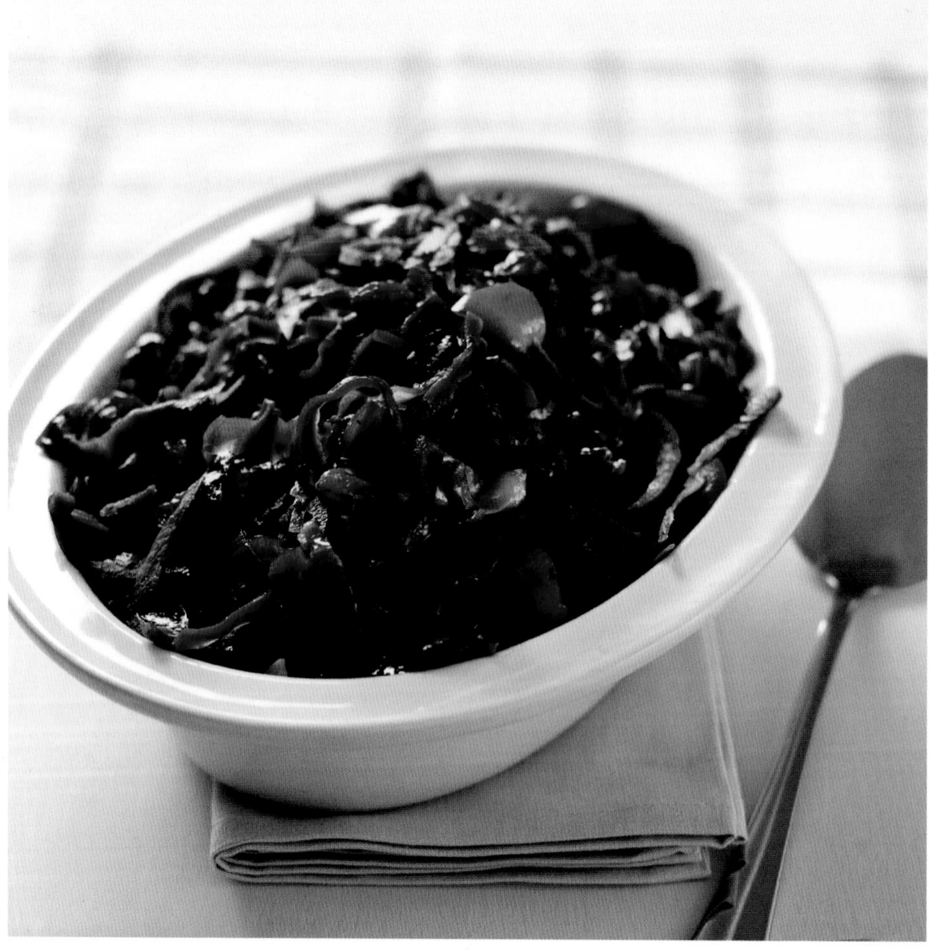

Summer peas and beans

SERVES 6–8 **CALS PER SERVING** 107–80

250 g (8 oz) shelled fresh broad beans (they must be young)
salt and black pepper
250 g (8 oz) shelled peas (they must be young)
250 g (8 oz) French beans, halved
30 g (1 oz) butter
2 tbsp chopped fresh mint
fresh mint, to garnish

1 Cook the broad beans in a saucepan of boiling salted water for a few minutes until just tender. Add the peas and French beans and cook for another 5–10 minutes or until tender (the timing depends on their freshness).

2 Drain all the vegetables, and return to the pan. Add the butter and mint and stir until the butter melts. Taste for seasoning, and serve hot, garnished with fresh mint.

Haricot bean cassoulet

SERVES 6 **CALS PER SERVING** 167

250 g (8 oz) dried haricot beans
30 g (1 oz) butter
1 small carrot, finely chopped
1 small onion, finely chopped
1 bouquet garni or bunch of fresh mixed herbs
salt and black pepper
2 tbsp chopped parsley

1 Put the beans into a large bowl, cover with cold water, then leave to soak for at least 8 hours.

2 Drain the beans. Rinse under cold water and drain again. Put the beans into a saucepan and cover with cold water. Bring to a boil and boil rapidly for 10 minutes. Drain.

3 Melt the butter in a heavy saucepan, add the carrot and onion, and cook, stirring, for 3–4 minutes until beginning to soften.

4 Add the beans and bouquet garni or fresh herbs, and pour in enough cold water to cover the beans generously. Bring to a boil, cover, and simmer gently for 1 hour or until the beans are soft but not breaking up.

5 Drain the bean mixture, reserving the cooking liquid. Discard the bouquet garni or herbs. Purée one-third of the bean mixture in a food processor.

6 Stir the purée back into the unpuréed bean mixture in the pan, adding a little of the reserved cooking liquid to make a sauce-like consistency. Season with salt and pepper. Reheat gently and serve hot, sprinkled with chopped parsley.

French-style peas

SERVES 4–6 **CALS PER SERVING** 237–158

1 small round lettuce, shredded
6 spring onions, chopped
60 g (2 oz) butter
1 tbsp chopped parsley
1 tsp caster sugar
500 g (1 lb) shelled fresh peas (they must be young)
4 tbsp water
salt and black pepper

1 Line the bottom of a saucepan with the lettuce. Add the spring onions, butter, parsley, and sugar, and top with the peas. Add the water, season with salt and pepper, and bring to a boil.

2 Simmer gently, uncovered, for 15–20 minutes until the liquid has evaporated and the peas are tender. Taste for seasoning and serve hot.

Pommes Anna

SERVES 6 **CALS PER SERVING** 205

750 g (1½ lb) floury potatoes
90 g (3 oz) butter, plus extra for greasing
salt and black pepper

1 Slice the potatoes very thinly, preferably with the slicing disc of a food processor.

2 Generously butter the base and sides of an ovenproof frying pan. Layer the potatoes in the frying pan, seasoning each layer with salt and pepper, and dotting with the butter.

3 Cover the pan tightly with buttered foil and the lid, and cook over a medium heat for about 15 minutes or until the base of the potato cake is light golden brown.

4 Transfer the pan to a preheated oven and cook at 190°C (170°C fan, Gas 5) for 30 minutes or until the potato cake is tender.

5 Invert a warmed serving platter over the pan, and turn out the potato cake so that the crisp layer is on the top. Serve at once, cut into wedges.

INDIVIDUAL POMMES ANNA

Layer the sliced potatoes in well-buttered individual patty tins, seasoning the layers and dotting with butter as in step 2. Omit the cooking on the hob in step 3, and bake, uncovered, in the hottest part of a preheated oven at 220°C (200°C fan, Gas 7) for 30–35 minutes or until the potatoes are tender and golden brown.

Cook's know-how

Arrange the potatoes in the frying pan as soon as they have been sliced. Don't leave them to soak in water or the starch in them will leach out and they will not hold together to make the cake.

Roast potatoes

SERVES 6 **CALS PER SERVING** 192

1 kg (2 lb) floury potatoes, cut into even-sized pieces
3 tbsp goose or duck fat, or sunflower oil
salt

1 Put the potatoes into a large saucepan, cover with cold water, and bring to a boil. Simmer for 1 minute, then drain thoroughly.

2 Return the potatoes to the saucepan and shake over a gentle heat to roughen the surfaces and dry the potatoes thoroughly.

3 Put the fat into a roasting tin, heat until very hot, then add the potatoes, turning to coat them in the fat. Roast the potatoes in a preheated oven at 220°C (200°C fan, Gas 7), turning and basting occasionally, for 45–60 minutes until tender, crisp, and golden. Sprinkle with salt, and serve at once.

Cook's know-how

Roughening the outside of blanched potatoes before roasting helps make them really crisp. If you like, you can also score them roughly with a fork.

Potatoes lyonnaise

SERVES 6 **CALS PER SERVING** 246

90 g (3 oz) butter, plus extra for greasing
1 large onion, sliced
1 kg (2 lb) floury potatoes, thickly sliced
salt and black pepper
chopped parsley, to garnish

1 Lightly butter a gratin dish. Melt the butter in a frying pan, add the onion, and cook gently, stirring occasionally, for 3–5 minutes until the onions are softened but not coloured.

2 Layer the potatoes and onion in the gratin dish, seasoning each layer with salt and pepper, and finishing with a neat layer of potatoes.

3 Pour any butter left in the frying pan over the potatoes. Bake in a preheated oven at 190°C (170°C fan, Gas 5) for 1–1½ hours until the potatoes are tender. Garnish with parsley, and serve hot.

Garlic creamed potatoes

SERVES 4 **CALS PER SERVING** 227

750 g (1½ lb) floury potatoes, cut into large chunks
4 garlic cloves, unpeeled
salt and black pepper
about 150 ml (¼ pint) milk
60 g (2 oz) butter
2 tbsp snipped fresh chives

1 Cook the potatoes and whole garlic cloves in boiling salted water for 20–30 minutes until tender. Drain thoroughly, and peel the skins off the garlic cloves.

2 Return the potatoes to the saucepan and toss over a gentle heat for a few seconds to dry thoroughly, shaking the saucepan so that the potatoes do not burn.

3 Mash the potatoes and garlic together, or work through a sieve for a finer purée, then push them to one side of the pan.

4 Pour the milk into the saucepan and heat until almost boiling. Beat the milk into the potatoes and garlic with the butter, and salt and pepper to taste. Sprinkle with chives, and serve hot.

HERB AND CHEESE CREAMED POTATOES

Omit the garlic, and add 2 tbsp chopped parsley and 60 g (2 oz) finely grated Cheddar cheese when you beat in the milk.

CREAMED POTATOES WITH SWEDE

Omit the garlic and fresh chives. Substitute 250 g (8 oz) swede, cut into small chunks, for 250 g (8 oz) of the potatoes, and add a pinch of grated nutmeg just before serving.

Hasselback potatoes

SERVES 8 **CALS PER SERVING** 183

8 large floury potatoes
60 g (2 oz) butter, melted, plus extra for greasing
salt and black pepper
4 tbsp grated Parmesan cheese
parsley, to garnish

1 Peel the potatoes, then slice them (see box, right).

2 Put the potatoes into a buttered roasting tin and brush with the melted butter, separating the slices slightly so a little of the butter goes between them. Season with salt and pepper.

3 Bake in a preheated oven at 220°C (200°C fan, Gas 7) for 45 minutes, then sprinkle with the Parmesan cheese and return to the oven for 10–15 minutes or until the potatoes are tender.

4 Transfer to a warmed serving platter, garnish with parsley, and serve at once.

Slicing the potatoes

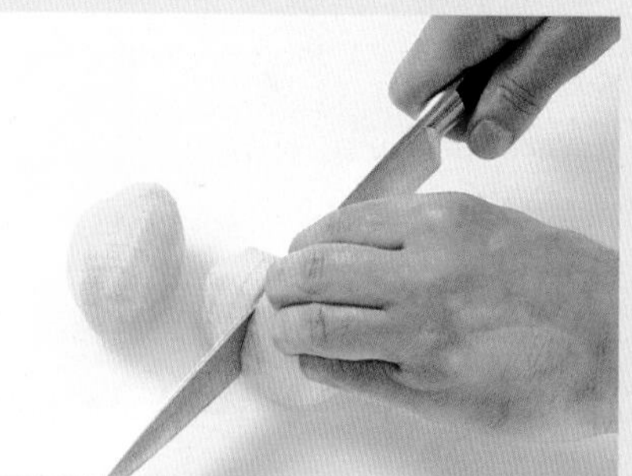

Cut a thin slice off one side of each potato, and place the potato cut-side down on a board. Make vertical cuts, three-quarters of the way through, at 5 mm (¼ in) intervals.

Cook's know-how

To make it easier to slice the potatoes, push a skewer lengthways through the lower part of each potato, and slice as far down as the skewer. Remove the skewer before cooking.

Swiss rösti

SERVES 8 **CALS PER SERVING** 230

1.5 kg (3 lb) large baking potatoes, scrubbed
black pepper
60 g (2 oz) butter
2 tbsp sunflower oil
fresh thyme, to garnish

1 Cook the potatoes in boiling salted water for about 10 minutes until just tender. Drain the potatoes thoroughly, leave to cool, then peel. Cover and chill for about 4 hours.

2 Coarsely grate the potatoes into a large bowl, season with pepper, and stir carefully to mix.

3 Melt 30 g (1 oz) of the butter with 1 tbsp of the oil in a frying pan, add the grated potato, and flatten into a cake with a fish slice. Cook over a low heat for about 15 minutes until the base is crisp and golden brown. Turn on to a large buttered plate.

4 Melt the remaining butter and oil in the frying pan, slide in the potato cake, and cook for 5–10 minutes to brown the second side. Turn out on to a warmed platter, garnish, and serve cut into wedges.

CELERIAC RÖSTI

Substitute 750 g (1½ lb) celeriac for half of the potato. Before boiling in step 1, peel the celeriac, and toss in lemon juice to prevent discoloration.

ONION RÖSTI

Heat 1 tbsp sunflower oil in a frying pan, add 1 large chopped onion, and cook for 3–5 minutes until softened but not coloured. Fork the onion into the grated potato in step 2, before seasoning with pepper.

Gratin dauphinois

SERVES 8 **CALS PER SERVING** 279

butter, for greasing
150 ml (¼ pint) single cream
150 ml (¼ pint) double cream
1 large garlic clove, crushed
1 kg (2 lb) main-crop potatoes
salt and black pepper
125 g (4 oz) Gruyère cheese, grated

1 Lightly butter a shallow gratin dish. Put the single and double creams into a bowl, add the garlic, and stir to mix.

2 Thinly slice the potatoes, preferably with the slicing disc of a food processor.

3 Prepare the gratin (see box, right).

4 Bake in a preheated oven at 160°C (140°C fan, Gas 3) for 1½ hours or until the potatoes are tender and the topping is golden brown. Serve at once.

Preparing the gratin

Arrange a layer of potatoes, slightly overlapping, in the bottom of the gratin dish. Season with salt and pepper.

Pour a little of the cream mixture over the potatoes, then sprinkle with grated cheese. Continue layering the potatoes, cream, and cheese, and adding salt and pepper, then finish with a layer of cheese.

Spinach and cheese baked potatoes

SERVES 4–8 **CALS PER SERVING** 291–146

4 baking potatoes, scrubbed
250 g (8 oz) spinach leaves
1 tbsp olive oil
1 small onion, finely chopped
125 g (4 oz) ricotta cheese
¼ tsp grated nutmeg
salt and black pepper

1 Prick the potatoes all over with a fork.Bake in a preheated oven at 220°C (200°C fan, Gas 7) for 1–1¼ hours until tender.

2 Meanwhile, wash the spinach and put it into a saucepan with only the water remaining on the leaves. Cook over a gentle heat for 1–2 minutes until the spinach has just wilted. Drain thoroughly, squeezing to remove excess water. Chop the spinach finely.

3 Heat the olive oil in a small saucepan, add the onion, and cook gently, stirring occasionally, for 3–5 minutes until softened but not coloured.

4 Cut the potatoes in half lengthways, scoop out the flesh and turn it into a bowl. Add the spinach, onion, any oil left in the pan, the ricotta cheese, and nutmeg. Season with salt and pepper, and mix thoroughly. Fill the potato skins with the mixture, return to the oven at the same temperature as before, and cook for 20 minutes or until piping hot. Serve hot.

SPRING ONION AND HUMMUS BAKED POTATOES

Bake the potatoes, cut in half lengthways, and scoop out the flesh. Mix with 4 finely chopped spring onions, 150 g (5 oz) hummus, and season with salt and pepper. Fill the potato skins and bake as in step 4.

Spiced yams

Serves 4 **cals per serving** 381

45 g (1½ oz) butter
2 garlic cloves, crushed
2 yams, total weight 1 kg (2 lb), trimmed but unpeeled, cubed
1 tsp mild chilli powder
¼ tsp paprika
¼ tsp ground cinnamon
1 x 200 g can chopped tomatoes
salt
plain yogurt and chopped parsley, to serve

1 Melt the butter in a large pan. When it is foaming, add the garlic, and cook gently, stirring occasionally, for 1–2 minutes until soft but not coloured.

2 Add the yams to the pan and toss over a medium to high heat for 1–2 minutes.

3 Stir in the chilli powder, paprika, and cinnamon, then add the tomatoes, and cook the mixture over a medium heat for 1–2 minutes.

4 Season with salt, cover, and simmer for 15–20 minutes until the yams are tender. Turn the yams occasionally with a palette knife, but do not stir or they will break up. Serve hot, topped with yogurt and parsley.

Roasted fennel and sweet potato gratin

SERVES 4–6 **CALS PER SERVING** 312–208

2 large fennel bulbs
500 g (1 lb) sweet potatoes
salt and black pepper
60 g (2 oz) butter
90 g (3 oz) Parmesan cheese, grated

1 Cut each fennel bulb lengthways in half, then cut each half lengthways into three pieces, keeping the root ends intact. Peel the sweet potatoes, and cut the flesh into 3.5 cm (1½ in) cubes.

2 Bring a saucepan of salted water to a boil. Add the fennel, bring back to a boil, and boil for 7 minutes. Add the sweet potatoes, and boil for a further 3 minutes. Drain the vegetables, rinse under cold running water, and dry well.

3 Melt the butter in the saucepan, and return the vegetables to the pan. Toss to coat in the butter, and season with salt and pepper.

4 Tip the mixture into a shallow ovenproof dish, level the surface, and sprinkle with the cheese. Roast in a preheated oven at 220°C (200°C fan, Gas 7) for 20–25 minutes until golden brown. Serve hot.

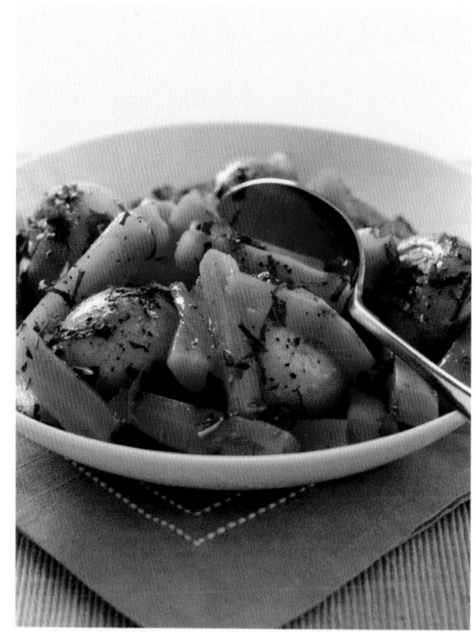

Glazed carrots and turnips

SERVES 4 **CALS PER SERVING** 115

375 g (12 oz) carrots, cut into 5 cm (2 in) strips
375 g (12 oz) baby turnips
300 ml (½ pint) chicken stock
30 g (1 oz) butter
1 tsp caster sugar
salt and black pepper
1 tbsp mixed chopped fresh mint and parsley

1 Put the vegetables into a pan with the stock, butter, and sugar. Season with salt and pepper, and bring to a boil. Cover and cook for about 10 minutes until the vegetables are almost tender.

2 Remove the lid and boil rapidly until the liquid in the pan has evaporated and formed a glaze on the vegetables. Stir in the herbs, and serve hot.

Italian fennel

SERVES 8 **CALS PER SERVING** 108

4 fennel bulbs, trimmed and quartered lengthways
salt and black pepper
butter for greasing
250 g (8 oz) mozzarella cheese, grated
chopped parsley, to garnish

1 Cook the fennel in boiling salted water for 3–5 minutes until just tender. Drain thoroughly.

2 Butter a shallow ovenproof dish. Add the fennel and season with salt and pepper. Sprinkle the grated mozzarella cheese on top.

3 Bake in a preheated oven at 200°C (180°C fan, Gas 6) for 15–20 minutes until the cheese topping is golden and bubbling. Sprinkle with chopped parsley, and serve hot.

Ginger parsnips

SERVES 8 **CALS PER SERVING** 249

1 kg (2 lb) parsnips, cut into matchstick-thin strips
salt and black pepper
60 g (2 oz) butter
2.5 cm (1 in) piece of fresh root ginger, peeled and grated
300 ml (½ pint) full-fat crème fraîche

1 Blanch the parsnips in a large saucepan of boiling salted water for 2 minutes. Drain the parsnips.

2 Melt the butter in the saucepan. Add the ginger and cook gently, stirring, for 2–3 minutes. Add the parsnips, tossing to coat in the butter. Season with salt and pepper, then turn the mixture into a large, shallow ovenproof dish.

3 Pour the crème fraîche over the parsnip mixture and bake in a preheated oven at 190°C (170°C fan, Gas 5) for 10–15 minutes until tender. Serve hot.

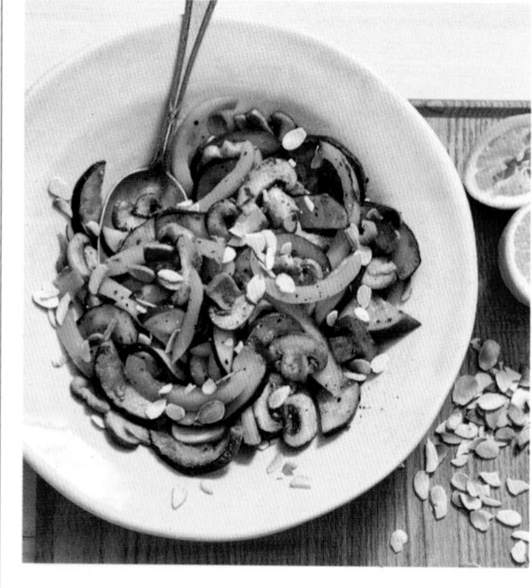

Mixed vegetable stir-fry

SERVES 4 **CALS PER SERVING** 155

1 tbsp olive oil
250 g (8 oz) courgettes, sliced thinly on the diagonal
1 yellow pepper, halved, deseeded, and thinly sliced
250 g (8 oz) mixed mushrooms, sliced
salt and black pepper
1 tbsp lemon juice
60 g (2 oz) flaked almonds, toasted

1 Heat the olive oil in a wok or large frying pan, add the courgettes, and stir-fry for 3–4 minutes until the courgettes are just beginning to colour.

2 Add the yellow pepper and mushrooms, and stir-fry for 2 minutes. Add salt and pepper, stir in the lemon juice, and leave the mixture to bubble for about 1 minute. Sprinkle with the toasted flaked almonds, and serve hot.

Ratatouille

SERVES 4–6 **CALS PER SERVING** 236–157

4 tbsp olive oil
1 large onion, sliced
1 large garlic clove, crushed
1 large aubergine, halved lengthways and cut into 1 cm (½ in) slices
4 courgettes, halved lengthways and sliced
6 juicy ripe tomatoes, sliced
1 large red pepper, halved, deseeded, and sliced
1 tsp caster sugar
salt and black pepper
1 tbsp chopped fresh basil, to garnish

1 Heat the olive oil in a large frying pan, add the onion and garlic, and cook gently, stirring occasionally, for 3–5 minutes until softened.

2 Add the aubergine slices, cover, and simmer gently for 20 minutes.

3 Add the courgettes, tomatoes, red pepper, and sugar. Season with salt and pepper. Cover and cook gently, stirring occasionally, for 30 minutes or until the vegetables are soft.

4 Taste for seasoning and serve hot or cold, sprinkled with the chopped fresh basil.

Okra with chilli

SERVES 4–6 **CALS PER SERVING** 152–101

3 tbsp sunflower oil
1 small onion, sliced
1 garlic clove, crushed
500 g (1 lb) okra, trimmed
1 large fresh red chilli, halved, deseeded, and diced
salt and black pepper

1 Heat the oil in a wok or large frying pan, add the onion, and stir-fry over a high heat for 3 minutes or until golden. Add the garlic and stir-fry for 1 minute.

2 Add the okra and chilli and stir-fry over a high heat for 5–10 minutes until the okra is tender, but still retains some crispness. Add salt and pepper to taste. Serve hot.

Cook's know-how

Because of its shape, okra is sometimes known as ladies' fingers. Trim the ends carefully so that the sticky juices and seeds are not exposed and released.

Sweet and sour beetroot

SERVES 4 **CALS PER SERVING** 242

3 tbsp olive oil
2 onions, chopped
2 garlic cloves, crushed
30 g (1 oz) caster sugar
4 cooked beetroot, diced
juice of 1 lemon
2 tsp chopped fresh mint
salt and black pepper
fresh mint, to garnish

1 Heat the olive oil in a large saucepan, add the onions and garlic, and cook gently, stirring occasionally, for 3–5 minutes until the onions are softened but not coloured.

2 Stir in the sugar, beetroot, half of the lemon juice, and the mint. Cook gently, stirring, for 10 minutes. Taste for seasoning, adding salt and pepper, and more lemon juice if needed.

3 Serve warm or cold, garnished with fresh mint.

Glazed shallots

SERVES 6 **CALS PER SERVING** 150

750 g (1½ lb) small shallots or pickling onions
90 g (3 oz) butter
1 tbsp caster sugar
1 tbsp chopped fresh thyme
salt and black pepper
chopped parsley, to garnish

1 Place the shallots in a single layer in a large frying pan. Add enough cold water to half-cover the shallots.

2 Add the butter, sugar, and thyme, and season with salt and pepper. Cover and bring to a boil. Uncover, and simmer gently for 10–15 minutes until the shallots are golden and the liquid almost evaporated. Shake the pan vigorously at intervals, to prevent the shallots sticking.

3 Garnish the shallots with parsley, and serve hot.

Herbed roasted tomatoes

SERVES 4 **CALS PER SERVING** 106

500 g (1 lb) cherry tomatoes
fresh herb sprigs, to garnish

Herb butter

45 g (1½ oz) butter, softened
2 tbsp chopped fresh herbs (e.g. coriander, basil, flat-leaf parsley)
1 garlic clove, crushed
½ tsp lemon juice
salt and black pepper

1 Arrange the tomatoes in a single layer in an ovenproof dish. Roast in a preheated oven at 230°C (210°C fan, Gas 8) for 15–20 minutes until the tomatoes are tender but still retain their shape.

2 Meanwhile, make the herb butter: put the butter into a small bowl and beat in the herbs, garlic, and lemon juice. Season with salt and pepper. Garnish and serve hot, dotted with the herb butter.

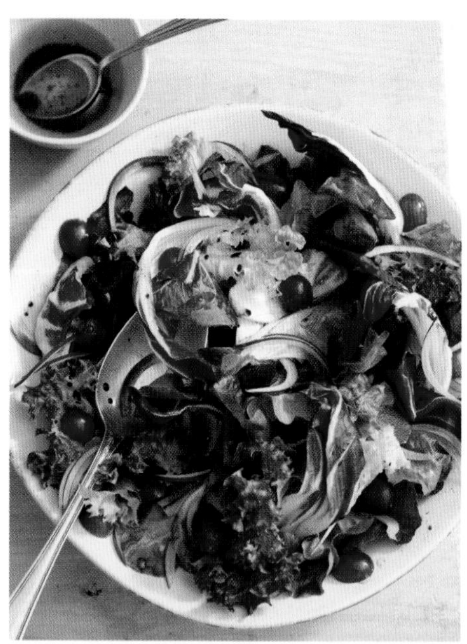

Red salad bowl

SERVES 4–6 **CALS PER SERVING** 387–258

1 small head of radicchio
1 small oak leaf lettuce
1 small lollo rosso lettuce
1 small red onion, thinly sliced
125 g (4 oz) seedless red grapes

Dressing

150 ml (¼ pint) olive oil
3 tbsp balsamic vinegar
1 garlic clove, crushed (optional)
½ tsp caster sugar, or to taste
salt and black pepper

1 Tear the radicchio leaves and the oak leaf and lollo rosso lettuce leaves into bite-sized pieces. Put them into a large salad bowl and mix together, then add the onion and grapes.

2 Make the dressing: combine the oil, vinegar, and garlic, if using, with sugar, salt, and pepper to taste.

3 Pour just enough dressing over the salad to cling to the leaves, toss gently, and serve at once.

Mixed leaf salad

SERVES 4–6 **CALS PER SERVING** 117–78

1 crisp lettuce, such as iceberg or romaine
1 bunch of watercress, tough stalks removed
60 g (2 oz) lamb's lettuce
60 g (2 oz) rocket
about 4 tbsp vinaigrette dressing (page 397)
1 tbsp snipped fresh chives

1 Tear the lettuce leaves into bite-sized pieces and put them into a large salad bowl. Add the watercress, lamb's lettuce, and rocket, and mix together.

2 Pour the dressing over the salad and toss gently. Sprinkle with the chives, and serve at once.

Crunchy coleslaw

SERVES 8 **CALS PER SERVING** 245

1 white cabbage, weighing about 750 g (1½ lb)
150 ml (¼ pint) vinaigrette dressing (page 397)
1 small onion, finely chopped
1 tsp Dijon mustard
salt and black pepper
3 celery stalks, thinly sliced
2 carrots, grated
60 g (2 oz) sultanas
75–90 ml (2½–3 fl oz) mayonnaise (page 397)

1 Cut the cabbage into quarters lengthways and cut out the core. Shred the cabbage finely, using either a sharp knife or the slicing blade of a food processor.

2 Put the cabbage into a large bowl, add the vinaigrette, onion, and Dijon mustard, and season with salt and pepper. Toss to mix thoroughly. Cover the bowl tightly, and leave to chill for about 8 hours.

3 Add the celery, carrots, and sultanas, and toss to mix thoroughly. Stir in the mayonnaise. Cover and chill until ready to serve. Toss the coleslaw well and taste for seasoning before serving.

Herb salad with orange and mustard dressing

SERVES 4–6 **CALS PER SERVING** 207–138

125 g (4 oz) fine asparagus
salt and black pepper
½ romaine lettuce
60 g (2 oz) lamb's lettuce
60 g (2 oz) rocket
1 small bunch of flat-leaf parsley, stalks removed
60 g (2 oz) pine nuts, toasted
60 g (2 oz) SunBlush or sun-dried tomatoes, snipped into small pieces

Dressing

1 orange
2 tbsp olive oil
1 tsp maple syrup
1 tsp wholegrain mustard

1 Trim the asparagus and cut into 2.5 cm (1 in) lengths. Cook in boiling salted water for about 3 minutes until just tender. Drain and refresh under cold running water.

2 Break the romaine lettuce into manageable pieces and mix with the lamb's lettuce, rocket, and parsley leaves in a salad bowl. Add the asparagus, pine nuts, and tomatoes, and toss gently.

3 Remove the zest of the orange with a zester and add the strips to the salad. Squeeze the juice from half of the orange to give about 3 tbsp, then mix with the remaining dressing ingredients and seasoning to taste. Toss the salad with the dressing just before serving.

Crunchy oriental salad

SERVES 6 **CALS PER SERVING** 141

1 iceberg or romaine lettuce
175 g (6 oz) ready-to-eat bean sprouts
6 spring onions, thinly sliced on the diagonal
1 green pepper, halved, deseeded, and thinly sliced
2 tbsp toasted sesame seeds

Dressing

3 tbsp sunflower or olive oil
1 tsp sesame oil
1 tbsp white wine vinegar
1 garlic clove, crushed
1 cm (½ in) piece of fresh root ginger, peeled and grated
½ tsp caster sugar, or to taste
salt and black pepper

1 Tear the lettuce leaves into bite-sized pieces. Put the lettuce, bean sprouts, spring onions, and pepper into a salad bowl and mix together.

2 Make the dressing: combine the oils, vinegar, garlic, and ginger, and season to taste with sugar, salt, and pepper.

3 Toss the salad with the dressing, sprinkle with the sesame seeds, and serve.

Caesar salad

SERVES 4 **CALS PER SERVING** 421

1 cos or romaine lettuce
4 tbsp olive oil
2 tbsp lemon juice
salt and black pepper
2 hard-boiled eggs, peeled
30 g (1 oz) Parmesan cheese, coarsely grated

Croûtons

3 large slices of thick-cut white bread, crusts removed
4 tbsp olive oil
1 garlic clove, crushed

1 Make the croûtons: cut the bread into small cubes. Heat the olive oil in a frying pan, add the garlic, and cook for 1 minute. Add the bread cubes and cook, stirring, for 1–2 minutes until crisp. Lift out and drain on paper towels.

2 Tear the lettuce leaves into bite-sized pieces and put them into a salad bowl. Whisk the olive oil and lemon juice, season with salt and pepper, and toss with the leaves.

3 Cut the hard-boiled eggs into quarters, and add to the salad. Add the croûtons and Parmesan cheese and toss gently. Serve at once.

CAESAR SALAD WITH ANCHOVIES

Coarsely chop 6 canned anchovy fillets and add to the salad with the hard-boiled eggs in step 3.

Cook's know-how

If you prefer a lighter salad, you can toast the bread to make the croûtons rather than frying it in oil. For a sophisticated change, use 4 hard-boiled quails' eggs, halved, instead of hens' eggs.

Spinach and bacon salad

SERVES 6 **CALS PER SERVING** 436

- 500 g (1 lb) baby spinach leaves, all stalks removed
- 3 large slices of thick-cut white bread, crusts removed
- 4 tbsp sunflower oil
- 1 garlic clove, crushed
- 12 streaky bacon rashers, rinds removed, cut into strips
- 4–5 tbsp vinaigrette or blue cheese dressing (page 397)
- salt and black pepper

1 Tear the spinach leaves into large pieces and put them into a salad bowl.

2 Make the croûtons: cut the bread into small cubes. Heat the sunflower oil in a frying pan, add the garlic, and cook for 1 minute. Add the bread cubes and cook, stirring, for 1–2 minutes until golden and crisp. Lift out the croûtons and drain on paper towels.

3 Add the bacon to the pan and fry for 5 minutes or until crisp. Lift out and drain on paper towels.

4 Sprinkle the bacon over the spinach. Spoon the dressing over the salad, season with salt and pepper, and toss gently. Scatter the croûtons over the salad, and serve at once.

Tomato and onion salad

SERVES 6 **CALS PER SERVING** 166

750 g (1½ lb) ripe but firm tomatoes, thinly sliced
1 mild onion, cut into thin rings
1 tbsp snipped fresh chives

Dressing

90 ml (3 fl oz) extra virgin olive oil
2 tbsp red wine vinegar
¼ tsp caster sugar
salt and black pepper

1 Overlap the tomato slices in circles of diminishing size in a large shallow dish. Arrange the onion rings on top.

2 Make the dressing: combine the olive oil, red wine vinegar, and caster sugar, and add salt and pepper to taste.

3 Spoon the dressing over the tomatoes and onions, cover, and leave to chill for about 2 hours. Sprinkle with the snipped chives before serving.

Tomato and basil salad

SERVES 4–6 **CALS PER SERVING** 146–97

2 beefsteak or slicing tomatoes
4 ripe salad tomatoes
125 g (4 oz) cherry tomatoes
1 yellow pepper, cored, deseeded, and cut into chunks
2 tbsp shredded fresh basil

Dressing

3 tbsp extra virgin olive oil
2 tsp balsamic vinegar
¼ tsp caster sugar
salt and black pepper

1 Make the dressing: combine the olive oil, vinegar, sugar, and salt and pepper to taste.

2 Cut the beefsteak or slicing tomatoes in half lengthways, cut out the cores, and cut each half into four wedges. Thickly slice the salad tomatoes. Halve the cherry tomatoes.

3 Put all the tomatoes and the yellow pepper into a salad bowl, and sprinkle with the dressing. Cover and leave to stand for 1 hour to let the flavours mingle. Sprinkle with the basil just before serving.

Cucumber salad

This Danish-style salad goes well with both grilled or baked fresh fish and smoked fish.

SERVES 4–6 **CALS PER SERVING** 75–50

1 cucumber, peeled and cut in half lengthways
1 tbsp chopped fresh dill

Dressing

2 tbsp hot water
2 tbsp white wine vinegar
1 tbsp sunflower oil
2 tbsp caster sugar
salt and black pepper

1 Scoop out the cucumber seeds. Cut the flesh crosswise into thin slices, and arrange in a serving dish.

2 Make the dressing: whisk together the water, white wine vinegar, oil, sugar, and salt and pepper to taste.

3 Pour the dressing over the cucumber and sprinkle with the dill before serving.

Greek salad

SERVES 4–6 **CALS PER SERVING** 503–335

4 beefsteak or slicing tomatoes
1 cucumber, sliced
250 g (8 oz) feta cheese, diced
24 black olives, pitted
125 ml (4 fl oz) extra virgin olive oil
4 tbsp lemon juice
salt and black pepper
2 tbsp chopped fresh oregano or flat-leaf parsley

1 Halve the tomatoes lengthways, cut out the cores, and cut each half into four wedges.

2 Put the tomatoes into a large salad bowl, and add the cucumber, feta cheese, and olives.

3 Spoon over the olive oil and lemon juice, and add salt and black pepper to taste (do not use too much salt as feta is a salty cheese), then toss gently to mix.

4 Sprinkle the salad with the oregano or parsley before serving.

Potato salad

SERVES 8 **CALS PER SERVING** 357

1 kg (2 lb) new potatoes, scrubbed
salt and black pepper
1 small mild onion, very finely chopped
4 tbsp vinaigrette dressing (page 397)
250 ml (8 fl oz) mayonnaise (page 397), or less if preferred
2 tbsp snipped fresh chives, plus extra to garnish

1 Put the potatoes into a large saucepan of boiling salted water and simmer for 15–20 minutes until tender. Drain the potatoes thoroughly. Cut them into even-sized pieces.

2 Put the potatoes into a large salad bowl and add the chopped onion.

3 While the potatoes are still quite warm, spoon the vinaigrette dressing over them and then toss gently to mix all the ingredients thoroughly.

4 Add the mayonnaise and the chives, and mix together gently. Add salt and pepper to taste, cover, and chill for about 30 minutes (the salad is best served not too cold). Garnish with extra chives before serving.

Carrot julienne salad

SERVES 4–6 **CALS PER SERVING** 79–53

5 carrots
salt and black pepper

Dressing

1 tbsp olive oil
1 tsp white wine vinegar
1 garlic clove, crushed
1 tsp chopped parsley
lemon and fresh chives, to garnish

1 Cut the carrots into matchstick strips. Blanch in a saucepan of salted boiling water for 2–3 minutes. Drain, refresh under cold running water, and drain again.

2 Make the dressing: combine the oil, white wine vinegar, garlic, and parsley, and season with salt and pepper.

3 Put the carrots into a salad bowl, pour over the dressing, and toss to coat evenly. Leave to cool. Garnish with lemon and chives before serving.

Celeriac remoulade

SERVES 4–6 **CALS PER SERVING** 100–66

500 g (1 lb) celeriac
juice of 1 lemon
sliced gherkin and chopped parsley, to garnish

Dressing

150 ml (1/4 pint) plain yogurt
2 tbsp mayonnaise (page 397)
1 tsp finely chopped capers
1/2 tsp Dijon mustard
salt and black pepper

1 Make the dressing: combine the yogurt, mayonnaise, capers, and Dijon mustard, and season with salt and pepper.

2 Peel the celeriac, cut into matchstick-thin strips, and place in a bowl of cold water. Add the lemon juice and toss to prevent discoloration.

3 Drain the celeriac and transfer to a salad bowl. Pour over the dressing and toss gently to mix. Garnish with the gherkins and chopped parsley, and serve at once.

Avocado salad

SERVES 6 **CALS PER SERVING** 240

60 g (2 oz) pine nuts
250 g (8 oz) mixed salad leaves
2 oranges
2 avocados

Dressing

finely grated zest of 1 orange
3 tbsp orange juice
1 tbsp walnut oil
1–2 tsp caster sugar
salt and black pepper

1 Spread the pine nuts on a baking tray, and toast under a hot grill for 2 minutes.

2 Put the salad leaves into a large salad bowl. Peel the oranges, removing the rind and pith, and separate into segments (page 519).

3 Halve, stone, and peel the avocados (page 395). Slice lengthways and mix with the orange segments and pine nuts.

4 Whisk together the dressing ingredients, and pour over the salad. Toss gently and serve.

Tricolore salad

SERVES 4 **CALS PER SERVING** 509

4 beefsteak or slicing tomatoes
salt and black pepper
250 g (8 oz) mozzarella cheese
2 avocados
2 tbsp lemon juice
3–4 tbsp extra virgin olive oil
basil sprigs, to garnish

1 Slice the tomatoes thinly, put into a bowl, and sprinkle with salt and pepper. Thinly slice the mozzarella.

2 Cut the avocados in half lengthways. Twist to loosen the halves and pull them apart. Remove the stones (page 395), score and peel off the skin, then cut the halves crosswise.

3 Cut the avocado quarters into slices lengthways, then sprinkle with lemon juice to prevent discoloration.

4 Arrange the tomato, mozzarella, and avocado slices attractively on a platter. Drizzle with the extra virgin olive oil and garnish with basil sprigs before serving.

Pepperata salad

SERVES 4–6 **CALS PER SERVING** 310–207

2 courgettes, sliced lengthways
1 tbsp olive oil
2 red peppers
2 yellow peppers
150 g (5 oz) watercress
vinaigrette dressing (page 397)

1 Brush the courgette slices on both sides with the olive oil, and cook under a hot grill, about 10 cm (4 in) from the heat, for 1–2 minutes on each side until golden. Leave to cool.

2 Halve the peppers lengthways and remove the cores and seeds. Roast and peel the peppers (see box, right). Cut the flesh into chunks. Cut the courgette slices crosswise.

3 Put the watercress into a large serving bowl. Mix in the peppers and courgettes, pour over the dressing, and toss to coat. Serve at once.

Roasting and peeling peppers

Cook the pepper halves, cut-side down, under a hot grill, 10 cm (4 in) from the heat, until the skin is black and blistered. Seal in a plastic bag and leave to cool. Peel off the skin, using your fingers.

Mushroom salad

SERVES 6 **CALS PER SERVING** 102

3 tbsp sunflower oil
½ tsp ground coriander
750 g (1½ lb) button mushrooms
salt and black pepper
4 celery stalks, thinly sliced
shredded fresh basil, to garnish

Dressing

150 ml (¼ pint) plain yogurt
1 tbsp lemon juice
1 tbsp white wine vinegar
1 tsp Dijon mustard
1 garlic clove, crushed

1 Heat the oil in a frying pan, add the ground coriander, and cook gently, stirring, for 1 minute. Add the mushrooms, season lightly, and cook over a high heat, stirring, for 5 minutes. Lift out with a slotted spoon. Leave to cool.

2 Make the dressing: combine the yogurt, lemon juice, vinegar, Dijon mustard, garlic, and salt and pepper to taste. Pour the dressing over the mushrooms, and toss to mix. Cover and chill for 8 hours. Stir in the celery and garnish with basil before serving.

Waldorf salad

SERVES 4 **CALS PER SERVING** 469

500 g (1 lb) crisp red-skinned apples, cored and diced
juice of ½ lemon
4 celery stalks, thickly sliced
150 ml (¼ pint) mayonnaise (page 397)
salt and black pepper
90 g (3 oz) walnut pieces, coarsely chopped
chopped parsley, to garnish

1 Put the diced apples into a bowl, pour the lemon juice over the top, and stir to coat thoroughly to prevent discoloration. Transfer to a salad bowl and add the celery.

2 Spoon the mayonnaise over the salad, season with salt and pepper, and toss gently to mix. Cover and chill until required. Stir in the walnut pieces and garnish with chopped parsley just before serving.

Potato, apple, and celery salad

SERVES 6 **CALS PER SERVING** 332

750 g (1½ lb) new potatoes, scrubbed
salt and black pepper
75 ml (2½ fl oz) vinaigrette dressing (page 397)
6 celery stalks, sliced
1 small red onion, very finely sliced
2 red-skinned apples, such as Red Delicious or Spartan, cored and diced
125 ml (4 fl oz) mayonnaise (page 397)
2 tbsp snipped fresh chives, to garnish

1 Put the potatoes into a large saucepan of boiling salted water and simmer gently for 10–15 minutes until just tender. Drain, leave to cool, then cut in half.

2 Put the potato halves into a large salad bowl, add the vinaigrette dressing, and toss gently while the potatoes are still warm. Leave to cool.

3 Add the celery, onion, and apples to the cold potatoes. Mix gently until all the ingredients are thoroughly coated with dressing, then season with salt and pepper. Cover and chill for at least 1 hour.

4 Gently stir in the mayonnaise, taste for seasoning, then sprinkle with the chives and serve at once.

Aubergine with fresh pesto

SERVES 4 **CALS PER SERVING** 499

1 large aubergine
75 ml ($2\frac{1}{2}$ fl oz) olive oil, plus extra for greasing
2–3 tsp balsamic or wine vinegar
fresh pesto (see box, right)
shredded fresh basil, to garnish

1 Cut the aubergine crosswise into thin slices and arrange in a single layer on a lightly oiled baking tray. Brush the slices with one-quarter of the oil, place under a hot grill, 7 cm (3 in) from the heat, and grill for 5 minutes or until lightly browned. Turn, brush with one-third of the remaining oil, and grill for 5 minutes more.

2 Sprinkle the remaining oil and the vinegar over the aubergine slices. Leave to cool. Spread pesto over one side of each slice, garnish with fresh basil, and serve at room temperature.

Fresh pesto

Purée 60 g (2 oz) grated Parmesan cheese, 1 garlic clove, 60 g (2 oz) pine nuts, 60 g (2 oz) fresh basil leaves, and salt and pepper to taste in a food processor until almost smooth.

Add 4 tbsp olive oil gradually, with the blades turning, scraping the side of the bowl occasionally with a rubber spatula to ensure that all of the mixture is incorporated.

Salade niçoise

SERVES 4 **CALS PER SERVING** 530

250 g (8 oz) French beans, cut in half crosswise
salt and black pepper
2 hard-boiled eggs
1 cos or romaine lettuce
½ cucumber, sliced
4 tomatoes, quartered
1 x 200 g can tuna, drained
1 small mild onion, very thinly sliced
1 x 50 g can anchovy fillets, drained
12 pitted black olives
chopped parsley, to garnish

Dressing
150 ml (¼ pint) olive oil
3 tbsp white wine vinegar
1 garlic clove, crushed
½ tsp Dijon mustard

1 Cook the French beans in boiling salted water for 4–5 minutes until just tender. Drain, rinse under cold running water, and drain again.

2 Peel the shells from the eggs, and cut the eggs into wedges lengthways.

3 Make the dressing: combine the oil, vinegar, garlic, and mustard, and season with salt and pepper.

4 Tear the lettuce leaves into pieces and place on a large serving plate. Arrange the cucumber and beans on top of the lettuce.

5 Arrange the tomatoes and eggs on the serving plate. Coarsely flake the tuna with a fork and place in the middle. Arrange the onion, anchovy fillets, and olives over the tuna. Pour over the dressing, garnish with parsley, and serve at once.

Three-bean salad

SERVES 4 **CALS PER SERVING** 315

250 g (8 oz) French beans, cut in half crosswise
salt and black pepper
1 x 400 g can chick peas, drained and rinsed
1 x 400 g can red kidney beans, drained and rinsed
10 pitted black olives, halved
chopped parsley, to garnish

Dressing
4 tbsp Greek-style yogurt
3 tbsp olive oil
3 tbsp red wine vinegar
2 tsp Dijon mustard
¼ tsp caster sugar, or to taste

1 Cook the French beans in boiling salted water for 4–5 minutes until just tender. Drain, rinse under cold running water, and drain again.

2 Make the dressing: combine the yogurt, oil, red wine vinegar, and mustard, and season with sugar, salt, and pepper to taste.

3 Put the chick peas, red kidney beans, and French beans into a large bowl. Pour the dressing over the beans and stir gently to mix. Cover and leave to stand for 1 hour. Add the olives, sprinkle with the chopped parsley, and serve at once.

THREE-BEAN SALAD WITH BACON

Substitute 250 g (8 oz) cooked, shelled and skinned broad beans for the chick peas, and omit the olives. Cut 60 g (2 oz) streaky bacon rashers into strips, and dry-fry until crisp and golden. Sprinkle over the salad just before serving.

Puy lentil salad

SERVES 6 **CALS PER SERVING** 181

250 g (8 oz) Puy lentils, rinsed
3 tbsp olive oil
2 tbsp balsamic vinegar
salt and black pepper
1 bunch of spring onions, trimmed and finely sliced
3 tbsp chopped fresh flat-leaf parsley

1 Pour the lentils into a medium saucepan, cover with plenty of cold water, and bring to a boil. Reduce the heat, cover, and simmer for 15 minutes or until the lentils are tender.

2 Drain the lentils well, tip into a serving bowl, and add the olive oil and vinegar, and plenty of seasoning (warm lentils absorb the flavours of the dressing better than cold lentils). Leave to cool, then mix in the spring onions and chopped parsley just before serving.

Italian pesto salad

SERVES 4–6 **CALS PER SERVING** 252–168

375 g (12 oz) broccoli, cut into bite-sized florets
375 g (12 oz) cauliflower, cut into bite-sized florets
about 12 black olives, pitted

Pesto

30 g (1 oz) fresh basil
1 garlic clove
1 tbsp pine nuts
30 g (1 oz) Parmesan cheese, grated
salt and black pepper
5 tbsp extra virgin olive oil

1 Make the pesto: put the basil, garlic, pine nuts, Parmesan and seasoning into a small food processor and process until the basil is finely chopped. With the machine running, add the oil in a fine stream until the paste is creamy. Check the seasoning.

2 Blanch the broccoli and cauliflower florets in boiling salted water for about 2 minutes (they should retain plenty of bite, so take care not to overcook them). Drain and refresh under cold running water. Drain again, then toss with the pesto. Scatter with the olives and chill before serving.

Tabbouleh

SERVES 4 **CALS PER SERVING** 193

125 g (4 oz) bulgur wheat
3 tbsp extra virgin olive oil
juice of 2 lemons
salt and black pepper
¼ bunch spring onions, finely sliced
½ cucumber, peeled, deseeded, and finely diced
6 tbsp chopped fresh mint
6 tbsp chopped fresh flat-leaf parsley

1 Soak the bulgur wheat in boiling water for 30 minutes. Drain well, tip into a serving bowl, and add the olive oil, lemon juice, and plenty of seasoning. Do this immediately while the wheat is still warm so that it absorbs the maximum amount of flavour.

2 Add the spring onions, cucumber, and freshly chopped herbs to the bowl. Stir well and check the seasoning. Chill before serving.

Rice salad

SERVES 6 **CALS PER SERVING** 345

250 g (8 oz) long grain rice
salt and black pepper
125 g (4 oz) frozen peas
125 g (4 oz) frozen sweetcorn kernels
1 red pepper, halved, deseeded, and diced
2 tbsp chopped fresh coriander

Dressing

90 ml (3 fl oz) olive oil
3 tbsp white wine vinegar
1 tsp Dijon mustard
1 garlic clove, crushed

1 Cook the rice in boiling salted water for 12–15 minutes until just tender, adding the peas and sweetcorn for the last 3 minutes. Drain, rinse in boiling water, and drain again. Transfer to a bowl.

2 Make the dressing: combine the olive oil, white wine vinegar, mustard, and garlic, and season with salt and pepper. Pour over the rice while still warm, stir gently, and leave to cool.

3 Add the red pepper, and coriander to the rice, and stir to combine. Serve at once.

Wild rice salad

SERVES 6 **CALS PER SERVING** 369

250 g (8 oz) mixed long grain and wild rice
salt and black pepper
175 g (6 oz) French beans, cut in half crosswise
2 tbsp chopped parsley
60 g (2 oz) button mushrooms, thinly sliced
60 g (2 oz) walnut pieces

Dressing

4 tbsp sunflower oil
2 tbsp walnut oil
2 tbsp white wine vinegar
1 tsp Dijon mustard

1 Cook the rice in boiling salted water for 15 minutes, or according to packet instructions, until just tender. Drain, rinse in boiling water, and drain again. Transfer to a large bowl.

2 Cook the beans in boiling salted water for 4–5 minutes until just tender. Drain, rinse in cold water, and drain again.

3 Make the dressing: combine the oils, white wine vinegar, mustard, and salt and pepper to taste. Pour over the rice while still warm, stir, and leave to cool.

4 Add the beans, parsley, mushrooms, and walnuts to the rice. Stir before serving.

Couscous salad

SERVES 6 **CALS PER SERVING** 280

½ tsp crushed dried red chillies
90 ml (3 fl oz) olive oil
250 g (8 oz) couscous
500 ml (16 fl oz) boiling water
3–4 tbsp sultanas
5 cm (2 in) piece of fresh root ginger, peeled and grated
salt and black pepper
3–4 tbsp white wine vinegar
5 ripe tomatoes, diced
1 onion, chopped
3 spring onions, thinly sliced
2 tbsp chopped fresh mint, plus extra to garnish

1 Combine the chillies and olive oil, and set aside.

2 Put the couscous into a bowl, stir in the measured water, sultanas, ginger, and a good pinch of salt. Cover and leave to stand for 10 minutes.

3 Stir in the chilli oil, white wine vinegar, tomatoes, onion, spring onions, and mint. Season with salt and pepper to taste, and garnish with chopped mint before serving.

Bulgur wheat salad

SERVES 4 **CALS PER SERVING** 280

175 g (6 oz) bulgur wheat
4–5 tbsp vinaigrette dressing (page 397)
juice of 1 lemon
3 tomatoes, diced
4 spring onions, chopped
3 tbsp chopped parsley
3 tbsp chopped fresh mint
salt and black pepper
parsley sprigs, to garnish

1 Put the bulgur wheat into a large bowl, cover with cold water, and leave to stand for 30 minutes.

2 Drain the bulgur wheat, pressing out as much of the liquid as possible. Transfer to a salad bowl, and mix in the vinaigrette dressing, lemon juice, tomatoes, spring onions, parsley, and mint. Season with salt and pepper, toss well, and garnish with parsley. Serve at room temperature.

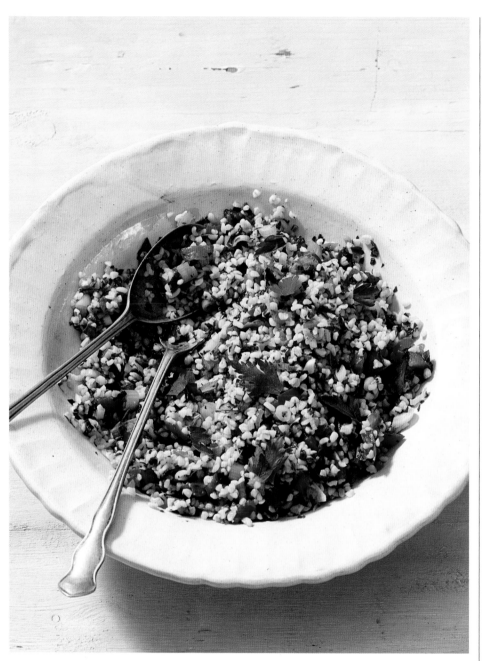

Pasta and mackerel salad

SERVES 6 **CALS PER SERVING** 643

500 g (1 lb) pasta shells
salt and black pepper
2 courgettes, sliced
125 g (4 oz) French beans, cut in half crosswise
2 oranges
375 g (12 oz) peppered smoked mackerel fillets
30 g (1 oz) walnut pieces

Dressing

juice of 1 orange
2 tbsp sunflower oil
1 tbsp walnut oil
2 tbsp chopped parsley

1 Cook the pasta shells in a large saucepan of boiling salted water for 8–10 minutes until just tender. Drain, rinse under cold running water, and drain again.

2 Cook the courgettes and French beans in another pan of boiling salted water for 4–5 minutes until tender. Drain, rinse, and drain again.

3 Peel and segment the oranges (page 519) and set aside. Remove the skin and any bones from the mackerel, then flake the flesh into large pieces.

4 Make the dressing: combine the orange juice, sunflower and walnut oils, and parsley, and season with salt and pepper.

5 Put the pasta, courgettes, French beans, orange segments, flaked mackerel, and walnut pieces into a large salad bowl. Add the dressing and toss gently so that the fish does not break up. Leave to chill in the refrigerator for at least 30 minutes before serving.

Pasta salad with peppers

SERVES 6 **CALS PER SERVING** 370

500 g (1 lb) pasta bows
salt and black pepper
1 red pepper, halved, deseeded, and diced
1 green pepper, halved, deseeded, and diced
3 spring onions, sliced diagonally
4 tbsp mayonnaise (page 397)
spring onion tops, sliced, to garnish

1 Cook the pasta bows in a large saucepan of boiling salted water for 8–10 minutes until just tender.

2 Drain, rinse under cold running water, and drain again. Leave to cool.

3 Put the pasta, peppers, and spring onions into a salad bowl, and season with salt and pepper. Add the mayonnaise, stir well to coat all the ingredients evenly, then chill for 30 minutes. Garnish with spring onions before serving.

PASTA SALAD WITH MANGETOUT AND SESAME SEEDS

Substitute 125 g (4 oz) blanched mangetout for the red and green peppers. Omit the mayonnaise. Mix together 2 tbsp white wine vinegar, 1 tbsp sunflower oil, and 1 tsp sesame oil, and pour over the salad. Taste for seasoning. Substitute 2 tbsp toasted sesame seeds for the spring onion garnish, and serve at once.

Yeast cookery

In this chapter...

Four seasons pizza
page 454

Pissaladière with Mediterranean vegetables
page 456

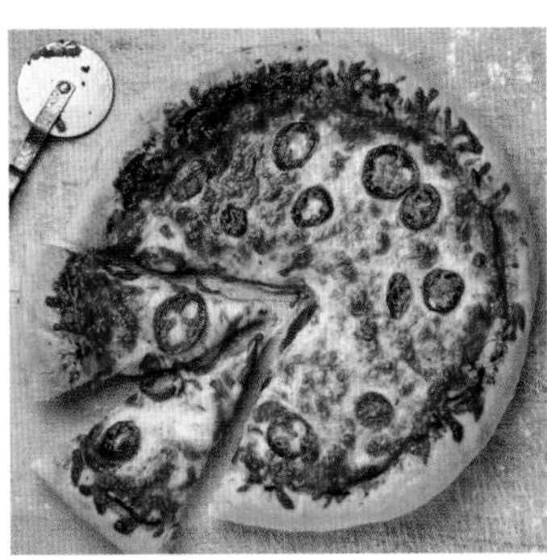
Spicy deep-pan pizza
page 456

Croissants
page 458

Cinnamon rolls
page 462

Brioches
page 459

Danish pastries
page 461

Hot cross buns
page 462

Chelsea buns
page 464

Griddled English muffins
page 464

Crumpets
page 466

Lardy cake
page 466

Yeast cookery know-how

The pleasure of baking bread is legendary. From making and kneading the dough to slicing a freshly baked loaf, the experience is a thoroughly satisfying one that cooks the world over have shared for centuries. Indeed, yeast cookery is perhaps the most popular of all kitchen crafts.

From this rich history comes a wide variety of recipes, both sweet and savoury, many of which are easily made; others are more time-consuming to prepare. Crumpets and hot cross buns, Danish pastries and croissants, wholemeal bread and crispy, thin-crusted pizzas are all equally delicious.

Yeast cookery ingredients

There is a large range of flours from which to choose, each with its own unique texture and flavour. The different types of yeast, on the other hand, vary simply in their method of preparation.

Flour

The best flours to use for yeast doughs are those labelled "strong". These are milled from hard wheat with a high gluten content and produce a good open-textured bread. Ordinary plain flour, which contains a higher proportion of soft wheat, can be used for yeast doughs, but the result will be a more close-textured and crumbly loaf.

The flour most commonly used for breadmaking is white wheat flour. Other wheat flours include wholemeal flour, also called whole wheat, which is milled from the entire wheat kernel, including the bran and germ; brown or wheatmeal flour, which contains more of the bran and wheat germ than white flour; granary flour, which is brown flour with malted wheat flakes and cracked and whole wheat grains added.

Other grains and cereals, such as barley, buckwheat, maize (corn), millet, oats, and rye, are milled into flour for bread-making. Soya beans are also ground into a flour-like powder. Most of these flours are low in gluten, or contain no gluten at all, so they are normally combined with wheat flour to prevent the bread from being too dense.

Fresh yeast

This form of yeast, which looks like creamy-grey putty, is perishable and so needs to be refrigerated (keep it in an airtight container for up to 4–5 days). You will find it at a bakery where they bake on the premises or at a healthfood shop. Fresh yeast should be almost odourless, with only a slightly yeasty smell, and it should break apart cleanly. It needs to be blended with warm liquid and "fed" with sugar, then left to become frothy before mixing with flour. To substitute fresh yeast for dried yeast, use double the weight, i.e. 15 g (½ oz) fresh yeast for 7 g (¼ oz) dried.

Dried yeast

Fast-action dried yeast (also known as easy-blend) is added directly to flour with other dry ingredients. Ordinary dried yeast needs to be blended with warm liquid and a little sugar before mixing with flour. After 5 minutes or so, the yeast should dissolve and the mixture should be foamy. If this is not the result, discard the yeast and start again. Dried yeast will keep for up to 6 months in a cool place.

Lukewarm water (40–43°C/105–110°F) should be used to blend and dissolve both fresh and ordinary dried yeast. If the water is too hot it will kill the yeast.

Bread machines

Although keen bakers maintain that bread made in a machine can never be as good to eat as a loaf made by hand, bread machines are increasingly popular, perhaps because they mean you can enjoy a freshly baked loaf at any time. Pop in the ingredients and the machine will mix, knead, raise, knock up, and bake for you. Just be sure to follow the manufacturer's recipes and instructions.

Freezing

It is a good idea to halve or quarter loaves before freezing so you can take out what you need. Pack in moisture-proof wrapping and seal well. Most loaves can be frozen for up to 4 months; if enriched with milk or fruit, storage time is 3 months. Thaw, still wrapped, at room temperature. Bread with a crust, such as baguette, does not freeze well as the crust lifts off.

Testing loaves

At the end of cooking, bread should be well risen, firm, and golden brown. To test if it is thoroughly cooked, tip out of the tin or lift off the baking tray and tap the base. The bread should have a hollow, drum-like sound. If it does not sound hollow, return it to the oven to bake for a further 5 minutes, then remove it and test again.

Successful home baking

The quantity of liquid given in a recipe can only be a guide because the absorbency of flour can vary. The quantity of liquid that flour can absorb depends on temperature and humidity, how much hard wheat the flour contains (proportions vary from one brand to another) and whether it is wholemeal or white.

Dough can be kneaded in a food processor or an electric mixer fitted with a dough hook, as well as by hand.

Dough rises quickest in a warm environment. A slow rise, such as in the fridge overnight, gives bread more flavour.

To test if dough has risen sufficiently, push in a finger; when withdrawn, an indentation should remain in the dough.

Glazes and toppings

Breads and rolls can be glazed before or after baking to add flavour and, depending on the glaze, to make the crust soft or shiny and crisp. Apply the glaze thinly, using a pastry brush. Here are a few suggestions for different glazes:

- water (before baking) for a crisp crust
- milk or cream (before baking) for a soft crust
- egg or egg yolk beaten with a pinch of salt (before baking) or butter (after baking) for a shiny crust
- sugar and water (after baking) for a shiny crust

Toppings such as wheat or barley flakes, woody herbs such as rosemary, sunflower or sesame seeds, poppyseeds, grated cheese, chopped nuts, and coarse sea salt can be sprinkled over glazed breads and rolls before baking. Sweetened breads are often sprinkled with sugar or a spice-and-sugar mixture after baking.

Making a yeast dough

Making bread is not difficult, nor does it take up a lot of time – the most lengthy parts of the procedure, the rising and baking, are done by the bread itself. Here are the basic techniques, using fast-action dried yeast.

1 Sift the flour into a large bowl, and then mix in the yeast and any other dry ingredients. Make a well in the middle and pour in almost all of the measured liquid (the precise amount is difficult to gauge).

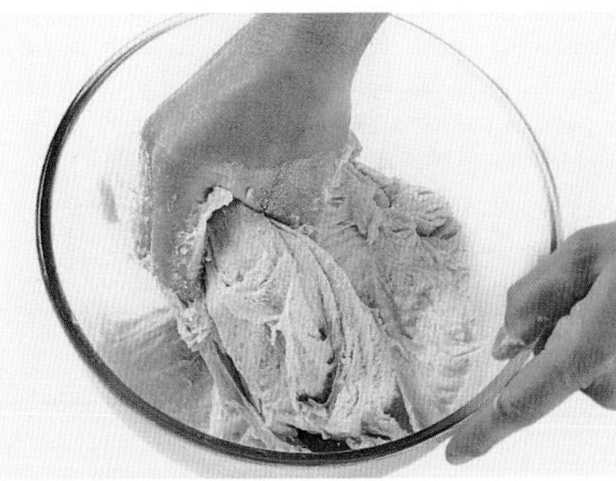

2 Using your fingers, mix the liquid ingredients together, then gradually incorporate the flour. Mix thoroughly until a soft, quite sticky dough is formed, adding the remaining liquid if it is needed.

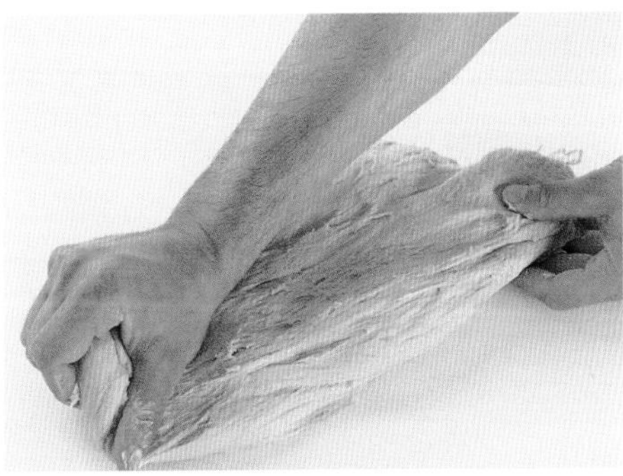

3 Turn the dough on to a lightly floured work surface and knead: fold it over towards you, then push it down and away with the heel of your hand. Turn the dough, fold it, and push it away again. Continue kneading for 5–10 minutes until the dough is elastic and smooth. Doughs made with strong wheat flour take longer to knead than those made with soft flour.

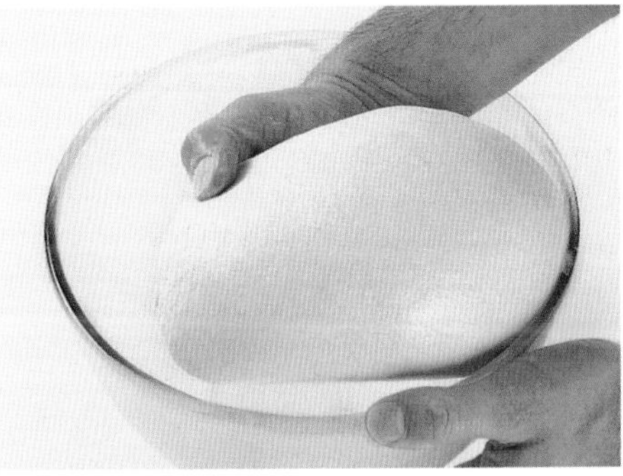

4 Shape the dough into a ball. Put the dough into a lightly oiled bowl and turn to coat it all over with oil. Cover with oiled cling film or a damp tea towel and leave to rise in a warm, draught-free place such as an airing cupboard (or in a cool place for a longer time).

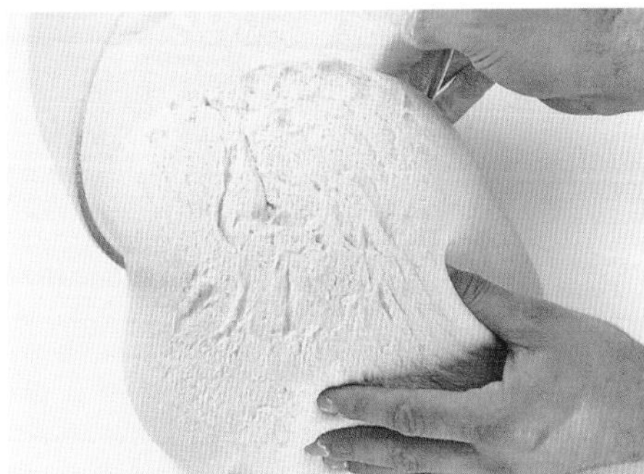

5 When the dough has doubled in size, turn it on to a lightly floured work surface and knock out the air by punching the dough gently. Knead the dough vigorously for 2–3 minutes until smooth and elastic.

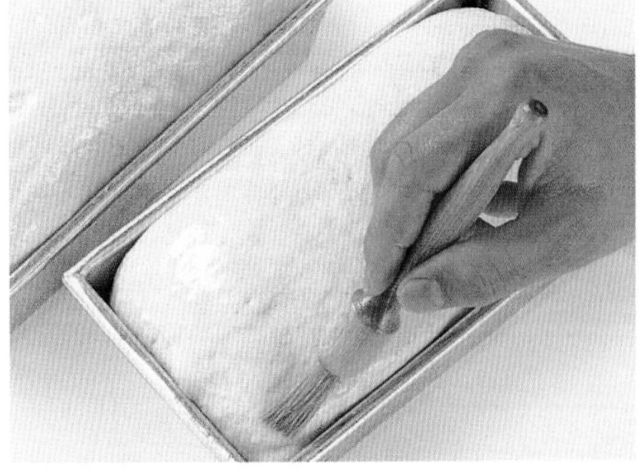

6 Shape the dough as directed. Cover loosely with cling film or a dry tea towel and leave in a warm, draught-free place to rise until doubled in size again. Bake according to the recipe.

Shaping loaves

Because of the elastic quality of dough, it can very easily be formed into a variety of different shapes. Here are some of the more traditional ones.

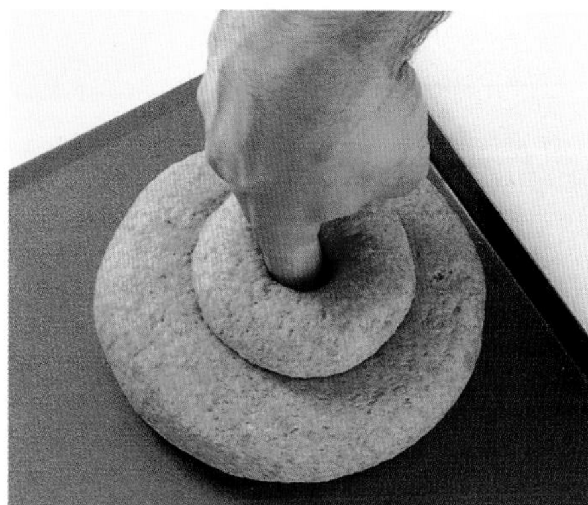

Cottage loaf

Cut off one-third of the dough. Roll each piece into a ball and put the small ball on top of the large ball. Push a forefinger through the middle all the way to the base.

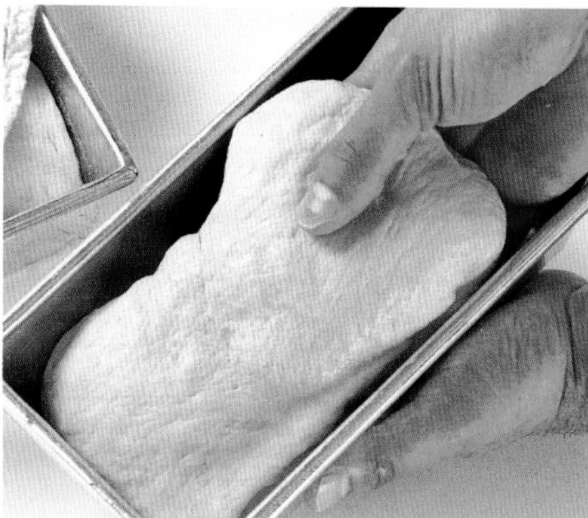

Tin loaf

Shape the dough into a cylinder a little longer than the tin, then tuck the ends under so the shape will just fit the tin. Place the dough in the tin, with the joins underneath.

Round loaf

Roll the dough into a ball, then pull up the sides of the ball to the middle, to make a tight, round ball. Turn the ball over and put on a baking tray.

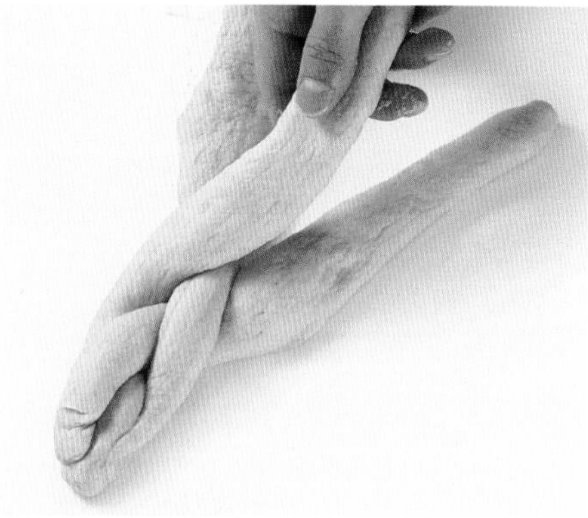

Plaited loaf

Divide the dough into three and roll each piece into a strand. Place them side by side and pinch together at one end. Plait the strands, pinching them together at the other end to secure.

Crown loaf

Divide the dough into nine even-sized pieces and shape each into a ball. Place eight balls around the side of a deep cake tin, then place one ball in the middle to form a crown. The balls will rise to fill the tin.

Butter shapes

When you are entertaining, butter looks much better if it is shaped rather than just being left in a block. These shapes can be prepared in advance, tray frozen, and packed in freezer bags, then thawed when needed. If you like, flavour the butter with herbs, garlic, or mustard to serve with savoury breads, and spices, honey, or sugar for sweet breads.

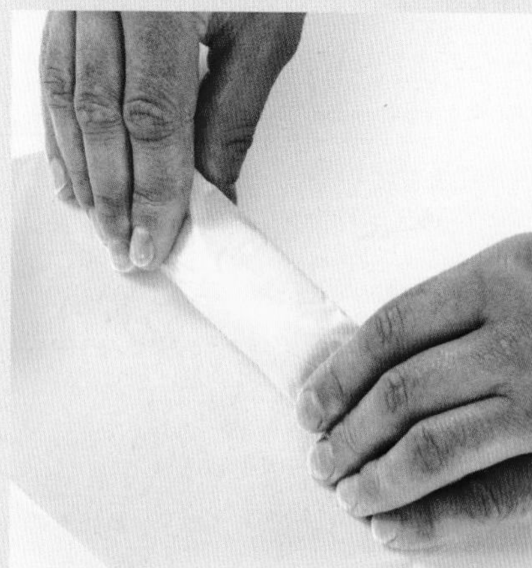

Discs Use butter at room temperature. Beat it with a wooden spoon until it is soft, then beat in any flavourings. Spoon on to a sheet of greaseproof paper and spread into a rough sausage, then roll in the paper until it forms a neat sausage shape. Wrap the butter tightly in the greaseproof paper and twist the ends to secure. Chill in the refrigerator until firm. Unwrap and slice the butter across into thin discs. Use immediately or keep chilled, or freeze until required.

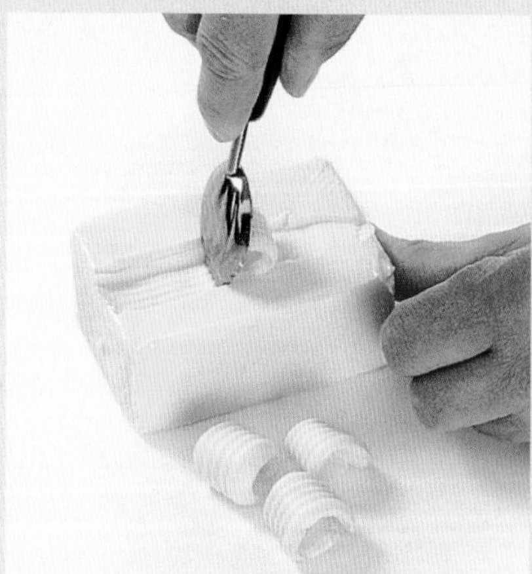

Curls Use a well-chilled block of butter. Warm a butter curler in hot water, then dry it. Pull the curler lengthways along the surface of the block, to shave off curls. Use the butter curls immediately, or keep them in iced water in the refrigerator until required.

Farmhouse loaf

MAKES 1 large loaf **CALS** 2790

750 g (1½ lb) strong white flour, plus extra for dusting
30 g (1 oz) butter or baking spread
2 tsp salt
1 x 7 g sachet fast-action dried yeast
about 450 ml (¾ pint) lukewarm water
sunflower oil, for greasing

1 KG (2 LB) LOAF TIN

1 Put the flour into a bowl, rub in the butter or baking spread with your fingertips until the mixture resembles breadcrumbs, then stir in the salt and yeast, and make a well in the middle. Add enough water to mix to a soft dough that is quite sticky.

2 Knead the dough on a lightly floured surface until smooth and elastic. Shape into a round and place in a lightly oiled large bowl.

3 Cover the bowl with oiled cling film and leave to rise in a warm place for 1–1½ hours or until the dough has doubled in size.

4 Turn out the dough on to a lightly floured surface and knock back with your fists. Knead vigorously for 2–3 minutes until the dough is smooth and elastic.

5 Lightly oil the loaf tin. Shape the dough to fit the tin, tucking the ends under to give a smooth top, and place in the tin. Cover loosely with oiled cling film and leave to rise in a warm place for 30 minutes or until the dough reaches the top of the tin.

6 Lightly dust the top of the loaf with flour and bake in a preheated oven at 230°C (210°C fan, Gas 8) for 30–35 minutes until golden. Turn the loaf out and tap the base: it should sound hollow if it is cooked. Leave the loaf to cool on a wire rack.

Wholemeal country loaf

MAKES 1 large loaf **CALS** 2975

750 g (1½ lb) strong wholemeal flour, plus extra for dusting
30 g (1 oz) butter or baking spread
1 tbsp caster sugar
2 tsp salt
1 x 7 g sachet fast-action dried yeast
about 450 ml (¾ pint) lukewarm water
sunflower oil, for greasing
milk, for glazing
cracked wheat, for sprinkling

20 CM (8 IN) ROUND CAKE TIN

1 Put the flour into a large bowl. Rub in the butter or baking spread with your fingertips, then stir in the sugar, salt, and yeast. Make a well in the middle and add enough water to mix to a soft, quite sticky, dough.

2 Knead the dough on a lightly floured surface until smooth and elastic, then shape into a round.

3 Place the dough in a lightly oiled large bowl, cover with oiled cling film, and leave to rise in a warm place for 1–1½ hours or until the dough has doubled in size.

4 Turn out the dough on to a lightly floured surface and knock back with your fists. Knead for 2–3 minutes until smooth.

5 Shape the dough into a round and put it into the lightly oiled cake tin. Flatten with your hand, then mark into eight wedges with a knife. Cover loosely with oiled cling film and leave to rise in a warm place for 1–1½ hours or until doubled in size.

6 Brush the loaf with milk and sprinkle with cracked wheat. Bake in a preheated oven at 230°C (210°C fan, Gas 8) for 20–25 minutes. Tap the base to see if the loaf is cooked: it should sound hollow. Leave to cool on a wire rack.

Dinner rolls

MAKES 18 **CALS EACH** 95

500 g (1 lb) strong white flour
1 tsp salt
1 x 7 g sachet fast-action dried yeast
about 350 ml (12 fl oz) lukewarm water
sunflower oil, for greasing

1 Put the flour into a large bowl, then stir in the salt and yeast. Make a well in the middle and pour in enough water to make a soft, quite sticky, dough.

2 Knead the dough on a lightly floured surface until smooth and elastic. Shape into a round and place in a lightly oiled large bowl. Cover with oiled cling film and leave to rise in a warm place for 1–1½ hours or until doubled in size.

3 Lightly oil two or three lined baking trays. Divide the dough into 18 pieces. Shape into balls, folding the sides to the middles to form round balls. Arrange on the trays, leaving room for expansion. Cover loosely with oiled cling film and leave to rise in a warm place for 20 minutes or until doubled in size.

4 Bake in a preheated oven at 190°C (170°C fan, Gas 5) for 20 minutes or until golden. Leave to cool on a wire rack.

Multi-grain loaf

MAKES 2 small loaves **CALS PER LOAF** 1495

150 g (5 oz) wheat flakes
45 g (1½ oz) linseed
300 ml (½pint) boiling water
500 g (1 lb) strong white flour, plus extra for dusting
125 g (4 oz) strong wholemeal flour
60 g (2 oz) sunflower seeds
20 g (3/4 oz) salt
1 x 7 g sachet fast-action dried yeast
about 350 ml (12 fl oz) lukewarm water
sunflower oil, for greasing
milk, for glazing
wheat flakes, to decorate

2 X 500 G (1 LB) LOAF TINS

1 Put the wheat flakes and linseed into a large bowl, pour the boiling water over, and stir. Cover and set aside for 30 minutes or until the water has been absorbed.

2 Stir the flours, sunflower seeds, salt, and yeast into the wheat-flake mixture. Make a well in the middle and add enough water to mix to a soft, quite sticky, dough.

3 Knead the dough on a lightly floured surface until smooth and elastic. Shape into a round and place in a lightly oiled large bowl. Cover with oiled cling film and leave to rise in a warm place for 1–1½ hours or until doubled in size.

4 Turn out the dough on to a floured surface and knock back with your fists. Knead for 2–3 minutes until smooth and elastic once again.

5 Oil the tins. Divide the dough in half, and shape into oblongs, tucking the ends under to give smooth tops. Place in the tins. Alternatively, shape into two rounds and place on oiled baking trays. Cover loosely with oiled cling film and leave to rise in a warm place for 20–30 minutes.

6 Brush the loaves with milk to glaze and sprinkle with wheat flakes. Bake in a preheated oven at 230°C (210°C fan, Gas 8) for 10 minutes; reduce the oven temperature to 200°C (180°C fan, Gas 6), and bake for 20–25 minutes. Tap the bases to see if the loaves are cooked: they should sound hollow. Leave to cool on a wire rack.

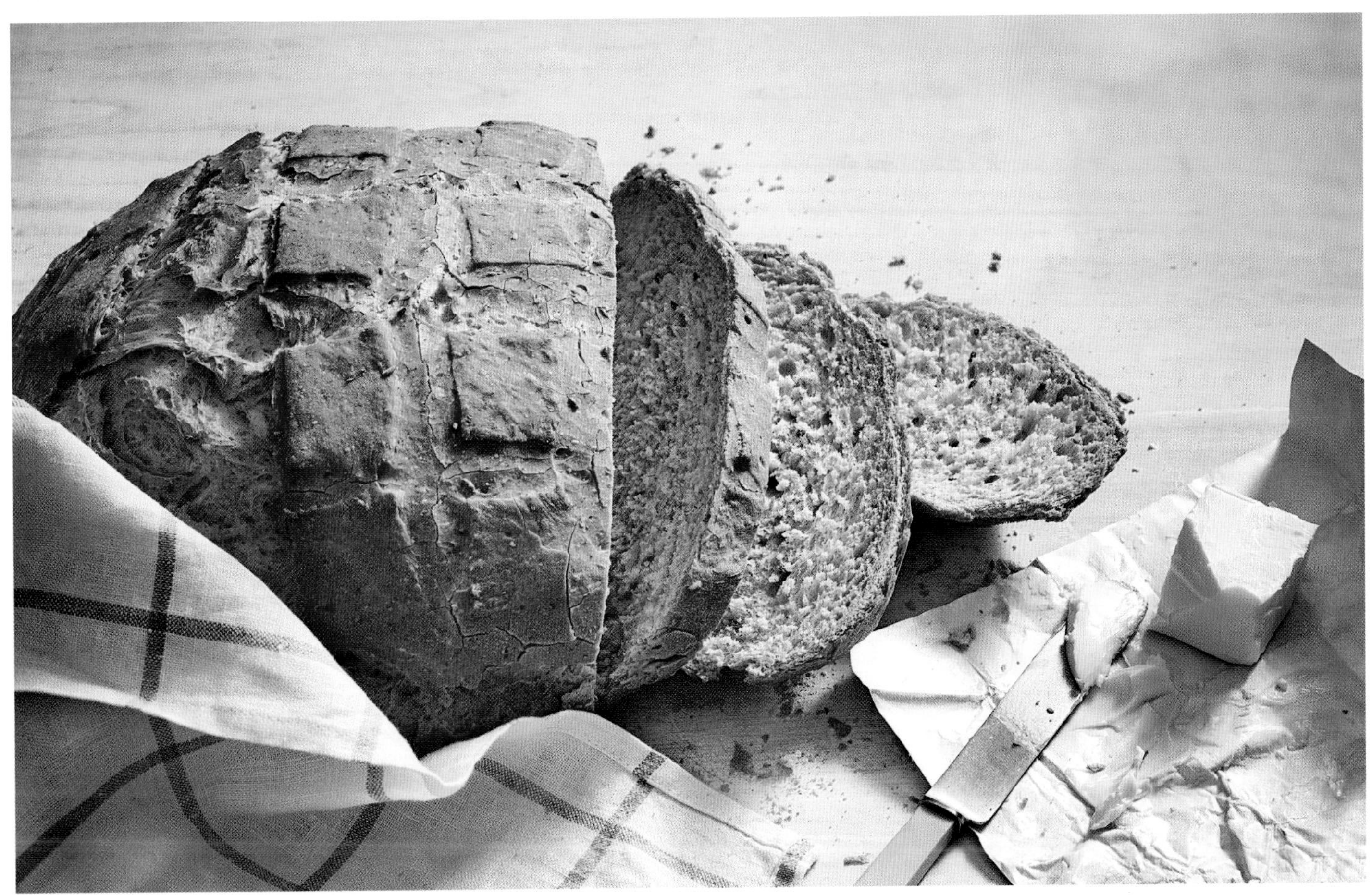

Sourdough rye bread

A satisfying and tasty country bread from Eastern Europe, this rye bread is not difficult to make but, because the starter has to be left to ferment for a couple of days, it does require a little forward planning.

MAKES 2 large loaves **CALS PER LOAF** 3329

- 1.5 kg (3 lb) strong white flour, plus extra for sprinkling
- 1 x 7 g sachet fast-action dried yeast
- 250 ml (8 fl oz) lukewarm water
- 3 tbsp caraway seeds (optional)
- 1 tbsp salt
- sunflower oil, for greasing
- polenta, for sprinkling

Sourdough starter

- 250 g (8 oz) strong white flour
- 1 tsp fast-action dried yeast
- 250 ml (8 fl oz) lukewarm water

Sponge

- 200 g (7 oz) rye flour
- 250 ml (8 fl oz) lukewarm water

1 Make the sourdough starter: put the flour into a large bowl and stir in the yeast. Make a well in the middle, pour in the lukewarm water, and mix together.

2 Cover tightly and leave at room temperature for 2 days. Alternatively, leave the starter in the refrigerator for up to 1 week.

3 Make the sponge: put the rye flour into a large bowl, add the sourdough starter and the lukewarm water, and stir to mix. Cover tightly and leave at room temperature for 8 hours or chill in the refrigerator for up to 2 days.

4 Put the flour into a bowl, add the sponge mixture, yeast, lukewarm water, caraway seeds (if using) and salt, and mix to a soft and slightly sticky dough.

5 Turn the dough into a large ungreased bowl, sprinkle the top with flour, cover loosely with oiled cling film, and leave to rise in a warm place for 2 hours or until doubled in size.

6 Lightly sprinkle two baking trays with polenta. Turn out the dough on to a lightly floured surface and knock back with your fists. Knead for 3–4 minutes until smooth and elastic. Halve the dough and form into two rounds. Score the tops with a sharp knife.

7 Place on the baking trays, cover loosely with oiled cling film, and leave to rise in a warm place for 45 minutes or until doubled in size.

8 Place the loaves in a preheated oven at 220°C (200°C fan, Gas 7). Fill a roasting tin with boiling water and place at the bottom of the oven. Bake the loaves for about 35 minutes until they are lightly browned. Tap the bases to see if the loaves are cooked: they should sound hollow. Leave to cool on wire racks.

Milk rolls

MAKES 18 **CALS EACH** 188

750 g (1½ lb) strong white flour, plus extra for dusting
60 g (2 oz) butter or white vegetable fat
2 tsp salt
1 x 7 g sachet fast-action dried yeast
about 450 ml (¾ pint) lukewarm milk
sunflower oil, for greasing
1 egg, beaten
poppy seeds and sesame seeds, for sprinkling

1 Put the flour into a large bowl, rub in the butter, then stir in the salt and yeast. Make a well in the middle and add enough milk to mix to a soft, quite sticky, dough.

2 Knead the dough on a lightly floured surface until smooth and elastic. Shape into a round and place in a lightly oiled large bowl. Cover with oiled cling film and leave to rise in a warm place for 1–1½ hours or until doubled in size.

3 Turn out the dough on to a lightly floured surface and knock back with your fists. Knead for 2–3 minutes until smooth and elastic.

4 Divide the dough into 18 even-sized pieces and shape into balls, folding the sides to the middles to form tight round balls, or shape as required (see box, opposite).

5 Lightly oil two or three baking trays. Arrange the rolls on the baking trays, leaving enough room between them for the dough to expand, cover loosely with oiled cling film, and leave to rise in a warm place for 15–20 minutes or until doubled in size.

6 Brush the rolls with the beaten egg to glaze and sprinkle with poppy seeds and sesame seeds. Bake in a preheated oven at 230°C (210°C fan, Gas 8) for about 15 minutes until golden brown. Leave to cool on a wire rack.

Shaping milk rolls

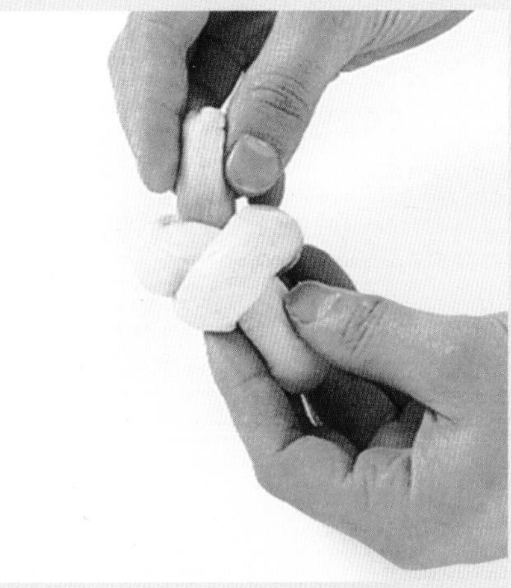

Form each piece of dough into a long rope and tie into a single knot.

Roll each piece of dough into a thin strand. Fold in half and twist together, sealing the ends well to form a twist. Shape each piece of dough into a ball or an oval. Snip tops with scissors.

Potato bread

MAKES 2 small loaves **CALS PER LOAF** 1002

500 g (1 lb) strong white flour, plus extra for dusting
1 tsp salt
15 g (½ oz) butter
1 x 7 g sachet fast-action dried yeast
250 g (8 oz) cold mashed potato
about 250 ml (8 fl oz) lukewarm water
sunflower oil, for greasing

2 X 500 G (1 LB) LOAF TINS

1 Put the flour and salt into a large bowl, rub in the butter, then stir in the yeast. Add the potato, rubbing it loosely into the flour. Make a well in the middle of the ingredients and add enough water to mix to a soft, quite sticky, dough.

2 Knead the dough on a floured surface until smooth and elastic, then shape into a round. Place in a lightly oiled large bowl, cover with oiled cling film, and leave to rise in a warm place for 1 hour or until doubled in size.

3 Turn out the dough on to a lightly floured surface and knock back with your fists. Knead until smooth and elastic.

4 Lightly oil the loaf tins. Divide the dough in half, and shape to fit the tins, tucking the ends underneath. Place in the tins. Cover loosely with oiled cling film and leave in a warm place to rise for 30 minutes or until the dough reaches the tops of the tins.

5 Bake in a preheated oven at 230°C (210°C fan, Gas 8) for 10 minutes; reduce the oven temperature to 200°C (180°C fan, Gas 6), and bake for 20–25 minutes until golden. Tap the bases of the loaves to see if they are cooked: they should sound hollow. Serve warm or cold.

Cook's know-how

Always add the measured liquid gradually when making dough. Recipes cannot specify exact amounts because flours vary in how much liquid they will absorb.

Devon flat baps

SERVES 16 **CALS EACH** 135

500 g (1 lb) strong white flour, plus extra for dusting
45 g (1½ oz) butter
1 tsp salt
1 x 7 g sachet fast-action dried yeast
about 150 ml (¼ pint) very hot water
about 150 ml (¼ pint) milk
1 tsp clear honey
sunflower oil, for greasing

1 Put the flour into a large bowl. Add the butter and rub in with the fingertips until the mixture resembles fine breadcrumbs. Stir in the salt and yeast, and make a well in the middle. Mix the water, milk, and honey together and add to the flour until a soft, quite sticky, dough is formed.

2 Knead the dough on a lightly floured surface until smooth and elastic. Shape into a round and place in a lightly oiled large bowl. Cover with oiled cling film and leave to rise in a warm place for 1–1½ hours or until doubled in size.

3 Turn out the dough on to a lightly floured surface and knock back with your fists. Knead for 2–3 minutes until the dough is smooth and elastic.

4 Lightly oil two baking trays. Divide the dough into 16 even-sized pieces. Knead and roll into rounds and place well apart on the baking trays. With the heel of your hand, flatten each round so that it measures 7 cm (3 in) across.

5 Cover loosely with oiled cling film and leave to rise in a warm place for about 30 minutes or until the dough has doubled in size.

6 Lightly flour the baps and bake in a preheated oven at 200°C (180°C fan, Gas 6) for 15–20 minutes until golden. Leave to cool on a wire rack.

Cook's know-how

If you are short of time, just mix and shape these baps, omitting the first rise in step 2 and giving them just one rise in step 5. The texture of the bread will not be quite as light, but it will still be good.

Cheese and herb bread

MAKES 1 medium loaf **CALS** 2707

500 g (1 lb) strong white flour, plus extra for dusting
90 g (3 oz) mature Cheddar cheese, grated
30 g (1 oz) Parmesan cheese, grated
2 tsp mustard powder
2 tbsp chopped parsley
1½ tsp salt
1 x 7 g sachet fast-action dried yeast
about 350 ml (12 fl oz) lukewarm milk
sunflower oil, for greasing
beaten egg, for glazing
2 tbsp grated Cheddar cheese, for sprinkling

1 Put the flour into a large bowl and stir in the cheeses, mustard powder, parsley, salt, and yeast, mixing thoroughly. Make a well in the middle and add enough milk to mix to a soft, quite sticky, dough.

2 Knead the dough on a lightly floured surface until smooth and elastic.

3 Shape the dough into a round and place in a lightly oiled bowl. Cover with oiled cling film, and leave to rise in a warm place for 1–1½ hours or until doubled in size.

4 Turn the dough on to a floured surface and knock back. Knead for 2–3 minutes until smooth and elastic.

5 Lightly flour a baking tray. Shape the dough into a 15 cm (6 in) round and place on the baking tray. Cover loosely with oiled cling film and leave to rise in a warm place for 20–30 minutes.

6 Brush with the egg to glaze, cut a shallow cross in the top, and sprinkle with the grated Cheddar cheese. Bake in a preheated oven at 230°C (210°C fan, Gas 8) for 10 minutes; reduce the oven temperature to 200°C (180°C fan, Gas 6), and bake for 20 minutes, covering the loaf loosely with foil halfway through baking if it is browning too much. Leave to cool on a wire rack before slicing.

Walnut bread

MAKES 2 small loaves **CALS PER LOAF** 1657

650 g (1 lb 5 oz) strong white flour, plus extra for dusting
2 tsp salt
30 g (1 oz) butter or baking spread
125 g (4 oz) walnut pieces, coarsely chopped
2 tbsp chopped parsley
1 x 7 g sachet fast-action dried yeast
about 400 ml (14 fl oz) lukewarm water
sunflower oil, for greasing

1 Put the flour and salt into a large bowl. Rub in the butter, then stir in the walnuts, parsley, and yeast. Make a well in the middle and add enough water to mix to a soft, quite sticky, dough.

2 Knead the dough on a lightly floured surface until smooth and elastic. Shape into a round and place in a lightly oiled large bowl. Cover loosely with oiled cling film and leave in a warm place for 1–1½ hours or until doubled in size.

3 Lightly oil two baking trays. Knock back the dough with your fists, then knead for 2–3 minutes until smooth and elastic.

4 Divide the dough in half, shape each half into a round, and then place on a baking tray.

5 Cover the rounds loosely with oiled cling film, and leave to rise in a warm place for 20–30 minutes.

6 Dust each loaf with flour, slash the tops in a criss-cross pattern, and bake in a preheated oven at 220°C (200°C fan, Gas 7) for about 10 minutes; reduce the oven temperature to 190°C (170°C fan, Gas 5), and bake for 20 minutes or until the bread is golden brown.

7 Tap the bases to see if the loaves are cooked: they should sound hollow. Best eaten while still warm.

Olive and sun-dried tomato breads

MAKES 2 small loaves **CALS PER LOAF** 1139

400 g (13 oz) strong white flour
60 g (2 oz) buckwheat flour
1 tsp salt
1 x 7 g sachet fast-action dried yeast
black pepper
about 300 ml (½ pint) lukewarm water
1 tbsp olive oil, plus extra for greasing
125 g (4 oz) pitted black olives, coarsely chopped
125 g (4 oz) sun-dried tomatoes in oil, drained and chopped
1 tbsp chopped parsley
1 tbsp chopped fresh basil
1 tbsp coarse sea salt

1 Put the flours into a large bowl. Stir in the salt and yeast and season with black pepper. Make a well in the middle. Pour in the water and oil and mix to a soft but not sticky dough.

2 Knead until smooth and elastic, shape into a round, and place in a lightly oiled large bowl. Cover with oiled cling film, and leave to rise in a warm place for 1–1½ hours or until doubled in size.

3 Lightly oil a baking tray. Knock back the dough, then knead for 2–3 minutes. Divide the dough into two pieces. Roll out each piece until about 23 x 25 cm (9 x 10 in). Spread one of the pieces with the olives and the other with the sun-dried tomatoes, parsley, and basil.

4 Roll up each piece of dough from one long end and place, seam-side down, on the tray. Make 4–5 diagonal slashes on the top of each loaf, cover loosely with oiled cling film, and leave to rise in a warm place for 20–30 minutes.

5 Brush the top of each loaf with water and lightly sprinkle with sea salt. Bake in a preheated oven at 230°C (210°C fan, Gas 8) for 15 minutes; reduce the oven temperature to 190°C (170°C fan, Gas 5), and bake for a further 15 minutes or until golden.

6 Tap the bases to see if the loaves are cooked: they should sound hollow. Leave to cool on a wire rack.

Focaccia

MAKES 1 large loaf **CALS** 2989

750 g (1½ lb) strong white flour, plus extra for dusting
1 x 7 g sachet fast-action dried yeast
3–4 tbsp chopped fresh rosemary
3 tbsp olive oil, plus extra for greasing
about 450 ml (¾ pint) lukewarm water
2 tsp coarse sea salt

1 Put the flour into a bowl, and add the yeast and rosemary. Make a well in the middle, add the oil and enough water to make a soft but not sticky dough. Knead the dough until smooth and elastic, then shape into a round.

2 Place the dough in a lightly oiled large bowl, cover loosely with oiled cling film, and leave to rise in a warm place for about 1 hour or until the dough has doubled in size.

3 Turn out the dough on to a lightly floured surface and knock back with your fists. Knead for 2–3 minutes until smooth. Roll out the dough to a round 5 cm (2 in) thick. Cover loosely with oiled cling film and leave in a warm place for 1 hour or until doubled in size.

4 Brush with olive oil and sprinkle with sea salt. Bake in a preheated oven at 190°C (170°C fan, Gas 5) for 20 minutes until golden. Best eaten warm.

Calzone

MAKES 4 **CALS EACH** 899

3 tbsp olive oil
2 large onions, sliced
1 tsp balsamic vinegar
3 Romano peppers, halved, deseeded, and chopped
250 g (8 oz) chestnut mushrooms, thickly sliced
salt and black pepper
1 x 400 g can chopped tomatoes, drained
4 tbsp tomato purée
30 g (1 oz) pitted black olives, halved
175 g (6 oz) mature Cheddar cheese, grated

Dough

500 g (1 lb) strong white flour
1 x 7 g sachet fast-action dried yeast
3 tbsp olive oil, plus extra for greasing
300 ml (½ pint) lukewarm water
beaten egg, to seal and glaze

1 Make the dough: put the flour, yeast, olive oil, and water into an electric mixer, and mix with the dough hook for about 5 minutes until a dough forms. If making the dough by hand, put the dry ingredients into a large bowl, add the oil and water, and mix with the hands until combined.

2 Knead the dough on a lightly floured surface for 5–10 minutes until smooth, shape into a ball, and place in a lightly oiled large bowl. Cover with oiled cling film, and leave to rise in a warm place for 1–1½ hours or until doubled in size.

3 Knock back the dough on a lightly floured surface, and knead until smooth. Cut into four equal pieces, and roll out each piece to a 23 cm (9 in) round.

4 Make the filling: heat 2 tbsp of the olive oil in a frying pan, add the onions, and fry over a high heat for 1 minute. Turn the heat down to low, cover, and cook for 15 minutes or until the onions are soft. Remove the lid, increase the heat to high, and fry for a few minutes, stirring frequently, to evaporate any liquid. Transfer the onions to a bowl with a slotted spoon, add the vinegar, and stir to mix. Heat the remaining 1 tbsp olive oil in the frying pan, add the peppers, and fry for 4 minutes. Add the mushrooms, and fry for 2–3 minutes until just cooked, then drain off any liquid. Mix the peppers and mushrooms with the onions, season with salt and pepper, and leave to cool.

5 Mix the drained tomatoes and tomato purée together in a bowl. Spread one-quarter of this mixture over one half of each piece of dough. Top with one-quarter of the vegetable mixture, and one-quarter of the olives and cheese. Season well. Brush the edges of the dough with beaten egg, and fold each round in half to enclose the filling. Press and crimp the edges together to seal (see box, below).

6 Lay the calzone on an oiled baking tray, and brush with beaten egg. Bake in a preheated oven at 240°C (220°C fan, Gas 9) for about 15 minutes until light golden brown and crisp. Serve hot or warm.

Filling the calzone

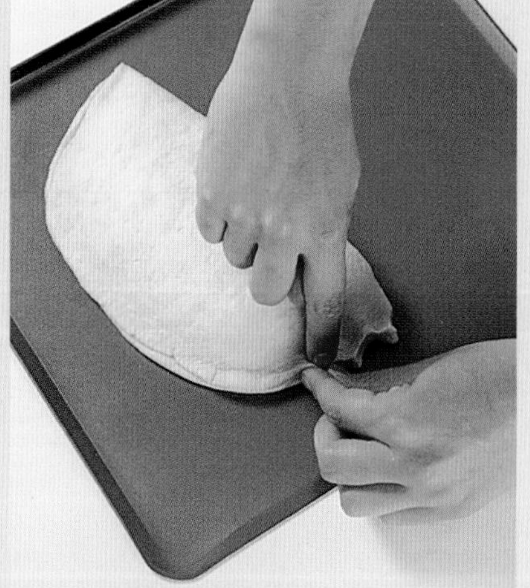

Put one-quarter of the filling on to half of each dough round.

Brush the edges of the dough with beaten egg and fold over to enclose the filling. Seal the edges and crimp as shown, then brush the top with egg.

Making the thin-crust pizza base

1 Sift 250 g (8 oz) strong white flour on to a work surface and add a heaped ½ tsp fast-action dried yeast and ½ tsp salt. Make a well in the middle and add about 150 ml (5 fl oz) lukewarm water and 1 tbsp olive oil. Draw in the flour with your fingertips or a pastry scraper and work to form a smooth dough.

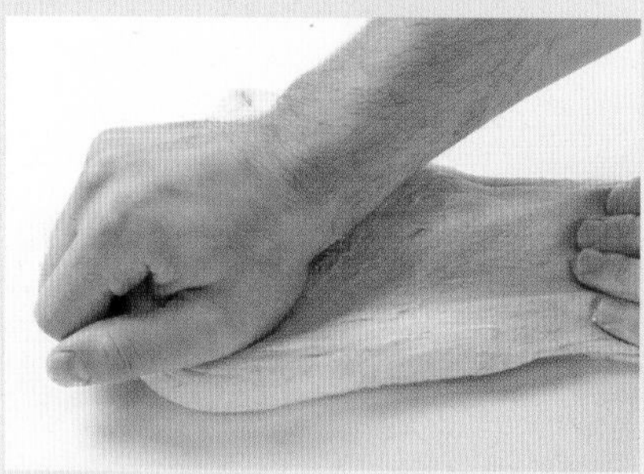

2 Lightly oil a large bowl. Knead the dough for 10 minutes until smooth. Shape into a round and put in the bowl. Cover loosely with oiled cling film and leave in a warm place to rise for about 1 hour or until doubled in size. Turn out of the bowl and knead for 2–3 minutes on a lightly floured surface until smooth.

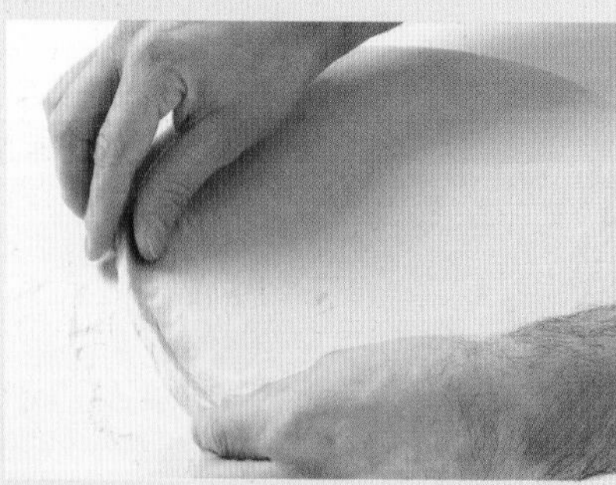

3 Roll and stretch the dough until it is about 35 cm (14 in) round and about 1 cm (½ in) thick. Make a rim around the edge. Put on a baking tray, add the toppings, and bake in a preheated oven at 220°C (200°C fan, Gas 7) for 20–30 minutes. Bake mini pizzas for only 12–15 minutes.

Mini pizzas

MAKES 12 **CALS EACH** 458

1 x 400 g can passata, drained
1 quantity pizza dough (see box, left), shaped into 12 x 7 cm (3 in) rounds
salt and black pepper
2 tbsp olive oil

Goat's cheese topping

8 sun-dried tomatoes in oil, diced
6 pitted black olives, diced
2 garlic cloves, crushed
60 g (2 oz) goat's cheese, diced

Parma ham topping

2 thin slices of Parma ham, diced
6 artichoke hearts in oil, drained and sliced

1 Spread the tomatoes over the pizza dough rounds and season to taste.

2 Top half the rounds with the sun-dried tomatoes, olives, garlic, and goat's cheese, and half with the Parma ham and artichokes. Sprinkle with the oil.

3 Bake the mini pizzas, following the instructions in step 3 (see box, left).

Napoletana pizza

MAKES 1 large pizza (serves 4)
CALS PER SLICE 404

1 x 400 g can passata, drained
1 pizza base (see box, left)
1 x 60 g can anchovy fillets, drained
125 g (4 oz) mozzarella cheese, chopped
2 tbsp olive oil

Spread the tomatoes over the pizza base. Halve the anchovies and arrange them on top with the remaining ingredients. Bake, following the instructions in step 3 (see box, left).

Tuna and caper pizza

MAKES 1 large pizza (serves 4)
CALS PER SLICE 466

1 x 400 g can passata, drained
1 pizza base (see box, left)
1 x 200 g can tuna, drained
2 tbsp capers
125 g (4 oz) mozzarella cheese, chopped
1 tsp oregano
2 tbsp olive oil

Spread the tomatoes over the pizza base. Top with the remaining ingredients. Bake, following the instructions in step 3 (see box, left).

Four seasons pizza

MAKES 1 large pizza (serves 4)
CALS PER SLICE 457

1 x 400 g can passata, drained
1 pizza base (see box, left)
salt and black pepper
60 g (2 oz) thinly sliced salami
½ tsp oregano
60 g (2 oz) small button mushrooms, sliced
30 g (1 oz) mozzarella cheese, chopped
30 g (1 oz) anchovy fillets, drained
12 pitted black olives
2–3 pieces of bottled red peppers (in oil), thinly sliced
2 tbsp olive oil
grated Parmesan cheese and fresh basil leaves, to finish

1 Spread the tomatoes over the pizza base and season to taste.

2 Put salami and oregano on one quarter of the pizza, the mushrooms and mozzarella on a second quarter, the anchovies and olives on a third, the peppers on the fourth. Lightly sprinkle with olive oil. Bake, following the instructions in step 3 (see box, left). Sprinkle with Parmesan and basil after baking.

Opposite, clockwise from top right: Mini pizzas, Four seasons pizza, Tuna and caper pizza, Napoletana pizza

Pissaladière with Mediterranean vegetables

SERVES 6 **CALS PER SERVING** 434

2 aubergines, cut into 2 cm (¾ in) cubes
salt and black pepper
3 tbsp olive oil
2 red peppers, halved, deseeded, and cut into 2 cm (¾ in) cubes
2 large onions, roughly chopped
pinch of sugar
125 g (4 oz) Emmental or Gruyère cheese, grated
2 tsp balsamic vinegar
2 tsp olive oil
leaves from 1 small bunch of basil

Dough

175 g (6 oz) self-raising flour
1 tsp baking powder
½ tsp salt
60 g (2 oz) butter, cubed
60 g (2 oz) Parmesan cheese, grated
1 large egg
about 100 ml (3½ fl oz) milk

1 Make the topping: spread the aubergine cubes out in a large roasting tin, season with salt and pepper, and drizzle with 1 tbsp of the olive oil. Spread the peppers out in another large roasting tin, season with salt and pepper, and drizzle with another 1 tbsp of the olive oil.

2 Roast the aubergines and peppers in a preheated oven at 200°C (180°C fan, Gas 6) for about 25 minutes until the vegetables are tender and the aubergine is golden.

3 Meanwhile, heat the remaining olive oil in a frying pan, and fry the onions over a high heat for 1 minute. Lower the heat, cover the pan, and cook for about 10 minutes until the onions are soft. Add the sugar, increase the heat, and fry for a few minutes more.

4 Tip the onions into a bowl, add aubergines and peppers, and stir gently to combine. Leave the oven on.

5 Make the dough: mix the flour, baking powder, and salt in a large bowl. Add the butter, and rub in with the fingertips until the mixture resembles fine breadcrumbs. Stir in the Parmesan. Beat the egg in a measuring jug with a fork, then pour in enough milk to make up to 150 ml (¼ pint). Gradually add the egg and milk to the flour, mixing with the hands to form a soft dough – not all of the liquid may be necessary.

6 Turn the dough on to a floured large baking tray. Knead lightly, roll out to a 28 cm (11 in) round, and flute the edge. Bake for 15 minutes or until the edge of the dough just begins to colour.

7 Spoon the vegetables over the dough, and sprinkle with the cheese. Bake for a further 15 minutes or until the cheese is light golden and the base is cooked. Transfer to a serving plate, drizzle with the vinegar and olive oil, and top with the basil leaves. Cut into six wedges and serve.

Spicy deep-pan pizza

SERVES 4 **CALS** 899

125 g (4 oz) tomato purée
1 x 400 g can chopped tomatoes, drained
60 g (2 oz) pepperoni sausage, sliced
300 g (10 oz) mozzarella cheese, grated
60 g (2 oz) Parmesan cheese, grated
2 tbsp sliced pickled green chillies (from a can or jar)

Dough

500 g (1 lb) strong white flour
1 x 7 g sachet fast-action dried yeast
½ tsp salt
2 tbsp olive oil, plus extra for greasing
about 300 ml (½ pint) lukewarm water

DEEP DISH 35 CM (14 IN) ROUND PIZZA PAN

1 Make the dough: mix the flour, yeast, salt, and 2 tbsp oil in a large bowl. Add enough water to mix to a soft, quite sticky, dough. Knead on a lightly floured surface for 5–10 minutes until smooth and elastic.

2 Put into an oiled large bowl, turn to coat with the oil, cover with oiled cling film and leave to rise in a warm place for 1 hour or until doubled in size.

3 Lightly oil the pizza pan. Knock back the dough on a floured surface, roll out, and shape into a 35 cm (14 in) round. Put into the pan and shape the edge to form a rim.

4 Spread the tomato pureé over the base. Top with the tomatoes and pepperoni. Sprinkle over the mozzarella, Parmesan, and green chillies.

5 Bake in a preheated oven at 240°C (220°C fan, Gas 9) for 10–15 minutes until the crust is golden and the cheese topping melted. Serve hot.

Croissants

Croissant is the French word for crescent, the traditional shape for this classic breakfast roll. The dough for croissants is made with butter and milk, so they are rich enough to be served just as they are, but they are even more delicious served warm with butter and jam, or marmalade.

MAKES 12 **CALS EACH** 352

500 g (1 lb) strong white flour
½ tsp salt
300 g (10 oz) butter, at room temperature
1 x 7 g sachet fast-action dried yeast
30 g (1 oz) caster sugar
about 150 ml (¼ pint) milk
about 150 ml (¼ pint) very hot water
sunflower oil, for greasing
beaten egg, for glazing

1 Put the flour and salt into a large bowl, add 60 g (2 oz) of the butter, and rub in with your fingertips until the mixture resembles fine breadcrumbs. Stir in the yeast and sugar.

2 Make a well in the middle of the dry ingredients. Mix the milk and water together, pour into the well, and mix with a wooden spoon until smooth.

3 Cover the bowl with oiled cling film and chill the dough for 2 hours.

4 Meanwhile, on a sheet of baking parchment, spread out the remaining butter into a 12 x 20 cm (5 x 8 in) rectangle. Cover with another sheet of baking parchment and chill.

5 Roll out the dough on a floured surface into an 18 x 35 cm (7 x 14 in) rectangle, and place the chilled butter on top so that it covers the top two-thirds of the rectangle.

6 Fold the bottom third of the dough over the middle third, and fold the top third, with the butter, over the top to form a neat parcel. Seal the edges with the edge of your hand. Wrap and chill for 30 minutes.

7 Roll out the dough parcel into an 18 x 35 cm (7 x 14 in) rectangle, fold into 3 as before, and seal the edges. Wrap and chill for a few hours until firm enough to roll and shape.

8 Shape the croissants (see box, opposite). Place on 2 baking trays and leave for about 30 minutes until almost doubled in size.

9 Lightly brush the croissants with the beaten egg and bake in a preheated oven at 220°C (200°C fan, Gas 7) for 12–15 minutes until crisp and golden brown. Leave to cool slightly before serving.

CHOCOLATE CROISSANTS

Make the dough. Before rolling the triangles into sausage shapes, sprinkle them with 90 g (3 oz) plain chocolate chips.

Shaping the croissants

Shape the dough into a 35 x 53 cm (14 x 21 in) rectangle, and cut into 12 triangles.

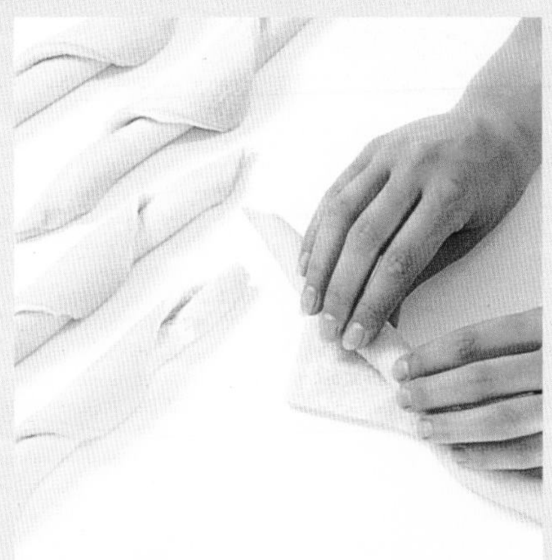

Roll each triangle into a sausage shape, starting from the long side and ending with the point of the triangle.

Bend the ends of each croissant to give the traditional shape.

Brioches

MAKES 12 **CALS EACH** 149

275 g (9 oz) strong white flour, plus extra for dusting
30 g (1 oz) caster sugar
60 g (2 oz) butter
1 x 7 g sachet fast-action dried yeast
2 eggs, beaten
about 3 tbsp lukewarm milk
sunflower oil, for greasing
beaten egg, for glazing

12 INDIVIDUAL BRIOCHE MOULDS

1 Sift the flour and sugar into a large bowl. Rub in the butter until the mixture resembles fine breadcrumbs, then stir in the yeast. Make a well in the middle, then pour in the eggs and enough milk to mix to a soft dough.

2 Knead the dough on a lightly floured surface until smooth and elastic. Shape into a round and place in a lightly oiled large bowl. Cover with oiled cling film and leave to rise in a warm place for 1–1½ hours or until doubled in size.

3 Turn out the dough on to a lightly floured surface and knock back with your fists. Knead the dough for 2–3 minutes until smooth.

4 Lightly oil the brioche moulds. Shape the brioches (see box, right).

5 Cover loosely with oiled cling film and leave to rise in a warm place for 20 minutes or until doubled in size.

6 Brush the brioches with a little beaten egg and bake in a preheated oven at 200°C (180°C fan, Gas 6) for 10–12 minutes until golden brown. Tap the bases to see if the brioches are cooked through: they should sound hollow. Leave to cool on a wire rack.

Shaping brioches

Divide the dough into 12 pieces, then cut one-quarter from each. Shape each piece into a ball. Place the large balls in the moulds, and press a hole in the middle of each. Place the small balls over the holes and press down to seal.

Danish pastries

These melt-in-the-mouth, flaky pastries are quick and easy to make and are particularly good for breakfast. Vary the fillings, bake them ahead, and freeze. Warm the pastries, loosely covered with foil, in a low oven, and serve for a special breakfast or brunch.

MAKES 16 **CALS EACH** 480

- 500 g (1 lb) strong white flour, plus extra for dusting
- ½ tsp salt
- 375 g (12 oz) butter, plus extra for greasing
- 1 x 7 g sachet fast-action dried yeast
- 60 g (2 oz) caster sugar
- 150 ml (¼ pint) tepid milk
- 2 eggs, beaten, plus extra to glaze

Filling and topping

- 250 g (8 oz) white almond paste (page 576)
- 4 apricot halves, canned or fresh
- about 2 tsp water
- 125 g (4 oz) icing sugar
- 60 g (2 oz) flaked almonds
- 60 g (2 oz) glacé cherries

1 Put the flour and salt into a bowl and rub in 60 g (2 oz) of the butter. Stir in the yeast and sugar. Make a well in the middle, add the lukewarm milk and eggs, and mix to a soft dough.

2 Turn out the dough on to a floured surface and knead for 10 minutes or until smooth. Shape into a round and place in an oiled bowl. Cover with oiled cling film and leave in a warm place to rise for 1 hour or until doubled in size.

3 Turn out the dough on to a lightly floured work surface and knead for 2–3 minutes until smooth. Roll out into a 20 x 35 cm (8 x 14 in) rectangle. Dot the top two-thirds of the dough with half of the remaining butter. Fold the bottom third up and the top third down to form a parcel. Seal the edges, then give the dough a quarter turn so the folded side is to the left.

4 Roll out the dough into a 20 x 35 cm (8 x 14 in) rectangle as before. Dot with the remaining butter, fold, and chill for 15 minutes. Roll, fold, and chill twice more.

5 Divide the dough into four pieces. Shape and fill the pastries (see box, below). Arrange on buttered baking trays and leave to rise in a warm place for 20 minutes. Brush with beaten egg and bake in a preheated oven at 220°C (200°C fan, Gas 7) for 15 minutes or until golden brown. Transfer to a wire rack.

6 Mix the water and icing sugar and spoon a little over each pastry while still warm. Decorate kites with flaked almonds and pinwheels with glacé cherries. Leave to cool.

Shaping Danish pastries

Crescents

1 Roll out the dough into a 23 cm (9 in) round. Cut into quarters. Place a small roll of almond paste at the wide end of each piece.

2 Starting from the wide end, roll up each dough quarter loosely around the almond paste, then curve the ends to form a crescent.

Kites

1 Roll out the dough into a 20 cm (8 in) square. Cut into four squares. Make cuts around two corners of each square, 1 cm (½ in) in from the edge.

2 Place a round of almond paste in the middle of each square. Lift each cut corner and cross it over the almond paste to the opposite corner.

Pinwheels

Roll out dough and cut into four squares as for kites. Put almond paste in the middle of each. Cut from the corners almost to the middle. Fold in alternate points.

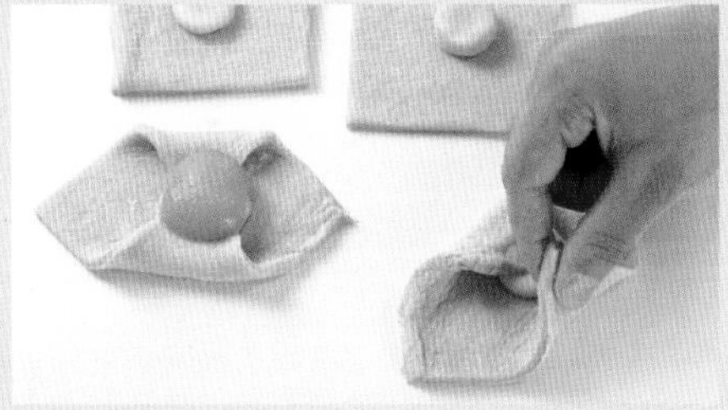

Envelopes

Roll out the dough, cut into four, and fill as for pinwheels. Fold two opposite corners into the middle. Top with a half apricot, cut-side down.

Hot cross buns

MAKES 12 **CALS EACH** 279

500 g (1 lb) strong white flour
60 g (2 oz) caster sugar
1 x 7 g sachet fast-action dried yeast
1 tsp salt
1 tsp ground mixed spice
1 tsp ground cinnamon
½ tsp grated nutmeg
about 150 ml (¼ pint) milk
about 75 ml (2½ fl oz) very hot water
60 g (2 oz) butter, melted and cooled slightly
1 egg, beaten
90 g (3 oz) currants
60 g (2 oz) chopped mixed peel
sunflower oil, for greasing
60 g (2 oz) shortcrust pastry

Glaze
2 tbsp caster sugar
2 tbsp water

1 Sift the flour into a large bowl, stir in the sugar, yeast, salt, mixed spice, cinnamon, and nutmeg, and make a well in the middle. Mix the milk and water together and add to the bowl with the butter, egg, currants, and mixed peel. Mix to a soft dough.

2 Knead the dough on a lightly floured surface until smooth and elastic, then shape into a round.

3 Put into an oiled large bowl, cover with oiled cling film, and leave to rise in a warm place for 1–1½ hours or until doubled in size.

4 Knock back the dough with your fists, then turn on to a lightly floured surface and knead for 2–3 minutes until smooth and elastic. Divide the dough into 12 pieces and shape into round rolls.

5 Roll out the shortcrust pastry to 5 mm (¼ in) thickness, cut it into 24 narrow strips, and press two strips in the form of a cross on each bun. Secure with a little water.

6 Lightly oil two baking trays, arrange the buns on the trays, and cover with oiled cling film. Leave to rise in a warm place for 30 minutes or until doubled in size.

7 Bake the buns in a preheated oven at 220°C (200°C fan, Gas 7) for 15 minutes or until golden brown. Transfer the buns to a wire rack, brush with the glaze, and serve warm or cold with butter to spread.

Cinnamon rolls

MAKES 16 **CALS EACH** 450

1 kg (2 lb) plain flour
60 g (2 oz) caster sugar
1 x 7 g sachet fast-action dried yeast
1 tsp salt
about 350 ml (12 fl oz) lukewarm milk
2 eggs, lightly beaten
30 g (1 oz) butter, melted
250 g (8 oz) raisins
1 tbsp ground cinnamon
sunflower oil, for greasing
milk, for glazing

Sugar glaze
200 g (7 oz) icing sugar
4 tbsp water
1 tsp vanilla extract

1 Sift the flour and 30 g (1 oz) of the sugar into a bowl, then stir in the yeast and salt. Make a well in the middle, pour in the milk, eggs, and butter, and stir to make a sticky dough.

2 Knead the dough on a lightly floured surface until smooth and elastic.

3 Knead in the raisins and half of the cinnamon, then divide the dough into 16 even-sized pieces. Shape each piece into a 20–25 cm (8–10 in) strand, then flatten.

4 Combine the remaining sugar and cinnamon, sprinkle the mixture over the strips of dough, then roll up tightly into spirals.

5 Lightly oil two baking trays. Arrange the rolls on the trays, cover loosely with oiled cling film, and leave to rise in a warm place for about 1 hour or until doubled in size.

6 Brush the rolls with milk to glaze, then bake them in a preheated oven at 190°C (170°C fan, Gas 5) for 30–40 minutes until lightly browned. Transfer the rolls to a rack.

7 Meanwhile, make the sugar glaze: in a small bowl, combine the icing sugar, measured water, and vanilla extract. As soon as the cinnamon rolls come out of the oven, brush them with the glaze. Serve the rolls warm or cold with butter.

Chelsea buns

MAKES 12 **CALS EACH** 298

500 g (1 lb) strong white flour
1 tsp salt
60 g (2 oz) butter
1 x 7 g sachet fast-action dried yeast
30 g (1 oz) caster sugar
about 200 ml (7 fl oz) lukewarm milk
1 large egg, beaten
sunflower oil, for greasing
4 tbsp clear honey

Filling

60 g (2 oz) butter
30 g (1 oz) light muscovado sugar
60 g (2 oz) sultanas
60 g (2 oz) currants
grated zest of 1 orange
1 tsp ground mixed spice

1 Put the flour into a large bowl and stir in the salt. Rub in the butter and yeast. Stir in the sugar. Make a well in the middle, pour in the milk and egg, and mix to a soft dough.

2 Knead the dough on a lightly floured surface until smooth and elastic, then shape into a round and place in a lightly oiled large bowl. Cover with oiled cling film and leave in a warm place for 1–1½ hours or until doubled in size.

3 Make the filling: cream the butter with the muscovado sugar. In another bowl, combine the sultanas, currants, orange zest, and mixed spice.

4 Lightly oil an 18 x 28 cm (7 x 11 in) roasting tin. Turn out the dough on to a lightly floured surface, and knock back with your fists. Knead for 2–3 minutes until smooth.

5 Roll out into a 30 cm (12 in) square and dot with the butter mixture. Fold in half and roll out into a 30 cm (12 in) square. Sprinkle with the fruit mixture, then roll up.

6 Cut the roll into 12 pieces and arrange cut-side up in the roasting tin. Cover with oiled cling film. Leave in a warm place to rise for about 30 minutes or until the pieces are touching.

7 Bake in a preheated oven at 220°C (200°C fan, Gas 7) for 20–25 minutes, covering the buns loosely with foil after about 15 minutes to prevent them from browning too much. Transfer to a wire rack.

8 Warm the honey in a small pan and brush over the buns to glaze. Pull the buns apart, and serve warm.

Griddled English muffins

MAKES 12 **CALS EACH** 158

500 g (1 lb) strong wholemeal flour, plus extra for dusting
1 tsp salt
1 x 7 g sachet fast-action dried yeast
about 250 ml (8 fl oz) milk
about 125 ml (4 fl oz) very hot water
sunflower oil, for greasing

7 CM (3 IN) PASTRY CUTTER

1 Put the flour into a large bowl, stir in the salt and yeast, and make a well in the middle. Mix the milk and water together, pour in all at once, and mix to a soft dough.

2 Knead on a lightly floured surface until smooth and elastic, then shape into a round. Place the dough in a lightly oiled large bowl, cover with oiled cling film, and leave to rise in a warm place for 45–60 minutes until doubled in size.

3 Knock back the dough, then turn out on to a lightly floured surface and knead for 2–3 minutes until smooth and elastic.

4 Roll out the dough until 1 cm (½ in) thick. Using the cutter, cut into 12 rounds, re-rolling and kneading the dough as necessary.

5 Lightly dust two baking trays with flour, arrange the rounds on the trays, and cover loosely with oiled cling film. Leave to rise in a warm place for about 30 minutes or until doubled in size.

6 Lightly oil a griddle or frying pan, and cook the muffins over a medium heat, three or four at a time, for about 7 minutes on each side until golden and cooked through. Do not allow the griddle to get too hot or the outside of the muffins will burn before the inside is cooked.

Crumpets

MAKES 20 **CALS EACH** 73

375 g (12 oz) strong white flour
½ tsp salt
1 x 7 g sachet fast-action dried yeast
about 250 ml (8 fl oz) milk
about 300 ml (½ pint) very hot water
sunflower oil, for greasing

4 CRUMPET RINGS OR 4 X 7 CM (3 IN) PASTRY CUTTERS

1 Put the flour into a large bowl, stir in the salt and yeast, and make a well in the middle. Mix the milk and water together, pour in, and beat to form a smooth, thick batter.

2 Cover and leave in a warm place to rise for 1 hour or until the surface is bubbling.

3 Beat the batter mixture for 2 minutes, then pour into a jug. Lightly oil the crumpet rings or pastry cutters and oil a griddle or frying pan. Place the rings or cutters on the griddle and then leave for 1–2 minutes to heat through.

4 Pour 2 cm (¾ in) of batter into each ring and cook for 5–7 minutes until the surface is dry and full of holes, and the crumpets are shrinking away from the sides of the rings.

5 Lift off the rings, turn the crumpets over, and cook for 1 minute until pale golden. Transfer the crumpets to a wire rack and leave to cool.

6 Repeat with the remaining batter, lightly greasing the griddle and rings between each batch. Serve warm.

Lardy cake

MAKES 1 large loaf **CALS** 8186

500 g (1 lb) strong white flour, plus extra for dusting
1 tsp salt
1 x 7 g sachet fast-action dried yeast
15 g (½ oz) white vegetable fat
about 300 ml (½ pint) lukewarm water
sunflower oil, for greasing

Filling

90 g (3 oz) lard or white vegetable fat
60 g (2 oz) butter, plus extra for greasing
90 g (3 oz) currants
90 g (3 oz) sultanas
60 g (2 oz) chopped mixed candied peel
90 g (3 oz) light muscovado sugar

Glaze

1 tbsp caster sugar
1 tbsp boiling water

23 X 30 CM (9 X 12 IN) ROASTING TIN

1 Mix the flour, salt, and yeast in a bowl. Rub in the fat. Make a well in the middle and pour in enough water to mix to a soft dough.

2 Knead on a lightly floured surface until smooth and elastic, place in a lightly oiled large bowl, and cover with oiled cling film. Leave to rise in a warm place for 1–1½ hours.

3 Turn out the dough on to a lightly floured surface and roll out to a rectangle about 5 mm (¼ in) thick. Dot with one-third each of the vegetable fat and butter. Sprinkle over one-third each of the dried fruit, mixed peel, and sugar.

4 Fold into three, folding the bottom third up and the top third down on top of it. Seal the edges to trap the air, then give the dough a quarter turn. Repeat the rolling and folding twice more, with the remaining fat, fruit, peel, and sugar.

5 Lightly butter the roasting tin. Roll out the dough to fit the tin, and lift it into the tin. Cover with oiled cling film and leave to rise in a warm place for about 30 minutes or until doubled in size.

6 Score the top of the dough in a criss-cross pattern, and bake in a preheated oven at 200°C (180°C fan, Gas 6) for about 30 minutes or until golden brown. Leave to cool in the tin for about 10 minutes.

7 Meanwhile, make the glaze: dissolve the sugar in the measured water. Brush the glaze on top of the warm cake and leave to cool.

Pies, tarts, and hot desserts

In this chapter...

Magic chocolate pudding
page 485

Steamed jam pudding
page 485

Christmas pudding
page 486

Rice pudding
page 486

French apple tart
page 487

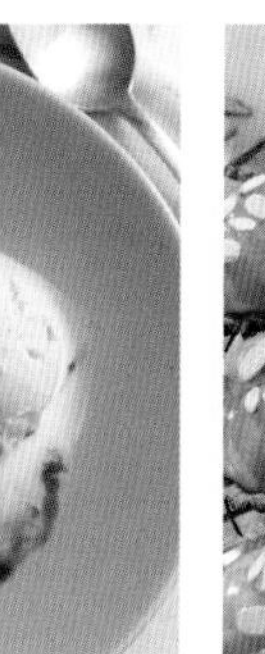
Jamaican bananas
page 487

Tropical tartlets
page 488

Blueberry puffs
page 491

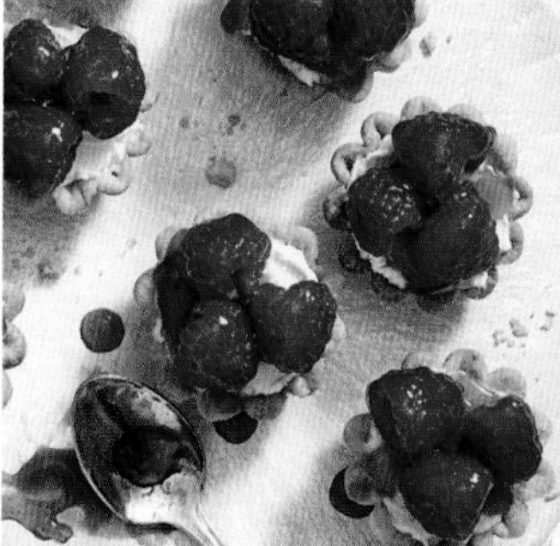
Raspberry tartlets
page 488

Tarte au citron
page 491

In this chapter... *continued*

Apple strudel
page 504

Strawberry and rhubarb pie
page 505

Lemon meringue pie
page 506

Mille-feuille
page 506

Baklava
page 508

Cherries Jubilee
page 509

Summer berry soufflés with berry compote
page 509

Crêpes Suzette
page 510

Hot chocolate soufflés
page 511

French pancakes
page 511

Chocolate fudge fondue
page 512

White chocolate fondue
page 512

Dark chocolate fondue
page 512

Pies, tarts, and hot desserts know-how

Puddings may no longer be a feature of every family meal, but few people can say that they don't enjoy something sweet from time to time, be it a traditional steamed pudding or comforting bread and butter pudding – one of the nation's favourites – or a glamorous golden pastry filled with fresh fruit or a rich custard. Hot pastry desserts can take very little time to make these days as bought pastry, especially the ready-rolled varieties, is so good. But if you have the time, and you enjoy it, then it's very satisfying to make your own, and you can try all the different types of pastry.

Types of pastry

All pastries are based on a mixture of flour, fat, and a liquid to bind them. Plain white flour is usually used, although wholemeal or a mixture of the two gives a "nuttier" pastry. The liquid used for binding may be water, milk, or egg; the fat may be butter, baking spread, lard, white vegetable fat, or a combination.

Shortcrust pastry

A blend of two parts flour, one part fat, and usually water, shortcrust pastry (opposite) is used for sweet and savoury pies and tarts.

Pâte sucrée

Bound with egg yolks, pâte sucrée (opposite) is richer than shortcrust pastry and is used for sweet tarts and tartlets. The classic method for mixing the dough is on a flat marble work surface.

Puff pastry

This light, flaky pastry is made by rolling and folding the dough many times to make paper-thin layers of dough and butter. Ready-made fresh or frozen pastry is very convenient, but not all brands are made with butter. Puff pastry is often used as a top crust for sweet and savoury pies, to wrap beef Wellington, and for mille-feuille.

Flaky pastry

This is a short-cut version of puff pastry. The rolling and folding process is repeated only a few times. It is used for pies and tarts.

Rough puff pastry

Like puff and flaky pastry, this is rolled and folded, but the butter is added all at once, in large cubes. Rough puff pastry can be used in the same ways as flaky pastry and for dishes normally made with puff pastry.

Filo and strudel pastry

These are similar types of pastry made from a pliable dough that is stretched and rolled until extremely thin. It is then rolled around a filling or layered with melted butter. Filo and strudel pastries are difficult to make at home, but ready-made varieties are available fresh and frozen. Common uses include strudel and baklava.

Freezing

Most puddings freeze well, particularly baked sponge and steamed suet puddings (before or after cooking), bread and butter pudding (before cooking), crumbles (before or after cooking), and pancakes. Custard-based and milk puddings are not as successful because they tend to separate.

Pastry dough is an excellent freezer standby; thaw before rolling out. Unbaked pastry shells are ideal for last-minute desserts as they can be baked from frozen. It's not a good idea to freeze baked pastries.

Microwaving

The microwave can be a helpful tool when preparing pies, tarts, and hot desserts. For baking pastry-based pies and tarts, however, there really is no substitute for the conventional oven.

The microwave is perfect for cooking fruit fillings for pies and tarts. The fruit remains plump and colourful. It can also be used to melt or soften butter and to heat liquids in which fruit is left to soak. Under careful watch, the microwave can be used to melt chocolate and to make caramel.

Decorating pies and tarts

Keep pastry trimmings to make small decorative shapes. Cut them freehand or use cutters. They can be fixed to the edge of a pastry shell or arranged on a lid. If the pastry has a glaze, attach the shapes with water, then apply the glaze all over the pie, brushing it on gently so the shapes are not disturbed.

A pastry lid can be brushed with a glaze before baking. A little milk or beaten egg will give a shiny finish, as will egg white alone – this is a good way to use up whites when the pastry is made with egg yolks. Sprinkle a pastry lid with sugar for a crisp, sweet glaze.

Decorative edges

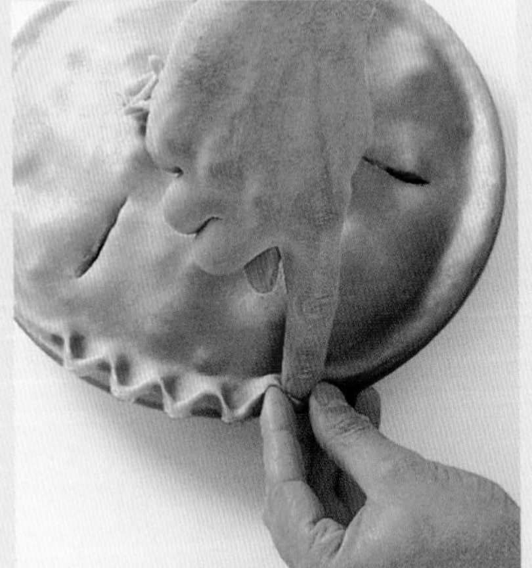

A simple way to give a decorative finish to a pie is to crimp the edge. Place the tips of the thumb and forefinger of one hand against the outside rim of the dish. With the forefinger of your other hand, gently push the pastry edge outwards between the thumb and finger, and pinch the pastry to make a rounded V shape. Repeat this action all around the pastry lid. Alternatively, push and pinch in the opposite direction, working from the outside of the edge inwards.

Shortcrust pastry

You can also make shortcrust in a food processor: pulse the flour with the fat until like breadcrumbs, then add the water and pulse again briefly (do this briefly or the pastry will be tough). Tip on to a floured surface and knead lightly to mix to a smooth dough. These quantities make sufficient pastry to line a 23–25 cm (9–10 in) flan dish, flan tin, or pie dish.

1 Sift 175 g (6 oz) plain flour into a bowl. Cut 90 g (3 oz) well-chilled butter, baking spread, or other fat into small pieces and add to the bowl. Stir to coat the fat with flour.

2 Using your fingertips, quickly and lightly rub the fat into the flour, lifting the mixture to incorporate air, until it resembles fine breadcrumbs. Sprinkle over about 2 tbsp cold water and stir gently with a table knife to mix. If the mixture seems too dry to bind together, add a little more water.

3 Gather the mixture together and knead very briefly until smooth (handle the dough as little as possible or the pastry will be tough). If the dough feels at all sticky, add a little more flour. Shape into a ball, wrap, and chill for 30 minutes.

Pâte sucrée

This French sweet pastry is traditionally made on a marble surface. These quantities make sufficient pastry to line a 25 cm (10 in) flan dish, tin, or pie dish.

1 Sift 200 g (7 oz) plain flour on to a work surface. Make a well in the middle and add 90 g (3 oz) softened butter, 60 g (2 oz) caster sugar, and 3 egg yolks (for a less rich pastry, use just 1 egg yolk). With your fingertips blend together the butter, sugar, and egg yolks.

2 Using your fingertips, gradually work the sifted flour into the blended butter mixture until the mixture resembles coarse crumbs. If the mixture seems too sticky, work in a little more flour.

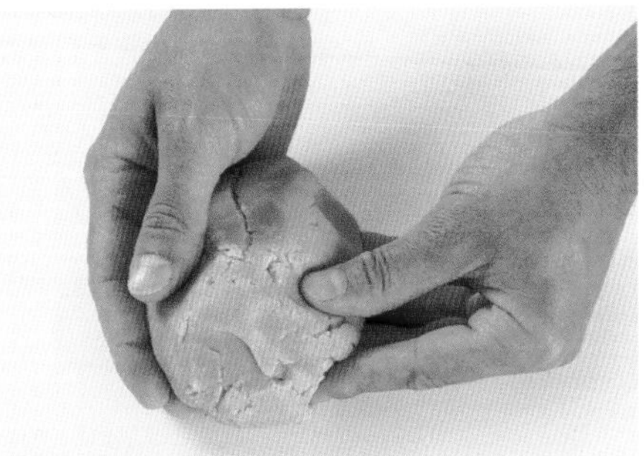

3 With your fingers or a pastry scraper, gather the dough into a ball, then knead briefly until it is smooth and pliable. Shape the dough into a ball again, wrap, and chill for 30 minutes or until it feels just firm.

Rough puff pastry

Ideal for both sweet and savoury pies. These quantities make sufficient pastry for a 25 cm (10 in) double-crust pie.

1 Sift 250 g (8 oz) plain flour into a bowl. Add 90 g (3 oz) each of cubed butter and white vegetable fat, and stir to coat in flour. Add 150 ml (¼ pint) cold water and, with a table knife, bind to a lumpy dough.

2 Roll out the dough into a rectangle three times as long as it is wide. Fold the bottom third up and the top third down. Press the edges to seal. Wrap and chill for 5 minutes, then place so the folded edges are to the sides.

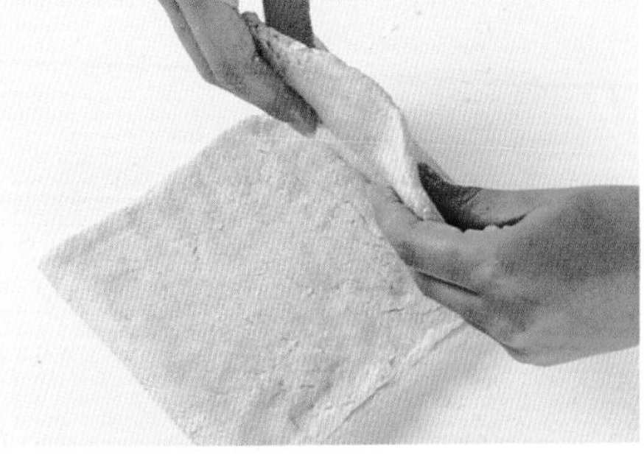

3 Roll out the dough into a rectangle and fold as before. Turn the dough so the folded edges are to the sides again. Repeat the rolling, folding, and turning twice more. Wrap and chill for 30 minutes.

Making a pastry shell

Careful handling of pastry dough should ensure that the shell does not shrink or distort when baking.

1 Put the pastry dough on a floured work surface and flour the rolling pin. Roll out into a round, starting in the middle each time and lifting and turning the pastry round a quarter turn after each roll.

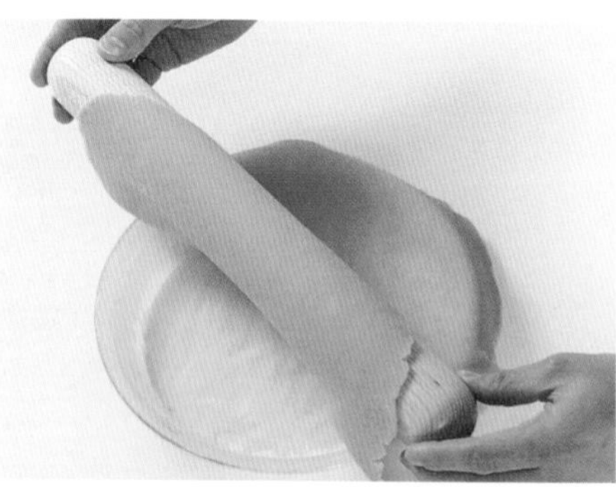

2 If lining a pie dish, roll out the pastry dough to a round 5 cm (2 in) larger than the top of the dish; a pastry lid should also be 5 cm (2 in) larger. Roll the pastry up loosely around the rolling pin, and unroll over the dish.

3 Gently ease the pastry into the dish, pressing it firmly and neatly into the bottom edge. Be very careful not to stretch the pastry. Carefully trim off the excess pastry with a table knife. If there are any holes, patch them with bits of pastry dough.

Baking blind

A pastry shell may be partly baked before adding a filling, to help it stay crisp, or it may be fully baked if the filling itself does not need to be cooked. The shell is filled with baking beans to weigh down the pastry.

1 Prick the pastry shell all over with a fork. Line with a piece of foil or greaseproof paper, allowing it to come high above the rim so that it can be lifted out easily after baking.

2 Fill the shell with ceramic baking beans, dried pulses, or uncooked rice, and bake in a preheated oven at 190°C (170°C fan, Gas 5) for 10 minutes.

3 Remove the beans and foil. Return the shell to the oven and bake for 5 minutes (partbaked) or 15 minutes (fully baked). If the pastry rises during baking, gently press it down with your hand.

Steamed puddings

Light sponges and rich suet mixtures can both be gently cooked by steaming. Be sure to make the seal tight so moisture cannot get inside. It is important to keep the water in the saucepan topped up, so boil some water ready to add to the pan when needed.

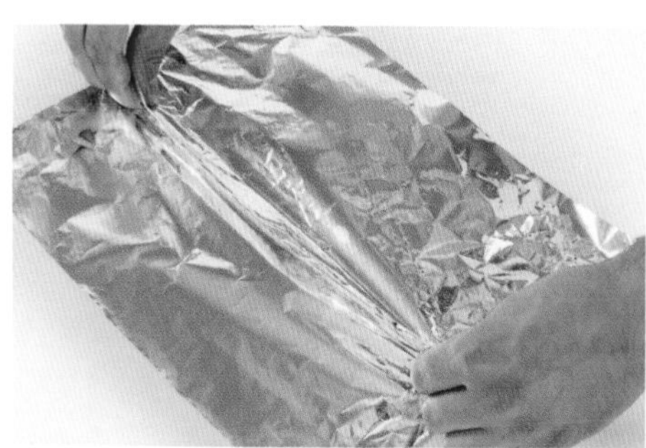

1 Turn the mixture into a greased, heatproof bowl. Layer a piece of greaseproof paper with a piece of foil and make a pleat across the middle, to allow for the pudding's expansion during cooking. Butter the paper.

2 Place the foil and paper, buttered-side down, over the top of the bowl. Secure by tying a string tightly under the rim. Form a handle with another string. Trim away excess paper and foil.

3 Put a trivet or upturned saucer or plate in the bottom of a saucepan and half fill with water. Bring to a simmer. Lower the bowl into the saucepan; add more boiling water to come halfway up the side of the bowl. Cover tightly and steam for the required time. Make sure that the water stays at simmering point and top up when necessary.

Eve's pudding

SERVES 6 **CALS PER SERVING** 414

butter, for greasing
500 g (1 lb) cooking apples, quartered, cored, peeled, and sliced
90 g (3 oz) demerara sugar
grated zest and juice of 1 lemon

Sponge topping

125 g (4 oz) baking spread, straight from the refrigerator
125 g (4 oz) caster sugar
2 eggs, beaten
125 g (4 oz) self-raising flour
1 tsp baking powder

1.25 LITRE (2 PINT) OVENPROOF DISH

1 Lightly butter the ovenproof dish and arrange the apples in the bottom. Sprinkle over the demerara sugar and the lemon zest and juice.

2 Make the sponge topping: put the baking spread, sugar, eggs, flour, and baking powder in a large bowl, and beat until smooth and well blended. Spoon on top of the apple slices, and level the surface.

3 Bake in a preheated oven at 180°C (160°C fan, Gas 4) for about 45 minutes until the sponge topping is well risen, golden, and springy to the touch. Serve hot.

SPICED EVE'S PUDDING

Add 1 tsp ground cinnamon to the sponge topping, and 60 g (2 oz) raisins, 1 tsp ground cinnamon, and 1 tsp ground mixed spice to the apple mixture.

Apple Charlotte

SERVES 8 **CALS PER SERVING** 321

1 kg (2 lb) cooking apples, quartered, cored, peeled, and sliced
125 g (4 oz) caster sugar
3 tbsp water
2 tbsp apricot jam
125 g (4 oz) butter, softened, plus extra for greasing
12 slices of bread, crusts removed

15 CM (6 IN) SQUARE CAKE TIN

1 Put the apples, sugar, and measured water in a saucepan and cook over a medium heat for about 10–15 minutes until the apples are soft but still holding their shape. Stir in the apricot jam.

2 Spread the butter on one side of each slice of bread. Lightly butter the cake tin and assemble the pudding (see box, right).

3 Bake in a preheated oven at 200°C (180°C fan, Gas 6) for about 40 minutes until crisp and golden. Serve hot.

Assembling the Charlotte

Use eight of the bread slices to line the tin, cutting them into strips or squares as necessary, and placing them buttered-side down. Spoon in the apple mixture. Cut the remaining slices of bread into quarters diagonally. Arrange the quarters, buttered-side up, on top of the apple mixture.

Baked apples

SERVES 6 **CALS PER SERVING** 235

6 cooking apples
90 g (3 oz) light muscovado sugar
90 g (3 oz) butter, diced
3 tbsp water

1 Wipe the apples, and remove the cores using an apple corer. Make a shallow cut through the skin around the equator of each apple.

2 Put the apples into an ovenproof dish and fill their middles with the sugar and butter. Pour the water around the apples.

3 Bake in a preheated oven at 190°C (170°C fan, Gas 5) for 40–45 minutes until the apples are soft. Serve hot, spooning all the juices from the dish over the apples.

CITRUS BAKED APPLES

Add the finely grated zest of 1 orange or 1 lemon to the muscovado sugar.

BAKED APPLES WITH MINCEMEAT

Use 125 g (4 oz) mincemeat instead of the sugar and butter.

Apple Brown Betty

SERVES 6 **CALS PER SERVING** 284

30–45 g (1–1½ oz) butter
175 g (6 oz) stale breadcrumbs
1 kg (2 lb) cooking apples, quartered, cored, peeled, and thinly sliced
125 g (4 oz) caster sugar, plus extra for sprinkling
1 tbsp lemon juice
1–2 tsp ground cinnamon

DEEP 1.5–2 LITRE (2½–3½ PINT) OVENPROOF DISH

1 Melt the butter in a frying pan. Add the breadcrumbs and stir over a medium heat for 5 minutes or until the crumbs are crisp and golden. Remove from the heat.

2 Toss the apples with the caster sugar, lemon juice, and ground cinnamon.

3 Press one-quarter of the crisp breadcrumbs over the bottom of the dish. Cover with half of the apple mixture and sprinkle with a further one-quarter of the breadcrumbs.

4 Arrange the remaining apple mixture on top of the breadcrumbs, spoon over any juices, and cover with the remaining breadcrumbs. Sprinkle the top of the pudding lightly with caster sugar.

5 Cover the dish with foil. Bake in a preheated oven at 200°C (180°C fan, Gas 6) for about 20 minutes.

6 Remove the foil and continue baking for a further 20 minutes or until the apples are tender and the top is golden brown. Serve warm.

APPLE AND CRANBERRY BROWN BETTY

Add 175 g (6 oz) fresh or thawed frozen cranberries to the apple mixture. Add a little more sugar if necessary.

PEACH MELBA BROWN BETTY

Substitute 3 peeled, stoned, and sliced peaches, and 250 g (8 oz) raspberries for the apples. Omit the lemon juice and cinnamon.

Cook's know-how

White or brown bread can be used for the breadcrumbs. Wholemeal gives a nutty flavour, and granary gives an interesting texture. For best results, the bread should be about 2 days old.

Classic apple crumble

SERVES 6 **CALS PER SERVING** 404

900 g (2 lb) cooking apples, e.g. Bramley's
175 g (6 oz) granulated sugar
finely grated zest of 1 lemon
6 tbsp water

Topping

175 g (6 oz) plain flour
90 g (3 oz) butter
60 g (2 oz) demerara sugar

20 CM (8 IN) OVENPROOF DISH

1 Quarter, peel, and core the apples, then slice them fairly thinly. Toss the slices in the sugar, lemon zest, and water and layer in the dish.

2 Make the topping: put the flour in a bowl and rub in the butter until the mixture resembles fine breadcrumbs, then stir in the sugar.

3 Sprinkle the topping evenly over the apple mixture in the dish and bake in a preheated oven at 180°C (160°C fan, Gas 4) for 40–45 minutes until golden brown and bubbling. Serve at once.

Cook's know-how

For a crunchier crumble topping, use 125 g (4 oz) wholemeal flour and 60 g (2 oz) porridge oats or muesli instead of the plain flour. To sweeten cooking apples, especially windfall apples that are not at their best, use apricot jam instead of some – or all – of the sugar. Apricot jam gives a gentle sweetness, and it improves the texture of the apples, especially if you are using them for a purée or a pie.

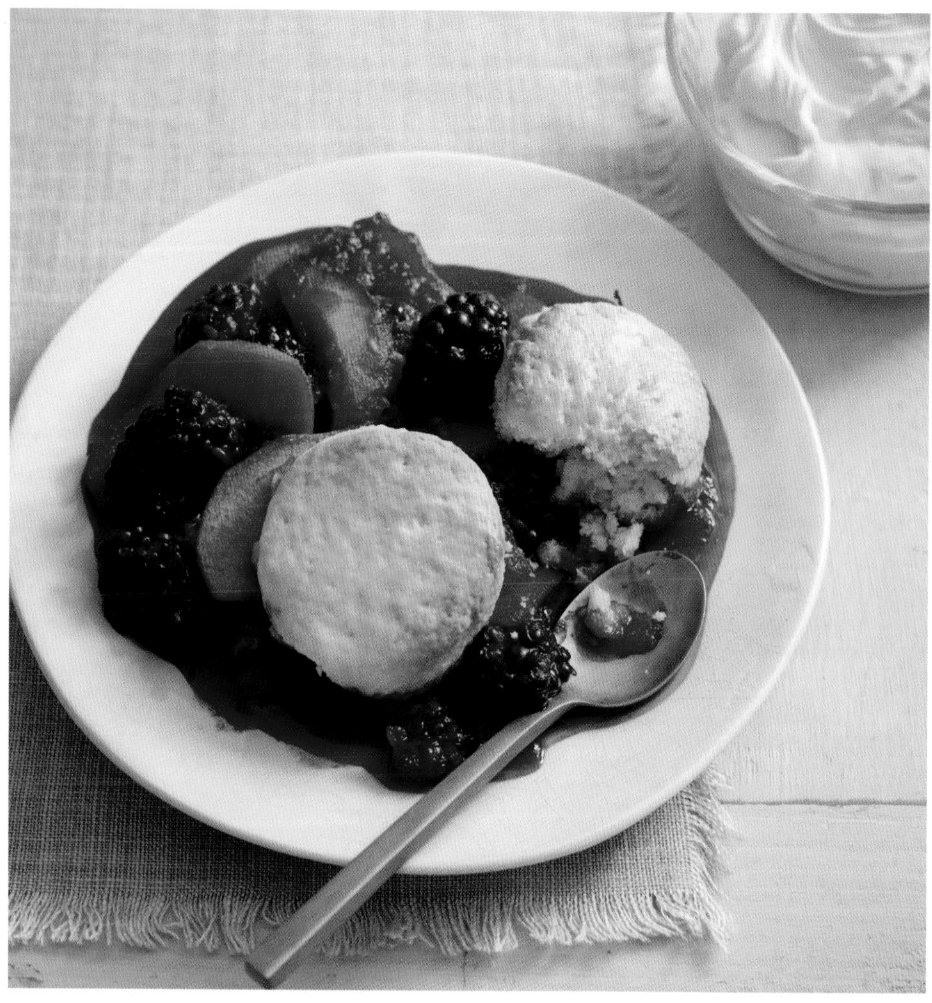

Blackberry and apple cobbler

SERVES 4 **CALS PER SERVING** 538

2 cooking apples, e.g. Bramley's
500 g (1 lb) blackberries
60 g (2 oz) caster sugar
finely grated zest and juice of 1 lemon

Cobbler topping
250 g (8 oz) self-raising flour
60 g (2 oz) butter, cubed
90 g (3 oz) caster sugar
90 ml (3 fl oz) milk, plus extra for glazing

5 CM (2 IN) ROUND FLUTED BISCUIT CUTTER

1 Quarter, peel, and core the apples, then cut the apples into large slices, about 1 cm (½ in) thick.

2 Put the apples into a saucepan with the blackberries, sugar, and lemon zest and juice. Cover and simmer gently for 10–15 minutes until the apple pieces are tender but not broken up.

3 Meanwhile, make the cobbler topping: put the flour into a bowl, add the cubes of butter, and rub in with the fingertips until the mixture resembles fine breadcrumbs. Stir in the sugar, add the milk, and mix to form a soft dough.

4 Roll out the dough on a lightly floured surface until 1 cm (½ in) thick. Cut out as many shapes as you can with the biscuit cutter, then re-roll the trimmings and cut out more. If you do not have a biscuit cutter, stamp out rounds with the rim of a glass or coffee mug.

5 Transfer the fruit to an ovenproof dish, arrange the pastry shapes on top and brush with milk to glaze.

6 Bake in a preheated oven at 220°C (200°C fan, Gas 7) for 15–20 minutes until the cobbler topping is golden. Serve at once.

Plum crumble

SERVES 6 **CALS PER SERVING** 436

1 kg (2 lb) plums, halved and stoned
60 g (2 oz) light muscovado sugar
1 tsp ground cinnamon

Crumble topping
250 g (8 oz) plain flour
125 g (4 oz) butter
90 g (3 oz) light muscovado sugar

1 Put the plums into a shallow ovenproof dish and sprinkle with the sugar and cinnamon.

2 Make the topping: put the flour into a bowl, and rub in the butter with the fingertips until the mixture resembles fine breadcrumbs. Stir in the sugar.

3 Sprinkle the topping evenly over the plums, without pressing it down, and bake in a preheated oven at 180°C (160°C fan, Gas 4) for 30–40 minutes until golden. Serve the crumble hot.

CRUNCHY APRICOT CRUMBLE

Substitute fresh apricots for the plums, and omit the cinnamon. Substitute porridge oats or muesli for half of the flour in the crumble topping, or use up to 125 g (4 oz) chopped toasted hazelnuts. You can also use half white and half wholemeal flour.

RHUBARB AND GINGER CRUMBLE

Substitute 1 kg (2 lb) rhubarb, cut into 2.5 cm (1 in) pieces, for the plums. Put into a saucepan with the sugar, 2 tbsp water, and 1 tsp ground ginger instead of the cinnamon, and cook gently until the rhubarb is soft.

Queen of puddings

SERVES 6 **CALS PER SERVING** 386

4 egg yolks
600 ml (1 pint) milk
30 g (1 oz) butter, plus extra for greasing
60 g (2 oz) caster sugar
grated zest of 1 orange
90 g (3 oz) fresh white breadcrumbs
3 tbsp strawberry or raspberry jam

Meringue topping

4 egg whites
175 g (6 oz) caster sugar

SHALLOW 1.25 LITRE (2 PINT) OVENPROOF DISH

1 In a large bowl, lightly beat the egg yolks. Set aside. Heat the milk in a small saucepan until bubbles appear around the edge. Add the butter, sugar, and orange zest, and heat gently until the butter has melted and the sugar dissolved.

2 Lightly butter the ovenproof dish and set aside. Gradually add the hot milk mixture to the egg yolks, whisking all the time.

3 Stir in the breadcrumbs, then pour into the ovenproof dish. Leave to stand for 15 minutes.

4 Bake the pudding in a preheated oven at 180°C (160°C fan, Gas 4) for about 30 minutes until just set. Remove from the oven and set aside.

5 Warm the jam in a small saucepan until melted. Spread the warmed jam evenly over the surface of the pudding.

6 Make the meringue topping: whisk the egg whites until stiff but not dry. With an electric mixer, whisk in the caster sugar, 1 tsp at a time, keeping the mixer at full speed.

7 Spoon the meringue on top of the pudding, spreading it to the edge and pulling it up to form peaks.

8 Return the pudding to the oven and bake for a further 10–15 minutes until the top of the meringue is crisp and golden brown. Serve at once.

Treacle pudding

SERVES 4–6 **CALS PER SERVING** 619–413

butter, for greasing
90 ml (3 fl oz) golden syrup
125 g (4 oz) self-raising flour
125 g (4 oz) shredded vegetable suet or grated chilled butter
60 g (2 oz) caster sugar
125 g (4 oz) fresh white breadcrumbs
about 125 ml (4 fl oz) milk

900 ML (1½ PINT) PUDDING BOWL

1 Lightly butter the bowl and spoon the golden syrup into the bottom.

2 Put the flour, suet or butter, sugar, and breadcrumbs into a bowl and stir to combine. Stir in enough milk to give a dropping consistency. Spoon into the bowl on top of the syrup.

3 Cover the bowl with buttered baking parchment and foil, both pleated in the middle. Secure by tying string under the rim of the bowl (page 476).

4 Put the bowl into a steamer or saucepan of simmering water, making sure the water comes halfway up the side of the bowl if using a saucepan. Cover and steam, topping up with boiling water as needed, for about 3 hours. Turn out the pudding, and serve with hot vanilla pouring custard (page 502).

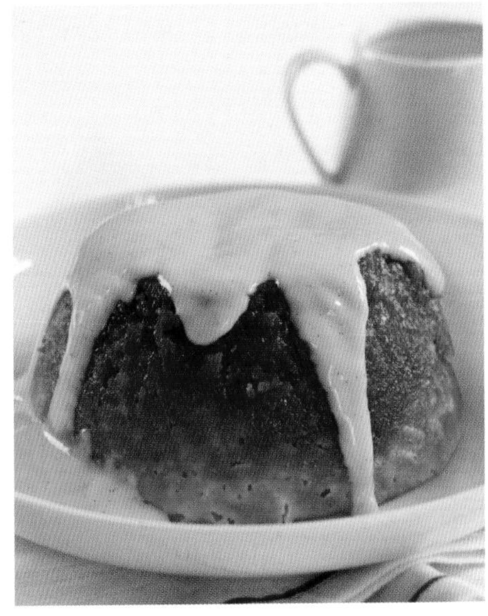

Sticky toffee pudding

SERVES 8 **CALS PER SERVING** 690

90 g (3 oz) butter, softened, plus extra for greasing
150 g (5 oz) light muscovado sugar
2 eggs, beaten
1 tbsp coffee extract
175 g (6 oz) self-raising flour
1 tsp baking powder
175 g (6 oz) stoned dates, roughly chopped
90 g (3 oz) walnuts, roughly chopped
175 ml (6 fl oz) hot water

Toffee sauce

125 g (4 oz) butter
175 g (6 oz) light muscovado sugar
6 tbsp double cream
60 g (2 oz) walnuts, roughly chopped

DEEP 18 CM (7 IN) SQUARE CAKE TIN

1 Butter the cake tin and line the bottom with baking parchment.

2 Put the butter, sugar, eggs, coffee extract, flour, and baking powder into a large bowl. Beat well until smooth and thoroughly blended.

3 Stir in the dates and walnuts, and then the measured hot water. Pour the mixture into the tin.

4 Bake in a preheated oven at 180°C (160°C fan, Gas 4) for 45–50 minutes until the pudding is well risen, browned on top, and springy to the touch.

5 About 10 minutes before the pudding is ready, make the toffee sauce: put the butter and sugar into a small saucepan, and heat gently, stirring, until the butter has melted and the sugar dissolved. Stir in the cream and walnuts and heat gently to warm through.

6 Cut the pudding into eight even-sized pieces, and transfer to serving plates. Spoon over the toffee sauce, and serve at once.

Cook's know-how

Serve the toffee sauce with other hot or cold desserts, such as steamed puddings or ice cream.

Pineapple upside-down pudding

SERVES 8 **CALS PER SERVING** 375

60 g (2 oz) butter, softened, plus extra for greasing
60 g (2 oz) light muscovado sugar
1 x 225 g can pineapple rings in natural juice, drained, and juice reserved
4 ready-to-eat dried apricots, coarsely chopped

Sponge

125 g (4 oz) butter, softened
125 g (4 oz) caster sugar
2 eggs, beaten
175 g (6 oz) self-raising flour
1 tsp baking powder

18 CM (7 IN) ROUND CAKE TIN

1 Lightly butter the tin and line the bottom with baking parchment. Cream together the butter and sugar and spread evenly over the baking parchment.

2 Arrange the pineapple rings on top of the butter and sugar mixture, and sprinkle the chopped dried apricots among the pineapple rings.

3 Make the sponge: put the butter, caster sugar, eggs, flour, and baking powder into a bowl with 2 tbsp of the reserved pineapple juice. Beat for 2 minutes or until smooth and well blended. Spoon the mixture on top of the pineapple rings and level the surface.

4 Bake in a preheated oven at 180°C (160°C fan, Gas 4) for about 45 minutes until the sponge is well risen and springy to the touch. Invert the sponge on to a warmed serving plate, and serve at once.

APRICOT UPSIDE-DOWN PUDDING

Substitute 1 x 400 g can apricot halves for the pineapple, and 2 tbsp chopped stem ginger for the dried apricots.

Bread and butter pudding

SERVES 6 **CALS PER SERVING** 516

12 thin slices of white bread, crusts removed
about 125 g (4 oz) butter, softened, plus extra for greasing
175 g (6 oz) mixed dried fruit
grated zest of 2 lemons
125 g (4 oz) demerara sugar
600 ml (1 pint) milk
2 eggs

1.7 LITRE (3 PINT) OVENPROOF DISH

1 Spread one side of each slice of bread with a thick layer of butter. Cut each slice of bread in half diagonally. Lightly butter the ovenproof dish and arrange 12 of the triangles, buttered-side down, in the bottom of the dish.

2 Sprinkle over half of the dried fruit, lemon zest, and sugar. Top with the remaining bread, buttered-side up. Sprinkle over the remaining fruit, lemon zest, and sugar.

3 Beat together the milk and eggs, and strain over the bread. Leave for 1 hour so that the bread can absorb some of the liquid.

4 Bake in a preheated oven at 180°C (160°C fan, Gas 4) for about 40 minutes until the bread slices on the top of the pudding are a golden brown colour and crisp, and the custard mixture has set completely. Serve at once.

Magic lemon pudding

SERVES 4 **CALS PER SERVING** 295

60 g (2 oz) butter, softened, plus extra for greasing
grated zest and juice of 1 large lemon
90 g (3 oz) caster sugar
2 eggs, separated
30 g (1 oz) plain flour
175 ml (6 fl oz) milk

600 ML (1 PINT) OVENPROOF DISH

1 Put the butter, lemon zest, and sugar into a bowl and beat together until pale and fluffy.

2 Add the egg yolks, flour, and lemon juice, and stir to combine. Gradually stir in the milk until evenly mixed.

3 Whisk the egg whites until stiff but not dry. Gradually fold into the lemon mixture.

4 Lightly butter the ovenproof dish. Pour the lemon mixture into the dish, and put the dish into a roasting tin. Add enough hot water to the roasting tin to come almost to the rim of the dish. Bake in a preheated oven at 160°C (140°C fan, Gas 3) for 40 minutes or until the sponge feels springy and serve hot. Leftovers are good cold.

Cook's **know-how**

This "magic" pudding separates during cooking to form a sponge topping with a tangy lemon sauce beneath.

Magic chocolate pudding

SERVES 4 **CALS PER SERVING** 361

60 g (2 oz) caster sugar
60 g (2 oz) fine semolina
30 g (1 oz) cocoa powder
1 tsp baking powder
30 g (1 oz) butter, melted, plus extra for greasing
2 eggs, beaten
2–3 drops of vanilla extract
icing sugar, for dusting

Sauce

90 g (3 oz) light muscovado sugar
2 tbsp cocoa powder
300 ml (½ pint) hot water

1 LITRE (1¾ PINT) OVENPROOF DISH

1 Mix together the sugar and semolina in a large bowl. Sift the cocoa powder and baking powder into the bowl, and mix thoroughly.

2 In a separate bowl, whisk together the melted butter, eggs, and vanilla extract with an electric whisk. Add this mixture to the dry ingredients and stir with a wooden spoon until well blended.

3 Lightly butter the ovenproof dish. Pour the mixture into the dish.

4 Make the sauce: mix together the muscovado sugar and cocoa powder, and gradually stir in the measured hot water. Pour the liquid over the pudding.

5 Bake the pudding in a preheated oven at 180°C (160°C fan, Gas 4) for 30 minutes or until the liquid has sunk to the bottom and the sponge is well risen and springy to the touch. Sprinkle with icing sugar, and serve at once.

NUTTY CHOCOLATE PUDDING

Add 60 g (2 oz) chopped pecan nuts or walnuts to the dry ingredients in step 1.

Steamed jam pudding

SERVES 4–6 **CALS PER SERVING** 573–382

125 g (4 oz) soft butter or baking spread, plus extra for greasing
3 tbsp jam
125 g (4 oz) caster sugar
2 eggs, beaten
175 g (6 oz) self-raising flour
1 tsp baking powder
about 1 tbsp milk

1.25 LITRE (2 PINT) PUDDING BOWL

1 Lightly grease the pudding bowl, and spoon the jam into the bottom.

2 Put the butter or baking spread, sugar, eggs, flour, and baking powder into a large bowl, and beat until smooth and thoroughly blended. Add enough milk to give a dropping consistency.

3 Spoon the mixture into the pudding bowl, and smooth the surface. Cover with greased greaseproof paper and foil, both pleated in the middle. Secure with string (page 476).

4 Put the bowl into a steamer or saucepan of simmering water, making sure the water comes halfway up the side of the bowl. Cover and steam, topping up with boiling water as needed, for about 1½ hours. Turn the pudding out on to a warmed plate, and serve hot.

Christmas pudding

This is a rich, dark pudding, laden with dried fruit, spices, and alcohol – the traditional way to finish the festive meal. A delicious cold alternative is the Iced Christmas pudding on page 555.

SERVES 8–10 **CALS PER SERVING** 522–418

- 90 g (3 oz) self-raising flour
- 125 g (4 oz) shredded vegetable suet or grated chilled butter
- 30 g (1 oz) blanched almonds, shredded
- 125 g (4 oz) carrot, grated
- 250 g (8 oz) raisins
- 125 g (4 oz) currants
- 125 g (4 oz) sultanas
- 125 g (4 oz) fresh breadcrumbs
- ¼ tsp grated nutmeg
- 60 g (2 oz) mixed candied peel, chopped
- 90 g (3 oz) light muscovado sugar
- grated zest and juice of 1 lemon
- 2 eggs, beaten
- butter, for greasing
- 75 ml (2½ fl oz) dark rum or brandy
- brandy butter (see box, below right), to serve (optional)

1.25 LITRE (2 PINT) PUDDING BOWL

1 In a large bowl, combine the flour, suet or butter, almonds, carrot, raisins, currants, sultanas, breadcrumbs, nutmeg, candied peel, sugar, and lemon zest. Add the lemon juice and eggs, and stir until well combined.

2 Lightly butter the pudding bowl. Spoon in the pudding mixture and level the surface.

3 Cover with buttered greaseproof paper, then foil, both pleated in the middle. Secure the paper and foil in place by tying string under the rim of the bowl (page 476).

4 Put the bowl into a steamer or saucepan of simmering water, making sure the water comes halfway up the side of the bowl. Cover and steam, topping up with boiling water as needed, for about 6 hours.

5 Remove the bowl from the steamer or pan and leave to cool. Remove the paper and foil covering. Make a few holes in the pudding with a fine skewer, and pour in the rum or brandy.

6 Cover the pudding with fresh greaseproof paper and foil. Store in a cool place for up to 3 months.

7 To reheat for serving, steam the pudding for 2–3 hours. Serve at once, with brandy butter if you like.

Brandy butter

Make your own brandy butter by creaming together 250 g (8 oz) each of unsalted butter and caster sugar or icing sugar, and 90 ml (3 fl oz) brandy. The brandy butter can be frozen for up to 3 months.

Rice pudding

SERVES 4 **CALS PER SERVING** 210

- 15 g (½ oz) butter, plus extra for greasing
- 60 g (2 oz) short grain (pudding) rice
- 600 ml (1 pint) milk
- 30 g (1 oz) caster sugar
- 1 strip of lemon zest
- ¼ tsp grated nutmeg

900 ML (1½ PINT) OVENPROOF DISH

1 Lightly butter the ovenproof dish. Rinse the rice under cold running water and drain well.

2 Put the rice into the dish and stir in the milk. Leave for about 30 minutes to allow the rice to soften.

3 Add the caster sugar and lemon zest to the rice mixture, and stir to mix. Sprinkle the surface of the milk with freshly grated nutmeg and dot with small knobs of butter.

4 Bake in a preheated oven at 150°C (130°C fan, Gas 2) for 2–2½ hours until the skin of the pudding is brown. Serve at once.

CHILLED RICE WITH PEARS

Let the pudding cool, then lift off the skin. Chill the pudding and serve in glass dishes, topped with slices of poached fresh or canned pears, and drizzled with melted strawberry jam.

French apple tart

SERVES 10 **CALS PER SERVING** 474

90 g (3 oz) butter
1.5 kg (3 lb) cooking apples, quartered, cored, and cut into chunks
3 tbsp water
6 tbsp apricot jam
125 g (4 oz) caster sugar
grated zest of 1 large lemon

Pastry

250 g (8 oz) plain flour, plus extra for dusting
125 g (4 oz) chilled butter, cubed
125 g (4 oz) caster sugar
4 egg yolks

Apple topping and glaze

375 g (12 oz) eating apples, quartered, cored, peeled, and sliced
juice of 1 lemon
1 tbsp caster sugar
6 tbsp apricot jam

28 CM (11 IN) LOOSE-BOTTOMED FLUTED FLAN TIN
BAKING BEANS

1 Make the pastry: put the flour into a bowl and rub in the butter until the mixture resembles fine breadcrumbs. Stir in the sugar, then the egg yolks and a little cold water, if needed, to make a soft dough. Wrap and chill for 30 minutes.

2 Melt the butter in a large saucepan, and add the cooking apples and water. Cover and cook very gently for 20–25 minutes until the apples are soft.

3 Rub the apple chunks through a nylon sieve into a clean pan. Add the jam, sugar, and lemon zest. Cook over a high heat for 15–20 minutes, stirring constantly, until all the liquid has evaporated and the apple purée is thick. Leave to cool.

4 Roll out the pastry on a lightly floured surface and use to line the flan tin. Bake blind (page 476) in a preheated oven at 190°C (170°C fan, Gas 5) for 10–15 minutes. Remove the beans and foil and bake for another 5 minutes. Allow to cool.

5 Spoon the apple purée into the shell. Arrange the apple slices on top, brush with lemon juice, and sprinkle with caster sugar. Return to the oven and bake for 30–35 minutes until the apples are tender and their edges lightly browned.

6 Heat the jam, work through a sieve, then brush over the apples to glaze. Serve the tart warm or cold.

Jamaican bananas

SERVES 4 **CALS PER SERVING** 269

30–45 g (1–1½ oz) unsalted butter
2–3 tbsp dark muscovado sugar
½ tsp ground cinnamon
60 ml (2 fl oz) dark rum
4 firm but ripe bananas, cut in half lengthwise
vanilla ice cream, to serve

1 Put the butter and sugar into a large heavy frying pan, and heat gently until the butter has melted and sugar dissolved. Stir to blend together, then cook gently, stirring, for about 5 minutes.

2 Stir the cinnamon and rum into the caramel mixture, then add the banana halves. Cook for 3 minutes on each side until warmed through.

3 Transfer the bananas and hot sauce to serving plates. Serve at once, with scoops of vanilla ice cream.

Tropical tartlets

MAKES 10 **CALS EACH** 286

about 600 ml (1 pint) ready-made thick custard
1 x 200 g can mandarin oranges in natural juice, well drained
1 x 200 g can apricot halves in natural juice, well drained and cut into pieces
about 3 tbsp apricot jam
about 60 g (2 oz) toasted flaked almonds

Almond pastry

60 g (2 oz) ground almonds
125 g (4 oz) plain flour
2 tbsp caster sugar
90 g (3 oz) chilled butter, cut into cubes
about 3 tbsp cold water

10 X 7 CM (3 IN) ROUND TARTLET TINS OR BOAT-SHAPED TINS (BARQUETTE MOULDS)

1 Make the pastry: combine the almonds, flour, and sugar in a bowl. Add the butter and rub in with the fingertips until the mixture resembles fine breadcrumbs. Add enough cold water to make a soft pliable dough. Wrap and chill for 1 hour.

2 Put the pastry on a floured surface and flatten slightly. Place a large sheet of baking parchment on top and roll out the pastry, beneath the parchment, until about 3 mm (⅛ in) thick. Line the tartlet tins with pastry and chill for 2 hours.

3 Prick the pastry all over and bake in a preheated oven at 190°C (170°C fan, Gas 5) for 10 minutes. Leave the shells to cool in the tins for 10 minutes. Remove and transfer to a wire rack. Leave to cool.

4 Spoon some custard into each shell, then top with the mandarin oranges and apricots. Melt the jam in a small pan, sieve, then spoon over the fruit. Sprinkle with the almonds and leave to set before serving.

Raspberry tartlets

MAKES 16 **CALS EACH** 209

250 g (8 oz) full-fat mascarpone
2 tbsp caster sugar
350 g (12 oz) raspberries
3 tbsp redcurrant jelly
1–2 tsp lemon juice, to taste

Pastry

250 g (8 oz) plain flour
125 g (4 oz) chilled butter, cut into cubes
2 tbsp caster sugar
3–4 tbsp cold water

7 CM (3 IN) PASTRY CUTTER
16 X 6 CM (2½ IN) ROUND TARTLET TINS

1 Make the pastry: put the flour into a bowl, add the butter, and rub in with the fingertips until the mixture resembles fine breadcrumbs. Stir in the sugar, then add enough cold water to bind to a soft pliable dough. Wrap and chill for at least 30 minutes.

2 On a lightly floured surface, roll out the pastry thinly. Using the pastry cutter, cut out 16 rounds.

3 Gently press the rounds into the tartlet tins. Prick all over with a fork and bake in a preheated oven at 190°C (170°C fan, Gas 5) for 12–15 minutes until golden. Leave in the tins for 10 minutes, then remove and transfer to a wire rack. Leave to cool completely.

4 Beat together the mascarpone and sugar and spoon into the pastry shells. Top with the raspberries, pressing them gently into the filling.

5 Melt the jelly with lemon juice to taste in a small pan, then spoon over the fruits. Leave to set before serving.

Tarte au citron

SERVES 10–12 **CALS PER SERVING** 572–476

5 eggs
125 ml (4fl oz) double cream
grated zest and juice of 4 lemons
225 g (8 oz) caster sugar
icing sugar, for dusting

Pastry
250 g (8 oz) plain flour
125 g (4 oz) chilled butter, cut into cubes
60 g (2 oz) caster sugar
1 egg
1–2 tbsp water

28 CM (11 IN) LOOSE-BOTTOMED FLUTED FLAN TIN
BAKING BEANS

1 Make the pastry: put the flour into a large bowl. Add the butter and rub in with the fingertips until the mixture resembles fine breadcrumbs.

2 Stir in the caster sugar, then bind together with the egg and water to make a soft, pliable dough. Wrap in cling film and chill for 30 minutes.

3 Roll out the dough on a lightly floured surface and use to line the flan tin. Bake blind (page 476) in a preheated oven at 220°C (200°C fan, Gas 7) for 10 minutes.

4 Remove the baking beans and foil and bake the pastry shell for 10 minutes or until the base is lightly browned. Remove from the oven, let cool, and reduce the oven temperature to 150°C (130°C fan, Gas 2). Trim the overhanging pastry edges with a sharp knife.

5 Beat the eggs in a bowl and add the cream, lemon zest and juice, and caster sugar. Stir until smooth, and pour into the pastry shell.

6 Bake for 35–40 minutes until the lemon filling has set. Cover the tart loosely with foil if the pastry begins to brown too much.

7 Leave the tart to cool a little, then dust with icing sugar. Decorate with lemon twists, and serve warm or at room temperature.

Blueberry puffs

MAKES 8 **CALS EACH** 375

500 g (1 lb) ready-made puff pastry
beaten egg
100 g (4 oz) blueberries
150 ml (5 fl oz) double or whipping cream
1 tbsp caster sugar
1 ripe nectarine or peach, stoned and sliced
icing sugar, for dusting

1 Roll out the pastry until 5 mm (¼ in) thick on a lightly floured surface. Cut into strips 7 cm (3 in) wide, then cut the strips diagonally into eight diamond shapes.

2 With a sharp knife, score each pastry diamond 1 cm (½ in) from the edge, taking care not to cut all the way through. Place on a dampened baking tray and glaze with beaten egg.

3 Bake in a preheated oven at 230°C (210°C fan, Gas 8) for 10–15 minutes until golden. Transfer to a wire rack. Remove the pastry centres, reserving them for lids if desired. Leave to cool.

4 Divide half of the blueberries among the pastry shells. Whip the cream and sugar and divide among the shells. Top with nectarine or peach slices, and the remaining blueberries. If using the pastry lids, dust with icing sugar and place on top of the filled shells before serving.

Treacle tart

SERVES 8 **CALS PER SERVING** 386

375 g (12 oz) golden syrup
about 200 g (7 oz) fresh white or brown breadcrumbs
grated zest and juice of 1 large lemon

Pastry

175 g (6 oz) plain flour
90 g (3 oz) chilled butter, cut into cubes
about 2 tbsp cold water

25 CM (10 IN) LOOSE-BOTTOMED FLUTED FLAN TIN

1 Make the pastry: put the flour into a large bowl, add the butter, and rub in with the fingertips until the mixture resembles fine breadcrumbs. Mix in enough water to make a soft, pliable dough.

2 Wrap the dough in cling film and leave to chill in the refrigerator for about 30 minutes.

3 Roll out the dough on a lightly floured surface and use to line the flan tin.

4 Gently heat the golden syrup in a saucepan until melted, and stir in the breadcrumbs and lemon zest and juice. Pour into the pastry shell.

5 Bake in a preheated oven at 200°C (180°C fan, Gas 6) for 10 minutes; reduce the oven temperature to 180°C (160°C fan, Gas 4), and bake for a further 30 minutes or until the pastry is golden and the filling firm.

6 Leave to cool in the tin for a few minutes. Serve warm, cut into slices with a spoonful of cream and a little grated lemon zest.

Apple tarte au citron

SERVES 10 **CALS PER SERVING** 463

4 eggs
250 g (8 oz) caster sugar
finely grated zest and juice of 2 lemons
125 g (4 oz) butter, melted
2 large cooking apples, e.g. Bramley's, quartered, cored, and peeled – about 350 g (12 oz) prepared weight
2 red eating apples, quartered, cored, and thinly sliced (leave the red skin on)
about 30 g (1 oz) demerara sugar
double or whipping cream, to serve

Pastry

250 g (8 oz) plain flour
30 g (1 oz) icing sugar
125 g (4 oz) butter, cubed
1 egg, beaten
1–2 tbsp water

25 CM (10 IN) DEEP LOOSE-BOTTOMED FLUTED FLAN TIN

1 Make the pastry: sift the flour and icing sugar into a bowl and rub in the cubes of butter until the mixture resembles breadcrumbs. Stir in the egg and water, and bring together to form a dough. (If making the pastry in a food processor, process the flour, icing sugar, and butter until like breadcrumbs, pour in the beaten egg and water, and pulse until the dough forms a ball.) Form the pastry into a smooth ball, put inside a plastic bag, and chill in the refrigerator for at least 30 minutes.

2 Roll out the chilled dough on a lightly floured surface and use to line the flan tin. Chill again for 30 minutes.

3 Prepare the filling: beat the eggs, caster sugar, and lemon zest and juice in a bowl. Stir in the warm melted butter, then coarsely grate the cooking apples directly into the mixture and mix well.

4 Spread the runny lemon mixture in the chilled pastry case. Level the surface with the back of a spoon and arrange the red-skinned apples around the outside edge. Sprinkle over the demerara sugar.

5 Bake on a hot baking sheet in a preheated oven at 200°C (180°C fan, Gas 6) for about 40–50 minutes or until the centre feels firm to the touch and the apples are tinged brown. Serve at once with fresh double or whipping cream.

Tarte Tatin

SERVES 6 **CALS PER SERVING** 511

90 g (3 oz) butter
90 g (3 oz) demerara sugar
1 kg (2 lb) Cox's apples or similar firm eating apples
grated zest and juice of 1 lemon

Pastry

175 g (6 oz) plain flour
125 g (4 oz) chilled butter, cut into cubes
30 g (1 oz) icing sugar
1 egg yolk
about 1 tbsp cold water

SHALLOW 23 CM (9 IN) ROUND CAKE TIN

1 Make the pastry: put the flour into a large bowl and add the butter. Rub in until the mixture resembles fine breadcrumbs. Stir in the icing sugar, then mix in the egg yolk and enough water to make a soft, but not sticky, dough. Wrap and chill for 30 minutes.

2 Put the butter and sugar into a pan and heat very gently until the sugar dissolves. Increase the heat and cook gently for 4–5 minutes until the mixture turns dark golden brown and is thick, but pourable. Pour evenly over the bottom of the tin.

3 Peel, core, and slice the apples. Toss them with the lemon zest and juice. Arrange in the cake tin (see box, right).

4 Roll out the pastry on a lightly floured surface into a round slightly larger than the tin. Lay the pastry over the apples, tucking the excess down the side of the tin.

5 Bake in a preheated oven at 200°C (180°C fan, Gas 6) for 25–30 minutes until the pastry is crisp and golden. Invert a serving plate on top of the tin, turn the tin and plate over, and lift the tin to reveal the caramelized apples. Serve warm or cold.

Arranging the apples in the cake tin

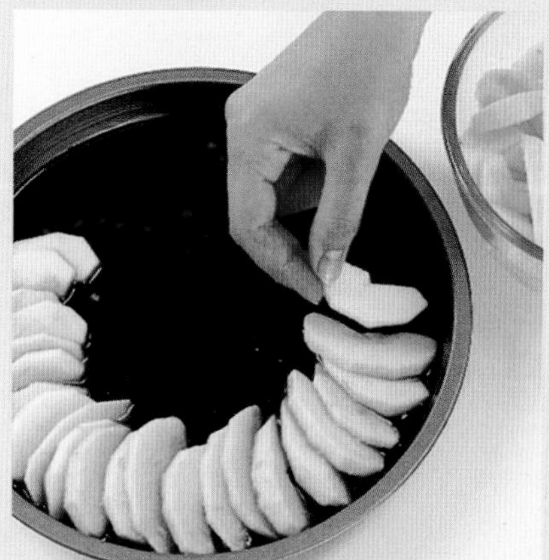

Arrange a single layer of the best apple slices in a circular pattern on top of the caramel mixture. Cover evenly with the remaining apple slices.

French apricot and almond tart

So often the star of French pâtisserie, this golden fruit tart is easy enough to make at home.

SERVES 10 **CALS PER SERVING** 398

crème pâtissière (see box, right)

Topping

1 kg (2 lb) fresh apricots, halved and stoned
juice of 1 lemon
125 ml (4 fl oz) water
75 g (2½ oz) caster sugar
1 tsp arrowroot
1 tbsp brandy
30 g (1 oz) toasted flaked almonds

Pastry

250 g (8 oz) plain flour
125 g (4 oz) chilled butter, cubed
60 g (2 oz) caster sugar
1 egg, beaten
1–2 tbsp water

28 CM (11 IN) LOOSE-BOTTOMED FLUTED FLAN TIN
BAKING BEANS

1 Make the pastry: sift the flour into a large bowl. Add the butter and rub in until the mixture resembles fine breadcrumbs.

2 Stir in the sugar, then mix in the egg and water to make a soft, pliable dough. Wrap in cling film and chill for 30 minutes.

3 Roll out the pastry on a lightly floured surface and use to line the flan tin. Bake blind (page 476) in a preheated oven at 200°C (180°C fan, Gas 6) for 10 minutes until the pastry shell is beginning to brown at the edge. Remove the beans and foil and bake for another 5–10 minutes. Leave to cool.

4 Put the apricots, cut-side down, in a shallow pan with the lemon juice, measured water, and sugar. Cover tightly and bring to a boil. Lower the heat and simmer gently for 3 minutes or until just soft.

5 Remove the apricots with a slotted spoon, reserving the juices. Drain on paper towels, and leave to cool.

6 Remove the pastry shell from the flan tin and put on a serving plate. Spread the crème pâtissière over the pastry shell, and smooth the surface.

7 Arrange the apricots, cut-side down, on the crème pâtissière. Combine the arrowroot and brandy in a small bowl and stir in the reserved apricot juices.

8 Return the mixture to the pan and bring to a boil, stirring until thick. Add the toasted flaked almonds.

9 Spoon the glaze over the apricots, making sure they are evenly coated. (Add a little water to the glaze if it is too thick.) Leave to stand until the glaze has cooled and set. Serve the tart cold.

Crème pâtissière

Put 3 eggs, 90 g (3 oz) vanilla sugar, and 60 g (2 oz) plain flour into a large bowl, add a little milk taken from 400 ml (14 fl oz), and mix until smooth. Pour the remaining milk into a heavy saucepan and bring almost to a boil. Pour on to the egg mixture, whisking well.

Rinse out the saucepan to remove any milk residue. Return the egg mixture to the pan, and cook over a gentle heat, stirring continuously, until thickened.

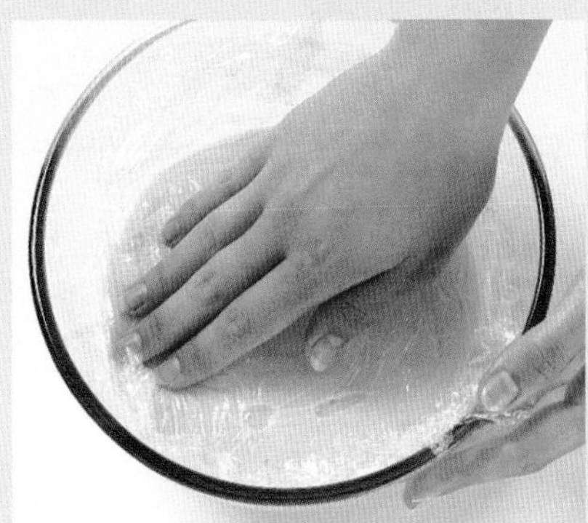

Pour into a bowl and cover with cling film, gently pressing it over the surface of the custard to prevent a skin from forming. Leave to cool.

Mincemeat and almond tart

This is a rich dessert, ideal for a Christmas dinner party. For an everyday pudding you could use less mincemeat and add some stewed apple, which will give a lighter texture and flavour.

SERVES 10 **CALS PER SERVING** 685

175 g (6 oz) butter, softened
175 g (6 oz) caster sugar
4 eggs
175 g (6 oz) ground almonds
1 tsp almond extract
about 8 tbsp good-quality mincemeat

Pastry

250 g (8 oz) plain flour
125 g (4 oz) chilled butter, cut into cubes
60 g (2 oz) caster sugar
1 egg, beaten
1–2 tbsp water

Topping

175 g (6 oz) icing sugar, sifted
juice of ½ lemon
1–2 tbsp water
60 g (2 oz) flaked almonds

DEEP 28 CM (11 IN) LOOSE-BOTTOMED FLUTED FLAN TIN

1 Make the pastry: put the flour into a large bowl. Add the butter and rub in with the fingertips until the mixture resembles fine breadcrumbs. Stir in the sugar, then mix in the egg and water to bind to a soft, pliable dough. Wrap the dough in cling film and chill for about 30 minutes.

2 Roll out the dough on a lightly floured surface and use to line the tin. Prick the bottom with a fork. Cover and chill while preparing the filling.

3 Put the butter and sugar into a large bowl and cream together until pale and fluffy. Add the eggs one at a time, beating well after each addition, then mix in the ground almonds and almond extract.

4 Spread the mincemeat evenly over the bottom of the pastry shell. Pour the almond mixture over the mincemeat.

5 Bake in a preheated oven at 190°C (170°C fan, Gas 5) for about 40 minutes until the filling is golden and firm to the touch. Cover loosely with foil if it is browning too much.

6 Meanwhile, make the topping: stir together the icing sugar, lemon juice, and enough water to make a thin glacé icing. Spread evenly over the tart, then sprinkle with the almonds.

7 Return to the oven for 5 minutes or until the icing is shiny and the almonds lightly coloured. Serve warm or cold.

Bakewell tart

SERVES 6 **CALS PER SERVING** 560

125 g (4 oz) butter
125 g (4 oz) caster sugar
1 egg, lightly beaten
125 g (4 oz) ground rice or semolina
½ tsp almond extract
2 tbsp raspberry jam
icing sugar, for dusting

Pastry

175 g (6 oz) plain flour
45 g (1½ oz) chilled butter, cut into cubes
45 g (1½ oz) chilled white vegetable fat, cut into cubes
about 2 tbsp cold water
milk, for glazing

19 CM (7½ IN) LOOSE-BOTTOMED FLUTED FLAN TIN

1 Make the pastry: put the flour into a large bowl. Rub in the butter and vegetable fat until the mixture resembles fine breadcrumbs. Mix in enough water to make a soft, pliable dough. Wrap in cling film and chill for 30 minutes.

2 Roll out the pastry on a lightly floured work surface and use to line the flan tin. Reserve the trimmings.

3 Melt the butter in a saucepan, stir in the caster sugar, and cook for about 1 minute. Remove from the heat, leave to cool a little, then gradually stir in the egg, ground rice or semolina, and almond extract.

4 Spread the jam evenly over the bottom of the pastry shell, and pour the almond mixture on top.

5 Roll out the reserved pastry trimmings, and cut into thin strips, long enough to fit across the tart. Arrange the strips on top of the almond filling to form a lattice, attaching them to the edge of the pastry shell with a little milk.

6 Bake in a preheated oven at 200°C (180°C fan, Gas 6) for 45–50 minutes until the filling is well risen and golden and springs back when lightly pressed with a finger. If the pastry is browning too much, cover the tart loosely with foil.

7 Remove the tart from the oven. Sprinkle with icing sugar and serve the tart warm or cold.

Plum and almond tart

SERVES 6 **CALS PER SERVING** 549

175 g (6 oz) golden marzipan, grated
500 g (1 lb) ripe plums, halved and stoned
icing sugar, for sifting

Pastry

250 g (8 oz) plain flour
125 g (4 oz) icing sugar, sifted
125 g (4 oz) butter, cubed
1 small egg, beaten
1–2 tbsp water
a little milk, for glazing

23 CM (9 IN) FLUTED FLAN TIN

1 Put a baking tray in the oven, and preheat the oven to 200°C (180°C fan, Gas 6).

2 Make the pastry: put the flour into a bowl, and rub in butter with your fingertips. Stir in the sugar, egg, and water, and bring together to form a ball. (If making the pastry in a food processor, pulse together the flour, sugar, and butter until the mixture resembles fine breadcrumbs. Add the egg, and pulse again until the dough holds together in a ball.) Knead the dough on a lightly floured surface until smooth, then wrap in cling film and chill for 10 minutes.

3 Remove a little less than half of the pastry for the top of the tart, and return it to the refrigerator. Roll out the remaining pastry on a lightly floured surface, and use to line the bottom and side of the flan tin, making a rim around the top edge. If the pastry cracks, press it together again, and patch it with rolled-out pastry trimmings if necessary.

4 Prick all over the bottom of the pastry with a fork, and scatter with the grated marzipan. Arrange the plums cut-side down on top. Brush the pastry rim with water. Roll out the reserved pastry to a round that is slightly larger than the diameter of the tin, and place over the plums. Press the pastry edges together to seal, and trim off any excess. Brush with a little milk to glaze.

5 Place the tin on the hot baking tray, and bake for 30–35 minutes until pale golden. Sift icing sugar over the tart, and serve warm.

Key lime pie

SERVES 8 **CALS PER SERVING** 489

300 ml (½ pint) double cream
1 x 400 g can full-fat sweetened condensed milk
grated zest and juice of 2 limes
lime slices, to decorate

Pastry

175 g (6 oz) plain flour
90 g (3 oz) chilled butter, cut into cubes
about 2 tbsp cold water

23 CM (9 IN) LOOSE-BOTTOMED FLUTED FLAN TIN
BAKING BEANS

1 Make the pastry: put the flour into a large bowl, add the butter, and rub in until the mixture resembles fine breadcrumbs. Add enough cold water to make a soft pliable dough.

2 Wrap the dough in cling film or foil and chill in the refrigerator for 30 minutes.

3 Roll out the dough on a lightly floured surface and use to line the flan tin.

4 Bake the pastry shell blind (page 476) in a preheated oven at 200°C (180°C fan, Gas 6) for about 10 minutes. Remove the baking beans and foil and return the shell to the oven for 5 minutes. Cool slightly.

5 Whip the cream to soft peaks in a large bowl and mix together with the condensed milk. Slowly stir in the lime zest and juice until the mixture thickens.

6 Pour the mixture into the shell and smooth the top, or create a pattern with a palette knife. Chill in the refrigerator for at least 2 hours or until the filling is set firm.

7 Serve the pie chilled, decorated with lime slices.

Mississippi mud pie

SERVES 12 **CALS PER SERVING** 553

200 g (7 oz) plain chocolate
125 g (4 oz) butter
1 tbsp coffee extract
3 eggs
150 ml (1/4 pint) single cream
175 g (6 oz) dark muscovado sugar
150 ml (1/4 pint) whipping cream, to decorate

Pastry

250 g (8 oz) plain flour
125 g (4 oz) chilled butter, cut into cubes
about 2–3 tbsp cold water

25 CM (10 IN) LOOSE-BOTTOMED FLUTED FLAN TIN
BAKING BEANS

1 Make the pastry: put the flour into a large bowl. Add the butter and rub in until the mixture resembles fine breadcrumbs. Add enough cold water to make a soft, pliable dough.

2 Wrap the dough and chill for 30 minutes.

3 Roll out the dough on a lightly floured surface and use to line the flan tin.

4 Bake the pastry shell blind (page 476) in a preheated oven at 200°C (180°C fan, Gas 6) for about 10 minutes until the pastry edge begins to brown.

5 Remove the baking beans and foil, and bake for a further 5 minutes or until the base has dried out. Remove the pastry shell from the oven, and reduce the oven temperature to 190°C (170°C fan, Gas 5).

6 Break the chocolate into pieces, and place in a heavy pan with the butter and coffee extract. Heat gently, stirring occasionally, until the chocolate and butter have melted. Remove from the heat. Leave the mixture to cool slightly.

7 Beat the eggs, then add to the saucepan with the cream and sugar. Stir thoroughly to mix.

8 Pour the filling into the pastry shell. Bake for 30–35 minutes until the filling has set. Leave to cool.

9 Pipe whipped cream rosettes around the edge of the pie before serving.

Pecan pie

SERVES 8 **CALS PER SERVING** 458

150 g (5 oz) pecan nut halves
30 g (1 oz) unsalted butter
60 g (2 oz) light muscovado sugar
30 g (1 oz) caster sugar
125 ml (4 fl oz) golden syrup
3 tbsp brandy
1 tsp vanilla extract
2 tbsp single cream
¼ tsp ground cinnamon
pinch of grated nutmeg
1 large egg, lightly beaten
2 egg yolks

Pastry

175 g (6 oz) plain flour
90 g (3 oz) chilled butter, cubed
about 2 tbsp cold water
1 egg white, lightly beaten

23 CM (9 IN) LOOSE-BOTTOMED FLUTED FLAN TIN
BAKING BEANS

1 Make the pastry: put the flour into a bowl, add the butter, and rub in with the fingertips until the mixture resembles fine breadcrumbs. Add enough water to make a soft dough. Leave to chill for about 30 minutes.

2 Roll out the pastry on a lightly floured work surface and line the flan tin. Bake blind (page 476) in a preheated oven at 180°C (160°C fan, Gas 4) for 10 minutes.

3 Remove the beans and foil, lightly brush the pastry shell with egg white, and return to the oven for 1–2 minutes. Remove from the oven and set aside.

4 Spread the pecans out on a baking tray, and roast in the oven, turning occasionally, for 10–15 minutes. Reserve a few pecan halves and coarsely chop the remainder. Leave the oven on.

5 Put the butter into a heavy saucepan and cook over a gentle heat until it turns golden brown. Add the sugars and golden syrup, and heat gently until the sugars dissolve. Add the brandy, bring to a boil, and cook for 5 minutes.

6 Remove from the heat and stir in the vanilla extract, cream, cinnamon, and nutmeg.

7 Whisk together the egg and egg yolks. Whisk a little hot syrup into the eggs. Add half of the syrup, little by little, then add the remainder. Leave to cool.

8 Arrange the chopped pecans and pecan halves in the pastry shell. Pour the syrup and egg mixture over them. Bake in the oven for about 40 minutes until golden brown and set. Leave to cool before serving.

Banoffi pie

SERVES 8 **CALS PER SERVING** 816

90 g (3 oz) butter, plus extra for greasing
90 g (3 oz) light soft brown sugar
1 x 397 g can caramel condensed milk

Biscuit crust

90 g (3 oz) butter
175 g (6 oz) digestive biscuits, finely crushed

Topping

2 bananas
200 ml (7 fl oz) double or whipping cream, lightly whipped
cocoa powder or chocolate curls

20 CM (8 IN) SPRINGFORM OR LOOSE-BOTTOMED CAKE TIN

1 Lightly grease the cake tin, and line the bottom with baking parchment.

2 Make the biscuit crust (see box, below right) and place in the refrigerator to set.

3 Meanwhile, make the filling: put the butter and sugar into a saucepan, and stir over a low heat until melted and combined. Add the condensed milk, and stir until smooth. Bring to a boil over a high heat, stirring. Boil for 1 minute only, then pour immediately over the biscuit crust in the tin. Chill for at least 30 minutes, until set. (The pie can be made up to this stage the day before serving.)

4 Peel the bananas, cut into chunky slices, and arrange over the set toffee base. Spread the whipped cream over the bananas to cover them completely so they do not discolour. Chill the pie for at least 2 hours until firm enough to cut (it will keep in the refrigerator for up to 6 hours). Before serving, sift cocoa powder over the cream or decorate with chocolate curls.

Making the biscuit crust

Melt the butter in a saucepan, add the crushed biscuits, and stir well to combine. Press on to the bottom and side of the flan tin. Chill.

Double crust apple pie

For a successful double crust pie, the pastry underneath should be properly cooked and not soggy. Putting the dish on a hot baking tray at the start of baking is the key.

SERVES 6 **CALS PER SERVING** 432

500 g (1 lb) cooking apples, preferably Bramley's, quartered, cored, peeled, and sliced
250 g (8 oz) Cox's apples, quartered, cored, peeled, and sliced
about 30 g (1 oz) caster sugar, plus extra for sprinkling
2 tbsp water
rough puff pastry (page 475)
milk, for glazing

24 CM (9½ IN) PIE DISH

1 Put the apples into a large pan and add the sugar and water. Cover and cook gently, stirring, for about 10 minutes until the apples are soft and fluffy. Taste for sweetness and add more sugar if necessary. Turn into a bowl and leave the apples to cool.

2 Divide the pastry into two portions, one portion slightly larger than the other. Roll out the larger portion on a lightly floured surface and use to line the pie dish.

3 Spoon the apple filling on to the pastry shell, spreading it almost to the edge and then doming it in the middle.

4 Roll out the remaining pastry. Brush the edge of the pastry shell with a little water, then lay the pastry lid over the apple filling. Trim the edge, then crimp to seal. Make a small hole in the pastry lid to allow the steam to escape.

5 Put a baking tray in the oven and preheat to 220°C (200°C fan, Gas 7). Meanwhile, use the pastry trimmings to make leaves to decorate the pie, attaching them with milk. Brush the pastry lid with milk and sprinkle with sugar.

6 Remove the hot baking tray from the preheated oven and place the pie dish on it (this helps ensure a crisp pastry base). Bake for 25–30 minutes until the pastry is golden. Serve with hot vanilla pouring custard (see box, right).

ST CLEMENT'S APPLE PIE

When cooking the apples, add the grated zest and juice of 1 large lemon, and 3 tbsp fine-cut orange marmalade to the apples.

Sauces for puddings

Pouring custard Blend together 3 eggs, 30 g (1 oz) caster sugar, and 1 tsp cornflour. Heat 600 ml (1 pint) milk to just below boiling and stir into the egg mixture. Return to the pan and heat gently, stirring, until thickened. Strain into a cold bowl to prevent further cooking, and serve warm or cold.

Sweet white sauce Blend 1 tbsp cornflour with 1 tbsp caster sugar, and a little milk taken from 300 ml (½ pint). Bring the remaining milk to a boil and stir into the cornflour mixture. Return to the saucepan and heat gently, stirring, until thickened. If preferred, add flavourings such as grated orange zest, brandy, rum, or vanilla extract to the sauce. Serve warm.

Sabayon sauce Put 4 egg yolks, 60 g (2 oz) caster sugar, and 150 ml (¼ pint) dry white wine into a bowl over a saucepan of gently simmering water. Whisk for 5–8 minutes or until the mixture is frothy and thick. Remove from the heat and whisk in the grated zest of 1 orange. Serve at once or, to serve cool, continue whisking the mixture until cool.

Baked apple dumplings

SERVES 4 **CALS PER SERVING** 781

4 cooking apples, peeled and cored
60 g (2 oz) demerara sugar
½ tsp ground cinnamon
milk, for glazing

Shortcrust pastry
375 g (12 oz) plain flour
90 g (3 oz) chilled butter, cut into cubes, plus extra for greasing
90 g (3 oz) chilled white vegetable fat, cut into cubes
3–4 tbsp cold water

1 Make the pastry: put the flour into a large bowl. Add the butter and white vegetable fat, and rub in with the fingertips until the mixture resembles fine breadcrumbs. Mix in enough water to make a soft, pliable dough. Wrap the dough in cling film and chill for about 30 minutes.

2 Divide the dough into four pieces. Roll out each piece on a lightly floured surface and cut into an 18 cm (7 in) round. Reserve the trimmings. Put an apple in the centre of each round and make four dumplings (see box, right).

3 Cut leaf shapes from the pastry trimmings, and use to decorate the tops of the dumplings, attaching them with a little water. Make a hole in the top of each dumpling, and lightly brush all over with milk.

4 Bake in a preheated oven at 200°C (180°C fan, Gas 6) for 35–40 minutes until the pastry is golden and the apples tender. Serve hot.

Making the apple dumplings

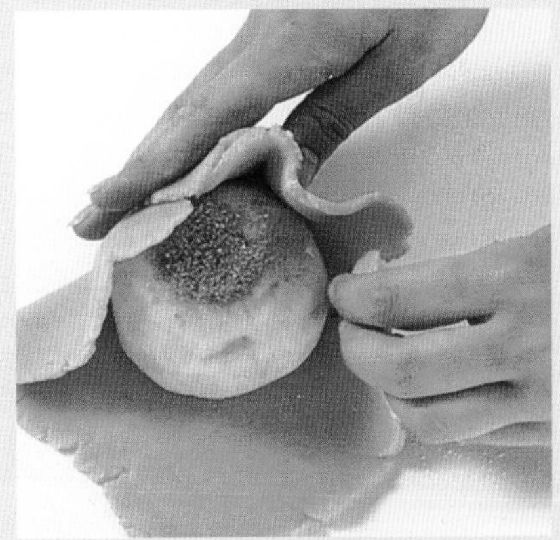

Fill the apples with the demerara sugar and cinnamon. Draw up a pastry round to enclose each apple, sealing the joins with a little water. Place, with the joins underneath, on a baking tray.

Apple strudel

SERVES 8 **CALS PER SERVING** 278

four 25 x 45 cm (10 x 18 in) sheets of filo pastry
60 g (2 oz) butter, melted
30 g (1 oz) fresh white breadcrumbs
15 g (½ oz) flaked almonds
icing sugar, for dusting

Filling

750 g (1½ lb) cooking apples, quartered, cored, peeled, and sliced
grated zest and juice of 1 lemon
3 tbsp light muscovado sugar
½ tsp ground mixed spice
½ tsp ground cinnamon
125 g (4 oz) sultanas
60 g (2 oz) blanched almonds, roughly chopped

1 Make the filling: mix together the apples, lemon zest and juice, sugar, mixed spice, cinnamon, sultanas, and almonds.

2 Lightly brush one sheet of filo pastry with melted butter. Cover with the remaining sheets, brushing each with butter. Add the filling and finish the strudel (see box, below).

3 Brush the strudel with the remaining melted butter and sprinkle with the almonds. Bake in a preheated oven at 190°C (170°C fan, Gas 5) for 40–45 minutes until the pastry is crisp and golden. Dust with the icing sugar. Cut into pieces and serve warm or cold.

Finishing the strudel

Sprinkle the breadcrumbs over the pastry. Spoon the apple mixture along the middle of the pastry.

Fold the pastry to enclose the filling, turn over on to a baking tray, and bend into a horseshoe shape.

Strawberry and rhubarb pie

SERVES 6–8 **CALS PER SERVING** 371–278

150 g (5 oz) caster sugar, plus extra for sprinkling
45 g (1½ oz) cornflour
750 g (1½ lb) rhubarb, cut into 1 cm (½ in) slices
1 cinnamon stick, halved
375 g (12 oz) strawberries, hulled and halved
whipped cream or crème fraîche, to serve

Shortcrust pastry

175 g (6 oz) plain flour
90 g (3 oz) chilled butter, cut into cubes
about 2 tbsp cold water

23 CM (9 IN) FLAN DISH OR TIN

1 Make the pastry: put the flour into a large bowl, add the butter, and rub in with the fingertips until the mixture resembles fine breadcrumbs. Add enough water to bind to a soft, but not sticky dough. Wrap the pastry in cling film and leave to chill in the refrigerator for about 30 minutes.

2 Meanwhile, combine the sugar with the cornflour and toss with the rhubarb, cinnamon, and strawberries. Leave to soak for 15–20 minutes.

3 On a lightly floured surface, divide the dough in half and roll out one half into a thin round to line the bottom and sides of the flan dish.

4 Put the soaked fruit into the pastry shell, removing the cinnamon.

5 Roll out the second half of pastry to the same size as the first round. Cut a 1 cm (½ in) strip from around the edge of the pastry.

6 Cut the remaining pastry into 1 cm (½ in) strips and arrange in a lattice on top of the pie. Brush the ends with water and attach the long strip around the rim of the pie. Sprinkle with 1–2 tbsp sugar.

7 Bake in a preheated oven at 220°C (200°C fan, Gas 7) for 10 minutes; reduce the oven temperature to 180°C (160°C fan, Gas 4), and bake for a further 30–40 minutes until the fruit is just cooked, and the pastry golden. Serve warm or cold, with whipped cream or crème fraîche.

Lemon meringue pie

SERVES 8–10 **CALS PER SERVING** 537–430

grated zest and juice of 4 large lemons
90 g (3 oz) cornflour
600 ml (1 pint) water
4 egg yolks
175 g (6 oz) caster sugar

Meringue

5 egg whites
250 g (8 oz) caster sugar

Pastry

250 g (8 oz) plain flour
30 g (1 oz) icing sugar
125 g (4 oz) chilled butter, cut into cubes
1 egg yolk
2 tbsp cold water

25 CM (10 IN) LOOSE-BOTTOMED FLUTED FLAN TIN
BAKING BEANS

1 Make the pastry: sift the flour and icing sugar into a large bowl. Add the butter and rub in with the fingertips until the mixture resembles fine breadcrumbs.

2 Mix in the egg yolk and enough cold water to make a soft, pliable dough. Wrap the dough in cling film and chill in the refrigerator for about 30 minutes.

3 Roll out the dough on a lightly floured surface and use to line the flan tin. Bake blind (page 476) in a preheated oven at 200°C (180°C fan, Gas 6) for 10 minutes.

4 Remove the baking beans and foil and bake the pastry shell for 5 minutes or until the base has dried out. Remove from the oven and reduce the temperature to 150°C (130°C fan, Gas 2).

5 Mix the lemon zest and juice with the cornflour. Bring the water to a boil, then stir into the lemon mixture. Return to the pan and bring back to a boil, stirring, until the mixture thickens. Remove from heat.

6 Leave to cool slightly, then stir in the egg yolks mixed with the sugar. Return to a low heat and cook, stirring, until just simmering. Pour into the pastry shell.

7 Whisk the egg whites with a hand-held electric mixer on maximum speed until stiff but not dry. Whisk in the sugar 1 tsp at a time. Pile on top of the filling and spread over evenly. Bake for 45 minutes or until crisp and brown. Serve the pie warm or cold.

Mille-feuille

SERVES 6 **CALS PER SERVING** 486

250 g (8 oz) puff pastry, thawed if frozen
3 tbsp raspberry jam
150 ml (1/4 pint) double or whipping cream, whipped

Crème pâtissière

2 eggs, beaten
60 g (2 oz) vanilla sugar or 1 tsp vanilla extract
30 g (1 oz) plain flour
300 ml (1/2 pint) milk

Icing

125 g (4 oz) icing sugar
about 1 tbsp water

1 Make the crème pâtissière (page 495), using the quantities listed above.

2 Roll out the pastry on a floured surface to make a thin, 28 x 33 cm (11 x 13 in) rectangle. Lay it over a dampened baking tray.

3 Prick the pastry with a fork. Bake in a preheated oven at 220°C (200°C fan, Gas 7) for 10–15 minutes until the pastry is crisp and golden.

4 Remove from the oven and leave to cool. Reduce the oven temperature to 180°C (160°C fan, Gas 4).

5 Trim the edges of the pastry to a rectangle, then cut into three equal rectangles, 10 cm (4 in) wide. Crush the pastry trimmings and set aside.

6 Mix the icing sugar and enough water to make a smooth glacé icing. Spread over one of the rectangles, and place on a baking tray.

7 Bake for 2 minutes or until the icing has just set and has a slight sheen. Leave to cool.

8 Place a second pastry rectangle on a serving plate. Spread evenly with the jam and then the whipped cream. Set the third rectangle on top and cover with the crème pâtissière.

9 Top with the iced pastry rectangle. Decorate the long edges of the rectangle with thin rows of crushed pastry trimmings.

10 Chill the mille-feuille in the refrigerator until ready to serve.

Baklava

MAKES 20 squares **CALS EACH** 249

250 g (8 oz) walnuts, finely chopped
60 g (2 oz) light muscovado sugar
1 tsp ground cinnamon
175 g (6 oz) butter, melted, plus extra for greasing
24 sheets of filo pastry, weighing about 500 g (1 lb)
90 ml (3 fl oz) clear honey
2 tbsp lemon juice

SHALLOW 18 X 23 CM (7 X 9 IN) RECTANGULAR CAKE TIN

1 Mix together the walnuts, sugar, and cinnamon.

2 Lightly butter the cake tin and lay one sheet of filo pastry in the bottom of the tin, allowing the pastry to come up the sides. (If necessary, cut the sheets in half to fit in the tin.) Brush the pastry with a little melted butter.

3 Repeat with five more filo sheets, layering and brushing each one with the butter. Sprinkle with one-third of the nut mixture.

4 Repeat this process twice, using six more sheets of filo pastry each time, brushing each sheet with butter and sprinkling the nut mixture over each sixth sheet. Finish with six buttered sheets of filo pastry, and lightly brush the top with melted butter.

5 Trim the edges of the filo, then, using a sharp knife, cut about halfway through the pastry layers to make 20 squares.

6 Bake in a preheated oven at 220°C (200°C fan, Gas 7) for 15 minutes, then reduce the oven temperature to 180°C (160°C fan, Gas 4) and bake for 10–15 minutes until the pastry is crisp and golden brown. Remove the baklava from the oven.

7 Heat the honey and lemon juice in a heavy saucepan until the honey has melted.Spoon over the hot baklava. Leave to cool in the tin for 1–2 hours. Cut into the marked squares, and serve the baklava at room temperature.

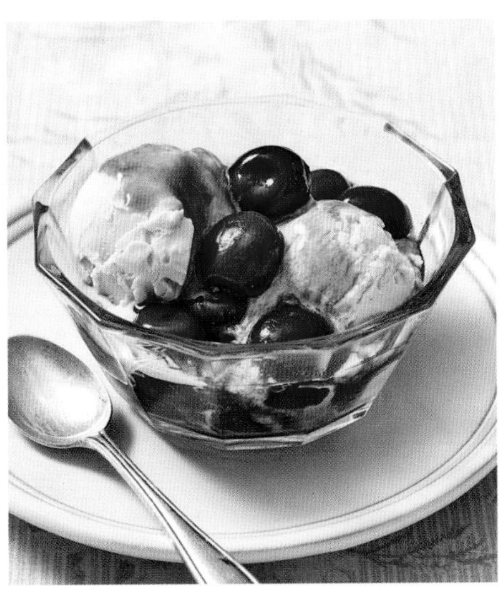

Cherries Jubilee

SERVES 4 **CALS PER SERVING** 162

1 x 425 g jar or can Morello cherries in syrup
2–3 tbsp caster sugar
75 ml (2½ fl oz) brandy
a few drops of almond extract
vanilla ice cream, to serve

1 Drain the cherries, reserving 125 ml (4 fl oz) of the syrup. Put the cherries into a saucepan with the measured syrup and the sugar.

2 Heat gently, stirring, until the sugar has dissolved, then bring to a boil. Simmer for about 5 minutes until the liquid has thickened and reduced by about half.

3 Pour the brandy over the cherries, and add the almond extract. Boil to evaporate the alcohol, then spoon the hot cherries and syrup over scoops of vanilla ice cream, and serve at once.

FRESH CHERRIES JUBILEE

Replace the Morello cherries with 500 g (1 lb) fresh cherries. Pit the cherries and poach them in 250 ml (8 fl oz) red wine and 100 g (3½ oz) caster sugar until tender. Substitute the poaching liquid for the syrup.

Summer berry soufflés with berry compote

SERVES 6 **CALS PER SERVING** 180

400 g (13 oz) frozen mixed summer berries
1 heaped tbsp cornflour
2 tbsp cassis (blackcurrant liqueur)
butter, for greasing
3 large egg whites
175 g (6 oz) caster sugar

6 X 150 ML (¼ PINT) RAMEKINS

1 Measure half of the berries into a saucepan, and heat gently for a few minutes until the fruit is soft.

2 Put the cornflour and cassis into a small bowl, and mix until smooth. Add a little of the hot berry juices to the cornflour mix, stir, and pour back into the saucepan. Heat, stirring, until thickened, then press through a sieve into a bowl, leaving just the pips behind in the sieve. Set the berry purée aside to cool.

3 Put a baking tray in the oven, and preheat the oven to 190°C (170°C fan, Gas 5). Butter the ramekins.

4 Put the egg whites into a large bowl, and beat with an electric whisk on high speed until stiff but not dry. Add 100 g (3½ oz) of the sugar a teaspoon at a time, and keep beating until stiff and shiny. Stir a little of the whites into the berry purée, then carefully fold in the remainder until evenly combined.

5 Spoon the mixture into the prepared ramekins, level the tops, then run your finger inside the rim of each dish – this will ensure the soufflés rise evenly. Place the ramekins on the hot baking tray, and bake for 8–10 minutes until the soufflés are well risen and light golden on top.

6 Meanwhile, make the compote: heat the remaining berries and sugar in a pan over a low heat, stirring until the sugar has dissolved and the fruit has defrosted. Check for sharpness, and add a little more sugar if the fruit does not taste sweet enough.

7 Serve the soufflés as soon as they come out of the oven, with the warm compote.

Crêpes Suzette

SERVES 4 **CALS PER SERVING** 604

juice of 2 oranges
125 g (4 oz) unsalted butter
60 g (2 oz) caster sugar
3–4 tbsp orange liqueur or brandy

Crêpes

125 g (4 oz) plain flour
1 egg
1 tbsp oil, plus extra for frying
300 ml (½ pint) milk

18–20 CM (7–8 IN) FRYING PAN

1 Make the crêpes: sift the flour into a bowl. Make a well in the middle. Mix together the egg, 1 tbsp oil, and the milk, and pour into the well. Gradually beat in the flour, to make a fairly thin batter.

2 Heat a little oil in the frying pan, then wipe away the excess oil. Add 2–3 tbsp batter to the pan, tilting it to coat the bottom evenly. Cook for 45–60 seconds, then turn over, and cook the other side for about 30 seconds. Slide the crêpe out on to a warmed plate.

3 Repeat to make seven more crêpes. Stack the crêpes on top of each other as soon as they are cooked (they will not stick together).

4 Make the orange sauce and add and fold the crêpes (see box, right). Heat to warm through.

Making the sauce and folding the crêpes

Put the orange juice, butter, sugar, and liqueur or brandy into a large frying pan, and boil for 5 minutes until reduced. Place one crêpe in the pan, coat with sauce, fold in half, then in half again. Move to one side of the pan. Add another crêpe. Coat with the sauce, and fold as before. Repeat with the remaining crêpes.

Hot chocolate soufflés

SERVES 4 **CALS PER SERVING** 494

125 g (4 oz) plain chocolate
2 tbsp water
300 ml (½ pint) milk
45 g (1½ oz) butter, plus extra for greasing
45 g (1½ oz) plain flour
2–3 drops of vanilla extract
60 g (2 oz) caster sugar
4 egg yolks
5 egg whites
sifted icing sugar, for dusting

4 X 300 ML (½ PINT) SOUFFLÉ DISHES

1 Break the chocolate into pieces, and put into a small saucepan with the measured water and a few tablespoons of the milk. Heat gently, stirring, until the chocolate has melted. Add the remaining milk, stirring to blend.

2 Melt the butter in a pan, add the flour, and cook, stirring, for 1 minute. Remove from the heat, and gradually add the chocolate and milk mixture. Bring to a boil, stirring, until the sauce has thickened. Stir in the vanilla extract and caster sugar, and leave to cool.

3 Beat the egg yolks into the cooled chocolate mixture. Lightly butter the individual soufflé dishes and set aside.

4 Whisk the egg whites until stiff but not dry. Stir 1 large spoonful of the egg whites into the chocolate mixture, then carefully fold in the remainder. Divide the mixture among the four soufflé dishes.

5 Place on a hot baking tray and bake in a preheated oven at 190°C (170°C fan, Gas 5) for 40–45 minutes until the soufflés are well risen and firm. Dust with sifted icing sugar. Serve the soufflés at once.

Cook's know-how

If you prefer, you can make one large soufflé instead of individual soufflés. Simply use 1 x 1.25 litre (2 pint) soufflé dish and bake in the oven for 45–50 minutes. Another alternative is to make eight small soufflés, ideal for a dinner party after a rich main course. If you use 8 x 150 ml (¼ pint) dishes they will take about 20–30 minutes to bake in the oven.

French pancakes

SERVES 4 **CALS PER SERVING** 378

60 g (2 oz) butter, softened, plus extra for greasing
60 g (2 oz) caster sugar
2 eggs, beaten
60 g (2 oz) self-raising flour
300 ml (½ pint) milk
apricot jam and caster sugar, to serve

8-HOLE BUN TIN WITH 7 CM (3 IN) CUPS

1 Combine the butter and sugar in a bowl and cream together until soft. Beat in the eggs, a little at a time, then fold in the flour.

2 In a small saucepan, heat the milk to just below boiling point. Stir into the creamed mixture.

3 Lightly butter the bun tin cups, and divide the batter equally among them. Bake in a preheated oven at 190°C (170°C fan, Gas 5) for about 20 minutes until the pancakes are well risen and golden brown.

4 Slide the pancakes out of the cups, and serve with apricot jam and caster sugar. To eat, place a little jam in the middle of each pancake, fold in half, and sprinkle with sugar.

Chocolate fudge fondue

SERVES 6 **CALS PER SERVING** 416

1 x 125 g (4 oz) bar caramel-filled chocolate
90 g (3 oz) good-quality dark chocolate
125 g (4 oz) butter
60 g (2 oz) golden syrup
4 tbsp double cream
dippers of your choice (see box, right)

1 Roughly chop the caramel-filled chocolate bar and the dark chocolate, and put the pieces into a small saucepan. Cut the butter into small cubes and drop them into the pan, then pour in the golden syrup.

2 Melt the mixture over a very low heat, stirring only once or twice, for 10–12 minutes. Remove from the heat and whisk together until smooth, then whisk in the cream.

3 Pour the chocolate fondue into a fondue pot and place over a low flame to keep warm. Serve with dippers of your choice.

White chocolate fondue

SERVES 6 **CALS PER SERVING** 278

175 g (6 oz) good-quality white chocolate
150 ml (¼ pint) double cream
dippers of your choice (see box, above right)

1 Roughly chop the chocolate and put the pieces into a heatproof bowl. Sit the bowl on top of a small saucepan of gently simmering water, making sure the bottom of the bowl does not touch the water or the chocolate may get too hot and "seize" into a ball. Heat very gently, stirring only once or twice, until the chocolate has just melted, then remove the bowl from the pan and set aside.

2 Pour the cream into a heavy-based saucepan and bring almost to boiling point (you should see bubbles beginning to break around the edge of the cream). Slowly pour the hot cream on to the melted chocolate, stirring gently.

3 Pour the chocolate fondue into a fondue pot and place over a low flame to keep warm. Serve with dippers of your choice.

Dark chocolate fondue

SERVES 6 **CALS PER SERVING** 208

200 g (7 oz) good-quality dark chocolate
30 g (1 oz) caster sugar
125 ml (4 fl oz) water
finely grated zest of 2 oranges (optional)
dippers of your choice (see box, right)

1 Break the dark chocolate into small pieces and put them into a heatproof bowl. Sit the bowl on top of a small saucepan of gently simmering water, making sure that the bottom of the bowl does not touch the water, or the chocolate may get too hot and "seize" into a ball. Heat the chocolate very gently, stirring only once or twice, until the chocolate has just melted, then remove the saucepan from the heat, keeping the bowl over the hot water.

2 Put the sugar into another saucepan, pour in the measured water, and bring to a boil. Simmer for 5 minutes, then slowly stir this sugar syrup into the melted chocolate and whisk until smooth. Stir in the orange zest, if using.

3 Pour the chocolate fondue into a fondue pot and place over a low flame to keep warm. Serve with dippers of your choice.

Dippers

Increase the fun of your fondue by offering as wide a choice as possible of ingredients for dipping and dunking. You can be as creative as you like, but bear in mind that the ingredients need to be speared on small forks so they should not be too hard or crisp. Conversely, if the texture of the dippers is soft and crumbly, they will drop into the pot and spoil the fondue. Here is a selection of tried-and-tested dippers.

- Strawberries with hulls intact, either whole fruits or halved if large
- Cherries, still on their stalks if possible
- Banana slices (slightly under-ripe)
- Fig wedges
- Apricots and peaches, stoned and cut into quarters
- Kiwi fruits, cut lengthways into eighths
- Pears, cut into chunky wedges and tossed in lemon juice
- Grapes, the large seedless variety
- Dried fruits, such as apricots, peaches, or mangoes
- Panettone cake, cut into cubes
- Brioche, cut into squares
- Long biscuits, such as Viennese fingers, langues de chats, or cigarettes russes

Opposite, clockwise from top: Chocolate fudge fondue, White chocolate fondue, Dark chocolate fondue

Chilled desserts

In this chapter...

Chilled lemon soufflé
page 537

Chocolate and brandy mousse
page 538

Mango and lime mousse
page 538

The ultimate chocolate roulade
page 540

Helen's pudding
page 540

Summer pudding
page 541

Pots au chocolat
page 542

Orange pannacotta with boozy oranges
page 542

Tiramisu
page 543

Cherry cheesecake
page 544

Tropical fruit cheesecake
page 544

Marbled raspberry cheesecake
page 547

Chocolate chip cheesecake
page 548

Cassata
page 549

Quick vanilla ice cream
page 549

Frozen lemon flummery
page 549

Rich vanilla ice cream
page 550

Chocolate and meringue bombe
page 550

Raspberry sorbet
page 552

Lime sorbet
page 552

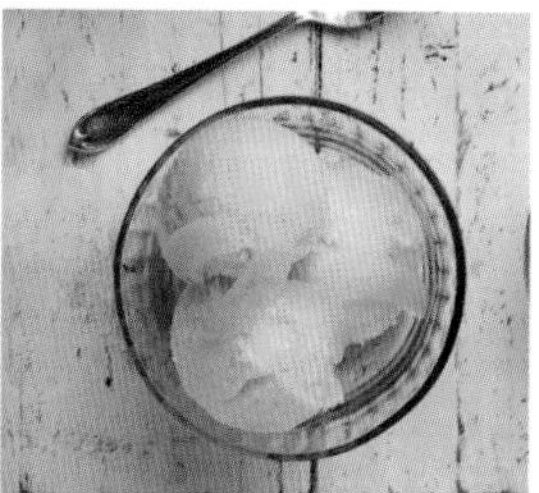
Apricot sorbet
page 552

Pear and ginger sorbet
page 552

Peach Melba
page 554

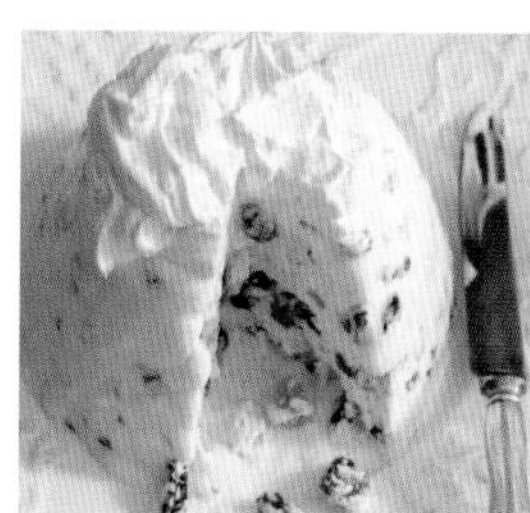
Iced Christmas pudding
page 555

Chilled desserts know-how

Chilled desserts can be made well in advance so are great for dinner parties. Fruit salads and fools, trifles, creamy mousses and light chilled soufflés, meringue baskets, gâteaux, rich cheesecakes, layered terrines, ice creams, and sorbets – all can be kept in the refrigerator or freezer, to be served when you're ready.

Freezing

Many completed desserts, as well as ingredients and accompaniments for desserts, can be stored in the freezer. Freeze chocolate, caramel, or fruit sauces; thaw at room temperature, or reheat from frozen if serving warm. Tray freeze piped rosettes of cream, then pack in a freezer bag; pack chocolate decorations in rigid containers. Both can be used frozen – they will thaw in minutes. Freeze citrus zest, and thaw, unwrapped, at room temperature. Tray freeze baked meringue shells, gâteau layers, and cheesecake; unwrap and thaw in the refrigerator. Crème caramel can be frozen uncooked in the mould and baked from frozen, allowing extra time.

Dissolving gelatine

Gelatine is a flavourless setting agent used in chilled desserts such as fruit jellies. It is most commonly available as a powder, in sachets. Leaf gelatine can also be used (four sheets in place of one sachet): soften in cold water for 5 minutes, then drain and melt in the hot dessert mixture, whisking well.

1 Put the given quantity of cold water or other liquid into a small heatproof bowl and sprinkle the given quantity of gelatine over the surface. Leave to soak for about 10 minutes until the gelatine has absorbed the liquid and become spongy.

2 Put the bowl of gelatine into a pan of hot water and heat until the gelatine has dissolved and is clear. Use a metal spoon to check that there are no granules left. Use the gelatine at the same temperature as the mixture it is setting.

Egg safety

Some of the chilled desserts in this book, such as mousses and soufflés, contain uncooked eggs. Because of the risk of salmonella poisoning, it is usually recommended that those in vulnerable groups should not eat raw or undercooked eggs.

Preparing citrus fruits

When taking the zest from citrus fruits (even if they are unwaxed), first scrub the fruit with hot soapy water, rinse well, and dry.

Grating
Hold the grater on a plate. Rub the fruit over the medium grid of the grater, removing just the zest and leaving behind the bitter white pith. Use a pastry brush to remove all the zest from the grater.

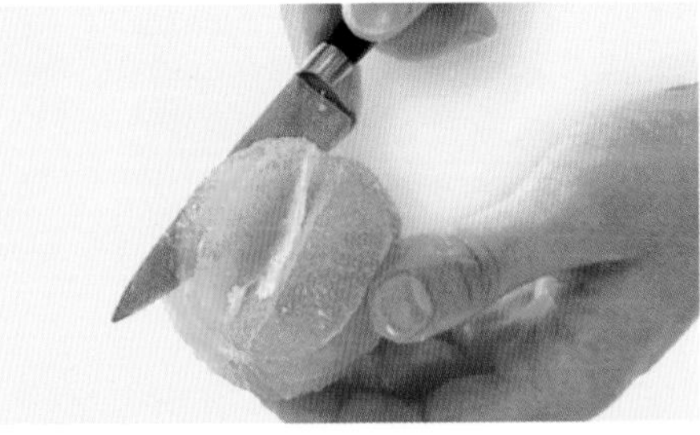

Segmenting
Hold the peeled fruit over a bowl to catch the juice. With a sharp knife, cut down one side of a segment, cutting it from the dividing membrane. Cut away from the membrane on the other side, and remove the segment. Continue all around the fruit.

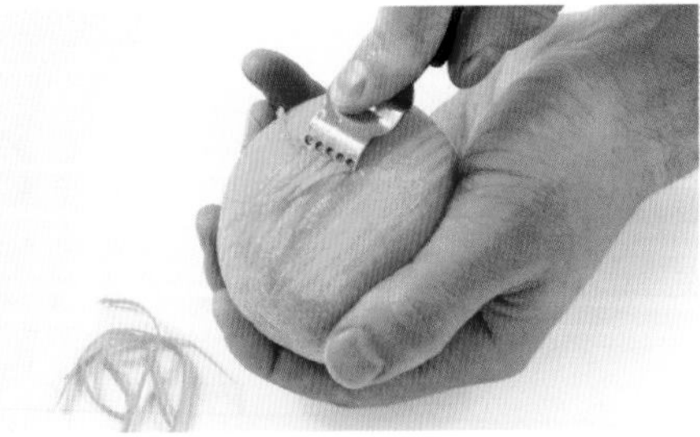

Zesting
For speedy removal of zest in tiny strips, use a citrus zester or a flat ultra-sharp grater.

Peeling
Use a small sharp knife. Cut off a slice of peel across the top and the base, cutting through to the flesh. Set the fruit upright on a chopping board and cut away the peel from top to bottom, following the curve of the fruit and cutting away the white pith as well.

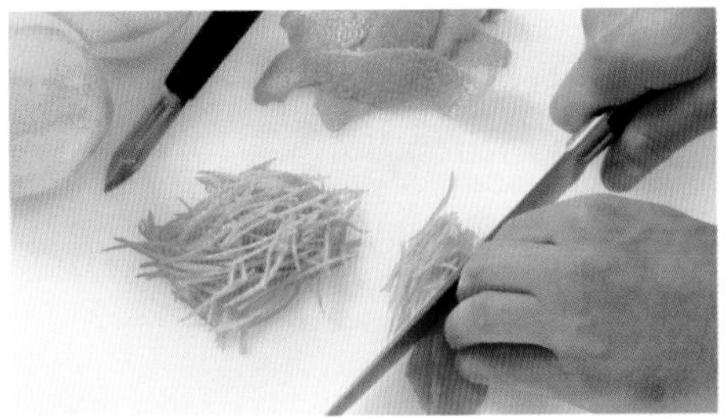

Paring
Use a vegetable peeler or small knife to pare off strips of zest, trying not to take any of the white pith with the zest. Cut the pieces of zest lengthways into very fine strips or "julienne".

Citrus tips

To get the maximum juice from citrus fruits, first roll the fruit gently on a work surface, pressing lightly. Or heat in the microwave, on HIGH (100% power) for 30 seconds, just until the fruit feels warm.

If a recipe includes citrus zest, add it immediately after grating or zesting, preferably to any sugar in the recipe. Then the zest won't discolour or dry out, and all the flavoursome oils from the zest will be absorbed by the sugar.

Preparing mangoes

Mangoes have a large, flat central stone and the flesh clings to it tightly. There are two methods of preparation, depending on how the flesh is to be used.

Slicing

For flesh to be used sliced or puréed, cut the flesh from each side of the stone with a sharp knife. Also cut the flesh from the edges of the stone. Then peel and slice or purée.

Dicing

1 Cut the unpeeled flesh away from each side of the stone. With a sharp knife, score the flesh in a criss-cross pattern, cutting just to the skin but not through it.

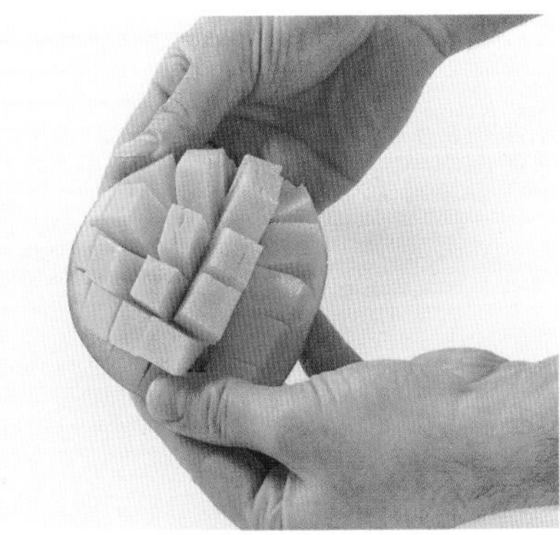

2 Press in the middle of the skin to open out the cubes of flesh, then cut them away from the skin with a sharp knife.

Preparing a pineapple

When peeling pineapple, cut away the skin in strips, taking out all the "eyes". If there are any left after peeling, cut them out with the tip of a knife.

Wedges or cubes

1 Cut off the green crown, then cut a slice from the base. Set the pineapple upright on a chopping board and slice away strips of skin, cutting from top to bottom.

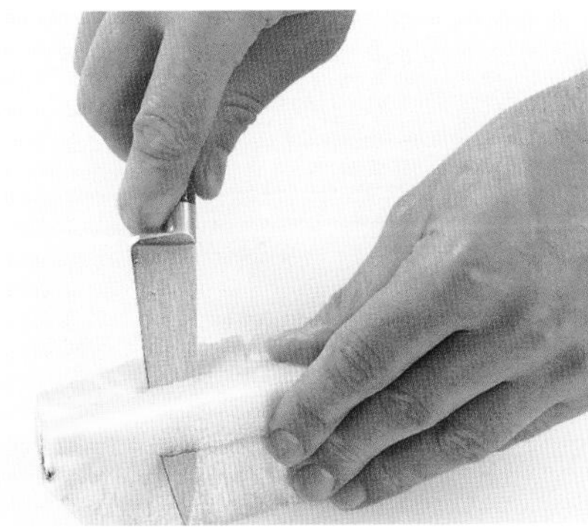

2 To remove the core, cut the pineapple into quarters lengthways. Cut the central core from each quarter. Cut the quarters into wedges or cubes as required.

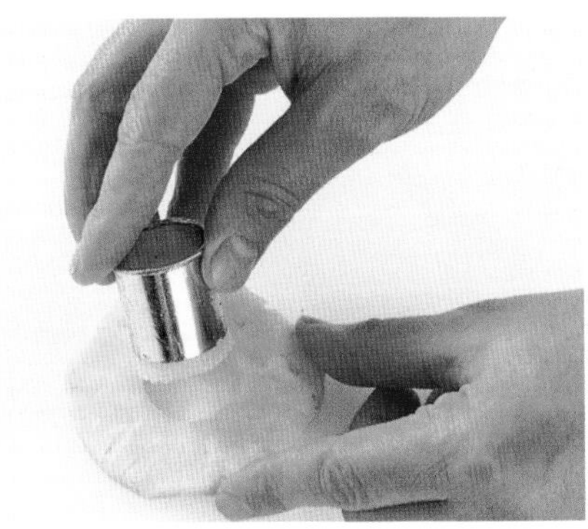

Rings

Do not cut the pineapple lengthways, but cut crosswise into 1 cm (½ in) slices. Stamp out the central core from each slice using a biscuit or pastry cutter.

Whisking egg whites

A balloon whisk is the classic tool for whisking egg whites, but an electric mixer saves time and effort. Ensure all your equipment is clean, dry, and grease-free, and that the egg whites are at room temperature.

Whisk the whites as forcefully as possible (on maximum speed if using an electric mixer) right from the start. When they look like a cloud, add any sugar little by little. The mixture will get stiffer and stiffer as you add sugar and whisk.

Folding egg whites

To retain as much air as possible, egg whites should be folded gently and quickly into a mixture.

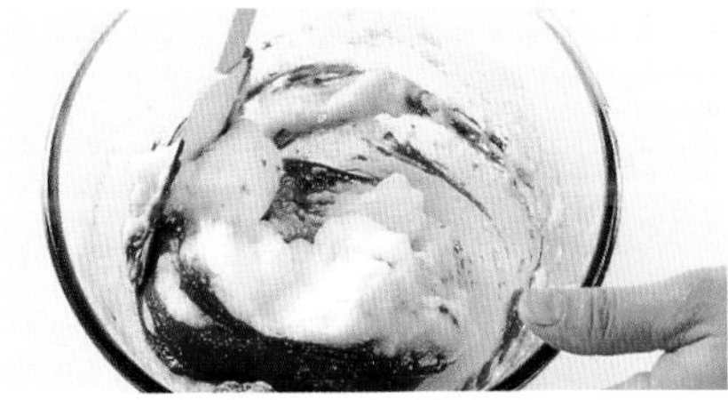

Mix a spoonful of the whites into the heavy mixture to lighten it. Using a rubber spatula or metal spoon, fold in the remaining whites using a "figure of eight" motion, cutting straight through the mixture, then turning it over until well blended.

Preparing a soufflé dish

To give a chilled soufflé the appearance of having risen above the rim of the dish, it is set with a raised collar.

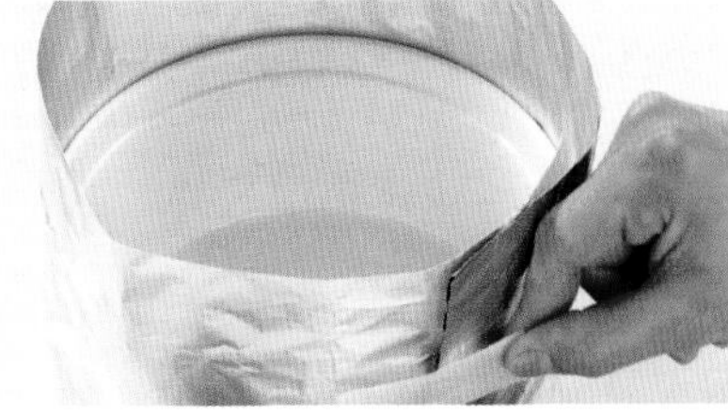

Cut out a piece of foil or greaseproof paper 5 cm (2 in) longer than the circumference of the dish and wide enough to stand 5 cm (2 in) above it when folded. Fold in half. Wrap around the dish and secure with tape or string. Remove before serving.

Decorating with chocolate

Chocolate decorations can transform a dessert, and you don't have to reserve them for desserts made only from chocolate – fruit fools and mousses can also benefit from a contrasting finishing touch.

Grating chocolate

Use chilled chocolate and hold it firmly in a piece of greaseproof paper. Hold the grater on a sheet of greaseproof paper and rub the chocolate over the large grid of the grater.

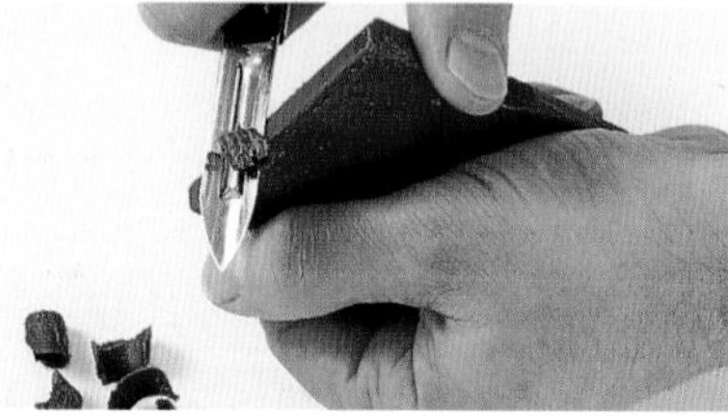

Chocolate curls

Keep the chocolate at room temperature, and use a vegetable peeler to shave off long curls on to a sheet of greaseproof paper. Lift the paper to tip the curls on to the dessert.

Chocolate caraque

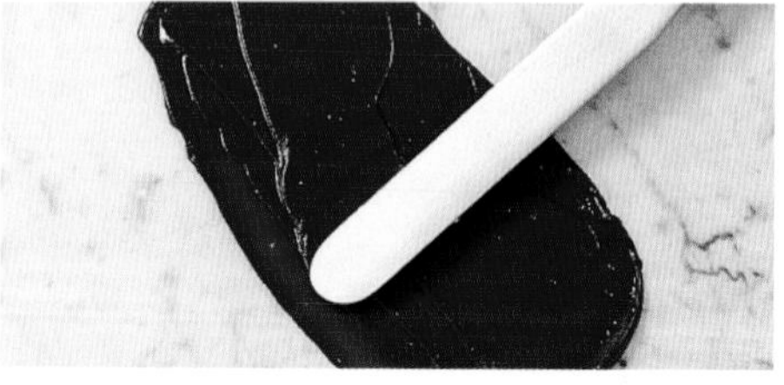

1 Spread a smooth, thin layer of melted chocolate, about 1.5 mm (1/16 in) thick, on to a cool work surface (preferably marble), and leave to cool until nearly set.

2 Using a long, sharp knife held at an angle, push across the chocolate with a slight sawing action, to shave it into "caraque" curls. Use a cocktail stick to pick up the caraque.

Melting chocolate

Care is needed when melting chocolate, especially white chocolate. Don't allow it to overheat or come into contact with any steam as this could cause it to scorch or harden.

Chop the chocolate and put it into a heatproof bowl set over a pan of hot, not boiling, water. The base of the bowl should not be touching the water. Heat gently, without stirring, until the chocolate becomes soft. Remove from the heat, but leave the bowl over the water. Stir until the chocolate is very smooth and creamy.

Decorating with cream

Piped whipped cream adds a professional touch to desserts and cakes, and with a little practice and some confidence this is not difficult to do. A star-shaped nozzle is the most useful.

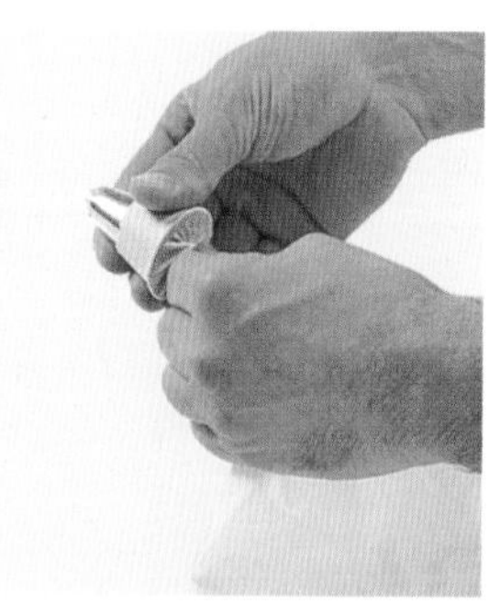

1 Drop the nozzle into the piping bag, then tuck the lower half of the piping bag into the nozzle, to prevent the cream from leaking out when filling the bag.

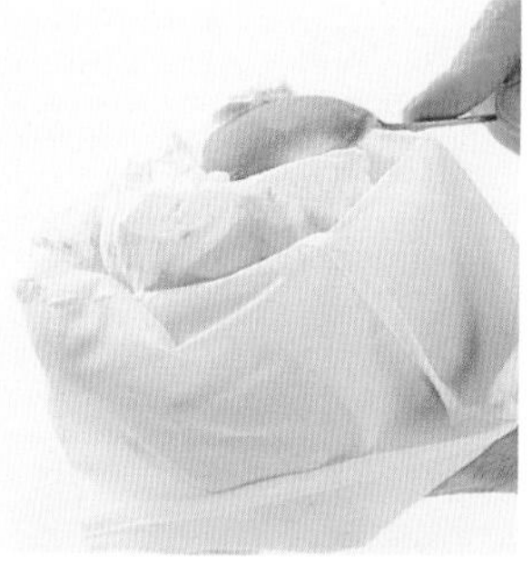

2 Hold the bag in one hand, folding the top of the bag over your hand. Spoon in the whipped cream.

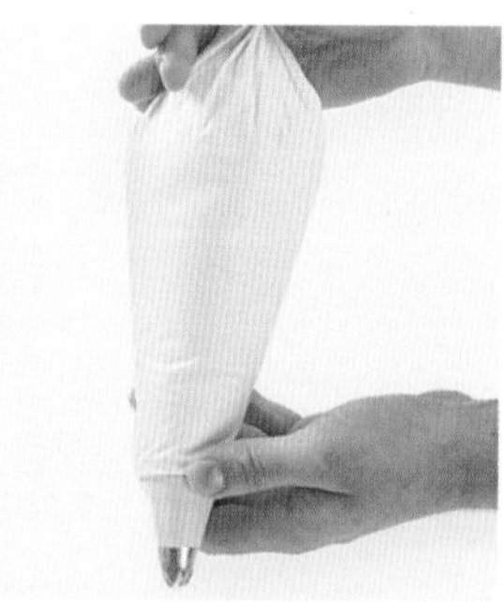

3 When the bag is full, twist the top until there is no air left. Pipe the cream as desired, gently squeezing the twisted end to force out the cream in a steady stream.

Rosette

Hold the bag upright, just above the surface of the cake. Squeeze gently, moving the bag in a small circle. Stop squeezing and lift the nozzle away.

Swirl

Hold the bag upright, just above the surface of the cake. Squeeze the bag and pipe the cream in a steady stream, guiding the nozzle in an "S" shape.

Rope

Hold the bag at a 45° angle. Pipe a short length of cream to one side. Pipe another length of cream to the opposite side, overlapping the first one.

Caramelized oranges

SERVES 4 **CALS PER SERVING** 388

250 g (8 oz) granulated sugar
150 ml (¼ pint) cold water
150 ml (¼ pint) lukewarm water
3 tbsp orange liqueur
8 thin-skinned oranges

1 Put the sugar and measured cold water into a heavy pan and heat gently until the sugar dissolves.

2 When all the sugar has dissolved, bring to a boil and boil steadily until a rich golden-brown colour. (If the caramel is too light in colour it will be very sweet, but be careful not to let it burn.)

3 Protect your hand by covering it with a cloth, and remove the pan from the heat. Pour the measured lukewarm water into the caramel.

4 Return the pan to the heat and stir to melt the caramel. Pour the caramel into a heatproof serving dish. Leave to cool for 30 minutes. Stir in the orange liqueur.

5 Pare the zest from one of the oranges, using a vegetable peeler. Cut the zest into very thin strips (page 518). Cook for 1 minute in boiling water, drain, rinse thoroughly under cold running water, and set aside.

6 Using a sharp knife, remove the peel and pith from each orange, catching any juice to add to the caramel in the dish. Cut each orange into slices crosswise, then reassemble the oranges, holding the slices together with cocktail sticks.

7 Place the oranges in the dish of caramel and spoon the caramel over them. Scatter the strips of orange zest over the top. Chill for about 30 minutes. Remove the cocktail sticks before transferring the oranges to individual bowls to serve.

Tropical island fruit salad

SERVES 6 **CALS PER SERVING** 155

1 small ripe pineapple
1 ripe charentais or cantaloupe melon
1 ripe mango
250 g (8 oz) seedless black grapes
150 ml (¼ pint) pineapple and coconut juice or pineapple juice
125 g (4 oz) physalis (cape gooseberries)
2 ripe guavas, preferably pink-fleshed
2 Asian (nashi) pears

1 Cut the top and bottom off the pineapple. Remove the skin with a sharp knife, then cut out the brown eyes. Cut the pineapple lengthways into four and remove and discard the hard inner core. Cut the flesh into chunks and put into a large glass serving bowl.

2 Cut the melon into quarters, remove and discard the seeds with a spoon. Cut each melon quarter in half, remove the skin with a sharp knife, and cut the flesh into chunks. Add to the pineapple.

3 Peel the mango, cut either side of the large flat stone, and neatly cut the mango flesh into pieces. Add to the bowl with the grapes. Pour over the fruit juice, cover, and chill in the refrigerator for about 4 hours, or overnight.

4 Peel back the paper lanterns on the physalis. Remove the fruits from about half of the physalis, wipe gently with kitchen paper, and add to the bowl.

5 Peel the guavas, halve the fruits, and remove the seeds. Cut the flesh into neat pieces and add to the bowl. Peel and quarter the pears, remove the cores, and slice the flesh neatly into the bowl.

6 Stir the fruits gently together, making sure the pear is submerged in juice or it will discolour. Cover and chill in the refrigerator for about 1 hour. Transfer to small serving bowls and serve chilled, decorated with the remaining physalis.

Cranberry and vodka sparkle

SERVES 4 **CALS PER SERVING** 66

2 sheets of leaf gelatine
250 ml (9 fl oz) cranberry juice
50 ml (1 ¾ fl oz) vodka
squeeze of lime juice
fresh berries (e.g. raspberries, strawberries, and blueberries), to serve

4 X 100 ML (3 ½ FL OZ) GLASSES

1 Put the sheets of gelatine into a medium bowl and cover with cold water. Leave to soak for about 5 minutes until softened.

2 Heat the cranberry juice in a pan. Lift the gelatine out of the water, squeeze it, then add to the cranberry juice and stir until the gelatine has dissolved. Cool slightly, then add the vodka and lime juice. Cool completely, then pour into glasses, cover and chill until set, for about 6 hours. Serve topped with fresh berries.

Fruits of the forest salad

SERVES 6 **CALS PER SERVING** 94

250 g (8 oz) fresh cranberries
60 g (2 oz) caster sugar
250 g (8 oz) strawberries, hulled and halved if large
125 g (4 oz) blueberries
250 g (8 oz) raspberries
250 g (8 oz) blackberries
250 g (8 oz) loganberries, or increase the amount of the other berries if loganberries are unavailable
2–3 tbsp balsamic vinegar
1 tsp green peppercorns in brine or oil, rinsed and lightly crushed
crème fraîche, to serve (optional)

1 Put the cranberries into a stainless steel pan with 5 tbsp water. Cook gently for about 5–10 minutes or until the cranberries pop and are just soft. Remove from the heat, stir in the sugar, and leave until the sugar has dissolved and the mixture has cooled slightly (do not add the sugar at the beginning or it will make the cranberry skins tough).

2 Put the remaining fruit into a serving bowl, add the cooled cranberries and juice, and mix gently together.

3 Add the balsamic vinegar and green peppercorns and mix gently. Cover and chill in the refrigerator for at least 4 hours (or overnight) to allow the juices to develop and the flavours to mellow. Serve, topped with crème fraîche if you like.

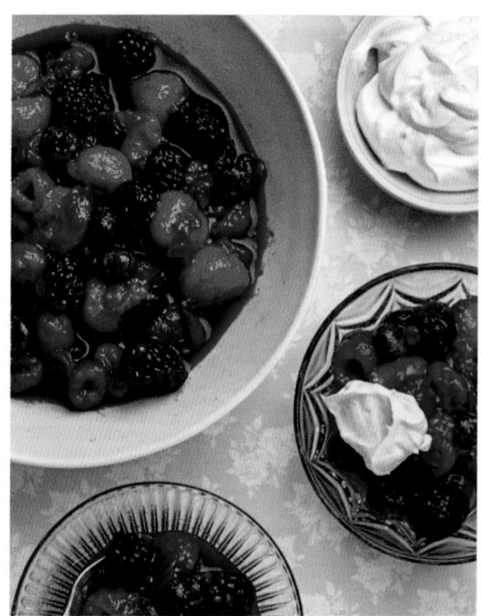

Spiced fruit salad

SERVES 4 **CALS PER SERVING** 460

500 g (1 lb) mixed ready-to-eat dried fruits, e.g. pears, peaches, mango, prunes, pineapple, figs, apple
about 900 ml (1½ pints) apple juice
2–3 star anise, to taste
1 vanilla pod
75 g (2½ oz) dried cranberries
75 g (2½ oz) dried cherries

1 Put the mixed fruits into a saucepan with 900 ml (1½ pints) apple juice, the star anise, and vanilla pod. Bring to a boil and simmer gently for about 15 minutes.

2 Add the dried cranberries and cherries to the pan and continue cooking for about 15 minutes, adding more apple juice (or water) if necessary. Serve hot or cold.

Mango and passion fruit meringue

SERVES 6 **CALS PER SERVING** 503

4 egg whites
250 g (8 oz) caster sugar

Filling

1 ripe mango
1 passion fruit
300 ml (½ pint) whipping cream, whipped until thick
125 g (4 oz) strawberries, sliced

Decoration

150 ml (¼ pint) double or whipping cream, whipped until stiff
a few strawberries

1 Mark 2 x 20 cm (8 in) circles on two sheets of non-stick baking parchment, turn the paper over, and use to line two baking trays.

2 Whisk the egg whites with a hand-held electric mixer on maximum speed until stiff but not dry. Add the sugar, 1 tsp at a time, and continue to whisk until all the sugar has been incorporated and the mixture is stiff and glossy.

3 Pipe the meringue, in concentric circles, inside the marked circles on the paper-lined baking trays.

4 Bake the meringue rounds in a preheated oven at 140°C (120°C fan, Gas 1) for 1–1¼ hours until crisp and dry. Leave to cool, then carefully peel off the paper.

5 Dice the mango very finely (page 519). Halve the passion fruit and scoop out the pulp.

6 Spread the whipped cream over one of the meringue rounds. Arrange the mango, passion fruit pulp, and strawberries on top, and cover with the remaining meringue round.

7 Decorate with piped rosettes of whipped cream (page 520), strawberry slices, and a whole strawberry.

PEACH MERINGUE

Substitute 2 peeled and sliced peaches for the mango, and 125 g (4 oz) raspberries for the strawberries. Decorate the top of the peach meringue with a few whole raspberries.

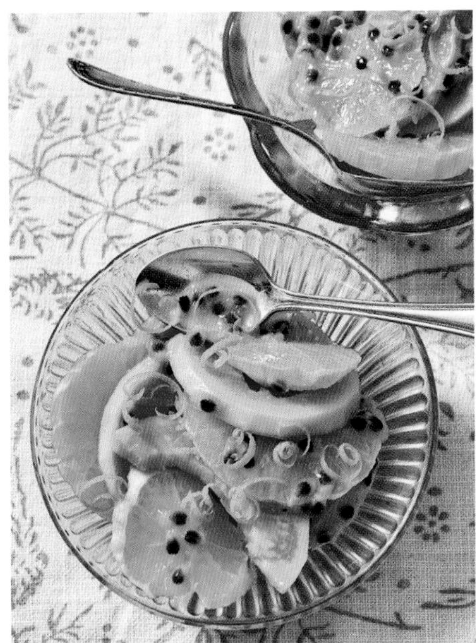

Orange passion salad

SERVES 6 **CALS PER SERVING** 89

8 thin-skinned oranges
juice of 1 small lime
2 ripe papayas
3 ripe passion fruit

1 Remove the thin orange skin from two of the oranges with a zester and set the strips of zest aside. Peel all the oranges and remove all the skin and pith. Slice into rounds and remove any pips.

2 Put the orange slices into a fairly shallow glass bowl with any juice from the oranges and the lime juice.

3 Halve the papayas lengthways and scoop out the seeds. Peel the halves, cut crosswise into fairly thick slices, and add to the bowl. Cut the passion fruit in half crosswise and scoop the juice and pips over the fruit in the bowl. Top the salad with the orange zest, cover, and chill in the refrigerator for at least 2 hours. Stir before serving – there is no need for sugar.

Winter fruit salad

SERVES 6 **CALS PER SERVING** 173

60 g (2 oz) caster sugar
90 ml (3 fl oz) water
pared zest of ½ lemon
2 pink grapefruit
2 oranges
250 g (8 oz) seedless green grapes, halved
2 ripe pears, peeled, cored, and sliced
2 bananas, sliced

1 Put the sugar and measured water into a saucepan and heat gently until the sugar has dissolved. Add the lemon zest and bring the syrup to a boil. Boil for 1 minute, then strain into a serving bowl. Leave to cool.

2 Using a sharp serrated knife, cut the peel and pith from each grapefruit and orange. Remove the segments by cutting between each membrane. Add the segments to the bowl.

3 Add the grapes, pears, and bananas to the serving bowl and gently mix to coat all of the fruit in the sugar syrup.

4 Cover and chill the fruit salad for up to 1 hour before serving.

SUMMER BERRY SALAD

Cut 750 g (1½ lb) strawberries in half, then mix them with 250 g (8 oz) raspberries and 250 g (8 oz) blueberries. Sift 3 tbsp icing sugar over the fruit, and pour the juice of 2 oranges on top. Stir gently, cover, and chill for 1 hour.

Cook's know-how

If you are short of time you can just sprinkle the fruit with caster sugar to taste rather than making a sugar syrup. To prevent the pears and bananas from discolouring when sliced and exposed to the air, toss the pieces in lemon juice.

Baked Alaska

SERVES 8 **CALS PER SERVING** 256

250 g (8 oz) raspberries, sliced strawberries, or other summer fruits
450 ml (3/4 pint) vanilla ice cream
2 egg whites
125 g (4 oz) caster sugar
whole berries, to decorate

1 X 20 CM (8 IN) SPONGE FLAN CASE

1 Put the sponge flan case into a shallow ovenproof serving dish. Arrange the fruits in the case.

2 Put the ice cream on top of the fruits and put in the freezer to keep the ice cream frozen while making the meringue.

3 Whisk the egg whites (an electric mixer can be used) until stiff but not dry.

4 Add the caster sugar, 1 tsp at a time, and continue to whisk until the sugar has been incorporated and the meringue mixture is stiff and glossy. Pipe or spoon the meringue over the ice cream, covering it completely.

5 Bake immediately in a preheated oven at 230°C (210°C fan, Gas 8) for 3–4 minutes until the meringue is tinged with brown. Serve at once, decorated with berries.

Cook's know-how

Firm ice cream is needed for this recipe – do not use soft scoop. Make sure the ice cream is completely covered by the egg white, which stops the ice cream melting.

Hazelnut meringue gâteau

Crisp meringues made with toasted hazelnuts are sandwiched with a whipped cream filling. The attractive decoration is easy to create: piped rosettes of cream are topped with hazelnuts and raspberries, and the gâteau is accompanied by a raspberry sauce.

SERVES 12 **CALS PER SERVING** 286

125 g (4 oz) shelled hazelnuts
4 egg whites
275 g (9 oz) caster sugar
1/2 tsp white wine vinegar
300 ml (1/2 pint) whipping cream, whipped until thick
icing sugar, for dusting

Raspberry sauce

250 g (8 oz) raspberries
about 4 tbsp icing sugar, sifted

1 Mark 2 x 20 cm (8 in) circles on two sheets of non-stick baking parchment. Turn the paper over and use to line two baking trays.

2 Spread the hazelnuts on another baking tray and toast in a preheated oven at 190°C (170°C fan, Gas 5) for about 10 minutes. Remove from the oven, then turn the temperature down to 160°C (140°C fan, Gas 3).

3 Tip the hazelnuts on to a clean tea towel and rub together inside the towel to remove the skins. Reserve six whole nuts for decoration and grind the remaining nuts in a food processor.

4 Whisk the egg whites until stiff but not dry (if using an electric mixer turn it to high speed). Add the caster sugar, 1 tsp at a time, and continue to whisk, still at high speed, until all of the caster sugar has been incorporated and the mixture is stiff and glossy.

5 Whisk in the white wine vinegar, then fold in the ground hazelnuts.

6 Divide the hazelnut meringue mixture equally between the baking trays, spreading it out evenly within the marked circles.

7 Bake in the oven for about 30 minutes until the top of each meringue round is crisp and a pale beige colour. The insides of the meringues should still be soft like marshmallow.

8 Lift the meringue rounds off the baking trays and peel the lining paper from the bases. Leave to cool on a wire rack.

9 Make the raspberry sauce: reserve eight whole raspberries for decoration, and put the remainder in a food processor. Blend until smooth, then push through a sieve to remove the seeds. Gradually whisk in icing sugar to taste.

10 Use two-thirds of the whipped cream to sandwich the meringue rounds together. Sift icing sugar on top and decorate with rosettes (page 520) of the remaining whipped cream. Top the rosettes with the reserved whole hazelnuts and raspberries. Serve with the raspberry sauce.

Sauces for desserts

Hot chocolate sauce Heat 175 g (6 oz) plain chocolate, broken into pieces, 2 tsp instant coffee granules, 125 ml (4 fl oz) hot water, and 90 g (3 oz) caster sugar in a pan until the chocolate has melted. Serve hot.

Chocolate marshmallow sauce Heat 60 g (2 oz) chopped plain chocolate, 100 g (3 1/2 oz) marshmallows, 75 ml (2 1/2 fl oz) double cream, and 75 ml (2 1/2 fl oz) honey in a pan until the chocolate and marshmallows have melted. Serve hot.

Butterscotch sauce Heat 60 g (2 oz) butter, 150 g (5 oz) light muscovado sugar, and 150 g (5 oz) golden syrup in a pan until melted. Remove from the heat and add 150 ml (1/4 pint) double cream and a few drops of vanilla extract, stirring until smooth. Serve hot.

Peach sauce Put 1 x 400 g can peaches and their juice into a food processor or blender with 1/4 tsp almond extract. Work to a smooth purée. Serve chilled.

Basic meringue

MAKES 24 **CALS EACH** 43

4 egg whites
250 g (8 oz) caster sugar

1 Whisk the egg whites in a scrupulously clean large bowl, with an electric hand mixer on maximum speed, until the whites are stiff and look like clouds.

2 Keeping the mixer on maximum speed, add the caster sugar a teaspoon at a time and continue whisking until the mixture is stiff and shiny.

3 Pipe, spoon, or spread the meringue as preferred and bake as in the recipes below. All ovens vary, so baking times cannot be exact. You will know the meringues are cooked when they can be lifted easily from the parchment.

Piping meringue shapes

Baskets Mark 8 x 10 cm (4 in) circles on non-stick baking parchment; turn over. Spoon the meringue into a piping bag fitted with a medium star nozzle, and pipe inside the circles, building up the sides to form baskets.

Shells Spoon the meringue into a piping bag fitted with a medium star nozzle. Pipe 24 even-sized shells, about 5 cm (2 in) in diameter at the base, on to non-stick baking parchment.

Fresh fruit baskets

MAKES 8 **CALS EACH** 303

1 quantity Basic meringue (see above)
250 ml (8 fl oz) double cream
berries and mint sprigs (optional), to decorate

Raspberry sauce
250 g (8 oz) fresh or frozen raspberries
2 tbsp icing sugar
a squeeze of lemon juice, to taste

1 Make the raspberry sauce: purée the raspberries in a blender or food processor, then push the purée through a sieve with a spoon into a bowl (discard the seeds in the sieve). Stir in the sugar and lemon juice to taste. Chill in the refrigerator until ready to use.

2 Pipe eight meringue baskets (see box, above right). Bake in a preheated oven at 120°C (100°C fan, Gas ½) for 1–1½ hours until firm. Leave to cool.

3 Whip the cream until it forms stiff peaks. Fill the baskets with the cream, top with berries, and decorate with mint sprigs if you like. Serve with the chilled raspberry sauce.

Mocha meringue mille-feuilles

MAKES 6 **CALS EACH** 537

1 quantity Basic meringue (see above left)
125 g (4 oz) slivered almonds
icing sugar, for dusting

Coffee Chantilly cream
250 ml (8 fl oz) double cream
1 tsp instant coffee, dissolved in 1 tbsp water
2–3 tbsp caster sugar

1 Spoon 18 mounds of meringue on to non-stick baking parchment, then spread them flat with a palette knife until they are very thin and about 7.5 cm (3 in) in diameter. Sprinkle over the almonds. Bake in a preheated oven at 120°C (100°C fan, Gas ½) for 1–1½ hours until firm. Cool.

2 Make the coffee Chantilly cream: whip the cream until it forms soft peaks. Add the coffee and sugar to the cream and whip until stiff peaks form.

3 Sandwich the meringue discs together in threes, with the coffee Chantilly cream in between. Dust with a little icing sugar and a few left-over almonds before serving.

Chocolate meringue shells

MAKES 12 **CALS EACH** 231

1 quantity Basic meringue (see above left)
60 g (2 oz) plain chocolate, chopped

Chocolate ganache
125 g (4 oz) plain chocolate, chopped
125 ml (4 fl oz) double cream

1 Pipe 24 shells (see box, above). Bake in a preheated oven at 120°C (100°C fan, Gas ½) for 1–1½ hours until firm. Leave to cool. Put the chocolate into a heatproof bowl over a pan of hot water and heat until melted. Drizzle over the meringues and leave to set.

2 Make the ganache: put the chocolate and the cream into a heavy-based saucepan and heat gently, stirring occasionally, until the chocolate has melted.

3 Remove the pan from the heat and whisk the ganache for about 5 minutes until the mixture is fluffy and cooled. Sandwich the meringues together with the chocolate ganache.

Opposite, clockwise from top right: Fresh fruit baskets, Mocha meringue mille-feuilles, Chocolate meringue shells.

Strawberry meringue roulade

SERVES 8 **CALS PER SERVING** 349

sunflower oil, for greasing
4 egg whites
250 g (8 oz) caster sugar
45 g (1½ oz) flaked almonds
icing sugar, for dusting

Filling

300 ml (½ pint) double or whipping cream, whipped until thick
250 g (8 oz) strawberries, quartered

23 X 33 CM (9 X 13 IN) SWISS ROLL TIN

1 Lightly oil the Swiss roll tin and line with a sheet of baking parchment.

2 Whisk the egg whites until stiff but not dry. Add the sugar, 1 tsp at a time, and continue to whisk, until all the sugar has been incorporated and the mixture is stiff and glossy.

3 Spoon the meringue into the lined tin and tilt to level the surface. Sprinkle over the flaked almonds.

4 Bake near the top of a preheated oven at 200°C (180°C fan, Gas 6) for about 8 minutes until the top is golden brown.

5 Reduce the oven temperature to 160°C (140°C fan, Gas 3), and continue baking for 10 minutes or until the meringue is firm to the touch.

6 Remove the meringue from the oven and turn out on to a sheet of baking parchment. Peel the lining paper from the base and leave the meringue to cool for 10 minutes.

7 Spread the whipped cream evenly over the meringue, and scatter the strawberries over the cream.

8 Roll up the meringue from a long side, using the lining paper to help lift it. Wrap the roulade in baking parchment and leave to chill in the refrigerator for about 30 minutes.Lightly dust with sifted icing sugar before serving.

Floating islands

SERVES 4 **CALS PER SERVING** 412

butter, for greasing
3 eggs, separated
30 g (1 oz) vanilla sugar
1 tsp cornflour
600 ml (1 pint) milk
175 g (6 oz) caster sugar
30 g (1 oz) flaked almonds, toasted

1 Butter four individual serving dishes. Line a baking tray with a sheet of baking parchment.

2 In a large bowl, mix together the egg yolks, vanilla sugar, and cornflour. In a heavy saucepan, bring the milk to a boil. Add the boiling milk to the egg-yolk mixture, stirring constantly, then pour the mixture back into the pan.

3 Return to the heat and cook gently, stirring constantly, until the froth disappears and the custard is thickened. Pour the custard into the buttered dishes, and leave to cool.

4 Whisk the egg whites until stiff but not dry. Add the caster sugar, 1 tsp at a time, and continue to whisk until all the sugar has been incorporated and the mixture is stiff and glossy.

5 Shape the meringue into eight ovals by scooping it up between 2 tablespoons.Place the ovals on the baking tray.

6 Cook in a preheated oven at 160°C (140°C fan, Gas 3) for 20 minutes until the meringues are set and no longer sticky. Leave to cool, then arrange on top of the custard. Sprinkle with almonds before serving.

Cook's know-how

This classic dessert is called *îles flottantes* in French, although you may also see it described as *oeufs à la neige*, or "snow eggs". They are one and the same thing. You can buy vanilla sugar, or make it yourself.

Pavlova with pineapple and ginger

Pavlova meringue is crisp on the outside, soft and slightly chewy like marshmallows inside. This pineapple and ginger topping is good in winter, but if you want to make a summer pavlova, use sweetened fresh red berries instead – and omit the ginger.

SERVES 6–8 **CALS PER SERVING** 504–378

4 egg whites
250 g (8 oz) caster sugar
1½ tsp cornflour
1½ tsp white wine vinegar

Topping

375 ml (13 fl oz) double or whipping cream
60 g (2 oz) stem ginger in syrup, cut into matchstick-thin strips
1 x 400 g can pineapple rings, drained

1 Preheat the oven to 160°C (140°C fan, Gas 3). Mark a 23 cm (9 in) circle on a sheet of non-stick baking parchment, turn the paper over, and line a baking tray.

2 Whisk the egg whites with a hand-held electric mixer on maximum speed until stiff, then add the sugar, 1 tsp at a time, whisking the mixture constantly.

3 Blend the cornflour and vinegar and whisk into the egg white mixture.

4 Spread the mixture inside the circle on the baking parchment, building the sides up so that they are higher than the middle. Place in the oven, then immediately reduce the heat to 150°C (130°C fan, Gas 2).

5 Bake the meringue for 1 hour or until firm to the touch. Turn off the oven and leave the meringue inside for another hour.

6 Peel the lining paper from the meringue, and transfer the meringue to a serving plate. Leave to cool.

7 Before serving, whip the cream until stiff, and stir in half of the stem ginger strips. Spoon the mixture into the middle of the meringue. Top with the pineapple rings and the remaining stem ginger strips.

Cook's know-how

Keep the oven door closed when you leave the meringue to dry out, but if you have a fan-assisted oven, you should leave the door slightly open. The meringue base can be made a day in advance and kept in an airtight container in a cool place until needed. Add the cream and fruit topping just before serving.

Crème caramel

SERVES 6 **CALS PER SERVING** 255

175 g (6 oz) granulated sugar
150 ml (¼ pint) water
4 eggs
30 g (1 oz) caster sugar
600 ml (1 pint) full-fat milk
1 tsp vanilla extract

6 SMALL RAMEKINS

1 Combine the sugar and water in a saucepan and heat gently until all the sugar has dissolved. Bring to a boil, and cook without stirring, until golden. Pour into the ramekins.

2 Whisk the eggs and vanilla sugar in a bowl. Heat the milk until just warm, then add the vanilla extract and pour into the egg mixture, stirring well. Strain into the ramekins.

3 Put the ramekins in a roasting tin and add enough hot water to come halfway up the sides of the ramekins. Bake in a preheated oven at 160°C (140°C fan, Gas 3) for about 40 minutes until just set and firm to the touch but not solid. Cool, then chill for 8 hours.

4 Turn the chilled desserts out on to individual plates to serve.

Crème brûlée

SERVES 6 **CALS PER SERVING** 302

butter, for greasing
4 egg yolks
30 g (1 oz) vanilla sugar
600 ml (1 pint) single cream
60 g (2 oz) demerara sugar

6 SMALL RAMEKINS OR SHALLOW CRÈME BRÛLÉE DISHES

1 Lightly butter the ramekins or crème brûlée dishes.

2 In a large bowl, beat the egg yolks with the vanilla sugar. Heat the cream to just below boiling point, then slowly pour into the egg-yolk mixture, stirring all the time.

3 Carefully pour the custard into the ramekins or dishes. Set in a roasting tin and add enough hot water to come halfway up the sides of the ramekins or dishes.

4 Bake in a preheated oven at 160°C (140°C fan, Gas 3) for about 25 minutes, or until just set and firm to the touch. Leave to cool.

5 Sprinkle the demerara sugar evenly over the top of the set custard. Place under a very hot grill until the sugar melts and caramelizes to a rich golden brown colour.

6 Chill the crème brûlées for no more than 2 hours before serving.

Gooseberry fool

SERVES 6 **CALS PER SERVING** 396

500 g (1 lb) gooseberries, topped and tailed
1 tbsp water
60 g (2 oz) butter
2 elderflower heads (optional)
sugar, to taste
300 ml (½ pint) double cream, whipped until thick
strips of blanched lime zest, to decorate

1 Put the gooseberries into a pan with the measured water, butter, and elderflowers, if using. Cover and cook gently for 5–10 minutes until the gooseberries are soft.

2 Beat with a wooden spoon until smooth, and add sugar to taste. Leave to cool.

3 Fold mixture into the cream. Turn into serving glasses and chill for 30 minutes. Decorate with lime zest.

RHUBARB AND ORANGE FOOL

Substitute 500 g (1 lb) chopped rhubarb for the gooseberries and omit the elderflowers. Cook the rhubarb until soft with sugar to taste and the finely grated zest and juice of 1 large orange.

Jubilee trifle

SERVES 6 **CALS PER SERVING** 417

8 trifle sponges
about 7 tbsp black cherry jam
1 x 420 g can pear quarters in natural juice, drained and juice reserved
1 x 420 g can red cherries, drained and juice reserved
4 tbsp kirsch or other cherry liqueur
500 ml (18 fl oz) custard (ready-made or see page 502 and use double the amount of cornflour)
150 ml (¼ pint) whipping cream

6 INDIVIDUAL GLASS DISHES, OR A 1.5 LITRE (2⅔ PINT) SHALLOW GLASS DISH, ABOUT 20 CM (8 IN) IN DIAMETER

1 Split the trifle sponges in half, spread generously with about 4 tbsp jam, and sandwich together again. Place four in the bottom of six individual glass dishes, cutting them to fit.

2 Chop each pear quarter into small pieces, and put some of the pieces around the edges of the dishes, and some in between the sponges. Dot with the cherries.

3 Mix 5 tbsp of the pear juice with the kirsch, and pour half of it over the sponges. Arrange the last four sponges in the dishes, again cutting them to fit, then pour over the remaining juice and kirsch. Leave for a few minutes, then gently squash flat with the back of a spoon. Pour over the custard, level gently, and chill for 1 hour.

4 Lightly whip the cream – it should still be soft and floppy – and spread over the custard. Cover and chill for at least 4 hours (or up to 24 hours).

5 To serve, warm 3 tbsp cherry jam in a small pan with 2 tbsp of the reserved cherry juice until the jam has dissolved. Leave to cool, then sieve to remove any lumps, and drizzle over the trifles.

Lemon syllabub

SERVES 4 **CALS PER SERVING** 470

150 ml (¼ pint) dessert wine or sweet white wine
2 large lemons
90 g (3 oz) caster sugar
300 ml (½ pint) double cream
2 egg whites

1 Put the wine into a bowl with the grated zest and juice of one of the lemons, and the sugar. Stir to mix, then leave to stand for about 15 minutes, stirring occasionally, until the sugar has dissolved.

2 Meanwhile, remove the zest from the remaining lemon in long, very thin strips. Blanch the strips in a small saucepan of boiling water for 1 minute. Drain, rinse under cold running water, and pat dry.

3 In a medium bowl, whip the cream until it just holds its shape. Add the wine mixture very slowly, whisking well between each addition to ensure that the mixture remains thick.

4 In a separate bowl, whisk the egg whites until stiff but not dry. Carefully fold into the cream and wine mixture. Spoon into four tall syllabub glasses. Decorate the top of each syllabub with a strip of lemon zest, and serve at once.

Scotch mist

SERVES 6 **CALS PER SERVING** 446

450 ml (¾ pint) double or whipping cream
4 tbsp whisky
90 g (3 oz) meringues, coarsely crushed
30 g (1 oz) flaked almonds, toasted

1 Whip the cream with the whisky until it just holds its shape. Fold in the crushed meringues.

2 Spoon the mixture into six serving glasses, cover, and chill for about 20 minutes or until firm.

3 Scatter the toasted flaked almonds over the desserts just before serving.

ETON MESS

Substitute 4 tbsp brandy for the whisky, and add 500 g (1 lb) chopped strawberries to the cream mixture. Decorate with strawberry halves and mint leaves instead of the almonds.

Zabaglione

SERVES 6 **CALS PER SERVING** 114

4 egg yolks
75 g (2½ oz) caster sugar
125 ml (4 fl oz) Marsala
savoiardi (Italian sponge fingers) or boudoir biscuits, to serve

1 Whisk the egg yolks and sugar in a heatproof bowl until light and foamy. Add the Marsala, and whisk to blend.

2 Put the bowl over a pan of simmering water, making sure it does not touch the water. Heat gently, whisking the mixture until it becomes thick and creamy and stands in soft peaks.

3 Remove from the heat and whisk until cool. Pour into serving glasses and serve at once, with savoiardi.

Old English trifle

SERVES 8 **CALS PER SERVING** 401

1 x 400 g can peach or pear halves
6 trifle sponges
4 tbsp red fruit jam
60 g (2 oz) ratafia biscuits or macaroons
75 ml (2½ fl oz) sherry
3 egg yolks
30 g (1 oz) caster sugar
1 tsp cornflour
300 ml (½ pint) milk
300 ml (½ pint) double or whipping cream
30 g (1 oz) flaked almonds, toasted, to decorate

1 Drain and slice the fruit, reserving the juice.

2 Cut the trifle sponges in half horizontally and sandwich the halves together with the jam.

3 Line the bottom of a glass serving bowl with the trifle sponges, and arrange the fruit and biscuits on top. Drizzle over the sherry and reserved fruit juice, and leave to soak while you make the custard.

4 In a bowl, mix together the egg yolks, sugar, and cornflour. Warm the milk in a heavy saucepan, then pour it into the egg yolk mixture, stirring constantly. Return the mixture to the pan and cook over a low heat, stirring constantly, until the custard thickens. Leave the custard to cool slightly.

5 Pour the custard over the sponges, fruit, and biscuits in the glass bowl. Cover the surface of the custard with a sheet of cling film, to prevent a skin from forming, and chill until set, preferably overnight (to let the flavours mingle).

6 Whip the cream until thick and spread over the custard. Scatter the almonds over the top to decorate. Serve chilled.

APRICOT AND GINGER TRIFLE

Use 1 x 400 g can apricot halves. Sandwich the sponges with apricot jam and sprinkle with 1 piece of stem ginger in syrup, chopped, instead of the almonds.

Raspberry passion

SERVES 6 **CALS PER SERVING** 196

3 ripe passion fruit
500 g (1 lb) plain yogurt
200 ml (7 fl oz) half-fat créme fraîche
375 g (12 oz) raspberries
90 g (3 oz) light muscovado sugar

6 X 300 ML (½ PINT) STEMMED GLASSES

1 Using a teaspoon, scoop the seeds and flesh from the passion fruit into a bowl, and mix with the yogurt and crème fraîche.

2 Put an equal quantity of raspberries in each glass, then fill with the crème fraîche mixture. Cover and refrigerate for up to 8 hours.

3 An hour or so before serving, sprinkle with sugar and return to the refrigerator until ready to serve.

Chilled lemon soufflé

SERVES 4 **CALS PER SERVING** 883

3 tbsp cold water
15 g (½ oz) powdered gelatine
3 large eggs, separated
250 g (8 oz) caster sugar
grated zest and juice of 3 lemons
300 ml (½ pint) double or whipping cream, whipped until thick

Decoration

30 g (1 oz) nibbed almonds, lightly toasted
150 ml (¼ pint) double or whipping cream, whipped until stiff

1 LITRE (1¾ PINT) SOUFFLÉ DISH

1 Prepare the soufflé dish: tie a band of double thickness greaseproof paper or foil around the outside so that it stands about 5 cm (2 in) above the top of the dish (page 519).

2 Put the water into a small bowl and sprinkle the gelatine over the top. Leave for about 10 minutes until it becomes spongy. Stand in a pan of hot water and heat until dissolved.

3 Put the egg yolks and sugar into a heatproof bowl and put over a pan of gently simmering water. Do not let the bottom of the bowl touch the water. Using an electric hand-held mixer, whisk together. Add the lemon zest and juice and whisk at full speed until the mixture is pale and thick.

4 Fold the whipped cream into the lemon mixture, then fold in the dissolved gelatine.

5 In a separate large bowl, whisk the egg whites until stiff but not dry. Fold into the lemon mixture, and carefully pour into the prepared soufflé dish. Level the surface, then chill for about 4 hours until set.

6 Carefully remove the paper collar. Decorate the outside edge of the soufflé with the lightly toasted almonds and sprinkle some in the middle. Pipe the cream (page 520) around the edge of the soufflé, and serve chilled.

Chocolate and brandy mousse

SERVES 6 **CALS PER SERVING** 585

250 g (8 oz) plain dark chocolate, broken into pieces
3 tbsp brandy
3 tbsp cold water
15 g (½ oz) powdered gelatine
4 eggs, plus 2 egg yolks
90 g (3 oz) caster sugar
150 ml (¼ pint) whipping cream, whipped until thick

Decoration

150 ml (¼ pint) double or whipping cream, whipped until stiff
chocolate curls or caraque (page 520), to decorate

1 Put the chocolate into a heatproof bowl with the brandy over a pan of hot water. Heat gently until melted. Leave to cool.

2 Put the cold water into a heatproof bowl and sprinkle the gelatine over the top. Leave for about 10 minutes until spongy. Stand the bowl in a pan of hot water and heat gently until dissolved.

3 Combine the eggs, egg yolks, and sugar in a large heatproof bowl, and put over a saucepan of simmering water. Whisk with a hand-held electric mixer until the egg mixture is very thick and mousse-like. Whisk in the dissolved gelatine.

4 Fold the whipped cream into the cooled chocolate, then fold into the egg mixture. Carefully pour into a glass serving bowl, cover, and leave in the refrigerator until set.

5 Decorate with piped rosettes of cream and chocolate curls or caraque (page 520). Serve the mousse chilled.

Cook's know-how

Buy a good-quality plain dark chocolate. For the best flavour, look for a brand with at least 70% cocoa solids.

Mango and lime mousse

SERVES 6 **CALS PER SERVING** 354

2 large ripe mangoes
grated zest and juice of 2 limes
15 g (½ oz) powdered gelatine
3 eggs, plus 1 egg yolk
45 g (1½ oz) caster sugar
150 ml (¼ pint) double or whipping cream, whipped until thick

Decoration

150 ml (¼ pint) double or whipping cream, whipped until thick
zest of 1 lime

1 Slice the mango flesh away from the stones (page 519). Peel the flesh, then purée in a blender or food processor. Add the lime zest to the purée.

2 Put the lime juice into a small bowl, sprinkle the gelatine over the top, and leave for 10 minutes until it becomes spongy.

3 Stand the bowl in a pan of hot water and heat until the gelatine has dissolved.

4 Combine the eggs, egg yolk, and sugar in a large bowl and whisk vigorously for about 10 minutes until the mixture is pale and very thick. Gradually add the mango purée, whisking between each addition to keep the mixture thick.

5 Fold the whipped cream into the mango mixture. Add the dissolved gelatine in a steady stream, stirring gently to mix. Pour the mixture into a glass serving bowl and chill until set.

6 To decorate, add a dollop of whipped cream on top of the mousse, sprinkle with lime zest, and serve chilled.

The ultimate chocolate roulade

SERVES 8 **CALS PER SERVING** 469

butter, for greasing
175 g (6 oz) plain dark chocolate, broken into pieces
6 large eggs, separated
175 g (6 oz) caster sugar
2 tbsp cocoa powder, sifted
300 ml (½ pint) double or whipping cream
icing sugar, for sifting

23 X 33 CM (9 X 13 IN) SWISS ROLL TIN

1 Lightly grease the tin, then line with baking parchment, pushing it into the corners.

2 Put the chocolate into a heatproof bowl. Put the bowl over a pan of hot water, and heat gently until the chocolate has melted, stirring occasionally. Remove the bowl from the pan, and allow the chocolate to cool slightly until warm.

3 Put the egg whites into a large bowl, and beat with an electric whisk on high speed until stiff but not dry. Put the sugar and egg yolks into another large bowl, and beat with the same whisk (no need to wash) on high speed until light, thick, and creamy. Add the chocolate to the egg yolk mixture, and stir until blended.

4 Stir two large spoonfuls of the egg whites into the chocolate mixture, then carefully fold in the remaining egg whites followed by the cocoa powder. Turn into the prepared tin, and gently level the surface.

5 Bake in a preheated oven at 180°C (160°C fan, Gas 4) for 20–25 minutes until risen. Remove from the oven, and leave the cake to cool in the tin (it will dip and crack a little).

6 When the cake is cold, whip the cream in a bowl until it just holds its shape. Sift icing sugar over a large sheet of baking parchment. Turn the cake out on to the paper with one of the short edges facing you, and peel off the lining paper. Spread the whipped cream over the cake, then make a shallow cut through the cream and cake along the short edge nearest to you, about 2 cm (¾ in) in from the edge. Roll up the roulade away from you, tightly to start with, and using the paper to help. Don't worry if it cracks – this is quite normal, and how it should be. Sift icing sugar over the roulade before serving.

Cook's know-how

If you like, add some fresh or frozen raspberries to the filling, and scatter lots of fresh raspberries around the roulade on a serving platter – it will look stunning. The filled roulade can be made a day ahead and kept in the refrigerator. It can also be frozen, wrapped in foil or cling film, for up to 2 months. Defrost overnight in the refrigerator, and bring to room temperature before serving.

Helen's pudding

SERVES 6 **CALS PER SERVING** 510

125 g (4 oz) fresh brown breadcrumbs
90 g (3 oz) demerara sugar
75 g (2½ oz) drinking chocolate powder
2 tbsp instant coffee
300 ml (½ pint) double cream
150 ml (¼ pint) single cream
60 g (2 oz) plain dark chocolate, grated

1 In a bowl, mix together the breadcrumbs, sugar, drinking chocolate, and coffee granules. In another bowl, whip the creams together until they form soft peaks.

2 Spoon half of the cream into six glass serving dishes. Cover with the breadcrumb mixture and then with the remaining cream. Chill for at least 6 hours, or overnight for best results.

3 Sprinkle generously with the grated chocolate just before serving.

Cook's know-how

To make grating chocolate easy, chill it well in the refrigerator before you grate it, and use the largest holes on the grater.

Summer pudding

This classic English summer-time treat is very easy to make, and not at all high in calories. For a perfect, evenly coloured result, reserve half of the cooking juices and pour them over any pale patches of bread after unmoulding the pudding.

SERVES 6 **CALS PER SERVING** 240

- 8 slices of stale medium-sliced white bread, crusts removed
- 875 g (1¾ lb) mixed summer fruits such as strawberries, redcurrants, blackcurrants, cherries, and raspberries
- 150 g (5 oz) caster sugar
- 75 ml (2½ fl oz) water
- 2 tbsp framboise or crème de cassis liqueur
- crème fraîche or Greek-style yogurt, to serve

1.25 LITRE (2 PINT) PUDDING BOWL

1 Set two slices of bread aside for the top of the pudding, then use the remaining slices to line the bowl (see box, right).

2 Hull and halve the strawberries if large, strip the currants from their stalks, and pit the cherries.

3 Place the redcurrants, blackcurrants, and cherries in a saucepan with the sugar and measured water. Heat gently until the juices begin to run. Stir until the sugar has dissolved, and cook until all of the fruit is just tender.

4 Remove from the heat and add the strawberries, raspberries, and liqueur.

5 Spoon the fruit and half of the juice into the lined bowl, reserving the remaining juice. Cover the top of the fruit with the reserved bread slices.

6 Stand the bowl in a shallow dish to catch any juices that may overflow, then put a saucer on top of the bread lid. Place a kitchen weight (or a can of food) on top of the saucer. Leave to chill for 8 hours.

7 Remove the weight and saucer and invert the pudding on to a serving plate. Spoon the reserved juices over the top, paying particular attention to any pale areas, and serve with either crème fraîche or Greek-style yogurt.

Lining the pudding bowl

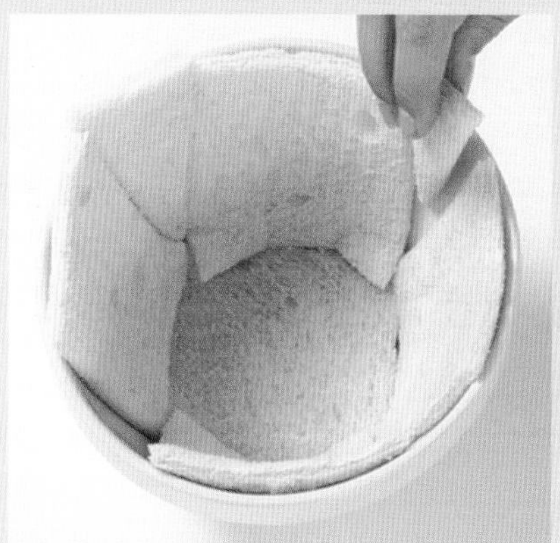

Put a slice of bread in the bottom of the bowl, cutting it to fit if necessary, then use the remainder to line the sides. The slices should fit snugly together.

Pots au chocolat

SERVES 6 **CALS PER SERVING** 324

175 g (6 oz) plain dark chocolate, broken into pieces
3 tbsp strong black coffee
15 g (½ oz) butter
a few drops of vanilla extract
3 eggs, separated
150 ml (¼ pint) double cream, whipped until stiff, to decorate

1 Put the chocolate pieces into a saucepan with the strong black coffee. Heat gently, stirring, until the chocolate melts.

2 Leave the chocolate mixture to cool slightly, then add the butter, vanilla extract, and egg yolks and stir until well blended.

3 Whisk the egg whites until stiff but not dry. Fold gently but thoroughly into the chocolate mixture.

4 Pour the mixture into six small custard pots, ramekins, or other serving dishes, and leave to chill for about 8 hours.

5 Decorate each pot of chocolate with a piped rosette of whipped cream (page 520) before serving.

Orange pannacotta with boozy oranges

SERVES 4 **CALS PER SERVING** 782

sunflower oil, for greasing
3 tbsp cold water
2 tsp powdered gelatine
600 ml (1 pint) whipping cream
60 g (2 oz) caster sugar
5 oranges
4 tbsp orange liqueur

4 X 150 ML (¼ PINT) METAL PUDDING OR DARIOLE MOULDS

1 Brush the moulds with oil, and stand them on a tray. Measure the water into a small bowl, sprinkle the gelatine over the top, and leave to become spongy.

2 Meanwhile, pour the cream into a saucepan, and add the sugar. Finely grate the zest from the oranges, and add to the pan with 2 tbsp of the liqueur. Heat the cream until bubbles appear around the edge, stirring until the sugar has dissolved and the cream is smooth. Remove from the heat, and leave to cool slightly.

3 Add the sponged gelatine to the warm cream, and whisk until completely dissolved and smooth. Pour the cream into the prepared moulds. Chill for about 6 hours, ideally overnight, until set.

4 Using a serrated knife, peel and segment the oranges, working over a bowl to catch the juice. Tip the segments into the bowl, and squeeze the thick, white membranes over the bowl to extract the remaining juice. Stir in the remaining liqueur. Chill until serving time.

5 To serve, dip each mould briefly into very hot water, then loosen the pannacotta away from the top of the mould with your fingertips, and carefully turn the pannacotta out on to a plate. Serve chilled, with a spoonful of boozy oranges alongside.

Tiramisu

SERVES 8 **CALS PER SERVING** 508

1 heaped tsp instant coffee granules
125 ml (4 fl oz) boiling water
3 tbsp brandy
2 eggs
65 g (2½ oz) caster sugar
250 g (8 oz) full-fat mascarpone cheese
300 ml (½ pint) double cream, whipped until thick
1 packet trifle sponges
60 g (2 oz) plain dark chocolate, coarsely grated
30 g (1 oz) white chocolate, coarsely grated, to decorate

1 Dissolve the coffee in the measured boiling water and mix with the brandy.

2 Combine the eggs and caster sugar in a large bowl and whisk together until thick and light, and the mixture leaves a trail on the surface.

3 Put the mascarpone into a bowl and stir in a little of the egg mixture. Fold in the rest, then fold in the cream.

4 Cut the trifle sponges horizontally in half. Layer the tiramisu (see box, right) with half the sponges, half the coffee and brandy mixture, half the mascarpone mixture, and half the plain chocolate.

5 Repeat the layers with the remaining ingredients, decorating the top with the grated white chocolate and the remaining grated plain chocolate. Cover and chill for at least 4 hours before serving.

Layering the tiramisu

Line the bottom of a large glass serving bowl with half of the sponge pieces. Drizzle half of the coffee and brandy mixture over the sponges.

Cherry cheesecake

SERVES 8 **CALS PER SERVING** 530

375 g (12 oz) full-fat soft cheese
125 g (4 oz) caster sugar
2 eggs, beaten
a few drops of vanilla extract
1 tbsp lemon juice

Biscuit shell

175 g (6 oz) digestive biscuits, crushed
90 g (3 oz) butter, melted
2 tbsp demerara sugar

Topping

1 tsp arrowroot
1 x 400 g can pitted black cherries
1 tbsp kirsch

23 CM (9 IN) SPRINGFORM CAKE TIN

1 Make the biscuit shell: mix together the crushed biscuits, melted butter, and sugar, and press evenly over the bottom and up the side of the cake tin.

2 Put the soft cheese into a bowl and beat until smooth. Add the caster sugar and beat until well blended. Add the eggs, vanilla extract, and lemon juice. Mix until smooth and creamy.

3 Pour the filling into the biscuit shell. Bake in a preheated oven at 180°C (160°C fan, Gas 4) for 25–30 minutes until just set. Leave to cool completely, then transfer to the refrigerator and leave to chill.

4 Make the topping: dissolve the arrowroot in a little of the cherry juice. Put the cherries and their juice into a small pan and add the arrowroot mixture with the kirsch. Bring to a boil, stirring, until thick. Leave to cool completely.

5 Spoon the cherries on top of the cheese filling. Chill. Use a knife to loosen the side of the cheesecake from the tin, then remove the cheesecake. Serve chilled.

Tropical fruit cheesecake

SERVES 10 **CALS PER SERVING** 396

2 ripe mangoes
150 ml (1/4 pint) mango and apple fruit juice
15 g (1/2 oz) powdered gelatine
250 g (8 oz) full-fat soft cheese, at room temperature
125 g (4 oz) caster sugar
2 eggs, separated
150 ml (1/4 pint) whipping cream, whipped until thick

Biscuit base

125 g (4 oz) coconut or digestive biscuits, crushed
60 g (2 oz) butter, melted
30 g (1 oz) demerara sugar

Decoration

2 kiwi fruit, peeled and sliced
1 x 250 g can pineapple pieces in natural juice, drained

23 CM (9 IN) LOOSE-BOTTOMED OR SPRINGFORM CAKE TIN

1 Make the biscuit base: mix together the biscuits, melted butter, and sugar, and press over the bottom of the tin.

2 Slice the mango flesh away from the stones (page 519). Peel, then purée in a food processor.

3 Pour the fruit juice into a heatproof bowl, and sprinkle the gelatine over the top. Leave for about 10 minutes until it becomes spongy. Stand the bowl in a small pan of hot water, and heat gently until the gelatine has dissolved.

4 In a large bowl, beat the soft cheese until smooth and creamy. Beat in half of the caster sugar, the egg yolks, and the mango purée. Gradually beat in the gelatine mixture.

5 In a separate bowl, whisk the egg whites until stiff but not dry. Whisk in the remaining sugar, 1 tsp at a time, and continue to whisk at high speed until the sugar is incorporated and the mixture is stiff and glossy.

6 Fold the whipped cream into the cheese and mango mixture, then fold in the egg whites. Pour on to the biscuit base and chill until set.

7 Use a knife to loosen the side of the cheesecake, then remove from the tin. Slide on to a serving plate. Decorate the top with slices of kiwi fruit and pieces of pineapple before serving.

Marbled raspberry cheesecake

The crunchy base of this cheesecake, made with crushed oat biscuits and walnuts, provides a delicious contrast to the creamy filling, marbled with streaks of fresh raspberry purée.

SERVES 10 **CALS PER SERVING** 439

3 tbsp cold water
15 g (½ oz) powdered gelatine
500 g (1 lb) raspberries
4 tbsp framboise (raspberry liqueur)
250 g (8 oz) full-fat soft cheese, at room temperature
150 ml (¼ pint) soured cream
2 eggs, separated
125 g (4 oz) caster sugar

Biscuit base

125 g (4 oz) sweet oat or digestive biscuits, coarsely crushed
60 g (2 oz) butter, melted
30 g (1 oz) demerara sugar
45 g (1½ oz) walnuts, chopped

Decoration

150 ml (¼ pint) whipping cream, whipped until stiff
a few raspberries
mint sprigs (optional)

23 CM (9 IN) LOOSE-BOTTOMED OR SPRINGFORM CAKE TIN

1 Make the biscuit base: mix together the biscuits, butter, demerara sugar, and walnuts and press evenly over the bottom of the tin.

2 Put the measured water into a heatproof bowl, sprinkle the gelatine over the top, and leave for about 10 minutes until spongy.

3 Meanwhile, purée the raspberries in a food processor, then push them through a sieve to remove the seeds. Stir in the liqueur. Set aside.

4 Put the soft cheese into a large bowl, and beat until soft and smooth. Add the soured cream and egg yolks, and beat until well blended.

5 Stand the bowl of gelatine in a saucepan of hot water and heat gently until it dissolves. Stir into the cheese mixture.

6 Make the filling (see box, below).

7 Use a knife to loosen the side of the cheesecake from the tin, then remove the cheesecake. Slide on to a serving plate. Pipe whipped cream (page 520) around the edge and decorate with raspberries and mint sprigs, if you wish.

Cook's know-how

This is a delicate no-bake cheesecake, set with gelatine. For best results, be sure to chill it well before slicing and serving.

Making the filling

Whisk the egg whites until stiff but not dry. Add the caster sugar, 1 tsp at a time, and keep whisking until all the sugar is incorporated and the meringue mixture is stiff and glossy.

Turn the cheese mixture into the meringue and fold together, blending well. Leave the mixture to thicken slightly.

Fold in the raspberry purée, swirling it in just enough to give an attractive marbled effect.

Pour the mixture carefully on to the biscuit base and chill until set.

Chocolate chip cheesecake

This delicious dessert, with its crunchy muesli base and rich chocolate filling, is ideal for parties. It can be prepared up to a month in advance and frozen in foil. Thaw, wrapped, in the refrigerator for 8 hours, then decorate.

SERVES 8 **CALS PER SERVING** 628

- 125 g (4 oz) plain dark chocolate, broken into pieces
- 3 tbsp cold water
- 15 g (½ oz) powdered gelatine
- 250 g (8 oz) full-fat soft cheese
- 2 eggs, separated
- 60 g (2 oz) caster sugar
- 150 ml (¼ pint) soured cream
- 30 g (1 oz) plain dark chocolate chips, coarsely chopped

Base

- 125 g (4 oz) muesli
- 90 g (3 oz) butter, melted
- 30 g (1 oz) demerara sugar

Decoration

- 300 ml (½ pint) whipping cream, whipped until stiff
- chocolate curls or caraque (page 520)

20 CM (8 IN) LOOSE-BOTTOMED OR SPRINGFORM CAKE TIN

1 Make the base: mix together the muesli, melted butter, and sugar, and press evenly over the bottom of the tin. Chill.

2 Meanwhile, put the chocolate into a small heatproof bowl over a pan of hot water. Heat gently to melt the chocolate, stirring occasionally. Leave to cool.

3 Put the measured water into a heatproof bowl and sprinkle the gelatine over the top. Leave for 10 minutes until spongy. Stand the bowl in a pan of hot water and heat gently until the gelatine has dissolved.

4 Beat the cheese until smooth. Add the egg yolks and sugar and beat until blended. Stir in the soured cream, melted chocolate, chocolate chips, and gelatine. Mix well.

5 In a separate bowl, whisk the egg whites until stiff but not dry. Fold carefully into the chocolate mixture until evenly mixed. Pour on to the muesli base and chill until set.

6 Use a knife to loosen the side of the cheesecake from the tin, then remove the cheesecake. Slide on to a serving plate. Pipe rosettes of whipped cream (page 520) on top and decorate with chocolate curls or caraque.

Cook's know-how

Chocolate chips are convenient, but if you don't have any to hand, simply chop up a bar of plain dark chocolate.

Cassata

SERVES 8 **CALS PER SERVING** 364

30 g (1 oz) candied angelica, rinsed, dried, and chopped
30 g (1 oz) glacé cherries, rinsed, dried, and chopped
30 g (1 oz) chopped mixed candied peel
2 tbsp dark rum
600 ml (1 pint) raspberry sorbet
150 ml (¼ pint) double cream, whipped until thick
600 ml (1 pint) vanilla ice cream

900 ML (1½ PINT) TERRINE

1 Chill the terrine. Put the angelica, glacé cherries, and candied peel in a bowl.

2 Add the rum and stir well, then leave to soak while preparing the ice-cream layers.

3 Allow the sorbet to soften, then spread it evenly over the bottom of the chilled terrine. Chill in the freezer until solid.

4 Fold the fruit and rum mixture into the whipped cream. Spoon into the terrine and level the surface. Return to the freezer until firm.

5 Allow the vanilla ice cream to soften, then spread it evenly over the fruit layer. Cover and freeze for 8 hours.

6 To turn out, dip the terrine into warm water and invert the cassata on to a large serving plate. Slice, and serve at once.

Quick vanilla ice cream

SERVES 4–6 **CALS PER SERVING** 799–533

6 eggs, separated
175 g (6 oz) vanilla sugar or 175 g (6 oz) caster sugar and 1 tsp vanilla extract
450 ml (¾ pint) double cream, whipped until thick

1 Whisk the egg whites (at high speed if using an electric mixer) until stiff but not dry. Add the sugar, 1 tsp at a time, and continue whisking until the sugar has been incorporated and the egg-white mixture is very stiff and glossy.

2 Put the egg yolks into a separate bowl and whisk at high speed with an electric mixer until blended thoroughly.

3 Gently fold the whipped cream and egg yolks into the egg-white mixture. Turn into a large shallow freezerproof container, cover, and leave the mixture to freeze for 8 hours.

4 Transfer the ice cream to the refrigerator for about 10 minutes before serving so that it softens slightly. Serve with crisp wafers.

CAPPUCCINO ICE CREAM

Substitute caster sugar for the vanilla sugar, and add 3 tbsp each coffee extract and brandy when folding the mixtures in step 3.

LEMON ICE CREAM

Substitute caster sugar for the vanilla sugar, and add the finely grated zest and juice of 3 large lemons when folding the mixtures in step 3.

Frozen lemon flummery

SERVES 4 **CALS PER SERVING** 391

150 ml (¼ pint) double cream
finely grated zest and juice of 1 large lemon
175 g (6 oz) caster sugar
300 ml (½ pint) milk
thinly pared zest of 1 lemon, cut into strips, to decorate

1 Whip the cream until it forms soft peaks. Add the lemon zest and juice, caster sugar, and milk, and mix until evenly blended.

2 Pour into a shallow freezerproof container, cover, and freeze for at least 6 hours or until firm.

3 Cut the mixture into chunks, then transfer to a food processor and work until smooth and creamy. Pour into four individual freezerproof dishes and freeze for about 8 hours.

4 Blanch the strips of lemon zest in a pan of boiling water for 1 minute only. Drain, rinse, and pat dry.

5 Decorate the flummery with the strips of lemon zest and serve.

FROZEN ORANGE FLUMMERY

Substitute the finely grated zest and juice of 1 orange for the lemon, and reduce the caster sugar to 125 g (4 oz). Decorate with blanched strips of orange zest.

Rich vanilla ice cream

Home-made ice cream tastes better than commercially made ice cream, and it keeps for up to a month in the freezer. If you have an electric ice-cream maker, you will get a smoother result.

SERVES 4–6 **CALS PER SERVING** 577–385

4 egg yolks
125 g (4 oz) caster sugar
300 ml (½ pint) milk
300 ml (½ pint) double cream
1½ tsp vanilla extract
strawberries, to serve

1 Put the egg yolks and sugar into a bowl and whisk until light in colour.

2 Heat the milk in a heavy pan to just below boiling point. Add a little of the hot milk to the egg-yolk mixture and stir to blend, then pour in the remaining milk.

3 Pour back into the pan and heat gently, stirring, until the froth disappears and the mixture coats the back of a spoon. Do not boil.

4 Leave the custard to cool, then stir in the cream and vanilla extract.

5 Pour into a container and freeze for 3 hours. Tip into a bowl and mash to break down the ice crystals. Return to container. Freeze for 2 hours. Mash and freeze for another 2 hours. Remove from the freezer 30 minutes before serving, and serve with strawberries.

CHOCOLATE ICE CREAM

In step 2, heat the milk with 125 g (4 oz) chopped dark chocolate. Let it melt before adding to the egg-yolk mixture.

CHOCOLATE CHIP ICE CREAM

In step 2, heat the milk with 125 g (4 oz) chopped white chocolate. Let it melt before adding to the egg-yolk mixture. Stir 60 g (2 oz) dark chocolate chips into the custard with the cream in step 4.

BANANA AND HONEY ICE CREAM

Mash 500 g (1 lb) bananas with 3 tbsp lemon juice and 2 tbsp honey. Add to the custard with the cream in step 4.

Chocolate and meringue bombe

SERVES 8 **CALS PER SERVING** 413

600 ml (1 pint) vanilla ice cream
600 ml (1 pint) chocolate ice cream
150 ml (¼ pint) whipping cream
1 tbsp brandy
125 g (4 oz) meringues, coarsely crushed

1.5 LITRE (2½ PINT) BOMBE MOULD OR PUDDING BOWL

1 Chill the bombe mould in the refrigerator. Layer the mould with the chocolate and vanilla ice creams (see box, below).

2 Whip the cream with the brandy until it just holds its shape. Gently fold in the crushed meringues. Use the cream mixture to fill the cavity in the mould. Cover and freeze overnight.

3 Dip the mould into cold water and invert the chocolate and meringue bombe on to a large serving plate. Slice and serve.

Filling the mould

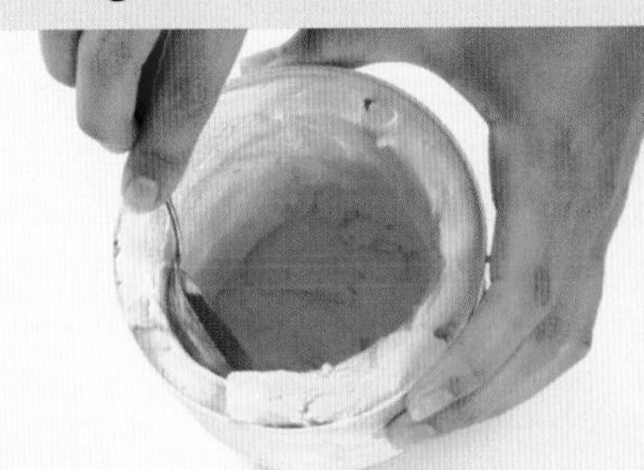

Allow the vanilla ice cream to soften at room temperature for about 20 minutes. Spread it over the base and up the side of the mould. Chill in the freezer until solid.

Soften the chocolate ice cream, then spread it evenly over the vanilla ice cream to make a hollow inner layer. Return to the freezer until solid.

Lime sorbet

SERVES 6 **CALS PER SERVING** 169

250 g (8 oz) granulated sugar
600 ml (1 pint) water
finely grated zest and juice of 6 limes
2 egg whites
strips of lime zest, to decorate

1 Put the sugar and measured water into a saucepan and heat gently until the sugar dissolves. Bring to a boil and boil for 2 minutes. Remove from the heat, add the lime zest, and leave to cool completely. Stir in the lime juice.

2 Strain the lime syrup into a shallow freezerproof container and freeze for about 2 hours until just mushy. Turn the mixture into a bowl and whisk gently to break down any large crystals.

3 Whisk the egg whites until stiff but not dry, then fold into the lime mixture. Return to the freezer, and freeze until firm. Transfer the sorbet to the refrigerator to soften for about 30 minutes before serving, and top with strips of lime zest.

Raspberry sorbet

SERVES 6 **CALS PER SERVING** 152

500 g (1 lb) raspberries
175 g (6 oz) granulated sugar
600 ml (1 pint) water
juice of 1 orange
3 egg whites
raspberries and mint sprigs, to decorate

1 Purée the raspberries in a food processor, then push through a sieve to remove the seeds. Put the sugar and measured water into a saucepan and heat gently until the sugar dissolves. Bring to a boil and boil for 5 minutes. Pour into a bowl and cool.

2 Stir in the raspberry purée and orange juice. Pour into a freezerproof container, then follow steps 2 and 3 of Lime sorbet (above). Decorate with raspberries and mint sprigs before serving.

Apricot sorbet

SERVES 6 **CALS PER SERVING** 104

90 g (3 oz) granulated sugar
300 ml (½ pint) water
juice of 1 lemon
750 g (1½ lb) apricots, halved and stoned
2 egg whites

1 Put the sugar, measured water, and lemon juice into a saucepan and heat gently until the sugar has dissolved. Bring to a boil, add the apricots, and simmer for 15 minutes or until very tender. Cool.

2 Peel and slice a few apricots for decoration, and set aside. Press the remainder through a sieve. Mix with the syrup in a freezerproof container, then follow steps 2 and 3 of Lime sorbet (left). Decorate with the sliced apricots before serving.

Pear and ginger sorbet

SERVES 6 **CALS PER SERVING** 128

90 g (3 oz) granulated sugar
300 ml (½ pint) water
1 tbsp lemon juice
750 g (1½ lb) pears, peeled and cored
1 piece of stem ginger in syrup, finely chopped
2 egg whites
strips of stem ginger, to decorate

1 Put the sugar, measured water, and lemon juice into a saucepan and heat gently until the sugar dissolves. Bring to a boil, add the pears, and poach gently, basting with the sugar syrup from time to time, for 20–25 minutes until the pears are tender. Cool, then purée in a food processor.

2 Add the chopped stem ginger to the pear purée. Pour the pear mixture into a freezerproof container, then follow steps 2 and 3 of Lime sorbet (above, left). Decorate with stem ginger before serving.

Granitas

Italian granitas are similar to sorbets but even easier to make: they are simply flavoured ice crystals.

Coffee
Put 60 g (2 oz) caster sugar and 4 tbsp instant coffee granules into a pan with 750 ml (1¼ pints) water and bring to a boil. Simmer for about 5 minutes. Leave to cool, then pour into a freezerproof container. Freeze, stirring occasionally, for 5 hours.

Lemon
Put 200 g (7 oz) caster sugar into a saucepan, add 500 ml (16 fl oz) water, and bring to a boil. Simmer for 5 minutes. Leave to cool. Add 2 tsp finely grated lemon zest and the juice of 4 lemons to the sugar syrup. Pour into a freezerproof container and freeze, stirring occasionally, for 5 hours.

Watermelon
Remove and discard the rind and seeds from 1 kg (2 lb) watermelon. Purée the flesh in a food processor. Pour into a freezerproof container and mix in 30 g (1 oz) icing sugar and 1½ tsp lemon juice. Freeze, stirring occasionally, for 5 hours.

Opposite, clockwise from top
Raspberry sorbet, Lime sorbet, Apricot sorbet, Pear and ginger sorbet

Peach Melba

SERVES 4 **CALS PER SERVING** 273

4 ripe peaches, peeled, stoned, and sliced
8 scoops of vanilla ice cream
mint sprigs, to decorate

Melba sauce

375 g (12 oz) raspberries
about 4 tbsp icing sugar

1 Make the Melba sauce (see box, right).

2 Arrange the peach slices in four glass serving bowls. Top each with two scoops of ice cream and some sauce. Decorate with mint sprigs and the remaining raspberries.

Making Melba sauce

Purée 250 g (8 oz) of the raspberries. Push through a sieve to remove the seeds.

Sift the icing sugar over the purée and stir in.

Iced Christmas pudding

SERVES 8 **CALS PER SERVING** 437

175 g (6 oz) mixed dried fruit
60 g (2 oz) ready-to-eat dried apricots, chopped
60 g (2 oz) glacé cherries, halved
3 tbsp brandy
3 eggs
125 g (4 oz) caster sugar
450 ml (¾ pint) milk
450 ml (¾ pint) double cream
150 ml (¼ pint) single cream

1.75 LITRE (3 PINT) PUDDING BOWL

1 Combine the dried fruit, apricots, glacé cherries, and brandy. Cover and leave to soak for 8 hours.

2 In a large bowl, whisk together the eggs and sugar. Heat the milk in a heavy saucepan to just below boiling point. Pour into the egg mixture, stirring.

3 Pour back into the pan. Cook gently, stirring with a wooden spoon, until the froth disappears and the mixture thickens. Do not boil. Remove from the heat and leave to cool.

4 Whip 300 ml (½ pint) double cream and the single cream together until they are just beginning to hold their shape. Fold into the custard with the fruit and brandy mixture.

5 Turn into a shallow freezerproof container and freeze for 2 hours or until beginning to set but still slightly soft.

6 Remove the pudding from the freezer and mix well to distribute the fruit evenly. Spoon into the pudding bowl, cover, and return to the freezer. Freeze for 3 hours or until firm.

7 Remove from the freezer about 20 minutes before serving to soften. Turn out on to a serving plate, and spoon the remaining cream, lightly whipped, on top. Slice and serve at once.

Cakes and teabreads

In this chapter...

Viennese fingers
page 580

Dundee cake
page 579

Ginger snaps
page 580

Brandy snaps
page 580

Coconut macaroons
page 582

Almond tuiles
page 582

Pink almond macarons
page 583

Simnel cake
page 584

Mincemeat buns
page 584

Fork biscuits
page 585

Pinwheel biscuits
page 585

Shortbread
page 586

Potato farls
page 586

Bara brith
page 587

Irish soda bread
page 587

Devon scones
page 588

Wholemeal drop scones
page 588

Welsh cakes
page 589

Cornbread
page 589

Religieuses
page 590

Chocolate profiteroles
page 590

Coffee éclairs
page 590

Cakes and teabreads know-how

Cake-making is often seen as the test of a cook's skills, but there are lots of cakes and teabreads, as well as scones, biscuits, cookies, and American-style muffins that are really quite simple to make and just as delicious as more elaborate creations. If you are a beginner, just remember to follow recipes carefully, and make sure your weighing and measuring is accurate. Use the right equipment and tins, and take the time to prepare cakes properly, and you'll achieve perfect results every time. You'll find that once you've gained confidence, you'll be able to experiment with more difficult recipes.

Storing

Most cakes are best eaten freshly made, particularly sponge cakes that don't contain fat, but if you do want to keep a cake, be sure to store it in an airtight container. Put the cake on the upturned lid of the cake tin, then put the tin over the top. This makes it easy to remove the cake from the tin. Fruit cakes and cakes made by the melting method, such as gingerbread, will improve with keeping (store in an airtight tin). Wrap fruit cake in greaseproof paper and then overwrap in foil. Don't put foil directly in contact with a fruit cake as the acid in the fruit may react with the foil. Any cake that has a filling or icing of whipped cream, butter-icing, or soft cheese should be kept in the refrigerator. Scones, American-style muffins, and most teabreads are best eaten freshly made.

Most biscuits can be stored in an airtight tin for a few days; if they soften, crisp them up in a warm oven. Allow cakes and biscuits to cool completely on a wire rack before putting them into a tin. Do not store cakes and biscuits together as the moisture from the cake will soften the biscuits.

Freezing

If baked goods are not eaten immediately freezing is a good way to keep them fresh. Cakes, teabreads, biscuits, American-style muffins, and scones all freeze well.

Wrap plain cakes, fruit cakes and teabreads in foil or freezer wrap. If a cake has been iced or decorated, tray freeze it, then place in a rigid container or freezer bag. Fruit cakes can be stored for up to 12 months; un-iced cakes for 4–6 months; iced cakes for 2–3 months. Unwrap decorated cakes before thawing, but leave other cakes in their wrapping.

Biscuits, muffins, and scones can be stored for 6 months. Interleave biscuits with foil or freezer wrap to keep them separate. Thaw biscuits and muffins at room temperature. Scones can be successfully reheated or toasted from frozen.

Microwaving

Microwave-baked cakes and biscuits can be disappointingly pale in colour and gluey in texture. Instead, in baking the microwave comes into its own when used as an accessory to the conventional oven. Here are good things to use it for:

- melting chocolate: break chocolate into small pieces, put into a bowl, and cook on LOW for 3–5 minutes until melted and shiny; stir halfway
- melting crystallized honey or syrup: heat on HIGH for 1–2 minutes. If kept in the jar, take off the lid
- softening hardened, set sugar: cook on HIGH for 30–40 seconds
- skinning and toasting hazelnuts: place them on paper towels and cook on HIGH for 30 seconds, then remove skins. Cook until golden

Baking ingredients

In baking it is important to use the ingredients specified in a recipe. Choose the best quality available.

Flour

Both plain and self-raising flours are used in baking, either white or wholemeal. Self-raising flour includes a raising agent (usually a mixture of bicarbonate of soda and cream of tartar), so if you want to substitute plain flour, add 2 tsp baking powder per 250 g (8 oz) flour.

Raising agents

Baking powder and bicarbonate of soda are used to raise cakes, teabreads, and biscuits. When a mixture contains baking powder, or self-raising flour, be sure to bake without delay, while the chemicals are still active.

Butter and other fats

In simple cakes, biscuits, and teabreads, where flavour is important, always use butter. In other cakes, baking spread is acceptable. For all-in-one mixtures soft baking spread is best as it is made up of 80% fat and blends easily. Low-fat spreads are not suitable for baking because of their high water content, so check before you buy. If oil is called for, use a mild, light one such as sunflower or sweeter corn oil.

Sugar

For most mixtures, it is essential to use a sugar that dissolves easily, such as caster sugar or soft, fine muscovado sugar. Granulated sugar can be used in rubbed-in mixtures. Coarse demerara sugar is fine for melted mixtures and is ideal for sprinkling on the top of cakes, as is icing sugar. Other sweeteners used in baking include golden syrup, honey, molasses, and malt extract, as well as concentrated fruit purée or juice.

Eggs

Eggs at room temperature are more easily aerated than cold eggs taken straight from the refrigerator. Cold eggs can also cause some cake mixtures to curdle.

Baking biscuits

When arranging biscuits on prepared baking sheets, leave enough space between them to allow for spreading, if necessary. As biscuits cook quickly, they can easily be baked in batches if you don't have enough baking sheets.

At the end of the baking time, many biscuits will still feel a little soft in the middle: they will continue to bake on the hot sheet after being removed from the oven. If the recipe directs, leave them to firm up for 1–2 minutes before transferring to a wire rack. Avoid letting biscuits cool completely on the sheet or they may stick.

Creamed cakes

The creaming method is used for both cakes and biscuits. A wooden spoon, rubber spatula, or electric mixer are all suitable. Be sure to soften the butter or baking spread first.

1 Cream the fat and sugar together until the mixture is pale in colour and fluffy in texture. Keep scraping the side of the bowl with a spoon or spatula to incorporate all of the mixture.

2 Lightly beat the eggs. Gradually add the eggs to the creamed mixture, beating well between each addition. If the mixture curdles, which will result in a dense-textured cake, beat in a spoonful of the flour.

3 Sift over the flour and any other dry ingredients. Using a wooden spoon, gently fold in the flour until well combined. Any liquid ingredients should also be added at this stage.

Whisked cakes

Light, fatless sponges are raised by air whisked into eggs. Use a hand-held electric mixer or a large, table-top mixer. If using a hand-held mixer, set it at high speed.

1 Whisk the eggs, or egg yolks, with the sugar until the mixture is light, pale, and thick enough to leave a trail on the surface when the beaters are lifted out.

2 Gently fold in the flour and any other ingredients. If the eggs have been separated, the whisked egg whites should be folded into the mixture last of all.

All-in-one cakes

Be sure to use a soft baking spread for this quick, simple technique.

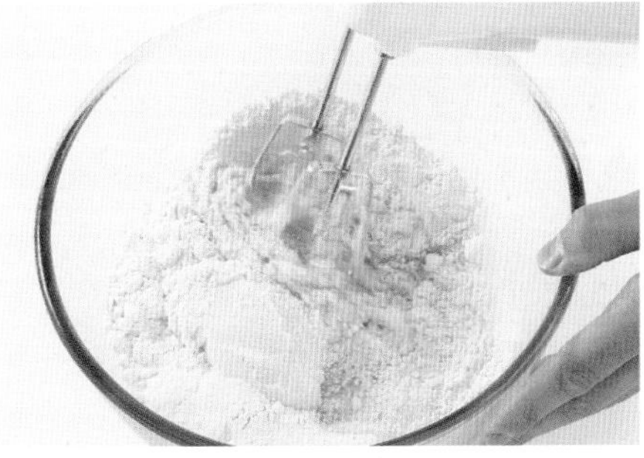

Put all the ingredients into a large bowl and beat together with a hand-held electric mixer until combined. You can also mix in a food processor or by hand.

Preparing cake tins

Lightly greasing the tin ensures a cake will turn out easily. Some recipes also call for the tin to be floured or lined with greaseproof paper or baking parchment.

Greasing and flouring

Use melted or softened butter or baking spread, or oil, according to the recipe. Brush over the bottom and side of the tin using a pastry brush or paper towels. If flouring, add a spoonful of flour and tilt the tin to coat it with a thin layer. Tip out any excess flour.

Lining

1 Set the cake tin on a sheet of greaseproof paper or parchment and mark around the base with a pencil or the tip of a knife.

2 Cut out the shape, cutting just inside the line, then press smoothly over the bottom of the tin. Lightly grease if directed in the recipe.

Baking, testing, and cooling cakes

Before baking cakes, teabreads, and biscuits, be sure to preheat the oven to the correct temperature. If you need to, adjust the position of the shelves before you turn on the oven.

1 As soon as the mixture is prepared, turn it into the tin and level the surface. Tap the tin on the work surface to break any large air bubbles. Transfer immediately to the oven.

2 When cooked, a cake will shrink slightly from the side of the tin. To test, lightly press the middle with a fingertip; the cake should spring back. Rich cakes should feel firm to the touch.

3 Set the cake tin on a wire rack and leave to cool for about 10 minutes. Run a knife around the side of the cake to free it from the tin.

4 Place a tea towel over a wire rack and hold over the cake tin. Invert the rack and tin so that the cake falls on to the tea towel. Carefully lift the tin away from the cake.

5 Peel off the lining paper. With a light-textured cake, turn it over again so the base is on the rack; this will prevent the rack marking the top.

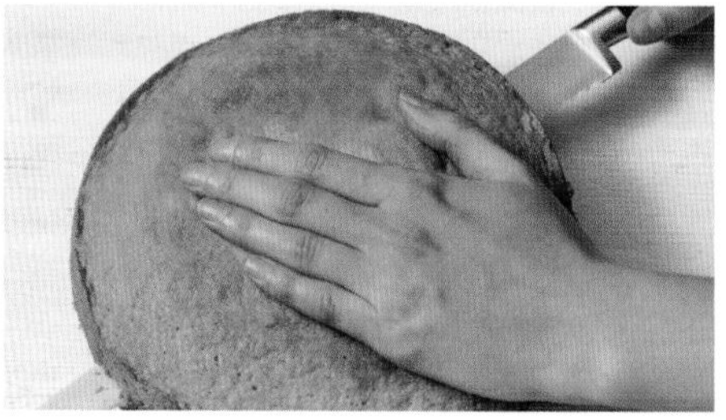

6 To cut the cake in half, steady it by setting one hand gently on top. Cut the cake horizontally, using a gentle sawing action.

Baking know-how

When measuring ingredients with a spoon, don't hold the spoon directly over the bowl or you may accidentally add too much.

Be sure to use the correct size tin, as stated in the recipe. To check the dimensions of a cake tin, measure inside the top rim. To work out the depth, measure from the bottom to the top rim on the inside of the tin. To check the capacity of a tin, measure how much water is needed to fill it to the brim.

Bake for the minimum time given in the recipe before opening the oven door. If the door is opened too soon it may cause some cakes to deflate.

If a cake looks as though it is browning too quickly, cover the top loosely with foil.If baking several cake layers, stagger them on the oven shelves so one is not directly beneath another.

Filling and icing cakes

There are many simple ways to fill or decorate cakes. Whipped cream, jam, or chocolate spread make quick and easy fillings. Butter-icing can be made in a variety of flavours, to complement the flavour of the cake.

Chocolate butter-icing

In a bowl, soften 150 g (5 oz) butter. Add 30 g (1 oz) cocoa powder and 250 g (8 oz) sifted icing sugar, and beat together until smooth. Add a little milk if necessary to give a spreading consistency. For a citrus icing, omit the cocoa powder and add finely grated orange or lemon zest.

Spreading icing

Only ice a cake when it has cooled completely. Use a large palette knife and spread the icing with long, smooth strokes over the top and side of the cake. Dip the palette knife in warm water if the icing sticks to it.

Testing fruit cakes

For fruit cakes and fruited teabreads, insert a metal skewer or long wooden cocktail stick into the middle: the skewer or stick should come out clean, without any moist crumbs sticking to it.

Wimbledon cake

CUTS INTO 8 slices **CALS EACH** 260

butter, for greasing
3 eggs
90 g (3 oz) caster sugar
90 g (3 oz) self-raising flour

Filling and topping

300 ml (½ pint) whipping cream, whipped until thick
125 g (4 oz) strawberries, sliced
1 passion fruit, halved
strawberries, halved, to decorate

2 X 18 CM (7 IN) SANDWICH CAKE TINS

1 Lightly butter the cake tins, line the bottoms with baking parchment, then butter the parchment.

2 Put the eggs and sugar into a large bowl. Whisk with an electric mixer at high speed until the mixture is pale and thick enough to leave a trail when the whisk is lifted out.

3 Sift in half of the flour and fold in gently. Repeat with the remaining flour.

4 Divide the mixture between the tins. Tilt to spread the mixture evenly.

5 Bake in a preheated oven at 190°C (170°C fan, Gas 5) for 20–25 minutes until well risen, golden, and beginning to shrink away from the sides of the tins. Turn out on to a wire rack, peel off the lining paper, and leave to cool.

6 Spread half of the whipped cream over one of the sponges. Top with the sliced strawberries and passion fruit pulp. Put the other sponge on top and press down gently.

7 Spread the remaining cream on top of the cake, smoothing it neatly with a palette knife. Decorate with the strawberry halves.

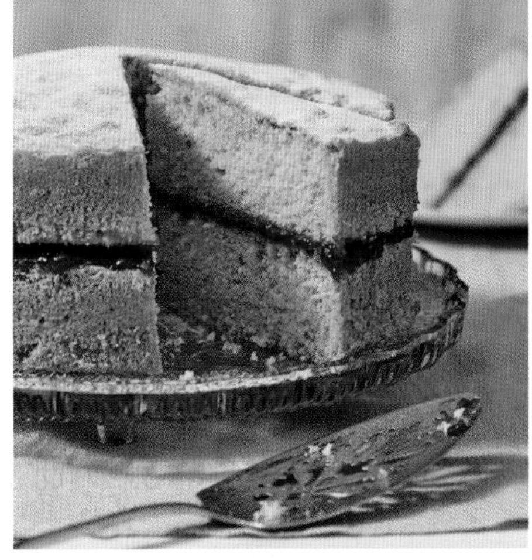

Victoria sandwich cake

CUTS INTO 8 slices **CALS EACH** 386

225 g (8 oz) soft butter or baking spread, plus extra for greasing
225 g (8 oz) caster sugar, plus extra for sprinkling
4 large eggs
225 g (8 oz) self-raising flour
1 tsp baking powder
4 tbsp raspberry or strawberry jam

2 X 20 CM (8 IN) SANDWICH TINS

1 Lightly grease the sandwich tins, line the bottoms with baking parchment, then grease the parchment.

2 Combine all the cake ingredients in a large bowl. Beat well for about 2 minutes until smooth.

3 Divide the mixture between the prepared tins and level the surfaces. Bake in a preheated oven at 180°C (160°C fan, Gas 4) for about 25 minutes or until the cakes are well risen, golden, and springy to the touch.

4 Turn out on to a wire rack, peel off the lining paper, and leave to cool.

5 Sandwich the two sponges together with jam and sprinkle the top of the cake with caster sugar.

LEMON SANDWICH CAKE

Add the finely grated zest of 1 lemon to the cake ingredients before beating. Sandwich the cakes together with lemon curd and 150 ml (¼ pint) whipping cream, whipped until thick. Dust with sifted icing sugar.

Swiss roll

CUTS INTO 8 slices **CALS EACH** 195

butter, for greasing
4 large eggs
125 g (4 oz) caster sugar, plus extra for sprinkling
125 g (4 oz) self-raising flour
about 4 tbsp raspberry jam
icing sugar, for sprinkling

23 X 33 CM (9 X 13 IN) SWISS ROLL TIN

1 Lightly butter the Swiss roll tin, line with baking parchment, then lightly butter the parchment.

2 Put the eggs and caster sugar into a large bowl. Whisk together with an electric mixer at high speed until the mixture is pale and thick enough to leave a trail when the whisk is lifted out.

3 Sift the flour into the egg mixture and fold in gently but thoroughly.

4 Turn the mixture into the prepared tin and tilt to spread the mixture evenly, particularly into the corners.

5 Bake in a preheated oven at 220°C (200°C fan, Gas 7) for 10 minutes or until the sponge is golden and starting to shrink away from the side of the tin.

6 Invert the sponge on to a large piece of baking parchment which has been liberally sprinkled with caster sugar. Peel off the lining paper and trim the edges of the sponge with a sharp knife.

7 Roll up the sponge and the baking parchment together, from one of the short ends. Leave to stand for 2–3 minutes.

8 Unroll the sponge, and remove the baking parchment. Spread the sponge with warmed jam and roll up again. Wrap tightly in baking parchment and leave to cool. Unwrap, dust with icing sugar, and serve in slices.

Gingerbread

MAKES 12 squares **CALS EACH** 436

250 g (8 oz) butter or baking spread, plus extra for greasing
250 g (8 oz) dark muscovado sugar
250 g (8 oz) black treacle
375 g (12 oz) plain flour
5 tsp ground ginger
2 tsp ground cinnamon
2 eggs, beaten
3 pieces of stem ginger in syrup, drained and roughly chopped
300 ml (½ pint) milk
2 tsp bicarbonate of soda

23 X 30 CM (9 X 12 IN) CAKE TIN

1 Lightly grease the tin and line the bottom with greaseproof paper.

2 Heat the butter, sugar, and treacle in a pan, stirring, until smooth. Cool slightly.

3 Sift in the flour and ground spices. Stir well, then beat in the eggs and stem ginger.

4 Warm the milk in a small heavy saucepan, and add the bicarbonate of soda. Pour into the gingerbread mixture and stir gently until thoroughly blended.

5 Pour the mixture into the prepared tin. Bake in a preheated oven at 160°C (140°C fan, Gas 3) for about 1 hour until well risen and springy to the touch.

6 Leave to cool in the tin for a few minutes, then turn out on to a wire rack, and peel off the paper. Leave to cool completely, then store in an airtight container for 2–3 days (it improves with keeping). Cut into squares to serve.

Best-ever brownies

MAKES 24 **CALS EACH** 336

250 g (8 oz) baking spread, plus extra for greasing
375 g (12 oz) plain chocolate, broken into pieces
2 tsp instant coffee
2 tbsp hot water
2 eggs
250 g (8 oz) caster sugar
1 tsp vanilla extract
90 g (3 oz) self-raising flour
175 g (6 oz) walnut pieces
250 g (8 oz) plain chocolate chips

23 X 30 CM (9 X 12 IN) TRAYBAKE TIN

1 Lightly grease the tin and line the bottom with greaseproof paper. Grease the paper.

2 Put the chocolate and baking spread in a bowl and sit the bowl on top of a small saucepan of gently simmering water. Melt the chocolate slowly, then remove the bowl from the pan and let the chocolate cool.

3 Put the coffee in another bowl, pour in the hot water, and stir to dissolve. Add the eggs, sugar, and vanilla extract. Gradually beat in the chocolate mixture. Fold in the flour and walnuts, then the chocolate chips.

4 Pour the mixture into the prepared tin and bake in a preheated oven at 190°C (170°C fan, Gas 5) for about 40–45 minutes or until firm to the touch. Don't overcook – the crust should be dull and crisp, but the middle should still be gooey. Leave to cool in the tin, then cut into 24 pieces.

Cook's **know-how**

For brownies to be good they must not be overcooked. The secret is to take them out of the oven just before you think they are done – the middle should be soft and squidgy, not set firm. Do not worry if there is a dip in the middle or any cracks on top. This is how it should be, and you will find the mixture firms up on cooling.

Date and walnut loaf

CUTS INTO 12 slices **CALS EACH** 269

90 g (3 oz) soft butter or baking spread, plus extra for greasing
250 g (8 oz) dates, stoned and roughly chopped
150 ml (¼ pint) boiling water
90 g (3 oz) caster sugar
1 egg
250 g (8 oz) self-raising flour
1 tsp baking powder
90 g (3 oz) walnuts, roughly chopped

1 KG (2 LB) LOAF TIN

1 Lightly grease the loaf tin with butter and line with greaseproof paper.

2 Put the dates into a bowl, pour over the measured boiling water, and leave for about 15 minutes.

3 Combine the butter, sugar, egg, flour, and baking powder in a large bowl and beat until well blended. Add the walnuts and dates, plus the soaking liquid, and stir to mix.

4 Spoon into the prepared loaf tin and bake in a preheated oven at 180°C (160°C fan, Gas 4) for 1¼–1½ hours until well risen and firm to the touch. A fine skewer inserted into the middle of the loaf should come out clean.

5 Leave to cool in the loaf tin for a few minutes, then turn out on to a wire rack, and peel off the lining paper. Leave to cool completely. Serve sliced and buttered, if wished.

CHERRY AND BANANA LOAF

Omit the dates and walnuts, and add 125 g (4 oz) quartered glacé cherries and 2 mashed large ripe bananas in step 3.

Courgette loaf

CUTS INTO 12 slices **CALS EACH** 331

250 g (8 oz) courgettes
2 eggs
125 ml (4 fl oz) sunflower oil, plus extra for greasing
250 g (8 oz) caster sugar
¼ tsp vanilla extract (optional)
375 g (12 oz) self-raising flour
1 tsp ground cinnamon
60 g (2 oz) walnuts, coarsely chopped

1 KG (2 LB) LOAF TIN

1 Coarsely grate the courgettes, put them into a sieve, and leave for about 30 minutes to drain.

2 Beat the eggs until light and foamy. Add the sunflower oil, sugar, vanilla extract (if using), and courgettes and mix lightly until combined.

3 Sift the flour and cinnamon into a large bowl. Make a well in the middle, pour in the courgette mixture, and stir to mix thoroughly. Stir in the chopped walnuts.

4 Pour the mixture into the greased loaf tin and bake in a preheated oven at 180°C (160°C fan, Gas 4) for about 50 minutes until firm. Turn out and cool.

Cook's know-how

For best results, the courgettes should be thoroughly drained. Press into the sieve with your hand or the back of a spoon to extract the excess juices.

Fruity banana bread

CUTS INTO 12 slices **CALS EACH** 334

125 g (4 oz) butter or baking spread, plus extra for greasing
250 g (8 oz) self-raising flour
175 g (6 oz) caster sugar
125 g (4 oz) sultanas
60 g (2 oz) walnuts, roughly chopped
125 g (4 oz) glacé cherries, quartered, rinsed, and dried
2 large eggs, beaten
500 g (1 lb) bananas, weight with peel, peeled and mashed

1 KG (2 LB) LOAF TIN

1 Grease the loaf tin and line the bottom with greaseproof paper.

2 Put the flour into a bowl, add the butter, and rub in with the fingertips until the mixture resembles fine breadcrumbs. Mix in the caster sugar, sultanas, chopped walnuts, and glacé cherries.

3 Add the eggs and mashed bananas and beat the mixture until well blended. Spoon into the prepared tin.

4 Bake in a preheated oven at 160°C (140°C fan, Gas 3) for about 1¼ hours until well risen and firm to the touch. A fine skewer inserted into the middle of the loaf should come out clean.

5 Leave the loaf to cool slightly in the tin, then turn out on to a wire rack, and peel off the lining paper. Leave the loaf to cool completely before slicing and serving.

Carrot cake

CUTS INTO 9 squares **CALS EACH** 458

150 ml (¼ pint) sunflower oil, plus extra for greasing
250 g (8 oz) wholemeal self-raising flour
2 tsp baking powder
150 g (5 oz) light muscovado sugar
60 g (2 oz) walnuts, coarsely chopped
125 g (4 oz) carrots, grated
2 ripe bananas, mashed
2 eggs
1 tbsp milk

Topping

250 g (8 oz) low-fat soft cheese, at room temperature
2 tsp clear honey
1 tsp lemon juice
chopped walnuts, to decorate

18 CM (7 IN) SQUARE CAKE TIN

1 Lightly grease the cake tin and line the bottom with baking parchment.

2 Combine all the cake ingredients in a large bowl. Mix well until thoroughly blended. Turn into the prepared cake tin and level the surface.

3 Bake in a preheated oven at 180°C (160°C fan, Gas 4) for about 50 minutes until the cake is well risen, firm to the touch, and beginning to shrink away from the sides of the tin.

4 Leave the cake to cool in the tin for a few minutes. Turn out on to a wire rack, peel off the lining paper, and leave to cool completely.

5 Make the topping: mix together the cheese, honey, and lemon juice. Spread on top of the cake and sprinkle the walnuts over the top. Store the cake in the refrigerator until ready to serve.

Blueberry and vanilla muffins

MAKES 12 **CALS EACH** 249

250 g (8 oz) plain flour
2 tsp baking powder
150 g (5 oz) caster sugar
175 ml (6 fl oz) milk
1 tsp vanilla extract
2 large eggs
150 ml (¼ pint) sunflower oil
90 g (3 oz) blueberries

DEEP 12-HOLE MUFFIN TIN AND 12 PAPER CASES

1 Line the muffin tin with the paper cases.

2 Put all the ingredients, except the blueberries, into a bowl. Beat with an electric whisk until evenly combined and smooth (it is quite a thin mixture). Stir in the blueberries.

3 Divide the mixture among the paper cases. Bake in a preheated oven at 180°C (160°C fan, Gas 4) for 25–30 minutes until well risen and light golden. Serve warm.

Cook's know-how

These traditional American muffins have a dense texture and are not too sweet. They are perfect for breakfast, and to serve with morning coffee or afternoon tea – or whenever you like.

Lemon cup cakes with lemon icing

MAKES 12 **CALS EACH** 332

125 g (4 oz) soft butter
125 g (4 oz) self-raising flour
125 g (4 oz) caster sugar
2 tbsp milk
2 large eggs
finely grated zest of 1 small lemon

Lemon icing

125 g (4 oz) soft unsalted butter
250 g (8 oz) icing sugar, sifted
juice of 1 small lemon
edible silver balls or glitter, to decorate

DEEP 12-HOLE MUFFIN TIN AND 12 PAPER CASES

1 Line the muffin tin with the paper cases. Put all the cake ingredients into a bowl, and beat with an electric whisk until evenly combined and smooth.

2 Divide the mixture among the paper cases. Bake in a preheated oven at 180°C (160°C fan, Gas 4) for 20–25 minutes until well risen and light golden brown. Transfer the cakes in their cases to a wire rack, and leave to cool.

3 Make the icing: put the butter and half of the icing sugar into a bowl, and beat with an electric whisk until evenly combined and smooth. Add the lemon juice and the remaining icing sugar, and beat again until light and fluffy. Spread the icing over the cold cup cakes, and decorate with silver balls or glitter.

Battenberg cake

CUTS INTO 8 slices **CALS EACH** 425

125 g (4 oz) soft butter or baking spread, plus extra for greasing
125 g (4 oz) caster sugar
2 large eggs
60 g (2 oz) ground rice
125 g (4 oz) self-raising flour
½ tsp baking powder
a few drops of vanilla extract
1½ tsp cocoa powder
3 tbsp apricot jam
250 g (8 oz) almond paste

SHALLOW 18 CM (7 IN) SQUARE CAKE TIN

1 Lightly grease the cake tin with butter. Fold an 18 cm x 30 cm (7 in x 12 in) piece of baking parchment to create a pleat 6cm (2 ½ in) high. Place inside the tin to form two equal sections.

2 Beat the butter, sugar, eggs, ground rice, flour, baking powder, and vanilla extract in a large bowl for 2 minutes or until the mixture is smooth and evenly combined.

3 Spoon half of the mixture into one half of the prepared tin. Dissolve the cocoa in a little hot water to make a thick paste and add to the remaining cake mixture in the bowl. Mix well, then spoon into the other half of the tin.

4 Bake the mixture in a preheated oven at 160°C (140°C fan, Gas 3) for 35 minutes or until the cake is well risen and springy to the touch. Turn out on to a wire rack, peel off the lining paper, and cool.

5 Trim the edges of the cake. Cut it into four equal strips down the length of the two colours.

6 Warm the apricot jam in a small saucepan. Stack the cake strips, alternating the colours to give a chequerboard effect and sticking them together with the apricot jam.

7 Roll out the almond paste into an oblong that is the same length as the cake and wide enough to wrap around it. Put the cake on top, then brush with jam. Wrap the paste around the cake (see box, right).

8 Score the top with a crisscross pattern and crimp the edges with your fingertips to make a decorative effect.

Wrapping the cake

Wrap the almond paste around the cake, pressing it on gently and making the join in one corner. Turn to hide the join.

Chocolate cup cakes

MAKES 24 **CALS EACH** 198

40 g ($1\frac{1}{2}$ oz) cocoa powder
about 4 tbsp boiling water
3 eggs
175 g (6 oz) baking spread
175 g (6 oz) caster sugar
115 g ($4\frac{1}{2}$ oz) self-raising flour
1 rounded tsp baking powder

Icing
60 g (2 oz) butter
30 g (1 oz) cocoa powder
about 3 tbsp milk
250 g (8 oz) icing sugar

2 X 12-HOLE MUFFIN TINS AND 24 PAPER CASES

1 Line two 12-hole muffin tins with paper cases. Sift the cocoa powder into a bowl, pour in the boiling water, and mix into a thick paste. Add the remaining cake ingredients and mix with an electric hand whisk (or beat well with a wooden spoon).

2 Divide the mixture equally among the 24 paper cases. Bake in a preheated oven at 200°C (180°C fan, Gas 6) for about 10 minutes until well risen and springy to the touch. Cool in the cases on a wire rack.

3 Make the icing. Melt the butter, then pour it into a bowl. Sift in the cocoa powder and stir to mix. Stir in the milk and then sift in the icing sugar a little at a time to make a glossy, spreadable icing. Spread the icing over the cakes and leave to set before serving.

Heavenly chocolate cake

CUTS INTO 8 slices **CALS EACH** 615

125 g (4 oz) butter,
plus extra for greasing
200 g (7 oz) plain dark chocolate, broken into pieces
2 tbsp water
3 eggs, separated
125 g (4 oz) caster sugar
90 g (3 oz) self-raising flour
60 g (2 oz) ground almonds

Fudge icing
125 g (4 oz) butter
60 g (2 oz) cocoa powder
about 6 tbsp milk
500 g (1 lb) icing sugar, sifted
white chocolate curls (page 520), to decorate

DEEP 20 CM (8 IN) CAKE TIN

1 Lightly butter the tin and line the bottom with baking parchment.

2 Put the chocolate into a heatproof bowl with the butter and water. Put the bowl over a pan of hot water and heat gently, stirring, until the mixture has melted. Set aside to cool.

3 Combine the egg yolks and caster sugar in a large bowl and whisk together with an electric whisk until fluffy and very light in colour. Stir in the cooled chocolate mixture. Carefully fold in the flour and ground almonds.

4 In a separate bowl, whisk the egg whites until stiff but not dry. Fold into the sponge mixture, gently but thoroughly. Pour the mixture into the prepared tin. Bake in a preheated oven at 180°C (160°C fan, Gas 4) for 50 minutes or until well risen and firm to the touch.

5 Leave the cake to cool in the tin for a few minutes, turn out on to a wire rack, and peel off the lining paper. Cool completely. Make the fudge icing: melt the butter in a pan, add the cocoa powder, and cook, stirring, for 1 minute. Stir in the milk and icing sugar. Beat well until smooth. Leave to cool until thickened.

6 Split the cake in half horizontally and sandwich the layers together with half of the fudge icing. With a palette knife, spread the remaining icing over the top and sides of the cake. Decorate with white chocolate curls.

Double chocolate muffins

MAKES 12 **CALS EACH** 262

2 eggs, lightly beaten
125 g (4 oz) full-fat plain yogurt
125 ml (4 fl oz) strong brewed coffee
125 ml (4 fl oz) milk
250 g (8 oz) self-raising flour, sifted
250 g (8 oz) caster sugar
75 g (2½ oz) cocoa powder
pinch of salt
100 g (3½ oz) plain chocolate chips
melted butter, for greasing

12-HOLE MUFFIN TIN

1 Combine the eggs, yogurt, coffee, and milk in a large bowl.

2 Sift together the flour, sugar, cocoa powder, and salt, and stir into the milk mixture. Mix well. Stir in the chocolate chips.

3 Butter each cup of the muffin tin, then spoon in the muffin mixture, filling the cups almost to the tops.

4 Bake the muffins in a preheated oven at 200°C (180°C fan, Gas 6) for about 10 minutes; reduce the oven temperature to 180°C (160°C fan, Gas 4), and continue to bake for about 15 minutes until the muffins are golden and firm. Serve warm.

White chocolate gâteau

CUTS INTO 14 slices **CALS EACH** 391

90 g (3 oz) butter, melted and cooled slightly, plus extra for greasing
6 large eggs
175 g (6 oz) caster sugar
125 g (4 oz) self-raising flour
30 g (1 oz) cocoa powder
2 tbsp cornflour

Filling and topping

300 ml (½ pint) double or whipping cream, whipped until thick
white chocolate curls (page 520)

DEEP 23 CM (9 IN) ROUND CAKE TIN

1 Lightly butter the cake tin and line the bottom of the tin with baking parchment.

2 Put the eggs and sugar into a large bowl and whisk together with an electric mixer on high speed until the mixture is pale and thick enough to leave a trail on itself when the whisk is lifted out.

3 Sift together the flour, cocoa powder, and cornflour, and fold half into the egg mixture. Pour half of the cooled butter around the edge; fold in gently.

4 Repeat with the remaining flour mixture and butter, folding gently.

5 Turn the mixture into the prepared cake tin and tilt the tin to level the surface. Bake in a preheated oven at 180°C (160°C fan, Gas 4) for 35–40 minutes until the sponge is well risen and firm to the touch. Turn out on to a wire rack, peel off the lining, and cool.

6 Cut the cake in half horizontally and sandwich the layers together with half of the whipped cream. Cover the cake with a thin layer of cream, press the chocolate curls over the top and side of the cake, then pipe the remaining cream around the top edge.

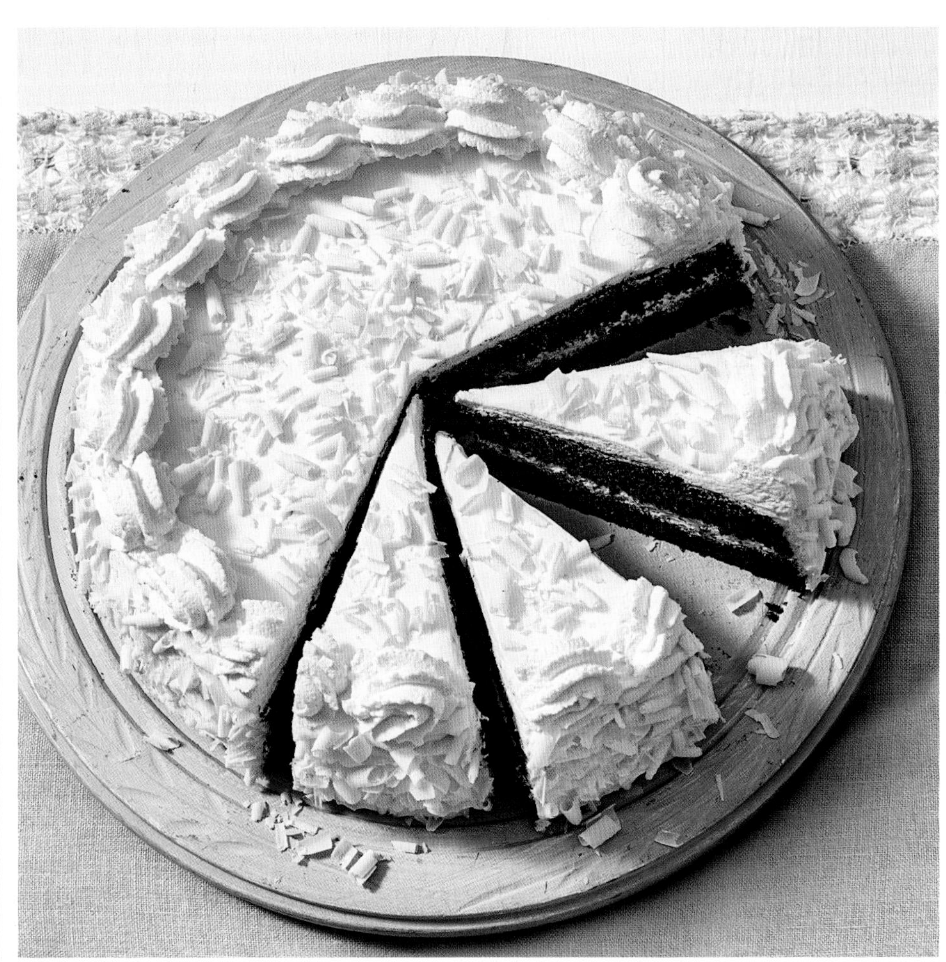

Chocolate and orange mousse cake

This cake is made of chocolate sponge layers sandwiched together with a deliciously fluffy chocolate and orange mousse. When making the mousse, do not overwhisk the egg whites; when they just flop over at the tip they are ready to fold into the chocolate mixture.

CUTS INTO 12 slices **CALS EACH** 417

butter, for greasing
4 eggs
125 g (4 oz) caster sugar
90 g (3 oz) self-raising flour
30 g (1 oz) cocoa powder

Mousse

175 g (6 oz) plain dark chocolate, broken into pieces
grated zest and juice of 1 orange
1 tsp powdered gelatine
2 eggs, separated
300 ml (½ pint) double cream, whipped until thick

Decoration

300 ml (½ pint) double or whipping cream, whipped until thick
strips of orange zest, blanched

DEEP 23 CM (9 IN) SPRINGFORM CAKE TIN

1 Lightly butter the tin and line the bottom with baking parchment. Make the sponge (see box, opposite).

2 Bake the sponge in a preheated oven at 180°C (160°C fan, Gas 4) for 40–45 minutes until the sponge is well risen and beginning to shrink away from the sides of the tin. Turn out on to a wire rack, peel off the lining paper, and leave to cool.

3 Cut the cake in half horizontally. Put one half back into the clean tin.

4 Make the mousse: put the chocolate into a heatproof bowl set over a pan of hot water. Heat gently, stirring occasionally, until the chocolate has melted. Leave to cool slightly.

5 Strain the orange juice into a small heatproof bowl and sprinkle over the gelatine. Leave for 3 minutes or until spongy, then stand the bowl in a saucepan of gently simmering water for 3 minutes or until the gelatine has dissolved.

6 Stir the egg yolks and orange zest into the cooled chocolate. Slowly stir in the dissolved gelatine, then fold in the whipped cream. In a separate bowl, whisk the egg whites until stiff but not dry, then gently fold into the chocolate mixture until well blended.

7 Pour the mousse on top of the cake layer in the tin. Put the remaining cake layer on top. Cover and chill in the refrigerator until the mousse filling is set.

8 Remove the side of the tin and slide the cake on to a serving plate. Cover the cake with a layer of cream, then decorate with orange zest.

Making the sponge

Combine the eggs and sugar in a large bowl and whisk with an electric mixer at high speed until the mixture is pale and thick enough to leave a trail on itself when the whisk is lifted out.

Sift the flour and cocoa powder over the surface.

Fold in the flour and cocoa until blended.

Turn the mixture into the prepared tin and tilt to level the surface.

Devil's food cake

CUTS INTO 12 slices **CALS EACH** 513

175 g (6 oz) soft butter or baking spread, plus extra for greasing
90 g (3 oz) plain dark chocolate, broken into pieces
175 ml (6 fl oz) hot water
300 g (10 oz) light muscovado sugar
3 eggs, beaten
300 g (10 oz) plain flour
1½ tsp bicarbonate of soda
1½ tsp baking powder
1 tsp vanilla extract
150 ml (¼ pint) soured cream

American-style frosting

400 g (13 oz) caster sugar
2 egg whites
4 tbsp hot water
pinch of cream of tartar

3 X 20 CM (8 IN) SANDWICH CAKE TINS

1 Grease the tins with butter and line the bottoms with baking parchment.

2 Put the chocolate into a pan with the water. Heat gently, stirring, until the chocolate melts. Cool.

3 Combine the butter and sugar in a bowl and beat until light and fluffy. Gradually add the eggs, beating well.

4 Stir in the melted chocolate. Sift together the flour, bicarbonate of soda, and baking powder. Fold into the chocolate mixture until evenly blended, then fold in the vanilla extract and soured cream.

5 Divide the mixture evenly among the prepared tins. Bake in a preheated oven at 190°C (170°C fan, Gas 5) for about 25 minutes until well risen, springy to the touch, and just shrinking away from the sides of the tins.

6 Turn out the cakes on to a wire rack, peel off the lining paper, and leave to cool.

7 Make the American-style frosting: combine all the ingredients in a heatproof bowl. Set the bowl over a pan of hot water and whisk with an electric mixer for 12 minutes or until the mixture is white, thick, and stands in peaks.

8 Use half of the American frosting to sandwich the layers together, then spread the remainder over the top and side of the cake, swirling it decoratively and pulling it into peaks with the flat of a small palette knife. Cut into slices and serve.

Chocolate and beetroot cake

CUTS INTO 8 slices **CALS EACH** 641

150 g (5 oz) soft butter, plus extra for greasing
250 g (8 oz) light muscovado sugar
3 large eggs
60 g (2 oz) cocoa powder
200 g (7 oz) self-raising flour
2 tsp baking powder
4 tbsp milk
250 g (8 oz) cooked beetroot, peeled and coarsely grated

Chocolate fudge icing

60 g (2 oz) butter
30 g (1 oz) cocoa powder, sifted
3 tbsp milk
250 g (8 oz) icing sugar, sifted

23 CM (9 IN) SPRINGFORM OR LOOSE-BOTTOMED CAKE TIN

1 Lightly grease the tin, and line the bottom with baking parchment.

2 Combine all the cake ingredients, except the beetroot, in a large bowl. Beat with an electric whisk until smooth, then fold in the beetroot. Spoon the mixture into the prepared tin.

3 Bake in a preheated oven at 180°C (160°C fan, Gas 4) for 45–55 minutes until the cake is well risen and shrinking away from the side of the tin. Set aside to cool a little, then remove the side of the tin (leaving the cake on the base), and leave to cool completely.

4 Make the icing: melt the butter in a saucepan, add the cocoa powder, and stir over a high heat for 1 minute. Add the milk and icing sugar, and stir to combine. Remove from the heat, and set aside to cool and thicken.

5 Remove the cake from the base of the tin, and peel off the lining paper. Using a serrated knife, slice the cake in half to make two equal layers. Spread one-third of the icing on the bottom half of the cake, and place the other half on top. Spread the remaining icing over the top and side of the cake to give a thin layer. Serve at once, or keep in the refrigerator for up to 3 days.

Marbled coffee ring cake

CUTS INTO 12 slices **CALS EACH** 471

250 g (8 oz) soft butter, plus extra for greasing
250 g (8 oz) caster sugar
4 eggs
250 g (8 oz) self-raising flour
2 tsp baking powder
2 tsp instant coffee
1 tbsp hot water
30 g (1 oz) white chocolate

Icing

60 g (2 oz) butter, softened
3 tbsp milk
2 tbsp instant coffee
250 g (8 oz) icing sugar, sifted

1.75 LITRE (2¾ PINT) RING MOULD

1 Lightly grease the ring mould with butter.

2 Combine the butter, sugar, eggs, flour, and baking powder in a large bowl. Beat until smooth.

3 Put half of the mixture into another bowl. Dissolve the instant coffee in the measured hot water and stir into one half of the cake mixture.

4 Drop tablespoonfuls of the plain mixture into the ring mould, then tablespoonfuls of the coffee mixture on top of the plain mixture. Marble by swirling together with a skewer.

5 Bake in a preheated oven at 180°C (160°C fan, Gas 4) for 40 minutes or until well risen and firm to the touch. Leave to cool for a few minutes, then turn out on to a wire rack set over a tray, and cool completely.

6 Make the icing: combine the butter, milk, and coffee in a pan and heat, stirring,until smooth. Remove from the heat and beat in the icing sugar until smooth and glossy.

7 Leave to cool, then pour over the cake, spreading it over the sides to cover completely. Leave to set.

8 Melt the white chocolate in a heatproof bowl over a pan of hot water. Cool slightly, then spoon into a plastic bag. Snip off a corner of the bag and drizzle the chocolate over the cake. Leave to set.

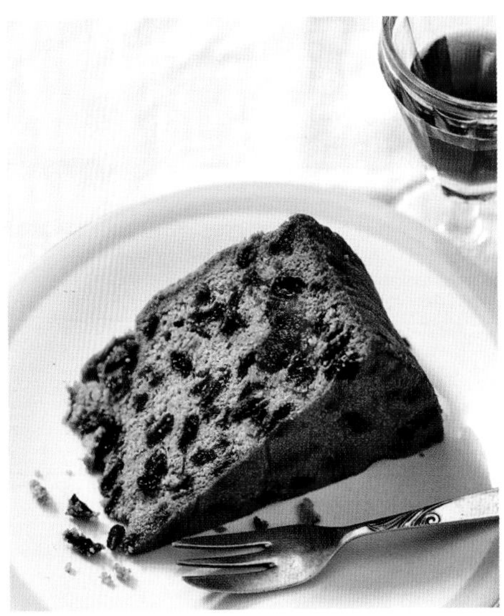

Rich fruit cake

CUTS INTO 10 slices **CALS EACH** 570

250 g (8 oz) soft butter or baking spread, plus extra for greasing
250 g (8 oz) light muscovado sugar
4 eggs
250 g (8 oz) self-raising flour
250 g (8 oz) raisins
250 g (8 oz) sultanas
125 g (4 oz) glacé cherries, halved and rinsed
½ tsp ground mixed spice
1 tbsp brandy

DEEP 20 CM (8 IN) ROUND CAKE TIN

1 Lightly grease the tin and line the bottom with greaseproof paper.

2 Combine all the ingredients in a large bowl and mix well until combined. Turn the mixture into the prepared cake tin and level the surface.

3 Bake in a preheated oven at 140°C (120°C fan, Gas 1) for 2–2¼ hours. Cover the top of the cake with foil after about 1 hour to prevent the top becoming too brown.

4 When cooked, the cake should be firm to the touch and a fine skewer inserted in the middle of the cake should come out clean. Leave the cake to cool in the tin before turning out. Store in an airtight container.

Rich fruit Christmas cake

CUTS INTO ABOUT 30 slices **CALS EACH** 316

425 g (14 oz) currants
250 g (8 oz) sultanas
250 g (8 oz) raisins
300 g (10 oz) cherries, quartered, rinsed, and dried
150 g (5 oz) ready-to-eat dried apricots, snipped into small pieces
75 g (2½ oz) mixed candied peel, roughly chopped
4 tbsp brandy, plus extra for soaking
300 g (10 oz) plain flour
1 tsp ground mixed spice
½ tsp grated nutmeg
300 g (10 oz) soft butter, plus extra for greasing
300 g (10 oz) dark muscovado sugar
5 eggs
60 g (2 oz) whole unblanched almonds, roughly chopped
1 tbsp black treacle
finely grated zest of 1 large lemon
finely grated zest of 1 large orange

DEEP 23 CM (9 IN) ROUND OR 20 CM (8 IN) SQUARE CAKE TIN

1 Combine the fruits and candied peel in a large bowl. Add the brandy, and stir to mix well. Cover and leave overnight.

2 Put the remaining ingredients into a large bowl and beat well with an electric mixer until thoroughly blended. Stir in the soaked fruits and any liquid.

3 Grease the cake tin with butter, line the bottom and sides with a double layer of greaseproof paper, and grease the paper. Spoon the mixture into the prepared tin. Level the surface and cover the top of the cake with greaseproof paper. If baking the Candied fruit cake (see Cake decorations, below right), gently press the fruits into the levelled surface in the desired pattern.

4 Bake in a preheated oven at 140°C (120°C fan, Gas 1) for 4¾–5 hours. Keep an eye on the cake through the oven door as it bakes: if it is browning too quickly, cover the surface with tin foil. The cake is ready when it is firm to the touch, and a skewer inserted into the middle of the cake comes out clean. Leave the cake to cool in the tin.

5 When the cake has cooled, pierce it in several places with a fine skewer and pour over a little brandy. Remove the cake from the tin, but leave the lining paper on. Wrap the cake in more greaseproof paper, then overwrap with foil. Store the cake in a cool place for up to 3 months to mature, unwrapping and spooning over more brandy (1–2 tbsp) occasionally.

6 If making the Snow white cake (see Cake decorations, below right) decorate the cake with almond paste and royal icing (see below). Tie a ribbon around the cake, if wished.

Marzipan (Almond paste)

MAKES enough for a 23 cm (9 in) round or 20 cm (8 in) square cake

250 g (8 oz) ground almonds
250 g (8 oz) caster sugar
250 g (8 oz) icing sugar, sifted, plus extra for dusting
6 drops of almond extract
about 4 egg yolks, or about 2 whole eggs

1 Mix the ground almonds in a bowl with the two different types of sugar until evenly combined. Lightly beat together the extract and egg yolks or whole eggs. Add almost all of this mixture to the dry ingredients and mix together until a stiff paste forms; it is best to do this with your hands. Add the remaining egg if needed so that the mixtures comes together well.

2 Dust a flat surface lightly with icing sugar, turn out the mixture on to it, and knead with your hands to make a stiff paste. Take care not to over-knead or the paste will be oily. Wrap in cling film and store in the refrigerator until required.

Royal icing

MAKES enough for a 23 cm (9 in) round or 20 cm (8 in) square cake

2 egg whites
500 g (1 lb) icing sugar, sifted
4 tsp lemon juice

1 Whisk the egg whites in a large bowl lightly with a fork until bubbles begin to form on the surface. Add about half the icing sugar and all of the lemon juice and beat well with a wooden spoon for about 10 minutes until brilliant white.

2 Gradually stir in the remaining icing sugar until the consistency is just right for spreading or piping. If not using immediately, keep the bowl covered with a damp cloth to prevent the icing drying out.

Cake decorations

Whichever cake you choose, you need to melt and sieve about 90 g (3 oz) apricot jam before you apply any of the decorations or icing. The jam prevents the cake from drying out and suppresses any crumbs.

Candied fruit cake
This looks most dramatic if it is made in a square tin. Before baking, arrange nuts and whole or sliced candied fruits in a decorative pattern on the surface of the cake mixture. Once baked and matured, brush and leave until set firmly in place before tying a ribbon around the sides of the cake.

Snow white cake
Brush the jam over the top and sides of the cake. Roll out the marzipan and use it to cover the cake completely, then smooth it in place with your hands and trim off any excess. Let the marzipan dry out for a few days before covering with royal icing. Use a palette knife to rough up the icing into peaks, immediately after you have spread it all over the cake. If you are using decorations for the top of the cake (here, fresh holly leaves and candied cranberries), you need to gently press them in before the icing sets hard.

Iced lime traybake

MAKES 12 squares **CALS EACH** 340

175 g (6 oz) soft butter or baking spread, plus extra for greasing
175 g (6 oz) caster sugar
250 g (8 oz) self-raising flour
1½ tsp baking powder
3 eggs
3 tbsp milk
finely grated zest of 2 limes, plus extra to garnish

Icing
250 g (8 oz) icing sugar
juice of 2 limes

23 X 30 CM (9 X 12 IN) TRAYBAKE TIN

1 Lightly grease the tin and line the bottom with baking parchment.

2 Combine all the cake ingredients in a large bowl and beat well for about 2 minutes or until smooth and thoroughly blended.

3 Turn into the prepared tin and level the surface. Bake in a preheated oven at 180°C (160°C fan, Gas 4) for 35–40 minutes until the cake is well risen, springy to the touch, and beginning to shrink away from the sides of the cake tin.

4 Leave to cool slightly in the tin, then turn out on to a wire rack, peel off the lining paper, and cool.

5 Make the icing: sift the icing sugar into a bowl. Mix in enough of the lime juice to give a runny consistency. Pour over the cooled cake, spreading carefully with a palette knife, and leave to set. When cold, cut into squares, and serve with a little lime zest grated over the top.

CHOCOLATE AND MINT TRAYBAKE

Mix 4 tbsp cocoa powder with 4 tbsp hot water and leave to cool. Add to the basic cake ingredients with 4 tbsp chopped fresh mint. For the icing, break 250 g (8 oz) plain dark chocolate into pieces and put into a heatproof bowl with 90 g (3 oz) butter and 4 tbsp hot water. Put the bowl over a saucepan of hot water and heat gently until the chocolate has melted. Beat together until smooth and shiny, then spread over the top of the cooled cake.

Fridge cookies

MAKES 50 **CALS EACH** 59

250 g (8 oz) plain flour
1 tsp baking powder
125 g (4 oz) butter, plus extra for greasing
175 g (6 oz) caster sugar
60 g (2 oz) walnuts, finely chopped
1 egg, beaten
1 tsp vanilla extract

1 Sift the flour and baking powder into a bowl. Rub in the butter with the fingertips until the mixture resembles breadcrumbs. Mix in the sugar and walnuts. Add the beaten egg and vanilla extract, and stir to form a smooth dough.

2 Shape the dough into a cylinder about 5 cm (2 in) in diameter. Wrap in foil, roll to give smooth sides, and refrigerate for about 8 hours.

3 Lightly butter several baking trays. Cut the cylinder into thin slices and place the biscuits on the baking trays. Bake in a preheated oven at 190°C (170°C fan, Gas 5) for 10–12 minutes until golden.

Flapjacks

MAKES 24 **CALS EACH** 102

125 g (4 oz) butter, plus extra for greasing
90 g (3 oz) golden syrup
90 g (3 oz) light muscovado sugar
250 g (8 oz) rolled oats

ROASTING TIN OR SHALLOW TRAYBAKE TIN, ABOUT 20 X 30 CM (8 X 12 IN)

1 Lightly butter the roasting tin or cake tin.

2 Combine the butter, syrup, and sugar in a saucepan and heat gently until the ingredients have melted and dissolved. Stir in the oats and mix well.

3 Spoon into the prepared tin and smooth the surface with a palette knife. Bake in a preheated oven at 180°C (160°C fan, Gas 4) for about 30 minutes.

4 Leave to cool in the tin for about 5 minutes, then mark into 24 fingers. Leave to cool completely, then cut and remove from the tin.

Dundee cake

CUTS INTO 12 slices **CALS EACH** 384

150 g (5 oz) butter, at room temperature, plus extra for greasing
150 g (5 oz) light muscovado sugar
3 eggs
250 g (8 oz) plain flour
1 tsp baking powder
175 g (6 oz) sultanas
90 g (3 oz) currants
90 g (3 oz) raisins
60 g (2 oz) glacé cherries, quartered, rinsed, and dried
60 g (2 oz) chopped mixed candied peel
2 tbsp ground almonds
grated zest of 1 large lemon
60 g (2 oz) whole almonds, blanched and halved, to decorate

DEEP 20 CM (8 IN) ROUND LOOSE-BOTTOMED CAKE TIN

1 Lightly butter the cake tin and line the bottom with greaseproof paper.

2 Combine the butter, sugar, eggs, flour, and baking powder in a bowl and beat for 2 minutes or until well blended. Stir in the fruit, mixed peel, ground almonds, and lemon zest.

3 Spoon the mixture into the prepared tin. Level the surface and arrange the halved almonds neatly in concentric circles on top.

4 Bake in a preheated oven at 160°C (140°C fan, Gas 3) for 1½ hours or until well risen, golden, and firm to the touch. A fine skewer inserted into the middle of the cake should come out clean. Cover the cake with foil halfway through baking if it is browning too quickly.

5 Leave the cake to cool in the tin for a few minutes, then turn out on to a wire rack and leave to cool completely. Store in an airtight container for about 1 week before eating.

Ginger snaps

MAKES 15 **CALS EACH** 81

60 g (2 oz) butter, plus extra for greasing
90 g (3 oz) golden syrup
125 g (4 oz) self-raising flour
2 tsp ground ginger
1 tsp ground cinnamon
½ tsp bicarbonate of soda
1 tbsp caster sugar

1 Lightly grease two baking trays with butter. Combine the butter and golden syrup in a small saucepan and heat gently until melted. Leave the mixture to cool slightly.

2 Sift the flour, spices, and bicarbonate of soda into a bowl, and stir in the sugar. Add the cooled syrup mixture, and stir to mix to a soft but not sticky dough.

3 Roll the dough into balls about the size of walnuts and place well apart on the baking trays. Flatten the dough balls slightly with the heel of your hand.

4 Bake in a preheated oven at 190°C (170°C fan, Gas 5) for about 15 minutes. Leave the biscuits to cool on the baking trays for a few minutes, then transfer them to a wire rack and leave to cool completely.

Brandy snaps

MAKES 15 **CALS EACH** 107

90 g (3 oz) butter
90 g (3 oz) demerara sugar
90 g (3 oz) golden syrup
90 g (3 oz) plain flour
¾ tsp ground ginger
¾ tsp lemon juice

1 Line a baking tray with baking parchment. Combine the butter, sugar, and syrup in a saucepan and heat gently until the ingredients have melted and dissolved. Cool slightly, then sift in the flour and ginger. Add the lemon juice and stir well.

2 Place 3–4 teaspoonfuls of the mixture on the baking tray, leaving plenty of room for the biscuits to spread out.

3 Bake in a preheated oven at 160°C (140°C fan, Gas 3) for about 8 minutes until the mixture spreads out to form large, thin, dark golden rounds. While the biscuits are baking, oil the handles of four wooden spoons.

4 Remove the biscuits from the oven and leave for 1–2 minutes to firm slightly.

5 Lift a biscuit from the paper using a fish slice or palette knife, turn the biscuit over so that the rough side is on the outside, and wrap around an oiled wooden spoon handle. Repeat with the remaining biscuits. Transfer to a wire rack and cool until firm. Slip from the spoon handles.

6 Continue baking, shaping, and cooling the remaining mixture in batches.

Viennese fingers

MAKES 12 **CALS EACH** 215

175 g (6 oz) butter, plus extra for greasing
60 g (2 oz) caster sugar
175 g (6 oz) self-raising flour
90 g (3 oz) plain dark chocolate, broken into pieces

1 Lightly butter two baking trays. Combine the butter and sugar in a bowl and cream together until pale and fluffy. Stir in the flour and beat until well combined.

2 Spoon the mixture into a piping bag with a medium star nozzle. Pipe into 7 cm (3 in) lengths on the baking trays. Bake in a preheated oven at 160°C (140°C fan, Gas 3) for about 20 minutes until golden. Cool on a wire rack.

3 Put the chocolate into a heatproof bowl. Set the bowl over a pan of hot water and heat gently until the chocolate has melted. Dip both ends of each biscuit into the chocolate. Leave to set on the wire rack.

Coconut macaroons

MAKES 26 **CALS EACH** 116

3 egg whites
175 g (6 oz) icing sugar
175 g (6 oz) ground almonds
a few drops of almond extract
175 g (6 oz) desiccated coconut
about 13 whole almonds, blanched and halved

1 Line two baking trays with baking parchment.

2 Whisk the egg whites thoroughly until stiff but not dry. Sift in the icing sugar and fold it in gently. Fold in the ground almonds, almond extract, and desiccated coconut.

3 Put teaspoonfuls of the coconut mixture on to the baking trays. Top each with an almond half.

4 Bake in a preheated oven at 150°C (130°C fan, Gas 2) for about 25 minutes until golden brown and crisp on the outside and soft in the middle.

5 Leave the macaroons to cool on a wire rack. Best served on the day of making.

Almond tuiles

MAKES 30 **CALS EACH** 45

2 egg whites
125 g (4 oz) caster sugar
60 g (2 oz) plain flour
½ tsp vanilla extract
60 g (2 oz) butter, melted and cooled
30 g (1 oz) flaked almonds

1 Line a baking tray with baking parchment. Put the egg whites into a bowl and beat in the sugar until frothy. Stir in the flour and vanilla extract, then add the melted butter.

2 Put six teaspoonfuls of the mixture on to the baking tray, spacing them well apart to allow for spreading. Flatten each with a fork.

3 Sprinkle with the almonds. Bake in a preheated oven at 180°C (160°C fan, Gas 4) for about 6 minutes until golden brown around the edges but still pale in the middle.

4 Allow the biscuits to cool on the baking tray for a few seconds, then lift off with a fish slice and gently lay them over a greased rolling pin to give the traditional curved shape.

5 Allow the biscuits to set, then lift off on to a wire rack and leave to cool.

6 Cook and shape the remaining mixture in batches, baking one batch while another is setting on the rolling pin.

Pink almond macarons

MAKES 40 **CALS EACH** 113

200 g (7 oz) icing sugar, sifted
200 g (7 oz) ground almonds
200 g (7 oz) caster sugar
4 tbsp cold water
4 large eggs, separated
1 tsp almond extract
red food colouring

Filling

90 g (3 oz) soft butter
150 g (5 oz) icing sugar, sifted
raspberry jam

PIPING BAG FITTED WITH 1 CM (½ IN) PLAIN NOZZLE

1 Line two baking trays with baking parchment. Combine the icing sugar and almonds in a bowl, and set aside.

2 Put the caster sugar and water into a stainless steel pan. Heat gently over a low heat, stirring, until the sugar has dissolved. Bring to a boil, and boil for a few minutes without stirring, until you have a shiny, clear syrup, the consistency of single cream. If you have a sugar thermometer it should read 110°C (230°F), no more. Remove from the heat, and leave to cool slightly.

3 Put two of the egg whites into a bowl, and beat with an electric whisk on high speed until stiff but not dry. Slowly pour in the sugar syrup in a thin, steady stream, beating constantly until all the syrup is used and you have a shiny meringue.

4 Add the remaining two unbeaten egg whites to the sugar and almonds, and mix to a very thick paste with a wooden spoon. Add the almond extract, and stir in just enough food colouring to make the mixture pink. Add a heaped tablespoonful of the meringue, beat well, then carefully fold in the remaining meringue until the mixture is an even pink colour. Do not overmix or it will be too runny.

5 Fill the piping bag with the mixture. Pipe 80 small rounds, each about 3.5 cm (1½ in) in diameter, on to each baking tray. Set aside to dry for about an hour until a skin forms on top.

6 Bake in a preheated oven at 150°C (130°C fan, Gas 2) for about 25 minutes until firm and glossy on top. Turn the oven off, and leave the macarons to cool in the oven for about an hour. Transfer to a wire rack with a damp palette knife, and leave to cool completely.

7 Make the filling: cream the butter and half of the icing sugar in a bowl, beating until pale and fluffy. Beat in the remaining sugar a little at a time until the mixture is smooth. Using a small palette knife, spread a little jam and butter cream over the bottom of 40 macarons, then sandwich together with the remaining macarons.

Simnel cake

This is now a traditional Easter cake, but originally it was given by girls to their mothers on Mothering Sunday. The almond paste balls represent the 11 disciples of Christ, excluding Judas Iscariot.

CUTS INTO 12 slices **CALS EACH** 494

175 g (6 oz) soft butter or baking spread, plus extra for greasing
175 g (6 oz) light muscovado sugar
3 eggs
175 g (6 oz) self-raising flour
175 g (6 oz) sultanas
90 g (3 oz) currants
90 g (3 oz) glacé cherries, quartered, rinsed, and dried
30 g (1 oz) candied peel, roughly chopped
grated zest of 1 large lemon
1 tsp ground mixed spice

Filling and decoration

500 g (1 lb) almond paste
2 tbsp apricot jam
1 egg white

DEEP 18 CM (7 IN) ROUND LOOSE-BOTTOMED CAKE TIN

1 Roll out one-third of the almond paste. Using the base of the cake tin as a guide, cut out an 18 cm (7 in) round.

2 Grease the cake tin and line the bottom and side with greaseproof paper.

3 Combine all the cake ingredients in a bowl. Beat well until thoroughly blended. Spoon half of the cake mixture into the prepared tin and smooth the surface. Top with the round of almond paste.

4 Spoon the remaining cake mixture on top and level the surface.

5 Bake in a preheated oven at 150°C (130°C fan, Gas 2) for 2¼ hours or until golden brown and firm to the touch.

6 Cover the top of the cake with greaseproof paper if it is browning too quickly. Leave to cool for 10 minutes, then remove from the tin, and leave to cool completely.

7 Warm the jam and use to brush the top of the cake.

8 To decorate the cake, roll out half of the remaining almond paste and use the tin to cut out an 18 cm (7 in) round. Put on top of the jam and crimp the edges. Roll the remaining almond paste into 11 even-sized balls. Place around the edge of the cake, attaching them with egg white.

9 Brush the tops of the balls and the almond paste with egg white. Place under a hot grill for 1–2 minutes, until the balls are golden.

Mincemeat buns

MAKES 32 **CALS EACH** 137

375 g (12 oz) mincemeat
250 g (8 oz) currants
2 eggs
150 g (5 oz) caster sugar
150 g (5 oz) soft butter or baking spread
250 g (8 oz) self-raising flour

32 PAPER CAKE CASES

1 Combine all the ingredients in a large bowl and beat well for about 2 minutes.

2 Divide the cake mixture evenly among the paper cases, putting them into bun tins if preferred.

3 Bake in a preheated oven at 160°C (140°C fan, Gas 3) for 25–30 minutes until golden and springy to the touch. Transfer the cases to a wire rack and leave to cool.

Cook's know-how

Mincemeat is traditionally made with beef suet. If you want a vegetarian version, use vegetable suet or grated chilled butter. Home-made mincemeat is best, but you can improve on commercial ones by adding finely chopped nuts, angelica, dried apricots, peaches, or pears.

Fork biscuits

MAKES 32 **CALS EACH** 104

250 g (8 oz) butter, at room temperature, plus extra for greasing
125 g (4 oz) caster sugar
300 g (10 oz) self-raising flour

1 Lightly grease two baking trays with butter. Put the butter into a large bowl and beat with a wooden spoon to soften it. Gradually beat in the caster sugar, then stir in the flour. Use your hands to gather the mixture together into a soft but not sticky dough.

2 Roll the dough into balls about the size of walnuts and place well apart on the baking trays. Dip a fork into cold water and press on top of each ball to flatten it and imprint the fork pattern.

3 Bake in batches in a preheated oven at 180°C (160°C fan, Gas 4) for 15–20 minutes until the biscuits are a very pale golden colour. Transfer the biscuits from the baking tray to a wire rack and leave to cool completely.

Pinwheel biscuits

MAKES 18 **CALS EACH** 98

Vanilla dough

60 g (2 oz) butter, at room temperature
30 g (1 oz) caster sugar
90 g (3 oz) plain flour
a few drops of vanilla extract
about 1 tbsp water

Coffee dough

60 g (2 oz) butter, at room temperature
30 g (1 oz) caster sugar
90 g (3 oz) plain flour
1 tbsp coffee extract
milk, for brushing

1 Combine the ingredients for the vanilla dough in a bowl and mix well, adding just enough water to bind. Knead lightly, then wrap and chill for at least 2 hours until very firm.

2 Mix the ingredients for the coffee dough, using the coffee extract to bind. Wrap and chill for at least 2 hours until very firm.

3 On a lightly floured work surface, roll out each dough to a rectangle about 18 x 25 cm (7 x 10 in).

4 Brush the coffee dough with a little milk, then place the vanilla dough on top. Roll up together like a Swiss roll, starting at a narrow end.

5 Wrap the roll tightly in foil and leave to chill in the refrigerator for about 30 minutes or until firm.

6 Lightly grease 1–2 baking trays. Cut the dough roll into about 18 thin slices and place them well apart on the baking trays.

7 Bake in a preheated oven at 180°C (160°C fan, Gas 4) for about 20 minutes until the vanilla dough is a very pale golden colour.

8 Leave the biscuits to cool on the baking trays for a few minutes, then lift off on to a wire rack and leave to cool completely

Cook's know-how

If the doughs become too soft and difficult to roll out, put each piece of dough between sheets of greaseproof paper before rolling.

Shortbread

MAKES 8 wedges **CALS EACH** 233

125 g (4 oz) plain flour
60 g (2 oz) semolina or cornflour
125 g (4 oz) butter, plus extra for greasing
60 g (2 oz) caster sugar, plus extra for sprinkling

1 Mix the flour with the semolina or cornflour in a bowl. Add the butter and rub in with the fingertips. Stir in the sugar. Knead the mixture lightly until it forms a smooth dough.

2 Lightly butter a baking tray. Roll out the dough on a lightly floured work surface into an 18 cm (7 in) round. Lift on to the baking tray. Crimp the edges to decorate, prick all over with a fork, and mark into eight wedges with a sharp knife. Chill until firm.

3 Bake in a preheated oven at 160°C (140°C fan, Gas 3) for 35 minutes or until a pale golden brown colour. Mark the wedges again and sprinkle the shortbread with sugar.

4 Allow the shortbread to cool on the baking tray for about 5 minutes, then lift off carefully with a palette knife and transfer to a wire rack to cool completely. Cut into wedges to serve.

Potato farls

MAKES 12 **CALS EACH** 113

175 g (6 oz) plain flour
1 tbsp baking powder
60 g (2 oz) butter, plus extra for greasing
45 g (1½ oz) caster sugar
125 g (4 oz) freshly boiled and mashed potato
3 tbsp milk

1 Sift the flour and baking powder into a bowl. Rub in the butter until the mixture resembles fine breadcrumbs. Stir in the sugar and mashed potato. Add enough milk to bind to a soft, but not sticky, dough.

2 Turn out the dough on to a floured surface and knead lightly until blended. Roll out until 1 cm (½ in) thick and cut into rectangles or triangles.

3 Place the farls on a buttered baking tray and bake in a preheated oven at 220°C (200°C fan, Gas 7) for 12–15 minutes until risen and golden. Leave to cool on a wire rack. Serve, buttered if you wish, on the day of making.

Bara brith

CUTS INTO 12 slices **CALS EACH** 257

375 g (12 oz) mixed dried fruit
250 g (8 oz) light muscovado sugar
300 ml (½ pint) strong hot tea, strained
butter, for greasing
300 g (10 oz) self-raising flour
1 egg, beaten

1 KG (2 LB) LOAF TIN

1 Combine the dried fruit, sugar, and hot tea in a large bowl. Stir the mixture, then cover and leave to steep for at least 8 hours.

2 Lightly butter the loaf tin and line the bottom with greaseproof paper. Stir the flour and egg into the dried fruit and tea mixture, mixing thoroughly. Turn the mixture into the loaf tin and level the surface.

3 Bake in a preheated oven at 150°C (130°C fan, Gas 2) for 1½–1¾ hours until well risen and firm to the touch. A fine skewer inserted into the middle should come out clean.

4 Leave to cool in the tin for about 10 minutes, then turn out on to a wire rack, and peel off the lining paper. Leave to cool completely. Serve sliced and buttered, if you like.

Irish soda bread

CUTS INTO 8 **CUTS INTO** **CALS EACH** 227

500 g (1 lb) plain white flour, plus extra for dusting
1 tsp bicarbonate of soda
1 tsp salt
300 ml (½ pint) buttermilk, or half milk and half plain yogurt
90 ml (3 fl oz) lukewarm water
sunflower oil, for greasing

1 Sift the flour, bicarbonate of soda, and salt into a large bowl. Pour in the buttermilk, or milk and yogurt, and the measured water. Mix with a wooden spoon or your hands to form a very soft dough.

2 Lightly oil a baking tray. Turn out the dough on to a lightly floured work surface and shape into a round measuring 18 cm (7 in) in diameter.

3 Place the loaf on the prepared baking tray and cut a deep cross in the top.

4 Bake in a preheated oven at 200°C (180°C fan, Gas 6) for 30 minutes. Turn the bread over and bake for a further 10 minutes or until the loaf sounds hollow when tapped on the base. Cool on a wire rack. Serve on the day of making.

Devon scones

MAKES 12 **CALS EACH** 133

60 g (2 oz) butter, plus extra for greasing
250 g (8 oz) self-raising flour
2 tsp baking powder
30 g (1 oz) caster sugar
1 egg
about 150 ml (¼ pint) milk, plus extra for glazing
butter and jam, to serve

5 CM (2 IN) PASTRY CUTTER

1 Lightly butter a large baking tray.

2 Sift the flour and baking powder into a bowl. Rub in the butter with the fingertips until the mixture resembles fine breadcrumbs. Stir in the sugar.

3 Break the egg into a measuring jug and make up to 150 ml (¼ pint) with milk. Beat lightly to mix. Add to the bowl and mix to a soft dough.

4 Lightly knead the dough until smooth. Roll out until 1 cm (½ in) thick, cut into rounds with the pastry cutter, and put on the baking tray. Brush with milk.

5 Bake in a preheated oven at 220°C (200°C fan, Gas 7) for about 10 minutes until risen and golden. Cool on a wire rack. Serve on the day of making, if possible, with butter and jam.

CHEESE SCONES
Omit the sugar, and add 125 g (4 oz) grated mature Cheddar cheese and ½ tsp mustard powder to the dry ingredients before mixing in the egg and milk. Roll out the dough into a 15 cm (6 in) round and cut it into wedges. Brush with milk and sprinkle with finely grated cheese. Bake as directed.

Wholemeal drop scones

MAKES 20 **CALS EACH** 55

175 g (6 oz) wholemeal self-raising flour
1 tsp baking powder
45 g (1½ oz) caster sugar
1 large egg
200 ml (7 fl oz) milk
sunflower oil, for greasing
golden syrup or butter and jam, to serve

1 Combine the flour, baking powder, and sugar in a bowl, and stir to mix. Make a well in the middle of the dry ingredients and add the egg and half of the milk. Beat well to make a smooth, thick batter.

2 Add enough milk to give the batter the consistency of thick cream.

3 Heat a flat griddle or heavy frying pan and grease with oil. Drop spoonfuls of batter on to the hot griddle or pan, spacing them well apart. When bubbles rise to the surface, turn scones over and cook until golden brown.

4 As each batch is cooked, wrap the scones in a clean tea towel to keep them soft. Serve warm, with syrup or butter and jam.

PLAIN DROP SCONES
Substitute plain self-raising flour for the wholemeal self-raising flour, and use a little less milk.

Welsh cakes

MAKES 12 **CALS EACH** 204

250 g (8 oz) self-raising flour
1 tsp baking powder
125 g (4 oz) butter
90 g (3 oz) caster sugar
90 g (3 oz) currants
½ tsp ground mixed spice
1 egg, beaten
about 2 tbsp milk
sunflower oil, for greasing

7 CM (3 IN) PASTRY CUTTER

1 Sift the flour and baking powder into a large bowl. Add the butter and rub in with the fingertips until the mixture resembles fine breadcrumbs.

2 Add the sugar, currants, and mixed spice, and stir to mix. Add the egg and enough milk to form a soft, but not sticky, dough.

3 On a lightly floured work surface, roll out the dough to a thickness of 5 mm (¼ in). Cut into rounds with a pastry cutter.

4 Heat a flat griddle or a heavy frying pan and grease with a little oil. Cook the Welsh cakes on the hot griddle or pan over a low heat for about 3 minutes on each side until cooked through and golden brown.

5 Leave to cool on a wire rack. Serve on the day of making, if possible.

Cornbread

MAKES 9 squares **CALS EACH** 230

sunflower oil, for greasing
175 g (6 oz) polenta or fine yellow cornmeal
125 g (4 oz) plain flour
2–3 tbsp brown sugar
2 tsp baking powder
1 tsp salt
300 ml (½ pint) lukewarm milk
2 eggs, lightly beaten
60 g (2 oz) butter, melted and cooled slightly

18 CM (7 IN) SQUARE CAKE TIN

1 Lightly oil the cake tin. Put the polenta, flour, sugar, baking powder, and salt into a large bowl and make a well in the middle. Pour in the milk, eggs, and butter, and beat the ingredients to form a batter.

2 Pour the mixture into the cake tin and bake in a preheated oven at 200°C (180°C fan, Gas 6) for 25–30 minutes until golden. Leave to cool, then cut into squares before serving.

Religieuses

MAKES 10 **CALS PER SERVING** 366

butter, for greasing
1 quantity choux pastry (see box, below)
1 egg, beaten
300 ml (½ pint) whipping cream, whipped
1 quantity Chocolate icing (Chocolate profiteroles, right)

1 Butter a lined baking tray and sprinkle with water. Spoon the choux into a piping bag fitted with a 1 cm (½ in) plain nozzle, pipe 10 small and 10 slightly larger balls, and brush with beaten egg. Bake in a preheated oven at 220°C (200°C fan, Gas 7) for 10 minutes, then bake at 190°C (170°C fan, Gas 5) for 20 minutes. Split one side of each bun and cool on a rack.

2 Reserve about 3 tbsp of the whipped cream. Fill the balls with the remaining whipped cream, spooning it in the sides.

3 Dip the tops of a large and small ball in chocolate icing. Fit a piping bag with a 1 cm (½ in) star nozzle and pipe the reserved cream on top of the large ball. Gently press the small ball on top of the cream, with the icing facing up. Repeat with the other balls.

Chocolate profiteroles

MAKES 12 **CALS PER SERVING** 306

butter, for greasing
1 quantity choux pastry (see box, below)
1 egg, beaten
300 ml (½ pint) whipping cream, whipped

Chocolate icing

150 g (5 oz) 38% cocoa solids plain chocolate, chopped
150 ml (¼ pint) double cream

1 Butter a lined baking tray and sprinkle with water. Put 12 tablespoonfuls of choux on the tray and brush with beaten egg. Bake in a preheated oven at 220°C (200°C fan, Gas 7) for 10 minutes, then bake at 190°C (170°C fan, Gas 5) for 20 minutes. Split each profiterole in half and cool on a rack.

2 Make the chocolate icing: gently melt the chocolate with the double cream in a bowl over a pan of simmering water, stirring until smooth and shiny (take care not to let it get too hot).

3 Sandwich the profiteroles together with the whipped cream, place on individual plates, and drizzle with the chocolate icing.

Coffee éclairs

MAKES 10–12 **CALS EACH** 263–219

butter, for greasing
1 quantity choux pastry (see box, below)
1 egg, beaten
300 ml (½ pint) whipping cream, whipped

Coffee icing

1 tsp instant coffee
15 g (½ oz) butter
2 tbsp water
90 g (3 oz) icing sugar

1 Butter a lined baking tray and sprinkle with water. Spoon the choux into a piping bag fitted with a 1 cm (½ in) plain nozzle, pipe into 7 cm (3 in) lengths, and brush with beaten egg. Bake in a preheated oven at 220°C (200°C fan, Gas 7) for 10 minutes, then bake at 190°C (170°C fan, Gas 5) for 20 minutes. Split in half and cool on a rack.

2 Spoon the whipped cream into the bottom halves of the éclairs.

3 Make the coffee icing: put the coffee, butter, and water in a bowl over a pan of water. Heat gently until the butter melts. Remove from the heat and beat in the icing sugar. Dip the top half of each eclair in the icing, then place on top of the cream. Leave the icing to cool before serving.

Basic choux pastry

1 Put 60 g (2 oz) butter, cut into cubes, into a heavy saucepan with 150 ml (¼ pint) water and heat until the butter melts. Bring to a boil.

2 Remove from the heat and add 75 g (2½ oz) sifted plain flour and a pinch of salt, if preferred. Stir vigorously until the mixture forms a soft ball.

3 Leave to cool slightly, then gradually add 2 lightly beaten eggs, beating well between each addition, to form a smooth, shiny paste.

Opposite, clockwise from top:
Religieuses, Chocolate profiteroles, Coffee éclairs

Index

Entries in **bold** indicate techniques.
Entries in *italics* indicate variations.

A

B

C

M

Q

R

Cook's notes

All the recipes in this book have been carefully tested to ensure that they produce successful results. When selecting a dish, shopping for ingredients, and making a recipe at home, bear in mind the following essential points:

- Use either all metric or all imperial measurements. Metric and imperial measurements are not interchangeable, so never combine the two.
- Tablespoons are 15 ml, and teaspoons are 5 ml. Spoon measurements are always level unless otherwise stated.
- Eggs are medium unless otherwise stated.
- To replace fresh herbs with dried, substitute 1 teaspoon dried herbs for 1 tablespoon chopped fresh herbs.
- Always preheat the oven before the food goes in to ensure successful results. Recipes in this book have been tested (where appropriate) in a preheated oven.
- No two ovens are alike, so temperatures and cooking times may need to be adjusted to suit your oven.
- When a dish is cooked in the oven, always use the middle shelf unless otherwise stated.
- Calorie counts are approximate and given for guidance only.
- Serving suggestions and accompaniments given with the recipes are optional, for guidance only, and are not included in the calorie counts.

Oven temperatures conversion table

Celsius	Fan	Fahrenheit	Gas	Description
110°	90°	225°	¼	Cool
120°	100°	250°	½	Cool
140°	120°	275°	1	Very slow
150°	130°	300°	2	Very slow
160°	140°	325°	3	Cool
180°	160°	350°	4	Moderate
190°	170°	375°	5	Moderate
200°	180°	400°	6	Moderately hot
220°	200°	425°	7	Hot
230°	210°	450°	8	Hot
240°	220°	475°	9	Very hot

Linear measures conversion table

Metric	Imperial
5 mm	¼ in
1 cm	½ in
2.5 cm	1 in
5 cm	2 in
7 cm	3 in
10 cm	4 in
12 cm	5 in
15 cm	6 in
18 cm	7 in
20 cm	8 in
23 cm	9 in
25 cm	10 in
28 cm	11 in
30 cm	12 in

Volume conversion table

Metric	Imperial
125 ml	4 fl oz
150 ml	¼ pint
175 ml	6 fl oz
250 ml	8 fl oz
300 ml	½ pint
350 ml	12 fl oz
400 ml	14 fl oz
450 ml	¾ pint
500 ml	16 fl oz
550 ml	18 fl oz
600 ml	1 pint
750 ml	1¼ pints
900 ml	1½ pints
1 litre	1¾ pints

Weight conversion table

Metric	Imperial
15 g	½ oz
30 g	1 oz
60 g	2 oz
90 g	3 oz
125 g	4 oz
175 g	6 oz
250 g	8 oz
300 g	10 oz
375 g	12 oz
400 g	13 oz
425 g	14 oz
500 g	1 lb
750 g	1½ lb
1 kg	2 lb

Acknowledgments

Author's acknowledgments

A huge thank you goes to Lucy Young, my assistant of 27 years, for her dedication throughout the updating of this book. Recipes and liaising with the publishers is down to her, so I thank you Lucy, for your work and friendship. Big thanks too to Lucinda McCord who tests our recipes – we discuss, taste, and discuss some more, to make the recipes foolproof. Thank you to the wonderful Mary-Clare Jerram, who is our guiding light at DK, and to Amy Slack, Stephanie Farrow, and the fantastic team.

Publisher's acknowledgments

The first edition of this book was created by Carroll & Brown Limited for Dorling Kindersley. Subsequent editions were created by Dorling Kindersley.

For this 2017 edition, DK would like to thank the following people for their help:
Photography art direction: Sara Robin
Photography: Stuart West, Mary Wadsworth, and William Reavell
Food styling: Jane Lawrie, Janet Brinkworth, Maud Eden, Sal Henley, Catherine Hill, Penny Stephens, and Kate Wesson
Prop styling: Linda Berlin
Art direction: Nicky Collings and Penny Stock
Author photography: Georgia Glynn-Smith
Author hair and make-up: Jo Penford
Author stylists: Arabella Boyce and Alicia Ellis
Design assistance: Philippa Nash
Proofreading: Rosamund Cox

NOTE: The author and publisher advocate sustainable food choices, and every effort has been made to include only sustainable foods in this book. Food sustainability is, however, a shifting landscape,and so we encourage readers to keep up to date with advice on this subject, so that they are equipped to make their own ethical choices.

Editor Amy Slack
Senior art editor Sara Robin
Senior jacket designer Nicola Powling
Pre-production producer Catherine Williams
Producer Stephanie McConnell
Creative technical support Sonia Charbonnier
Managing editor Stephanie Farrow
Managing art editor Christine Keilty
Art director Maxine Pedliham
Publishing director Mary-Clare Jerram

DK INDIA
Project editor Janashree Singha
Editors Sugandh Juneja, Shreya Sengupta
Senior art editor Ivy Sengupta
Project art editor Vikas Sachdeva
Managing editor Soma B. Chowdhury
Managing art editors Arunesh Talapatra, Navidita Thapa
Pre-production manager Sunil Sharma
DTP designers Manish Upreti, Rajdeep Singh

First published in Great Britain in 1995
Second edition published in 2003
Third edition published in 2012
This updated edition published in 2017 by Dorling Kindersley Limited, 80 Strand, London WC2R 0RL

2 4 6 8 10 9 7 5 3 1
001 – 299173 – September/2017

A CIP catalogue record for this book is available from The British Library
ISBN 978-0-2412-8612-8

Printed and bound in China

A WORLD OF IDEAS
SEE ALL THERE IS TO KNOW
www.dk.com